A University Course in

ENGLISH GRAMMAR

Angela Downing
and Philip Locke

London and New York

First published 1992 by Prentice Hall International (UK) Ltd

This edition first published 2002
by Routledge
11 New Fetter Lane, London EC4P 4EE

Simultaneously published in the USA and Canada
by Routledge
29 West 35th Street, New York, NY 10001

Routledge is an imprint of the Taylor & Francis Group

Typeset in Cheltenham Light
Printed and bound in Great Britain by
TJ International Ltd, Padstow, Cornwall

British Library Cataloguing in Publication Data
A catalogue record for this book is available from the British Library

Library of Congress Cataloging in Publication Data
A catalog record for this book has been requested

ISBN 0-415-28810-X (pbk)

Contents

5 *Interaction between speaker and hearer:*
Mood structures of the clause   163

6 *Organising the message:*
Thematic and information structures of the clause   219

7 *Expanding and projecting the message:*
The clause complex   273

8 *Talking about events:*
The Verbal Group   313

Preface

Over recent years functional and communicative approaches to English language teaching have left advanced students, particularly, in need of a more explicit analysis of English grammar to improve their control and understanding of language use in context. What is now needed is a description of English which, in keeping with many of those learning materials, starts out from a social and interactive perspective on language as discourse and shows in a consistent way how lexicogrammar acts to enable speakers and writers to encode their purposeful messages appropriately in text.

'Placing meaning firmly in the context of grammar' (the authors' words) is characteristic of the systemic-functional model of grammar to emerge from the research and writings of Michael Halliday. His influence on English language teaching and learning has been immense. In the teaching of English as a mother tongue and as a second language, his writings have been a practical inspiration to teachers and learners. Yet for many practitioners in English as a Foreign Language the theory has often proved difficult to introduce into the classroom.

In **A University Course in English Grammar**, Angela Downing and Philip Locke have drawn on their detailed knowledge of Halliday's theory to provide a clear descriptive account of sentence grammar but in addition and more importantly an account that offers a means of analysing texts. This is realised through varied practice tasks which both exemplify the grammatical description and provide authentic texts for further analysis.

I am confident that teachers, learners, and syllabus designers will find the rich and detailed content in harmony with their functional and communicative goals, to be a means by which the exploration of grammar in a discoursal context can become a central part of language learning.

Professor Christopher N Candlin
Macquarie University
Sydney

Table of notational symbols

Most of the symbols used in this book follow current conventions, but since conventions vary, the following list indicates the meanings assigned to them here. Some are used for more than one purpose, but their meanings, including their everyday senses, are always clear from the content.

Classes of units

Cl	clause
Clf	finite clause
Clnf	non-finite clause
Cl-*ing*	-ING clause
Cl-*en*	-EN clause
Clinf	infinitive clause
Cl *to*-inf	*to*-infinitive clause
VG	verbal group
NG	nominal group
AdjG	adjectival group
AdvG	adverbial group
PrepG	prepositional group
v	verb
n	noun
pron	pronoun
adj	adjective
adv	adverb
prep	preposition
conj	conjunction
det	determinative

Unit boundaries

///	sentence/clause-complex
//	clause
/	group

Tonicity

‖	boundary of tone unit
		onset of tone unit
\	falling tone
/	rising tone
–	level tone
∧	rising-falling tone
∨	falling-rising tone
		next syllable is stressed
↑	next syllable is stressed with step-up in pitch
‖	extra strong stress

Syntactic elements and relations

S	subject
p	predicator
Od	direct object
Oi	indirect object
Oprep	prepositional object
Cs	subject complement
Co	object complement
Cp	predicator complement
A	adjunct
D	disjunct
C	conjunct
h	head
m	modifier
q	qualifier
d	determiner
e	epithet
cl	classifier
c	completive
o	operator
x	auxiliary
v	main verb
+	coordination, addition
×	dependency
→	right-branching dependency
←	left-branching dependency
[ ]	embedded unit

Pauses from brief to long

·   –   – –   – – –

Other symbols

*	unacceptable form
(?)	doubtfully acceptable
/	alternative form
†	keyed task

C.O.D. = Concise Oxford Dictionary
L.D.C.E. = Longman Dictionary of Contemporary English

Introduction

Aims of the course

This book has been written primarily for students of English as a foreign or second language in higher education. It assumes an intermediate standard of knowledge and operational ability in the language and, from this point of departure, seeks to fulfil the following aims:

1 to further students' knowledge of English through exploration and analysis;
2 to help students acquire a global vision of English, rather than concentrate on unrelated areas;
3 to see a grammar as providing a means of understanding the relation of form to meaning and meaning to situation;
4 to provide a basic terminology which, within this limited framework, will enable students to make these relationships explicit.

While not pretending to be comprehensive, its wide coverage and functional approach may be found appropriate not only in first degree courses but also in background courses for literature and discourse studies.

A functional approach to grammar

Following the systemic-functional tradition, we distinguish several ways in which grammar is functional. In the first place we base our approach on the assumption that all languages fulfil two higher-level or meta-functions in our lives. One is to express our interpretation of the world as we experience it (sometimes called the 'ideational' or the 'representational' function); the other is to interact with others in order to bring about changes in the environment (the 'interpersonal' function). The organisation of the message in such a way as to enable representation and interaction represents a third (the 'textual' meta-function), and this, too, is given its place in a functional grammar.

In the second place, the regular patterns of different kinds that can be distinguished reflect the uses which a language serves. For instance, the structural patterns known as 'declarative', 'interrogative' and 'imperative' serve the purposes of expressing a multitude of types of social behaviour, while the Nominal Group pattern enables us to encode a good deal of information about entities: people, things, events and abstractions.

When we come to describe the more detailed mechanisms of English, we also make use of the notion of 'function' to describe syntactic categories such as Subjects and Objects, semantic roles such as Agent and informational categories such as Theme. These different types of function constitute autonomous dimensions of analysis, so that there is no one-to-one relationship between them. Rather, we shall find that they can conflate together in different ways, the choice of one or other being determined by such factors as context, co-text, particularly what has gone before in the message, and the speaker–hearer relationship.

Third, this type of grammar is functional in that each linguistic element is seen not in isolation but in relation to others, since it has potential to realise different functions. Structural patterns are seen as configurations of functions, whether of participants and processes, or of modifiers and qualifiers of a head, or of Subject, verb and Complements, among others. Speakers are free, within the resources a particular language displays, to choose those patterns which best carry out their communicative purposes at every stage of their interaction with other speakers.

With these considerations in mind, the present course has been designed to place meaning firmly within the grammar and, by stressing the meaningful functions of grammatical forms and structures, to offer a description of English sentences which will serve as a bridge to courses dealing with the analysis, interpretation and organisation of whole texts.

Presentation of content

The grammatical content of the course is presented in three blocks: (a) a first chapter giving a bird's-eye view of the whole course and defining the basic concepts and terms used in it; (b) six chapters describing clause structures and clause complexes from semantic, syntactic and functional points of view; (c) six chapters dealing similarly with group units. Chapter titles attempt to reflect, as far as possible, the angles from which the description is made.

The chapters are divided into 'modules' (sixty in all), each one being conceived as a teaching and learning unit with appropriate practice tasks grouped at the end of each chapter.

Each module begins with a boxed summary which presents the main matters of interest. It is designed to assist both tutor and students in class preparation and to offer a review for study purposes.

Exemplification

Most of the examples which illustrate each grammatical point have been drawn from or are based on actual occurrences observed by the authors.

Inevitably, it would be impractical to contextualise each example. To offset this limitation and to make it clear that we are describing a living language, we have made regular use of short excerpts of connected speech and writing from a wide variety of authentic sources. Our intention here is to illustrate the natural use of the features being described, not to offer a method of discourse analysis.

Practice tasks

Each of the sixty modules which make up the course is accompanied by a varying number of practice tasks. Some involve the observation and identification of syntactic elements and their semantic functions, or of the relations between them; others call for the manipulation or completion of sentences in various meaningful ways; grammatical topics are sometimes proposed for discussion between pairs or groups of students; mini-projects are suggested for individual research by students based on their own reading or experiences outside the class; topics are proposed for the writing of original letters, short articles, advertisements, instructions, narratives and descriptions, dialogues for social purposes. Some tasks involve the interpretation of meanings and intentions which are to be inferred from the use of particular forms and structures within certain contexts. The different areas of grammar lend themselves to a wide variety of practical linguistic tasks limited only by the time factor. Those proposed here can be selected, adapted, amplified or omitted, according to need.

A 'key' is provided at the end of the book for those tasks which have a single solution. There are many tasks, however, that have no solution of this kind: for example, those requiring original composition or open discussion and explanation of grammar topics. Tasks involving the interpretation of meanings or those whose solution is variable are either not keyed at all or are accompanied by a suggested solution, since it is felt that they are more appropriately left to classroom discussion.

It is the opinion of the authors that university study should not attend solely to the attainment of certain practical end-results. Its value lies to a great extent in the thinking that goes on in the process of ensuring the results, not only in the results themselves. It is rather in the performance of a task that the learning takes place. The premature reference to a key negates the whole purpose of the tasks and should be resisted at all costs.

Suggestions for using the book

When this book is used as a basis for classroom teaching of English language at universities, it may be treated as a resource book by approaching it in the following way:

(a) *either*: by presenting the 'Summary' outlined at the beginning of each module and amplifying it according to the time allotted, with occasional reference to appropriate parts of the module; *or*: by taking an illustrative text as starting-point, and drawing out the meanings, forms and functions dealt with in the module.

(b) The complete module can then be read by the students out of class and any suggested tasks prepared. Some tasks may be assigned to different students and discussed collectively. Others may more usefully be prepared by all members of the class. Alternatively, for assessment purposes, students may be allowed to build up a dossier of tasks of their own choice. Certain tasks can be done collectively and orally in class, without previous preparation. Students should be encouraged to bring in selections of their own texts, whether self-authored or collected from specific genres, for presentation and discussion within a group.

(c) A further session may be devoted to clarification of points raised as a result of students' reading and of carrying out the tasks.

(d) Although the content of this book is organised as a coherent course, universities vary considerably in the entry standard of their students, in the amount of class time allotted to English language, in time for reading and practice, in the number of students in a class and the aims of the syllabus. Such factors determine the rate of progression through the course. In some cases the course may be spread over two years; in others it may be studied more rapidly, for enrichment or as a bridge to the study of texts.

Whether the book is studied with or without guidance, access to the grammatical terms and topics treated in it is facilitated in three ways:

1   by the initial list of chapter and module headings;
2   by the section and subsection headings listed at the beginning of each chapter;
3   by the alphabetical list of items, terms and topics given in the general Index at the end of the book.

Acknowledgements

All the material in this book appears with the permission of those who hold the copyright. The authors and publishers thank the following for their permission to reproduce extracts of the copyright material:

Aitken and Stone for *Confessions of a Storyteller*, Copyright © Paul Gallico 1961; Arrow and Warner Books Inc. for *The Complete Hip and Thigh Diet*, Rosemary Conley; BBC Enterprises Ltd for *The Complete Yes Prime Minister*, edited by Jonathan Lynn and Antony Jay; the excerpt from *Testament of Experience* by Vera Brittain is included with the permission of Paul Berry, her literary executor, and Virago Press; Blackwell Ltd for *Oxford Today: Volume 1 Number 3*, pp 37 and 58 published in *Oxford Today* and reprinted with the permission of the Chancellor and Scholars of Oxford University; The Bodley Head for *Don't Fall Off The Mountain*, Shirley MacLaine and *Zen and The Art of Motorcycle Maintenance*, Robert Pirsig; Cambridge University Press for *The Universe Around Us*, James Jeans; Casarotto Company Ltd for extracts from J. G. Ballard; Chatto and Windus for *Just Between Ourselves*, Alan Ayckbourn, *A Fairly Honourable Defeat* and *The Sea The Sea*, Iris Murdoch; Curtis Brown London Ltd for permission to reproduce *Doctor on the Boil*, Copyright Richard Gordon 1973; Express Newspapers Plc for an extract from *The Daily Express* dated 18 June 1990; David Higham Associates for *Under Milkwood* and *Quite Early One Morning*, Dylan Thomas, *Akenfield*, Ronald Blythe and *The Spy Who Came In From The Cold*, John le Carré; the Estate of the late Sonia Brownwell Orwell and Martin Secker and Warburg Ltd for *A Hanging* and *England Your England* in *Collected Essays, Journalism and Letters Volume 1*, G. Orwell; Faber & Faber Ltd and The Putnam Publishing Group for *Lord of the Flies*, William Golding; George Weidenfeld and Nicolson Ltd for *Bandits*, E. J. Hobsbaum and *Valparaiso*, Nicolas Freeling; Hamish Hamilton Ltd for *The New Confessions*, William Boyd; Hamish Hamilton Ltd and Houghton Mifflin Company for *The Long Goodbye*, Raymond Chandler; Harcourt Brace Jovanovich Ltd for *North to the Orient*, Copyright 1935 and renewed 1963 by Anne Morrow Lindbergh; Harper Collins Publishers for *Beat Jet Lag*, Kathleen Mayes; Harrap Publishing Group Ltd for *The Boundaries of Science*, Magnus Pike; Hodder and Stoughton Ltd for *Polaris* and *Christmas List* in *Polaris and Other Stories*, Fay Weldon; Hogarth Press and Random

Century Group for *Cider with Rosie*, Laurie Lee and *Mrs Dalloway*, Virginia Woolf; *The Independent* for an article by Jim White, first published in *The Independent*, 13 January 1991 and for an article by Peter Popham first published in *The Independent Magazine*, 24 November 1990; The Institute of Linguists for an article from *The Linguist Vol 29 No 5*, 1990; John Murray (Publishers) Ltd for *A Winter in Arabia*, Freya Stark; Jonathan Cape and Harper Collins Publishers for *Under the Volcano*, Malcolm Lowry; Laurence Pollinger Ltd and the Estate of Frieda Lawrence Ravagli for *England, My England* and *The Lost Girl*, D. H. Lawrence; Laurence Pollinger Ltd and The William Saroyan Foundation for *The Human Comedy*, William Saroyan; Longman Group UK for *Advanced Conversational English*, Crystal & Davy and *Metals and Alloys*, H. Moore; The MacDonald Group for Futura Publications' *Lightning in May*, Gordon Parker; Martin Secker & Warburg Ltd and Octopus Publishing Group Library for *The Children of Sanchez*, Oscar Lewis, *The British Museum is Falling Down* and *How Far Can You Go*, David Lodge and *The Wedding Jug* from *Twenty Stories*, Philip Smith; Methuen and Octopus Publishing Group Library for *Time Pieces* in *Plays by Women Volume 3*, Lou Wakefield and *Find me* in *Plays by Women Volume 2*, Olwyn Wymark; Methuen and Sheil Land Associates Ltd for *The Secret Diary of Adrian Mole*, Copyright © Sue Townsend 1983; Methuen and Radio Films UK for *No Quarter*, Barry Bermange; *The Observer* for extracts from *The Sunday Observer*, 25 November 1990 and 18 August 1991; Oxford University Press for *Varieties of Spoken English*, Dickinson and Mackin; Peters Fraser & Dunlop for *Brideshead Revisited*, Evelyn Waugh and *The Long-Distance Piano Player*, Alan Sharp; Penguin Books for *Success with English: Outlook: Artists talking*, Anthony Schooling, *Hypnosis: Fact and Fiction*, F. L. Marcuse. *Billy Phelan's Greatest Game*, Copyright © 1975 by William Kennedy, used by permission of Viking Penguin, a division of Penguin Books USA Inc and Penguin Books. Penguin Books and Peters Fraser & Dunlop for *A Particular Friendship*, Dirk Bogarde; Penguin Books and The British Museum Press for *The Innocent Anthropologist*, Nigel Barley; The Society of Authors on behalf of the Bernard Shaw Estate for *Candida, A Sunday on the Surrey Hills* and *Too True to be Good*, G. B. Shaw; Thomas Nelson & Sons Ltd for *Human Types*, Sir Raymond W. Firth; Thames & Hudson Ltd for *Recollections and Reflections*, Bruno Bettelheim; The Times Newspapers Ltd © 1985 for an extract from *The Times Higher Education Supplement*, 27 December 1985; Copyright 1990 The Time Inc Magazine Company, reprinted by permission 'Education: doing bad and feeling good', Charles Krauthammer, 5 February 1990; Copyright 1986 Time Warner Inc., reprinted by permission, 'Turning brown, red and green', 15 December 1986; Victor Gollancz Ltd for *The Citadel*, A. J. Cronin and *Malicious Mischief*, Lesley Egan; Virago Press for *Nothing Sacred*, Angela Carter; A. P. Watt Ltd on behalf of The Literary Executors of the Estate of H. G. Wells for *A Short History of the World*, H. G. Wells; A. P. Watt Ltd for *No Place Like Home*, Nadine Gordimer; William Heinemann Ltd and David Higham Associates for *The Heart of the Matter*, © 1948 Verdant SA, Graham

Greene; William Heinemann Ltd and The Octopus Publishing Group Library for *The Godfather*, Mario Puzo, *The Grapes of Wrath*, John Steinbeck, *The Balkan Trilogy*, Olivia Manning and *Ripley's Game*, Patricia Highsmith; William Heinemann Ltd for *Making a New Science*, James Gleick; The World Health Organization, Geneva for Glossary of Terms used in the *Health for All* series, No. 9, 1984.

Every effort has been made to trace and acknowledge ownership of copyright. The publishers will be glad to make suitable arrangements with any copyright holders whom it has not been possible to contact.

Our Thanks to ...

Our debts to our predecessors in writing this book are many and various. No present-day students' grammar could fail to draw on the wealth of information and accurate detail of the various grammars by Randolph Quirk, Sydney Greenbaum, Geoffrey Leech and Jan Svartvik. In addition, and within the systemic-functional tradition, we have been most influenced by some of the works of M. A. K. Halliday, in particular *An Introduction to Functional Grammar*. Many of Halliday's insights, together with the organisation of a great part of the book, and in particular his view of the clause and clause complex, have been adopted extensively; certain modifications, which Halliday might not agree with, have been made in order to suit the rather different learning objectives of our readers.

Other works on which we have drawn in the course of writing this grammar include Flor and Jan Aarts, *English Syntactic Structures*, Keith Allan, *Nouns and Countability*, D. J. Allerton, *Essentials of Grammatical Theory*, Margaret Berry, *Introduction to Systemic Linguistics*, D. Bolinger, *This and That*, and *Meaning and Form*, especially Chapter 2, E. K. Brown and J. E. Miller, *Syntax: A Linguistic Introduction to Sentence Structure*, Penelope Brown and Stephen C. Levinson, *Politeness: Some Universals in Language Usage*, C. S. Butler, *Systemic Linguistics, Theory and Practice*, F. Daneš, *Functional sentence perspective and the organization of the text*, Simón Dik, *The Theory of Functional Grammar*, Robin Fawcett, *Some Proposals for Systemic Syntax*, Talmy Givón, especially *Syntax, Volume I*, Georgia Green, especially *Pragmatics and Natural Language Understanding*, M. A. K. Halliday and Ruquaiya Hasan, *Cohesion in English*, Rodney Huddleston, *Introduction to the Grammar of English*, M. Leonetti Jungl, *Referencia y Sintagmas Nominales Genericas*, John Lyons, *Semantics*, Louise Ravelli, *Grammatical Metaphor: An Initial Analysis*, Sandra Thompson, especially 'Grammar and written discourse: initial v. final purpose clauses in English', David Young, *The Structure of English Clauses*.

This book therefore makes no claim to originality in its content. We hope to have made accessible to our students the kind of knowledge which may help them to become aware of the resources which English offers, and which may sharpen their curiosity to extend their reading to more comprehensive grammars and specialised works.

We have not considered it necessary, in a course-book of this kind, to indicate the source of every detail of our description, but if any writer feels that an acknowledgement is due, future rectification will be made.

We wish to thank David Haines and Isobel Fletcher de Téllez of Prentice Hall International for their unfailing patience and confidence in us; our friends and colleagues, especially Patricia Shaw (University of Oviedo), Carmen Olivares Rivera (University of Zaragoza), Vicente López Folgado (Universities of León and Córdoba), José Simón Granda (University of Alcalá de Henares), Joyce Greer (Instituto Universitario de Lenguas Modernas y Traductores, Universidad Complutense de Madrid), and Rachel Whittaker (Universidad Autónoma de Madrid), all of whom read and commented on parts of the manuscript; Ann Farrow and Juana Marín (Universidad Complutense de Madrid), who commented on the tasks; and Emilio Lorenzo Criado, of the Real Academia Española, who encouraged us to start in the first place. Thanks also to Jean Smears for allowing personal letters of hers to be published as illustrative texts, and to John Hollyman for spontaneous conversations recorded with some of his students at the University of Bristol.

We owe a special debt to Chris Butler for the generous sharing of his time and knowledge as our consultant in the final version of the manuscript. We are especially grateful for his suggestions for tightening up our description of the grammar, particularly in the syntactic areas. Needless to say, any deficiencies in the course-book are entirely our own responsibility.

We must also acknowledge our debt to our long-suffering families for their unending help and support.

Finally, we would not wish to forget our students, who have collaborated unwittingly with their many comments over the years in the elaboration of this book.

Angela Downing
Philip Locke

*Universidad Complutense
Madrid*

1

Basic concepts

MODULE 1
Language and meaning

1.1 Communicative acts

Let us start from the basic concept that language is for communication. Here is part of a recorded conversation taken from a sociological project of the University of Bristol. The speakers are Janice, a girl who runs a youth club and disco in an English town, and Chris, one of the boys in the club, who is 19 and works in a shop. In the dialogue, we can distinguish various types of communicative act, or **illocutionary act**, by which people communicate with each other: making statements, asking questions, giving directives with the aim of getting the hearer to carry out some action, making an offer or promise, thanking or expressing an exclamation.

Offer	J:	If you like, I'll come into your shop tomorrow and get some more model aeroplane kits.
Directive	C:	O.K. Don't forget to bring the bill with you this time.
Promise	J:	I won't.
Question		Do you enjoy working there?
Statements	C:	It's all right, I suppose. Gets a bit boring. It'll do for a while.
Statement	J:	I would have thought you were good at selling things.
Statement	C:	I don't know what to do really. I've had other jobs. My Dad keeps on at me to go into his business. He keeps offering me better wages,
Exclamation		but the last thing to do is to work for him!
Question	J:	Why?
Echo question	C:	Why? You don't know my old man! I
Exclamations		wouldn't work for him! He always
Statement		wanted me to, but we don't get on. . . .
Question		D'you think it's possible to get me on a part-time Youth Leadership Course?
Offer/Promise	J:	I'll ring up tomorrow, Chris, and find out for you.
Thanking	C:	Thanks a lot.

In a communicative exchange between speaker and hearer such as this, there are two basic kinds of **speech roles**: that of giving and that of demanding. The thing given or demanded may be essentially something linguistic, such as information, an opinion (e.g. *Do you enjoy working there? It's all right, I suppose.*) or it may be something non-linguistic, some type of 'goods or services', such as handing over the aeroplane kits, which may be verbalised but need not be. Typically, however, when goods and services are exchanged, verbal interaction takes place too; for instance, asking a favour (*D'you think it's possible to get me on a part-time Youth Leadership Course?*) or giving a promise (*I'll ring up tomorrow, Chris, and find out for you.*) are carried out verbally.

It can be appreciated that the kind of meaning expressed by the categories outlined here is **interpersonal** meaning. The grammatical forms in which these and other types of interpersonal communication are expressed are described, in this book, in Chapter 5.

1.2   The content of communication

Every illocutionary act, whether spoken or written, takes place in a social context. A telephone conversation, writing a letter, buying a newspaper, giving or attending a lecture, are all contexts within which the different illocutionary acts are carried out. Such contexts have to do with our own or someone else's experience of life and the world at large, that is the doings and happenings in which we are involved or which affect us.

Any happening or state in real life, or in an imaginary world of the mind, can be expressed through language as a **situation** or **state of affairs**. Used in this way, the terms 'situation' or 'state of affairs' do not refer directly to an extralinguistic reality which exists in the real world, but rather to the speaker's conceptualisation of it. The components of this conceptualisation of reality are **semantic roles** or **functions** and may be described in very general terms as follows:

1   **processes**: that is, actions, events, states, types of behaviour;
2   **participants**: that is, entities of all kinds, animate and inanimate, concrete and abstract, that are involved in the processes;
3   **attributes**: that is, qualities and characteristics of the participants;
4   **circumstances**: that is, any kind of contingent fact or subsidiary situation which is associated with the process or the main situation.

The following example from the text shows one possible configuration of certain semantic roles:

I	'll come	into your shop	tomorrow
participant	process	circumstance	circumstance

The kind of meaning expressed by these elements of semantic structure is experiential meaning or meaning that has to do with the content of the message. The types of process, participants, attributes and circumstances are dealt with in Chapter 4.

1.3   Three ways of interpreting clause structure

The basic unit for the expression of interpersonal and experiential meanings is the independent clause, equivalent to the traditional 'simple sentence'. There is also a third type of component, the textual, which enables the experiential and interpersonal components to cohere as a message, not simply as a sentence in isolation, but in relation to what precedes it in the linguistic co-text. Each kind of meaning is expressed by its own structures; the three types of structure combining to produce one single realisation in words.

To summarise, the three kinds of meaning and structure derive from the consideration of a clause as: (a) the linguistic representation of our experience of the world; (b) a communicative exchange between persons; (c) an organised message or text.

1.3.1   The clause as representation: transitivity structures

The experiential meaning of the clause is realised through the transitivity structures, whose elements of structure or functions include: Agent, Recipient, Affected, Process, Attribute and Circumstance, as described in Chapter 4. Some of these make up the semantic structure of the following example:

Janice	will give	Chris	the address	tomorrow
Agent	Process (action)	Recipient	Affected	Circumstance (time)

With a process of 'doing' such as the action of giving, the Agent is that participant which carries out the action referred to by the verb; the Recipient is that participant to whom the action is directed and who receives the 'goods' or 'information' expressed as the Affected. Circumstances attending the process are classified as locative, temporal, conditional, concessive, causal, resultant, etc.

1.3.2   The clause as exchange: mood structures

When a speaker interacts with others to exchange information or to influence their behaviour and get things done, he adopts for himself a certain role, such as 'questioner' and, in doing so, assigns a complementary role, such as 'informant', to his addressee. Unless the conversation is very one-sided, the roles of 'questioner' and 'informant' tend to alternate between the interlocutors engaged in a conversation, as can be seen in the exchange of speech roles between Chris and Janice in the text on page 2.

The clause is the major grammatical unit used by speakers to ask questions, make statements and issue directives. The exchange of information is typically carried out by the indicative mood, as opposed to directives, which are typically expressed by the imperative. Within the indicative, making a statement is associated characteristically with the declarative, and asking a question with the interrogative. More exactly, it is one part of these structures, which we call the 'Mood element', which carries the syntactic burden of the exchange. The rest of the clause remains unchanged, and can therefore be called the Residue, as is shown below for declarative and interrogative:

Declarative

Janice	will	give	Chris	the address	tomorrow
Subject	Finite				
Mood element		Residue			

Interrogative

Will	Janice	give	Chris	the address	tomorrow?
Finite	Subject				
Mood element		Residue			

It can be seen that the mood structures are characterised by the presence or absence of a Subject element and by the relative positions of the Subject and the Finite, the Finite being that element which relates the content of the clause to the speech event. It does this by specifying a time reference, through tense, or by expressing an attitude of the speaker, through modality. Also associated with finiteness, although less explicitly in many cases in English, are person and number. The Finite element is realised in the examples above by the modal auxiliary *will*.

Mood structures and the meanings they convey are treated in Chapter 5.

1.3.3   The clause as message: thematic structures

Here, the speaker organises the informational content of the clause so as to establish whatever point of departure is desired for the message. This is called the 'Theme', which in English coincides with the initial element or elements of the clause. The rest of the clause is the Rheme:

Janice	will give	Chris	the address	tomorrow
Theme	Rheme			

The Theme may coincide with one of the participants, as in this example, or it may 'set the scene' by coinciding with an initial expression of time, place, etc. These possibilities are illustrated in 1.3.4.

1.3.4 Combining the three types of structure

The three types of structure we have briefly introduced are examined more closely in Chapters 4, 5 and 6. Here, they are mapped simultaneously on to the example clause, in order to show the tripartite nature and analysis of English clauses from a functional point of view. Predicator, Indirect and Direct Objects and Adjunct are included as clause elements which fall within the Residue:

	Janice	will give	Chris	the address	tomorrow
Experiential	Agent	Process	Recipient	Affected	Circumstance
Interpersonal	Subject	Finite + Predicator	Indirect Object	Direct Object	Adjunct
Textual	Theme	Rheme			

In a typical declarative clause such as this, Agent, Subject and Theme coincide and are realised in one wording, in this case *Janice*. But in natural language use, a situation can be expressed in different ways, in which the order of clause elements can vary, since different elements of structure can be moved to initial position. Our present example admits at least the following possible variants:

1 Chris   will be given the address by Janice tomorrow.
2 The address   will be given to Chris tomorrow by Janice.
3 The address   Janice will give Chris tomorrow.
4 The address   Janice will give it to Chris tomorrow.
5 Tomorrow,   Chris will be given the address (by Janice).
6 Tomorrow,   the address will be given to Chris by Janice.

It can be seen that the three types of structural elements do not coincide (vertically) in the same way as they do in the typical canonical clause. For example:

(a) Theme coincides with Subject in 1 and 2, with Direct Object in 3 and 4 and with Adjunct in 5 and 6.
(b) Agent no longer coincides with Theme in any of the variants. In 1 the Recipient is Theme; in 2, 3 and 4 the Affected is Theme.

The configurations for 1 are illustrated below:

Chris	will be given	the address	by Janice	tomorrow
Recipient	Process	Affected	Agent	Circumstance
Subject	Finite + Predicator	Direct Object	Adjunct	Adjunct
Theme	Rheme			

The configurations for 6 are as follows:

Tomorrow,	the address	will be given	to Chris	by Janice
Circumstance	Affected	Process	Recipient	Agent
Adjunct	Subject	Finite + Predicator	Oprep	Circumstance
Theme	Rheme			

The motivation for this and the other variants is not to be sought in the clause in isolation, but in its relationship to that part of the discourse at which it is located. The speaker organises the content of the clause in order to establish the point of departure of the clausal message and to highlight that constituent which is presented as New information, usually at the end of the clause. By choosing 1, for example, *Chris* becomes the point of departure while *tomorrow* is still in final position, with the Agent nearing final position. By using the passive, the Agent could be omitted altogether, leaving the Affected, *the address*, in final position if the Adjunct is fronted, as in 5. By means of such reorganisations of the clausal message, the content of the clause can be made to relate to the rest of the discourse and to the communicative context in which it is produced.

The textual motivations outlined in the previous paragraph and the syntactic strategies which serve to produce different kinds of clausal message are examined in Chapter 6.

We will now look at the full range of grammatical units on a scale in which the clause is central. We will then look briefly at the unit above the clause, the 'clause complex', and the units immediately below the clause, the 'groups'.

MODULE 2
Linguistic forms and syntactic functions

2.1   Syntactic categories and relationships

In this module we shall outline the basic syntactic concepts on which our structural analysis is based. These include the structural **units** which can be arranged on a scale of **rank**, the **classes** into which these units can be divided, and the **elements** of which they are composed. We shall also consider the relationship of **realisation** by means of which the units of one rank are related to those of another.

2.2   Testing for constituents

Before attempting to see how a stretch of language can be broken down into units, it is useful to be able to reinforce our intuitions as to where boundaries lie. This can be done by applying certain tests in order to identify whether a particular stretch of language is a constituent of a higher unit or not.

For instance, the following stretch of language is ambiguous:

> Muriel saw the man in the service station

Two interpretations are possible, according to how the units are grouped into constituents. In version (i) the Prepositional Group *in the service station* forms part of the constituent whose head word is *man* (*the man in the service station*) and tells us something about the man; whereas in version (ii) the same Prepositional Group functions separately as a constituent of the whole stretch of language in question and tells us where Muriel saw the man. Evidence for this analysis can be sought by such operations as (a) coordination, (b) *WH*-questions, (c) clefting, (d) passivisation and (e)fronting. Tests (b) to (e) involve moving the stretch of language around and observing its syntactic behaviour. Testing by coordination involves adding a conjoin which realises the same function; only stretches of language which realise the same function can be conjoined.

(a) It can be seen that different types of conjoin are required according to the function of *in the service station*:

> (i)   Muriel saw *the man in the service station* and *the woman in the shop.*

(ii)   Muriel saw the man *in the service station* and *in the shop.*

(b) The *WH*-question form and the appropriate response will be different for the two versions:

(i)   *Who* did Muriel see? – *The man in the service station.*
(ii) *Where* did Muriel see the man? – *In the service station.*

(c) Clefting by means of *it* + *that*-clause highlights a clause constituent (see 30.1) and thus yields two different results:

(i)   It was *the man in the service station* that Muriel saw.
(ii) It was *in the service station* that Muriel saw the man.

WH-clefting (see 30.2) gives the same result:

(i)   The one Muriel saw was *the man in the service station.*
(ii) Where Muriel saw the man was *in the service station.*

The form *the one (that …)* is used in this construction since English does not admit *who* (**Who Muriel saw was the man in the service station*).

(d) Passivisation likewise keeps together those units or bits of language that form a constituent:

(i)   *The man in the service station* was seen by Muriel.
(ii) The man was seen by Muriel *in the service station.*

(e) A constituent can be fronted, that is brought to initial position:

(i)   *The man in the service station* Muriel saw.
(ii) *In the service station* Muriel saw the man.

It is not always the case that a stretch of text responds equally well to all five types of test. Certain types of unit may resist one or more of these operations; for instance, the frequency adverbs *often* and *usually* resist clefting (**It's often / usually that Muriel saw the man in the service station)*, whereas the verbal element of a clause resists fronting (**Saw Muriel the man in the service station*). Nevertheless, if two or more of the operations can be carried out satisfactorily, we can be reasonably sure that the stretch of language in question is a constituent of a larger unit.

We now turn to the description of units, their classes and the relationship holding between them.

2.3   Units and rank of units

The moving around of bits of language, as carried out in 2.2, suggests that language is not a series of words strung together like beads on a string. Language is patterned, that is, certain regularities can be distinguished throughout every linguistic manifestation in a text. A **unit** will be defined as any stretch of language which constitutes a semantic whole and which has a recognised pattern that is repeated regularly in speech and writing. For instance, the previous sentence is a unit containing other units such as *a recognised pattern* and *in speech and writing*. Sequences such as *defined as any* and *repeated regularly in* which also occur in the same sentence do not constitute units since they have no semantic whole and no syntactic pattern. The following stretch of language which comments on the effects of a nuclear accident constitutes one syntactic unit which is composed of further units:

> The effects of the accident are very serious.

In English, it is useful to recognise four structural units which can be arranged in order of magnitude on what is called a **rank-scale**:

Unit	Boundary marker	Example
Clause:	//	// the effects of the accident are very serious //
Group:	/	/ the effects of the accident / are / very serious /
Word:	a space	the effects of the accident are very serious
Morpheme:	+	{EFFECT} + {PLURAL}, realised by the morphs *effect* and -*s*.

For the initial stages of analysis it may be helpful to mark off the boundaries of each unit by a symbol, such as those adopted in the example. The symbol for 'clause boundary' is //, that for 'group boundary' is /, that for 'word boundary' is simply a space, as is conventionally used in the written language. The independent clause is the equivalent of the traditional 'simple sentence'. Combinations of clauses, the boundaries symbolised by ///, are introduced in 3.1.1 and treated more fully in Chapter 7.

The relationship holding between the units is, in principle, as follows: each unit consists of one or more units of the rank below it. Thus, a clause consists of groups, a group consists of words and a word consists of morphemes. For instance, *Wait!* consists of one clause, which consists of one group, which consists of one word, which consists of one morpheme. More exactly, we shall say that the elements of structure of each unit are realised by units of the rank below.

However, as we shall see in 3.1.2 and in later chapters, units may be 'embedded' within other units, such as the clause *who live in the north* within the Nominal Group *people who live in the north*. Similarly, the Prepositional Group *of the accident* is embedded in the Nominal Group *the effects of the accident*.

We shall be concerned in this book mainly with the units clause and group. The structure and constituents of these units will be described in later sections, together with their functions and meanings.

2.4 Classes of units

At each rank of linguistic unit mentioned in 2.3, there are various classes of unit.

2.4.1 Classes of clauses

At the rank of 'clause', the first distinction to be made is that between **independent** and **dependent** clauses. An independent clause (indep.cl) is complete in itself, whereas a dependent clause (dep.cl) is necessarily related to an independent clause. This is illustrated in:

> They locked up the house (indep.cl), before they went on holiday (dep.cl).

A further necessary distinction is that between **finite** and **non-finite** clauses, and this depends on the form of the verb chosen. If the speaker wishes to express tense, person or number, a 'finite' form of the verb is chosen, such as *is, eats, locked, went* and the clause is then called a finite clause (Clf). For example, all the verbs, and therefore the clauses, in the following paragraph are finite:

> /// I *had* a farm in Africa, at the foot of the Ngong hills. [1] /// The Equator *runs* across these highlands, a hundred miles to the north, [2] // and // the farm *lay* at an altitude of over six thousand feet. [3] //// In the daytime you *felt* that you *had got* high up, near to the sun, [4] // but // the early mornings and evenings *were* limpid and restful, [5] // and // the nights *were* cold. [6] ////
>
> Karen Blixen, *Out of Africa*.

If the verb-form does not express this type of information about the verbal 'process', the verb and the clause are classified as 'non-finite' (Clnf). The non-finite verb forms are: (a) the **infinitive** (inf.) (*be, eat, lock, go*), which may be preceded by *to* and is then called the ***to*-infinitive** (*to*-inf), the participial *-ing* form (*-ing*) (*being, eating, locking, going*) and the past participial form, symbolised in this book as *-en* (*been, eaten, locked, gone*). Most of these non-finite verb forms are illustrated in the following passage:

> Three men, *cramped* [1] together on their bellies in a dead end, were doing their best *to revive* [2] another man who lay in a huddled attitude, his body *slewed* [3] sideways, one shoulder *pointing* [4] backwards, *lost*, [5] seemingly, in the mass of rock behind him.
>
> A. J. Cronin, *The Citadel*.

All independent clauses are finite, as can be seen in the examples above. Dependent clauses can be either finite or non-finite. In our earlier example

They locked up the house before they went on holiday, the finite dependent clause *before they went on holiday* can be replaced by a non-finite clause *before going on holiday*.

In a sentence such as *He saw that the bottles were empty*, the clause [*that the bottles were empty*] is embedded as a constituent of the clause *he saw x*. In such cases the clause without the embedded constituent is called the **superordinate** clause.

A subsidiary type is composed of **minor** clauses (Clm). These are clauses which lack all or part of the Mood element (Subject + Finite) and are therefore 'moodless'. The omitted verb is typically a form of *be* and is recoverable from the context or the co-text; e.g.

> Take travellers' cheques abroad, *whenever possible*. (= whenever *it is* possible)
> *Though rather too rich for some of us*, the food was excellent.
> (= Though *it was* rather too rich for some of us)

Further instances occur in the following extract:

> Man, apes and monkeys can all be observed to cry out *when in pain*, flush *when enraged*, yawn *when tired*, glare *when defiant*, grin *when tickled*, tremble *when afraid*, embrace *when affectionate*, bare their teeth *when hostile*, raise their eyebrows *when surprised*, and turn their heads away *when offended*.
>
> Elaine Morgan, *The Descent of Woman*.

We shall also classify as minor, 'moodless' clauses many irregular constructions such as the following:
(a) *WH*-questions without a finite verb:

> Why not sell your car and get a new one?
> How about a nice glass of beer?
> What if the roof leaks while we're away?

(b) Adjuncts with the force of a command, sometimes with a Subject:

> Hands off!
> Into the shelter, everybody!

(c) Proverbs of the type *Out of sight, out of mind*.

Finally, we shall call **abbreviated clauses** those such as *can you? I won't, has she?* which consist of the Mood element alone, with the rest of the clause ellipted because it is known. These clauses typically occur as responses or initiators in conversational exchanges (see 22.3), but may express illocutionary acts such as reprimand (*Must you?*), given an appropriate social context.

2.4.2 Classes of groups

Groups are classified according to the class of word operating as the main or 'head' element. That is to say, we can identify the following classes:

Nominal Groups	(NG)	*films,*	wonderful *films* by Fellini
Verbal Groups	(VG)	*return,*	is going to *return*
Adjectival Groups	(AdjG)	*good,*	very *good* at languages
Adverbial Groups	(AdvG)	*fluently,*	more *fluently* than before

Units such as groups, which centre round one main element which proto-typically cannot be omitted, are said to be 'endocentric'. We shall, however, recognise as a group one structure which is not endocentric, but 'exocentric', that is, consisting of two elements neither of which is subordinate to the other. This is the Prepositional Group (PrepG) as in *just around the corner.*

In an endocentric structure, the main element can replace the whole structure: *films, good* and *fluently* can have the same syntactic functions as the whole group of which each is head. In a PrepG, by contrast, neither the preposition (e.g. *round*) nor its completive (e.g. *the corner*) can have the same syntactic functions as the whole unit *round the corner.* However, since the two elements combine to function as a single element, we are justified in giving the combination the grammatical status of a 'group'. Moreover, since it is the preposition which characterises this particular combination of words, we shall regard it as the main element and use its name as the name of the group.

2.4.3 Classes of words

Words are classified grammatically according to the traditional terminology, which includes **noun, verb, adjective, adverb, preposition, pronoun, article** and **conjunction**. Words are made up of morphemes.

2.4.4 Classes of morphemes

We shall consider the morpheme to be an abstract category which has either a lexical or a grammatical meaning. We have already indicated in 2.3 that a word such as *effects* can be considered as formed from the lexical mor-pheme {Effect} + the {PLURAL} morpheme. These abstract categories are realised by **morphs** such as *effect* and −s or /ifekt/ and /s/, the actual segments of written and spoken language, respectively.

Since the study of words and morphemes takes us out of syntax and into morphology and phonology, the scope of this book does not allow for further treatment of these units.

2.5   The concept of unit structure

The term 'structure' refers to the relationships that exist between the small units that make up a larger unit. For example, the basic components of a table are a flat board and four long thin pieces of wood or metal, but these elements do not constitute a structure until they are related to each other as a horizontal top supported at the corners by four vertical legs. In this way, each 'element' is given its position and its 'function', which together we may call the 'grammar' of all those members of the general class of objects called 'table'.

Everything in our lives has structure. A house may be built of bricks, but its structure consists of rooms having different formal, functional and distributional characteristics. Tables, chairs, cars, all objects are composed of functionally related 'formal items'; and the same applies to activities (speeches, conversations, plays, concerts, football matches) or events (explosions, accidents, heart attacks). It is natural that languages, which are the spoken and written representation of our experience of all these things, are also manifested in structured forms. Linguistic structures are described in terms of the semantic functions of their various elements and the syntactic forms and relationships which express them.

We have seen in 1.3 a brief preview of the main semantic elements of the clause, together with some of the possible configurations produced by the combinations of these elements. Groups, whose function it is to express the things, processes, qualities and circumstances of our experience, also have semantic elements and structures. These are different for each type of group and are treated in the relevant chapter on each of these classes of unit. Here we shall briefly present the syntactic elements of all ranks of unit.

2.5.1   Syntactic elements of clauses

Clauses have the greatest number of syntactic elements of all classes of unit. The criteria for their identification, the syntactic features and the realisations of each are examined in Chapter 2. Here we simply list and exemplify the clause elements within basic clause structures. The type of structure used in order to express a 'situation' or 'state of affairs' depends to a great extent on the verb chosen. Verb complementation types are treated in Chapter 3.

Subject (S)	*Fog* is dangerous on motorways.	SPCsA
Predicator (P)	The election campaign *ended* today.	SPA
Direct Object (Od)	Ted has bought *a new motorbike.*	SPOd
Indirect Object (Oi)	They sent *their friends* postcards.	SPOiOd
Prepositional Object (Oprep)	You must allow *for price increases.*	SPOprep
Subject Complement (Cs)	He is *powerless to make any changes.*	SPCs
Object Complement (Co)	We consider the situation *alarming.*	SPOdCo

Predicator	She tiptoed *out of the room.*	SPCp
Complement (Cp)		
Adjunct (A)	The news reached us *on Tuesday.*	SPOdA
Disjunct (D)	*Unfortunately,* it was too late	
	to get to Newcastle in time.	DSPCs
Conjunct (Conj)	*However,* other friends were	ConjSPA
	there.	

2.5.2   Syntactic elements of groups

Nominal Groups, Adjectival Groups and Adverbial Groups are composed of three primary elements: a head **(h)** preceded by a modifier **(m)** and followed by a qualifier **(q)**. These last two elements are sometimes called 'premodifier' and 'postmodifier'. The term 'qualifier' is preferred here, because the two elements tend to express different types of information about the 'head', and also because this permits the use of two different symbols **(m** and **q)** in the structural notation.

In the case of **Nominal Groups**, we also distinguish between 'modifiers', which describe or classify the head, and 'determiners' **(d)** which specify it in terms of definiteness, quantity, possessiveness, etc. Thus, we give the determiner, the modifier and the qualifier equal syntactic status as primary elements of Nominal Groups. The following are examples of these group structures:

NG:	dmhq:	those / beautiful / paintings / by Goya
AdjG:	mhq:	extremely / difficult / to translate
AdvG:	mhq:	very / carefully / indeed

In **Verbal Groups**, the lexical verb is regarded as the main element **(v)**, which either functions alone, in both finite or non-finite forms, as in the example ***Walking*** *along the street, I* ***met*** *a friend of mine*, or is preceded by auxiliaries **(x)**, as in *will go* or *has been reading*. The first auxiliary (or the auxiliary if there is only one) is called the 'operator' **(o)**. It is the element that contributes information about tense, modality, number and person, and so helps to make the VG finite and fully 'operative'. It is also the element that operates in the Mood structures to make the clause interrogative, and to make ellipted responses:

Have you been driving for many years? – Yes, I *have.*
Do you enjoy driving? – Yes, I *do.*

Verbal Group structures are illustrated as follows:

v:	plays
ov:	has / played
oxv:	will / be / playing
oxxv:	must / have / been / played

The lexical verb is sometimes followed by an adverbial particle (symbolised by '**o**') as in *ring up, break out, take over*. Although the particle frequently forms an integral part of the meaning of the lexical verb, and in fact can often be replaced by a simple verb form (*ring up* = *telephone*; *break out* = *escape, erupt*), it can be separated from the verb as in *I'll ring you up, They've taken it over*, and we therefore analyse the particle as a separate element of structure. Phrasal verbs and other multi-word combinations are discussed in Chapter 8.

In **Prepositional Groups** there are two obligatory elements: the prepositional head **(h)** and the complement or 'completive' **(c)**. There is also an optional modifier **(m)** usually realised by an adverb of degree (e.g. *right, quite*). The structure of PrepGs is illustrated as follows:

mhc:　right / across / the road
　　　quite / out of / practice

2.5.3　Componence, realisation and function

Any structure can be considered to be composed of elements which form a configuration of 'functions', whether semantic functions such as Agent–Process–Affected or syntactic functions such as the clause configuration Subject–Predicator–Direct Object or the modifier–head–qualifier structure of the Nominal Group.

Each of these functions is in turn realised by a unit which is itself, at least potentially, a configuration of functions, and these in turn are realised by others until the final stage is reached and abstract categories such as Subject, head, modifier, etc., are realised by the segments of the spoken or written language. The following 'structural tree' diagrams this model of analysis at the three unit ranks of clause, group and word, to illustrate the clause *The bus strike will affect many people tomorrow*:

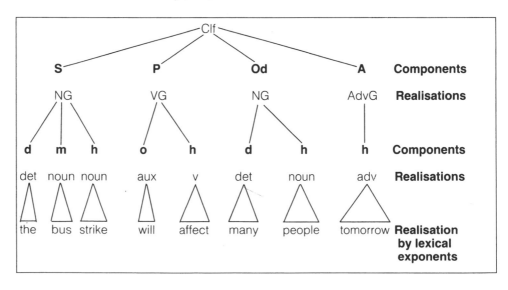

An important property of language is the fact that there is no one-to-one correspondence between the class of unit and its function. While it is true that certain classes of unit *typically* realise certain functions, Nominal Groups at Subject and Object functions, for instance, it is nevertheless also true that many classes of unit can fulfil many different functions, and different functions are realised by many different classes of unit. For instance, the NG *next time* can fulfil the following clause functions, among others:

Subject: *Next time* will be better.
Adjunct: I'll know better *next time*.
Direct
  Object: We'll enjoy *next time*.

The nearest to a one-to-one relationship in the grammar is that between the verbal process, realised by the Predicator, which is then realised by a Verbal Group. But even this relationship can be disturbed by the alternative realisation of semantic functions known as 'grammatical metaphor' (see Module 21). Common occurrences of this phenomenon are nominalisations (see 50.10) such as *our evening walk along the river*, which expresses the action of walking as if it were an entity, consequently producing a slightly different effect from the basic realisation *we walked in the evening along the river*.

This many-to-many relationship is fundamental for the understanding of the relationship of the grammar of English to text. By this it is not implied that a text is a kind of super-sentence, a grammatical unit that is simply 'larger' than a sentence and with the same kind of relationship holding between its parts as that which holds between grammatical units. A text is quite different in kind from a grammatical unit. It is, rather than grammatical, a semantic unit of whatever length, spoken or written, and which forms a unified whole, with respect both to its internal properties and to the social context in which it is produced. A text is encoded by or realised by various types of semantic unit, which in turn are realised by syntactic units. In this book, although we start from the grammar rather than from the text, the relationship between the two is of primary interest.

MODULE 3
Expanding linguistic units

3.1   Simple and complex

Each of the linguistic units outlined above has been illustrated by single occurrences of that unit, for instance, one Nominal Group functioning at Subject or Direct Object, one modifier of an adjective or an adverb. Sometimes our everyday communication requires no more. But each unit can be expanded in more than one way, to enable the speaker or writer to add further information which is, nevertheless, contained within the chosen structure at any point in the discourse. In this module we give a brief overview of the ways in which linguistic units can be expanded.

3.1.1   Unit complexes

One way of expanding a unit is to repeat that unit more than once, producing what we shall call a **unit complex,** + symbolising a paratactic relationship, × a hypotactic relationship. Examples of each unit complex are as follows:

Clause **+/× clause = clause complex**

> /// While many citizens are suffering from stress and anxiety // × the effects of the accident are less serious than many had feared.///

group +/× group = group complex

NG + NG	many citizens and a number of agricultural workers
VG + VG	had feared and had suspected
AdjG × AdjG	happy though poor
AdvG × AdvG	slowly if rather painfully
PrepG + PrepG	over the wall and into the garden

word +/× word = word complex

> *can though need not* stay
> had *feared or suspected*
> *if* and *when* you have time

morpheme + morpheme = morpheme complex

pre- and post-operative care
pro- and anti-abortionists

'Sentence' is the term traditionally used to denote the highest grammatical unit on a scale of rank. While not rejecting this term, we shall prefer, however, to use the term 'clause complex' to refer to units of two or more related clauses such as those of the example above. 'Sentence' can then be used as the orthographical unit which comes between full stops. Discussion of the terms 'sentence' and 'clause complex' and their usefulness for linguistic analysis is to be found in Module 31.

The concept of unit complexes facilitates the reading of long units that might otherwise appear complicated, as can be seen with the following clause complex:

Over the next decade, automation and the mechanisation of production [1] will improve and transform [2] farming, industrial plants and service industries [3] and also make our leisure time more productive, creative and interesting.[4]

[1] group complex (NG + NG); [2] word complex (main verb + main verb); [3] group complex (NG + NG + NG); [4] word complex (adj. + adj. + adj.).

In the case of clause complexes, if the various conjoined clauses share the same Subject or the same operator, these elements are regularly ellipted because they are recoverable (see 29.3), and the rest of the predication may be analysed as a clause. This occurs in the above example where the sequence *automation and the mechanisation of production* is ellipted, as is *will*, before the Predicator *make*.

Ellipsis similarly occurs in group structures, as in the above example, where in one interpretation of (4), the modifier *more* is ellipted before *creative* and *interesting*.

3.1.2   Expanding units by coordination, subordination and embedding

Looking at the linguistic expansion of the message from another angle, we can say that each element of structure can be realised more than once. This property of language to repeat any unit indefinitely is sometimes called **recursion**. It accounts to a great extent for our everyday creative use of language, although it is clear that it can also be abused. One might say but not write the following:

(a)   I left the house at 9 a.m. and went to the bus-stop and got on a bus, but I had forgotten my purse so I had to get off and go back home for it and then I went to the market and did some shopping and after that ... *ad infinitum*

It would, however, be natural if divided into utterances composed of three elements, as in version (b):

(b)   I left the house at 9 a.m., went to the bus-stop and got on a bus. However, I had forgotten my purse, so I had to get off and go back home for it. Then I went to the market, did some shopping and returned home. After that ...

There are two types of relationship which link elements: a coordinating relationship, if the elements are of equal grammatical status; or a subordinating relationship if the elements are of unequal grammatical status, one being subordinate to or dependent on the other. The first type may be called 'paratactic expansion', the second 'hypotactic expansion'. Both relationships may be realised syndetically (by a conjunction) or asyndetically (without a conjunction, but by a comma in writing and a slight pause in speech).

The following are examples of coordination of various classes of elements:

dependent clauses:
I will take a holiday *when the course is over* + *and if I pass the exam* + *and also provided I can afford it.*
modifier in a NG
She says she is looking for a *handsome,* + *intelligent* + *and, above all,* + *rich* husband.
modifier in an AdjG
He says he is *really* + *and truly* sorry for what happened.
Adjuncts in a clause
You can put in the application *now* + *or in a month's time* + *or else next year.*

Similarly, the following are examples of subordination of various classes of elements:

dependent clauses
I'll let you borrow the tapes (*as soon as I've finished*) (*provided you bring them back (when I need them)*).

In this clause complex the fourth clause *when I need them* is dependent on the third clause *provided you bring them back*; these together form a block which is dependent on the block formed by the first (independent) clause *I'll let you borrow the tapes* and its dependent clause *as soon as I've finished*.

Cs in a clause
He is *quite brilliant (though totally unreliable).*
modifier in a NG
A *very lovable, (if rather dirty),* small boy
(((Passenger) train) speed) regulations
determiner in a NG
(((Tom's) sister's) husband's) mother

Adjuncts in a clause
We arrived (*late (though not too late)*) for the wedding.

A third way of expanding the content and the structure of a linguistic unit is to realise one or more of its elements by a unit of the same rank as itself (a clause as element of a clause, or a group as element of a group), or by a unit of higher rank (a clause as element of a group). This type of expansion, known as 'embedding', and indicated by enclosure in square brackets, is found in elements such as the following:

clause at **S:**   [*That he left so abruptly*] doesn't surprise me.
clause at **Od:**   I don't know [*why he left so abruptly*].
clause at **c:**   I'm pleased about [*Jane winning a prize*].
clause at **q:**   Thanks for the card [*you sent me*].

Parallel to the exaggerated example of coordination quoted above, the following equally exaggerated sequence illustrates the theoretical possibility of infinite expansion by progressive embedding:

I couldn't get out of the house because of the snow [piled up against the back door [that opens on to the path [leading down to a road [which goes over a new bridge [near the town [where I live with my parents [who bought the house [we live in. . . .]]]]]]]]

The following news item contains a moderate amount of expansion by coordination, subordination and embedding:

In a Californian national park a crowd of anxious animal lovers recently gathered round a tree (to watch a humane rescue). [1] A black bear, [stuck up the tree], [2] had become distressed, (flapping its limbs alarmingly). [3] A squad of park rangers, [armed with tranquilliser darts and supervised by vets], [4] shot the unfortunate beast, (but the drugged animal remained [entangled in the branches]). [5] [6] (Only after ladders were called for and the creature was brought down into the comforting arms of the crowd), [7] [8] did they discover [that they had spent eight hours (watching the rescue of a black plastic rubbish bag)]. [9] [10].

Jim White, *The Independent*, 13 January 1991.

[1] main clause and subordinate clause *to watch a humane rescue*; [2] embedding of Clnf (*stuck up the tree*) as qualifier of *a black bear*; [3] main clause and subordinate clause (*flapping its limbs alarmingly*); [4] coordination of two non-finite clauses (*armed . . . and supervised . . .*), both embedded as qualifiers of *park rangers*; [5] coordination of two finite clauses by *but*; [6] embedding of Clnf (*entangled in the branches*) as Complement (Cs); [7] Clf *Only after . . .* subordinated to following main clause *did they discover . . .*; [8] this subordinate Clf itself coordinated with another Clf *and the creature . . .*; [9] embedding of *that*-clause as object of *discovered*; [10] subordinate clause within the *that*-clause, *watching. . . .*

TASKS ON CHAPTER 1
Basic concepts

Module 1

1   †*For each of the following clauses say whether a participant or a circumstance has been chosen as Theme:*
1) Main Street is usually crowded on late shopping nights.
2) The girls armed with hockey-sticks chased the burglar.
3) Quite by accident I came across a very rare postage-stamp.
4) Away in the distance you can see Mount Kilimanjaro.
5) What I am going to tell you must not be repeated.

2   †*In each of the following clauses say whether the Subject, the Direct Object or the Adjunct has been chosen as Theme:*
1) About fifty or sixty thousand years ago, there lived on earth a creature similar to man.
2) Skulls and bones of this extinct species of man were found at Neanderthal.
3) Where the first true men originated we do not know.
4) These newcomers eventually drove the Neanderthalers out of existence.
5) In Asia or Africa there may be still undiscovered deposits of earlier and richer human remains.

Module 2

3   †*Look at the stretches of language below and apply the tests outlined in Module 2.2 to answer the questions following them:*
1) The little boy in the red jersey is making a sand castle on the beach.
    (a) Is *the little boy* a constituent of the whole stretch of language?
    (b) Is *on the beach* a constituent?
    (c) Is *in the red jersey* a constituent?
    (d) Is *castle* a constituent?
2) Tom happened to take the road to the factory by mistake.
    (a) Is *the road* a constituent?
    (b) Is *to the factory* a constituent?
    (c) Is *by mistake* a constituent?
    (d) Is *happened* a constituent?

4   †*Identify each of the uncontextualised clauses listed below as*

(a) independent; (b) dependent finite; (c) dependent non-finite;
(d) abbreviated; (e) minor. Punctuation and capitals have been omitted.

1) the complacency of the present government amazes me
2) although presumed dead
3) not being a tele-viewer myself
4) as I am the principal at a large boarding-school for girls
5) her future husband she met on a course for playleaders
6) I certainly will
7) while on vacation in Bali
8) because he is over-qualified for this job
9) just when he was starting to get himself organised
10) we'll probably get only a fraction of the factory's worth

5 †*Say to which class of group each of the following belongs:*
1) the anti-terrorist laws
2) not quite hot enough
3) within three quarters of an hour
4) pretty soon
5) aren't playing
6) wide awake
7) the urban young
8) in spite of the bad weather
9) his departure from Moscow
10) over there

Module 3
6 †*Read the text below, and then answer the questions which follow:*

'Does she [1] or doesn't she?' [2] The fashionable answer nowadays is always a louder and louder yes. [3] From Manhattan to Los Angeles a sunburst of bold, exotic, and decidedly unnatural colors, is streaking, squiggling and dotting across the hairstyles of the nation's trendy younger set, [4] and even making inroads among more mature professionals. [5] The startling palette of reds and blues, golds and silvers, greens and purples comes from inexpensive temporary hair-coloring products, [6] that are easily applied at home [7] and almost as easily showered away. [8] Confrontational coloration, once a shocking British and American punk emblem, [9] is now celebrated as the sleek plumage of the up-and-coming yuppie generation. [10]
'Turning brown, red and green' in *TIME*, 15 December 1986.

1) Say which of the numbered clauses are (a) finite independent; (b) finite embedded; (c) abbreviated; (d) minor.
2) Which of the numbered clauses are in a coordinating relationship?
3) Which of these clauses have ellipted elements?
4) Identify as many recursive elements as you can in the text. Do you consider the choice of recursive elements to have any special importance in this article?

2

The skeleton of the message:
Introduction to clause structure

MODULE 4
Syntactic elements and structures of the clause

Summary

1   The independent clause (or simple sentence) has two basic constituents: Subject and Predicate.

2   The Predicate may consist simply of the Predicator realised by a Verbal Group such as *disappeared* in *Tom disappeared*, or of a Predicator followed by one or more nuclear constituents, as in *All the men wore dark suits*, *He handed me a telegram*, *Your idea sounds great*. These nuclear elements are the complements, using the term **complement** in a general sense.

3   Within this category we distinguish more specifically three types of Object (Direct, Indirect and Prepositional) and three types of Complement (Subject Complement, Object Complement and Predicator Complement).

4   In addition, the clause may contain optional, non-nuclear elements which express inessential circumstances. These are the Adjuncts, which are always omissible.

5   All Objects and Complements differ from Adjuncts in being conditioned by verb type and limited in number.

6   Less integrated in the clause are the Disjuncts and the Conjuncts.

7   The symbols used are as follows:

Subject S	Predicator P	Direct Object	Od
		Indirect Object	Oi
		Prepositional Object	OPrep
		Subject Complement	Cs
		Object Complement	Co
		Predicator Complement	Cp
Adjunct A	Disjunct D	Conjunct Conj.	

4.1   Elements of clause structure

Traditionally, the clause (or simple sentence) is divided into two basic constituents, Subject and Predicate, as in the examples:

Subject	Predicate
The plane	is landing.
Tom	disappeared suddenly after the concert.

For the purpose of analysing and creating texts it is helpful to see how the Predicate is made up, since this tends to be the most informative part of the clause. A first distinction can be made between elements that are obligatory or nuclear, and elements that are optional or non-nuclear. This can be seen from the example *Tom disappeared suddenly after the concert.*

In this clause *suddenly* and *after the concert* are not essential, syntactically or semantically, for the completion of the clause. Although they are to a certain extent integrated in the clause, they are optional elements and will be called Adjuncts.

We are left with *Tom disappeared*, which is complete in itself. Something is predicated of Tom, namely that he disappeared. The Predicator, realised by the VG *disappeared*, constitutes the whole predication.

In other cases what is predicated of the Subject must be made up by a Predicator together with one or more **complements**, as in the following examples:

All the men wore *dark suits*.	SPOd
She handed *me the telegram*.	SPOiOd
Your idea sounds *great*.	SPCs
They found *the test difficult*.	SPOdCo
He put *the letter in an envelope*.	SPOdCp

Without the various complements each of the above clauses would be incomplete or, as in the case of *they found the test*, have a different meaning. Complements are therefore nuclear constituents as opposed to Adjuncts, which are not. This means that we shall analyse as complement such items as *badly* in *He treated us badly* and *into trouble* in *He got us into trouble* since, although they express circumstances, these circumstances are inherent to the situation, not peripheral. *Badly* is, of course, an Adjunct in *He is sleeping badly these days*.

4.1.1 Complements and Adjuncts

The non-nuclear status of Adjuncts and the nuclear status of complements are related to certain other characteristics:

(a) Adjuncts are not conditioned by any particular type of verb, as are complements. *Suddenly*, for instance, can be used with intransitive verbs like *disappear* and transitive verbs like *find*.

(b) The number of complements that can occur is more grammatically determined than is the case with Adjuncts. Different structures, based on different verbs, require one, two or three complements (see Chapter 3). There is no limit to the number of Adjuncts that can be included in a clause.

(c) Complements are typically realised by NGs and AdjGs, whereas Adjuncts are typically realised by AdvGs and PrepGs. There is no one-to-one correspondence, however, between class of unit and its syntactic function. A PrepG realises Adjunct *at the weekend* in *Tom runs at the weekend* and a Predicator Complement *to work* in *Tom runs to work*. The difference between locative or directional Adjuncts and locative or directional Complements can be established by paraphrase:

> John runs. That happens at the weekend.
> John runs. *That happens to work.

4.1.2 Objects and other Complements

Within clause complements in general we shall want to distinguish between Objects and other types of complement. For this purpose, we shall make use of such features as number, position in relation to the verb, passivisation and the ability to be replaced by a pronoun. Complementation from the point of view of verb type is discussed in Chapter 3.

(a) Objects typically refer to participants in the event different from the Subject. The process expressed by the verb is 'extended' from the Subject through the verb to the Objects. This 'extensive' relationship is what is meant by 'transitivity'. Objects occur immediately after the verb in transitive clauses, and the most central type (the Direct Object) does so without the mediation of a preposition (The bomb killed *a policeman*). No prepositional paraphrase is possible with the Direct Object.

(b) Singular or plural number of the Object is therefore independent of the Subject. (*The bomb killed a policeman / two policemen*). Instances of number agreement as in *Bill hurt himself, Bill and Tom hurt themselves* are not exceptions, since *himself* and *themselves* are in paradigmatic contrast with other possible realisations of the Object function (*Bill hurt Tom, Bill and Tom hurt the cat*).

(c) Objects can normally become Subject in a passive clause, since the system of voice allows different semantic roles to be associated with Subject and Object functions (*The bomb killed the policeman / The policeman was killed by the bomb*).

(d) Since Objects refer to participants, they can be realised by objective-case pronouns (*The bomb killed him / them*).

(e) In clauses containing more than one Object we shall distinguish between Direct Object (Od) and Indirect Object (Oi). These distinctions are based on relative position in the clause, substitution by other forms and the semantic roles associated with each. These features are treated in Module 6 of this chapter. As a less prototypical Object, we shall treat elements such as *on Tom* in *You can rely on Tom* as Prepositional Object, since *Tom* can be considered an oblique Object, mediated by a preposition, and can become Subject in a passive clause (*Tom can be relied on*).

Complements which are not Objects will be classified as follows:

Complement of the Subject	Cs	(Bill is *a policeman*)
Complement of the Object	Co	(I found the map *helpful*)
Predicator Complement	PC	(The fare costs *$150*)
		(I wish you *success*)

In comparison with Objects, Complements can be seen to have the following features:

(a) Subject and Object Complements, rather than picking out a different participant, typically predicate something about the Subject or the Object. There is an 'intensive' relationship between the Subject and its Complement and between the Object and its Complement.

(b) Consequently, there is normally number agreement between the Subject or Object and its Complement. (*He is a policeman / They are policemen. They made him Inspector. *They made him Inspectors.*)

(c) Unlike Objects, Complements do not become Subject in passive clauses (**$150 was cost the fare; *Success is wished you*).

(d) Since Complements predicate rather than refer, many cannot be replaced by a personal pronoun (**Bill is he/him. *It cost it*).

(e) Predicator Complement is the term we shall use for those obligatory constituents which do not meet the criteria established for Objects and the other types of complement. (Strictly speaking, all complements are predicative in that they complete the predication made by the verb; however, as there is no generally accepted term to distinguish this type, **Predicator Complement** will be used in this restricted sense.) It includes the complements of verbs such as *have* and *cost* in one-complement predications (*He has no money*; *the fare cost $150*), and obligatory directional expressions such as *into the cave* in *They crawled into the cave*. It also covers the obligatory non-object constituent of two-complement predications such as *success* in *I wish you success* and *to see a doctor* in *They persuaded Tom to see a doctor*. None of these can become Subject in a passive clause.

4.2   Basic syntactic structures of the clause

Clausal elements or functions enter into varied relationships with each other to express different types of proposition concerning different states of affairs. These are exemplified as follows, and are treated further in Chapter 4.

SP	Tom / disappeared.
	The bells / rang.
	The marketing Manager's ingenious plan to promote sales / has failed.
SPOd	Tom / hired / a car.
	Doctors /recommend / a less stressful way of life.
SPOiOd	I / have sent / them / an invitation.
	The Ministry of Education / awarded / their son / a grant.
SPOprep	You / can rely / on Tom.
	The police / are looking / into the matter.
SPCs	My brother / has become / a ski instructor.
	Your exam results / were / better than mine.
SPOdCo	They / appointed / him / First Secretary.
	I / don't consider / Brenda / much of a friend.
SPOdCp	They / charged / him / with robbery.
	He / convinced / the jury / of his innocence.

4.3   Further optional additions

In addition to optional Adjuncts, which can be added freely to any of the above clause structures, other optional elements can be added to the basic clause, for the purpose either of commenting on its content or of connecting it to another clause. The three primary classes of optional elements that we shall establish, according to the types of functional relationship they realise, are therefore as follows:

Adjunct (A):   consisting in the expression of an optional
                  circumstance attending the process expressed
                  by the clause.

                  Tom / disappeared / *suddenly* / *after the*
                  concert.

Disjunct (D):   consisting in the addition of a unit which
                  expresses a comment by the speaker on the
                  clause or sentence as a whole or relating it to
                  something outside it. Strictly speaking, this unit
                  is outside clause structure.

                  Obviously, he'll rely on you even more now.
                  Salewise, the product is a success.

Conjunct (Conj.): consisting in the joining together of two
                  utterances, or parts of an utterance, together
                  with the semantic relationship holding between
                  them.

                  The hotel was rather noisy. *On the other hand*, it
                  wasn't expensive. (adversative)

The following extract illustrates some of the possible configurations of
clause elements:

At the hotel / I / paid / the driver / and / gave /
   A   S P   Oi   +   P

him / a tip. // The car / was / powdered with dust. //
 Oi   Od   S   P   Cs

I / rubbed / the rod-case / through the dust. //
S P   Od   A

It / seemed / the last thing that connected me with
S   P   Cs

Spain and the fiesta. // The driver / put / the car /
                S   P   Od

in gear / and / went / down the street. // I / watched /
 Co   +   P   Cp   S P

it / turn off to take the road to Spain. // I / went /
Od   Co   S P

into the hotel / and / they / gave / me / a room. //
   Cp   +   S   P   Oi   Od

It / was / the same room I had slept in when Bill and
S P   Cs

Cohn and I were in Bayonne. // That / seemed / a very
                S   P

long time ago. //
    Cs

            Ernest Hemingway, *Fiesta (The Sun Also Rises)*

In the remaining sections of this chapter we shall describe the syntactic features of each clausal element and the principal realisations of each, together with any relevant discourse characteristics. Reference will be made to the semantic roles associated with these elements, but these are dealt with more fully in Chapter 5.

4.4   Realisations of the elements

It is important to remember that with the exception of the Predicator function, there is no one-to-one correspondence between class of unit and syntactic function in English. So, whereas the Predicator is always realised by a VG, the other functions display a considerable range of possible realisations by different classes of group and clause. It is true that most functions are prototypically realised by a certain class of unit (for example, Subjects and Objects by NGs), but the versatility of the language is such that almost any group or clause can realise these functions. As we analyse texts, or create our own, we must be aware that each function can be realised by different classes of unit, and each class of unit can perform various functions. In the following pages, the realisations of each clause element are arranged in order of typicality. When the element is realised by the head-word of a group, the realisation is normally regarded as a group unit.

MODULE 5
Subject and Predicator

Summary

1   The Subject is identified syntactically by the features of position, concord, pronominalisation and reflection in tag questions. Semantically, almost all participant roles can be associated with the Subject. It can be realised by a wide variety of groups and clauses.

> 2   The Predicator is identified syntactically by position and concord. It indicates the process type and is associated with the meanings expressed by tense, aspect, modality, voice and phase. It is realised by Verbal Groups.

5.1   The Subject

5.1.1   Syntactic features

(a) The Subject is that element of which something is predicated in a clause and which, in English, must be present in declarative and interrogative clauses.

(b) The Subject is placed before the Predicator in declarative clauses:

> Unfortunately, *everyone* left early.
> *Passing through the sound barrier* doesn't affect the passengers.

and in *WH*-interrogative clauses where the *WH*-element is Subject:

> *Who* came in late last night?
> *How many* were left?
> *Which horse* won the first race this afternoon?

It is placed after the operator (the finite part of the Predicator) in polar (yes/no) interrogative clauses:

> Did *everyone* leave early?
> Does *passing through the sound barrier* affect the passengers?

and in *WH*-interrogative clauses in which the *WH*-element is Object or Adjunct:

> Who(m) did *you* see last night?
> How does *passing through the sound barrier* affect you?

(c) The Subject is that element which is picked up in a tag-question phrase and referred to anaphorically by a pronoun:

> *Your brother* goes in for skiing, doesn't *he*?
> *Not many people* would object to that suggestion, would *they*?

(d) The pronominal forms *I*, *he*, *she*, *we* and *they* are used to realise Subject function, in contrast to the objective forms *me*, *him*, *her*, *us* and *them*, which are used for Objects. The *who/whom* distinction is no longer made by all speakers. Possessive forms may stand as Subject:

> *Yours* was rather difficult to read.
> *Jennifer's* got lost in the post.

(e) Subjects determine number (singular or plural) and person concord with the verb. Concord is manifested only in those verb forms which show inflectional contrast:

The librarian / he / she has checked the book.
The librarians / I / you / we / they have checked the book.
Where *is my credit card*?
Where *are my credit cards*?

With verb forms which show no number or person contrast such as *had* in *the money had all been spent*, we can apply the criterion of paradigmatic contrast with a present form such as *has* (*the money has all been spent*).

When the Subject is realised by a collective noun, concord depends on how the referent is visualised by the speaker:

The committee is sitting late. (seen as a whole)
The committee have decided to award extra grants. (seen as a number of members)

(f) The Subject typically determines the number of the NG realising Subject Complement, and of reflexive pronouns at Cs, Oi and Od, together with person and gender:

Jean and Bill are *my friends.*
She cut *herself* with a piece of broken glass.
Why don't *you* give *yourself* a treat?

Some of the features which help to identify the Subject are illustrated in the following short extract from a fictitious diary:

I have decided to be a poet. My father said that there isn't a suitable career structure for poets and no pensions and other boring things, but I am quite decided. He tried to interest me in becoming a computer operator, but I said, 'I need to put my soul into my work and it is well known that computers haven't got a soul.' My father said, 'The Americans are working on it.' But I can't wait that long.

Sue Townsend, *The Secret Diary of Adrian Mole aged 13¾*

5.1.2 Semantic features

The Subject can be associated with almost every type of semantic role. These are treated in Chapter 4 and are merely exemplified briefly here:

Jones headed the ball into the net. (Agent)
The ball was headed into the net. (Affected)
Holes were made in the road by the hand grenades. (Effected)
I feel a little tired today. (Experiencer)
This key won't open the front door. (Instrument)
The secretary has been given some chocolates. (Recipient)

5.1.3 Realisations of the Subject

Subjects can be realised by various classes of groups and clauses:

nominal group
finite clause
non-finite clause
anticipatory *it* + extraposed finite or non-finite clause
prop *it*
presentative *there* + postposed NG
prepositional group (marginally)
adverbial group (marginally)
adjectival group (marginally)

(a) Nominal Groups

Nominal Groups are the most prototypical realisation of Subject and can range from simple heads (see 45.3.1) to the full complexity of **dmhq** structures (see 50.1):

> *Cocaine* can damage the heart as well as the brain.
> *The precise number of heart attacks from using cocaine* is not known.
> *It* is alarming.

(b) Finite clauses

Finite clauses at Subject are of two types: *that*-clauses and *WH*-clauses, the latter being either interrogative or nominal relative clauses (see 9.5.1). *That*-clauses are more acceptable in English if they are preceded by *the fact*, thus losing their status as clausal Subject, since the resulting combination is an appositive NG:

> *That he failed to turn up* surprised nobody. (*that*-clause)
> *The fact that he failed to turn up* surprised nobody. (NG)
> *Why the library was closed for months* was not explained. (*WH*-interrogative)
> *What he said* shocked me. (*WH*-nominal relative clause)
> *Whoever told you that* is sadly out of date. (nominal relative)
> *How they managed to survive* is a mystery. (nominal relative)

(c) Non-finite clauses

Non-finite clauses at Subject are of two types, depending on the VG they contain: *to*-infinitive, which can be introduced by a *WH*-word, and *-ing* clauses. 'Bare' infinitive clauses (without *to*) occur as Subject only in equative (*WH*-cleft) sentences (see 30.2.):

> *To take such a risk* was rather foolish. (*to*-inf. clause)
> *Where to leave the dog* is the problem. (*WH*- + *to*-inf. clause)
> *Run for President* is what he may do. (bare inf. clause)
> *Having to go back for the tickets* was a nuisance. (*-ing* clause)

To-infinitive and *-ing* clauses at Subject can have their own Subject; bare infinitive clauses cannot. A *to*-infinitive clause with its own Subject must be introduced by *for*:

For everyone to escape was practically impossible.
Sam having to go back for the tickets was a nuisance.

The pronominal Subject of an *-ing* clause can be in the possessive or the objective case. The objective form is the less formal:

Him / his having to go back for the tickets was a nuisance.

Of all embedded clauses, only *that*-clauses introduced by *the fact*, finite nominal relative clauses and non-finite *-ing* clauses are sufficiently nominal to be able to invert with the operator in interrogative clauses:

Did *what he said* shock you?
Was *Sam having to go back for the tickets* a nuisance?
*Was *to take such a risk* rather foolish?
*Did *that he failed to turn up* surprise nobody?
Did *the fact that he failed to turn up* surprise nobody?

(d) Anticipatory it + extraposed finite/non-finite clause

Examples such as *That he failed to turn up surprised nobody* and *For everyone to escape was practically impossible* have as an alternative structure the following:

It surprised nobody *that he failed to turn up.*
It was practically impossible *for everyone to escape.*

in which the finite or non-finite clause realising the Subject is said to be *extraposed* (30.5), that is, placed after the Complement or Object. The initial Subject position is filled, obligatorily, by the pronoun *it* (usually called 'anticipatory *it*'), acting as a kind of substitute for the 'postponed' Subject. It is commonly used in both speech and writing, especially when the Subject is longer than the Complement and is better placed at the end of the sentence, in accordance with the informational and stylistic principle of 'end-weight'. This principle can be appreciated in the following extract, in which many of the notional Subjects are extremely long:

In spite of the campaigns of a few thousand left-wingers, *it* is fairly certain *that the bulk of the English people were behind Chamberlain's foreign policy.* More, *it* is fairly certain *that the same struggle was going on in Chamberlain's mind as in the mind of ordinary people.* His opponents professed to see in him a dark and wily schemer, plotting to sell England to Hitler, but *it* is far likelier *that he was merely a stupid old man doing his best according to his very dim lights. It* is difficult otherwise *to explain the contradictions of his policy, his failure to grasp any of the courses that were open to him.*

George Orwell, *England Your England.*

Extraposed Subjects occur frequently in SPCs structures in which the Cs is realised by an adjective, as can be seen in our text.

The Cs can also be realised by a NG, as in the following examples:

It's *a pity* (that) you are leaving the company.
It's *a bore* when people can't make up their minds.
It's *a scandal* that the racket was allowed to go undetected so long.
It is not *the case* that he has a drinking problem.
It shouldn't come as *a surprise* that the firm has sold out.
It is *no concern of mine* what she does outside working hours.
It is *time* he stopped fooling around.

Clausal Subjects can be extraposed from other structures too:

SP   *Where you sit* doesn't matter.
           It doesn't matter *where you sit.*
SPOd   *That the number-plate had been changed* struck
           me.
           It struck me *that the number-plate had been
           changed.*
SPOdCo   *To see such poverty* makes one sad.
           It makes one sad *to see such poverty.*

For the apparently extraposed clause which follows *It is time* (or *It is high time* . . .) there is no corresponding pattern with the clause in initial position (**That he stopped fooling around is high time*).

Likewise, the clause following *it* + verbs of seeming (*seem, look, sound*) and happening (*happen, turn out, come about*), together with the passive of *say, hope* and *intend*, is obligatorily extraposed:

It seems that you were right after all. (**That you were right after all seems*)
It looks as though the weather is about to change.
It sounds as if someone is crying.
It so happened that the driver lost control.
It turned out that no-one was hurt.
It is said that the regulations will be changed.

The expressions *The thing is that* . . ., *it's not that* . . . and *it's just that* . . . function in a similar way. They act as 'introducers' in spoken discourse, as in the following invented exchange:

A. The thing is that I can't get him to understand how off-putting such remarks as that can be.
B. I know. It's not that he means to be hurtful. It's just that he doesn't seem to be able to put himself in the other person's place and so can't imagine what it's like to be on the receiving end of his remarks.

The examples shown so far have all been of clauses in active voice. Long clausal Subjects in passive sentences are frequently extraposed and replaced by anticipatory *it*:

It has been suggested *that age is an important factor in opinion polls.*

It is doubted *whether the troops will be withdrawn soon.*
It is now believed *that the vaccine will be commercialised within a year.*
It is proposed *to hold a summit meeting between the two Presidents.*

Certain extraposed *-ing* clauses in common use include:

It's no use *waiting any longer.*
It's no good *crying over spilt milk.*

(e) Prop *it*

Anticipatory *it* is usually distinguished from the obligatory use of *it* as empty or 'prop' Subject in expressions of time, atmospheric conditions and distance such as:

It's nearly three o'clock.
It's raining.
It was a dark, windy night.
It's often cold and damp in the north.
It is eight hundred kilometres from here to Barcelona.

Semantically, the situations expressed by such clauses do not contain any participant, only processes (*rain*) or attributes (*cold*, *damp*), locatives (*in the north*) or other circumstantials.

Syntactically, English requires the presence of a Subject even in such situations, in order to distinguish between declaratives and interrogatives:

Is *it* raining?   How far is *it* from here to Barcelona?

For many circumstantial expressions, however, there is a corresponding pattern with a NG or PrepG realising a locative or extent Subject:

The night was dark and windy.
The north is often cold and damp.
From here to Barcelona is eight hundred kilometres.

This fact would suggest that prop *it* in these instances is in fact a 'presentative' *it* similar to existential *there* (see 30.4) and to 'anticipatory' *it*. There is no corresponding alternative pattern for examples such as *it is raining*.

(f) Unstressed *there*

The Subject is regularly postponed in existential clauses (see 30.4), the normal initial position being occupied by unstressed *there*, which 'presents' the notional Subject:

There's plenty of time.
Are *there* any Maltese falcons?
There were only two fine days last week.

Presentative *there* fulfils several of the syntactic criteria for Subject: position, inversion with auxiliaries and repetition in tag phrases; but unlike normal Subjects it cannot be replaced by a pronoun. Concord, when made, is with the following NG:

> There *was only one fine day last week*, wasn't there?
> There *were only two fine days last week*, weren't there?

In informal spoken English plural concord is not always made with the present tense of *be*, and when the notional Subject is a series of proper names concord is never made:

> *There's several pages* of this book missing.
> How many are coming? Well, *there's Andrew and Silvia, and Jo and Pete.*
> * There *are* Andrew and Silvia and Jo and Pete.

Because of the lack of concord and pronominalisation, unstressed *there* can be considered as a Subject 'place-holder' or 'syntactic filler', rather than a full Subject, since the unit following the verb is clearly the notional Subject.

(g) Prepositional Groups

Prepositional Groups functioning at Subject usually specify spatial or temporal meanings of location or extent, but instrumental meanings can also occur.

> Will *up in the front* suit you? (spatial locative)
> *Before midday* would be convenient. (temporal locative)
> *By plane* costs more than by train. (instrumental)

(h) Adverbial Groups

Adverbial Groups headed by *now*, *here* and *there* can realise Subject function:

> *Now* is the time to act.
> *Just here* would be an ideal place for a picnic.
> *Over there* is where I'd put it.

Certain manner adverbs such as *slowly* and *gently* marginally function as Subject in stereotyped expressions:

> *Slowly / gently* does it!

(i) Adjectival Groups

The Adjectival Group as such does not function as Subject. However, certain adjectives preceded by a definite determiner, normally the definite article, and which represent (a) conventionally recognised classes of people, and (b) abstractions, can function as heads of (untypical) NGs (see 48.5.1), and so realise the S, Od and Oi elements:

> *The handicapped* are given special facilities in public places.
> *The very young and the very old* need State care.
> *The supernatural* attracts many people.

Pronouns account for a high percentage of Subjects in the spoken language, as can be seen in the following recorded dialogue about the mini-skirt. Several other types of Subject are also illustrated in the main and embedded clauses of this text, including two different functions of *it*:

Q. What about the mini-skirt itself? What was the origin of that?
A. *That*[1] started in the East End of London. *Mary Quant* [2] picked it up and then *a lot of other designers* [3] did too. *I* [4] think again *it* [5] was reaction against the long skirts of the 1950s. *It* [6] was smart *to get much, much shorter*. *I* [7] think that, partly, *it* [8] was fun *to shock your father and older people*, but *it* [9] was also a genuinely felt fashion, as *we*[10] can see by the fact that it spread nearly all over the world. *I* [11] think *it* [12] is a lovely look / *long leggy girls*. *The fact that fat legs are seen, too,* [13] is just bad luck. But *I* [14] still don't think that *the mini-skirt* [15] is going to disappear for some time. *I* [16] think *girls* [17] just love the feeling.

[1] deictic pronoun; [2] proper noun; [3] NG; [4] pronoun; [5] pronoun: [6] anticipatory *it* + *to*-infinitive; [7] pronoun; [8] anticipatory *it* + *to*-infinitive; [9] pronoun; [10] pronoun; [11] pronoun; [12] anticipatory *it* + NG; [13] *the fact* + *that*-clause; [14] pronoun; [15] NG; [16] pronoun; [17] NG.

Janey Ironside in *Artists Talking: five artists talk to Anthony Schooling*.

5.2   The Predicator

The Predicator is the verbal component of a clause. It tells us whether the situation expressed by the clause is a state, an action or an event. It relates the speech event to other points in time, through tense, and specifies whether the verbal process is visualised as on-going, as in *is dancing*, *are worrying*, by means of aspect (see 42.1); it can specify phases of the process, such as seeming, turning out to be (see 39.4). The speaker's viewpoint or assessment of the situation may be expressed, by means of modal verbs (see Module 44), and for the speaker's organisation of the message the active–passive voice alternative offers an important choice (see 30.3):

Our apartment in town *is being redecorated*. (Present tense, Progressive aspect, passive voice, material process *redecorate*)

You *must be joking*. (modality, progressive aspect, Present tense, active voice, verbal process *joke*)

5.2.1   Syntactic features

In English the Predicator typically follows the Subject in declarative clauses, as in the above examples, and precedes the Subject in polar interrogatives, if it is realised by *be* or *have* as main verbs:

Have you enough money?   *Is* that car yours?

Otherwise, the Predicator is discontinuous in polar interrogatives since the operator (the Finite in Mood structures) precedes the Subject:

> *Does* anyone here *know* how to give an injection?

5.2.2 Realisations of the Predicator

The Predicator is always realised by a VG, whose structure may consist of one single form or a number of forms (see 37.2). Single forms are either finite such as *ate*, *brings*, *talked*, or non-finite such as *saying*, *finished*, *to be*. Longer VGs consist of the main verb preceded by one or more auxiliaries:

> You *can't* possibly *have finished* already!
> This Underground station *must have been being repainted.*

The following extract from a conversation contains both simple forms, which carry the narrative forward, and longer VGs, which express combinations of tense, aspect and modality:

> A. So they *blew* in and I *was* at home and we *had* tea; and she *rang* up
>   last week and *said* she'd *got to come and supervise* this girl again,
>   and *could* they *come* to lunch. So they *did*.
> B. mm
> A. And then it *turned* out the girl *had gone and got* a chill or
>   something, *having heard* her supervisor *was coming*, so there *was*
>   no supervision to do, so they *stayed* for a nice long time and they
>   *may be coming* again tomorrow.
> B. Good God.

> Adapted from J. Svartvik and R. Quirk (eds.), *A Corpus of English*
> *Conversation.*

MODULE 6
Direct, Indirect and Prepositional Objects

Summary

1   The Direct Object is the single Object in a transitive clause, not mediated by a preposition and having no prepositional paraphrase. In clauses with two Objects, it follows the Indirect Object (Send them *a telegram*). It can become Subject in a passive clause (*The telegram* was sent). It represents a wide variety of semantic roles. Typically, the Direct Object is realised by Nominal Groups expressing entities; less typically by other classes of unit.

2   The Indirect Object is that clause constituent which immediately follows the Predicator in clauses with two Objects (Send *them* a telegram). It can become Subject in a passive clause (*They* were sent a telegram) and has a prepositional paraphrase (A telegram was sent *to them*). It is associated with the Recipient and Beneficiary roles. It is realised by Nominal Groups and nominal relative clauses.

3   The Prepositional Object is an Object mediated by a preposition (agree *on a plan*). The nominal element following the preposition can become Subject in a passive clause (*The plan was agreed on*). This property distinguishes the Prepositional Object from other clause constituents which may be realised by Prepositional Groups.

6.1   The Direct Object

6.1.1   Syntactic features

A single complement can be considered to function as Direct Object (Od) if the following criteria are fulfilled:

(a) It is placed immediately after the Predicator.
(b) The VG which realises the Predicator can occur in a passive clause. The Direct Object typically becomes Subject in the passive clause (more exactly, the semantic role realised by the Direct Object can be realised by the Subject in a passive clause, see 14.3).
(c) After passivisation, the meaning remains unchanged.

The police have identified *the victim*.
The victim has been identified by the police.

> I used to spend *all my money* on going to the cinema.
> *All my money* used to be spent on going to the cinema.
>
> Many people admire *his work.*
> *His work* is admired by many people.

The following examples have no passive counterparts:

> Tom hurt *himself.* *Himself was hurt by Tom.
> Tom waved *his hand.* *His hand was waved by Tom.

Nevertheless, we shall consider *himself* and *his hand* as Direct Objects, although not the most typical, since the verbs *hurt* and *wave* can occur in passive clauses which keep the same meaning; in addition, *himself* and *his hand* occur in paradigmatic contrast with other possible NG realisations of the Direct Object function:

> Tom hurt *their feelings. Their feelings* were hurt (by Tom).
> Tom waved *the flag. The flag* was waved (by Tom).

(d) In clauses with two Objects the Direct Object is placed after the Indirect Object:

> They gave me *my new timetable* today.
> All her friends sent her *cards* on her birthday.
> Perhaps someone could lend this girl *a pen.*

(e) No prepositional paraphrase is possible for the Direct Object.

6.1.2 Semantic features

The Direct Object is associated with a wide variety of semantic roles, some of which are illustrated in the following examples:

> He headed *the ball* into the net. (Affected)
> She writes *children's stories.* (Effected)
> The burglars used *an acetylene lamp* to break open the safe.
> (Instrument)
> I felt *a sudden pain in my arm.* (Phenomenon)
> Do you always tell *the truth*? (Verbiage)
> We sang *songs* round the camp fire. (Range)

6.1.3 Realisations of the Direct Object

The Direct Object can be realised by:

> a nominal group
> a finite clause
> a non-finite clause
> anticipatory *it* + finite/non-finite clause
> a prepositional group of time or place

(a) Nominal Group
The prototypical realisation of the Direct Object function is the Nominal

Group. The same varied range of Nominal Groups found at Subject can realise Direct Object; however, the principle of end-weight (see 7.3.2) makes for the frequent occurrence of longer and more complex NGs at Direct Object:

> He has lodged *a complaint.*
> Did you hear *anything*?
> She has made herself *an extraordinary fancy-dress in the shape of a balloon.*

(b) Finite clause

The two types of finite clause found at Subject also function at Direct Object: *WH*-clauses and *that*-clauses, *that* often being omitted in informal styles. For the passive construction with *that*-clauses, anticipatory *it* may be required with a verb of low communicative dynamism like *say*.

> Most people recognise *that some form of taxation is necessary.*
> *That some form of taxation is necessary* is recognised by most people.
> *It* is recognised by most people *that some form of taxation is necessary.*
>
> They say *that he is moving to New York.*
> It is said that he is moving to New York.

In accordance with the criteria established in 6.1.1 we say that the *that*-clauses are realisations of the Direct Object in both these examples. The *that*-clause is placed in each case after a verb (*recognise, say*) which can passivise while retaining the same meaning.

Clauses are less typical realisations of Direct Object than are NGs. An additional test for clauses which do not become Subject of a corresponding passive clause is to add a coordinate clause with a pronominal form such as the demonstrative pronoun *that* and then passivise:

> They say that he is moving to New York and his friends say that too.
> That is said by his friends.

Further examples of *that*-clauses functioning at Direct Object are:

> The authorities claim *that everything possible has been done.*
> They fear *that there may be no survivors.*
> Peter denied *that he had left the lights on all night.*
> We realise *that he is under great strain.*
> Officials argue *that their public image is unfair.*

Conversely, in the following case, the *WH*-clause is considered to be a Complement but not a Direct Object, since the verb *wonder* cannot normally be passivised:

> I wonder whether they know the truth.
> *Whether they know the truth is wondered.
> *It is wondered whether they know the truth.

WH-clauses are considered to be Direct Objects in the following example:

> You know very well *how difficult he can be.*
> *How difficult he can be* is well known.
> *It* is well known *how difficult he can be.*

Further examples of *WH*-clauses which realise Direct Object are:

> No-one knows *where he lives.*
> I can't imagine *why he should do such a thing.*
> Someone should explain *what kind of applicant they are looking for.*
> You can eat *whatever you like.*

Finite clauses realising the Direct Object function are illustrated in the following short text:

> Clarence had joined them to ask *what the excitement was all about.* [1]
> When she told him *that the Rumanians had been summoned to a conference at Salzburg* [2] he shrugged, having expected worse. She too felt *that in a world so full of dangers those that did not immediately affect them could be put on one side.*[3]

> Olivia Manning, *Fortunes of War.*

[1] *WH*-clause; [2] *that*-clause; [3] *that*-clause.

(c) Non-finite clause

Non-finite clauses realising Direct Object function are of two types: infinitive clauses with or without *to*, and *-ing* clauses.

> Many Londoners prefer *to travel by train.*
> Many Londoners prefer *travelling by train.*

We analyse such clauses as embedded at Direct Object on the strength of the following criteria:

(i) The non-finite clause can be replaced by a NG (*prefer the train*) or simply by *it* (*prefer it*).

(ii) The non-finite clause can be made the focus of a *WH*-cleft (equative) sentence (*What many Londoners prefer is to travel/travelling by train.*).

We do not analyse as embedded clauses at Direct Object catenatives (hypotactic or 'phased') Verbal Groups such as *He failed to appear*; *I ventured to raise an objection* (see 39.4).

Although superficially similar, catenatives do not fulfil these criteria. Taking the example *He failed to appear*, we cannot say **He failed it*, nor make a corresponding equative (**What he failed was to appear*). In both cases it would be necessary to add *to do* (*What he failed to do was appear*), which confirms the catenative nature of such VGs. As a full lexical verb, *fail* as in *He failed the driving test* does of course fulfil these criteria.

Many embedded clauses at Direct Object occur with an explicit Subject of their own; otherwise the implicit Subject is the same as that of the main clause:

(i) *to*-infinitive:

> The villagers want *to leave immediately.* (implicit Subject)
> The villagers want *the soldiers to leave immediately.* (explicit Subject)

(ii) *-ing*:

> Do you mind *waiting a few minutes*? (implicit Subject)
> Do you mind *me waiting a few minutes*? (explicit Subject)

(iii) *to*-infinitive or *-ing* clause:

> He hates *to tell/telling lies.* (implicit Subject)
> He hates *people to tell/telling lies.* (explicit Subject)
> He hates *there to be quarrelling.* (explicit *there* Subject)

Although we have considered such clauses as Direct Object, for the reasons explained above, they are even more marginal than finite clause realisations in that many do not passivise. Semantically, they are likewise untypical, since they represent situations rather than participants, and the verb which governs them is frequently not a process of 'doing'. For further discussion of non-finite complementation and the meanings expressed by such clauses, see Chapter 3. An alternative analysis of clauses as 'projections' of mental or verbal processes is given in Module 36.

(d) Anticipatory *it*

The semantically empty pronoun *it* is necessary as an 'anticipatory Direct Object' in SPOdCo structures in which the Od is realised by a finite or non-finite clause:

S	P	(Od)	Co	Od
I	find	*it*	strange	*that he refuses to come.*
He	considers	*it*	unlikely	*that the money will be refunded.*
She	might regard	*it*	insulting	*for you to leave now.*
You	must find	*it*	flattering	*having so many fans.*

(e) Prepositional Group

Prepositional Groups of time or place can realise Direct Object:

> I would prefer *before noon* for a meeting.
> Don't choose *by a swamp* for a picnic.

6.2 The Indirect Object

6.2.1 Syntactic features

When the Predicator is followed by two complements, each of which can typically become Subject in a passive clause, the first of these is considered the Indirect Object.

> The doctor gave *the injured man* treatment for shock.
> *The injured man* was given treatment for shock.
>
> Someone has sent *the bank manager* a letter-bomb.
> *The bank manager* has been sent a letter-bomb.
>
> Sammy Karanja is teaching *the students* Swahili.
> *The students* are being taught Swahili by Sammy Karanja.

Another feature of the Indirect Object is its ability to be replaced by a *to*-phrase complement which follows the Direct Object:

> The doctor gave treatment for shock *to the injured man*.
> Someone has sent a letter-bomb *to the bank manager*.
> Sammy Karanja is teaching Swahili *to the students*.

Unlike the Direct Object, the Indirect Object cannot be fronted in a passive *WH*-interrogative or in a relative clause. The prepositional alternative is used:

> *Who(m) has the letter-bomb been sent?
> To whom has the letter-bomb been sent?
> Who has the letter-bomb been sent to?
>
> *The man who(m) the letter-bomb was sent is here.
> The man to whom the letter-bomb was sent is here.
> The man who the letter-bomb was sent to is here.

The Indirect Object can generally be left unexpounded without affecting the grammaticality of the clause:

> The doctor gave treatment for shock.
> Someone has sent a letter-bomb.
> Sammy Karanja is teaching Swahili.

With some verbs (*show*, *tell*, *teach*, etc.) the Direct Object may be unexpounded. We still regard the single Object as Indirect Object, since a Direct Object could easily be added:

> Who told *you* (the answer)?
> Perhaps you could show *me* (how to do it.)
> He's teaching *immigrant children* (maths).

6.2.2   Semantic features

The semantic roles associated with the Indirect Object are more restricted than with the Subject and the Direct Object.

The Indirect Object is typically associated with the Recipient of the action (see 1.4.5). The process expressed by the verb is extended from the Subject to the Indirect and Direct Objects. All the examples seen so far have Recipient Indirect Objects.

Also associated with the Indirect Object is the Beneficiary, or 'intended Recipient' (see 14.5) as in the following examples:

> I'll get *you* some coffee.
> We've bought *the children* bicycles.
> Could you fetch *me* the scissors?
> Bill has saved *us* a place in the front row.

The Beneficiary appears to be a less integrated participant in the situation than is the Recipient, and this fact is reflected in the syntax.

Whereas Recipient Indirect Objects have as an alternative a *to*-phrase, with Beneficiary Indirect Objects the preposition is *for*:

> I'll get some coffee *for you*.
> We've bought bicycles *for the children*.
> Could you fetch the scissors *for me*?
> Bill has saved a place *for us* in the front row.

Moreover, most Beneficiary Objects do not easily become Subject in a passive clause, although this restriction is not absolute:

> *You'll be got some coffee.
> ?The children have been bought bicycles.
> *Could I be fetched the scissors?
> We have been saved a place in the front row.

6.2.3   Realisations of the Indirect Object

Both Recipient and Beneficiary Indirect Objects are prototypically realised by Nominal Groups and less typically by *WH*-nominal relative clauses:

> Ken has taught *his wife* to drive. (NG)
> Lend *whoever calls* the bicycle pump in the shed. (Nom.cl.)
> Phil has booked *all his friends* tickets for the show. (NG)
> Save *whoever comes* the trouble of ringing. (Nom.cl.)
> Give *whatever you think best* priority. (Nom.cl.)

Recipient Indirect Objects can also be realised by non-finite *-ing* clauses and by Prepositional Groups, but these options are not open to Beneficiary Indirect Object, since the latter always refers to an entity:

> I'm giving *reading magazines* less importance lately. (*-ing* cl.)
> Let's give *before lunch-time* priority. (PrepG)

6.3   The Prepositional Object

6.3.1   Syntactic features

A subsidiary type of Object is that which is mediated by a preposition. We shall call this the Prepositional Object (Oprep):

He agreed *to the change of plan*.
You can count *on Jane* to help make the sandwiches.
They have dealt *with the transport crisis*.

We do not consider *the change of plan*, *Jane* and *the transport crisis* to be Direct Objects of the prepositional verbs *agree to*, *count on* and *deal with* respectively, since (a) the Object is mediated by a preposition and (b) the cut-off point between the prepositional verb and its complement is before the preposition, not after it. This can be tested by inserting an adverb:

He agreed *wholeheartedly* to the change of plan.
*He agreed to *wholeheartedly* the change of plan.

They have dealt *successfully* with the transport crisis.
*They have dealt with *successfully* the transport crisis.

A contrary criterion is the intuitive view that the verb is closely cohesive with its preposition, and the fact that for some combinations there is an alternative one-word lexical item (e.g. *look after = tend*). With some such combinations, the adverb is felt to be awkward in separating verb and preposition (?*She is looking carefully after the old man*, as against *She is looking after the old man carefully*, which would support a Direct Object interpretation). However, in general, we feel that in most cases the Prepositional Object analysis is to be preferred. (For verbs which take Prepositional Objects see 9.2.2; for comparison with phrasal verbs see 40.4.)

A further criterion for Prepositional Object is its ability to passivise; more exactly, the NG completive of the preposition can become Subject in a passive clause, the preposition being 'stranded':

The change of plan was agreed to.
The transport crisis has been dealt with.
The old man is being looked after.

This criterion distinguishes Prepositional Objects from Predicator Complements realised by a Prepositional Group as in *This land belongs to the National Trust*; *The idea never occurred to me*. (see 7.3) Such clauses do not passivise.

6.3.2   Realisations of the Prepositional Object

The Prepositional Object is realised by a Prepositional Group. Just as with any PrepG, the completive of the preposition can be realised by Nominal Groups and by clauses:

Let's try to keep to *the schedule*. (Nominal Group)
This job calls for *great initiative*. (Nominal Group)

I strongly object to *what you are insinuating*. (nominal clause)
The party will have to draw on *whatever resources it can*. (nominal clause)

He believes in *getting things done as quickly as possible.* (*-ing* cl.)
They are all arguing about *how much to charge for admittance.* (*WH-
+ to*-inf.cl.)

Prepositional Groups and their meanings are described more fully in Chapter 13; for constraints on prepositions before *that*-clauses and *to*-infinitive clauses see 9.4.

The following extract illustrates some realisations of the different types of Objects described in these sections:

Telescopes
More than three centuries before Galileo, Roger Bacon, the inventor of spectacles, had explained *how a telescope could be constructed so as to 'make the stars appear as near as we please'.* [1] Yet, it was not until 1608 that the first telescope had been constructed by Lippershey, a Flemish spectacle-maker. On hearing *of this instrument,* [2] Galileo set to work to discover *the principles of its construction* [3] and by 1610 had made *himself* [4] *a telescope* [5] far better than the original. His telescope created *no small sensation* [6] in Italy. Such extraordinary stories had been told of its powers that he had been commanded to take *it* [7] to Venice and exhibit *it* [8] to the Doge and Senate. The citizens of Venice had then seen *the most aged of their senators* [9] climbing *the highest bell-tower* [10] to spy through the telescope *at ships which were too far out at sea to be seen at all without its help.* [11]

J. Jeans, *The Universe Around Us.*

[1] Od (*WH*-clause); [2] Oprep; [3] Od (NG); [4] Oi (NG); [5] Od (NG); [6] Od (NG); [7] Od (NG); [8] Od(NG); [9] Od (NG); [10] Od (NG); [11] Oprep.

MODULE 7
Subject, Object and Predicator Complements

Summary

1   The Subject Complement completes the predication after a copular verb by specifying an Attribute of the Subject, its identity, or a circumstance inherent to the predication. No passivisation is possible. The Subject Complement can be realised by AdjGs, by definite and indefinite NGs and by clauses.

2   The Object Complement completes the predication after a Direct Object with the same type of information as is provided by the Subject Complement: identifying, attributing or circumstantial. The clause can passivise with the Direct Object, but not the Complement, as Subject. The Object Complement is realised by AdjGs, definite and indefinite NGs and clauses.

3   These Complements are linked in an intensive relationship to the Subject and Object, respectively.

4   The Predicator Complement is the constituent necessary to complete the predication and which does not fulfil the criteria established for Objects and other Complements. There are various subtypes.

7.1   The Complement of the Subject or Subject Complement (Cs)

7.1.1   Syntactic features

The Subject Complement is the obligatory constituent which follows a copular verb and which cannot be made Subject in a passive clause. It is linked in an intensive relationship to the Subject:

> That journey was *a mistake.*
> Feel *free to ask questions*!
> Let's go home – I'm getting *rather tired.*
> He became *a tennis champion* at a very early age.

As well as *be* and *seem*, a wide range of verbs can be used to link the Subject to its Complement; these add meanings of transition (*become, get, go, grow, turn*) and of perception (*sound, smell, look*) among others and are discussed in Modules 12 and 17. The constituent following such verbs will be considered Subject Complement if the verb can be replaced by *be* and cannot be intransitive with the same meaning:

> His excuse *sounds* suspicious. (= *is* suspicious)
> *His excuse *sounds*.
>
> Daphne *looks* a wreck. (= *is* a wreck)
> *Daphne looks.

More problematic is the constituent following other verbs which could be used intransitively with the same meaning as in:

> He returned *a broken man.* (He returned.)
> He died *young.* (He died.)

We shall consider such constituents as Complements on the strength of the possible paraphrase containing *be* (*When he returned he was a broken man*; *When he died he was young.*). In addition, the relationship holding between the Subject and this element is intensive.

There is, typically, number agreement between the Subject and its Complement, and gender agreement with a reflexive pronoun at Complement as in *Janet isn't herself today*. There are, however, several common exceptions to number agreement:

> Joan and Lionel make *a good couple*.
> My neighbour's cats are *a nuisance/a joy*.
> Are these socks *wool*? No, they're *cotton*.
> The twins are *the same height*.

Complements of the type *a good couple* in *Joan and Lionel make a good couple* are explainable on semantic grounds, *couple* being inherently plural in meaning. Semantic criteria may also be invoked to explain the use of *a nuisance/a bore/a joy* in examples such as *Rainy days are a bore*; *My neighbour's cats are a nuisance/a joy*, since abstractions such as these are equally applicable to singular or plural Subjects.

A third type, exemplified by expressions such as *wool, cotton, rather an odd colour, the same height/length/shape*, etc., can all be paraphrased by a PrepG with *of* (*of wool, of rather an odd colour, of the same height*, etc.) which formerly had greater currency. They all express qualities of the Subject, and in present-day English the NG form without a preposition is the more common.

7.1.2 Semantic features

The Subject Complement completes the predication by providing information about the Subject with regard to its Attributes or its identity. The identifying type is typically reversible, the attributive not:

> The concert was *marvellous*.   (attributive)
> The concert was *a great success*.   (attributive)
> The orchestra was *the London Philharmonic*.   (identifying)
> (The London Philharmonic was the orchestra.)

The Subject Complement can also express an inherent circumstance which is in a copular, intensive relationship with the Subject, and not in an adjunctive relationship with the Predicator. The circumstance may be attributive or identifying:

> The concert was *on Friday*.   (attributive)
> Yesterday was *Friday*.   (identifying)

Sometimes a circumstantial Complement (e.g. *out of work*) is semantically equivalent to an attributive one (e.g. *unemployed*).

7.1.3 Realisations of the Subject Complement

Attributive Subject Complements are realised by Adjectival Groups and indefinite Nominal Groups. Identifying Subject Complements can be realised by definite Nominal Groups and by clauses.

(a) Attributive Complements

AdjG   Mountaineering can prove *very dangerous indeed.*
　　　　She is *twenty-two years old.*
　　　　The strikers are *determined to stay put.*

NG   　John is *a very lucky man.*
　　　　The two brothers are *pilots.*

(b) Identifying Complements

NG   　　　The Robinsons are *our next-door neighbours.*

Fin.cl.   　Ken's belief is *that things can't get any worse.*
　　　　　He has become *what he always wanted to be.*

Non-fin.cl.   The only thing I did was *tell him to go away.*
　　　　　My advice is *to withdraw.*
　　　　　The best plan is *for you to go by train.*
　　　　　What I don't enjoy is *standing in queues.*
　　　　　What most people prefer is *others doing the work.*

NGs and AdjGs can occur as attributive Subject Complement in passive clauses derived from SPOdCo structures:

Professor Biggs is considered *an authority on the subject.*
The gate was left *open* all night.

(c) Circumstantial Subject Complements

Circumstantial Subject Complements are realised by NGs, AdvGs, PrepGs or by finite *WH*-clauses:

NG   　The exam is *next Tuesday.*
AdvG   The amusement park is *over there.*
PrepG   The manager is *in a good mood.*
Fin.cl.   This is *how you should do it.*

Some realisations of Subject Complement are illustrated in the following passage from a university magazine, in which a graduate characterises the early stages of his career:

New College, poorest of the rich colleges, dullest of the clever colleges and so far down the river that we had to row on the Thames is *the place where I grew up* [1]. I loved it then and I love it now. But for me real life started in investment banking. It was called *merchant banking* [2] but was *just as fashionable then to pretentious young squirts as it is now* [3]. The pay on the other hand was *something else* [4]. Everyone apart from me seemed to have a private income. Worse still, they all had private shoots and invited the chairman. No shoot, no promotion. No promotion, no pay. No pay, no shoot. It was *circular* [5] and it was *vicious* [6]. Then there were the social duties. Clients tended to be *rich, foreign and important* [7]. We squirts were *the entertainment* [8] when their offspring hit town. Unfortunately, one of them was, to me, *quite*

beautiful[9]. I stumbled, flailed around a bit and fell. It was *ridiculous*[10].
I still drove my bubble car, she owned the bank that owned the factory.
It could not last. It didn't.

Steve Baker in Oxford Today, vol. 1, no. 3, 1989.

[1]NG (ident.); [2]NG (attrib.); [3]AdjG (attrib.); [4]NG (attrib.); [5]AdjG (attrib.); [6]AdjG (attrib.); [7]AdjG (attrib.); [8]NG (ident.); [9]AdjG (attrib.); [10]AdjG (attrib.).

7.2 The Complement of the Object or Object Complement (Co)

7.2.1 Syntactic features

The Object Complement is the constituent which completes the predication when the verb chosen leads us to specify some characteristic of the Direct Object. (For verbs which introduce this type of complementation see Module 11). The Object Complement is normally placed immediately after the Direct Object:

> We found the new secretary *very helpful.*
> They have appointed my brother *Managing Director of the firm.*
> I like my coffee *black.*

The Object Complement is linked in an intensive relationship with the Direct Object, similar to that holding between the Cs element and the Subject. Although it is not linked to the Object by a copula, this is understood. For example, in the above sentences it is implied that 'the new secretary *was* very helpful', 'my brother *is* Managing Director' and 'I like my coffee when it *is* black'.

There is typically number agreement between the Direct Object and the Nominal Group realising the Object Complement, as in:

> Circumstances have made *the brothers enemies.*

But there are occasional exceptions; expressions of size, shape, colour, height, etc., which are to be explained in the same way as those seen in 7.1.1:

> You haven't made the sleeves *the same length.*

7.2.2 Semantic features

The Object Complement provides the same type of information about the Direct Object as the Subject Complement does about the Subject. That is to say, it can characterise the Direct Object in terms of the following three semantic features: a qualitative or substantive Attribute, an entity which identifies it, or a circumstance which relates specifically to the Direct Object in the given situation:

Attribute:	We found the secretary *helpful.*
	Your work has made the show *a success.*
identity:	They appointed him *Manager.*
circumstance:	I like them *on toast.*

Just as with the circumstantial Cs, the inherent circumstantial Co is distinguished from an optional Adjunct, even though in some cases there is a grammatical SPOd structure without the Object Complement, as in *I like them*.

7.2.3   Realisations of the Object Complement

(a) Attributive Object Complements can be realised by:

AdjG	They found the dog *dead* by the roadside.
	The government's imports policy has made the farmers *furious.*
Indefinite NG	Does he consider himself *a genius?*

(b) Identifying Object Complements are realised by:

Definite NG	Can you imagine yourself *the owner of a luxury yacht?*
	They elected her *Miss Universe.*
Finite cl.	Our supporters' enthusiasm has made the club *what it is today.*

Nominal Co elements are sometimes introduced by *as* or *for*, and are then analysed as Prepositional Object Complements. Some verbs require this; with others it is optional:

as + NG	Party members regard him *as the only possible candidate.*
	I consider you *(as) my best friend.*
for + NG	Do you take me *for a complete idiot?*
	I'm sorry! I mistook you *for a friend of mine.*

(c) Circumstantial Object Complements can be realised by:

| PrepG | The burglars left the house *in a mess.* |
| | We found the Dean *in a good mood.* |

This type of realisation of Object Complement is distinguished from the superficially similar realisation of Adjunct (e.g. *in five minutes* in *The burglars left the house in five minutes*) by the intensive relationship linking the Direct Object and its Complement. This can be tested by paraphrase with *be* (*The house was in a mess*; **The house was in five minutes*).

| Finite cl. | We put our coats *where we could see them.* |
| | Dye your shoes *whatever colour you like.* |

Non-finite cl.	We'd better not leave the children *playing in the garden.*
	I regard that *as asking the impossible.*
	The authorities ordered hundreds of demonstrators *placed under house arrest.*
	His admirers believe him *to be a genius.*

7.3   The Predicator Complement (Cp)

The term 'Predicator Complement' is used by some grammarians to refer to any obligatory constituent that is not classed as an Object. Here we shall use it in a more restricted way to denote an obligatory constituent which does not fulfil the criteria used to define the three types of Object and the two types of Complement so far discussed.

7.3.1   Types of Predicator Complement

Certain verbs take an obligatory Complement but do not passivise or, if they do, the same relationship is not maintained. We shall distinguish the following types:

(a) The constituent following relational verbs

These include *have*, *possess*, *lack*, *suit*, *resemble*, *contain* and *fit*:

We have *plenty of time.*	*Plenty of time is had.
I don't possess *any valuables.*	*No valuables are possessed.
His argument lacks *force.*	*Force is lacked by his argument.
Will 5 o'clock suit *you*?	*Will you be suited by 5 o'clock?
This jar contains *nails.*	*Nails are contained in this jar.
These gloves don't fit *me.*	*I am not fitted by these gloves.

(b) The constituent following verbs of measure

These include such verbs as *measure*, *cost*, *take* and *weigh*:

The window measures 1m by 2m.	*1m by 2m was measured the window.
Each ticket cost two dollars.	*Two dollars were cost by each ticket.
This suitcase weighs 20 kilos.	*20 kilos are weighed by this suitcase.
The flight to Tokyo took 21 hours.	*21 hours were taken by the flight to Tokyo.

(c) The constituent following verbs of equal reciprocity
These are verbs such as *marry* and *resemble*:

Sam married *Susan* last May.	*Susan was married by Sam last May.
Joe resembles *his father*.	*Joe's father is resembled by him.

The reason for non-passivisation in examples such as these is that the relationships expressed by these verbs are by their very nature not extensive. Verbs of possession and non-possession (*lack*), of suitability, resemblance and measure are essentially processes of *being* (17.3), and the semantic structure shows that the nominals which follow them cannot be considered as Direct Objects. *Weigh* and *measure* can be used in an extensive sense with a Direct Object Complement as in:

The airport official weighed her suitcase.	Her suitcase was weighed by the airport official.
My assistant measured the room.	The room was measured by my assistant.

(d) Obligatory Directional Complements
Many verbs which express movement, in many cases together with the manner of moving (e.g. *creep*, *slip*, *slide*, *steal*, etc.), require a Complement which names the direction or destination of the action.

They crept *into the cave*.
I'll just slip *into something more comfortable*.
He tends to slide *over questions* without answering them.
We stole *out of the lecture-room*.
The hurricane brought disaster *to the crops*.

(e) Other obligatory Predicator Complements
With many verbs which do not passivise the predication is completed by means of a finite or non-finite clause. When this cannot be replaced by a Nominal Group or by *it* we classify it as Predicator Complement. Such verbs are exemplified here by *complain*, *wish*, *wonder*, *fancy* and *bother* in the senses illustrated below:

He complains *that he is never consulted about anything*.
I wish *he wouldn't speak with his mouth full*.
I wonder *if you would like to join us for tea*?
Fancy *getting into a panic over a silly thing like that*!
Don't bother *to clear away the dishes*.

Many verbs such as *force* and *urge* take one Object which can become Subject in a passive clause and a second obligatory constituent which cannot. Nor can this second Complement be replaced by a NG or *it*. We include this latter constituent in the category of 'Predicator Complement' as a subtype of ditransitive complementation (see 10.3.5).

They forced him *to turn out his pockets.*
I urged her *to see a psychiatrist.*
The physiotherapist encouraged the patient *to walk by herself.*
This kind of landscape reminds me *of Zimbabwe.*

7.3.2   **Realisations of the Predicator Complement**

The Predicator Complement can be realised by:

nominal group
prepositional group
finite clause
non-finite clause

NG	Smoke means *fire.*
	The tent sleeps *four.*
	I have *no money.*
PrepG	She dashed *into the child's bedroom.*
	He crawled *under the wire-netting.*
	They deprived him *of his rights.*
Finite cl.	He boasts *that no-one can beat him.*
	She complains *that he doesn't write.*
	I wonder *why they went to live in a place like that.*
Non-fin. cl.	I can't help *thinking he must be crazy.*
	He doesn't bother *changing the sheets/to change the sheets.*
	Tom trusts us *to let him know the result.*

Finite clauses such as those illustrated above can also be analysed, perhaps more satisfactorily, as 'projected' clauses after verbal or mental processes such as *boast*, *complain* and *wonder* (see Module 36).

In the following extract examples of the three types of Complement (Cs, Co and Cp) are numbered, together with the occurrences of Adjunct (A):

Next morning[1] it was *still*[2] snowing. The British couple left *their hotel*[3] *early*[4] *to find the right bus stop, which was at the other end of the city in a poor suburb.*[5] [6] [7] The snow fell *listlessly*[8] *from a low grey sky*[9] and fine shreds of dingy snow lay *sparse*[10] on the dark earth.[11] The bombs of the recent war had laid the streets *here*[12] *flat*[13] *for miles around.*[14] The streets were etched *in broken outlines*,[15] and the newly-laid railway lines ran *clean and shining*[16] *through them.*[17] The station had been bombed, and there was a wooden shed doing temporary duty *until another could be built.*[18] *Nearby*[19] a mass of workmen were *busy*[20] *on a new building that rose fine and clean and white out of the miles of damaged houses.*[21] [22] [23] They looked *like black and energetic insects at work*[24] *against the stark white of the walls.*[25]

Doris Lessing, *The Eye of God in Paradise*, in *Collected Stories.*

[1] A; [2] A; [3] Cp; [4] A; [5] (to end of sentence) A; [6] *at the other end of the city* Cs; [7] *in a poor suburb* Cs; [8] A; [9] A; [10] Cs; [11] Cs; [12] A; [13] Co; [14] A; [15] A; [16] Cs; [17] A; [18] A; [19] A; [20] Cs; [21] (to end of sentence) A; [22] *fine and clean and white* Cs; [23] *out . . . houses* A; [24] Cs; [25] A.

MODULE 8
Adjunct, Disjunct and Conjunct

Summary

1   Adjuncts, Disjuncts and Conjuncts are optional elements which can be added or omitted without producing an ungrammatical clause.

2   The Adjunct provides non-inherent circumstantial information and is realised by adverbs, AdvGs and PrepGs. In a constituency analysis, Adjuncts are also realised by clauses.

3   Disjuncts provide an attitudinal comment by the speaker on the content of the clause. They are realised by adverbs, PrepGs and clauses.

4   Conjuncts are not elements of structures, but connectors of structures. They reflect how the speaker intends the semantic connections to be made between one part of the discourse and another. They are realised by adverbs and AdvGs, PrepGs and clauses.

8.1   The Adjunct (A)

8.1.1   Syntactic and semantic features

The Adjunct is an optional element of clause structure which can be omitted without affecting the grammaticality of the clause. In the following example, the bracketed items are Adjuncts:

> (If at all possible) I'll see you (tomorrow) (after the show) (with Pete and Susan) (outside the main entrance).

Adjuncts can be added to any of the basic clause structures:

> SP(A)   The bells rang *all day long*.

SPOd (A)	Tom hired a car *at Doncaster.*
SPOprep(A)	You must allow for delays *in holiday periods.*
SPOiOd(A)	He sent me some flowers *through Interflora.*
SPOdCp(A)	He convinced the jury of his innocence *without much difficulty.*
SPCs(A)	The weather is rather unpredictable *in these parts.*
SPOdCo(A)	They elected her Miss Universe *in Miami.*

Whereas the more central elements of clause structure typically have fixed places in the clause, Adjuncts are characterised by their flexibility as regards position:

Hastily she hid the letter.
She *hastily* hid the letter.
She hid the letter *hastily.*

While the great majority occur at the end of the clause, they also occur frequently in initial and medial positions, these being determined to a great extent by semantic and pragmatic considerations (see 55.2).

Semantically, Adjuncts represent optional circumstances of many different types which are attendant on the process. A further type, the Mood Adjunct, relates to the operator in the verbal process and expresses modal or temporal meanings (*I'll willingly help*, *We've not yet finished*). These meanings of adverbs are described in 54.4. The semantic classification of circumstantial elements in general is found in Module 19.

A third characteristic of Adjuncts is the tendency of different types of circumstances to be expressed by different Adjuncts in a single clause, not as coordinated realisations of a single adjunctive element, but as separate, multiple Adjuncts:

He worked *for a while* (A1) *as a theatrical agent* (A2) *in London* (A3) *before moving into commercial television* (A4).

8.1.2   Realisations of the Adjunct

The Adjunct element is prototypically realised by PrepGs and AdvGs. NGs occur with spatial and temporal meanings. In grammars based on constituency, it is held that Adjuncts can be realised by almost any class of unit except the VG and the AdjG, and in traditional grammar great prominence is given to 'adverbial clauses'. Although this analysis appears satisfactory when applied to isolated sentences, in discourse it is often difficult to uphold the status of clauses as Adjuncts embedded in a single main clause. We shall prefer, in Chapter 7, to analyse dependent circumstantial clauses as part of a clause complex. It is true, however, that there is no systematic relation between the class of unit and the specific type of circumstance expressed. The following examples illustrate the wide range of forms and meanings traditionally associated with the Adjunct element in English:

PrepG

Set the video *for 9.00.* (time)
Did you do that *on purpose*? (intention)
I can't live *without you.* (accompaniment)
She married him *for his money.* (reason)
He was educated *in Scotland.* (place)
We take a week's holiday *from time to time.* (frequency)
I never travel *by air.* (means)
You'll never open the gate *with that key.* (instrument)
He spoke to me *in a very strange way.* (manner)

Closed-class adverbs

here, there, everywhere, abroad, upstairs, where (space)
then, now, tomorrow, yesterday, always, when (time)
thus, so, wrong, likewise, how, well (manner)

Open-class adverbs

probably, possibly, certainly, undoubtedly (modality)
quickly, carefully, cheaply, angrily, gently (manner)
hourly, daily, weekly, monthly, annually (frequency)
previously, subsequently, recently, presently (time)

AdvGs

It has been raining *very hard indeed.* (manner)
We were flying *due north.* (direction)
There's a good restaurant *quite near here.* (location in space)
Just then, I heard a loud bang. (location in time)
Do you bake your own bread *every other day*? (frequency)
I'm tired; I can't walk *much further.* (extent)

Finite clauses

According to a constituency analysis, in each of the following examples a circumstantial clause is adjunctive to a main clause. For an alternative and in many ways preferable analysis of such clauses as dependent but not embedded, see Chapter 7.

She has hidden the money *where no-one will ever find it.* (space)
Bring the books back *as soon as you've finished with them.* (time)
He talks *as if he owned the place.* (manner)
If you drop out, everyone will do the same. (condition)
Don't touch an abandoned bag, *even though it seems harmless.* (concession)
There was plenty to see, *so (that) no-one was bored.* (result)
Just because you're scared, you needn't make a fuss. (reason)
As one drives south, the landscape becomes more barren. (proportion)

Non-finite clauses

Non-finite clauses at Adjunct can occur with or without a Subject. When the Subject is not explicit, it is normally the same as that of the main clause. The semantic value of the non-finite clause is in many cases less clear than with finite clauses.

> He wrote quickly, *in order to finish in time.* (purpose)
> *Sitting at the window,* she watched the parade. (contingency)
> *Horrified at what he had done,* Phil phoned the police. (reason)

Explicit Subjects sometimes require an introductory word such as *with* or *for*. Others are optional:

> *(With) things being as they are,* it's no use asking them for support. (contingency)
> *For John to recover his sight,* every possible treatment was tried. (purpose)

Abbreviated clauses

Abbreviated clauses, especially verbless clauses, may or may not have an explicit Subject. Those without it may be introduced by a subordinator:

> *If in doubt,* count ten and think again. (condition)
> *When on holiday,* try to forget your problems. (time)
> *An expert philatelist,* he soon discovered the fake. (reason)

NGs

Nominal Groups as realisations of the Adjunct element refer mainly to circumstances of time and matter. They comprise a small number of relatively fixed expressions:

> Are you going abroad *this year*?
> Yes, we reserved our flight *last week.*
> Why don't you play it *the other way* for a change?
> No, I want to play it *my way.*

The following letter contains a number of Adjuncts realised by different types of units. [1] and [2] are adjunctive, not to the main clause but to the embedded clause *not to hear from you*:

1 Apr. 19–

Dear Mr Trevanny,
　　I was sorry not to hear from you *this morning* [1] or *so far this afternoon.* [2] But *in case you change your mind,*[3] I enclose a card with my address in Hamburg. *If you have second thoughts about my proposition,*[4] please telephone me *collect*[5] *at any hour.*[6] Or come to talk to me *in Hamburg.*[7] Your round-trip transportation can be wired to you *at once*[8] *when I hear from you.*[9]
　　In fact, wouldn't it be a good idea to see a Hamburg specialist *about*

your blood condition[10] and get another opinion? This might make you feel more comfortable.

I am returning to Hamburg *Sunday night.*[11]

Yours sincerely,
Stephen Wister

Patricia Highsmith, *Ripley's Game.*

[1] and [2] coordinated NGs (time); [3] finite clause (contingency); [4] finite clause (condition); [5] AdvG (manner); [6] PrepG (time); [7] PrepG (place); [8] PrepG (time); [9] finite clause (time); [10] PrepG (matter); [11] NG (time).

8.2 The Disjunct (D)

8.2.1 Features of the Disjunct

Disjuncts are optional additions to a clause or sentence. Syntactically, they remain somewhat separate from the clause, since their message refers to the whole of the clause or sentence. For this reason, they are usually found before the clause or after it:

Naturally, he spoke to me when he saw me.
He spoke to me when he saw me, *naturally*.

But they can also be placed parenthetically or between commas, within a clause or sentence:

He *naturally* spoke to me when he saw me.
He spoke to me, *naturally*, when he saw me.

Textually, Disjuncts represent a comment by the speaker or writer on the content of the clause as a whole. The semantic import of this comment is treated in Chapter 6 under modal and relational Themes. Briefly, three main types of comment may be distinguished:

(a) the subjective or objective attitude of the speaker:

Broadly speaking, the Health Service is satisfactory.

(b) the speaker's opinion regarding the validity of the content:

Undoubtedly, he is the finest pianist alive today.

(c) the relation of the clause with something outside it:

Medically, it has little to recommend it.

8.2.2 Realisations of the Disjunct

Disjuncts can be realised by adverbs, Prepositional Groups, finite and non-finite clauses:

adverbs:	frankly, honestly, confidentially, hopefully, truly
prepGs:	in fact, in reality, at a rough guess, by any chance
non-fin cl.:	to be frank, to tell the truth, strictly speaking
fin. cl.:	if I may be frank with you . . .; don't take this personally, but . . .

8.3   The Conjunct (Conj)

8.3.1   Features of the Conjunct

Whereas Adjuncts modify elements of clauses, and Disjuncts add a comment on whole clauses or sentences, Conjuncts tell us how the speaker or writer understands the semantic connection between two utterances, or parts of utterances. They are not, therefore, elements of structure, but connectors of structure:

between groups:	Lord Shaftesbury was a persuasive speaker and *furthermore* a great pioneer of social reform.
between clauses:	The students are on strike; *nevertheless*, the examinations will not be cancelled.
between sentences:	He has been undergoing treatment for asthma since he was a boy. *Consequently*, he never went in for sports.
between paragraphs:	*In addition to all this. . .* *First of all . . .* *In conclusion . . .*

That is to say, Conjuncts occur at some boundary established at a significant point in the organisation of the text.

The role played by Conjuncts differs from that of coordination in that coordination expresses a logical relationship whereas Conjuncts express textual relationships. The conjunctions *and*, *but* and *or* have typically the function of expressing logical connection, but they can also function as Conjuncts. Most Conjuncts, unlike conjunctions, are not tied to a fixed position in relation to the units they conjoin.

Semantically, many different types of connection can be expressed. Here, we shall briefly exemplify four main types (see also Chapters 6 and 9):

(a)   additive: and, furthermore, in other words, similarly . . .
(b)   adversative: but, instead, on the contrary, on the other hand . . .
(c)   causal: for, because, so , therefore, then, in that case . . .
(d)   temporal: then, next, after that, finally, at once, first . . .

In daily life, turns in conversation are often initiated by a common institutionalised Conjunct, such as *Well . . ., Now . . ., Oh . . ., So . . . .* Semantically, many different types of connection can be made, and these are treated in

Chapter 6 under the headings 'Conjunctive Themes' and 'Continuative Themes' and throughout Chapter 7 on the clause complex.

8.3.2   Realisations of the Conjunct

The Conjunct can be realised by various classes of units:

closed-class adverbs:	nevertheless, moreover, first, therefore, next, now
open-class adverbs:	namely, accordingly, consequently, alternatively
PrepGs:	in other words, by the way, on top of that
AdjGs:	last of all, better still
AdvGs:	more accurately
Fin. cl.:	that is to say, what is more
Non-fin.cl.:	to sum up, to cap it all

The following extract from Alan Ayckbourn's play *Just Between Ourselves*, in which Neil comes to Dennis's house to inspect a car for sale, contains examples of the 'expressive' function of Disjuncts and the 'logical' and 'continuative' functions of Conjuncts:

Dennis:	It's the pilot light, you see. It's in a cross draught. It's very badly sited, that stove. They should never have put it there. I'm planning to move it. *Right, now*.[1] You've come about the car, haven't you?
Neil:	*That's right.*[2]
Dennis:	*Well*,[3] there she is. Have a look for yourself. That's the one.
Neil:	Ah.
Dennis:	*Now*[4] I'll tell you a little bit about it, shall I? Bit of history. *Number one*,[5] it's not my car. It's the wife's. *However*,[6] *now*[7] before you say ah-ah – woman driver, she's been very careful with it. Never had a single accident in it, touch wood. *Well*[8], *I mean*[9] *look*[10], you can see hardly a scratch on it. *Considering the age*[11]. *To be perfectly honest*[12], *just between ourselves*[13], she's a better driver than me – when she puts her mind to it. *I mean*[14], *look*[15], *considering it's what – now – seven – nearly eight years old*[16]. Just look for yourself at that body work.
Neil:	*Yes, Yes*[17].

Alan Ayckbourn, Just Between Ourselves.

[1] Conjunct; [2] Conjunct; [3] Conjunct; [4] Conjunct; [5] Conjunct;
[6] Conjunct; [7] Conjunct; [8] Conjunct; [9] Conjunct; [10] Conjunct;
[11] Disjunct; [12] Disjunct; [13] Disjunct; [14] Conjunct; [15] Conjunct;
[16] Disjunct; [17] Conjunct.

TASKS ON CHAPTER 2
The skeleton of the message: Introduction to clause structure

Module 4

1 †*Bracket the non-essential constituent(s) in each of the following clauses*:
1) Many of the houses must have disappeared since my father's day.
2) The pace of development was rapid.
3) I explained briefly to Mrs Davies that there was a power cut.
4) It seemed a good idea at the time.
5) Can you tell me the way to the Post Office?
6) I felt my face turn red.
7) Somebody snatched my bag in the park.
8) They strode in silence to the car-park.
9) He helped the girl to her feet.
10) I drew a deep breath.
11) She seems to have altered.
12) He hesitated for a moment, wondering what to do.
13) The full text of the speeches at the symposium will be published in a special issue of *The Oxford Review of Education*.
14) The telephone began to ring insistently at six o'clock on a cold November morning.
15) Arsenal became League champions for the fifth time on Monday.
16) Sierra Leone is one of the world's biggest producers of diamonds.
17) The romantic lyrics of post-war songs reflected a general desire to return to normal life.
18) He happened to coincide with the Chicago wedding of his former secretary.
19) Their performance exceeded all expectations.
20) The film is just under 90 minutes long.

2 *In what ways do Objects differ from Complements, and both of these types of constituents from Adjuncts?*

Module 5

1 †*Check the criteria for identifying Subject. Then read again the extract from* The Secret Diary of Adrian Mole aged 13¾ *on page 33. Which of the criteria for Subject are clearly fulfilled? Which are not clear? Which do not occur at all? Add some tag questions and note the pronominal forms that occur.*

2   *Write an entry for today in your own diary.*

3   *†Identify the constituent which realises Subject function in each of the following clauses:*
   1)   The use of caves for smuggling is as old as the hills.
   2)   There were about half a dozen men seated in the bar.
   3)   The light of a torch flickered.
   4)   What the critics failed to understand is that his art was not sacrificed to popularity.
   5)   The list of people who she says helped her is long.
   6)   It was my great good fortune to meet him before he died.
   7)   The wind coming down from the snowfields above woke us every night as we lay in our tent.
   8)   It makes sense to tell the neighbours you are going away on holiday.
   9)   It is sometimes argued that there is no real progress.
   10)   There's no way of knowing what goes on in their minds.

4   *†Extrapose the Subject in the following clauses:*
   1)   That Pam is seeking a divorce surprised us.
   2)   To leave without saying goodbye was bad manners, really.
   3)   Who she goes out with doesn't interest me.
   4)   To swim in a cold lake is not my idea of fun.
   5)   That recognising syntactic categories at first sight is not easy is obvious.

5   *†Identify the different types of **it** Subjects in the clauses below:*
   1)   It costs £6,500 a day to hire a 40-seat marquee at Wimbledon during the tennis tournament.
   2)   Why spend so much to sit in the cold and watch tennis? – Ah, it's the place to be.
   3)   It was quite sunny and warm when we left the house, but by early afternoon it had started to rain.
   4)   For some people, it's a nightmare when they can't park their cars.
   5)   I don't much like the heat. – Oh, I do. I find it stimulating.

Module 6
1   *†Identify the constituent which functions as Direct Object in each of the following clauses, and the class of unit which realises this function:*
   1)   Shoppers are flouting the no-sales-on-Sunday trading laws.
   2)   He banged the door as he went out.
   3)   He pointed out that foreign doctors were not permitted to practise in that country.
   4)   The negotiations have achieved very little.
   5)   Don't expect a classical rendering of Shakespeare's text at this year's International Theatre Festival.
   6)   A team of divers have discovered what they believe to be sunken treasure.

7) One doubts that many will survive the long trek over the mountains.
8) You might ask what is the use of all this.
9) He shovelled a ton of gravel into the back garden.

2 †*Discuss the application of the criteria for identifying Direct Object in relation to the above examples. Can they, for instance, be passivised?*

3 †*Which of the following clauses contain a constituent which functions as Recipient Indirect Object and which contain a Beneficiary Indirect Object? Apply the passivisation and prepositional tests to distinguish between the two:*
1) They did not give the leaders time to establish contact.
2) Why should I write him his French essays?
3) I am going to make myself a nice cup of tea.
4) He is offering us a chance in a million.
5) Why did she refuse to lend me her mink coat?
6) Save your brother a piece of your birthday cake.
7) Her parents have told the doctors that they are grateful and thankful.
8) She has bought her boy-friend a butterfly pillow to use on long flights.
9) He left his daughter most of his fortune.
10) He'll paint you your portrait for a large sum.

Module 7

1 †*Some of the following clauses contain Subject Complements, others Object Complements. Identify each and state the class of unit which realises each of these constituents:*
1) Leave him alone.
2) They must prove themselves fit for the task.
3) Spying on firms has become a multi-million pound industry.
4) What will they call the baby?
5) Archie's bar is where it's at.
6) Life is a series of accidents. That's what he thinks.
7) He made his films accessible to a wide public.
8) He kept us laughing all evening with his jokes.
9) The weather has turned unexpectedly cold lately.
10) Make the coffee a bit stronger, would you?
11) I am an animal lover working in a department dedicated to cancer research.
12) I think you have mistaken the gentlemen's lavatory for the stage door.
13) They found Winston's sense of humour rather disconcerting.
14) What colour is she going to dye her hair?
15) Any attempt to re-establish control over the liberated areas would prove self-defeating.

2 †*Some of the clauses below contain a Predicator Complement and others contain a Prepositional Object. Underline these and apply the criteria in 7.3.1 to distinguish between them:*

1) His masterpieces equal any in Europe.
2) They don't approve of what we are doing.
3) The robot costs over a million pounds.
4) They accused him of illegal possession of fire-arms.
5) A burglar could not easily break into this house.
6) An attractive secret agent has confessed to snooping.
7) His work-mates are always getting at him.
8) I have no idea how to tackle this problem.
9) She lacks discretion.
10) Tom reached for his pipe.

Module 8

1 †*Distinguish between the occurrences of Adjunct and those of Predicator Complement in the clauses below:*
1) He was chairman of the English Tourist Board for five years.
2) We booked rooms for two nights at a magnificent hotel on the coast.
3) The soldier crawled under the barbed wire.
4) Our patients feel safe and secure in the nurses' hands.
5) Another dealer has knocked £300 off the standard price for this car.

2 †*Discuss the status of the constituents following the verb* **find** *in the two clauses below:*
1) The police found the gang's hide-out without much difficulty.
2) The police found the gang's hide-out more elaborately equipped with technology than they had expected.

3 †*Rewrite this text and mark the following: / each constituent of the clauses and (a) the function, (b) the class of unit which realises the function:*

The sun never sets on the tourist empire. But travel pictures, business contracts and sports programmes don't tell the full story: getting there may be no fun at all. Aircraft perform flawlessly, but what happens to passengers, flight crews and cabin staff? Jet lag. A mass phenomenon, almost as universal as the common cold.

Kathleen Mayes, *Beat Jet Lag*.

Write a few lines on the effects of jet lag. Then look again closely at your own text and see how it might be improved as regards realisations of clause elements and connectors.

4 *Read the following text closely, trying to relate the forms to the meanings expressed. Orthographic sentences are numbered for convenience:*

She was beautiful.[1] Everything you have ever imagined about a solid, mannish-looking writer with a sensible hair-cut and glasses is pure fiction.[2] As a young woman, and she was very young when she first achieved success, Agatha Christie was a tall, Scandinavian-looking blonde who was, on the one hand, secretive and introverted, and on the other, impulsive, passionate and sensitive.[3] She could have been a concert pianist if she hadn't suffered terribly with nerves.[4] She could have been a professional singer, so clear and perfect was her voice.[5] Instead, she became the best-known, best-selling detective writer in the world, outselling Shakespeare and only beaten in book sales figures by the Bible.[6] Yet her background was most unlikely for a writer.[7]

In Britain, August 1990.

(i) Identify the Subject, Objects (if any) and Complements in each of the clause structures that make up the numbered sentences.
(a) What class of unit realises the Subject in [2]?
(b) Which type of clause element, apart from Subject and Predicator, is most frequent in this text? How is it realised?

(ii) Identify the Conjuncts, or connectors, used throughout this text. What type of units do they connect – words, groups, clauses, sentences? How do these Conjuncts help to establish meaningful connections between the ideas and to guide the reader through the text?

3

The development of the message:

Complementation of the verb

Introduction

Verb complementation refers to the number and type of Objects and Complements that follow particular verbs or classes of verbs, and the syntactic structures that verbs enter into. The term **complement** is used in this grammar, as in others, when referring to complementation in general. When capitalised, **Complement** refers to specific elements of clause structure. Since Objects and Complements have been dealt with from the point of view of clause elements in Chapter 2, and are referred to as realisations of semantic functions in Chapter 4, this chapter aims to outline in a way that may be helpful to the student of English the main choices open to speakers from the standpoint of the verb.

There is rarely a one-to-one relationship between form and meaning, and clause structures are no exception. Configurations of clause elements into structures can express more than one meaning and, conversely, a meaning can be expressed in similar ways by more than one structure. Here we shall enumerate the complementation types based on the verb and attempt to relate each to its possible meanings – the converse of Chapter 4, where we start from the meanings.

We shall identify the following main types of complementation:

Type	Objects/ Complements	Example	Structure
Intransitive	no Object	Tom disappeared.	SP
	one Complement	He crept *into the cave*.	SPCp
Monotransitive	one Object	Tom bought *a car*.	SPOd
		You can rely *on Tom*.	SPOprep
Ditransitive	two Objects	Tom gave *her a ring*.	SPOiOd
	one Object + one Complement	Ask *someone the way*.	SPOdCp
Complex transitive	one Object + one Complement	Tom made *Susan angry*.	SPOdCo
Copular	one Complement	Susan is *unhappy*.	SPCs

Such an outline represents an oversimplification of the variety of complementation types which occur in English, and is intended at this stage simply to give an overall view of the main configurations. For this reason some of the minor types of complementation, particularly those involving Predicator Complements dependent on a small number of verbs, are not included here, but are dealt with in subsections.

The number of verbs in common use in English is very large, especially in certain constructions, such as the monotransitive. For these it is impossible to give more than a representative selection of those verbs most likely to be encountered by the student.

A further complication arises from the fact that many verbs, especially those of general meaning, such as *get, turn* and *make*, admit more than one type of complementation, each of which reflects a different type of situation. *Make*, for instance, can enter into all but intransitive and SPOprep structures:

I'll make some tea.	SPOd
It makes for good relations.	SPCp
I'll make you a pizza.	SPOiOd
I'll make the questions easy.	SPOdCo
They make a good couple.	SPCs

MODULE 9
No-complement verbs and verbs with one Object or Complement

Summary

1 Verbs which do not take Objects or intensive Complements are **intransitive**. Some are almost always intransitive (*snow, blink, vanish*). Others represent intransitive uses of basically transitive verbs (*eat, drive, read*). In some types there is a corresponding transitive use; in others, not.

2 Many intransitive verbs, particularly those which refer to location (*stand, lie*) or movement (*go, creep*), take a locative or directional Predicator Complement which is inherent to the situation expressed.

3 Verbs with one extensive Complement are called **monotransitive**. The Complement is a **Direct Object** or a **Prepositional Object**. Prototypically it represents an entity, less prototypically a fact or a situation within the main situation. Entities are typically realised by group structures, facts and situations by clauses.

4 Certain small groups of verbs which express non-extensive relationships (*have, lack, measure, fit, marry* among others) take a Predicator Complement.

9.1   Intransitive Verbs

When a verb has no Object or intensive Complement it is intransitive. Semantically, one participant only is involved in the action expressed by the verb.

Intransitive verbs can be divided into two main classes:

9.1.1   Pure intransitives

These are verbs which are almost exclusively intransitive, such as *arrive, elapse, fade, vanish, rise, materialise, rain, snow*.

> It is *snowing*. The sun *rose*. The clouds *disappeared*.
> Time *elapsed* but no-one *arrived* and the show didn't *materialise*.

Many pure intransitives express behaviour which is typically involuntary or semi-involuntary, as in the following list:

> *blink, blush, collapse, cough, cry, die, faint, fall, laugh, sleep, slip, smile, sneeze, scream, tremble, yawn*

Other intransitives, particularly verbs of position such as *stand, live, hang* and verbs of movement such as *walk, stroll, trudge, sail, slip*, typically require a spatial or temporal locative or directional Predicator Complement to complete their meaning:

> The National Theatre stands near the river.
> He is lying in a hammock.
> We have lived here for ten years.
> Your raincoat is hanging in the hall.
> The boys trudged up the steep path.
> He strolled towards the bar.
> The ship sailed out of the harbour.
> I'll slip into something more comfortable.

We can compare this verb *lie*, meaning to be in a prone position, with *lie*, a 'pure' intransitive, meaning to tell lies:

> He is lying in a hammock.   He is lying.

We can also contrast uses of the same verb, such as *run*, which can occur as a pure intransitive in the answer to *How does Tom keep fit? – He runs*, and with a directional Complement in *He runs to the bus-stop* (see 4.1.1).

9.1.2   Verbs used both transitively and intransitively

According to the degree of correspondence with a transitive use, and to the Subject–Predicator relationship in each, we can distinguish the following types:

(a) The Direct or Indirect Object may be left unexpounded when its referent is understood by social convention (*drive / park a car, wave one's hand, save money, drink alcohol*) or is not specific: one can *drive* various kinds of vehicles, *teach* different subjects and *write* different things:

> It is dangerous to *drive* if you have been *drinking*.
> They are *saving* to buy a house.
> She *teaches* and he *writes*.
> It's impossible to *park* in the city centre.
> He *waved* to them from the bridge.

Other Objects would not be left unexpounded, for example *wave a flag; save time; drink a glass of milk*.

Certain verbs are used in this way in more restricted social contexts such as *order* in *Have you ordered yet?* in a restaurant or *give* in *Many people gave generously* when what is given is a donation.

With certain verbs such as *tell* and *promise*, Direct and Indirect Objects may be ellipted when they represent something already mentioned, as in *I told him, You promised* for *I told him the truth, You promised me a bike*. This makes them appear to be monotransitive and intransitive respectively, but they are classed as ditransitive, three-place verbs.

(b) Verbs which have a corresponding causative use. The intransitive construction forms part of an 'ergative pair' (see 14.7):

> The door *opened*. (X opened the door.)
> The ball *rolled*. (X rolled the ball.)
> The bell *rang*. (X rang the bell.)

(c) 'Pseudo-intransitives', which express the properties or potential of an entity to undergo the action expressed by the verb (15.3). There is no corresponding transitive use.

> Your essay *reads* well.
> This material won't *wash*; perhaps it will *dry-clean*.

(d) Verbs with the meaning of 'reciprocal participation', such as *join, combine, disagree, meet* and *kiss*. There is a corresponding construction with a Predicator Complement:

> My sister and her boyfriend *met* at a dance. (... met each other)
> The two rivers *join* to form the Amazon. (One river joins the other.)
> We *disagreed* on almost every major point. (We disagreed with each other on almost every major point.)

9.2 One-Object verbs and complementation types

Monotransitive verbs are those which take one Object. Prototypically the Object is a Direct Object, less typically a Prepositional Object.

9.2.1 Verbs which take a Direct Object

This type is very numerous (*lose the tickets*; *win the race*; *break a cup*; *see the flames*). Direct Objects are also found as complements to phrasal verbs used transitively (*switch off the light*; *rub out a mistake*).

9.2.2 Verbs which take a Prepositional Object

These are prepositional verbs such as *see to, deal with* (*see to the plane tickets, deal with any emergency*), phrasal prepositional verbs such as *run out of* (*run out of petrol*), and multi-word combinations which end in a preposition, such as *get rid of* (*get rid of old newspapers*). Cohesion between verbs and prepositions is variable (see 6.3); in this book prepositional verbs are counted as monotransitive (i.e. what follows the verb is a Prepositional Object) if (a) their cohesion is such that without the preposition the verb is either meaningless (e.g. *account for*) or has a different meaning (e.g. *allow, allow for*); and (b) if the verb can passivise with the completive of the preposition at Subject (*The loss can't be accounted for*). In addition, such verbs can typically answer a question beginning with *what* or *who(m)* (*What/ who must I see to?*). A short list of some common verbs of this kind is given below. Many verbs, such as *think* and *hear*, admit more than one preposition with a slight difference of meaning:

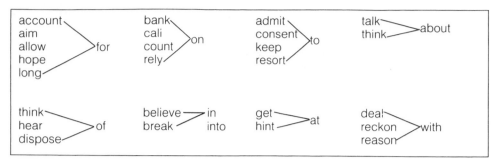

The Prime Minister can't account for the loss of votes.
We're banking on everyone's support for the rally.
He would never resort to cheating.
What are you hinting at?
The organisers hadn't reckoned with a strike.

In the episode related below, a deserter from the army enters a pub, hoping his accent will not give him away. The transitive verb *realise* introduces clauses containing intransitive verbs. These and other intransitives and transitives which express movement and perception carry the narrative forward and contribute to the tension of the situation described:

> I suddenly realised *that the accordion had stopped playing*[1] [2]. The singing *had ceased*[3]. So had [4] the click of the skittles. I *turned quickly*[5]. No-one *was talking*[6]. They were all *looking at me*[7]. I *was seized* [8] with a panic desire to *run*[9]. But my feet *seemed to be* [10] rooted to the floor. I *took a grip* [11] on myself. They *couldn't tell* [12] just by the look of me. 'Why do you *stare at me?*' [13] I *heard myself ask*[14].
>
> Hammond Innes, *The Killer Mine*.

[1] monotransitive + *that*-clause; [2] phased intransitive; [3] intransitive; [4] intransitive (ellipted); [5] intransitive; [6] intransitive; [7] monotransitive; [8] monotransitive (passive); [9] intransitive; [10] phased copula (see Ch. 9); [11] monotransitive; [12] monotransitive (Object unexpounded); [13] monotransitive; [14] complex transitive; [15] ditransitive (Indirect Object unexpounded).

The Object following a transitive verb is not necessarily a NG representing a person or thing (see Chapter 10), but can also be a clause which represents a fact, a report or a situation, makes a proposal or expresses an indirect question. The Recipient of these facts, proposals and indirect questions is not encoded in the syntax of a monotransitive clause: there is no Indirect Object. This is presumably because the clause simply 'projects' what someone has said or thought (see 36.3). Many monotransitive verbs such as *say* and *explain* reflect this and do not take an Indirect Object, although a Recipient can be added if necessary. We can say *He explained that you were ill* or *He explained to me that you were ill* but not **He explained me that you* *were ill*. On the other hand, non-finite embedded clauses may have their own Subject, which introduces a new participant in the subordinate situation (I want *you* to stay). The choices of clause types in monotransitive complementation are summarised below:

Clause as Complement with monotransitive verbs

finite *that*-clause:	He believes that *he's right*.
finite *WH*-clause:	He asked *what I meant*.
	He believed *what I told him*.
non-finite *to*-infinitive clause:	
− own Subject	He wants *to stay*.
+ own Subject	He wants *us all to stay*.
non-finite *-ing* clause:	
− own Subject	He doesn't enjoy *driving*.
+ own Subject	He doesn't enjoy *her driving*.

9.3　Meanings expressed by *that*-clause Complements

A single *that*-clause Complement can be used to express factual information which is reported, known, believed or perceived; it can be used to make proposals and suggestions and to describe situations which produce an emotive effect on the Subject. The choice of verb and the syntax of the *that*-clause contribute to these different meanings.

9.3.1　Facts

Facts are expressed by a *that*-clause containing an indicative. This represents an indirect statement and follows verbs of certain types:

(a) Verbs of knowing and perceiving such as *know, believe, think, imagine, dream, conclude, gather, infer, learn, find, discover, realise, observe, see, sense*.

> He always believes that he is right.
> I gather you have lived abroad for some time.
> We found that the last train had just left.
> Did you infer from her sudden departure that she was annoyed?
> I sensed that she was not at all happy.
> Have you ever dreamed that you were flying through the air?

(b) *Hope, expect* and *suppose*, when they refer to potential situations rather than facts, frequently take a modal auxiliary in the indicative *that*-clause:

> I expect you would like something to drink after your journey.
> We hope that you will visit us next time you are in Spain.
> I suppose he must have lost his way.

9.3.2   Reports

Reports encode things that people have said. They are introduced by verbs of communicating, such as *say* and *announce, answer, explain, mean, mention, report* and *state*, and performatives such as *admit, acknowledge* and *confess*. (Performatives carry out the action they name, in first person active or in third person passive clauses). *Tell* as a verb of communicating is ditransitive, but it is monotransitive when it means 'distinguish', as in the narrative text on p. 76. Reports are treated in Chapter 7 under 'indirect speech' as projected clauses in clause complexes.

> The Minister answered that he didn't know.
> You never mentioned that you had got married.
> A Government spokesman explained that fuel stocks were dwindling rapidly.
> Do you mean that there is no cure?
> It is admitted that a quick peace settlement is unlikely.
> I confess that I am totally at a loss for a solution.

9.3.3   Proposals

These are indirect directives which aim at getting someone to do something. They are, therefore, potential rather than factual, and this potentiality is expressed by means of a subjunctive or *should + infinitive*, in the *that*-clause. They follow verbs such as *propose, suggest, recommend* and *demand* (but not *command*, which takes two Complements):

> The chairman proposed *that a vote be taken.*
> > *that a vote should be taken.*
> Her friends suggested *that she see a psychiatrist.*
> > *that she should see a psychiatrist.*

The present subjunctive as in *see* is commonly used even in past environments. The subjunctive realisation is more widely extended in American English and the *should* alternative in British English, where the subjunctive sounds too formal for any but the most solemn occasions. In informal British English the indicative is used (*He suggested that she sees a psychiatrist*).

9.3.4   Decisions, intentions and resolutions

These are Complements which follow verbs such as *decide, intend* and *resolve*. These verbs describe mental processes of volition which take *that*-clauses containing a subjunctive or *should* when a new participant is introduced as the Subject of the subordinate clause. (For complementation by infinitive clause see 9.6.1):

> It has been decided *that she rest for a month.*
> > *that she should rest for a month.*
> The committee has resolved *that a coordinator be appointed.*
> > *that a coordinator should be appointed.*

9.3.5   Situations with emotive effect

These are expressed by means of *that*-clauses following verbs such as *feel* + adjective (*feel sorry / glad / ashamed / amazed*), the expression *it's a pity* and, in more formal registers, *regret* and *marvel*. The subordinate situation can be presented either as a fact, by means of a plain indicative, or as a potentiality by means of *should*. The subjunctive is not used:

> I am amazed that she *feels* so confident.
>   *should feel* so confident.
> Everyone regrets that he *left* the team.
>   *should be leaving* the team.

9.4   Prepositional verbs and *that*-clauses

That-clauses cannot follow prepositions and consequently do not occur as Prepositional Objects. With some prepositional verbs such as *insist on, agree to, admit to, see to* certain alternatives are possible:

(a) the preposition is dropped as in:

> We insist *that he is told the truth*. (*We insist on that he is told the truth.)
> They agreed *that there should be changes*. (*They agreed to that there should be changes.)

(b) the preposition is retained and is followed by anticipatory *it* before the *that*-clause:

> We insist on *it that he is told the truth*.
> They agreed to *it that there should be changes*.

With some other prepositional verbs *the fact* can be inserted before the *that*-clause, turning this into an appositional NG:

> You must *allow for the fact that he is severely depressed*.
> Several of the neighbours have *commented on the fact that the gates were left open all night*.

9.5   Meanings expressed by *WH*-clause Complements

Many verbs which express verbal or mental processes can also take a finite *WH*-clause as their Direct Object or Prepositional Object. The *WH*-clause can express a nominal entity or abstraction in the form of a clause (nominal relative), an indirect interrogative or an indirect exclamation:

> He insists on *what he believes is right*. (nominal relative)
> The tourist asked *why the museum was closed*. (indirect interrogative)
> She realised *what an opportunity it was*. (indirect exclamative)

It may be difficult to distinguish between nominal relative clauses and indirect interrogative clauses when these are introduced by an item such as *what, who* and *where*, which can function both as relative pronouns and as interrogative pronouns:

He explained *what I already knew.* (nominal relative)
He asked *what I knew.* (indirect interrogative)

9.5.1   Things or abstractions: nominal relative clauses

A nominal relative clause expresses an entity and can be considered as a NG qualified by a relative clause, except that the *WH*-element has merged with the NG head. It can therefore be identified by replacing the *WH*-word by a fuller NG such as *that which* (rarely used), *the person who, the place where,* as in:

Take *what you like.* (= *that which/the thing(s) you* like)
He beat *whoever opposed him.* (= *the person(s)* who opposed him)

The *WH*-item can be a determiner as in:

He gratefully accepted *what help was offered.* (= *whatever help/any help*)

9.5.2   Doubts and lack of knowledge: indirect interrogatives

Indirect interrogatives are those which express doubt or lack of knowledge, and as such contain an implicit question. They often follow such verbs as *ask, doubt, inquire, discuss, can't tell, don't know*. They include yes / no clauses introduced by *whether* and *if*. S–Finite inversion does not normally occur, as it does in independent interrogative clauses. Compare:

Indirect interrogative	Direct interrogative
Let's inquire *where the dining-car is.*	*Where is the dining-car?*
Ask *whether anyone rang.*	*Did anyone ring?*

9.5.3   Indirect exclamatives

The embedded *WH*-exclamative clause maintains the same *WH-* + S + Finite order of elements as the independent exclamative (see 27.1):

You'll never believe *what a good time we had.*
I said *how sorry I was.*

Certain utterances of this type may be ambiguous, either an interrogative or an exclamative interpretation being possible:

You can't imagine *how much he knows about explosives.*

exclamatory interpretation: *he knows a lot about explosives* interrogative interpretation: *the extent of his knowledge about explosives*

Facts, reports, doubts and implicit questions as Complements are extremely common in everyday conversation. They feature in this authentic dialogue between one person who has kept diaries for years and another who would like to have access to these diaries in order to complete a survey:

> 'I don't know *whether you have talked with Hilary about the diary situation.*' [1]
> 'Well, she has been explaining to me in rather more general terms *what you are sort of doing* [2] and *what it was all about.*'[3]
> 'I gather *you've been at it for nine years.*' [4]
> 'By golly, that's true, yes. It's not a long time of course in this sort of work, you know.'
> 'Well, no. But it's quite a long time by any standards.'
> 'Yes, suppose *so.*' [5]
> 'She told me *what you did* [6] and we decided *that we were both a bit out of date compared with present-day students ...*' [7]
> 'Well, I suppose *that's true.*' [8]
> 'But I don't know *that I'm going to be a* vast amount of help to you. [9] I was interested in your advertisements but I gather *you're after an enormous amount of information* [10] and I really don't know *that I've got ...,* [11] you know, *whether what I've got is of any help.* [12]

> Adapted from J. Svartvik and R. Quirk, *A Corpus of Spoken English*.

[1] lack of knowledge (indirect interrogative); [2] = the things that ... (nominal relative); [3] = the things that ... (nominal relative); [4] fact (*that*-clause); [5] *so* replaces ellipted *that*-clause; [6] = the things that (nominal relative); [7] fact (*that*-clause); [8] fact (*that*-clause); [9] doubt as fact (*that*-clause); [10] fact (*that*-clause); [11] doubt as fact; [12] doubt (indirect interrogative).

The relatively high number of 'doubts represented as facts' following *I don't know* are not to be interpreted as lack of information. They express, rather, the diary-writer's unwillingness to hand over his diaries without being reassured of the use that will be made of them.

9.6 Meanings expressed by non-finite clause Complements

Non-finite clauses which can be single Complements are infinitive clauses and *-ing* clauses. Participial *-en* clauses do not occur. Non-finite clause Complements represent subordinate situations which are integrated into the main situation.

> Most of us need *to get away for a while.*
> But we'll avoid *going to the coast in August.*

The criteria for analysing such clauses as Direct Objects are explained in Chapter 2, 6.1.3.

We do not analyse as embedded clauses at Direct Object catenatives (hypotactic or 'phased' Verbal Groups) such as *He failed to appear; I ventured to raise an objection*. (39.4)

Some verbs take *to*-infinitive complementation, others *-ing* complementation, while certain verbs can take either of these. Many non-finite clauses can occur with or without a Subject of their own. When the Subject of the non-finite clause is not explicitly mentioned, it is understood to be the same as the Subject of the matrix clause. We shall illustrate each type separately.

9.6.1　Potential situations as Complements: *to*-infinitive clauses

To-infinitive clauses tend to describe a situation which is potential in relation to the process represented by the verb. Verbs such as those in the following list introduce such a potentiality:

afford	agree	arrange	ask	attempt
decide	demand	deserve	expect	need
offer	promise	refuse	swear	undertake
vow	want			

Certain verbs do not take a subordinate clause Subject:

> You should *attempt* to answer every question.
> I *asked* to see the Minister himself.
> Has he *decided* to take early retirement?
> I *demand* to be told the truth.
> You *deserve* to be treated better.
> The man waiting outside *refuses* to give his name.
> He *swore* / *vowed* to give up smoking.
> I can't *promise* to be there before nine.
> We can't *afford* to be without a car.

Other verbs can take a sub-clause Subject:

> They *want* their children to have a good education.
> I'll *arrange for* Mary to see an optician.
> Would you *like* me to lend you a track-suit?

9.6.2　Actualised situations as Complements: *-ing* clauses

Non-finite *-ing* clauses as Complements tend to express a meaning of actualisation. The following verbs take only *-ing* clauses. Many of these admit a subordinate clause with its own Subject. *Can't help* is commonly followed by anticipatory *it* + finite *if*-clause when a new participant is introduced as Subject of the subordinate clause (*I can't help it if the typewriter is noisy*):

avoid	detest	dislike	enjoy
miss	resent	risk	can't help

You should avoid *travelling in the rush hour*.
They disliked *living in a big city*.
I can't help *splashing paint everywhere*.
I think he misses *someone taking care of him*.
We can't risk *you all missing the plane*.
Many people enjoy *sleeping in on Sunday mornings*.
Arthur resents *having to take the dog out every day*.

In most cases the Subject of the non-finite clause cannot be separated from its clause to become Subject in a passive clause (*The children are wanted to have a good education*; *You can't be risked missing the plane*). This criterion is often used to distinguish these SPOd structures from SPOdCp structures such as *I advised her to go* and SPOdCo structures such as *We found her lying on the floor*, which can passivise (*She was advised to go; She was found lying on the floor*).

9.6.3   Potential and actualised meanings contrasted: *to*-infinitive and *-ing* clauses

When both *to*-infinitive and *-ing* complementation are possible the difference of meaning between potentiality and actualisation is normally present. For this reason, the *to*-infinitive form is used when a specific occasion is referred to, often of a future or hypothetical kind, as in *I would like to go to Paris*; an *-ing* clause tends to be used when the implied reference is to repeated occasions, as in *I like going to Paris*. Contrasts of meaning vary, however, between different groups of verbs.

(a) **Emotive verbs** such as *like, love, hate* and *prefer* (but not *enjoy, detest* and *dislike* which admit only *-ing* clauses) establish this distinction clearly:

I like *listening to Mozart*.
I'd like *to buy a compact disc-player*.

Pepe loves *riding in taxis*.
Pepe would love *to go to the zoo by taxi*.

Most people hate *standing in queues*.
Most people would hate *there to be no public transport*.

There is a further distinction between *like* + *to*-infinitive and *like* + *-ing* indicative clauses. *Like* + *to*-infinitive can have the meaning of 'consider the action right or appropriate', and refers to a potential action, whereas *like* + *-ing* has an actualisation meaning similar to *enjoy*:

I don't like *to telephone him after midnight*. (= I don't think I should)
I don't like *telephoning people I don't know*. (= I don't enjoy it)

Dread always anticipates unpleasant states or events. When followed by a *to*-infinitive clause it usually occurs in the locution *I dread to think*, which means *I think with apprehension* as in *I dread to think what may happen*; otherwise, *dread* takes an *-ing* clause for either single or repeated situations:

> I dread / I have always dreaded *going to the dentist*.

(b) **Verbs of retrospection** such as *regret, remember, forget* but not *recall*, which takes only *-ing*, take non-finite Complements which mark a difference of time reference in relation to the main verb. With a *to*-infinitive clause, the action expressed is seen as *following* the mental process of remembering or forgetting, whereas an *-ing* form marks the action as *previous* to the mental process:

> I remembered *to lock up the house*. (= I remembered that I had to lock up the house, and did so.)
> I remembered *locking up the house*. (= I remembered that I had locked up the house.)
> I forgot *to give him the message*. (= I forgot that I had to give him the message, and so didn't give it.)
> I forgot about *giving him the message*. (= either: I forgot that I had given him the message; or: I forgot that I should give him the message.)
> I regret *telling / having told you the bad news*. (= I am sorry that I told you the bad news.)
> I regret *to tell you there is some bad news*. (= I am sorry to have to tell you / I tell you regretfully there is some bad news.)

Regret + *to*-infinitive is always followed by a verb of communication (*say, tell, announce, inform*, etc., which is performative), whereas *regret* + *-ing* has no such limitation (She regretted *going out without an umbrella*).

(c) **Verbs of intention and proposal** such as *mean, try* and *propose* have meanings which differ according to the type of non-finite clause complementation. Compare:

> My son means *to study oceanography*. (= intends)
> Studying oceanography means *going to a coastal region*. (= involves)
> Try *to go to bed early, for a change*. (= attempt)
> Try *going to bed early, for a change*. (= experiment)
> I propose *to make a donation to cancer research*. (= intend)
> I propose *making a donation to cancer research*. (suggest)

The *to*-infinitive clause after *mean, try* and *propose*, as after *regret*, is essentially part of a complex Verbal Group which describes an action carried out in two phases, and in this grammar is preferably analysed in this way. We would not consider such clauses to be Complements, strictly speaking, but part of a 'phased' VG. This analysis is supported by the corresponding WH-question, which appropriately contains an infinitive *What does he mean to do? What should I try to do? What do you propose to do?*

The *WH*-question without an infinitive *What does it mean? What shall I try? What do you propose?* corresponds to the verb + *-ing*, in which the non-finite *-ing* clause can be considered a Complement which expresses an action or a situation. With *propose* + *-ing*, the Subject is not even necessarily involved in the action, whereas with *propose* + *to*-infinitive it must be.

In accordance with these criteria, verbs of *starting, continuing* and *ending*, when followed by either *to*-infinitive or *-ing* clauses, are analysed as phased Verbal Groups. (39.4)

9.7   Verbs followed by a Predicator Complement

Certain small groups of verbs take an obligatory constituent which cannot become Subject in the passive and which we have called the Predicator Complement (see 7.3.1). Those which might be confused at first glance with transitive verbs include relational verbs (*have, lack, contain, resemble, fit* and *suit*), verbs of measuring (*measure, weigh, cost, take*) and verbs of equal reciprocity (*marry, resemble*) (see 7.3.1 for discussion and examples).

A further group which includes such verbs as *complain, fancy, mind, wish* and *wonder* are more satisfactorily analysed as verbs of mental or communicative meaning which project reported and sometimes quoted locutions and ideas in a clause complex (see 7.3.1, 36.3.1 and 36.3.2).

> # MODULE 10
> # Verbs with two Objects or Object and Complement

Summary

1   Under the heading 'Verbs with two Objects or Object and Complement' we include two main types of complementation: (a) **ditransitive verbs** (*give, send, fetch*, etc.) which take two Objects, **Indirect** and **Direct**, sequenced in that order, each of which can potentially become Subject in a passive clause (*give Esther a present*); and (b) verbs which take one **Object** followed by a **Predicator Complement** (e.g. *It reminds me of Italy*).

2   Ditransitive verbs are further classified into those which take a Recipient Indirect Object (e.g. *give*) and those which take a Beneficiary Indirect Object (e.g. *fetch*), these differences being reflected in the ability to passivise and in the preposition *to* or *for* used, respectively, in the semantically equivalent Prepositional Group.

3   The second type of complementation (P + Od + Cp) is included here because both the Object and the Complement are obligatory. The Object can become Subject in a passive clause (*I am reminded of Italy*) but lacks the prepositional equivalent which is characteristic of Indirect Objects (**It reminds to me*). We therefore treat it as a Direct Object. The Complement of the Predicator cannot become Subject in a passive clause (**Italy is reminded of*).

   The Predicator Complement can be realised by different NGs, PrepGs and clauses, with a considerable variety of meanings, representing as it can a thing, a fact, an indirect interrogative, an order, request or offer.

4   The types of complementation treated here express many interpersonal relationships based on actions such as those of *advising, fetching, giving, offering, paying, persuading, reminding, sending, showing, telling, writing.*

10.1   Two-complement patterns

There are two main patterns of complementation, based on the types of Objects or Object and Complement governed by the verb: (a) verbs which take two Objects, a Direct and an Indirect, and (b) verbs which take an Object followed by a Predicator Complement.

10.2   Verbs which take Indirect + Direct Objects: verbs of transferring and verbs of benefitting

This type of complementation expresses situations in which three participants are involved, encoded syntactically as the Subject and the two Objects. The verbs which occur are typically verbs of transferring and of benefitting. They are illustrated as follows:

> He gave Esther a present.
> He promised Bill a rise in salary.
> She told the children a story.

The Direct Object typically represents an entity such as a present, a rise in salary, a story. The Indirect Object typically represents a person, or at least an animate being, which is the Recipient or the Beneficiary of the action. For the distinction between Objects and Complements see 4.1.2. The syntactic and semantic features of the Direct and Indirect Objects are described more fully in Module 6.

   The person who receives the action or benefits from it is placed immediately after the verb as an Indirect Object (SPOiOd structure) or can often be placed after the Direct Object as a Prepositional Object (SPOdOprep structure):

> He showed *the policeman his driving-licence*. (SPOiOd)
> He showed *his driving-licence to the policeman*. (SPOdOprep)
>
> Will you order *me a taxi*, please? (SPOiOd)
> Will you order *a taxi for me*, please? (SPOdOprep)

The Prepositional Object contains *to* when the participant is Recipient and *for* when it is Beneficiary (14.5) and this difference is determined by the verb.

Verbs which take Recipient Indirect Objects and alternative *to* Opreps are typically verbs of transferring goods, services or information from one person to another. They include:

give	grant	hand	leave	offer	owe	pass
promise	read	send	show	teach	throw	write

We are offering *our clients* a unique opportunity. (. . . *to our clients*)
He owes *several people* money. (. . . *to several people*)
I handed *Jennifer* the pile of letters. (. . . *to Jennifer*)
He teaches *medical students* English. (. . . *to medical students*)
Do you send *your neighbours* Christmas cards? (. . . *to your neighbours?*)

Verbs which take Beneficiary Indirect Objects, with an alternative *for* construction, are verbs which carry out an action on someone's behalf. They include:

book	bring	build	buy	cash	cut	fetch
find	get	keep	leave	make	pour	reserve
save	spare	write				

Book *me* a seat on the night train. (. . . a seat *for me*)
Would you cash *me* these travellers' cheques? (. . . *for me*)
She cut *the boys* some slices of ham. (. . . *for the boys*)
I've kept *you* a place in the front row. (. . . *for you*)
He got *us* a very good discount. (. . . *for us*)
She made *all the family* a good paella. (. . . *for all the family*)

Certain verbs such as *bring, read* and *write* admit either *to* or *for* as alternatives, depending on the interpretation. With *to* as in *bring it to me, read it to me, write it to me*, I receive the thing, either physically or mentally. With *for* as in *bring it for me, read it for me, write it for me* the thing is brought, read or written on my behalf.

As has been explained in 6.2, SPOiOd structures with Recipient Indirect Objects (*They gave Tim a prize*) admit two passives, one with the Recipient at Subject (*Tim was given a prize*), the other with the Affected at Subject (*A prize was given to Tim*). These are useful alternatives when the active Subject is not known or is not important in the discourse, as can be seen in the following extract from an article in an American magazine under the heading 'Education: doing bad and feeling good:'

A standardized math test was given to 13-year-olds in six countries last year. Koreans did the best, Americans did the worst, coming in behind Spain, Britain, Ireland and Canada. Now the bad news. Besides *being shown triangles and equations, the kids were shown the statement 'I am good at mathematics'.* Koreans came last in this category. Only 23% answered yes. Americans were No. 1, with an impressive 68% in agreement.

American students may not know their math, but they have evidently absorbed the lessons of the newly fashionable self-esteem curriculum wherein *kids are taught to feel good about themselves.* . . . Judging by the international math test, . . . kids already feel exceedingly good about doing bad.

Charles Krauthammer in *Time*, 5 February 1990.

10.3 Verbs which take Direct Object + Predicator Complement

When the obligatory complement following the Object does not fulfil the criteria for Objects established in Modules 4 and 6, we call this constituent the Predicator Complement (see 7.3). There is a considerable variety of realisations of this type of structure, illustrated by the following examples:

We'll allow *everybody a ten-minute break.*
The shop assistant charged *me too much for the toothpaste.*
They are comparing *one theatre production with another.*
The nurse encouraged *the patient to eat.*

Here the Object typically describes a person or thing or abstraction while the Predicator Complement may refer indirectly to a person, an activity or a situation. Usually only the Object constituent can become Subject in a passive clause:

Everybody will be allowed a ten-minute break.
I was charged too much for the toothpaste.
One theatre production is being compared with another.
The patient was encouraged to eat.

Both Direct and Indirect Objects share this potential. However, this Object does not fulfil the second syntactic criterion for Indirect Objects, that of substitution by a phrase with *to* or *for*, which help to identify Recipient and Beneficiary roles. We will therefore call this Object a Direct Object:

*A ten-minute break will be allowed to everybody.
*Too much was charged to me for the toothpaste.

The verbs which take a Direct Object followed by a Predicator Complement can be grouped into several classes:

10.3.1 Type *cost, charge* + NG + NG

These are verbs such as *allow, ask, bet, charge, cost, deny, forgive, grudge, wish, refuse* and 'empty' uses of *give*. The second constituent after the verb cannot become Subject in a passive clause and there is no prepositional alternative to the Object. We would not say, for instance, *A great effort was cost John* nor *It cost a great effort to John* instead of *It cost John a great effort*. Other examples illustrate this feature:

He wished me a happy birthday.	*He wished a happy birthday to me.
He gave the door a push.	*He gave a push to the door.
Let's ask someone the way.	*Let's ask the way to someone.
The bank has refused me a loan.	*The bank has refused a loan to me.
They grudge him his pocket-money.	*They grudge his pocket-money to him.

Ask can take *of*, (= demand) = She asks too much of everyone.

10.3.2 Type *remind* + NG + PrepG

This type is illustrated by *remind someone of the time, deprive someone of their freedom*. The Direct Object is affected in some way by the action and the Predicator Complement may be an entity, an abstraction or a situation.

Some of the verbs taking this construction are listed here according to preposition:

for	from	of	to	with	on	in
blame	prevent	accuse	confine	charge	blame	interest
thank	protect	convict	help	compare	compliment	
		convince	introduce	supply	congratulate	
		deprive	refer			
		remind	sentence			
		rob	treat			

He *convinced* the jury *of his innocence*.
They *robbed* her *of her watch and jewels*.
The government should *inform* the public *of the consequences*.
Will you *introduce* us *to your friends*?
I *congratulated* Janet *on her success*.

Ditransitive prepositional verbs are frequently used in the passive, with the Direct Object constituent becoming Subject in the passive clause:

The jury was convinced of his innocence.
She was robbed of her watch and jewels.
The public should be informed of the consequences.
Janet was congratulated on her success.

Blame and *supply* have alternative structures based on different prepositions (*blame something on someone* / *blame someone for something; supply someone with something* / *supply something to someone*). As a result, they admit two passives:

> They *blamed* the fire *on the gardener*. They *blamed* the gardener *for the fire*.
> The fire was blamed *on the gardener*. The gardener was blamed *for the fire*.
> That firm *supplies* paper *to the university*. That firm supplies *the university with paper*.
> Paper is supplied *to the university* (by that firm).
> The university is supplied *with paper* (by that firm).

The Subject of the verb and the Recipient or Affected Object may refer to the same person, in which case a reflexive pronoun is used:

> *He* convinced *himself* of the rightness of his actions.
> Why don't *you* help *yourself* to wine?

10.3.3   Type *convince* + NG + *that*-clause

Many verbs of communicating (*assure, inform, tell, notify*), verbs of causing someone to think or believe or know something (*convince, persuade, remind, teach*) and the performative verbs *bet, promise* and *warn* can take a finite *that*-clause after the Direct Object:

> The doctor *assured us that she is in no danger*.
> I *bet you that no-one will accept the offer*.
> He finally *convinced the jury that he was telling the truth*.
> The police *notified my friend that his car had been found*.
> They *persuaded me that the plan was feasible*.
> *Remind your father that we have visitors tonight*.
> Experience *has taught them that a back-up copy is essential*.
> Has anyone ever *told you that you're beautiful?*

Bet can take a Direct Object expressing the sum wagered:

> I *bet you ten pounds that no-one will accept the offer*.

With certain verbs of communicating which are basically monotransitive such as *confess, point out, explain, prove* and *signal* a Recipient participant can be added, expressed by a Prepositional Group with *to* before the *that*-clause.

> He *confessed to me* that he was extremely alarmed.
> Sir Humphrey *explained to the Minister* that delays might be fatal.
> I *pointed out to John* that few people would agree.
> Can you *prove to the commission* that the effects are not harmful?
> He *signalled to us* that we should keep quiet.

Other verbs which admit *to* + Recipient PrepG include the following:

acknowledge	*admit*	*announce*	*declare*	*mention*	*propose*
recommend	*remark*	*report*	*state*	*suggest*	

These verbs do *not* take regular Indirect Objects nor can the Recipient become Subject in a corresponding passive clause. We cannot say, for instance,* *Sir Humphrey explained the Minister that delays might be fatal* nor* *The Minister was explained that delays might be fatal*. If a passive is required, perhaps to avoid mentioning the active Subject, in this case Sir Humphrey, some verbs (not including *answer*) allow an alternative structure with anticipatory *it* and extraposed Subject (see 30.5.1):

It was explained to the Minister that delays might be fatal.

This alternative corresponds to the structure containing the PrepG *Sir Humphrey explained to the Minister that delays might be fatal*.

10.3.4   Type *advise* + NG + *WH*-clause

Information based on *what, where, when* and *how* to do something is expressed by a *WH*-clause as second complement of a ditransitive verb (*tell someone what to do*). Some common ditransitive verbs which introduce indirect interrogatives are listed below. Most of these can take a *WH*-finite or non-finite clause; *remind* is commonly used with a non-finite.

advise	ask	remind	show	teach	tell

Can you advise *us what we should do / what to do*?
Tom will show *you where you can send it / where to send it.*
I'll ask *someone who we can give it to / who to give it to.*
The instructor taught *the dancers how they should breathe / how to breathe.*
Tell *me how I can switch it on / how to switch it on.*
Remind *me when to switch it off.*

10.3.5   Type *encourage* + NG + *to*-infinitive clause

Indirect commands, requests and other directives are introduced by the following ditransitive verbs, by which the Subject aims at getting someone to do something. They include verbs of causing, enabling, obliging, permitting and encouraging. The second complement is a non-finite *to*-infinitive clause. As with other ditransitives, passives are commonly used:

advise	allow	ask	beg	challenge	enable
encourage	forbid	force	get	help	lead
order	persuade	tell	trust	urge	

He advised her *to see a doctor.*
She'll probably ask you *to lend her some money.*
I challenge you *to disprove my argument.*
Passengers are forbidden *to talk to the driver.*

Can she be persuaded *to change her mind*?
Tell the children *to keep quiet*!
He urged his friend *to give up drugs*.
An unexpected clue led the police *to suspect a kidnap*.
This law will enable elderly people *to claim higher pensions*.
Tom's friends encouraged him *to enter the competition*.
I trust you *to keep these papers in a safe place*.
They got all the neighbours *to sign the petition*.

10.3.6   Type *make* + NG + infinitive clause

The causative verbs *have, let* and *make* take an infinitive clause without *to*. With *help* either a *to-* or a bare infinitive is possible:

I'll have my secretary *make you a reservation*.
They won't let you *visit the patient yet*.
They made the prisoners *stand against the wall*.
Can you help me (*to*) *move this piano*?

In passive clauses *let* is replaced by *allow* (*You won't be allowed to see the patient yet*); *make* takes a *to*-infinitive (*The prisoners were made to stand against the wall*). *Have* admits no passive at all.

The possible realisations of these two main complementation patterns can be summarised as follows:

Two-complement patterns		
Indirect Object	**Direct Object**	
NG +	NG	*He gave Esther a present.*
Direct Object	**Predicator Complement**	
NG +	NG	*It cost John an effort.*
NG +	PrepG	*He reminded her of the time.*
NG +	finite *that*-clause	*He assured her that he cared.*
NG +	finite *WH*-clause	*He asked me where the library was.*
NG +	non-finite *to*-infinitive clause	*He told us to sit down.*
NG +	non-finite bare infinitive clause	*He made them stand up.*

As can be seen, non-finite *-ing* clauses and *-en* clauses do not occur as ditransitive complements. Non-finite *-ing* clauses can, however, occur as completives of prepositions (*congratulate someone on winning a prize; prevent burglars from entering*).

Instead of a NG as Direct Object, a nominal relative clause can occur (tell *whoever calls* to leave the keys).

Some of the variety of two-complement patterns is illustrated in this extract from a magazine:

Sniffing food for about 30 seconds before you eat it *can help you lose weight* [1], says an expert in weight loss.

'You*'re* in fact *tricking the brain into thinking* [2] that you've already eaten,' explains Dr. Alan Hirsch, 'so you don't eat as much.'

In a study, Dr. Hirsch *had 20 people sniff their food* [3] before eating it – and the results were amazing. 'We found that they each lost between 10 and 12 pounds over a three-month period.'

So if you have an urge for a candy bar, *hold it up to your nose* [4] for 30 seconds, then *put it away*[5]. Usually you'll be able to resist the urge to eat it!

National Enquirer, 9 December 1989.

[1] *help* + Od + infinitive clause (potential action); [2] *trick* + Od + prep. + *-ing* clause (metaphorical direction); [3] causative *have* + Od + infinitive clause (action); [4] *hold* + Od + two directional Complements; [5] *put* + Od + directional Complement.

MODULE 11
Verbs with one Object and one intensive Complement

Summary

1   Verbs with one Object and one intensive Complement are called complex transitive. The Direct Object generally represents a person or thing, and the Object Complement adds information about this entity from the standpoint of the Subject, as in *I found the place empty.*

2   This information can **describe** or **identify** the referent of the Direct Object by means of some **attribute**; or express a **circumstance** or **situation** in which the referent is said to be. The participant encoded as Direct Object can typically be made Subject in a passive clause.

3   There is an extensive relationship between Subject, Predicator and Object, and an intensive relationship between the Object and its Complement.

4   The relationship between verb and Object Complement is either 'current' or 'resulting'.

11.1   Complex transitive meanings and complementation types

Complex transitive complementation enables us to say something about the person or thing encoded as the Direct Object in a way that relates it to the Subject and to the action described by the verb. What is said may be an Attribute (He keeps the garden *beautiful*), or an identification of the Direct Object (They elected her *Miss America*) or a circumstance (I found her *lying on the floor*) or the result of a causative action (They appointed him *chairman of the committee*).

The SPOdCo construction contains an extensive relationship, that between Subject and Direct Object, and an intensive relationship, that between Direct Object and Object Complement. This intensive relationship can often be brought out by paraphrase (*The garden is beautiful; she is Miss America; she was lying on the floor; he is chairman of the committee*). Taking the NG as the typical realisation of the Direct Object, the syntax of complex transitive complementation may be summarised as follows:

Complex transitive complementation types

Direct Object	+	Object Complement	
NG	+	AdjG	Hold your hands *steady*!
NG	+	NG	He called her *an angel*.
NG	+	PrepG	I prefer it *with water*.
NG	+	Finite clause	
			He made the team *what it is today*.
NG	+	Non-finite clause	
		(a) *-ing*	He kept us *waiting*.
		(b) *to*-inf.	He left it *to dry*.
		(c) *-en*	He left me *stunned*.

11.2   Expressing Attributes of the Direct Object

The Object Complement can express a state or characteristic of the person or thing named by the Direct Object. This type of Attribute is sometimes called a 'current Attribute'. It is introduced by verbs of the following types of meaning:

(a)   verbs of causing to remain in a certain state such as *leave, hold* and *keep*.

(b)   mental process verbs such as *believe, consider, think, find, imagine, judge, presume, hold*.

(c)   affection process verbs such as *want, like* and *prefer*.

> He *keeps* the garden *beautiful*.
> The news *left* me *speechless*.

I *imagined* him *much older.*
They *judged* him *fit for military service.*
I *hold* you *responsible for any breakages.*
His colleagues consider him *too old for the job.*
Do you *want* the chicken *hot or cold?*

An Attribute can also express a state caused by the action of the verb. It is then called a 'resulting Attribute'. Such verbs represent processes of doing and include *bake, drive, get, knock, make, paint, rub, send, serve, wipe* and verbs of declaring such as *appoint, call, brand, label, name, declare, report, turn* and *certify*, which confer an official status.

You've *baked* the cakes *hard.*
That barking dog *is driving / sending* me *mad.*
They *labelled* the contents *dangerous.*
The heat *has turned* the milk *sour.*
They *declared* the bridge *unsafe.*
Get your priorities *right!*
I've *made* the sauce *too thin.*
These windscreen wipers don't *rub* the windscreen *dry.*
No, they just *wipe* them *fairly clean.*
They *serve* the coffee *rather weak* in this place.

The Direct Object in complex transitive structures can easily be made Subject in a passive clause; in fact, with some verbs the passive is more common than the active, particularly when the Agent is unexpounded as in *he was presumed dead; he is reported missing; she was certified insane; the contents are labelled dangerous.*

With some of the verbs listed above, the Attribute is not essential to make a grammatical clause (*You've baked the cakes; they labelled the contents*). We include them here because, semantically, they fit the complex transitive structure; they are commonly used in everyday English, and they illustrate the economy of this structure which combines a process with the result of the process. Other examples include *You've cut your hair short; we got the books cheap; visitors' feet have worn the steps smooth.*

11.3   Identifying the Direct Object

The Direct Object can be followed by an identifier, which is realised by a NG, a PrepG or a *WH*-clause. It occurs after verbs which refer typically to public identifications such as *appoint, christen, crown, make, name* and *proclaim*:

They appointed him *chairman of the committee.*
The witch turned the prince *into a frog.*
The efforts of all have made the party *what it is today.*
The Pope crowned Charlemagne *Emperor.*
The referee proclaimed him *world champion.*

Certain verbs such as *call* and *make* are also used in ditransitive structures.

Consequently, ambiguous examples can be invented in which one type of unit can realise two different types of constituent:

He called her an angel.	SPOdCo
He called her a taxi.	SPOiOd
I'll make you First Secretary.	SPOdCo
I'll make you an omelette.	SPOiOd

11.4   Circumstance as Object Complement

Circumstantial Object Complements are illustrated by the following examples:

They found the cat *at the bottom of the well*.
Do you want your Scotch *on the rocks*?
No, I'll have it *with water*, please.

A further type of circumstance is that of the **role** of the Direct Object. This is expressed by *as* + NG or AdjG when introduced by such verbs as *regard, refer to* and *denounce*:

His friends regard him *as a genius at chess*.
They refer to him *as an outstanding leader*.
The M.P. denounced the proposal *as unconstitutional*.

11.5   Situations as Object Complement

Situations as Object Complement are realised by non-finite clauses. There are four types:

1	*to*-infinitive	We believe John *to be honest*.
2	bare infinitive	She saw them *enter the shop*.
3	*-ing*	They found her *lying on the floor*.
4	*-en*	I heard two shots *fired in the street*.

The verbs in these types are essentially monotransitive verb followed by a Direct Object, with the difference that the Direct Object of the main verbs is also the Subject of the verb in the non-finite clause. It is sometimes known as a 'raised' Object. The Object Complement describes some action or situation in which the referent of the Object is involved. The passive is commonly used, since the more important participant is the one *known to be honest, seen to enter the shop, found lying on the floor, fired in the street*.

The separability of the Direct Object constituent from its Complement when it becomes Subject in a passive clause identifies the Complement as a separate constituent. It also distinguishes this SPOdCo structure from the superficially similar realisation of an SPOd structure with a verb such as *like* or *want*; in the latter, the embedded *to*-infinitive or *-ing* clause with its own Subject make up one single constituent. Compare:

She saw them enter the shop. — They were seen to enter the shop.
She wanted them to enter the shop — *They were wanted to enter the shop.
He found Pete washing the car. — Pete was found washing the car.
He likes Pete washing the car. — *Pete is liked washing the car.

The verb types found in these structures are as follows:

Type 1: with *to*-infinitive clause
Mental process verbs such as *assume, believe, consider, understand, feel, imagine, know* (with optional *to*).

> I imagined him *to be older.*
> We assumed the elderly man *to be his grandfather.*
> I've never known him *(to) spend much on the lottery.*
> Do you consider her *to be suitable for the job?*
> I felt her *to be somehow unwilling to talk.*

Type 2: with bare infinitive clause
Verbs of perception: *see, hear, feel, notice, watch.*

> I felt a shiver *run down my spine.*
> We saw the car *skid on the icy road.*
> Did you notice anyone *come in?*
> We watched the boats *speed down the river.*

Type 3: with *-ing* clause
Verbs of perception: *see, hear, feel, notice, smell.*
Verbs of finding and leaving: *catch, discover, find, come across, leave.*

> I can smell something *burning.*
> Did you see anyone *hanging about the building?*
> They caught him *stealing from the till.*
> We discovered the tortoise *ambling out of the gate.*
> She left the child *sleeping peacefully.*

With verbs of perception we can make a distinction between a completed action, with the complement expressed by the bare infinitive, and an uncompleted action or action in progress, expressed by an *-ing* clause; compare *we watched the house burn down* and *we watched the house burning.*

Type 4: with *-en* clause
The causative verbs: *get* and *have.*
Volitional verbs: *want, need, like, prefer.*
Verbs of perception: *see, hear, feel, watch.*
Verbs of finding and leaving: *find, discover, leave.*

> We'll have the computer *repaired within a week.*
> The boss wants these letters *typed immediately.*
> Would you like *your shoes cleaned?*
> I felt my arm *grasped from behind.*

Airport officials have found an unidentified bag *abandoned in the duty-free shop*.

The following extract from the life-story of a Mexican girl contains two examples of complex transitive complementation:

One day my father gave Antonia a box of Max Factor face powder *which she had heard advertised on the radio*. [1] She had told him to bring a box for each of us and when *I saw him come home* [2] with one box and give it to her, it hurt me. Antonia took it and said, 'Look, Consuelo, you take from here too.' But I said contemptuously, 'No, what do I want it for? You use it.' Tonia was offended and went out.

Oscar Lewis, *The Children of Sanchez*.

It should be mentioned that the author has translated Consuelo's spoken account literally, using *take* intransitively, as its equivalent can be used in Spanish, with an ellipted Object. In English 'some' would be required.

MODULE 12
Copular verbs with one Complement

Summary

Verbs with one Complement serve as a link or copula to what the referent of the Subject is or becomes. The most common copula is *be*. Other verbs used as copulas in English provide additional meaning to the mere linking. This may be sensory (*look, feel, smell, sound, taste*); or situational (*stand, lie, stay, remain, keep*); or refer to a process of becoming (*become, get, go, grow, turn*).

A single Complement after a copular verb such as *be* characterises the Subject or identifies it, telling us what the Subject is or has become; it can also express a circumstantial state of the Subject. These and other characteristics of Subject Complements, and their realisations by various syntactic forms, are explained in 7.1.

The reason is *simple*. (characterising)

Mary is *the most beautiful girl I've ever met.* (identifying)
The truck drivers are *on strike.* (circumstantial)

Verbs of being and becoming in English carry, in addition, various shades of meaning. Some, such as *be, become, get, seem*, are followed by a wide range of adjectives. Others, such as *taste, smell, sound, fall, feel, come, grow* and *turn*, are followed by a more limited range of adjectives:

12.1   Verbs of being

Verbs of *being* are stative and introduce current or existing complements. They are illustrated by the following examples:

The city by night *looked* medieval and cosmopolitan.
Such behaviour *appeared* rather childish in someone his age.
The splendour *seems* decidedly less splendid by day.
I *felt* rather nervous all through the interview.
We have to *remain* optimistic about the results.
Fast food doesn't *taste* as good as a freshly prepared meal.
The kitchen *smells* pleasantly of roasting fowl.
$220 a night for a room *sounds* rather expensive to me.
He *kept* quiet about his win at the lottery.
The weather *stayed* fine throughout the games.

12.2   Verbs of becoming

Verbs of *becoming* are dynamic and introduce resulting complements. They are illustrated by the following examples:

His latest novel *has become* a best-seller.
The jokes my father makes usually *fall* flat.
Most of the labels *have come* unstuck.
People *are getting* tired of the constant rise in prices.
The author *might prove* more censorious than the censor.
The show *turned out* a success after all.
When I refused to give him my watch, the man *turned* nasty.
We began to *grow* uneasy when the skin-diver didn't appear.

An adjective as Complement may have its own *to*-infinitive clause qualifier (*anxious to hear from you; happy to get the good news*). The various meanings expressed by this clause are explained in 53.1.2.

12.3   Other linking verbs

A small number of verbs which are normally used without complementation (*fall, come, run, loom*) can function as copulas with specific adjectives or nouns as Complement:

The child *fell flat* on its face.

> The soldiers all *fell asleep / fell ill.*
> The label has *come unstuck.*
> Most of the streams in this area *run dry* in the summer.
> The coming examination *loomed large* in his mind.

The following extract from an interview gives an idea of how the verb and its complements contribute to the expression of interpersonal relations in a text. The young person interviewed is Kirsty Ackland, the daughter of an actor. The structures she chooses help to express the meanings she wants to convey. When she describes herself or another person she uses copular complementation. When she describes the interaction between herself and her actor father, or between herself and her schoolfriends, she uses ditransitive complementation. Her father's independence is perhaps suggested by the use of *help* with an unexpounded Direct Object.

> Until *I was about 13*[1], when *I became terribly shy*[2], *I was absolutely desperate to be an actress*[3]. My sister Sammy and I *would beg Dad to* [4] *let us go to drama school* [5] but there was no way he would *allow it* [6] until we'd been educated. I went *to Putney High School*[7]. *I was the only one in the family* [8] who didn't *get a scholarship*[9]. *Dad turned up* [10] for parents' evenings and things like that but *he never helped* [11] with the homework. I used to *help him!* [12] *I loved hearing his lines*[13]. But I *never told anyone I was the daughter of an actor*[14]. Most of the fathers of the girls at school *were 'something in the City'* [15] and I *pretended Dad was an interior decorator*[16].

The Sunday Times Magazine, 29 April 1990.

[1] copular (state); [2] copular (becoming); [3] copular (state); [4] indirect request + Od + clause; [5] indirect permission + Od + clause; [6] monotransitive + situation; [7] intransitive + Predicator Complement; [8] copular, state, identifying; [9] monotransitive + thing; [10] intransitive; [11] transitive (Od unexpounded); [12] monotransitive + person; [13] monotransitive + situation; [14] verb of communicating + fact; [15] copular (state); [16] copular (state).

TASKS ON CHAPTER 3
The development of the message:
Complementation of the verb

Module 9

1   †With the help of a monolingual dictionary, say whether the verbs in the examples below are (a) exclusively intransitive or (b) can be used either transitively or intransitively:

1) Women today *are achieving* in many professions which were previously open only to men.
2) Don't *panic*! There's no real danger.
3) He *has exhibited* in all the major art galleries over the last five years.
4) You *must be joking*!
5) Most of our students *baby-sit* two or three evenings a week.
6) Her eyes *glittered* as she saw the jewels.
7) My brother-in-law *ghost-writes* for at least two politicians.
8) Have you ever heard it said that horses *sweat*, men *perspire* and ladies *glow*?
9) She'll find it difficult to make him change the way he *dresses*.
10) The little bird *quivered* in my hands.
11) Pete doesn't *adapt* easily to new situations.
12) He thinks he can take me in, but I know when he's *bluffing*.
13) Those couples who have no children of their own are often eager to *adopt*.
14) Look at Howard, he's *been dozing* all through the lecture.
15) I don't seem to be able to *concentrate* lately.
16) The two companies *have merged*.

2   †*Of the verbs which could be used transitively in exercise 1, which can be considered to have an Object unexpounded by social convention, which have an ellipted Object because the referent has already been mentioned and which represent 'reciprocal participation'?*

3   †(a)*Choose the most appropriate prepositional verb from the list on page 76 for each of the sentences below. Then (b) put each sentence into the passive:*

1) You can't . . . . Cecil, he has such fixed ideas.
2) It is not easy to . . . . old broken furniture.
3) They will . . . . the Minister of Defence to explain the charges.
4) The target they are . . . . is too high.

5)   You should . . . . your schedule if you hope to deliver the goods on the agreed date.

4   *In the text on page 76 from 'The Killer Mine', clause 12 has an unexpounded Direct Object ('They couldn't tell just by the look of me'.). In the story, what the men in the pub couldn't tell (i.e. distinguish) about the first-person narrator was his nationality. Complete this sentence with as many types of Direct Object realisations as you think are possible and suitable. Check with the complementation diagrams on pages 72 and 77.*

5   †*Combine the following pairs of clauses so that the first clause can be analysed as an embedded constituent of the superordinate clause. Add or omit whatever is necessary. The first is done for you:*
1)   He has lived abroad for several years. I gather that from what he says. From what he says, I gather that he has lived abroad for several years.
2)   Have we enough petrol to reach Barcelona? I doubt it.
3)   Is there an emergency kit in the building? Who knows?
4)   Where is the nearest Metro station? I asked.
5)   You keep the keys. We have all agreed on that.
6)   Some of the documents are missing. The Under-Secretary can't account for it.
7)   Why doesn't he look in the safe? I suggest that.
8)   We have just heard that. The spokesman confirmed it.
9)   He has been under great strain lately. We must allow for that.
10)   These letters must be posted today. Will you see to it please?

6   †*Say which of the italicised clauses in the examples below are nominal relative clauses, which are indirect interrogative clauses and which are embedded exclamatives:*
1)   He asked *where I had been all afternoon*.
2)   The spokesman announced *what we had all been hoping to hear*.
3)   You've no idea *how cold it was in Granada at Easter*.
4)   They don't know *who wrote the graffiti on the Faculty walls*.
5)   They have agreed on *who should be given the first prize*.
6)   Let's inquire *which platform the train leaves from*.
7)   I mean *what I say*.
8)   We'd better find out *whether a visa is necessary*.
9)   I said *what a pity it was they couldn't be with us*.
10)   He's sure to fall in with *whatever you suggest*.

7   *Answer the following questions using embedded* **to***-infinitive clauses or* **-ing** *clauses to express situations within the main situation – at least to start off with!*
1)   What do you particularly dislike doing on Monday mornings?
2)   Is there anything you regret?
3)   If people go off on holiday without locking up the house, what do they risk?

4) How many things do you feel you can't afford?
5) Do you feel you deserve to have achieved something you haven't?
6) What kind of thing would you absolutely refuse to do?
7) Has anyone arranged for you to do something you positively hate?
8) Is there anything that you miss especially when you are away from home?
9) What kind of situation would you tell a friend to avoid on a first visit abroad?
10) Is there anything many people simply can't help doing?

Module 10

1 †*Mark the boundaries between the constituents of the clauses below and indicate the structure of each. The first one is done for you.*
1) I/ gave/ the haughty-looking secretary/ one of my cards.   SPOiOd
2) Most teenagers attach great importance to their peer group.
3) Support for the party dropped five points in May.
4) Has she made you one of those strange concoctions of hers?
5) His uncle has left him a large fortune.
6) I ran some cold water into the kettle.
7) They granted all the prisoners a reprieve.
8) She thanked the lost-property officer for the trouble he had taken.
9) They can pressurise you into doing what you'd rather not do.
10) The Olympic committee has commissioned a Japanese architect to build one of the stadiums.

2 (a) †*Insert a suitable verb into the spaces provided:*
1) This cream will . . . . . . you from sunburn.
2) The airline official . . . . . us that we would be given lunch vouchers.
3) Has the film director . . . . . . the actress to continue?
4) Would you be so kind as to . . . . me your invitation card?
5) I . . . . you not to say a word to anyone.
6) Shall I . . . . . . both of us a curry?
7) I . . . . the results to him over the phone.
8) Did you . . . . them of your capacity to carry out the plan?
9) The Personnel Manager . . . . . to the team that each project must have a project leader.
10) The usher . . . . . . to the bride's friends to sit on the left.

2 (b) †*Test for passivisation of the clauses in 2(a) and decide which constituents are Objects.*

3 *Answer the questions below and note the complementation patterns you use:*
1) Do you find it more difficult to spare someone your time than to lend them some money?

2) What kind of thing would you find it impossible to promise someone to do?
3) How would you go about booking yourself a safari holiday in Kenya?
4) Would you rather owe someone money or a favour or have money or a favour owed to you?
5) What kind of souvenirs do you buy for your friends and family when you are on holiday?
6) What would you advise an overweight friend to eat?
7) How would you encourage an oversensitive person to react?
8) How would you help someone to be assertive without being aggressive?
9) What would you recommend a bored housewife to do?
10) Has anyone ever urged you to give up something you don't want to give up?

4   *Read the following passage, which describes a journey by taxi on the island of Corfu, and then answer the questions below:*

> We climbed into the spacious car[1], and our driver hoisted his bulk behind the steering-wheel [2] and engaged his gears with a terrifying sound[3]. We shot through the twisted streets on the outskirts of the town[4], swerving in and out among the loaded donkeys, the carts, the groups of peasant women, and innumerable dogs[5], our horn honking a deafening warning[6]. During all this our driver seized the opportunity to engage us in conversation[7]. Each time he addressed us [8] he would crane his massive head round [9] to see our reactions[10], and the car would swoop back and forth across the road like a drunken swallow[11].

> Gerald Durrell, *My Family and Other Animals.*

1) Which of the numbered clauses in the text contain Direct Objects?
2) What do these Objects refer to – persons, things, abstractions, facts, proposals, or situations within a main situation?
3) Does any clause contain an Indirect Object?
4) Which clauses contain directional or locative Predicator Complements?
5) Is there any copular complementation? (see 7.1 and Module 12)
6) Check the frequency of occurrence of each type of complementation you have found.
7) Can you relate the frequency of occurrence of certain complementation patterns with the content of the text – what it describes?

Module 11
1   †*Say which of the following clauses have complex transitive complementation and which have some other type of complementation:*
    1) I consider the whole thing totally ridiculous.
    2) You'll find it very difficult to get tickets at this late date.

3)   He never allowed Thomas to drive the jeep in his absence.
4)   That kind of film leaves me cold.
5)   His powerful imagination makes him quite different from the others.
6)   Keep your shoulders straight.
7)   He left her sitting on the bridge.
8)   They like their next-door neighbours to come in for a drink occasionally.
9)   I have never known Mr. Lyons to keep a secret.
10)   They discovered gold in the local streams.
11)   Don't you find it odd that there has been no mail for days?
12)   My parents think me foolish to give up this job.
13)   They regard them as second-class citizens.
14)   I prefer Mike to drive you to the station.
15)   Do you find snobs unbearable, funny or pathetic?

2   If you are giving an opinion in English about a person, a place, a thing, an event, etc., from a rather subjective point of view, you will find yourself using monotransitive structures with *that*-clause complements (*I think she is rather silly*), complex transitive complementation (*Oh, I found her quite amusing*) and copular complementation (*She's certainly self-assured*).

Discuss among a group of friends a person, place or event known to you all. Tape your conversation (try to forget you are being recorded!) and then analyse what you have said.

Module 12
1   *Read the following extract and then answer the questions below:*

Dougal had taken Miss Merle Coverdale for a walk across the great sunny common of the Rye on a Saturday afternoon. Merle Coverdale was head of the typing pool at Meadows, Meade & Grindley. She was thirty-seven.

Dougal said, 'My lonely heart is deluged by melancholy and it feels quite nice.'

'Someone might hear you talking like that.'

'You are a terror and a treat,' Dougal said. 'You look to me like an Okapi,' he said.

'A what?'

'An Okapi is a rare beast from the Congo. It looks a little like a deer, but it tries to be a giraffe. It has stripes and it stretches its neck as far as possible and its ears are like a donkey's. It is a little bit of everything. There are only a few in captivity. They are very shy.'

'Why do you say I'm like it?'

'Because you're so shy.'

'Me shy?'

'Yes. You haven't told me about your love affair with Mr. Druce. You're too shy.'

'Oh, that's only a friendship. You've got it all wrong. What makes you think it's a love affair? Who told you that?'

'I've got second sight.'

Muriel Spark, *The Ballad of Peckham Rye.*

1) Find the clauses that (a) identify Merle Coverdale, (b) describe her, and (c) describe the Okapi. Make a note of the complementation patterns used and of their realisations. What is your opinion of Dougal's characterisation of Merle? In what ways does it differ from what the narrator tells us?

2) Imagine you are Merle Coverdale. Write a paragraph describing Dougal from Merle's point of view.

3) '*You've got it wrong*' is often heard in conversational exchanges to correct a previous speaker's opinion about something. What is its complementation pattern? *Wrong* can be replaced by other units such as *all mixed up, quite out of perspective.* Try using one of these in a dialogue.

Chapter tasks

1 *Describe the complementation pattern and verb type of each of the following headlines and advertisements from the Observer newspaper:*
   1) Get your hands on a phone.
   2) Now the danger is that no-one will hear a cry for help.
   3) AEG cookers won't cook fingers.
   4) Museum collection sale will cost county more than it saves.
   5) On paper it will save you a few seconds. On complete documents it will save you cancelling dinner.
   6) Our Prime Ministers have been a funny lot.
   7) It pays to be quick.

2 *Read the following passage carefully, mentally noting the main points made by the author:*

Unnecessary modesty has a great deal to do with envy. Modesty is considered a virtue, but for my part I am very doubtful whether, in its more extreme forms, it deserves to be so regarded. Modest people need a great deal of reassuring, and often do not dare to attempt tasks which they are quite capable of performing. Modest people believe themselves to be outshone by those with whom they habitually associate. They are, therefore, particularly prone to envy, and, through envy, to unhappiness and ill-will. For my part, I think there is much to be said for bringing up a boy to think himself a fine fellow. I do not believe that any peacock envies another peacock his tail, because every peacock is persuaded that his own tail is the finest in the world. The consequence of this is that peacocks are peaceable birds.

Bertrand Russell, *The Conquest of Happiness.*

1) Now, without looking at the text, summarise the points made in your own words. Then compare the result with the original.

2) Compare this text with the one in 10.2, 'Education: doing bad and feeling good'. In what way are the ideas expressed similar? Discuss to what extent the differences of expression can be described grammatically.

4

Expressing patterns of experience:

Processes, participants, circumstances

MODULE 13
Experiences expressed as situation types

Summary

1   Semantically, a clause represents a pattern of experience, conceptualised as a situation type.

2   Situation types consist of:
Processes: material, mental, relational.
Participants: animate, inanimate or abstract entities.
Attributes: qualities or circumstances of the participants.
Circumstances: time, place, manner, cause, etc., of the whole situation.

3   The type of process usually determines the type and number of the participants (verb valency):

one participant:	*The dog* barked.
two participants:	*The dog* bit *the postman*.
three participants:	*Mary* gave *the Red Cross a donation*.
participant unexpounded:	Do you drive? (*a car*)
no participant:	It is raining.

13.1   Processes, participants, circumstances

In this chapter we look at the clause as a grammatical means of expressing patterns of experience. A fundamental property of language is that it enables us to conceptualise and describe our experience, whether of the phenomena of the external world or of the internal world of our thoughts, feelings and perceptions. The clause is, here too, the most significant grammatical unit, since it permits us to encode, both semantically and syntactically, our mental picture of the physical world and the worlds of our imagination. In this mental picture we can think of a clause as being the linguistic expression of a pattern of experience, conceptualised as a situation type. 'Situation' and 'situation type' are, therefore, used here to refer to the conceptualisation of experience, as opposed to the social context or 'context of situation' in which illocutionary acts are produced by speakers, as described in Chapter 5.

Certain common experiences are typically not analysed in detail. We say *It's raining* rather than *Drops of water are falling from the sky*. But as language-users, we are usually interested in participants, especially when one or more of them is human; we are interested in the qualities we ascribe to them, in what they do, say and feel and the circumstances in which these happenings take place. The semantic framework for a situation, therefore, consists potentially of the following components:

> the process;
> the participants in the situation;
> the attributes ascribed to participants;
> the circumstances associated with the process.

The process
There is no satisfactory general term to cover that central part of a situation which is typically realised by the Predicator and which can be a state, an action, an event, a transition or change of state, a climatic phenomenon, a process of sensing, saying, behaving or simply existing. We here use the term 'process' to refer in a general sense to all these types.

The participant roles (semantic functions) involved in the situation
The entities represented by these can be persons, objects or abstractions; they can be the Agent of the action or be affected by it, benefit from it or receive its effects. They are typically realised by Subject, Direct Object and Indirect Object in the syntactic structure. They are the inherent semantic roles. There are also other, non-inherent participants; for instance, Instrument, such as *her handbag* in *She hit the burglar with her handbag*.

The Attributes ascribed to entities
These either identify or characterise the entity, or state its location in space or time. They are realised syntactically by the intensive Complements (Complement of the Subject and Complement of the Object).

The circumstantial roles associated with the process
These include expressions of time, place, manner, means, cause, condition, concession, accompaniment and role. They are typically optional in the semantic structure, in the same way as their adjunctive realisations are in the syntactic structure. Circumstances can, however, be inherent to the situation, and are then described as complements (see 4.1.1). Such is the case with the locative expression which, as well as the Object, is obligatory with *put* as in *Put the flowers in water*.

We have now outlined the framework which will serve to carry the different configurations of semantic functions that go to make up semantic structures. Not that any particular configuration is inherently given in nature. There are various ways of conceptualising a situation, according to what the lexico-grammatical resources of a language permit. In English we may say that *it's cloudy*, specifying simply a state (*is*) and an Attribute (*cloudy*); or that *the sky is cloudy*, adding a Carrier participant (*the sky*) for the Attribute; or that *clouds are gathering in the sky*, in which we represent the situation as consisting of an inanimate Agent (*clouds*), a dynamic process (*are gathering*) and a locative circumstance (*in the sky*).

There is no one-to-one correlation between semantic structures and syntactic structures; rather, the semantic categories cross-cut the syntactic ones, although with some correlation. Semantic structures and syntactic structures do not, therefore, always coincide; rather, they overlap. In both cases, however, it is usually the process, expressed by the verb, that determines the choice of participants in the semantic structure and of syntactic elements in the syntactic structure. In Chapter 3 the possible syntactic combinations are discussed from the point of view of verb complementation and clause type. In this chapter we shall start from the semantics; at the same time we shall try to relate the choice of semantic roles to their syntactic realisations.

One obvious problem in the identification of participants and processes is the vastness and variety of the physical world, and the difficulty involved in reducing this variety to a few semantic roles and processes. All we can attempt to do is to specify the paradigm cases, and indicate where more detailed specification would be necessary in order to account semantically for the varied shades of our experience.

13.1.1   Types of process

There are three main types of process:

(a) Material processes, or processes of 'doing' (e.g. *kick, run, paint, construct, dig, write, repair, send, give*).

(b) Mental processes, or processes of 'experiencing' or 'sensing' (e.g. *see, hear, know, feel, believe, think, like, hate, regret, forget*).

(c) Relational processes, or processes of 'being' or 'becoming' in which a participant is characterised, or identified, or situated circumstantially (e.g. *be, seem, stand, lie, become, turn, get*).

13.1.2   Inherent participants and actualised participants

Most of these processes are accompanied by one or more inherent participants; the nature of the process determines how many and what kind of participants are involved. The material process represented by the verb *die* for instance, has only one participant, whereas *kick* typically requires two: one participant is the Agent who carries out the action, and must be 'animate' and even typically 'human'; the other is the participant affected by the action of kicking, and is not required to be human, or even animate.

In the example *Ted kicked the ball* both the inherent participants are **actualised** as *Ted* and *the ball*. If we say *Ted kicked hard*, however, only one participant, the Agent who carries out the action, is actualised. The second participant, the one affected by the action, is **unactualised** or **unex-**

pounded. In everyday uses of English, speakers frequently find it convenient not to actualise certain inherent participants. *Give*, for instance, is typically a three-participant process as in *Mary gave the Red Cross a donation*; only two participants are actualised, however, in *Mary gave a donation* and only one in *Mary gave generously*.

Participants are unexpounded because they can be conventionally understood in the situational context. The unactualised participant is specific in:

> Do you drive (a car)?
> I'll wash and you dry (the dishes).
> Will you pour (the tea / coffee)?
> He's shaving (himself).

It is not specific in *electricity can kill, remarks like that can hurt*, and is perhaps not even known to the speaker in *she teaches, he writes*.

Processes with the meaning of 'reciprocal participation' such as *meet, join* and *kiss* can be represented with implicit reciprocity as in *your sister and I have never met* (each other).

Some processes have no participants; for example, statements about time, distance or weather such as *it is raining, it's a long walk to the beach, it's half past eleven*. In these the pronoun *it* is merely a surface form required to realise the obligatory Subject element.

Traditionally, the term **intransitive** has been used to refer to verbs which express one-participant processes such as *die* or no-participant processes such as *rain*, whose action does not extend to any Object; the term **transitive** has been used to refer to verbs and clauses in which the process is extended to one or more Objects. Following this convention, *give* is transitive in *Mary gave a donation* but intransitive in *Give generously!* In this book we shall use 'transitive' and 'intransitive' as syntactic terms, while referring semantically to one-, two- or three-participant processes, with 'actualised' or 'unactualised' inherent participants.

The number of participants involved in a process can also be referred to as its **valency**. A process with one participant is said to be **monovalent** as in *the dog died*. A process with two participants is **bivalent** as in *the dog bit the postman*; a process with three participants is **trivalent** as in *Mary gave the Red Cross a donation*. The valency is reduced from three to two, or from two to one when participants are not actualised, as in the examples above.

MODULE 14
Expressing processes of doing and causing

Summary

1   Material processes are actions carried out by a participant called Agent. They may or may not affect other participants. Examples of material processes are *do, run, paint, kick, hit, spoil, pay, bring, turn.*

2   Participant roles in material processes:

Agent:	*The Prime Minister* resigned.
Force:	*Lightning* struck the oak tree.
Affected:	An avalanche buried *the climbers.*
Effected:	Mary made *an omelette.*
Recipient:	They gave *the children* some sweets.
Beneficiary:	I'll pour *you* some coffee.
Causative Agent:	*Pat* boiled the water. ⎱ (ergative
	The water boiled. ⎰ pair)

14.1   Agent

Material processes express an action or an activity which is typically carried out by a 'doer' or **Agent**. By 'Agent' we mean any entity that is capable of operating on itself or others, usually to bring about some change in the location or properties of itself or others. Typical Agents are human, as in the following examples:

Agent		
The Prime Minister	resigned.	
The spectators	cheered.	
Ted	hit	Bill.
We	carried	our luggage.

We can test for Agent in material processes by questioning 'What did X do?' or 'Who did Z?' and by forming a 'thematic equative' (or 'pseudo-cleft') construction (see 15.2): What *the Prime Minister* did was resign. What *we* did was carry our luggage. Many two-participant material processes, in addition to these two tests, also answer the question 'What did X do to Y?' (*What did Ted do to Bill?*).

14.2   Inanimate Agent or 'Force'

The notion of **agency** is a complex one, which includes such features as animacy, intention, motivation, responsibility and the use of one's own energy to bring about an event or initiate a process. In central instances, all these features will be present. In non-central instances, one or more of these features may be absent. If we say, for example, that *the horse splashed us with mud as it passed* we do not imply that the horse did so deliberately. We do not attribute intentionality or responsibility or motivation to the horse in this situation. We might call it an 'unwitting Agent'. However, rather than devise a different term for every subtype of agency we will make just one further distinction: that between animate and inanimate Agents. This is useful in order to account for such natural phenomena as thunder, lightning, electricity, avalanches, the wind, tides and floods. As Agents they are inanimate, and their power or energy cannot therefore be intentional. These and many others we will call **Force** or simply **inanimate Agent**; we shall also include here such psychological states as anxiety, fear or joy.

Inanimate Agent (Force)	Process	Affected
Lightning	struck	the oak tree.
An avalanche	buried	the climbers.
The thunder	rolled.	
Anxiety	can ruin	your health.

In certain cultures, such phenomena may be interpreted as real animate Agents, or as Instrument of some divinity. In non-animistic cultures like ours, these roles are easily accepted as metaphoric transfers of the category 'normally animate' to 'inanimate'. In the following short text, the italicised Subjects realise the role of inanimate Agent:

> *The cold* crept in from the corners of the shanty, closer and closer to the stove. *Icy-cold breezes* sucked and fluttered the curtains around the beds. The little shanty quivered in the storm. But the steamy smell of boiling beans was good and *it* seemed to make the air warmer.
>
> Laura Ingalls Wilder, *The Long Winter*.

14.3   Affected

The Affected participant is that which is affected by the action expressed by the verb. (Other terms used are **Patient** and **Goal**.) The semantic structure of such two-participant situations can be illustrated as follows:

Agent	Material process	Affected
Ted My brother The child	kicked is painting ate	the ball. the house. the chocolate.
S	P	Od

Besides asking 'What did Ted / my brother / the child do?', or 'Who did Z?', identifying the Agent, we can also ask 'What happened to the ball / the house / the chocolate?', identifying the Affected. Consequently, if the process extends to an Affected participant, the representation can be made in two forms, either active, in which Agent is realised as Subject and Affected as Direct Object, as above, or passive, in which Subject realises Affected and Agent is realised as Adjunct:

Affected	Material process	Agent
The ball The house The chocolate	was kicked is being painted was eaten	by Ted. by my brother. by the child.
S	P	A

14.4 Effected

Our example *My brother is painting the house* admits two interpretations: one, that he is putting paint on the house; and the other, that he is painting a picture of the house. In the first, the house is affected by the process, and *the house* is an 'Affected participant'. In the second, the house is not affected by the process; rather it – in this case the picture of the house – is created, or brought into being, by the process of painting. In the latter case, *the house* is termed an **Effected participant**. Another term is **Resulting Object**. Other common situations that are interpreted in this way include such everyday occurrences as building a bridge, writing a letter, making an omelette, digging a hole. Syntactically, the Effected participant is realised by a Direct Object in an active clause, just as the Affected is; but semantically they are different; with an Effected Object the situation cannot be questioned by 'What did X do to Y', but rather by the thematic equative 'What was brought into being was *Y*'. Compare the Affected and Effected participants realised at Od in the following:

Agent	Process	Affected
Mary The gardener	fried dug Bring	an egg. the garden. who you like.
S	P	Od

Agent	Process	Effected
Mary The gardener	made dug Write	an omelette. a hole. what you can.
S	P	Od

14.5   Recipient and Beneficiary roles

When the action expressed by the verb extends to two inherent participants the additional participant is the **Recipient**. Processes of this type include *give, send, lend, grant, pay*:

> I'll give *the children* some sweets.
> Bill's father has lent *us* his car.
> The judge granted *the accused* bail.
> Someone has sent *Mary* a get-well card.
> Have you paid *the taxi-driver* the right amount?

The **Recipient** is the one to whom the action is directed and who receives the 'goods'. In processes of 'doing' it is typically realised in the syntax by the Indirect Object. It is typically animate and human, as in the examples above, but occasionally an inanimate Recipient occurs as in:

> We'll give *the unemployment question* priority.
> The classical porch lends *the house* an air of distinction.

There are two syntactic tests for Recipient in material processes:

(a) Recipient can become Subject in a corresponding passive clause:

> *The children* will be given some sweets.
> Has *the taxi-driver* been paid the right amount?
> *The accused* was granted bail.
> *Mary* has been sent a get-well card.
> *The unemployment question* will be given priority.

(b) There is usually a corresponding SPOdOprep construction, in which the Recipient is expressed by a Prepositional Object containing *to*. (Some verbs, such as *pay*, do not have this alternative.)

> I'll give some sweets *to the children*.
> The judge granted bail *to the accused*.
> Someone has sent a get-well card *to Mary*.
> *Have you paid the right amount *to the taxi-driver*?

Beneficiary is the optional, not inherent, participant for whom some service is done. This is not necessarily the same as receiving the goods. I can say I am knitting a sweater, without declaring who it is for. This difference is reflected in English in the syntax of verbs such as *fetch, make, buy, pour* and many verbs such as *cook, bake, mix, knit* which can be replaced by *make*. These represent services which are done *for* people rather than actions *to* people. Beneficiary is realised as optional Indirect Object in:

> Could you fetch *me* the newspaper?
> She mixed *James* a cocktail.
> I'll make *you* an omelette.
> Jane poured *all the guests* a cup of coffee.

Unlike Recipient, Beneficiary can rarely become Subject in a passive clause. The following are not acceptable: *ˈI could be fetched the newspaper, ˈJames was mixed a cocktail, ˈYou'll be made an omelette, ˈAll the guests were poured cups of coffee*.

In the alternative SPOdOprep construction the preposition is usually *for*. (*Could you fetch the newspaper for me? She mixed a cocktail for James. I'll make an omelette for you. Jane poured cups of coffee for all the guests.*)

Recipient and Beneficiary can occur together in the same clause, as in the following example, where *me* is Recipient and *my daughter* is Beneficiary:

> She gave *me* a bracelet for *my daughter*.

Both Recipient and Beneficiary may be involved in processes of an unbeneficial nature such as *they sent him a letter-bomb*, in which *him* is Recipient; and *they set him a trap* in which *him* is Beneficiary.

14.6 Causative processes

Causative processes are of various kinds, depending on the verb. We will deal here with causative material processes realised by SPOd and SPOdCo structures:

(a) Type: *They are making the road wider*. A **causative Agent** brings about a change of state in the Affected participant. The resulting state is expressed by an Attribute:

Causative Agent	Process	Affected	Resulting Attribute
They	are making	the road	wider.
This machine	will make	your tasks	simple.
Sea-water	rendered	the equipment	useless.
The heat	has turned	the milk	sour.
That noise	is driving	me	mad.
Pat	had	her face	lifted.
S	P	Od	Co

The resulting change of state in the Affected participant sometimes forms part of the meaning of a morphologically related causative verb: *widen* is the equivalent of *make wide* and *simplify* means *make simple*. With such verbs there are alternative SPOd causative structures: *They are widening the road; This machine will simplify your tasks*. For other adjectives such as *useless* there is no corresponding causative verb. Certain dynamic verbs such as *drive* and *turn* can be used in specific causative senses in English. *Have* introduces a passive sense, expressed by a participle (cause to be *-en*).

(b) Type: *Pat boiled the water*. A causative Agent causes the Affected participant to undergo or perform an action. A change of state or location of the Affected may also be involved:

Causative Agent	Process	Affected
Pat	boiled	the water.
I	rang	the bell.
The child	flew	the kite.
Peter	rolled	the ball.
A stone	broke	the window.
S	P	Od

Causative Agents initiate the causative process and are not necessarily human, but may be instrumental participants, such as *a stone* in *a stone broke the window*.

The Affected is, however, the essential participant, the one which is primarily involved in the action. It is the water that boils, the bell that rings, the kite that flies, the ball that rolls and the window that breaks.

14.7 Causatives with corresponding one-participant processes: ergative pairs

The situations described above with the causative Agent expressed as Subject can also be expressed with the causative Agent suppressed. The Subject is the Affected in a one-participant process:

Affected	Process
The water	boiled.
The bell	rang.
The kite	flew.
The ball	rolled.
The window	broke.
S	P

Processes such as *boil, ring, fly, stop, roll* and others listed below, in which the Affected Object in a transitive clause (I rang *the bell* twice) can be the

Affected Subject in an intransitive clause (*The bell* rang twice) are sometimes called **ergative pairs** in English. In some languages, such as Basque, ergativity is marked by a special case form on all Agentive Subjects of transitive clauses.

Within this type of causative processes it is also possible to distinguish a set of volitional activities (*walk, jump, march*) in which the Affected participant is involved (*I'll walk you home; He jumped the horse over the fence; The sergeant marched the soldiers along the road*).

It is also possible to have an additional agent and an additional causative verb in the transitive clauses of ergative pairs; for example, *The child got his sister to fly the kite, Mary made Peter roll the ball.*

Ergative pairs account for many of the most commonly used verbs in English, some of which are listed below, with examples:

burn	X burned the cakes. The cakes burned.
burst	X burst the balloon. The balloon burst.
change	X has changed the programme. The programme has changed.
close	X closed his eyes. His eyes closed.
cook	X cooked the rice. The rice cooked.
drop	X dropped the book. The book dropped.
join	X joined their hands. Their hands joined.
melt	X melted the ice. The ice melted.
move	X moved the glass. The glass moved.
open	X opened the door. The door opened.
run	X is running the bathwater. The bathwater is running.
shake	X shook the branches. The branches shook.
shut	X shut the window. The window shut.
stand	Stand the lamp here! The lamp stands here.
start	X started the car. The car started.
stretch	X stretched the elastic. The elastic stretched.
tighten	X tightened the rope. The rope tightened.
turn	X turned the doorknob. The doorknob turned.

Causatives and ergatives are illustrated in the following text:

The cold wind *made the horses eager to go*[1]. They *pricked their ears* forward and back [2] and *tossed their heads*[3], *jingling the bits*[4] and pretending to shy at their own shadows. They *stretched their noses* forward[5], pulling on the bits and prancing to go faster.

Laura Ingalls Wilder, *The Long Winter*.

[1] causing a change of state (*eager*) in the Affected participant (*horses*);
[2] causing the Affected (*their ears*) to undergo an action (*prick ...*);
[3] causing the Affected (*their heads*) to undergo an action (*toss*);
[4] causing the Affected (*the bits*) to undergo an action (*jingle*);
[5] causing the Affected (*their noses*) to undergo an action (*stretch ...*).

Clauses [2], [3], [4], and [5] contain ergative verbs and could also be expressed intransitively:

> Their ears pricked forward.
> Their heads tossed.
> The bits jingled.
> Their noses stretched forward.

In clause 1 *the cold wind* is the inanimate causative Agent which initiates the action. In the remaining clauses *they* (the horses) are the causative Agent, setting in motion parts of themselves or their harness. By choosing the two-participant, rather than the one-participant structure, the author is able to present the horses as lively, eager beings.

MODULE 15
One-participant processes: containing a Subject which acts or is acted upon

Summary

1 When the process is not extended to any other participant, the single participant is either an Agent Subject of a voluntary process (*Nobody turned up*), or an Affected Subject of an involuntary process (*The old lady collapsed*).

2 An Affected Subject occurs with certain verbs such as *break, wash*, when used to express a property or potentiality of the entity (*Glass breaks easily; That material won't wash*). A negative, modal or manner adverb is usually present.
   There are two main types of one-participant process to be considered here, both consisting of a Subject and Predicator. In one type the Subject is the Agent of the process; in the other type, it is affected by the process. The difference is therefore a semantic one, which depends on the relationship between participant and process.

15.1   Agentive Subject of a voluntary process

A voluntary one-participant process is carried out by an Agent:

Agent	Process
Birds	fly.
Nobody	turned up.
S	P

We have also seen that many natural phenomena are also represented intransitively, with inanimate, non-volitional Agents or 'Force' at Subject as in *lightning* flashed and *thunder* rolled, *the sun* rose and *the clouds* disappeared.

15.2   Affected Subject of an involuntary process

Not all material processes have a participant which carries out the action by means of its own energy, whether intentionally or not. In situations expressed as *the dog died, the old lady collapsed, the children have grown, the vase fell off the shelf*, the participant, even when animate, is neither controlling nor initiating the action. This is proved by the inappropriateness of the question 'What did X do?' and of the thematic equative test (*What the children did was grow.*). Rather, we should ask 'What happened to X?' The participant on which the action centres in such cases is, then, Affected. It is found in involuntary transitional processes such as *die, arrive* and *grow*, which represent the passage from one state to another, and in involuntary actions such as *trip* and *stumble*, which always have an animate participant. *Fall* and *slip* are accompanied by a participant which may be either animate or inanimate. A locative circumstance is also often present.

Affected	Non-Agent-controlled act or transition	Circumstance
The dog	died.	
The old lady	collapsed.	
The children	have grown.	
The government	has fallen.	
I	tripped	over the carpet.
He	slipped	on the ice.
S	P	A

Certain of these actions, such as *slip* and *fall*, lend themselves to two types of situation, one Agent-controlled, with an Agent participant, the other non-Agent-controlled, with Affected participant. A change from intransitive to transitive or causative may also be involved.

Agent at Subject	Affected at Subject
She dropped a hint.	She dropped dead.
She fell to her knees.	She fell down the stairs.
She slipped the money	She slipped on the ice.
into her pocket. (causative)	

A borderline area between agency and non-agency is provided by **behavioural** processes such as *cough, sneeze, yawn, blink, laugh* and *sigh*, which are usually one-participant. They are considered as typically involuntary; but it may be that there is a very slight agency involved. They can be deliberate, too, as in *he coughed discreetly, he yawned rudely*, in which the Adjunct element implies volition. Such volitional Adjuncts could not be used with *die, collapse* and *grow*, which are completely lacking in agency and volition.

In the following passage almost all the clauses are intransitive; the participant at Subject varies from Agentive (voluntary) to Affected (animate involuntary or inanimate).

Encounter between an Indian father and his son

So *I raced* out of my room[1], with my fingers in my ears, to *scream* [2] till *the roof fell* [3] down about their ears.

But *the radio* suddenly *went off* [4], *the door to my parents' room suddenly opened* [5] and *my father appeared* [6], bathed and shaven, . . *his white 'dhoti' blazing* [7], *his white shirt crackling* [8], *his patent leather pumps glittering* [9]. *He stopped* [10] in the doorway and *I stopped* [11] on the balls of my feet and *wavered* [12].

Anita Desai, Games at Twilight.

[1] Agentive Subject; [2] implicit Agentive Subject; [3] Affected inanimate Subject; [4] Affected inanimate Subject; [5] Affected inanimate Subject; [6] Agentive Subject; [7] Affected inanimate Subject; [8] Affected inanimate Subject; [9] Affected inanimate Subject; [10] Agentive Subject; [11] Agentive Subject; [12] animate diminished volition.

The high number of one-participant processes in this text helps to make us participate in the boy's apprehension. Inanimate objects (*radio, door, roof, 'dhoti', shirt, pumps*) appear to take on a life of their own, able to carry out actions which to him are potentially violent and threatening (*fall down, blaze, crackle, glitter*). Potentially threatening, too, are his father's actions, in this context. They are not extended to any other entity; he simply *appears* and *stops*. But the foreboding is there. The boy's actions are not directed towards anything except escape (*race out*). But this initial volition weakens, becomes semi-voluntary (*scream*) and is almost lost in the final intransitive (*wavers*).

15.3   Expressing the properties of an entity

A further type of Affected Subject occurs with certain processes (*break, read, translate, polish, wash, fasten, lock*, etc.) which are otherwise typically two-participant:

> Glass breaks easily.
> This box doesn't shut/close/lock/fasten properly.
> This novel reads like a government report.
> Colloquial language translates badly.
> Some synthetic fibres won't wash. Usually they dry-clean.
> Silver polishes better than plastic.

They differ from other intransitives in the following ways:

(a) They express a general property or a potentiality of the entity. Compare *the glass broke*, which refers to a specific event.

(b) Although no Agent is mentioned, the possible activity of an Agent is necessarily implicit; we do not mean that glass breaks spontaneously, or that the novel can be read without a reader.

(c) Related to this implicit agency is the fact that these intransitives are accompanied by a modal, negation or some adjunctive specification such as *properly, like a government report*.

(d) This type of intransitive is sometimes called 'pseudo-passive'. It is not possible in every case, however, to express these meanings by the passive voice, without some lexical or grammatical additions. The following are not equivalent:

> This box isn't shut properly.
> This novel is read like a government report.
> Colloquial language is translated badly.
> Some synthetic fibres won't be washed.
> Silver is polished better than plastic.

(e) There is no corresponding transitive construction with Agentive Subject, despite the fact that these verbs can normally be used transitively. It is not equivalent to say, for instance, *He reads the novel like a government report, He translates colloquial language badly*.

(f) Frequently, certain lexical changes or additions are necessary, in order to express the meaning in an alternative form (*This novel is written in the style of a government report. It is impossible to wash some synthetic fibres.*). The difficulty of paraphrasing this clause meaning shows how specific and how useful it is.

MODULE 16
Expressing what we perceive, think and feel

Summary

1   Mental processes are processes of perception (*see, hear,* etc.), of cognition (*know, understand,* etc.) and of affection (*like, fear,* etc.).

2   There is always a conscious participant, the **Experiencer**, who perceives, knows, likes, etc. There is usually a second participant, **Phenomenon** – that which is perceived, known, liked, etc.

3   Mental process verbs arc typically stative.

4   For certain types of mental process, English has both a stative verb (*see*) and a dynamic verb (*watch*). Dynamic mental processes such as *watch* take Progressive tense-aspect, whereas involuntary mental processes generally do not.

16.1   Mental Processes

Not all situations that we wish to express linguistically centre on who does what to whom. The processes of perception (*see, hear, feel,* etc.), of cognition (*know, think, believe, realise, recognise,* etc.) and of affection (*like, dislike, love, hate, please,* etc.) which we group together under the heading 'mental processes' are semantically different from material processes of 'doing', and these differences are reflected in the grammar in several ways:

(a)   There is typically one participant who is conscious, and can be called the **Experiencer**; this is the one who sees, feels, thinks, likes, etc., and is typically human, but may also be an animal. (*The rider heard a noise. The horse sensed danger.*) The use of a non-conscious entity as Experiencer in a mental process is often exploited for commercial ends:

> Your car knows what it needs.
> This airline cares for you.

(b)   There is usually a second participant in a mental process, that which is perceived, known, liked, etc., and which may be a 'thing' realised by a NG, but can also be a fact, a process or an entire situation, realised by a clause. This participant can be called the **Phenomenon**:

Experiencer	Mental process	Phenomenon
Who Phil We Children	saw knows believe like	what happened? the answer. that he is right. going to the circus.

(c) Verbs of mental process are typically stative verbs and consequently the unmarked tense-aspect form is the non-Progressive (*I know the answer*, not *I am knowing the answer*.). Material processes, on the other hand, are typically dynamic and take the Progressive as their unmarked tense-aspect (*What are you reading? I am reading this script*, not *What do you read? I read this script*.) (see Module 42).

(d) A mental process cannot be questioned by 'What did X do?' as can a material process. Compare: *What did Mary do with the gift? She gave it away.* *She liked it.*

16.2   Perception processes

As realised by the verbs *see* and *hear* in English, perception is an involuntary state which does not depend upon the agency of the perceiver, who in fact **receives** the visual and auditory sensations non-volitionally. The participant in such situations can be considered **Recipient Experiencer** (*We saw the accident. The rider heard a noise.*). Corresponding to *see* and *hear*, English has the dynamic verbs *look/watch* and *listen*, respectively. These are volitional material processes and consequently are accompanied by an Agentive, not a Recipient, Experiencer, and can take Progressive aspect (*We were watching the match ... Everyone was listening attentively.*).

The perception processes of 'feeling', 'smelling' and 'tasting' each make use of one verb (*feel, smell* and *taste*) to express both types of process, one dynamic, and volitional with an Agentive Subject (*Feel this cloth. Smell these roses. Taste this sauce.*), the other non-volitional with a Recipient Subject (*The child feels hot. I can smell gas. Can you taste the lemon in this sauce?*).

For the use of *look, feel, smell, taste* and *sound* in relational processes, see Module 17.

Perception processes can be summarised as follows:

(i) **Recipient Experiencer** S	**Non-volitional process** P	**Phenomenon** Od
Tom We I I The child	saw heard can smell can taste feels	a snake. a noise. gas. the lemon. hot.

(ii)**Agentive Experiencer** S	**Volitional process** P	**Phenomenon** Od
Tom He Pam Phil The mother	watched listened to smelled tasted felt	the snake. the noise. the roses. the sauce. the child's forehead.

In processes of seeing, hearing and feeling English allows the Phenomenon to represent a situation that is either completed or not completed. This aspectual distinction is realised by the type of non-finite clause chosen; a *to*-infinitive clause with its own Subject represents the situation as completed, whereas an *-ing* clause with its own Subject represents the Phenomenon as in the process of happening (see also 11.5). Compare:

Completed	Not completed
I saw *him cross the road.* We heard *the tree fall.* He felt *someone grasp his arm.*	I saw *him crossing the road.* We heard *the rain falling.* He felt *someone grasping his arm.*

In mental processes which are passivised, the Phenomenon is realised by the Subject (*A snake* was seen; *a noise* was heard).

16.3   Cognitive processes

Cognitive processes are realised by such stative verbs as *believe, doubt, guess, know, recognise, think, forget, mean, remember, understand*. Most verbs of cognition can have as their Phenomenon a wide range of things apprehended, including human, inanimate and abstract entities, realised by NGs, facts, and situations, realised by different types of clauses. The process expressed by the verb *realise* can take as its Phenomenon only a situation realised by a finite clause. A selection of examples is given below.

Experiencer	Cognitive process	Phenomenon
I He Everybody Nobody She Nobody My parents I	don't know can't understand remembered recognised has forgotten realised thought didn't think	what to do. their objections. his face. that he was a genius. to leave the key. how late it was. that you were coming. to see you here.

Cognitive processes are stative and almost invariably take the non-progressive tense-aspect, as in the above examples (*Think* is dynamic in the sense of 'ponder' as in *What are you thinking about?*). Many cognitive processes allow the Phenomenon to be unactualised when this is 'Given information' (*I don't know. Jill doesn't understand. Nobody will remember. Elephants never forget.*).

In the following short extract, the author has chosen processes of cognition, perception and affection to reflect the mental make-up of a meteorologist whose work contributed to chaos theory:

> Lorenz *enjoyed* [1] weather – by no means a prerequisite for a research meteorologist. He *savored* [2] its changeability. He *appreciated* [3] the patterns that come and go in the atmosphere, families of eddies and cyclones, always obeying mathematical rules, yet never repeating themselves. When he *looked* [4] at clouds he *thought* [5] he *saw* [6] a kind of structure in them. Once he had *feared* [7] that studying the science of weather would be like prying a jack-in-the-box apart with a screwdriver. Now he *wondered* [8] whether science would be able to penetrate the magic at all. Weather had a flavor that could not be expressed by talking about averages.

> James Gleick, *Chaos, Making a new science*.

[1] affection; [2] affection; [3] cognition; [4] perception; [5] cognition; [6] perception; [7] affection; [8] cognition.

The Phenomenon in processes of cognition can be an entity realised by a NG, a fact, or a whole situation realised by a finite *that*-clause or a nominal *WH*-clause:

> He knows *most of Spain.* (NG)
> He knows *that you are waiting.* (finite *that*-clause)
> He knows *what he wants.* (finite nominal *WH*-clause)

Remember and *forget*, in addition to finite clauses, can take as their Phenomenon either *-ing* or *to*-infinitive non-finite clauses:

> I remember *locking the door.* I remembered *to lock the door.*
> I forgot about *locking it.* I forgot *to lock it.*

The choice between these two reflects a difference in the time-relation of the Phenomenon to the process of remembering or forgetting (see 9.6.3).

The Phenomenon can include another participant and the Attribute of this:

> We know *Tom to be honest.*
> She believed *him to be sincere.*
> I understand *you to be the Director of this department.*

This SPOdCo structure is used as a formal alternative to the more widely used finite *that*-clause.

The cognitive processes described so far express **indirect thoughts** and for this reason their Phenomenon is typically realised by an indicative.

Mental processes such as *decide, intend* and *resolve* are processes of **volition** and a following *that*-clause as Phenomenon contains a verb in the subjunctive or else modal *should* + infinitive, both of which express an indirect directive (see 9.3.3).

> The court resolved that the child *be taken* into care.
> The court resolved that the child *should be taken* into care.

16.4   Affectivity processes

(a) Under the first type of affectivity process we include those expressed by such verbs as *like, love, enjoy, please, delight, dislike, hate, detest, want*.

In English most of these verbs in everyday use have a Recipient Experiencer Subject:

> *Cats* love sardines.
> *Many people* enjoy breakfast in bed.
> *I* detest hypocrisy.

With *please* and *delight* the Recipient Experiencer is Direct Object in active clauses; these verbs are more commonly used in the passive, however, and by this grammatical device Recipient is made to coincide with Subject, thus conforming to the predominant pattern:

Recipient	Recipient
The news pleased *us*. His success delighted *his wife*.	*We* were pleased by the news. *His wife* was delighted by his success.
Od	S

The Phenomenon in affectivity processes can be expressed by a NG, which represents an entity, or by a clause representing a process or a situation. Some NGs express processes (*a walk, a swim*) and these are often interchangeable with non-finite clauses, especially the *-ing* type, which is the most nominal in English. Some verbs, such as *enjoy, dislike, detest*, invariably take an *-ing* clause. Others such as *want, hope* and *long* take a *to*-infinitive clause. Others, particularly *like, love* and *hate*, admit either an *-ing* clause or a *to*-infinitive clause; the *-ing* clause suggests an interpretation of habituality or actuality, while the *to*-infinitive clause suggests potentiality. For this reason, the latter is used in hypothetical meanings (see also 9.6.3). The following examples will illustrate these differences:

NG / *-ing* clause	NG / *to*-infinitive clause
They love *a walk in the woods.* They enjoy *walking in the woods.* She likes *visiting her friends.* I hate *having a tooth out.*	They love *a walk in the woods.* They love *to walk in the woods.* She would like *to visit Janet.* I would hate *to have more teeth out.*

(b) A second type of affectivity process includes verbs which express such emotions as surprise, dismay, worry, depression. They can occur with a *that*-clause Phenomenon at Subject and Recipient Experiencer at Direct Object:

> That she initiated divorce proceedings surprised no-one.
> That their son never writes home depresses them.
> That the road works are paralysed dismays the public.

But most English speakers usually prefer either to extrapose the Phenomenon *that*-clause, with anticipatory *it* in Subject position as in (i), or to use a participial adjective (*surprised, depressed, dismayed*), bringing Experiencer to Subject position as in (ii) (see 5.1.3(d)):

> (i)   It surprised no-one that she initiated divorce proceedings.
>   It depresses them that their son never writes home.
>   It dismays the public that the road works are paralysed.

> (ii) No-one was surprised that she initiated divorce proceedings.
>   They are depressed that their son never writes home.
>   The public is dismayed that the road works are paralysed.

The indicative is used in the subordinate *that*-clause to present the Phenomenon as a **fact**. When the speaker wishes to present the Phenomenon **non-factually**, as an **idea**, modal *should* + infinitive is used instead, as in (iii) (see 9.3.5):

> (iii) No-one was surprised that she should initiate divorce
>   proceedings.
>   They are depressed that their son should never write home.
>   The public is dismayed that the road works should be
>   paralysed.

(c) A third type of mental affection process comprises the verbs *wish, suppose* (imperative) and *would rather* (*wish* and *suppose* are no doubt cognitive-affective). All three refer to unreal or hypothetical events or states, from the stand-point of speech time. This notion of unreality is expressed by a simple Past tense (or the Past subjunctive *were* if the verb is *be*) or a Past Perfect. These Past tenses have the effect of 'distancing' the event from speech time. *Wish* takes modal *would* + infinitive to refer to future time. The subordinating conjunction *that* is normally omitted (see 7.3.1(e)):

> **present-time reference** I wish Ted *were* here with us.
>   Suppose Ted *were* here with us.
>   I'd rather Ted *were* here with us.

past-time reference	I wish Ted *had been* here with us.
	Suppose Ted *had been* here with us.
	I'd rather Ted *had been* here with us.
future-time reference	I wish Ted *would come* soon.
	Suppose Ted *came / were to come* soon.
	I'd rather Ted *came / were to come* soon.

MODULE 17
Expressing processes of being and becoming

Summary

1   The third main category of processes, relational processes, expresses the notion of being something or somewhere, as in *Tom is generous, James is an M.P., The Post Office is over there*. Similar to processes of being are existential processes, which state that something exists or took place, as in *There are millions of stars*. These are treated from the point of view of information processing in 30.4.

2   The notion of being is reflected in languages in different ways. In English relational processes can be grouped into three types:

attributive: Tom is generous.
circumstantial: The Post Office is over there.
possessive: That car is mine.

3   The participant in a relational process is termed the **Carrier** (*Tom, the Post Office, that car*). The process itself appears to have less meaning than do material processes and mental processes, and serves merely to relate the Carrier to its **Attribute** (*generous*), to a **circumstance** (*over there*) or to the semantic function expressing **possession** (*mine*).

17.1   Attributive relational processes

There is an intensive relationship between the Carrier and its Attribute. That is to say, the Carrier *is* in some way the Attribute. The contribution of the Attribute is to characterise the Carrier or to identify it, as illustrated below:

Characterising Attribute		
The play	was	a success.
John	is	a good player.
The river		
we crossed	was	wide.
Silvia	is	thirteen.
S	P	Cs

Identifying Attribute		
The play	was	'Hamlet'.
John	is	the captain.
The river		
we crossed	was	the Thames.
Silvia	is	my cousin.
S	P	Cs

The difference between these two types of Attribute is reflected in the syntax in three ways: (a) Only the identifying type is reversible (*'Hamlet' was the play. *A success was the play*). (b) Only the characterising type can be realised by an adjective (*The river we crossed was wide*). (c) NGs which realise characterising Attributes are usually indefinite (*a good player*), while NGs which realise identifying Attributes are usually definite (*the captain*).

The process itself can be expressed either as a state or as a transition. With state verbs such as *be, keep, remain, stay, seem* and *appear* the Attribute is seen as existing at the same time as the process described by the verb and is sometimes called the **current Attribute**.

With dynamic verbs of transition such as *become, get, turn, turn out, grow, run, end up* the Attribute exists as the result of the process and can be called the **resulting Attribute**:

Current Attribute
We kept quiet.
He remained the leader.
The leaves are yellow.
She felt exhausted.
Your sister looks tired.
My boss is quite bald.
The steps are smooth.
The water feels cold.
My face was red.

Resulting Attribute
We fell silent.
He became the leader.
The leaves turned yellow.
She ended up exhausted.
She gets tired easily.
He went bald very young.
The steps have worn smooth.
The water has run cold.
My face turned red.

There is a wide variety of verbs in English to express both states and transitions (see Module 12). As states, the mental process verbs *look* (= *seem*), *sound, smell, taste* and *feel* can be used and lend an additional meaning of 'sensory perception' to the relational process in which they occur. A Recipient participant can be optionally added to this semantic structure:

Carrier	Process	Attribute	Recipient
This test	looks	easy	(to me)
His name	sounds	familiar	(to me)
That fish	smells	bad	(to me)
Mangos	taste	delicious	(to me)
The surface	feels	rather rough	(to me)
The child	feels	hot	(to me)
S	P	Cs	A

The verb *feel* can function in two types of semantic structure: (a) with a Recipient Carrier (*I feel hot; she felt exhausted*) and (b) with a neutral Carrier (*the surface feels rather rough*). The example *the child feels hot* is therefore ambiguous; according to one interpretation the child (Recipient) feels the heat; according to another, someone feels the heat (that is, the temperature) of the child, this meaning admitting the optional Recipient (see also 15.2 for volitional *feel*).

Other realisations of transitional processes with resulting Attributes include the following:

> Her dreams came true.
> The joke fell flat.
> The days are growing shorter.
> Only two university posts have fallen vacant this year.
> His results proved difficult to confirm.

We also analyse as Attribute expressions of temporary state, whether realised by an adjective such as *unemployed*, or by a Prepositional Group such as *out of work*. Some expressions which might appear to be locatives (*on top of the world* = 'happy', *in the clouds* = 'absent-minded') we would analyse as metaphorical realisations of the Attribute, when they express a temporary state, as these do. There is usually a one-word adjectival equivalent (*happy, absent-minded*).

In expressions referring to climatic phenomena such as *it is hot / cold / sunny / windy / frosty / cloudy / foggy* there is no Carrier and the greater part of the meaning is expressed by the Attribute.

17.2   Circumstantial relational processes

These are processes of being in which the circumstantial element is essential to the situation, not peripheral to it (see also 7.1.2). There are many types of circumstance which in this way stand in an intensive relationship with the Carrier:

location in space:	The museum is *round the corner.*
location in time:	Our next meeting will be *on June 10.*
extent in space:	The desert stretches as *far as the eye can see.*

extent in time:	The performance lasted *three hours.*
measurement:	The carpet measures *three metres by two.*
cost:	The tickets cost *five dollars each.*
weight:	My suitcase weighs *20 kilos.*
means:	Entrance to the exhibition is *by invitation.*
Agent:	This symphony is *by Mahler.*
Beneficiary:	These flowers are *for you.*
metaphorical meanings:	He's *off alcohol.* Everyone's *into yoga* nowadays.

Examples such as *Tomorrow is Monday; Yesterday was July 1st* are reversible and can therefore be considered as identifying circumstantial processes.

17.3   Possessive relational processes

In this type, the relationship between the two entities is one of possession: one owns the other. The notion of possession is expressed either by the Attribute, or by the process itself.

(a) Possession as Attribute: the verb is *be* and the Attribute is realised by a genitive pronoun (*mine, yours, his, hers, ours, theirs*) or by an *'s* genitive such as *John's* in *the car is John's.*

(b) Possession as process: English has several verbs to express possession. With *have, own* and *possess* the Carrier is the possessor and the Attribute is the possessed. With *be* and *belong* it is the other way round: the Carrier is the possessed, the Attribute the possessor.

Also included in the category of 'possessing' are the notions of not possessing (*lack, need*), of being worthy to possess (*deserve*), and the abstract relations of inclusion, exclusion and containment.

Examples of all types of relational processes of possession are seen below:

Carrier	Process	Attribute
Those socks	are	my brother's.
This glove	isn't	mine.
Neither of these	is	yours.
The house	belongs	to a millionaire.
Possessed		Possessor

Carrier	Process	Attribute
The baby	has	blue eyes.
His uncle	owns	a yacht.
I	don't possess	a gun.
He	lacks	confidence.
Plants	need	water.
You	deserve	a prize.
The price	includes	postage.
The price	excludes	breakfast.
That can	contains	petrol.
Possessor		Possessed

Relational processes are extremely common in all uses of English. The following extract is based on an interview with a young farmer who breeds pigs; he describes them, not by what they do, but as they are; this view is reflected in the large number of characterising Attributes:

> Pigs are *different*. [1] A pig is *more of an individual*, [2] *more human* [3] and in many ways *a strangely likeable character*. [4] Pigs have *strong personalities* [5] and it is easy to get *fond of them*. [6] I am always getting fond of pigs and feel a bit *conscience-stricken* [7] when I have to put them inside for their whole lives. Pigs are *very clean animals* [8] but, like us, they are all *different*; [9] some will need *cleaning out* [10] after half a day and some will be *neat and tidy* [11] after three days. Some pigs are always *in a mess* [12] and won't care. Pigs are *very interesting people* [13] and can leave quite a gap when they go off to the bacon factory.
>
> Ronald Blythe, *Akenfield*.

[1–4] characterising; [5] possessed; [6–9] characterising; [10] possessed; [11–13] characterising.

MODULE 18
Expressing processes of saying and existing

Summary

1   Processes of saying and communicating are verbal processes. The participant who communicates is the Sayer, and is typically human. That which is communicated is the Verbiage and may be a reported statement, a reported question or a reported directive. A Recipient may also be present in some verbal processes.

2   *Say* and *tell* are distinguished as verbs of communicating by certain semantic properties which are reflected in the syntax.

3   Processes of existing are existential processes. The single participant is the Existent, which may be an entity or an event. The process refers to the existence, location or happening of the Existent.

18.1   Verbal processes or processes of saying

Verbal processes are processes of 'saying' or 'communicating' and are realised by such verbs as *say, tell, announce, ask* and *report*. They have one participant which is typically human, but not necessarily so (the **Sayer**) and a second essential participant which is what is said or asked or reported (the **Verbiage**). A **Recipient** may also be present in some verbal processes:

Sayer	Verbal process	Recipient	Verbiage
Mary They That sign Big Ben Our correspondent	told announced says tells reports	me	a secret. the name of the winner. 'No entry'. the time in London. renewed fighting on the frontier.

The Sayer can be anything which puts out a communicative signal (*Mary, that sign, Big Ben, our correspondent*, etc.). The Verbiage is realised either by a NG, as in the examples above, or by a clause, as in the following table. Depending partly on the verb, the following clause can express a reported statement as in the examples in (a), a reported question as in (b) or a reported directive, as in (c) (see also 36.4 and 36.5).

(a)

Sayer	Verbal process	Recipient	Reported statement
She A voice No-one	said announced told	 us	that the film was good. that the train was arriving. that the match was cancelled.

(b)

Sayer	Verbal process	Recipient	Reported question
Sue We	asked enquired	the assistant of the clerk	how much it cost. if the museum was open.

(c)

Sayer	Verbal process	Recipient	Reported directive
John I She The notice The captain	told persuaded urged forbids asked	the boys my mother us children everyone	to be quiet. to see a doctor. to stay a little longer. to use the lift alone. to pay attention.

The verbs *say* and *tell* are distinguished by certain semantic properties which are reflected in the grammar:

(i) *Tell* typically requires a Recipient at Indirect Object, especially in its use as a directive. The Recipient is unrealised in stereotyped expressions such as *tell a story, tell the truth, tell lies*. *Say* does not have a Recipient at Indirect Object.

Mary told me a secret.	*Mary said me a secret.
Mary told us she would come.	*Mary said us she would come.
* Mary told she would come.	Mary said she would come.

(ii) Reported directives are expressed in two ways: *tell* + a *to*-infinitive clause, and *say* + a modalised *that*-clause:

He told us to leave at once.	He said that we must leave at once.
The red light tells you to stop.	The red light says that you are to stop.

(iii) The Verbiage after *say*, but not after *tell*, can be quoted direct speech (see 36.3.1):

*Mary told us 'Hello'.	Mary said 'Hello'.

Verbal processes and the clauses which follow them can be considered to form a clause complex, with the second clause dependent on the first. The clause complex is described in Chapter 7.

It is sometimes difficult to draw the line between verbal processes and others. *Wish* in *I wish you a merry Christmas* is both mental and verbal. Reading aloud and dictating may be counted as both verbal and material, since, while in both cases a communicative signal is emitted, they could be questioned by 'What is X doing?'. *Talk* and *chat* are verbal processes which have an implicit reciprocal meaning (*They talked / chatted to each other.*). There is no Verbiage participant except in the expressions *talk sense / nonsense*. *Speak* is not implicitly reciprocal and can take a Range participant, (see 20.1) (*She speaks Spanish. He speaks five languages.*).

In the following newspaper article, all the main verbs realise verbal processes. The Sayer is in each case the newspaper *The Mail on Sunday*:

> The Mail on Sunday *says* the government is in a panic over the poll tax[1].
>
> It *argues* that originally the poll tax seemed an 'elegant and rational way to levy local taxation', but it has turned into 'both a political and a bureaucratic nightmare which could easily destroy this government'[2].
>
> The newspaper *claims* the best points about the poll tax were its straightforwardness, its fiscal neutrality and its ease of comprehension[3].
>
> It *cautions* against 'tinkering' with it to allay public fears because 'that will simply produce more anomalies and greater injustices'[4].
>
> The only answer, it *concludes*, 'is to scrap it and start all over again'[5].
>
> *The Sunday Times*, 29 April 1990.

The Phenomenon in sentences [1], [2], [3] and [5] is a fact, an indirect statement realised by a *that*-clause. In sentence [4], *cautions* (= *warn*) expresses a warning against a possible circumstance. In sentence [5] the *that*-clause which realises the factual Phenomenon is discontinuous and the verbal process *concludes* is medial.

The repeated use of verbal processes to introduce the factual statements and the warning can be explained by the situation; in this article *The Sunday Times* is not reporting a series of facts but, rather, another paper's statements of certain facts. In other words, what is being reported is not a representation of reality but a representation of a representation.

18.2 Existential processes or processes of existing

Existential processes are processes of existing or happening (*There's a man at the door; there was a loud bang*). *There* is not a participant since it has no semantic content, although it has both a syntactic function as Subject (5.1.3(f)) and a textual function as 'presentative' element, since it pushes the true Subject to the right, placing it under stronger focus (see 30.4). The single participant is the **Existent**, which may refer to a countable entity (*There's a good film on in town*), an uncountable entity (*There's roast lamb for lunch*) or an event (*There was an explosion*).

The existential clause may simply state the existence, or non-existence, of something, as in *there are no fairies; there are many kinds of sea-birds*. More frequently it states the existence of something together with its location in time or place. A third type expresses an Attribute of the Existent, while a fourth type expands the Existent in some other way:

(a) with a locative circumstance:

There	is	some ice	in the refrigerator.
There	was	a storm	at sea.
There'	s	not a cloud	in the sky.

(b) with an Attribute characterising the Existent:

| There | are | some pages | blank. |
| There | were | few people | in favour. |

(c) expansion of the Existent by the addition of clauses:

There	are	few people who realise the danger.
There'	s	a strange-looking man waiting outside.
There	is	a wedding announced.

By means of the expansions in (c), a state of affairs is expressed linguistically as existential, which would in its more basic semantic structure be a process of another type, whether mental (*Few people realise the danger*), material (*Someone is waiting*) or verbal (*X announces a wedding*).

The process in existential clauses is typically expressed by *be*. Other intransitive verbs which can be used are *stand, lie, stretch, hang* and *remain*, which express positional states; as well as these there are a few intransitive dynamic verbs which express the notion of 'occurring', 'coming into view' or 'arrival on the scene' (*occur, follow, appear, arise, emerge, loom*). Both types are illustrated below:

> There remain many problems.
> Below the castle there stretches a vast plain.
> On the wall there hangs a mirror.
> There followed an extraordinary scene.
> There appeared on the stage six beautiful dancers.
> There emerged from the cave a huge brown bear.
> Out of the mist there loomed a strange shape.

Existential *there* may be omitted when a locative or directional Adjunct or a clause is in initial position:

> Below the castle stretches a vast plain.
> On the wall hangs a mirror.
> Standing at the door is a strange-looking man.

Such clauses are very close semantically to reversed relational processes. However, the addition of a tag question, with *there*, not a personal pronoun (*On the wall hangs a mirror, doesn't there?*), suggests that they are in fact existentials. On the other hand, the same clauses with SPCs order would clearly be analysed as relational, confirmed by *it* in the tag question (*A mirror hangs on the wall, doesn't it?*). Clearly, the expanded existential clause is more a textual device than a statement of existence since it shows the interaction of certain relational processes with the textual function of presenting a situation.

Both the presence and the omission of existential *there* are illustrated in the following extract. All the existential verbs are some form of *be*, except *stood* in [6]. All the Existents are useful objects; the location of these is obviously important and in four cases is specified in initial position, thus making for existential clauses without existential *there*:

> She looked at the room. There *was* a wooden settle in front of the hearth, stretching its back to the room[1]. There *was* a little table under a square, recessed window[2], on whose sloping ledge *were* newspapers, scattered letters, nails and a hammer[3]. On the table *were* dried beans and two maize cobs[4]. In the corner *were* shelves[5], with two chipped enamel plates, and a small table underneath, on which *stood* a bucket of water and a dipper[6]. Then there *was* a wooden chest, two little chairs and a litter of faggots, cane, vine-twigs, bare maize hubs, oak-twigs filling the corner by the hearth[7].
>
> D. H. Lawrence, *The Lost Girl*.
>
> [1] + *there*; [2] + *there*; [3] − *there*; [4] − *there*; [5] − *there*; [6] − *there*; [7] + *there*.

MODULE 19
Expressing the attendant circumstances

Summary

The circumstantial element in English covers a great variety of meanings, of which the most common are those related to space and time, manner, contingency, accompaniment, modality, degree, role and matter. They are described from the point of view of their syntactic function in 8.1 and also as group structures in 57.

Clauses expressing circumstances are treated as part of clause complexes (see Chapter 7).

19.1   Spatial and temporal circumstances

There are many parallel expressions of space and time, in many cases introduced by the same preposition:

	Space	Time
location direction direction + end-point starting-point extent extent + end-point relative distributive	at home, in the park, below towards the south to the south pole from the north for several miles as far as Granada here, there, nearby, in front, behind us, above our heads at intervals every 100 yards here and there	at 5 o'clock, in May, years ago towards midnight up to now since Christmas, since I saw you for several years until we meet again, by Tuesday now, then, recently, before, after tea at intervals every so often now and then, off and on

Locative, directional and relative meanings are questioned by *where*? and *when*?, starting-point meanings by *where ... from*? and *since when*?, extent by *how far*?, *how long*? and distribution by *how often*? (see also 59.1 and 59.5).

19.2   Manner

Under this heading we include, as well as manner in the sense of 'quality', the notions of means and comparison, illustrated by the following examples, to which the *WH*-question forms are added:

	WH-form	
manner as quality means comparison	how? how? what with? what ... like?	Don't do it *that way*; do it *gently*. It's cheaper *by bus*. He watered the garden *with a hose*. Snow lay *like a blanket* on the ground.

19.3   Contingency

The circumstantial element of contingency covers such meanings as cause, purpose, reason, concession and behalf:

cause	what cause?	The child took the pen *out of envy.*
		They are dying *of hunger.*
purpose	what . . . for?	He is studying *for a degree.*
		The team is training *to win.*
reason	why?	We stayed in *on account of the rain.*
		He stopped *because he was tired.*
concession	how?	*No matter how hard they train*, they won't
		beat our team.
		In spite of the delay, we reached the
		concert hall in time.
behalf	who/what for?	Give up smoking *for the sake of your*
		health.
		I'll speak to the Director *on your behalf.*
condition	*if*-clause	Send a telegram, *if necessary.*

19.4   Accompaniment

Accompaniment expresses a joint participation in the process, involving either the notion of 'togetherness' or that of 'additionality'. Each of these can be either positive or negative:

togetherness	positive	Tom came *with his friend.*
		Tom came *with a different haircut.*
togetherness	negative	Tom came *without his friend.*
		Tom came *without the car.*
additionality	positive	Tom came *as well as Paul.*
additionality	negative	Tom came *instead of Paul.*

19.5   Modality

Modality expresses the notions of possibility, probability and certainty (see 44.1):

possibility	His new novel will *possibly* come out next month.
probability	It will *probably* be well received.
certainty	It will *certainly* cause a lot of controversy.

19.6   Degree

Circumstantial expressions of degree either emphasise or attenuate the process:

| emphasis | I *completely* forgot to bring my passport. |
| attenuation | You can *hardly* expect me to believe that. |

19.7   Role

A role circumstance indicates in what capacity the participant is involved in the process:

capacity	I'm speaking to you *as a friend*. *As an actor* he's not outstanding, but *as a dancer* he's brilliant. He's *by way* of being an amateur inventor. The prince appeared *in the guise of* a beggar.

19.8   Matter

This element adds the notion of 'with reference to ...' and is realised by a wide variety of simple and complex Prepositional Groups, including those circumstantial Predicator Complements which follow certain verbs such as *deprive, rob* and *help oneself* (see 7.3.1 and 10.3.2):

> They are anxious *about* her health.
> Is there any news *of* the missing seamen?
> *With regard to* your order of July 17. ...
> *As for* that, I don't believe a word of it.
> The old lady was robbed *of* all she possessed.
> You shouldn't deprive yourself *of* vitamins.
> Help yourself *to* wine.

Some of the numerous types of circumstance available are illustrated in the following extract. This type of fiction tends to contain very detailed references to the circumstances accompanying each episode:

> He'd noticed it first *during the Riemick case*[1], *early last year*[2]. Karl had sent a message; he'd got something special for him and was making one of his rare visits *to Western Germany*[3]; some legal conference *at Karlsruhe*[4]. Leamas had managed to get an air passage *to Cologne*[5], and picked up a car *at the airport*[6]. It was *still* [7] quite *early in the morning* [8] and he'd hoped to miss most of the autobahn traffic *to Karlsruhe* [9] but the heavy lorries were *already* [10] on the move. He drove seventy kilometres *in half an hour*[11], weaving between the traffic, taking risks *to beat the clock*[12], when a small car, a Fiat *probably*[13], nosed its way out *into the fast lane* [14] *forty yards ahead of him*[15]. Leamas stamped on the brake, turning his headlights full on and sounding his horn, and *by the grace of God* [16] he missed it; missed it *by the fraction of a second*[17].

> John Le Carré, *The Spy Who Came In From The Cold.*

[1] extent: time; [2] location: time; [3] direction: space; [4] location: space; [5] direction: space; [6] location: space; [7] emphasis; [8] location: time; [9] direction: space; [10] emphasis; [11] extent: time; [12] purpose; [13] modality; [14] direction: space; [15] location: space; [16] cause; [17] degree.

MODULE 20
Two subsidiary participants: Range and Instrument

Summary

1   There are two further participant roles which are to be distinguished from circumstantial elements. These are **Range** and **Instrument**.

2   Range is the nominal concept implied by the process as its scope or range. It covers entities such as *life* in *lead a good life*, measurements such as *10 kilos* in *It weighs 10 kilos* and the real process after such verbs as *have* and *do* in e.g. *have a bath, do a dance*.

3   Instrument is the entity which a human Agent uses in order to carry out or initiate the process. It is typically associated with the preposition *with*. An Instrument participant can become Subject in an active clause. With verbs such as *elbow, head* the notion of Instrument is incorporated into the process itself.

20.1   Range

Range is the nominal concept which is implied by the process as its scope or range: *song* in *sing a song, games* in *play games, prize* in *win the prize, race* in *run a race*.

The Range element may refer to an entity which exists independently of the process (*the prize* is there whether it is won or not), and may be more specific (*the TV set* in *win a TV set*). But in many cases the Range element is an extension of the process itself. The nominals *song, game* and *race*, when used in the expressions *sing a song, play games* and *run a race*, are not conceived as independent entities but as extensions of the processes of singing, playing and running, respectively. In other semantic structures, such nominals could of course realise a different function, such as Effected in *compose a song, invent a new game*.

Certain Range elements are morphologically related to the verb, such as *sing* and *song*, and these are traditionally termed Cognate Objects. The term 'cognate' is, however, not applicable to items which are not morphologically related such as *play* and *game*, and for this reason the more comprehensive term Range is preferred. In present-day English truly cognate instances of Range often sound slightly archaic: *smile a mysterious smile, fight a clean fight, sleep a deep sleep*, although certain combinations such as *live a peaceful life, die a horrible death* continue to be heard. Most present-day instances of Range are not cognate. Such is the case with the numerous expressions of the type *have a chat / drink / rest / smoke; give a push / kick / nudge; take a bath / shower / walk; do a dance; give a smile / grin / laugh; make a mistake; ask a question*, etc. In all such expressions the process is realised by the nominal element, the Range, while the verb itself is lexically empty.

One reason for the popularity of this construction today is the potential that the noun has for being modified in various ways. It would be difficult to express through the Verbal Group the meanings of specificness, quantification and quality present in *she took a long, relaxing hot bath, they played two strenuous games of tennis, I had such a strange experience yesterday*.

Another reason for the proliferation of Range Objects and Complements is that the resulting Nominal Group is longer and heavier than the Verbal Group which precedes it, thus satisfying the principle of end-weight (see Module 5.1.3d).

Furthermore, the Range nominal can initiate a *WH*-cleft structure more easily than a verb can (see 30.2) as in *a good rest is what you need*; it can also occur as participant in other semantic and syntactic structures, such as causative Agent Subject in *the awkward questions he asked made him unpopular*.

The Range element is realised by the Direct Object or by the Predicator Complement in those structures that do not passivise (e.g. *The case weighs 10 kilos*). In a few infrequent cases, Range is realised by the Subject, which is cognate (*The frost froze hard; day dawned*).

20.2   Instrument

Instrument is the entity which a human Agent uses in order to carry out or initiate the process. The preposition which introduces the nominal realisation of the Instrument is *with*:

> The child broke the window *with a stone*.
> I can't open the door *with this key*.
> The builders levelled the site *with a bulldozer*.
> They polluted the water *with chemicals*.

The Instrument participant can become Subject in the same basic clause:

> A stone broke the window.
> This key won't open the door.
> A bulldozer levelled the site.
> Chemicals polluted the water.

Instrument differs in this respect from the circumstance Means, which cannot become Subject in the same basic clause:

> He watered the garden *with a hose*.   *A hose* watered the garden.

There is also a correspondence with clauses containing the verb *use*. However, as this verb emphasises the factor of motivation on the part of the Agent, the notion of agency in the two clauses may not be exactly equivalent; for instance, *they used chemicals to pollute the water* will be interpreted as a deliberate action, whereas *they polluted the water with chemicals* could be interpreted as not deliberate. This would be an instance of agency without motivation.

> The child used a stone to break the window.
> I can't use this key to open the door.
> The builders used a bulldozer to level the site.

In passive clauses the distinction between Agent and Instrument is sometimes hard to draw, since Instrument can occur in passives in a *by*-phrase. Compare:

> He was killed *by a fanatic*. (Agent)
> He was killed *by a hand-grenade*. (Instrument)

In *he was killed by a hand-grenade* the human Agent is silenced (see 30.3); this is even more obvious in *he was killed by a stray bullet*, in which the factor of motivation is absent. In such cases, Instrument is likely to be expressed by a *by*-phrase. If we say, however, *he was killed with a hand-grenade / with a bullet*, expressing the Instrument by means of a *with*-phase, the human agency is clearly implicit.

With some verbs the notion of Instrument is incorporated into the process itself; in this way *bulldoze* can be used as a material process: *the builders bulldozed the site*. Other examples include:

> He *elbowed* his way through the crowd. (by using his elbows)
> The player *headed* the ball into the net. (by using his head)
> They *levered* the rock into position. (by using a lever)

MODULE 21
Conceptualising experiences from a different angle: grammatical metaphor

Summary

1   In the semantic structures described so far, processes have been realised by verbs, entities by nouns and Attributes by adjectives. These are indeed the basic correspondences which are found in the language of children and in basic English. But any state of affairs can be expressed in more than one way. The first, or more basic realisation will be called the *congruent* one, as in *We walked in the evening along the river to Henley*; the other, or others, will be called *metaphorical*, as in *Our evening walk along the river took us to Henley*. This is not lexical metaphor, however, but grammatical metaphor.

2   Thus, process can be realised as Thing (*Take a deep breath*), Attribute as Thing (*Bigness is paid for by fewness*) and circumstances as Thing (*August 12 found them in Rome*). These alternative realisations of the semantic roles involve further adjustments in the correspondences between semantic roles and syntactic functions in the clause.

3   Grammatical metaphor is a feature of much written English and of spoken English in professional registers.

21.1   Congruent realisations and metaphorical realisations

In describing semantic structures throughout this chapter, we have seen that, in active clauses, the inherent participants such as Agent, Affected, Experiencer and Carrier are realised by NGs, processes are realised by VGs and circumstantials by PrepGs and by AdvGs. This correspondence between the semantics and the syntax of English structures is indeed the typical one, but it is by no means the only one. We have to beware of assuming that a one-to-one correspondence exists between any semantic function and any syntactic function. We have to beware of assuming that entities such as people and things are necessarily expressed by nouns, that actions are necessarily expressed by verbs and that qualities are necessarily expressed by adjectives. Except in the language of children and in very basic English, our linguistic representation of reality tends to be more complex. Any situation can be expressed in more than one way; the first or typical realisation may be called the 'congruent' one; the other, or others, the 'metaphorical'. The two forms may be illustrated by an example.

Suppose that I wish to tell you that my friends and I walked in the evening along the river as far as Henley. In the 'typical' or 'congruent' version, I first select the process type from the options 'material', 'mental' and 'relational' processes. The notion of walking is typically seen as a process of 'doing', so I select a material process *walk*. To accompany a process such as *walk* seen intransitively, I then select an Agent, or 'doer' of the action, and a number of circumstantial elements, of time, place and direction, to give the following semantic structure and its lexico-grammatical realisation:

Agent	Material process	Time circ.	Place circ.	Direction circ.
Subject	Predicator	Adjunct	Adjunct	Adjunct
NG	VG	PrepG	PrepG	PrepG
We	walked	in the evening	along the river	to Henley

This is not the only way of expressing this situation. Instead, I could have said *Our evening walk along the river took us to Henley*. In this 'metaphorical' interpretation the semantic functions are 'transferred' in relation to the syntactic functions. The material process *walk* has now become Agent, and the circumstances of time (*in the evening*) and place (*along the river*) have become classifier and qualifier, respectively, of the new Agent realised at Subject (*evening walk along the river*). The original Agent *we* is now divided into two; one part functions as possessor of the Subject entity (*our evening walk along the river*), the other as Affected (*us*) of a new material process expressed by the verb *took*. Only the directional circumstance *to Henley* is realised in the same way in both interpretations:

Agent	Material process	Affected	Direction circ.
Subject	Predicator	Direct O	Adjunct
NG	VG	NG	PrepG
Our evening walk along the river	took	us	to Henley

This second interpretation is a very simple instance of 'grammatical metaphor' or alternative realisations of semantic functions, and is a phenomenon which occurs all the time, in different degrees, in adult language, especially in certain written genres.

Even in everyday spoken language it sometimes happens that the metaphorical form has become the normal way of expressing a certain meaning.
We have seen that the Range element (20.1) *drink / chat / rest* in *have a drink
/ chat / rest* is the one which expresses the process, while the syntactic
function of Predicator now expresses a relation *have*. These are simple types
of transferred semantic functions which have been incorporated into everyday language. Slightly more complex but still used by adult speakers in
spoken English are examples such as the following:

> The large department stores *are within easy walking distance* of
> each other. (= The large department stores are so close to each
> other that you can easily walk from one to the other.) (Attribute
> realised as a circumstance, process (*walk*) realised as part of a
> thing)

> *Daylight saving time* starts at midnight tomorrow. (= Clocks are put
> forward / back at midnight tomorrow in order to get the maximum
> amount of daylight.) (circumstance of purpose realised as a
> classifier)

It is clear that a choice of transferred realisations such as these has as one
result an increase in lexical density: Nominal Groups become long and
heavy. For this reason nominalisation is the form of grammatical metaphor
most consistently recognised under different labels. When, for instance, a
process is realised by a nominal instead of by a verb, what we have is an
'event' or a 'happening'. In this way, a process such as *explode* can be
visualised as an entity (*explosion*), which can then carry out all the functions
realised by nominals, such as a Subject or Direct Object (*The explosion
occurred at 6 a.m.; leaking gas caused an explosion*). Languages abound in
nouns such as these, and this fact makes it no doubt impossible to carry the
notion of grammatical metaphor to its logical conclusions: it would be
awkward, for instance, to have to analyse *war* every time we come across the
word as a metaphorical interpretation of 'nations using arms to fight each
other', in which a whole situation is nominalised under an institutionalised
term 'war'. More accessibly, the English word *shopping* is a useful grammatical metaphor for the process expressed as 'going to the shops and buying
things', which then permits other useful combinations as *window shopping*
(=looking in shop windows but not buying anything) and *shopping centre*
(= area in which one can go to many shops), as well as the result of the
process itself (*bags of shopping*). Here, grammar borders on lexis, and
different languages have different means of visualising one semantic function
as if it were another. There is usually some slight difference in meaning, in
content or in emphasis between the metaphorical and the congruent forms in
any language, as there is when these are translated into another language.
Here we can do no more than briefly outline some of the transfers of semantic functions. In the following sections, metaphorical forms are given first,

with a congruent or basic corresponding form suggested in the right-hand column.

21.2   Process realised as Thing

This is by far the most common type of grammatical metaphor. Many are institutionalised nominalisations, such as the following.

(a) Without the slightest *hesitation.*	Without *hesitating* at all.
(b) Take a deep *breath.*	*Breathe* deeply.
(c) There was a sudden *outburst of laughter.*	X *burst out laughing* suddenly.
(d) The *exploration and mapping* of the world went on.	X continued to *explore and map* the world.
(e) *Communication* was difficult between the two groups.	The two groups *communicated* with difficulty.

Many others, however, represent a more original view of reality on the part of the speaker or writer, as in example (f):

(f) His conception of the drama has a very modern *ring.*	He conceives the drama in a way that *sounds* very modern to us.

21.3   Attribute realised as Thing

An Attribute can be realised as an entity by means of an abstract noun. The forms may be morphologically related, as in example (a), or not, as in (b).

(a) *Bigness* is paid for, in part, by *fewness*, and a decline in competition.	If firms are very *big, fewer* will exist and they will compete less.
(b) The *usefulness* of this machinery is dwindling.	This machinery is becoming less *useful.*

21.4   Circumstance realised as Thing

A circumstance realised as an entity frequently functions as a locative Subject, with either a spatial meaning, as in (a), or a temporal meaning, as in (b), (c) and (d):

(a) *His face* was streaming with sweat.	Sweat streamed *down his face.*
(b) *August 12* found the travellers in Rome.	The travellers were / arrived in Rome *on August 12.*
(c) *The last decade* has witnessed an unprecedented rise in agricultural technology.	*During the last decade* agricultural technology increased as never before.

(d) *The seventeenth century*   *In the seventeenth century*
   saw the development of   scientific works began to be
   systematic scientific   published systematically.
   publication.

Circumstantial Subjects often involve the introduction of a completely new process, which is usually realised by a verb of perception such as *see, witness* or *find*. As these new processes are transitive, typically taking a nominal Complement, further nominalisations are to be expected, such as *rise (or increase) in agricultural technology*, instead of *increase* as a verb, in (c), while in (d) *development* and *publication* instead of *develop* and *publish* follow the same pattern. It would not even be possible to use *that*-clauses after verbs such as *see*, as in **The seventeenth century saw that scientific works began to be published systematically*, even though *that*-clauses are considered nominalisations by some linguists, since the verb would then be interpreted with its literal meaning, which would be nonsense.

21.5   Process and circumstance as part of the Thing

When a process or a circumstance is visualised as an entity, the syntactic realisation of this entity is a noun, which can be modified in many ways. It often happens that the epithets, classifiers and quantifiers of these 'meta-phorical' NGs are also instances of transferred correspondences between the semantic and the syntactic functions. The choice of *rise* in (c) above, for instance, permits the modifier *unprecedented*, with the circumstantial meaning of *as never before*.

A process together with an accompanying circumstance can be realised as epithet or classifier by means of *-ing* and *-en* participles:

(a) his *best-selling* novel   His novel is selling better than
                                others.
(b) a *steadily increasing* series   More and more things and
   of inventions and devices   devices (are) being invented.

21.6   Dependent situation as Thing

A whole state of affairs, which in its congruent form would be realised as a subordinate clause, can be visualised as an entity and expressed by a nominal:

Fears of disruption to oil   Because people feared that oil
supplies from the Gulf helped   would not be supplied as usual
push crude oil prices above   from the Gulf, the price of crude
$20 a barrel.   oil rose to above $20 a barrel.

In this journalistic example the long NG at Subject is the Agent in a new process *helped push*. This process would normally be associated with a human Agent, while the Affected would typically be a concrete entity, followed by a locative expressing where the Object was pushed as in *he pushed me through the door*. The introduction of a verb such as *helped push* has the effect of presenting the situation as more dynamic, while the long nominal *fears* ... silences the true Agent, drawing the reader's attention instead to the emotionally charged word *fears*.

These few examples may serve to show that 'grammatical metaphor' is a very powerful option in the presenting of information. There is always more than one way of expressing what the speaker or writer perceives as a situation. The transfer of semantic functions as illustrated above presents the experiential and interpersonal content in a more abstract way, which is reflected syntactically in the density of the nominals. The organisation of the text is also greatly modified by the distribution of information in this way.

The concept of grammatical metaphor is useful since it helps us to become aware of non-institutionalised realisations which represent real options of expression for the speaker or writer. As such they have textual, stylistic and ideological implications which require further study. Many written genres of English, and no doubt of other languages, make great use of the semantic-syntactic transfers which result in the phenomena described here. When institutionalised within restricted social contexts, the concept of grammatical metaphor goes a long way towards explaining professional jargons such as journalese and officialese as written forms. Others, such as the language of business management, are not only written but spoken.

SUMMARY OF PROCESSES, PARTICIPANTS AND CIRCUMSTANCES

Process		Example	Participants	Attribute	Circumstances
Material	1	Tom kicked the ball into the goal.	Agent + Affected		Direction + end-point
	2	Lightning struck the oak tree.	Force + Affected		
	3	Mary made an omelette.	Agent + Affected		
	4	I gave the children some sweets.	Agent + Recipient + Affected		
	5	Will you bring me a newspaper?	Agent + Beneficiary + Affected		
	6	They're making the road wider.	Causative Agent + Affected	Resulting	
	7	Pat boiled the water.	Causative Agent + Affected		
	8	The water boiled.	Affected		
	9	Birds fly.	Agent		
	10	The bird died.	Affected		
	11	She slipped on the wet pavement.	Affected		Locative (space)
	12	Glass breaks easily.	Affected		Manner
	13	Do you drive?	Agent + Unactualised Affected		
Mental	14	Tom watched the snake.	Experiencer (volitional) + Phenom.		
	15	Tom saw the snake.	Experiencer (non-volitional) + Phenom.		
	16	Tom knows the answer.	Experiencer + Phenom.		Degree
	17	We were pleased by the news.	Recip. Experiencer + Phenom.		
	18	The news pleased us very much.	Phenom. + Recip. Experiencer.		
	19	I wish you were here.	Experiencer + Phenom. (unreal)		
Relational	20	The play was a success.	Carrier	Characterising	
	21	The play was 'Hamlet'.	Carrier	Identifying	
	22	The film lasted three hours.	Carrier	Circumstantial	
	23	Those gloves aren't mine.	Possessed	Possessor	
	24	Her dream came true.	Carrier	Resulting	
Verbal	25	Mary told me a secret.	Sayer + Recip. + Verbiage		
	26	I didn't say that.	Sayer + Verbiage		
Existential	27	There's a notice on the door.	Existent	Characterising	Locative (space)
	28	There are some pages blank.	Existent		
	29	There remains one problem.	Existent		

TASKS ON CHAPTER 4
Expressing patterns of experience: Processes, participants, circumstances

Modules 13 and 14

1   †*Identify each process in the following examples as a process of 'doing' (material), a process of 'experiencing' (mental) or a process of 'being' (relational)*:
   1) Bees make honey.
   2) I prefer ballet to opera.
   3) The ground is soggy after the heavy rain.
   4) Do you know the author's name?
   5) The wounded soldier staggered down the road.
   6) The abbey is now a ruin.
   7) I don't trust his judgement.
   8) She writes romances about rich and beautiful people.
   9) The weather has turned cold. The days are becoming longer.
   10) You don't seem convinced by his argument.

2   †*Say whether **it** in each of the following clauses refers to a participant or is merely a Subject-filler*:
   1) *It* rarely snows in the south of Spain.
   2) I can lend you 10 dollars. Will *it* be enough?
   3) Her baby is due next month and she hopes *it* will be a girl.
   4) *It* rained heavily last night.
   5) Where's your bicycle? *It*'s in the garage.
   6) *It*'s our first wedding anniversary today.
   7) The kiwi is a bird, but *it* can't fly.
   8) *It*'s too hot to play tennis.
   9) The brake pedal is between the clutch and the accelerator. Can you feel *it*?
   10) *It*'s two miles to the nearest supermarket.

3   †*Fill in the blank space with a suitable Force participant*:
   1) As we left the hotel, ... was blowing off the sea.
   2) Huge .... crashed onto the beach and broke against the rocks.
   3) Several bathers were caught by the incoming .... and had to be rescued by the coastguard patrol.

4) Further inland, a usually tranquil . . . . broke its banks and flooded the surrounding fields.

5) In the mountains above the village, campers were surprised by a sudden . . . . which threatened to engulf their tents. Fortunately, they were able to run to safety.

4 *Write a short paragraph on 'A forest fire', using Force participants and material processes.*

5 †*Identify the italicised participant as Affected or Effected:*
1) He paints *surrealist portraits of his friends.*
2) Don't pick *the flowers!*
3) My mother used to bake *delicious pies and bread.*
4) They carve *these figures* out of wood.
5) According to the Guinness Book of Records, Havergal Brian composed *the longest symphony ever.*
6) He angrily threw *a stone* at the barking dog.
7) Engineers are installing *a telephone box.*
8) The old man sat down on a bench and rolled *a cigarette.*
9) In their youth they wrote *pop-songs* and made *fortunes.*
10) Angry housewives attacked *the striking dustmen* with umbrellas.

6 (a) †*Identify the italicised participant as Recipient or Beneficiary:*
1) Don't forget to send *us* a postcard.
2) *My brother-in-law* has been offered a job analysing mud for an oil company.
3) Can I get *you* something to eat?
4) I think Sammy would like you to buy *him* an ice-cream.
5) *The tourists* were charged too much for the boat-trip.

(b) *Fill in the blank with a suitable Recipient or Beneficiary:*
1) Cut . . . . a couple of thin slices of ham, would you?
2) They deprived . . . . of his freedom.
3) They'll weave . . . . a rug for a moderate sum.
4) They succeeded in robbing . . . . of her share of the inheritance.
5) Provide . . . . . . with a good pair of boots!

7 †*Say which of the following clauses are ergative and write underneath these the corresponding intransitive constructions:*
1) The stress of high office ages most Prime Ministers prematurely.
    ....
2) The child blew up the balloon.
    ....
3) Smoking can damage your health.
    ....
4) Swarms of locusts darkened the sky.
    ....

5) They sprayed the crops with insecticide.

....

6) Pain and worry wrinkled his brow.

....

7) They are developing new techniques in pig-breeding.

....

8) The photographer clicked the camera.

....

9) The truck tipped a load of sand onto the road.

....

10) This year the company has doubled its sales.

....

8 *Imagine you are a copy-writer for a well-known cosmetic firm. You are told to write a brochure for a new range of cosmetics. Include in your description causative verbs such as* **soften, whiten, lighten, lessen, tighten, freshen, refresh, cleanse, smooth, moisturise** *and / or SPOdCo structures containing* **make** *or* **leave** *and an Attribute.*

9 *With the help of a good dictionary draw up a list of verbs which can be used in ergative pairs and compare them with their equivalents in another language.*

Module 15

1 †*Say whether the participant in the following one-participant situations is acting (Agent), is acted upon (Affected) or whether properties of the participant are being expressed:*
    1) This kind of material creases easily.
    2) The car broke down.
    3) Your letter got lost in the post.
    4) Glass recycles well.
    5) For Heaven's sake, don't dither!
    6) He ruled with an iron hand.
    7) This cream whips up in an instant.
    8) Peaches won't ripen in this climate.
    9) Two of the deputies arrived late.
    10) The chimney-pot crashed to the ground.

2 *Each of the following clauses describes the properties of some entity. Complete the (a) set by adding the entity, the (b) set by expressing a property of the entity given:*
    (a)
    1) .... doesn't rust but other types of steel do.
    2) .... irons well.
    3) .... breaks easily.
    4) .... doesn't spread as easily as margarine.
    5) .... won't rub out.

(b)
6) Plastic containers . . . .
7) That new suitcase of yours . . . .
8) Leather skirts . . . .
9) Squeezable sauce-bottles . . . .
10) Brass buttons . . . .

3   *Comment on the causative processes in the following quotation from Shakespeare's 'Antony and Cleopatra' (2.2.224):*

> Age cannot *wither* her, nor custom *stale*
> Her infinite variety: other women *cloy*
> The appetites they feed, but she *makes hungry*
> Where most she *satisfies*.

Module 16

1   † *Identify each of the processes in the main clauses of the following sentences as one of perception, cognition or affectivity. Say whether the Phenomenon is an entity, a fact or a situation:*
1) He recognised a group of fellow Americans by their accent.
2) Yesterday I saw a mouse in the supermarket.
3) The miner knew he wouldn't see the light of day again for many hours.
4) Most people hate going to the dentist.
5) Did you watch the World Cup final on television?
6) He wondered whether he had heard correctly.
7) He could hardly believe that what had happened to him was true.
8) I just love it when she dances like that.
9) With a cold like this I can't taste what I'm eating.
10) Jane won't relish having to wash up all those dishes.

2   † *Write an alternative construction for each of the following clauses so that Experiencer is made to coincide with Subject, as in (b) below:*
(a) The news delighted us.
(b) We were delighted with the news.

1) Neither of the proposals pleased the members of the commission.
. . . .
2) His presence of mind amazed us.
. . . .
3) The dramatic increase of crime in the cities is alarming the government.
. . . .
4) The fact that she seems unable to lose weight worries her.
. . . .
5) Will the fact that you forgot to phone annoy your wife?
. . . .

3   *Write two paragraphs, one on the things you enjoy doing most, the other on the things you dislike doing most.*

Module 17

1   †*Each of the following clauses contains at least one relational process. Say whether they are attributive, circumstantial or possessive and write out the structure for each:*
    1) One of the fringe benefits of this job is a company car.
    2) I haven't any change, I'm afraid.
    3) At that time Laura must have been eleven or twelve.
    4) This job requires concentration.
    5) Our special offer deckchairs are of superb quality.
    6) They'll last for years.
    7) The concert will be in the sports stadium, at nine o'clock.
    8) It smells rather musty in here.
    9) Many middle-aged singers own palatial mansions in the south of England.
    10) The atmosphere suddenly became oppressive.

2   *Add a suitable Attribute or circumstance to each of the following clauses and say whether it is current or resulting:*
    1) After wandering around in circles for more than an hour, we ended up . . . .
    2) Keep your money . . . . in this special travelling wallet.
    3) Growing coffee proved to be more . . . . than they had expected.
    4) Stand . . . . while I bandage your hand.
    5) Feel . . . . . to do as you like.
    6) From June to December nights gradually grow . . . . . .
    7) The festival turned out . . . . after all.
    8) The water in the pool felt deliciously . . . . to the tired climbers.
    9) His explanation doesn't sound . . . .
    10) It looks rather . . . . not going to your best friend's wedding.

3   *Here are two opposite opinions on the effects of television on viewers: the first is of an art specialist, the second of a psychologist. Elaborate on one – or both – of these opinions, expressing the characteristics of television programmes by at least a proportion of relational clauses:*

    Watching television easily becomes a compulsive and addictive occupation unlike watching ballet or looking at pictures.

    Our children are neither bored nor stultified; all of us need to dream the same daydream until we have had our fill of it . . . and the more frustrating reality is for us, the greater is our need.

Module 18

1   †*Complete each of the following sentences containing verbal processes and say whether the result is a reported statement, a reported question or a reported directive:*

1) Mounted policemen urged the crowd. . . . .
2) This notice says. . . . .
3) The usher at the House of Commons explained. . . . .
4) Let's enquire at the information desk . . . .
5) I have asked the nightwatchman . . . .
6) You'd better not tell the children. . . . .
7) A voice over the loudspeaker announced . . . .
8) Recent reports from the north confirm . . . .
9) The prince's advisers persuaded him . . . .
10) My business connections suggest . . . .

2 *Add a suitable Existent to each of the following existential clauses and say whether your Existent represents a countable entity, a non-countable entity or an event:*
1) There appeared on the horizon. . . . .
2) There was . . . . and all the lights went out.
3) There's . . . . in the next village, where you can get quite a good meal.
4) On the floor there lay . . . .
5) Just opposite the cinema there's . . . .; you can send a telegram from there.
6) There's no . . . . to lose; the taxi will be here in five minutes.

3 †*In which of the clauses in Task 2 could* **there** *be omitted and why?*

4 *Add expansions of three types (locative, attributive, clausal) to each of the following existentials:*
1) There was a plane. . . . .
2) There were a few members. . . . .
3) There's nothing. . . . .

5 *Study the text in 18.2 and then write a paragraph describing one of the following:*
1) the house of a friend who collects objects from all over the world
2) a fortune-teller's parlour
3) a five-star hotel in the middle of the Amazonian rain-forest

Use existential clauses with different types of expansion and omit **there** *sometimes.*

Modules 19 and 20
1 †*Identify the italicised circumstantial element in each of the following:*
1) Trains to Lancing run *every twenty minutes in off-peak periods*.
2) It's supposed to be quicker *by first-class mail*.
3) *In spite of the forecast for storms*, they set off in a rowing-boat to cross the lake.
4) Someone must have done it *out of spite*.
5) He speaks German *as well as French*.

6) Payments must be made *by the end of the month*.
7) The horse show was cancelled *on account of the epidemic*.
8) *As a do-it-yourself decorator*, I'm not the most enterprising.
9) Say it *with flowers*.
10) *As for the dog*, he'll have to go to a kennels *for a month*.

2   †*Say which of the following italicised items is Instrument and which is Range:*
1) They blocked the road *with dustbins*. .
2) We crossed *the Channel* by hovercraft.
3) Rita won *the jackpot*.
4) She managed to open the suitcase *with a hairpin*.
5) They lead *a quiet life*.

3   *Make up sentences to illustrate the following processes which include Instrument in their meaning:*
1) to *tape* a conversation / some music
2) to *spoon* something into something
3) to *book* a room / seats
4) to *pencil* a note in the margin

Module 21

1   †*Give a possible 'congruent' (i.e. basic) form for each of the following sentences. Comment on the semantico-syntactic changes involved. Provide a translation into another language of the 'metaphorical' (i.e. more nominalised) form, if possible.*
1) We had a long chat.
   ....
2) Bombing continued throughout the night.
   ....
3) Canada saw the launch of a 50-day election campaign last weekend.
   ....
4) His obvious intelligence and exceptional oratory won him (Franz Josef Strauss) a place in Konrad Adenauer's 1951 cabinet as minister without portfolio.
   ....
   ....
   ....
5) The release came after rising expectations in Washington throughout the day that Professor Steen, aged 48, would be the hostage to be freed.
   ....
   ....

2   †*Try to construct a more nominalised version of the following. The key words to be changed are italicised to help you.*
1) Most of the companies in the motor industry *are interested in*

manufacturing other things as well as *producing* cars, commercial
vehicles and components.
2) During the inter-war years a number of companies *gradually*
manufactured fewer and fewer of these other things, or else *stopped*
manufacturing vehicles.
3) In this way, *companies became more and more specialised*.
4) Because *companies have continued to do this* since 1945, *there are*
now fewer companies engaged in *manufacturing vehicles*.
5) Also *because many companies have either merged or been taken over*,
different products are now more concentrated in certain areas.

3   †*Recognising unactualised participants: Identify the unactualised*
participant or Attribute, and the process in which it is involved, in each
clause (some have more than one unactualised):
1) Do they pay well?
2) Milk doesn't keep in hot weather.
3) Navratilova serves and her opponent fails to return.
4) Gerald teaches, while his wife paints for a living.
5) I'm sorry, I can't hear.

4   *Analysing a text: 'Bonfire Night': This spoken text, a dialogue between two*
speakers, has to do with the preparations for bonfire night, November 5th, in
England, and also, with bonfires in general. What kind of processes and
participants would you expect to find in a conversation on such a topic?
Now read the text and then do the tasks underneath:

A We're looking forward to bonfire night, at least the children are. Do
you indulge in this?
B Oh, in Sussex we did. I went to one last week, but it was . . .
A That was a bit early, wasn't it?
B All the joy was taken out of it for me because it was a huge bonfire in
a garden the size of this room, with big houses all around, and the
bonfire was right under a big tree with its leaves all dry.
A Mm
B And I was so worried, the flames were going right up to the lower
branches of the tree, and I was so worried about everything catching
fire that I didn't really enjoy the flames very much.
A No, I don't think we can manage a large bonfire, but the fireworks
themselves – er – we have a little store of.
B Oh yes, they're quite fun.
A Yes, the children like them very much; so I think as long as one is
careful, very careful, oh yes, it's all right.
B Mm
A But I ban all bangers; we don't have any bangers, I can't stand those.
Just the pretty ones.
B Sparklers are my favourites.
A Catherine wheels are my favourites, but you know, we have anything
that's pretty and sparkly; and we have a couple of rockets, you know,

to satisfy Jonathan, who's all rockets and spacecrafts and things like this . . .

B   Mm

A   So that's Friday night; they can't wait for that and keep saying 'Well, couldn't we just have one, just now?', you see, trying to use them up before the actual night.

B   Yes.

A   But I don't know where we can get any wood from, apart from chopping down a few trees, which I wouldn't like to do. We don't seem to have very much wood.

B   Yes, that's a point.

A   Well, I suppose if we went into the park we might collect a few sticks, but it's not quite like having logs, is it? But I don't know where one would get this from here. If we were at home back in the Midlands we would know where we could go and get all these things from.

B   Yes, yes, in Sussex, in my village, they spent the whole of October building up the bonfire. They probably did it in yours.

A   They had a village one, did they?

B   Yes. All the local people helped with it, put their old armchairs and things on it. Used to be about twenty feet high.

A   Mm

Adapted from D. Crystal and D. Davy, *Advanced English Conversation.*

1)   Make a separate column for each type of process. Make columns for subtypes, such as mental processes of perception, cognition and affectivity.

2)   Go through the text again, assigning each process with its participants to a column. Include ellipted participants when these are clearly understood. Make a column for problematic processes. List the circumstantial elements.

3)   Make a numerical or statistical count of the number of instances of each type of process. List them in order of frequency. Discuss the problematic processes from the point of view of compound participants (see Task 4 for Module 17) and discuss how far it is possible to assign them to some category.

4)   Which type of process is the most frequent? Do you find this surprising? Which aspects of the bonfire are the speakers most concerned with? What do you think this tells us about the speakers? Would a dialogue in which you took part, on the same subject, be similar? Try it!

5

Interaction between speaker and hearer:

Mood structures of the clause

MODULE 22
Syntactic moods and illocutionary acts

Summary

1   Interpersonal meaning between speaker and hearer is expressed by choices from several different areas of the language which include modality, intonation and attitudinal lexical items.

   Here we examine interpersonal meaning as it is realised by the choice between declarative, interrogative and imperative clause types or 'moods'. These are realised in English by the presence or absence of Subject together with the Finite element, and the order in which these occur. A further mood type, the exclamative, is described here as a variation of the declarative.

2   Each mood type is basically associated with an illocutionary act: the declarative can be used to express a statement; the interrogative a question; the imperative a directive such as a command or request; and the exclamative an exclamation.

3 However, for social reasons, particularly that of politeness, indirect correspondences are often preferred. These are examined and illustrated throughout this chapter. The relationship between mood and illocutionary act is, therefore, not one-to-one but many-to-many. Thus, as well as expressing statements, positive declaratives can be used to ask questions, utter exclamations and give directives, in addition to other functions such as predictions, invitations, offers and warnings. Certain illocutionary acts, such as promising, warning and thanking, can be carried out by using a specific verb in the declarative.

22.1   The basic correspondences

The clause is the major grammatical unit which a speaker or writer uses when communicating with a hearer or reader, to give information, to ask for information or to give a directive (try to get the hearer to carry out some action, by means of an order, request or invitation, for instance). These three main illocutionary acts are realised grammatically in the following way: the indicative is the grammatical category typically used for the exchange of information, in contrast to the imperative, which realises a directive. Within the indicative, it is the declarative clause which typically expresses a statement and the interrogative clause a question. These basic clause types can be diagrammed as follows:

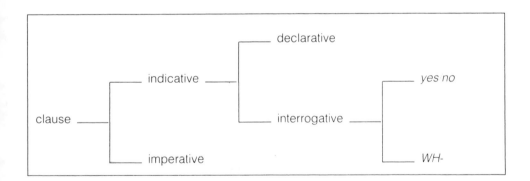

A further illocutionary act to which can be assigned a corresponding mood structure is that of expressing an exclamation. This is achieved structurally by modifying the declarative clause, which can therefore be either exclamative or non-exclamative. Interrogative clauses can be either polar (*yes/no* interrogatives) or non-polar (*WH*-interrogatives). The structures of these various clause types will be studied in later sections. For the moment, we can represent the basic correspondences between mood structures and illocutionary acts as follows:

Mood	Illocutionary act	Example
Declarative Interrogative Imperative Exclamative	making a statement asking a question giving a directive expressing an exclamation	We had a good time. Did you have a good time? Have a good time! What a good time we had!

It is important to separate the concepts of statement, question and directive, which are utterance categories, from the syntactic categories of declarative, interrogative and imperative which realise them. When a syntactic mood type is used to carry out the illocutionary act typically associated with it, it is considered to be a **direct illocution** or **direct speech act**. Thus, in a direct illocution the declarative has the **illocutionary force** of a statement, an interrogative has the illocutionary force of a question, an imperative has the illocutionary force of a directive, and an exclamation has the illocutionary force of an exclamation. The table above shows this basic or prototypical correspondence between the two sets of categories; and in the following invented dialogue based on an advertisement in *Time* magazine, each Mood structure in the independent clauses realises its prototypical illocutionary act:

> Is that you, Brad? [1] Simon here.
> Hi, Simon.
> Did the board reach a conclusion? [2]
> They've decided to launch the product, [3] if the terms are right.
> How do ours compare? [4]
> Very well. But are you sure you can put up the necessary capital? [5]
> We've got a massive loan from the Bank of England. [6]
> In that case, let's go. [7]
> Have we got the deal, then? [8]
> You've got it. [9]
> Fantastic. How soon do you expect to be able to sign? [10]

[1] question; [2] question; [3] statement; [4] question; [5] question; [6] statement; [7] directive; [8] question; [9] statement; [10] question.

In reality, however, the relationship is frequently more complex. In fact, almost any illocutionary act can be realised by almost any mood structure, and almost every mood structure can carry out different illocutionary acts. When a mood structure has any other but its typical illocutionary force, we consider it an **indirect illocutionary act**.

Some of the structures of the executives' simple dialogue may be rewritten so that the correspondences between syntactic form and utterance category illustrate indirect illocutionary acts:

> In that case, *shall we go ahead*? (interrogative) [7]
> So *we've got* the deal, then? (declarative) [8]

Fantastic. *Why don't we sign* in Paris? (interrogative) [10]

[7] directive; [8] question; [10] directive.

The motivation for using indirect illocutionary acts is that of tact, or politeness. By expressing the intended meaning in an indirect form, the speaker allows the hearer to make the necessary inferences in order to arrive at the correct interpretation. For instance, the interrogative in *Have you come by car today?* may lead the hearer to infer that the speaker is politely requesting to be given a lift.

In inferring the speaker's meaning the situational context and the linguistic co-text are all-important, as is the relationship between speaker and hearer. In different situations, or at different points in a conversation, any one utterance may take on a different illocutionary force. If an explosion has just been heard in the car-park, *Have you come by car today?* will suggest a very different intended meaning, perhaps that of a warning, or an injunction to look and see what has happened.

It is not always possible to make a clear-cut distinction between one type of indirect illocutionary act and another. *Sit over here by me* may be either a request or an invitation or a combination of the two. Similarly, Simon's response *We've got a massive loan from the Bank of England* is at once a statement and an assurance in answer to Brad's question. This indeterminacy of pragmatic meaning is not, in general, a disadvantage, since it allows the interlocutors in a situation to negotiate the outcome of any one utterance as they go along.

22.2   The Mood element

The three main illocutionary acts of stating, questioning and commanding are typically realised in English by variation in the order of one part of the clause, called the **Mood element**, while the rest of the clause, called the **Residue**, remains unchanged. The following dialogue, in which the Mood element is italicised, illustrates this:

A: *Tom is* training to become a tennis champion.
B: Who *is he* training with?
A: *I don't* know. *Does it* matter?
B: *It matters* more than anything else in that game. *Think* of all the
   trainers who were first-class players in their day!

The main elements of structure which together form the Mood element are Subject (S) and Finite (F). The structures of the declarative, interrogative and imperative moods are manifested by the presence or absence of Subject and the order in which the Subject and the Finite occur in relation to each other:

Mood	+/– Subject	Order	Example
Declarative	+ Subject	Subject + Finite	Jane sings.
Interrogative	+ Subject	Finite + Subject	Does Jane sing?
Imperative	– Subject	Predicator	Sing!

Certain modifications will have to be made later regarding the interrogative and imperative structures.

In most cases, it is not the whole Predicator which precedes the Subject to signal the interrogative mood, but only the finite part of it. Finiteness is expressed either by the verbal operator or by the simple Present and Past tense forms of the lexical verb, including *have*, *has*, *had*, *was*, *were* when these are used as main verbs.

The following examples show the different order of the elements in declarative and interrogative clauses:

Declarative mood: *Ben* writes letters.
                     Ben has written a letter.
Interrogative mood: *Does Ben* write letters?
                       Has Ben written a letter?

22.3   Minor clauses and abbreviated clauses

Only finite independent clauses have mood. Neither subordinate clauses nor minor clauses (see 2.4.1) present the alternative orderings of Subject and Finite which are essential to the Mood element as the expression of interpersonal interaction. We cannot say, in a subordinate *if*-clause for instance, **if are you sure* instead of *if you are sure*. Similarly, minor clauses such as *if possible* admit no variation. However, elliptical structures such as *It is*, *You can*, which consist of the Mood element, do have the alternative orderings of Subject and Finite (*Is it?*, *Can you?*) characteristic of this element. These we shall call *abbreviated* clauses.

Subordinate and minor clauses which function independently may have illocutionary force, however, as can be seen from the following two examples of minor clauses from the dialogue, to which we add an example of a moodless *-ing* clause:

Simon here. (minor clause) [11]
Fantastic! (minor clause) [12]
Looking forward to seeing you. (moodless clause) [13]

[11] self-identification; [12] exclamation; [13] anticipation.

In conversational exchanges in English, minor clauses and abbreviated clauses play an important part in their ability to realise initiations and responses to initiations.

Initiations can be expressed by moodless *WH*-questions with the illocutionary force of an invitation (*How about some lunch?*), an encouraging suggestion (*Why not give it another try?*), an inquiry (*Why this sudden urge to tidy up?*), etc. Initiations can also be expressed by subordinate clauses preceded by *well*, as in *Well, if it isn't the great man himself!*

Responses by means of subordinate clauses are frequently exclamations of regret (*If we had only thought of it earlier!*) and are exemplified further in the summary table of 27.4.

Responses realised by abbreviated clauses function within the framework of the basic correspondences which hold between the utterance categories and the mood structures outlined in 22.1.

In the interactive event between speaker and hearer that is realised by an independent clause, there are two basic kinds of speech role: that of giving and that of demanding. The thing that is given or demanded may be essentially verbal and linguistic (e.g. information, an opinion) or it may be essentially non-linguistic (e.g. passing the salt, asking for or giving a donation). In the latter case, what is given or demanded comes under the label of 'goods and services', and need not be verbalised at all, but may be carried out by non-verbal signals such as gestures. Typically, however, when goods or services are exchanged, verbal interaction takes place, with language reinforcing the act carried out by some non-verbal signal. When it is information which is required or given, the realisation of the exchange is necessarily linguistic. The interplay of these two dimensions gives the three basic categories described in 22.1, statement, question, directive, together with a fourth, offer:

```
goods and services  giving      = offer
                    demanding = command
information         giving      = statement
                    demanding = question
```

These illocutionary acts provide the speaker with options from which to choose when initiating a dialogue. Matched with each of these is a pair of possible types of response, one complying with the initiation, the other rejecting it:

Initiation	Complying response	Rejecting response
offer command statement question	acceptance undertaking acknowledgement answer	rejection refusal contradiction disclaimer
Examples: Would you like a beer? Bring me a beer! This is good beer. Whose is that beer?	Yes, I would. All right, I will. Is it? Yes, it is. Mine.	No, I wouldn't. No, I won't. No, it isn't. I don't know.

As has been seen in 22.1, three of these illocutionary acts have corresponding mood structures as direct in the sense of 'unmarked' realisations: the direct realisation of a command is the imperative clause, that of a statement is the declarative and that of a question is the interrogative. The illocutionary act of offering has, in English at least, no corresponding direct mood structure; instead of the interrogative *Will you have a beer?*, the imperative *Have a beer!* and the declarative *There's some beer for you* are equally unmarked; that is to say, offers have not become grammaticised to the extent that the other three speech act functions have.

Typical responses, of both the complying and rejecting types, are realised by abbreviated clauses which can consist of the Mood element without the Residue (*I would*, *Is it?*), or of ellipted clauses (*Mine*), together with a continuative element (*Yes*, *No*, etc.) as can be seen in the examples above.

Clause tags, which can also be considered abbreviated clauses consisting of the Mood element, are discussed in 27.3.

22.4   The Finite element

The Finite element serves to relate the proposition to a point of reference by specifying either the time reference by means of tense, or the speaker's judgement by means of modality. The proposition can in this way be affirmed, questioned, doubted, hypothesised or denied.

The positive/negative contrast, called polarity, is an essential semantic feature associated with finiteness. In order to be affirmed or denied, a proposition has to be either positive or negative. Polarity can be considered to belong to the interpersonal component of language, in so far as a negative clause often has the function of denying a prior assertion. In combining with the declarative, interrogative and imperative moods, polarity also represents a point of contact between the expression of our experience and the act of communicating it to other people.

In the following dialogue between two friends, finiteness is expressed by the words or morphs italicised:

> 'So what *did* you do at the weekend, Janet?'
> 'Well, Jeff and I *went* off to Whitby to visit our in-laws. We *took* the dog with us and we all *ended up* having a walk along the beach.'
> '*Can* you walk right along the cliffs to Robin Hood's Bay?'
> 'I *think* probably *could* do, but it'*s* quite dangerous. You *can* get through occasionally when the tide'*s* out, but it *doesn*'t stay out for very long and you *can* get caught.'

In English, Mood has to do with clause types rather than verb inflection. It leaves the subjunctive somewhat isolated, since the latter is not a clause type but a verb form which in present-day British English plays a very marginal role, although it is reputedly more common in American English.

In independent clauses the subjunctive can express a wish, but only in fossilised stereotyped expressions like *Long live the Queen!*, *So be it*, *Heaven be praised!*, *Far be it from me to doubt your word*. Even in subordinate clauses, a clearly identifiable present subjunctive is limited to the VG occurring with a third person singular subject in *that*-clauses after verbs of recommending and suggesting, as in: We recommend / urge / suggest *that he obtain permission first* (see 9.3.3). Even here, the indicative, in this case *obtains*, is now used by many speakers.

A past subjunctive can be identified only in the first and third persons singular of *be* (*If I were you* … *If he were alive today* …) in subordinate clauses of condition and concession. Most non-factual notions, such as the expression of doubt and hypothesis, are conveyed in English by other lexicogrammatical means, principally the modal auxiliaries.

22.5 Positive declarative clauses and illocutionary acts

The basic clause structures are all declarative, and so constitute the unmarked type. They can, however, be modified by thematisation (see 28.4) and by ellipsis (see 29.3).

Semantically, a declarative structure is used typically to express a statement and is accompanied by falling intonation (symbol \\):

It's r\aining.

The normal illocutionary force of a statement can, however, be overridden in various ways; for instance:

(a) If spoken with rising intonation, (symbol /), it will be interpreted as a question:

It's r/aining(?)

(b) If spoken with a high fall tone, it becomes exclamation:

It's r\aining!

Such, *so* and other intensifying items such as *terribly* also confer exclamative force on a declarative:

He's such a bore!   It's so tiring!
It's terribly hot!   It was extraordinarily beautiful!

(c) If the Finite element is a modal auxiliary (e.g. *can*, *shall*, *will*, *may*, *might*, *must*), the clause can be used with the illocutionary force of a directive:

You will report to Head Office tomorrow.
Dogs must be kept on a lead.
You might like to look at this new catalogue I've received.
Surely you can take your own decisions!

(d) A first person declarative with a modal can have the effect of committing the speaker to a course of action:

> I'll meet you at the entrance at about nine.
> I must rush off now to my aerobics class.

(e) With certain 'performative' verbs used in the first person singular or plural of the Present indicative tense, such as *I promise, I warn, I advise, I beg, I request, we thank, we order, we acknowledge, we apologise, we name*, etc., the declarative structure 'performs' the verbal action it denotes. It therefore has an illocutionary force different from that of statement:

> *I advise* you to see a doctor.
> *We warn* you that anything you say will be taken down and may be used as evidence against you.
> *Thank* you for taking such trouble.
> *We acknowledge* receipt of your letter of 20 May.

As long as the underlying Subject is the speaker or the writer, the passive forms, or an active one with an impersonal NG Subject, have the same effect:

> You *are warned* that anything you say . . .
> Passengers on flight 335 *are requested* to proceed to Gate 6.
> The Management *thanks* all members of the staff for their cooperation.

In addition, many other illocutionary acts can be expressed by the declarative, such as apology (*I'm sorry I'm late*), compliment (*you look beautiful*) and, by the addition of a modal, prediction (*her mother will know her age*).

Sometimes the performance of the verbal action is referred to indirectly by means of a modal auxiliary or other form preceding the performative verb:

> We *would like to* thank you for your kindness to our daughter.
> I *must* beg you not to tell anyone about this.
> I *am afraid I have to* request you to move to another seat.

The indirect reference, by means of *would like, must, am afraid I have to*, to the performative act of thanking, begging, requesting, is felt by the speaker to be the equivalent to producing the illocutionary act itself. Not only are indirect forms more polite than direct forms, but they may be felt to be more sincere, as seen in this reader's thank-you letter to a well-known dietician:

> *I must tell you* what really made me realise I was so overweight. All winter I went round the house in a bright green track suit (extra large). One day I opened the door to the milkman. 'You look smart in your green,' he said. 'Yes,' I said, 'kidding myself I'm the green goddess!' 'Well,' said he, 'I was thinking more of the Jolly Green Giant!' We both rolled up laughing but it made me think.
>
> *I would like to say a big thank you* for giving me the inspiration to do something about my shape.
>
> Rosemary Conley, *Complete Hip and Thigh Diet.*

(f) A clause which is, strictly speaking, declarative but which contains a displaced *WH*-element, will have the force of a question:

> So you took the documents to *which* Ministry office?
> And in the end you left them *where*?

MODULE 23
Assertion and non-assertion

Summary

1 In English, rather than distinguishing simply between **positive** and **negative** forms, we must establish a previous distinction between **positive** and **non-positive** (or, as they are commonly called, **assertive** and **non-assertive**) forms, although it is more correctly the context, rather than the form, which is assertive or non-assertive.

2 Assertive words such as *some* occur typically in assertive contexts. These are expressed by positive declarative clauses and are distinguished by having the feature of **factuality**.

3 Non-assertive words such as *any* occur in contexts which are non-positive or non-assertive. These contain the feature of **non-factuality**, which is a feature of interrogative, negative, conditional and comparative clauses, among others. It is, in fact, the general non-factual meaning, rather than any particular syntactic structure, which provides the context for non-assertive items to be used.

4 *Any* (and its compounds) have two meanings, which are usually differentiated by stress.

23.1   Factual and non-factual meaning

In addition to the types of mood structure which have been outlined, it is necessary to examine their meanings in the light of two concepts which are generally referred to as **assertion** and **non-assertion**. A clause will be uttered in a situational context which is presented by the speaker as **assertive** or **non-assertive**. Assertive forms such as *some, someone, somewhere* have **factual meanings** and typically occur in positive declarative clauses. Non-assertive words such as *any, anyone, anything, ever* are associated with **non-factual** meanings in the sense of **non-fulfilment** or **potentiality** and occur typically in many syntactic contexts, described in 23.5, of which interrogative clauses and negative clauses are perhaps the most common. It must be stressed, however, that non-assertion is a wider concept than either of these. Some common assertive and non-assertive items are summarised in the table below:

	Assertive	**Non-assertive**
determinative	some	any
pronoun	some	any
det. or pron.	one or the other	either
pronoun	someone	anyone
	somebody	anybody
	something	anything
adverb	somewhere	anywhere
adverb	somehow	anyhow/in any way
adverb	sometimes	ever
adverb	already	yet
adverb	still	any more/any longer
adverb	to some extent	at all
adverb	a lot/some (AmE)	much, any (AmE)

The assertive forms are used when a specific meaning is required, whereas non-assertive forms make for a non-specific interpretation. For example, the following positive declarative clauses have assertive meaning:

> We have *some* very good coffee.
> *Somebody* rang while you were out.
> I've left my car keys *somewhere*.
> We've heard the news *already*.
> She's *a lot* better today.
> I know London *to some extent*.
> Your call helped *a lot*.

These seven clauses refer to a factual specific object (*some coffee*) or person (*somebody*) or place (*somewhere*) or boundary of time (*already*) or degree (*to some extent*, *a lot*).

The negative declarative, interrogative and conditional clauses of the following examples express potential or unfulfilled situations which make for a non-specific interpretation, and so require non-assertive forms:

> Have you *any* good coffee?
> If *anyone* rings while I'm out ...
> Have you seen my glasses *anywhere*?
> No-one has heard the news *yet*.
> She is scarcely *any* better / not *much* better today.
> I hardly know London *at all*.
> His call didn't help *much* / *any*. (AmE)

23.2   Assertive *some* in a non-assertive context

A non-assertive, that is a non-factual, situation can, however, allow the use of a specific item, as in:

If *someone* rings while I'm out . . .
Will you have *some* coffee?

The difference between *someone ringing* and *anyone ringing* is, in the conditional clause, a matter of viewing the potential caller as specific (*someone*) or non-specific (*anyone*). This difference is brought out in the following text, slightly abbreviated, from a detective novel:

'Would it – Dad and I were wondering – do *any* [1] good, maybe, to offer a reward? To the public? *Any*[2] information leading to . . .'
   O'Connor stabbed out his cigarette. 'No, most of the citizenry, Mr. Mayse, are honest, well-intentioned people.' The kind cops didn't so often meet with on the job. 'If *anybody*[3] had *any*[4] information, they'd have come in with it by now. And if *somebody*[5] – say a garage owner *somewhere*[6] – was bribed to clean up the car, if it was *at all*[7] damaged, he isn't going to open his mouth now, to involve himself, for more money.
                         Lesley Egan, *Malicious Mischief*.

[1] non-specific; [2] non-specific; [3] non-specific; [4] non-specific; [5] specific; [6] specific; [7] non-specific.

An assertive item such as *some* in a hypothetical context reflects a positive attitude on the speaker's part towards the content of the clause, whereas a non-assertive item such as *any* reflects a neutral or negative attitude. Two clauses, identical except for the *some/any* alternative, may reflect the same state of affairs but have quite different illocutionary forces, as in (a) and (b) below:

(a) Bring some more old newspapers and I'll make a bonfire of them.
(b) Bring any more old newspapers and I'll make a bonfire of them.

In (a) the imperative clause *bring some more old newspapers* has the force of condition of promise, 'making a bonfire' being interpreted as something desirable. In (b) *bring any more . . .* will be interpreted as condition of threat, with 'making a bonfire' as something undesirable to the addressee.

23.3   The two meanings of *any*

The lexical item *any* has two different meanings in English, distinguished by stress and non-stress. In interrogative clauses like '*Have you any good coffee?*', *any* is inherently unstressed, whereas in positive declaratives, '*Any information would be useful*', *any* is inherently stressed (see also 47.3).
   The two different meanings of *any* are in some languages lexicalised by different word-forms. The meaning of stressed *any* is 'It doesn't matter which', as in:

Any child could tell you the answer to that question.

Choose *any* of the questions in section one.
Anybody with a bit of sense would have refused to go.
Anywhere south will be fine for a holiday.

Unstressed *any* refers to an indefinite thing or quantity, and means 'even the smallest number or amount', as in:

Can you give me *any* idea of the cost?
I'm afraid I haven't *any* idea.

It must be borne in mind that unstressed *any* can be intensified by being made to carry marked focus (see 29.7), but without meaning 'it doesn't matter which'. In such cases it is simply the notion of indefiniteness that is intensified:

Can't you give me *ANY* idea of the cost?
I'm sorry, I'm afraid I haven't *ANY* idea.
I can't find your car keys *ANYWHERE*.

Only stressed *any* meaning 'it doesn't matter which' can occur as determiner or pronoun in the NG at Subject:

Any car is better than no car.
Any of the dates you suggest will be acceptable.

Although such clauses as these may appear to be assertive, since they are neither negative, nor interrogative, nor conditional, they are in reality non-assertive in that they are non-factual, and refer to a potential or unfulfilled state of affairs.

The non-factual, non-specific nature of the context is frequently reinforced by the presence of a modal expression (*will*, *can*, *be sure to*, *be bound to*), or an imperative, which also refers to an as yet unrealised action.

You will have to wait until tomorrow to hear *anything* he *may* disclose. (potentiality reinforced by *may*)
Any concert by that group *is bound to* be good. (potentiality reinforced by *be bound to*)
Any friend of yours is a friend of mine. (no reinforcement)
I know I can rely on him at *any* time. (no reinforcement)

Ambiguity between the two meanings of *any* can occur in the written language as in: Can *anyone* go? The non-stressed form has the meaning 'one non-specific person among the total number of persons involved'; it could be replaced by *someone* with the illocutionary force of a request, as in 'Can someone go to the door, please'. A possible response might be 'Yes, I'll go'.

The stressed form in 'Can *anyone* go?' has the meaning 'no matter which non-specific person', its main feature being that of non-restrictedness. It can be intensified by *just*, as in 'Can *just anyone* go to that party?', but could not be replaced by *someone*. A possible answer to the stressed form would be 'Yes, *anyone* can go', whereas for the non-stressed form this is not possible.

23.4   *Any, every, either*

Stressed *any* differs from *every* in that *every* has a meaning of 'totality' or 'universality' and is specific, whereas *any* has a meaning of 'partiality' and is non-specific. *Every* can, in addition, be factual as in the example below. Compare:

> *Every* friend of his was a friend of mine. (factuality)
> *Any* friend of yours is a friend of mine. (potentiality)

Stressed *any* is also close to stressed *either*. The difference between them is that stressed *either* selects between two and has the 'restrictive' meaning of 'no matter which of the two', whereas stressed *any* selects from more than two and is 'unrestricted', meaning 'no matter which'. Compare:

> You can keep *any* (among any number) of the puppies.
> You can keep *either* (of the two) puppies.

Any can be intensified by *whatsoever*, whereas *either* and *every* cannot:

> *Any* day *whatsoever* will be suitable.
> **Either* day *whatsoever* will be suitable.
> **Every* friend of yours *whatsoever* is a friend of mine.

In comparison with stressed *any* and *either* in non-factual contexts, English has the corresponding stressed assertive forms *some* and *one*, which are used in factual contexts:

> *Some* papers were very good.
> *One* paper was very good.

23.5   Non-assertive contexts

Non-assertive contexts include the following:

1	Negative clauses:	He did*n't* say *anything*.
		No-one said *anything*.
2	Interrogative clauses:	*Did* you say *anything*?
3	Interrogative–negative	*Didn't* you say *anything*?
	clauses:	*Isn't* there *anyone* at home?
4	Negative imperative clauses:	Don't eat *any* more! (unstressed *any*)
5	Imperative with non-specific meaning:	Take *any* you like! (stressed *any*)
6	Comparative clauses:	She is singing *better than* she has *ever* done *yet*.
7	Conditional clauses:	If you *ever* need *any* advice about computers, consult Julian.
8	Clauses containing hypothetical *should*:	It's odd that you *should* find *any* evidence among the possessions of a total stranger.
		It's a pity he *should* feel so shy about asking *any* questions.

9	Universals:	*Every* student who has *ever* read *anything* about the subject knows ...

Many non-assertive contexts are introduced by a word which is negative, even if by implication:

10	Clauses after negative adjectives:	It is *untrue* / *unlikely* / *incredible* that Ed stole *anything* from the sports shop.
11	Infinitive constructions after *too*:	I am *too* tired to walk *any* further.
12	NGs introduced by *only*:	*Only* two people suffered *any* serious injury.
13	Completives in PrepGs introduced by *without*:	*Without any* doubt. *Without any* delay.

Non-finite constructions after verbs such as *fail to*, *prevent*, *stop*, *deny*, *dissuade*, *forget*, *refuse* and adjectives such as *hard*, *difficulty*, *reluctant*, *unwilling*, are all implicitly negative in meaning, as they are after *dare* and *need* as operators in negative and/or interrogative clauses:

I *fail to* see *any* need for a change of plan.
The watchman has orders to *stop anyone* from entering the building.
The lawyer *dissuaded* them from taking *any* further legal action.
John has either *forgotten* or *refused* to tell *anyone* his address.
It is *difficult* / *hard* to find *anything* helpful to say.
We are *reluctant* / *unwilling* to do *anything* about it.
Dare you go *any* further?
Need we spend *any* more time on this?

In addition, many clauses functioning at Subject or Direct Object provide non-assertive contexts if they contain an indirect question and/or a negative implication:

Whether he has *anything* important to contribute remains to be seen.
Ask if *anyone* wants *any* more icecream.
I doubt whether *anything* can be done.
I wonder why he *ever* accepted such a job.

Non-assertive forms can occur in minor clauses dependent on a main clause:

It is not known when, *if ever*, the cathedral will be completed.
It would be interesting to find out who, *if anyone*, would support the plan.

Summary of assertion and non-assertion combined with mood types

1	Declarative positive assertive:	I'll buy some cakes.
2	Declarative positive non-assertive:	I'll buy any cakes they've got.
3	Declarative negative assertive:	....

4	Declarative negative non-assertive:	I won't buy any cakes.
5	Interrogative positive assertive:	Will you buy some cakes?
6	Interrogative positive non-assertive:	Will you be buying any cakes?
7	Interrogative negative assertive:	Won't you buy some cakes?
8	Interrogative negative non-assertive:	Won't you be buying any cakes?
9	Imperative positive assertive:	Buy some cakes!
10	Imperative positive non-assertive:	Buy any cakes you like!
11	Imperative negative assertive:	....
12	Imperative negative non-assertive:	Don't buy any cakes!

Numbers (3) and (11) have no assertive forms, since these are logically incompatible with negation.

The compounds of *any*, just as *any* itself, have two meanings expressed by a stressed and an unstressed form respectively. They have not been treated here in detail for reasons of space.

MODULE 24
Negative declarative clauses and illocutionary acts

Summary

1   Negation of clauses can be carried out in English in two ways:
   (a) by negating the Finite element (*isn't* going; *doesn't* want) or the non-finite verb in a dependent clause (*not wishing* to disturb them); or
   (b) by using a non-verbal 'nuclear negative' item (e.g. *never, nobody, no, nothing*).

2   Since non-assertive forms such as *any* are not in themselves negative, they cannot be used as nuclear negatives.

3   The 'scope of negation' marks the limits to which the semantic notion of negation extends in the clause. Assertive items such as *some* can be used outside the scope of negation.

4   Negative declaratives typically express a negative statement; but they can also be used to ask tactful questions, utter exclamations, and give commands, among other illocutionary acts.

24.1   Nuclear negatives

Many negative declarative structures can be formed in two ways:

(a) by negating the Finite element (*aren't* waiting, *don't* care) or the non-finite verb in a dependent clause (*not expecting* a reply);

(b) by negating a non-verbal element, using words sometimes called 'nuclear negatives':

Negative pronoun at S:	*Nobody* came. *Nobody* knows.
	None of the passengers were hurt.
Negative pronoun at Od:	I saw *nothing*.
Negative modifier of adj.:	I felt *none* the worse for it.
Negative determiner:	She felt *no* pain.
	Expecting *no* reply.
	Neither parent was informed.
Negative coordinators:	*Neither* today *nor* tomorrow is suitable.
Negative modifier of determiner:	*Not* much whisky was left.
	Not many people turned up.
	Not enough time was allowed.
	Not one student failed.
Negative modifier of adverb:	*Not* even the President was told.
Negative Adjunct:	Elephants *never* forget.
	We found *nowhere* to stay.
	Under no circumstances must you touch a live wire.

24.2   Implied or semi-negative forms

These include the use of *scarcely*, *hardly*, *barely*, *rarely* as Adjunct, and *little* and *few* as quantifying determiners:

Adjuncts	Determiners
He *scarcely* opened his mouth.	There is *little* news to report.
You *hardly* feel the jab.	*Few* people survived. (negative)
The chairman *rarely* intervenes.	cf. A *few* people survived. (positive)
The students *seldom* complain.	

24.3   Non-assertive forms and negation

Unlike some languages, standard national forms of English (British, American, Canadian, Australian, etc.) do not favour multiple negation, that is, a succession of nuclear negative items in one clause (although this is a feature of some dialects of English). Instead, the first negative item is followed throughout the rest of the clause by one or more non-assertive forms, such as *any*, *either*, *ever* as in:

We're *not* going *anywhere* with *either* of our parents.
I have*n't* said *anything* to *anybody yet*.
He *hardly ever* writes Christmas cards to *anyone any* more.

Two alternative negative structures, corresponding to one positive declarative, are therefore often available, one containing a negated operator, the other some other negated element:

Positive structures	Negative structure 1	Negative structure 2
There's *some* bread left.	There is*n't any* bread left	There's *no* bread left.
There's *some* left.	There is*n't any* left.	There's *none* left.
He met *someone* at the pub.	He did*n't* meet *anyone* at the pub.	He met *no-one* at the pub.
I know *something* about it.	I do*n't* know *anything* about it.	I know *nothing* about it.
They go *somewhere* at the weekends.	They do*n't* go *anywhere* at the weekends.	The go *nowhere* at the weekends.
They *sometimes* open on Sundays.	They do*n't ever* open on Sundays.	They *never* open on Sundays.
He *always* wins.	He *doesn't ever* win.	He *never* wins.
It's six o'clock *already*.	It is*n't* six o'clock *yet*.	–
He *still* plays golf.	He does*n't* play golf *any more* / *any longer*.	He *no longer* plays golf.
My son will go *too* / *as well*.	My son wo*n't* go *either*.	*Neither* will my son go.

Although they are semantically equivalent, the two negative structures are rarely appropriate in the same stylistic register. The nuclear forms occur more in formal and written language, while the non-assertive forms are more informal. The nuclear negative *no* with determiner function is, however, frequently used in the spoken language to give prominence to the negation:

There's *no* time to be lost.   He's *no* friend of mine.

When the negative item stands in initial position only the nuclear form is possible. The reason for this lies mainly in what is called the scope of negation (see 24.4).

Occasionally, sentences with double negation occur in English, such as the following:

Not many Spaniards have *no* knowledge of bull-fighting.
Nobody here has *never at any time* told a lie.
Neighbours should *not* be *un*cooperative.

Such double negatives are possible because each negative element negates its own part of the sentence. A paraphrase of the whole sentence will give the same meaning with a positive value:

Most Spaniards have *some* knowledge of bull-fighting.
Everybody here *has* at some time *told a lie*.
Neighbours *should* be *cooperative*.

24.4   The scope of negation

By the scope of negation we mean the semantic influence that a negative word has on the rest of the clause that follows it. Typically, all that follows the negative form to the end of the clause will be non-assertive and within the scope of negation. Thus, in *Some people don't have any sense of humour*, *some* is outside the scope of negation whereas *any* is inside it.

As the non-assertive forms are not in themselves negative, they cannot initiate the scope of negation by standing in initial position in the place of a nuclear negative form. Compare the following examples of acceptable and non-acceptable forms:

Acceptable	Not acceptable
Nobody turned up. No invitations were sent. None of them arrived. Never say die! Nothing simpler can you find.	*Anybody didn't turn up. *Any invitations weren't sent. *Any of them arrived/didn't arrive. *Ever say die! *Anything simpler can you find.

Assertive forms such as *some* and its compounds can occur after a negative word, but they must necessarily stand outside the scope of negation. Compare the difference in meaning between the two following clauses:

(a) He didn't reply to any of my letters.
(b) He didn't reply to some of my letters.

The non-assertive form *any* in the (a) clause expresses the scope of negation as extending to the end of the clause. *None of the letters received a reply*. The (b) example, on the other hand, implies that some letters received a reply, while others didn't. *Some* must be interpreted as outside the scope of negation.

The scope of negation is closely related to the function of Adjuncts in the clause. Compare the difference in meaning between the (a) and (b) examples below, in which the manner Adjunct *clearly* is within the scope of negation in (a), whereas the attitudinal sentence Adjunct *clearly* in (b) is outside it:

(a) She didn't explain the problem *clearly*.
(b) She *clearly* didn't explain the problem.

24.5   Illocutionary acts performed by negative declarative clauses

The typical speech act function of a negative declarative clause is to make a negative statement:

Dogs don't eat grass.
Not everyone enjoys skin-diving.

Just as with positive declarative utterances, other types of illocutionary force are possible in appropriate contexts:

(a) With a rising tone, the utterance will be interpreted as a question. Such questions may carry negative expectations; however, the indirectness is frequently motivated by tact, since a request or invitation may be inferred, and the hearer is given an opportunity to decline gracefully:

> Bill hasn't said anything about the weekend?
> You don't know anyone in the Defence Ministry, by chance?
> You won't sit down for a moment?

You don't suppose followed by a *that*-clause can express a request, either for a service to be done or for information or reassurance on the part of the hearer:

> *You don't suppose* I could borrow your lawn-mower?
> *You don't suppose* anything has happened to him?

(b) With a high fall tone, the utterance will be interpreted as exclamation, but the force of a directive may also be present:

> You're not going out in this weather!
> I never heard such nonsense!

(c) With *must, shall, should, ought, can* and *may*, the utterance can have the force of a directive, expressing strong or attenuated obligation not to do something, or lack of permission:

> You must never cross without looking both ways. (strong obligation)
> Children should not be left unattended. (attenuated obligation)
> Your car ought not to be parked outside the hospital gates.
> (attenuated obligation)
> We can't take more than one free bottle each. (lack of permission)
> Card-holders may not transfer their membership cards. (lack of
> permission)
> I wouldn't ring the bell, if I were you. (advice)

(d) With the performative verb *promise*, negation attenuates the illocutionary act of promising, or the reported act:

> I don't promise you that I'll convince him.
> He didn't promise to come.

The negation of *advise*, and other similar verbs such as *recommend*, present instances of **transferred negation**. The negative particle is transferred from the subordinate clause where it belongs semantically, to the main clause:

> I don't advise you to buy those shares. (= I advise you not to buy
> those shares)

Certain verbs expressing mental processes, such as *think, believe, expect* (but not *hope*), *want* and *like* also show transferred negation:

> I don't think we'll get there in time. (= I think we won't . . .)
> The P.M. doesn't believe that inflation will increase. (= The P.M. believes that inflation won't increase.)
> I don't want you to think that I'm indifferent. (= I want you not to think that I'm indifferent.)

(e) Some negated modal verbs are used by speakers to avoid committing themselves to an opinion. The responses *I wouldn't know, I wouldn't like to say, I can't think* and *I can't say* have this pragmatic function, which is called a **hedge**.

In the following text from a detective story, negative declarative clauses are used with different illocutionary forces by the two speakers. Those spoken by the police inspector have the force of a question and are part of the indirect probing technique characteristic of the police – in detective novels at least. The person questioned replies mostly with straight negative statements, adding in [2] the expression of polite regret *I'm afraid*, but in [8] she avoids total commitment:

> *'You don't know the actual name of the firm or association that employed her?'*[1]
> 'No, *I don't,*[2] I'm afraid.'
> 'Did she ever mention relatives?'
> 'No. I gather she was a widow and had lost her husband many years ago. A bit of an invalid he'd been, but *she never talked much about him.'*[3]
> *'She didn't mention where she came from*[4] – what part of the country?'
> *'I don't think she was a Londoner.*[5] Came from somewhere up north, I should say.'
> *'You didn't feel there was anything – well, mysterious about her?'*[6]
> Lejeune felt a doubt as he spoke. If she was a suggestible woman – but *Mrs. Coppins did not take advantage of the opportunity offered to her.*[7]
> 'Well, *I can't really say*[8] that I did. *Certainly not from anything she ever said.*[9] The only thing that perhaps might have made me wonder was her suitcase. Good quality it was, but not new.'

> Agatha Christie, *The Pale Horse.*

[1] question; [2] negative statement; [3] negative statement; [4] question;
[5] transferred negation; [6] question; [7] negative statement; [8] hedge;
[9] negative statement.

MODULE 25
Interrogative clauses and illocutionary acts

Summary

1   Interrogative structures in English are of two main types: polar, asking for an answer which is either 'Yes' or 'No' (*Can you swim?*), and non-polar, asking for information referred to by the *WH*-word (*Where are you from?*). A further type, the alternative interrogative, consists of two polar interrogatives joined by *or* (*Do you want it or don't you?*).

2   *WH*-units can function as elements of a clause which is embedded in a main clause (*How far* did he say (that) he walked?).

3   Interrogatives can reflect the positive, neutral or negative expectation of the speaker by including assertive, non-assertive or negative items respectively.

4   The typical illocutionary act associated with the interrogative is that of seeking information from the hearer. Many other social meanings are possible, however. Appropriate intonation will produce an exclamation, while modalised interrogatives express a great variety of directives.

25.1   Types of Interrogation

Interrogative structures are either **polar**, **alternative** or **non-polar**:

> Did you remember to buy the paper? (polar)
> Shall I buy a paper or would you prefer a magazine? (alternative)
> Which one do you like best? (non-polar)

In polar interrogatives, also called **yes/no questions**, it is simply the polarity that is in question; what the speaker wants to know is: 'Is the answer 'yes' or 'no'?' In non-polar interrogatives, also called **WH-questions** or **information questions**, it is some other element embodied in the *WH*-word that is in question and that the speaker wants to know.

A *WH*-interrogative can be embedded as a constituent of a polar interrogative, in which case the *WH*-interrogative has the order of a declarative clause, as in *Do you know what time it is?* rather than **Do you know what time is it?* (see also 9.5). There are two questions involved in such cases: (a) the polarity of the main clause, in this example whether the addressee knows the answer to the *WH*-question; and (b) the content embodied in the *WH*-element. The intention of the speaker, together with the context, will 'weight' one or other in importance. For example, if the addressee is slowly packing a suitcase to catch a train shortly, (a) is likely to be more important; on the other hand, if the speaker's watch has stopped, (b) is likely to be of greater interest to the speaker.

25.2 Polar interrogatives

Polar interrogatives, when they ask questions, are generally accompanied by rising intonation and have the structure Finite + Subject + Residue:

Finite	Subject	Residue
Did	you	remember to buy the paper?
Has	everybody	left?
Is	that man over there	a doctor?
Do	many people	come here on Sunday?

The Finite element is always realised by an operator, or by *have* or *be* fused with the main verb (*has*, *had*, *is*, *are*, *was*, *were*). In the following text an eager applicant for a job is asked a great many unexpected questions by the interviewer Miss Piffs. All Miss Piffs' questions are of the polar type; those beginning *would you say* are not *WH*-questions, but polite *yes/no* questions. The applicant Lamb shows his perplexity and surprise by uttering echo questions (see 27.2), and finally an alternative interrogative:

Piffs: *Would you say* you were an excitable person?
Lamb: Not – unduly, no. Of course, I –
Piffs: *Would you say* you were a moody person?
Lamb: *Moody?* No, I wouldn't say I was moody – well, sometimes
        occasionally I –
Piffs: *Do you* ever *get* fits of depression?
Lamb: Well, I wouldn't call them depression exactly.
Piffs: *Do you* often *do* things you regret in the morning?
Lamb: *Regret? Things I regret?* Well, it depends what you mean
        by often, really – I mean when you say often –
Piffs: *Are you* often puzzled by women?
Lamb: *Women?*
Piffs: Men.
Lamb: Men? Well, I was just going to answer the question about
        women –
Piffs: *Do you* often *feel* puzzled?
Lamb: *Puzzled?*
Piffs: By women.
Lamb: *Women?*
Piffs: Men.

Lamb: Oh now, just a minute I.... *Do you want separate*
        answers or a joint answer?

> Harold Pinter, *Applicant*, in Mark Shackleton (ed.), *Double Act*.

25.3   Alternative interrogatives

These consist of two polar interrogatives joined by *or*:

Do you want to stay a bit longer *or* would you prefer to go home?

The expected answer to such a question is obviously no longer simply *Yes* or *No*; the answer is to be found in the question itself, no other information is sought outside that contained in the question. The expected answer will be similar to one of the interrogative structures, or part of it:

I'll stay a bit longer.   I'll stay.
Stay a bit longer.   Stay.

Such disjunctive interrogatives sometimes have the Mood element of the second clause ellipted as in *Is it a boy or a girl?* (= Is it a boy or is it a girl?)
    A further variant of the alternative interrogative presents an open list, each item accompanied by rising intonation:

Would you like gin, or vodka, or whisky, or ...?

Sometimes, the two can have different polarity, as in *Are you staying or aren't you?* (= Are you staying or aren't you staying?)

25.4   Non-polar interrogatives

Non-polar, or *WH*-interrogatives, are generally accompanied by falling intonation. The structural order differs according to whether the Subject or some other element is being questioned. If it is the identity of the subject that is questioned, the *WH*-unit conflates with the Subject and the Subject + Finite order prevails:

Subject	Finite	Residue
Who	wants	a chocolate?
What	happened?	
Which horse	came	first?
Whose car	was	stolen?

This order of elements, which is typical of declarative structures, is therefore an exception to the normal order prevailing for interrogative structures in English, as it is likewise in many other languages. If any other clause element is questioned (Object, Complement or Adjunct) this is placed in initial position and the normal interrogative order prevails:

Element questioned	*WH*-word	Finite	Subject	Residue
Od	What	did	you	buy?
Od	Who(m)	have	your friends	invited?
Oprep	Who(m)	did	he	send it to?
Cs	What	is	he	in the Council?
Co	What	have	they	appointed him?
A	How	is	it	pronounced?
A	How often	do	the children	watch TV?

In *WH*-questions the recipient can only be expressed by a Prepositional Object with *to*, and not by an Indirect Object. The objective form *whom* is used only in formal style nowadays. *Who* is used for both Subject and Object functions in neutral style. However, *whom* is obligatory as a completive placed immediately after a preposition, as in (a) below. But this, too, is formal. Ordinary everyday usage favours a discontinuous structure with the preposition postposed as in (b):

(a) (formal) *From whom* did you obtain this report?
(b) (neutral) *Who* did you get this report *from*?

In the following dialogue from a radio play, one woman questions the other about the pianist; she uses two *WH*-forms and one polar form with *won't*:

He is going to play all week –
How do you mean play all week –
All week, he's going to play all week –
What's he doing it for, *what's it for?* –
It's a record if he plays all week, he's trying to beat the record –
And he's going to play all week, in there –
They have to feed him everything, his meals and all that –
Won't he stop for anything then? –
There wouldn't be much point if he could stop, that's the whole point not to stop –
I suppose so –

Alan Sharp, *The Long-distance Piano-player.*

The *WH*-interrogative words sometimes combine with the word *-ever*, which acts as an intensifier expressing the surprise, perplexity or disbelief of the speaker:

Whoever would believe such a story?
Wherever did you hear that?
Why ever didn't he let us know he was coming?
How ever could you say a thing like that?

Why ever is always spelt as two words, the other items as either one or two.

Besides the *-ever* combinations, *WH*-interrogative words can be intensified informally by certain lexical items which include *on earth*, *in heaven's name*, *in the world*, and other colloquialisms such as *the devil*, *the hell*, *in God's name*:

> What on earth has the dog found?
> Who the hell said that?
> Why in heaven's name didn't you get in touch?

When the interrogative clause contains a PrepG, the *WH*-word may function, either as the completive itself as in:

> *Which* did you vote for?

or as part of the completive as in:

> *Which party* did you vote for?

In both cases the *WH*-word is then functioning at a lower level of structure. It has been 'pushed down' the rank scale of structure, as follows:

> 1 element of a clause: *Which* do you want?
> 2 element of a PrepG in a clause: *Which* do you vote for?
> 3 element of a NG embedded in a   *Which* party did you vote for?
>   PrepG in a clause:

In examples (2) and (3), the *WH*-units *which* and *which party* are completive elements of PrepGs functioning as Adjuncts in a clause. Such a PrepG may itself be 'pushed down' to a lower rank of structure, by being embedded in a NG as a qualifier:

> *Which country* is this the flag of? (qualifier of *flag*)
> *What author* do you want a novel by? (qualifier of *novel*)

WH-units sometimes function as elements of a clause which is embedded in a main clause:

> 1 at A in *that*-clauses: *How far* did he say (that) he walked?
> 2 at Oprep in V-inf clause: *Who* would you like me to introduce you *to*?
> 3 at Od in V-*ing* clause: *What kind of questions* do you avoid answering?

In informal speech the *WH*-element can be 'pushed down' even further, by operating within a unit which functions in another unit which expounds some element of structure in the main clause:

> 4 at Od in a clause which is at *q* in an AdjG which is at Cs in a main clause:
>
>   *How much* are you willing to lend us?
>
> 5 at *c* in a PrepG operating at *q* in a NG which functions at Cs in a clause embedded in the main clause:
>
>   *Which company* does the paper say he is the director *of*?

25.5   Orientation in interrogative structures

Interrogative structures, like declarative structures, are either positive or negative:

> Have you accepted the job? Haven't you accepted the job?
> Why did you accept the job? Why didn't you accept the job?

The questions expressed by interrogative structures can be oriented according to the kind of answer the speaker expects, and are said to have **neutral**, **positive** or **negative** orientation. This is achieved by the addition of **non-assertive** forms (*any*, *anybody*, *ever*, *yet*, etc.), **assertive** forms (*some*, *somebody*, *always*, *already*, etc.) and **negative** forms (*no*, *nobody*, *never*, etc.) respectively.

A neutral attitude or expectation is expressed by a positive interrogative together with non-assertive forms:

> Have you *ever* been to India?
> Do you know *anyone* in Brighton?
> Is the bank open *yet*?

A positive orientation is given by adding assertive forms to the positive interrogative:

> Do you know *someone* in Brighton?
> Is the bank open *already*?
> Is John coming *too*?

Even in a negative interrogative, assertive forms can be added to reflect a positive orientation:

> Isn't there *some* butter *somewhere*?
> Don't you know *someone* in Brighton?
> Isn't John coming *too*?

The positive orientation of *Isn't John coming too?* can be compared with the negative orientation of *Isn't John coming either?*

Negative interrogative clauses, like negative declaratives, can generally be structured in two ways: either with the negative particle *not* and non-assertive forms, or with the nuclear negative word. Compare:

> Have*n't* you *ever* been to India?   Have you *never* been to India?
> Did*n't* she speak to *anyone*?   Did she speak to *no-one*?

The nuclear negative item always carries tonic stress, with the result that the negation in such interrogatives appears stronger. In non-emphatic speech, the *not any* form is the more frequent one.

The two alternative structures are possible even when the negative item is Subject, as opposed to the single possible structure in negative declarative clauses. Compare:

Declarative negative: *Nobody* has given back their books.

Interrogative negative: *Has nobody* given back their books?
Hasn't anybody given back their books?

25.6   Illocutionary acts performed by interrogative clauses

Interrogative structures display a variety of speech act functions:

(a) Information-seeking

The intention of the speaker in asking a question is, typically, to obtain information which he or she believes the hearer knows. The vast majority of interrogatives in daily use fulfil this function; however, it is not the only one. The following other types of illocutionary force are also possible.

(b) Exclamation

> Isn't it a lovely day!
> Was that some party!
> Was my face red!
> Aren't they slow! – Aren't they though!
> Was that ever a good meal! (AmE)

When polar interrogatives such as these take on exclamatory force they typically combine with falling intonation.

(c) Equivalence to a negative statement

> Do you expect me to wait here all day?
> What wouldn't I do for an opportunity like that?

Questions of this type are to be interpreted as meaning 'You can't expect me to wait here all day' and 'There is nothing I wouldn't do for an opportunity like that', respectively. They are often described as 'rhetorical questions', since the answer is so obvious as to be unnecessary. In their emotive content they are similar to exclamatives and, like exclamatives, they depend on the context of situation or on the preceding discourse for their interpretation, signalled here anaphorically by *here* and *like that*.

(d) Directive

> Must you make so much noise? (command/request)
> Can you pass me that hammer? (request)
> Would you mind signing here? (request)
> Will you have some more icecream? (offer)
> Why don't you help yourself? (invitation)
> Why don't you apply for that job? (suggestion)

In none of these questions is the speaker seeking information or expecting any in reply. Some kind of response is expected, however, in all cases. Interrogative exclamations, unlike basic exclamatives, call for agreement or disagreement from the hearer: A. *Isn't it a lovely day*! B. *Yes, it is*. Commands call for acquiescence, or for the non-verbal response of carrying out the order. Requests are sometimes responded to by a standard phrase: A. *Would you mind signing here?* B. *Not at all / Certainly / Sure.* Of these, *certainly* and *sure* clearly respond to the pragmatic meaning of 'request' rather than to the sentence meaning, since they are not to be taken as *certainly / sure I mind signing.* Offers can be accepted by *Yes, please*, or *Oh, thanks* or refused by *No, thanks.* Suggestions are responded to in many different ways. Again, as was mentioned in 22.1, many utterances combine more than one illocutionary act; *Why don't you help yourself*, for instance, in the right context, could be at once an invitation and a suggestion, while *Why don't you apply for the job?* combines suggestion with advice.

(e) In yet another illocutionary act performed by the interrogative, the speaker asks *himself* or *herself* the question, and then proceeds to answer it. This type occurs frequently in public speaking and in academic writing:

> And what have we achieved in the last 18 months? I think we can
> truly say we have achieved a great deal.

(f) A 'push-down' element used with the verb *suppose* can be used as a topic introducer which creates suspense in the hearer:

> *Who* do you *suppose* I saw last week at the races?

MODULE 26
Imperative clauses and illocutionary acts

Summary

1   The basic structure of the imperative consists of the Predicator alone (*Sit down!*). This can be preceded by the Finite *do*, and the negative form *don't*.

2   A second person Subject (stressed *you*) can be added, usually for purposes of contrast with another person (*You sit down and I'll stand*). A third person Subject (*somebody, everybody, nobody*) can also be used.

3   Directives to be carried out by the speaker are preceded by *Let me* or *Let's*, the negative of which is now usually *Don't*, as for all imperatives.

> 4   Since the imperative can express a strong command, this is not always socially
> acceptable in English, even when accompanied by *please*. In many social
> contexts strong directives are preferably made indirectly, by means of other mood
> structures. In contexts of urgency (*Help!*, *Stop!*) the imperative can be used, as in
> others in which the hearer's welfare is referred to (*Sleep well! Have fun!*).

26.1   The basic imperative structure

Imperative mood structures differ from declarative and interrogatives in three ways:

(a)   There may be no Mood element at all (*Stop! Wait a moment!*), the imperative structure consisting of the Residue only; or there may be an imperative marker + Subject (*let's go*), a Finite (*Do stay!*) or a Finite + Subject (*Don't you say a word!*). A Finite element can always occur in a clause tag (see 27.3), as in the examples below:

Wait	a moment	will	you
Predicator	Adjunct	Finite	Subject
Residue		Mood tag	

Do	come	in	won't	you
Finite	Predicator	Adjunct	Finite	Subject
Mood	Residue		Mood tag	

Let's	have	a swim	shall	we
Subject	Predicator	Complement	Finite	Subject
Mood	Residue		Mood tag	

Don't	you	say	a word
Finite	Subject	Predicator	Complement
Mood		Residue	

(b) Typically, imperatives have no Subject; when a Subject is added, the result is a marked form of this mood structure.

(c) As a base form, the imperative Predicator does not indicate tense, number or modality, although a Perfect form occasionally occurs (*Have finished that essay by next week*!). It does, however, relate speaker and addressee in the here and now, signalling a mood that is different from the declarative and interrogative.

The rest of the imperative clause is structurally the same as that of any basic declarative:

Clause structure	Predicator	Residue
PA	Stop	at the traffic lights!
PCs	Be	careful!
POiOd	Pass	me the scissors!
POdCO	Make	yourself comfortable!

This structure occurs consistently in many kinds of instructional texts, such as driving regulations, machine assembly and servicing, repair manuals and books of recipes:

> Shark's Fin Soup
> *Wash* the shark's fin and *soak* it for 6–8 hours. *Place* the shark's fin in a large saucepan and *cover* with fresh water. *Bring* to the boil, *cover* and *simmer* for 2–3 hours. *Drain*. *Chop* very finely 1 piece of fresh ginger, 1 cup crab meat and 2 spring onions. *Slice* 6 bamboo shoots. *Heat* oil in a saucepan, *add* the vegetables, chicken stock and shark's fin. *Simmer* for 20 minutes. *Add* 1 tablespoon cornflour mixed with soy sauce, monosodium glutamate and seasoning. *Simmer* for 3 minutes. *Add* the crab meat and bamboo shoot. *Serve* very hot.

The Finite is rarely realised by other auxiliaries but *do*, since the stative, aspectual and attitudinal meanings expressed by auxiliaries are incompatible with directives to perform an action. However, *be* and *get* are occasionally used in the imperative followed by a present or past participle with dynamic meaning:

> *Be waiting* outside when I leave the office!
> *Don't be watching* television when your parents get back!
> *Don't be taken in* by his pleasant manner!
> *Get started*! *Let's get going*!
> *Get dressed*! *Don't get lost*!

26.2   Imperative clauses with and without a Subject

In its unmarked or more typical form, the Imperative has no Subject. The reason for this is that the most obvious recipient of a directive to carry out an action is the addressee, syntactically filled by the second person singular or plural *you*. The fact that *you* is the implicit Subject of an imperative clause can be demonstrated by the addition of (i) a tag question, (ii) the pronoun *yourself / yourselves*, (iii) the intensifying phrase *of your own*. In all these cases, no other pronominal form can occur:

> Sit down, will *you*?   Be a bit more careful, can't *you*?
> Help *yourself*!   Enjoy *yourselves*!
> Buy a house of *your* own!   Use *your* own toothbrush!

In the marked imperative structure, a grammatical Subject appears as the potential performer of the action. It can be second person *you*, or third person, like *somebody*; in both cases, the Subject is the addressee, whether listener or reader. A second person Subject is either contrastive or emphatic:

> contrastive: *You* stay here until I come back.
> emphatic: *You* go on ahead and get the tickets!
>   *You* keep quiet!
>   *You* tell me the solution if you can!

An imperative structure with *you* is syntactically identical to a declarative one, and can only be distinguished from the latter in the spoken language by the stress on *you*. In a declarative clause, the *you* is not stressed. Compare:

> A. How do we get tickets for this show?
> B. You go and stand in the queue. (unstressed, declarative)
> A. What shall we do then?
> B. *You* go and stand in the queue while I park the car. (stressed, imperative)

There is, however, a distinction between declarative and imperative when the verb is *be*. Compare:

> You be the doctor and I be the nurse. (imperative)
> You're the doctor and I'm the nurse. (declarative)

A third person Subject (*everybody, somebody, nobody*) is used when the speaker wishes the action to be carried out by a group of persons (*everybody*) or by a single unspecified member of the group (*somebody*). The lack of a third person concord with the verb (*somebody call a doctor*! and not *somebody calls ...*) indicates that these Subjects are addressees and not Subjects of declarative clauses. Compare:

Imperative	Indicative
Somebody call a doctor!	Somebody calls a doctor.
Everybody sit down, please!	Everybody sits down.
Nobody say a word!	Nobody says a word.
Jane stay here and Bill come with me!	Jane stays here and Bill comes with me.

If the Subject is plural, the verb form is the same in both moods, and only the situation can disambiguate the meaning, for example, by intonation, pause, gesture or common sense:

Ticket-holders come this way!   Ticket-holders come this way.
Those in agreement raise their   Those in agreement raise their
hands!   hands.

Explicit imperative Subjects are not **vocatives**. Vocatives are identified by their ability to stand not only in initial position but also in the middle and at the end of the clause:

Bill, stand by with the camera! *You over there*, shut up!
Stand by, *Bill*, with the camera! Shut up, *you over there*!
Stand by with the camera, *Bill*!

The use of vocative *you* is less polite than a vocative noun such as *Bill*, *Professor Jones*, *doctor*, *operator*, *waiter* or an honorific such as *Your Highness*.

Vocatives in initial position have a separate tone unit (see 29.1), which is typically fall–rise, whereas imperative Subjects fall within the same tone unit as the rest of the clause.

Finally, both vocative and imperative Subjects can occur together:

|*BILL* | *you* stand by with the camera! |
|*You* stand by with the Camera, *Bill*! |

26.3   Imperative structures with *let*

If the action is to be carried out by the speaker, or by the speaker and some other participant, usually the addressee, the structures *let me*, *let's* (= *let us*) or *let + name* are used:

Let me see, how many shall we need? ('I must consider this')
Let me think a moment. ('I must reflect for a moment')
Let's try to finish before 6. ('We must try to finish . . .')
Let Bill and me get the tickets. ('I suggest that Bill and I get the tickets')

This use of *let's* must be kept separate from the imperative use of the lexical verb *let* meaning *permit, allow* as in *Please let me go! Please let us go!* In a first person imperative structure *let* is simply an imperative marker, with *let us* being reduced to *let's* as in *let's wait*. The non-reduced form *let us* is used only in very formal registers as in *Let us pray*. By contrast, lexical *let* cannot fuse with *'s*, but requires a full Direct Object pronoun *us*: *Let us wait* = *Permit us to wait*. Obviously, both the imperative marker *let* and the lexical verb *let* can occur in the same clause, as in *Let's let them in now*.

The potential performer may be a third person who is not even present. If a personal pronoun is used, it will be in the objective case:

Let *Arnold* get the tickets.
Let *someone else* do it.
If he thinks he can turn us out of the house, *let him* just try!

However, in isolated examples and even sometimes when contextualised, this use is potentially ambiguous, since the interpretation of *let* as 'permit' is sometimes possible.

Imperatives with impersonal reference are relatively rare in present-day English:

> We mean to stay here and let *no-one* imagine otherwise.
> Let *it* not be said that we didn't try to solve the problem.

The forms of the Subject element of imperative clauses can be summarised as follows:

Potential performer of action	Introducer	Subject
Addressee only:	–	–/ you
Speaker only:	Let	me
Speaker + addressee:	Let	's
Neither speaker nor addressee	Let	him, etc.

Advertising nowadays uses many linguistic resources, but large colour advertisements with a minimum of text still sometimes put part of the verbal message across by means of imperative clauses. Here are some typical examples:

> Discover gold. (Benson & Hedges in *Oxford Today*)
> Steer your vacation course towards Austria. (Austrian Tourist Office)
> Strike it rich and become a millionaire overnight. (German State Lottery)
> Get 'em before they're hot. (summer book offer in *Premiere*)
> Take an early summer break, but without breaking the bank.
> (Mark Warner in *The Sunday Times Magazine*)

26.4   Negative imperative structures

Imperatives without *let*, with or without a Subject, are negated by adding *Don't* (*Do not* in formal English registers) in initial position. This applies even if the verb is *be*:

> *Don't* say a word.   *Don't* you say a word.
> *Don't* be too long.   *Don't* you be too long.

Someone / somebody is replaced by the non-assertive form *anyone / anybody* or the nuclear negative form *no-one / nobody*:

> *Someone* say *something*.   Don't *anyone* say *anything*.
>   *Nobody* say *anything*.

Let imperatives are negated by adding the particle *not* or another negative word after the Subject:

Let me not get caught in a traffic jam!
Let's not stay until the end of the show!
Let no-one say I didn't warn you.
Let nothing more be said about the matter.

However, the negation of *let* by *don't* is gradually becoming very common in informal spoken English, despite the possible ambiguity it produces with lexical *let*:

Don't let me get caught in a traffic jam.
Don't let's stay till the end of the show.
Don't let anyone say I didn't warn you.

26.5   Illocutionary acts performed by the imperative

Although the basic illocutionary act associated with imperative clauses is commonly held to be that of expressing a command, the imperative is used more frequently in English for less mandatory purposes. It can imply attitudes and intentions which are not actually formulated in the clause, and which can only be interpreted through a knowledge of the background context and of the relationships that exist between the persons involved. In fact, the difference between commands and other directives such as requests, invitations and advice is, as we have already seen, not clear cut; it depends on such factors as the relative authority of the speaker towards the addressee and whether the addressee is given the option of complying or not with the directive: in the case of a command there is no option, whereas with a request there is. Other factors include which of the two interlocutors is judged to benefit from the fulfilment of the action: a piece of advice benefits the addressee, whereas a request benefits the speaker. Politeness is also a major factor. The more the action is likely to benefit the addressee, the more socially acceptable an imperative will be. Otherwise, an imperative is likely to sound curt or demanding in English.

Other factors override politeness, however, such as emergency (*Help!*), or attention-seeking in conversation (*Look, what I meant was ...*); the imperative can also be used when the speaker and hearer are carrying out a task together (*Pass me the spanner*), when the hearer's interests are put first (*Don't worry! Cheer up! Take care!*), and even as a discourse initiator or topic introducer (*Guess who I saw this morning at the bank*). The social meaning of imperatives has, therefore, to be worked out by the addressee from the logical meaning of the sentence combined with the inferences made on the basis of context and the speaker–hearer relationship. Isolated examples can simply illustrate some typical interpretations:

Quick march!	command
Keep off the grass	injunction
Do not pick the flowers.	injunction
Please close the window!	request

Don't tell me you've passed your driving test!	disbelief
Do that again and I'll smack you!	condition of threat
Pass your exams and we'll buy you a motor-bike.	condition of promise
See a doctor then!/Don't forget your umbrella!	advice
Mind the step!/Be careful with that hot plate!	warning
Feel free to take as many leaflets as you like.	permission
Just listen to this!	urgency
Try one of these!	offer
Let's go jogging!	suggestion
Come on now, don't cry!/Go on, have a go!	encouragement
Sleep well. Have a good time.	good wishes
Have a safe journey	
Suppose he doesn't answer.	considering a possible happening
More people read magazines than, *let's say*, historical treatises.	giving a possible example
Think nothing of it.	rejecting thanks

Some of the non-mandatory functions of the imperative are illustrated in the following dialogue between two men who find themselves in a dark room in a hotel. In addition, a minor and therefore moodless clause (*Light!*) is used with the illocutionary force of a command or urgent request:

Fat man: There must be a window in here.
Quiet man: Doesn't seem to be.
Fat man: There must be.
Quiet man: Ouch!
Fat man: *Light!* (Another match is struck. Pause.)
                (Woebegone) There isn't.
Quiet man: *Don't worry*. It will be all right.
Fat man: It's the thought of being trapped in a windowless
                room . . .
Quiet man: *Try* not to think about it.
Fat man: I can't help myself.
Quiet man: *Try*.
Fat man: It's no use. I can't help myself.

         Barry Bermange, *No Quarter*, in *New English Dramatists*, 12.

MODULE 27
Exclamations, echoes and tags

Summary

1   True exclamative structures are formed by fronting an Object, Complement or Adjunct of a declarative and preceding this element by *What* (+NG) (*What a fine dancer she is!*) or by *How* (+ AdjG or AdvG) (*How cold it is!*, *How fast you walk!*). The exclamative clause can be abbreviated, leaving only the *WH*-element + a NG (*What a mess! What nonsense!*) or an AdjG (*How dreary!*).

Appropriate intonation can be imposed on any type of unit, including a single word, to express an exclamation (*Splendid!*).

2   Echoes repeat all or part of what a previous speaker has said. The motivation may be that of surprise, disbelief or agreement.

3   Tag questions are interrogative signals added after declaratives or imperatives. There are two main types, distinguished by features of intonation and polarity. An important function of tags is to elicit a response from the hearer; for this purpose, other one-word tags are also used.

27.1   Exclamative structures

Exclamative structures are not so much a distinct mood option as an emotive element superimposed onto the declarative. The **Subject + Finite** order of elements is the same as for the declarative structure: however, in true exclamative mood structures the S+F sequence is preceded by *What* or *How*, which gives prominence to some element of the message. If the highlighted element is a Complement, an Object or an Adjunct, it is brought forward to initial position:

Declarative mood structure	Highlighted element	Exclamative structure
A lot of people live here.	Subject	*What a lot of people* live here!
Few understood the problem.	Subject	*How few* understood the problem!
She is a fine singer.	Complement of the Subject	*What a fine singer* she is!
She has a lovely voice.	Predicator Complement	*What a lovely voice* she has!

Sometimes the *WH*-item does not merely highlight exclamatively one of the clause constituents, but is itself a clause constituent:

He talks *a lot.* These children of mine can eat a lot.	Adjunct Direct Object	*How* he talks! *What* these children of mine can eat!

The emotive effect of an exclamation can be achieved non-grammatically by imposing an appropriately emphatic intonation contour (high fall–rise or high rise–fall) on any type of clause, whether major or minor, or even on group structures and words:

Isn't it a beautiful day!
How dare you! How could you!
Swim at this time of year!
Quick! the fire extinguisher!
All hands on deck!
Disgusting!
Rubbish!

27.2   Echo structures

This type of structure refers back to all or part of a previous utterance (made by someone else), which the hearer either does not understand or finds difficult to believe; or on the other hand wishes to agree or disagree with:

Previous utterance	Echo
1 I've bought an electric tooth-brush. 2 We'd better leave at half-past six. 3 I'm going to give my golf clubs away. 4 Would you mind putting the cat out? 5 Did the Vice-Dean leave a message? 6 Isn't it hot! 7 Throw some salt over your left shoulder. 8 What a glorious day!	You've bought a what? Half-past six! Give them away! Putting the cat out? Did who leave a message? Isn't it! Throw it where? A *glorious* day?

The first utterance of each pair can have any type of mood structure: declarative (1, 2, 3), interrogative (4, 5, 6), imperative (7) or exclamative (8), in this case a minor clause. Note that the interrogative structure of (6) has an exclamative function. The echo itself is likewise of any type of clause, but its illocutionary force is that of a question or of an exclamation. An echo with an interrogative structure can be a question about a question (sometimes called a second order question) as (5) and:

What did you say to him?   What did I say to him?
Have you finished with the hair-dryer?   Have I finished with it?

27.3   Clause tags

Tag questions are structurally polar interrogatives; however, they are not interrogative clauses, but only an interrogative signal appended to one of the other types of clause:

a declarative clause tag: It was quiet in there, *wasn't it?*
an exclamative clause tag: How quiet it was in there, *wasn't it?*
an imperative clause tag: Be quiet for a moment, *will you?*

Of these three types, the declarative clause tag is by far the most common. Tags in English are characterised by the three features of 'structure', 'polarity' and 'intonation', and are exemplified in declarative clauses as follows.

27.3.1   Structural features of clause tags

As interrogatives, tags have the mood structure **Finite + Subject** in which Finite is always realised by an operator, and Subject by a pronoun (*will you? can he? don't they?*). The Subject in a tag question is either the same as or is co-referential with the Subject of the preceding main clause, maintaining concord with it in number, person and gender:

1   *You* thought we were trying to get away, didn't *you?*
2   *It's* not the first time he has failed to turn up, is *it?*
3   *Most people* enjoy a beach holiday, don't *they?*
4   *An air stewardess* must know several languages, mustn't *she?*
5   *There* won't be room for everyone, will *there?*

With a main clause verb such as *think*, *suppose* or *expect*, which can be expressed parenthetically, followed by an embedded *that*-clause, the tag refers to the embedded clause, not to the main one:

I think he left before lunch, *didn't he?* (not **don't I?*)
(He left, I think, before lunch, didn't he?)
I suppose you'd prefer a coke *wouldn't you?* (not ˙*don't I?*)
(You'd prefer a coke, I suppose, wouldn't you?)
I expect she'll be all right, *won't she?* (not **don't I?*)
(She'll be all right, I expect, won't she?)

Indefinite human singular pronouns take *they* in the tag:

Everybody seemed to enjoy themselves, didn't *they?*
Nobody will agree to that, will *they?*
Somebody should be told, shouldn't *they?*

If the VG in the main clause contains an operator, this is reflected in the tag, as in examples (2), (4) and (5) above. If no operator is present, *do*-support is required, as in examples (1) and (3).

Used to + V-inf. takes *do*-support in the tag:

She *used to* go out with Paul, *didn't* she?

Ought can be followed by either *ought* or *should* in the tag:

It *ought to* be dry now, *oughtn't* it / *shouldn't* it?

Mayn't is rarely used and is sometimes replaced by *might* in the tag:

He *may* be right after all, *mightn't* he?

27.3.2   Polarity features of clause tags

There are two types of declarative mood tag, distinguished by polarity sequence. In **Type 1** (the more common) the polarity of the main clause and the polarity of the tag are reversed, that is to say, a negative tag follows a positive main clause and vice versa:

You *won't* say a word, *will* you?
You'll tell the truth, *won't* you?

In **Type 2** the tag has the same polarity as the main clause; this appears to be always positive in Standard BrE; negative forms are not found. However, in some dialects such as South Wales English, negative tags are found on negative clauses, as in *So you haven't done it, haven't you?* Type 2 tags express a conclusion drawn by the speaker, and occasionally an attitude of irony, or sincere interest, or thoughtful consideration:

So you *believe* in democracy, *do you*?
Oh, that's what you believe, *is it*?
And you*'ve* lived in this village all your life, *have you*?

The following extract from a play parodies a doctor's questioning of a patient, who is not allowed time to reply:

Falling hair, loss of weight, gain of weight, tenseness, got a drink problem *have you*, smoking too much, hallucinations, palpitations, eructations, on drugs *are you*, can you read the top line, overdoing it at work perhaps, worrying about the work, about the spouse, about where to go for your holiday, about the mortgage, about the value of the pound, about the political situation, about your old mother, about the kids, kids playing up *are they*, not doing well at school, got a drink problem *have they*, smoking, on drugs *are they*, suffering from loss of weight, falling hair, got any worries *have you*?

Yes!

James Saunders, *Over the Wall*.

27.3.3   Intonation features of clause tags

Type 1 tags can have either rising or falling intonation. There are thus four possibilities:

Negative rising tag: You've got a car, *haven't you*?

Negative falling tag: You've got a car, *hàven't you?*
Positive rising tag: You háven't got a car, *háve you?*
Positive falling tag: You hàven't got a car, *háve you?*

A rising tone indicates doubt, and expects the hearer to clarify whether the statement is true or not. It combines with either a positive or a negative assumption, expressed in the statement, to give the following meanings:

Positive assumption (in the statement) + **doubt** (in the tag)

You've got a car,   háven't you?

meaning: I think you have a car. Am I right?

Negative assumption (in the statement) + **doubt** (in the tag)

You haven't got a car,   háve you?

meaning: I don't think you have a car. Am I right?

A falling tone in the tag indicates a greater degree of certainty regarding the truth of the statement, and simply expects the hearer to agree with the statement.

Positive assumption (in the statement) + **certainty** (in the tag)

You've got a car,   hàven't you?

meaning: I think you have a car; please confirm that.

Negative assumption (in the statement) + **certainty** (in the tag)

You haven't got a car,   hàve you?

meaning: I believe that you haven't a car; please confirm that.

Type 2 tags typically have a rising tone on the tag, and the statement is often preceded by a discourse marker such as *Oh*, *So* or *Well now* which indicate that the speaker is expressing a conclusion or inference drawn from the situation or from what has been said before.

Oh, so you're the new assistant, *áre you?*
So your father is a doctor, *ís he?*
Well now, this is the Norman chapel, *ís it?*

27.3.4   Tags with imperative clauses

Second person positive imperatives (*Read it! Sit down! Turn the light off!*) can be followed by positive or negative tags containing one of the modal auxiliaries *will/won't/would/can/can't/could* accompanied, according to the meaning to be conveyed and the modal chosen, by either rising or falling intonation. Rising intonation is typically polite and persuasive, falling intonation more insistent. The following examples illustrate some of the meanings conveyed by imperative tags. The first four could have rising intonation, the last two falling intonation.

Check this for me, will you?   *polite, anticipates willingness*
Sign this for me, would you?   *polite, anticipates willingness*
Keep this for me, can you?   *familiar, anticipates willingness*
Hold this for me, could you?   *less familiar, anticipates willingness*
Keep quiet, can't you?   *insistent, anticipates unwillingness*
Do make yourself at home,   *polite, insistent*
won't you?

Second person imperatives with an explicit Subject *you* can be followed by tags spoken with a rising tone:

You take the umbrella, will   *contrastive, polite*
you, and I'll carry the cases.

Negative imperatives are followed only by the positive tag *will you*, which is a persuasive softener spoken with a falling tone:

Don't be late, will you? Don't say a word, will you?

More insistent is the intensifier *mind*, spoken as a tail to the falling intonation on *late* and *word* in the following examples:

Don't be late, mind.   Don't say a word, mind.

First person plural imperatives take the positive tag *shall we* spoken with a rising tone:

Let's take a taxi, shall we?   Let's not walk any further, shall we?

27.3.5 Tags with exclamative clauses

Exclamative clauses can be followed by tags, which are always negative and with falling intonation:

What a good time we had, didn't we?
How cold it is in here, isn't it?

27.3.6 Tags with minor clauses

Independent minor clauses which are either abbreviated declaratives or abbreviated exclamatives can likewise take tag questions with the tag tone rising or falling for question or exclamation respectively:

Question: In New York, isn't he? (= X is in New York)
Question: Five dollars, didn't it? (= X cost five dollars)
Exclamation: What lovely roses, aren't they!
Exclamation: What a waste of time, wasn't it!

Subordinate minor clauses, such as *if possible, while on holiday*, do not take tag questions.

27.3.7 The discourse functions of clause tags

Tags are characteristic of the spoken language and appear to fulfil the following important interpersonal functions:

(a) As they are different in mood type from the clause which precedes them, they allow a speaker to alter the initial mood choice (from declarative or imperative to interrogative), and consequently to modify the illocutionary force of the utterance. A motivation for doing this may be that of forestalling possible silence or non-compliance on the part of the hearer.

(b) Tag questions are questions and so require an answer. They are an important means of carrying the conversation forward, and enable a speaker to elicit a response from the hearer, where a tagless declarative or exclamative would not necessarily achieve this end.

(c) After an imperative, a tag acts as an intensifier, either softening or heightening the insistence of the directive.

(d) With certain speech act functions of the declarative and the imperative, such as good wishes and warnings, a tag question is not used. Instead, these meanings are reinforced by other tag forms such as the following:

> Take care, *then*! Have a good journey, *then*!
> That plate is hot, *mind*!
> Look out, *there*! Come on, *now*!

(e) A form which has become popular in recent years is *Right?*, now often used instead of a polarity tag as in:

> The train doesn't leave until ten o'clock, right?
> So Tom's your younger brother, right?

27.4 Mood structures and illocutionary force: summary table

Mood structure	Illocutionary force	Example
DECLARATIVE	Statement	The sky is cloudy.
	Explicit performative	I beg you to reconsider your decision.
	Hedged performative	We would like to thank you for all your help.
	Question (*yes/no*)	You're ready?
	Question (*WH-*)	You took the documents to which ministry?
	Exclamation	It was so hot!
	Directives:	
	command	Papers are to be in by April 15. Off you go! In you get!

Mood structure	Illocutionary force	Example
	request	I wonder if you would . . . I'm terribly sorry but, could you . . . ? I suppose you haven't got any change on you.
	advice warning offer	I'd sell if I were you. That plate's hot! You must try one of these.
EXCLAMATIVE	Exclamation	What an angel you've been!
INTERROGATIVE	Question Demanding an explanation Exclamation	Who is that man over there? How come there's no lunch? Isn't it wonderful! How dare you speak to her like that!
	Statement Directives: command request suggestion/advice offer/invitation	Who will believe that story. Will you please be quiet! Would you mind signing here? Would it be inconvenient if . . .? Why don't you see a doctor? Won't you sit down?
IMPERATIVE	Directives: command request offer warning instructions Statement	Shut up! Save some for me! Have a drink! Mind your head! Twist off Don't tell me you've passed!

This table illustrates some of the more conventional correspondences between mood types and their illocutionary force. Many illocutionary acts can also be expressed by units both larger and smaller than the clauses, as well as by non-linguistic means such as gestures.

Clause combinations

Combinations of clauses can be used in English to express a polite request. The greater the imposition on the hearer, the longer the combination is likely to be, and may be preceded by an apology:

> I'm terribly sorry to bother you. I wonder if you could possibly write me a testimonial.
> If it's not too inconvenient, perhaps you could let me have it back by tomorrow.

Moodless clauses

Moodless clauses, when they stand independently, carry illocutionary force (see 22.3). They include the following:

Moodless *WH*-clauses	
moodless *WH*-questions as invitation/suggestion	How about a swim? How about going for a ride? Why not start again?
verbless *Why*-questions as inquiry	Why so downcast? Why all the jubilation?
WH-to-inf. clauses as directive headings	What to do in case of fire Who to contact on arrival How to boost your self-esteem
WH-if-clauses as suggestions or invitations	What if we all go for a swim? What if you stay a bit longer

Subordinate clauses	
to-infinitive clauses as exclamations or as friendly advice	To think that it should come to this! To think what we might have missed! Not to worry!
negative *if*-clauses, preceded by *Well,* indicating teasing surprise	Well, if it isn't the great man himself!
if only clauses, indicating regret	If only I had taken his advice! If only we had thought of booking a week ago!

Groups and words with illocutionary force	
Adverbial/Prepositional Groups or heads as directives	On your way! Out of my way! Straight ahead! Home, James! On with the show! Down with war!
Adjectival/Nominal Groups or heads as directives	Quiet! Careful! Silence! Scissors!

The following text illustrates the many-to-many relationship between mood types and illocutionary force:

The Patient: Mother, *take* this hateful woman away[1]. *She wants* to kill me[2].

The Elderly Lady: Oh no, dear: *she has been* so highly recommended[3]. *I can't* get a new nurse at this hour[4]. *Won't you try*, for my sake, to put up with her until the day nurse comes in the morning?[5]

The Nurse: *Come!*[6] *Let me arrange* your pillows and *make* you comfortable[7]. *You are* smothered with all this bedding.[8] Four thick blankets and an eiderdown![9] No wonder you feel irritable[10].

The Patient: (screaming) *Don't touch* me[11]. *Go* away[12]. *You want* to murder me[13]. *Nobody cares* whether I am alive or dead[14].

The Elderly Lady: Oh, darling, *don't keep on saying* that[15]. *You know* it's not true[16] and *it does* hurt me so[17].

The Nurse: *You must* not mind what a sick person says, madam[18]. *You had better* go to bed and leave the patient to me[19]. *You are* quite worn out[20].

G. B. Shaw, *Too True To Be Good* in *Plays Extravagant*.

[1] imperative = command/request; [2] declarative = statement/accusation; [3] declarative = exclamation; [4] declarative = statement; [5] interrogative = plea; [6] imperative = encouragement; [7] imperative = offer; [8] declarative = statement; [9] minor clause = exclamation; [10] minor clause = exclamation; [11] and [12] imperative = command; [13] and [14] declarative = statement/accusation; [15] imperative = plea; [16] declarative = statement; [17] declarative = exclamation; [18] declarative = injunction; [19] declarative = suggestion; [20] declarative = statement.

TASKS ON CHAPTER 5
Interaction between speaker and hearer:
Mood structures of the clause

Module 22

1   *Discussion: Answer the following questions, giving examples where you can*:
   1)   What are the main Mood types and the illocutionary act which corresponds basically to each?
   2)   What is a 'direct illocution'?
   3)   What is an 'indirect illocution'?
   4)   What is the motivation for indirect illocutions?
   5)   Why is it not always possible to make a sharp distinction between one type of indirect illocution and another?
   6)   Which part of the clause undergoes variation according to the mood structure chosen, and which part remains the same?
   7)   Explain the importance of the Finite element.
   8)   Explain the function of ellipted clauses as responses to initiations in conversational exchanges.
   9)   What kinds of intonation contour can modify the typical illocutionary force of a positive declarative clause?
   10) In what other ways can this typical illocutionary force be overridden?

2   †*Identify the mood type of each of the following clauses and suggest what illocutionary force would conventionally be assigned to each of these utterances. Is there indeterminacy in any of them? (Final punctuation is omitted.)*
   1)   Isn't that amazing
   2)   The Vice-President is not likely to resign
   3)   What an extraordinary dancer she is
   4)   Do you feel harassed by the congestion of city life
   5)   The Sultan's biographer presents him as what kind of figure
   6)   You're sure you won't have any more
   7)   Drop that gun
   8)   Members will refrain from smoking in the dining-room
   9)   You're leaving already
   10) I warn you that a villa in that area is not cheap

3   †*According to your analysis of Task 2, which are direct illocutions and which are indirect?*

4   †*The background of the following dialogue is a psychiatric hospital, where Jean and Edward have brought their daughter. For each numbered stretch of the text, say whether it has a Mood element or not and, if so, the Mood type. Discuss possible illocutionary acts carried out by each:*

Mood	**Type**	**Illoc. act**	
1)	____	_____	_____ Nurse: Who sent you in here?[1]
2)	____	_____	_____ Edward: The porter at reception.[2]
3)	____	_____	_____ Jean: We've been waiting nearly half an hour.[3]
4)	____	_____	_____ Nurse: I'm sorry.[4] We're very
5)	____	_____	_____ understaffed today.[5] It's
6)	____	_____	_____ the bank holiday.[6]
7)	____	_____	_____ Edward. Yes.[7]
8)	____	_____	_____ Nurse: He should have sent you straight to Admissions.[8]
9)	____	_____	_____ If you'll just come this way. [9]

Olwen Wymark, *Find Me*, in *Plays by Women*, vol. 2.

5   †*Discuss whether the exchange of 'goods or services' or of 'information' is involved in each of the utterances below. Make a suitable response, (a) complying, and (b) rejecting:*
   1)   Here's a cage for your birds.
   2)   You don't mean it, do you?
   3)   Come on, Bridget, give me a kiss!
   4)   Bus fares have gone up again.
   5)   I wonder what she is doing now.

6   †*Positive declarative clauses can carry out a wide variety of illocutionary acts. Suggest one or more for the utterances below, specifying who the speakers might be and a possible social context in which these utterances might take place:*
   1)   That's awfully sweet of you.
   2)   We're supposed to be on holiday! We're supposed to be getting some rest and relaxation!
   3)   I'll call you back.
   4)   We'd better be careful.
   5)   You did check that the gas is turned off?

6) There's a football international on television, you know.
7) I'm not going to have you buying such trash.
8) You won't let them put me in a home, will you?
9) Surely it's on the wrong way round.
10) That's very clever of you, Laura, I would never have thought of that myself.

Module 23

1 *Discussion:*
1) What semantic feature is associated with non-assertive contexts?
2) What semantic feature distinguishes an assertive item such as *some* from a non-assertive item such as *any*?
3) What is the meaning of stressed *any*?
4) In which semantic features does stressed *any* differ from *every* and *either*?
5) Besides negative and interrogative clauses, there are many other 'non-assertive' contexts. Name as many as you can.

2 †*Fill in the blanks with the appropriate non-assertive item. Decide whether it would be possible to have a 'specific' interpretation by inserting an assertive item.*
1) She hardly . . . . . complains about . . . . . . he does.
2) 'How's your house plant?' 'Still alive, I think. I gave it a little of your rose food. Can't do . . . . . harm.'
3) It's useless to search . . . . further, I feel.
4) I'm sorry I took the bag. It was just an ordinary bag, the same as . . . . you get at the supermarket, and I mistook it for mine.
5) He denied having . . . . . to do with the smear campaign.
6) I fail to find . . . . justification for these expenses.
7) That's a pretty kitten you have there. Got . . . . . more like it?
8) It's wonderful to live out here, far away from . . . . connected with the party, you know.
9) I don't remember seeing . . . . talking to Milly.
10) I don't think I could honestly recommend . . . . within ten miles of the coast.

3 †*Underline the non-assertive items used in the following text. Then, identify the type of syntactic contexts in which they are used and comment on their possible equivalents in your own or another language.*

Should NATO ever approve the development and production by the United States of the new tactical nuclear weapons and fail to offer any concrete proposals for talks with the Warsaw pact countries, the latter will have every right to question the general possibility of taking any concerted measures for disarmament in conjunction with NATO.

Module 24

1   *Discussion*:
   1)   Give some examples of 'nuclear negatives'.
   2)   What do you understand by 'the scope of negation'?
   3)   What is the typical illocutionary force of a negative declarative clause?
         What type of intonation accompanies this function?
   4)   In what ways can this typical illocutionary force be modified?
   5)   What do you understand by 'transferred negation'? Give an example.

2   †*Account for acceptability of the non-starred forms and the unacceptability
   of the starred forms *in each of the following sets*:
   1)   (a)   He has never lied to anyone.
         (b)   He hasn't ever lied to anyone.
         (c)   *He has never lied to anyone.

   2)   (a)   Nobody was able to work out the puzzle.
         (b)   There wasn't anybody able to work out the puzzle.
         (c)   *Anybody was able to work out the puzzle.

   3)   (a)   Nothing was left standing after the tornado.
         (b)   *Anything was left standing after the tornado.
         (c)   *Anything wasn't left standing after the tornado.

3   †*Discuss the possible illocutionary force(s) of each of the utterances below,
   suggesting a possible social context*:
   1)   She didn't leave a message with anyone?
   2)   You don't know anyone who has a spare video tape, I suppose?
   3)   You can't mean that you're throwing me out.
   4)   You don't know what you're talking about.
   5)   There'll be no trouble, at least as far as I'm concerned.
   6)   It never cools off enough to sleep properly at night.
   7)   I wouldn't worry, if I were you.
   8)   I don't think it's likely to be a success.
   9)   You won't get another, if you break this one.
   10)   I couldn't help it. It wasn't my fault.

Module 25

1   *Discussion*:
   1)   Outline the mood structure of the polar interrogative.
   2)   Outline the mood structure of the *WH*-interrogative.
   3)   What is in question in each of these interrogative types?
   4)   Explain what you understand by 'alternative interrogatives' and give
         some examples.
   5)   What do you understand by a 'push-down element' in an interrogative
         clause? Give an example.
   6)   What is meant by 'neutral orientation' of the interrogative?

7) What does the inclusion of an assertive item such as *some* indicate about the speaker's orientation of the interrogative?
8) Account for the fact that it is possible to have an assertive item such as *some* in a negative interrogative, as in *Isn't there someone outside*?
9) What is the unmarked illocutionary force of the interrogative mood?
10) What intonation patterns accompany the interrogative structures in their unmarked meanings?

2　†*Suggest possible illocutionary acts carried out by each of the utterances below*:
1) Is the coffee made?
2) Could you tell me the way to the nearest Tube station, please?
3) Must you leave your bike out in the rain?
4) Won't you have some more Passion-fruit Cake?
5) Isn't this exciting!
6) Would you mind moving your car so that I can get mine out?
7) Is that your umbrella dripping on to the sofa?
8) Do you know where I can find an English newspaper?
9) Would you be interested in doing something for our radio show?
10) What could I say?
11) Where would we be without tin openers?
12) How should I know?
13) Would it be very inconvenient if I popped round to borrow Jill's Chinese cookery book this evening?
14) Why don't you try a short hair-cut, for a change?
15) Would you believe it!

3　*If a person comes up to you and says 'Have you change of a pound?' and you say 'Yes' without bringing out the change, you are reacting to the conceptual meaning of the interrogative, but not to the pragmatic meaning, the illocutionary force of 'request'. Such a response is uncooperative or impolite. Suggest (a) an uncooperative and (b) a cooperative response for the utterances (2), (3), (6), (7) and (8) above.*

4　*Read the following extract, and then give your interpretation of the illocutionary force of each intervention and of the extract as a whole*:

Dr. Patrick (laughs):	Why don't you . . run away from home, Lizzie?
Lizzie (laughs):	Why don't you 'run away' with me?
Dr. Patrick:	Where'll we go?
Lizzie:	Boston.
Dr. Patrick:	And when will we go?
Lizzie:	Tonight.
Dr. Patrick:	But you don't really mean it, you're havin' me on.
Lizzie:	I do mean it.
Dr. Patrick:	How can you joke – and look so serious?

Lizzie: It's a gift.
Dr. Patrick (laughs):   Oh, Lizzie …

Sharon Pollock, *Blood Relations*, in *Plays by Women*, vol. 3.

Module 26

1 *Discussion*:
1) What is the basic mood structure of the imperative?
2) Which types of Subject can be present in an imperative clause?
3) How can a Subject in an imperative clause be distinguished from a vocative?
4) Explain the use of *let* as an imperative marker.
5) Give examples to illustrate (a) the difference between the imperative marker *let* and the lexical verb *let*, and (b) possible ambiguity between the two.
6) If the unmarked illocutionary force of the imperative is that of a directive, why is the imperative mood so often replaced by another mood structure in interpersonal interaction?
7) In what circumstances and with what kinds of illocutionary act is the imperative socially acceptable?

2 †*Decide whether the italicised item is a Subject or a vocative*:
1) Keep still, *Edward*, there's a good boy.
2) 'I'll read it later.' 'Oh, all right, *you* please yourself.'
3) *Somebody* pass me the insect repellent, quick! Thank you, *dear*. Now *you* take some.
4) Say hello to Uncle Arthur, *children*!
5) *Everybody* lift at the same time! Right, up she goes, *everybody*!
6) Do shut up, *Helen*, you're making a fool of yourself.
7) *You all* wait here, that will be best, I'll be back in a moment.
8) *You* just leave him alone, do you hear?

3 †*Discuss possible illocutionary acts carried out by each of the utterances below and suggest suitable social contexts*:
1) Tell me what the problem is, I'm sure we can fix it.
2) Don't try it, eh? Just don't try it.
3) Break the habit! Go on, break it today.
4) Don't give me orders. Don't tell me what I can do.
5) Assert yourself, for Heaven's sake!
6) Oh, now let's get this straight.
7) Take some more pictures like that and I'll reward you.
8) Take any more pictures like that and I'll report you.
9) Look, just give me the key, will you?
10) Calm down, darling, it's only a game.
11) Right, let's not waste time.
12) Suppose there's no-one at home.

4   *In pairs, take turns to carry out a series of directives, with the aim of getting your hearer to do something, first by means of a direct directive, and then by means of an indirect directive. Notice how your hearer reacts in each case. Remember that the greater the imposition on the hearer, and the greater the social distance which separates speaker and hearer, the more polite, i.e. indirect, the speaker will have to be. Try some of the suggestions below, or, even better, think of contexts you have actually experienced. (This exercise could be taped for further analysis.)*

1)   e.g. You want to borrow your father's car to take your camping gear to be repaired.
(a) Dad, lend me your car to go to Davy's.
(b) Oh, by the way, Dad, I've got to take all my camping gear to be repaired and it weighs a ton. If you're not using your car on Saturday morning I wondered if you could lend it to me.

2)   Your sister is always borrowing your clothes. You don't like this.

3)   Your son keeps a fierce dog as a pet. You ask your next-door neighbour to feed it when you go on holiday.

4)   You need a testimonial from your tutor in order to apply for a grant at a foreign university. The letter must reach the university in not later than a fortnight.

5)   Your botany lecturer has borrowed your collection of wild flowers which took you years to collect. You want it back.

6)   The people in the flat above yours switch on their very noisy washing-machine late at night. They also have a dog which barks all night. The result is you can't sleep.

Module 27

1   *Discussion*:
1)   How is the exclamative mood structure formed?
2)   What is an abbreviated exclamative mood structure?
3)   How can the effect of an exclamation be achieved non-grammatically?
4)   What are the psychological motivations for using echo structures?
5)   What speech act functions do echo structures always have?
6)   Which mood structures can have clause tags, in Standard BrE?
7)   Explain the structure of the clause tag.
8)   What are the two polarity types of tag? Which is the more common?
9)   How does intonation combine with polarity in tags to produce four types of meaning when appended to declarative clauses?
10)   What kind of meaning does the Type 2 tag convey? Can you suggest how these meanings are conveyed in your own or another language?
11)   Outline the characteristics of tags used with imperative clauses.
12)   What functions do tags fulfil in interpersonal interaction?

2   †*As speaker, add a tag to each of the following clauses, indicating the intonation type that would accompany the tag. Then, as hearer, add (a) a confirming and (b) a disconfirming response. This can be done in pairs*:

1) You'll do anything for me.
2) There's nothing to be done but go back.
3) What a dreadful climate.
4) So you're the new secretary.
5) You haven't by chance got Alastair's address.
6) Let's sit down here.
7) I suppose there's no likelihood of getting our money back.
8) He didn't approve of the plan.
9) Let's not say any more about it.
10) It might be difficult to find anywhere to stay in the village.

3 †*Try to assign an illocutionary act to each of the abbreviated clauses below. Then add the necessary constituents in order to make them finite independent clauses and say to which type of mood structure they belong*:
1) Now then, to business!
2) Anything in the paper tonight?
3) Sounds nasty to me.
4) Why apologise?
5) What awful weather!

4 *In pairs, take turns to give a set of oral instructions for guidance on one of the topics below. The hearer may interrupt to ask for clarification*:
1) how to connect and disconnect the burglar alarm in your house;
2) how to make your favourite pudding;
3) how to record a television programme on video;
4) how to start a car.

Tape your dialogue, listen to it afterwards and analyse the structures you used. Were they mostly imperatives? With or without a Subject? Or declaratives? Did the hearer use echo questions?

5 *Read the following imaginary letter from an airman in the Second World War to his girlfriend and decide which illocutionary acts are illustrated in each paragraph*:

Ted's letter, May 1943

Mary (reads):
Darling Mary,
Thank you for your letter. Your trip to Hammersmith Palais sounded fun – I'm surprised Aunt Annie didn't stop you. Don't get too carried away with those Canadians and Americans – they can spin a good yarn or two.[1]

Training is nearly finished, and we'll soon be put in our air crews and ready to fly on raids. They are a grand bunch of lads to be with. Last week the warning sounded and our drome got off thirty-three aircraft in twenty-seven minutes to fly on a thousand bomber raid. Quite a few didn't come back.[2]

The food is terrible as ever. We always know when fish is on the menu – there are no servers. The fish is so high it just flies on to the plates.[3]

Mary, it is hard to say this in a letter, but I have a forty-eight hour leave at the end of June. Could we get married then? I know it's a rush, but we needn't have any fuss – just the two of us and friends – and Aunt Annie, of course. Please say yes.[4]

All my love,
Ted

Lou Wakefield, *Time Pieces* in *Plays by Women*, vol. 3.

1) How many different illocutionary acts have you identified in each paragraph?
2) Which type of illocutionary act occurs most frequently?
3) Which illocutionary act do you consider the most important in this letter?
4) Which illocutionary acts are expressed by Ted directly, and which are expressed indirectly?
5) For the expression of which illocutionary act does Ted introduce further illocutionary acts?
6) From this analysis, what inferences do you draw about Ted and Mary, and about Aunt Annie?

6 *In pairs, carry out the illocutionary acts specified below, choosing whatever structures you feel are most appropriate to the social context. Tape your exchanges and analyse your reactions.*
1) You have taken part in a competition and a person you don't like much has won the first prize, while you have won nothing. You have to congratulate the winner.
2) You have borrowed your brother's / sister's best white shirt / blouse without asking permission and someone has spilt red wine all over it. You have to apologise.
3) You are at the annual staff party and inadvertently spill black coffee onto the General Manager's clothes. You have to apologise.
4) You are invited at the last minute to the theatre by your parents, but you have already arranged to go out with someone else. So you refuse.
5) Someone has repeatedly been scrawling graffiti on the wall of your house. One day you unexpectedly catch him/her in the act. You decide to complain.

6

Organising the message:
Thematic and information structures of the clause

Introduction

In this chapter we turn to the third type of meaning expressed by the clause: this is the clause as message.

Messages are organised units of information. When a speaker structures a message, the information is processed into units and ordered in such a way as to produce the kind of message that is desired. As well as variations produced by phonological means, several syntactic alternatives exist for arranging information into a series of alternative messages. For instance, the proposition 'A waiter brought them cocktails' can be processed in English into different combinations such as the following:

1 A waiter brought them cocktails.
2 A WAITER brought them cocktails.
3 They were brought cocktails by a waiter.
4 Cocktails they were brought by a waiter.
5 It was cocktails that a waiter brought them.
6 What the waiter brought them was cocktails.
7 Bring them cocktails, the waiter did.
8 There was a waiter who brought them cocktails.

All of these clauses – and there are still further alternatives – can be said to have the same propositional meaning, but not the same communicative significance. For this reason, the various alternatives are not equally appropriate at any given point in the discourse. To illustrate this we can start by making sentence (1) form part of a text:

> They arrived at the hotel and sat on the terrace. The sun was hot but the canopies gave a pleasant shade. There was a glimpse of the sea through the palm-trees. A waiter brought them cocktails.

Of the eight alternatives listed above, only (3) *They were brought cocktails by a waiter* and (8) *There was a waiter who brought them cocktails* are reasonable alternatives, and even these are not as satisfactory as (1) since they seem to give more importance to the waiter than to the cocktails.

Even more striking is the lack of coherence which is produced by using the alternative forms indiscriminately. In the following version of the text, no structure is appropriate at the point at which it occurs:

> At the hotel they arrived and on the terrace they sat. It was the sun that was hot, but what the canopies gave was a pleasant shade. A glimpse of the sea was through the palm-trees. Brought them cocktails, the waiter did.

The appropriateness of alternative structures can also be tested by providing questions. For instance, in answer to the question '*Who brought them cocktails?*' the alternatives (5), (6) and (7), would not be appropriate. While the others would be possible, the most common reply would be '*A waiter did*', in which the recoverable information has been elliptted. In answer to the question '*Was there anyone else on the terrace?*' the only really appropriate alternative would be (8). The factors which condition the choice of one alternative rather than another are pragmatic and include the following:

(a) which element of the proposition represents the main topic, what the clause is about;
(b) which part of the message the speaker considers most important;
(c) which part of the message the speaker treats as known to the hearer, and which is presented as new;
(d) what information, if any, is presupposed at any given point in the discourse;

(e) which element the speaker chooses as the point of departure of the message.

These choices combine together to produce such informational structures as those exemplified in (1) to (8) above. We shall be describing them in more detail in terms of 'Theme, Rheme and Topic' (Module 28), 'Given information, New information and information focus' (Module 29), and finally, in Module 30, the clause structures which are used in English to express a message in different communicative ways. It is important to realise, however, that the choices operate in conjunction to produce certain configurations of meaning in each case.

MODULE 28
Theme: the point of departure of the message

Summary

1   Theme is an element of the thematic structure of a clause, of which the other element is Rheme. It is therefore a different category from the syntactic Subject and from Topic – what the message is about – although these three tend to coincide in one wording.

2   It is convenient to think of Topics as organised hierarchically according to their level of operation: superordinate Topics are what the whole text is about, basic-level Topics refer to the main participants, and subordinate Topics are related to these. There are certain devices to introduce new Topics into the discourse, to maintain topic continuity and to reactivate Topics which have languished.

3   Theme is the point of departure for the message and is realised in English by the first clause constituent. It is unmarked when it coincides with the expected element such as Subject in a declarative clause. When some other element is fronted to initial position it is a marked Theme, and carries some additional significance in the discourse. Objects, Complements and Adjuncts can be fronted. Whole clauses can be fronted in complex sentences.

4   Other items whose normal position is at the beginning of the clause such as conjunctions (*and, or, but*), Conjuncts such as *however*, Disjuncts such as *personally*, vocatives (*Doctor!*) and discourse markers such as *Well* may be considered to be part of the Theme. In this way we can talk of 'multiple Themes'. A subordinate clause in initial position may be considered as Theme of a sentence.

28.1   The meaning of Theme

In this book we shall say that the Theme of a clause is what speakers or writers take as their 'point of departure' in that clause. It is realised in English by the first clause constituent, and the rest of the message constitutes the Rheme. Together, Theme and Rheme are the elements which make up the functional configuration of the clause as message. The semantic choice associated with the Theme/Rheme structure is 'What notion will I use as my point of departure in this clause?' From this, the rest of the clause proceeds. In the following clauses, which represent the same propositional content, a different element has been chosen as the initial constituent in each case:

Theme	Rheme
I	can't stand the noise.
The noise	I can't stand.
It's the noise	I can't stand.
What I can't stand	is the noise.
The noise,	I can't stand it.

The choice of Theme is important because it represents the angle from which the speaker projects his/her message, and partially conditions how the message develops. The initial element acts as a signal to the hearer, directing expectations regarding the structure that is likely to follow, or about the mental representation of what the message is likely to be. For this reason, a Theme which coincides with the clause Subject prepares the hearer for a declarative structure (*I can hear a noise*), while an auxiliary in initial position signals that the clause will be interrogative (*Can you hear a noise?*). Presentative *there* introduces information that is considered new to the hearer (*There was a loud noise*) while certain openings such as *Once upon a time* condition the hearer to expect a certain type of narrative.

Another factor which affects the choice of initial element concerns the speaker's assumptions regarding what the hearer knows or doesn't know about the state of affairs described; in other words, whether anything is necessarily involved or presupposed. In the examples above, the first clause *I can't stand the noise* seems to involve no particular supposition about the situation on the part of the hearer, apart from the definiteness of the noise, signalled by the definite article *the*, as opposed to noise in general. The second, *The noise I can't stand*, seems to imply a contrast with something else (*though the people are friendly*). The third, *It's the noise I can't stand*, seems to presuppose a shared belief on the part of the speaker and hearer that I can't stand something, and identifies that entity; while the fourth *What I can't stand is the noise* seems to restrict what I can't stand among other things imagined by the hearer. The fifth, *The noise, I can't stand it*, might be said in answer to the question *Don't you mind the noise from the bar downstairs?*

From these considerations, it is clear that the Theme of a clause represents a choice, both as the absolute starting-point and also as the point of departure of each subsequent clause and of each paragraph. It permits the speaker the choice of taking as point of departure one or other participant in the situation described, or something else, such as a circumstance. It can serve to link up with what has gone before in the discourse and it helps push the message forward. Because of the presuppositions involved in certain thematic structures, not all choices will be appropriate from the point of view of creating a coherent whole.

28.2   Theme, Subject and Topic

Theme is to be distinguished from Subject and Topic. Theme, as we have seen, is an element of the **thematic** structure, of which the other element is Rheme. **Subject** is a **syntactic** element of clause structure, of which the other elements are Predicator, Complements, Objects and Adjunct. **Topic**, as we see it, is a **discourse category** representing the notion 'what the text, or part of the text, is about'. This notion of 'aboutness' is, thus stated, too wide to be useful when applied to a text. It is helpful, therefore, to classify Topics according to the level at which they operate into superordinate Topics, basic-level Topics and subordinate Topics.

Superordinate Topics are cognitive schemata (the organisation of thoughts into schemes of things) and could be the Topic of a whole text, such as *buying a caravan* or *six ways to combat inflation*. Superordinate Topics are typically reflected in the titles of books, articles, lectures and so on. Basic-level Topics are individual participants within the scene; for instance, in the scene *buying a caravan* the Topic participants would be the buyer, the seller, the caravan and the money. Subordinate Topics are aspects or parts of basic-level Topics, for instance, some part of the caravan, if this is mentioned in the discourse. Any of the three levels of Topic can function as current clause Topic.

Topics are at some point introduced into the discourse for the first time. These are new Topics. As the discourse proceeds, they are either maintained as old or known Topics, sometimes for a considerable stretch, or they drop out. A Topic which has been allowed to languish can be reintroduced into the discourse.

English has no morphological device for introducing new Topics. Syntactically, however, various devices exist, including the following:

(a) Presentative adverbs such as *here, there, up, out* which push the Topic, which is also Subject, to end-position in the clause as in *Out went the light*.

(b) Unstressed *there* with *be* or a presentative verb such as *emerge* or *appear* which have the same effect, as in *There emerged from the cave a huge bear*. Fronted spatial or temporal Adjuncts also occur: *Once upon a time, in a dark forest, there lived an old witch*.

(c) When the Subject is known, the Direct Object or Predicator Complement often introduces a new Topic: *What did you make of Elsa's behaviour?*

(d) A statement which explicitly informs the hearer what the Topic is going to be as in *You can describe this kind of behaviour in one of two ways* or *Today I want to talk to you about genetic engineering*.

(e) Inversion of relational clauses as in *Worst of all was the lack of fresh water*. (28.6)

Topics are maintained by what is known as 'topic continuity' (30.3.4). This is mainly achieved by anaphora, a form of presupposition which points back to some item which has occurred previously in the discourse. Anaphora involves the use of pronouns (or *zero anaphora*, with no pronoun) and lexical variation to refer back to the previous item. In the opening paragraph of James Joyce's story *The Boarding House*, given below, *she, herself* and *his wife* refer anaphorically to *Mrs Mooney*, while *he, him* and *Mr Mooney* refer back to *her father's foreman*:

> *Mrs Mooney* was a butcher's daughter. *She* was a woman who was quite able to keep things to *herself*: a determined woman. *She* had married her father's foreman, and opened a butcher's shop near Spring Gardens. But as soon as his father-in-law was dead *Mr Mooney* began to go to the devil. *He* drank, plundered the till, ran headlong into debt. It was no use making *him* take the pledge: *he* was sure to break out again a few days after. By fighting *his wife* in the presence of customers and by buying bad meat *he* ruined his business. One night *he* went for *his wife* with the cleaver, and *she* had to sleep in a neighbour's house.
>
> James Joyce, Dubliners.

The part of the message that is referred to anaphorically may be not simply an item, but a whole sentence or stretch of discourse. In the opening sentence of the second paragraph of Joyce's story *that* refers back to the events related in the last part of the first paragraph:

> After *that* they lived apart.

Topics can be reactivated into the discourse by such expressions as *as regards, as for, what about* ... and the conjunctive adverb *now*. They are generally followed by full NGs rather than pronouns:

> 'We've been talking about all the things that have to be done before we go on holiday: fill in our income tax forms, get the roof mended, find a suitable kennels for the dog ...' (long digression about the dog).
> '*As regards the income tax return forms*, you'd better fill them in straight away.' (discussion about income tax forms)
> '*Now, the roof, what about the roof* – suppose it rains.'

Not all Topics are pushed to end-position, however. They can be introduced initially, coinciding with Theme and Subject and receiving considerable pitch prominence, as in the following example in which *Eddoes* is point of departure of the message, syntactic Subject and new Topic:

Eddoes, who was a driver, was admired by all the boys.
Subject Theme New Topic

When this happens, the speaker takes the new Topic – what the clause is about – as the point of departure. But they do not necessarily coincide; a circumstance, such as an expression of place or time, may be taken as Theme, with an old Topic in second position as in:

In my village, all the boys admired Eddoes, who was a driver.		
Theme Adjunct	old Topic Subject	new Topic Direct Object

Topic is not easy to identify unequivocally, even in a coherent text. Topics are usually entities and, if new, they are introduced into the discourse by one or other of the devices described above. An interpretation is suggested for the following text, in which Topics are italicised:

> After midnight, there were *two regular noises in the street*[1]. At about two o'clock you heard *the sweepers*[2]; and then, just before dawn, *the scavenging-carts* [3] came and you heard *the men* [4] scraping off *the rubbish the sweepers had gathered into heaps*[5].
>
> *No boy in the street* [6] particularly wished to be a sweeper. But if you asked *any boy* [7] what he would like to be, *he* [8] would say, 'I going be a cart-driver.'
>
> There was certainly *a glamour to driving the blue carts*[9]. *The men* [10] were aristocrats. *They* [11] worked early in the morning, and had the rest of the day free. And then *they* [12] were always going on strike. *They* [13] didn't strike for much. *They* [14] struck for things like a cent more a day; *they* [15] struck if someone was laid off. *They* [16] struck when the war began; *they* [17] struck when the war ended. *They* [18] struck when India got Independence. *They* [19] struck when Gandhi died.
>
> V. S. Naipaul, *Miguel Street*.

28.3   Unmarked and marked Theme

Theme is a meaningful choice and, as in other parts of the grammar, speakers can choose between a **marked** and an **unmarked** option. Unmarked Theme coincides with the first constituent of each mood structure, as follows:

Subject in a declarative clause:	*Alice* went home.
Finite + Subject in a polar interrogative clause:	*Did Alice* go home?
WH-element in a *WH*-interrogative:	*Where* did Alice go?
Predicator or *let* + Subject in an imperative clause:	*Go* home!
	Let's go home!

In such cases as these, the starting-point of the clause is the expected one, the one that announces the mood type of the clause. Theme is marked when any other element of structure but the expected one is brought to initial position, as can be done by rearranging our examples:

Cp. in a declarative clause:	*Home* went Alice.
Cp. before Finite in a polar interrogative:	*Home did* Alice go?
Non-*WH*- Subject in a *WH*-interrogative:	*Alice* went where?
Subject in an imperative:	*You* go home!

Utterances of the type *Alice went where?* have the unmarked order of a declarative clause which corresponds to unmarked Theme, but this can be overridden by such factors as intonation and movement of the *WH*-element.

28.4   Marked Theme in the declarative clause

When a clause constituent is moved to initial position this is called **thematic fronting** and the fronted element is a marked Theme. Fronting, or **thematisation**, is an important process in that it affects the structural ordering of the declarative clause. The thematised element does not change its grammatical function, however. Compare the unmarked and the marked versions of the following clauses:

Unmarked Theme	Rheme
You	'll never meet a nicer girl.
His name	is Archibald.
It	made me very angry.
The frightened villagers	ran out into the fields.

Marked Theme	Rheme
(Od) *A nicer girl*	you'll never meet.
(Cs) *Archibald*	his name is.
(Co) *Very angry*	it made me.
(Cp) *Out into the fields*	ran the frightened villagers.

A fronted Predicator is not usually possible in English, except when it is non-finite and is followed by the remaining part of the predication as in '*Get an answer* I will'. In some journalistic styles, the non-finite *-ing* part of the Predicator, together with its predication, are fronted as in:

> *Coming up to the stage now* is this year's winner of the Oscar. . . .

The discourse motivation for this fronting appears to be two-fold: that of pushing a new Topic to end-position while adopting a striking point of departure. In journalism, not only non-finite but also finite Predicators are now fronted when the rest of the predication is quoted speech:

> *Snapped* back the 18-year-old princess: 'No comment'.

28.5   Themes which provoke Subject–Finite inversion

Thematised elements which have the most marked effect are those which provoke inversion of the Subject and the Finite part of the Predicator. There are two main types: expressions of direction and expressions with negative meaning.

28.5.1   Expressions of direction

These are Predicator Complements which accompany verbs of directional movement (see 7.3.1d). They are semantically and syntactically integrated into the clause structure, and include adverbs such as *home, here, there, up, down, in, out, off, away*, Prepositional Groups such as *across the campus*, or adverbs followed by Prepositional Groups as in *down to the bottom of the sea*:

> Home *went Alice.*
> There *goes my last dollar.*
> Across the campus *raced the students.*
> Down to the bottom of the sea *plunged the diver.*

When used as Themes, these Predicator Complements accompany simple tenses (*goes, raced*), not expanded forms such as *is going, have raced*. This means that the Subject inverts with the whole Predicator. The effect is emphatic, partly because the directional meaning is taken as the point of departure of the message, and partly because the Subject participant, which is likely to be also Topic, is pushed to end-position where it is given maximum focus. The result is that the inverted declarative has what amounts to exclamatory force, and certain everyday situations seem to call for this rhetorical effect (*Here comes the bus! Off they go!*). In such cases the non-thematised form would sound odd (*The bus comes here. They go off.*) since the effect produced is simply that of a statement.

When the Subject is a pronoun, inversion is avoided (*Across the campus raced they*), since a pronoun expresses known information and therefore is not appropriately placed so as to receive end-focus (29.7).

28.5.2   Expressions with negative meaning

These are fronted negative Adjuncts such as *never, nowhere, on no account, under no circumstances, not only* and negative NGs such as *not a soul, not a thing* functioning as fronted Direct Objects:

Never	*have I* seen such a sight.
Under no circumstances	*must medicines* be left within reach of children.
Not often	*do you* get an opportunity like this.
Not a soul	*did the travellers* see.
Not a thing	*could the patient* remember.

Implicit negatives introduced by *hardly, scarcely, seldom* and *rarely* provoke the same inversion when they are placed initially:

Hardly a soul	*did the travellers* see.
Seldom	*does one find* such generosity.
Scarcely	*had the show started* than fire broke out.

In this type the Subject inverts not with the whole Predicator but with the finite operator.

28.5.3 Other Themes which provoke inversion

Apart from these two main types, there are other units which, when thematised, provoke Subject–Finite auxiliary inversion:

(a) *So, neither, nor* introducing elliptical clauses:

> Ed passed the exam and *so did Mary.*
> Ed didn't pass the exam and *neither / nor did Mary.*

(b) *Such* and *so* as modifiers of Objects, Complements or Adjuncts:

> *So depressed did he feel* that nothing would cheer him up.
> *Such a bad time did we have* that we'll never forget it.

(c) Subordinate clauses of condition and concession. This inversion is used in rather formal language:

> *Had I* known the facts, I would not have employed him.
> *Should you* decide to change your mind, please let us know.
> *Were he* alive today, he would be horrified.

28.6 Attributes as Themes

It is possible to make an Attribute the point of departure of the message by fronting a Complement, accompanied sometimes by S-P inversion:

> And *very pretty* she is too.
> *Quite riotous* the party became in the end.
> *Very handy* we found the multi-use tool you lent us.
> *Bluer than velvet* was the night.

Circumstantial Attributes with verbs expressing position are more easily thematised, since this type of structure is reversible. The function of this thematised element is, as in other inversions, probably that of introducing a new Topic in end-position. Compare:

> The castle stands on a hill.   On the hill stands a castle.
> The hotel is five minutes'   Five minutes' walk from the
> walk from the beach.   beach is the hotel.

28.7   Circumstantial Adjuncts as Themes

Probably the most common elements as Themes, after clause Subjects, are Adjuncts which express time, duration, extent and other attendant circumstances as in:

> *Only ten years ago*, this coastline was quite unspoilt.
> *A mile further on*, we came upon a single-line railway track.

Unlike directional Predicator Complements, these are not semantically or syntactically integrated into clause structure and for this reason are easily moved around. They are not themselves Topics, since they are not participants, nor do they identify or describe a participant. Their function is to 'set the scene' by setting up a framework of time, place or some other circumstance within which the situation unfolds. Circumstantials in other, non-initial positions do not have this scene-setting effect.

The language of travel advertisements achieves some of its heightened effects by means of thematised circumstantial elements. Here is an example:

> *Three hours by boat from the Ionian island of Kerkyra (Corfu)* [1] lies
> Paxos. *As a holiday destination* [2] it was discovered by the Italians a
> few years ago, following in the steps of the Venetians. *Thus far,* [3] the
> rugged islanders have succeeded in defending the tranquil simplicity of
> the island, of its small harbour town and fishing villages. *A short motor
> boat trip from the harbour town of Gaios,* [4] is Antipaxos, with
> turquoise waters and beaches 'softer than silk'.

> *Oxford Today*, vol. 1, no. 3 (1989).

[1] circumstantial Attribute of extent in time; [2] circumstantial Adjunct of role; [3] circumstantial Adjunct of extent in time; [4] circumstantial Attribute of extent.

28.8   Direct Objects as Themes

Thematised Direct Objects can represent participants in the situation and therefore qualify as possible Topics in the discourse. Three types of realisation are common, all typically containing some item which is retrospective in the discourse:

28.8.1   Nominal Groups representing entities

One half she ate herself, *the other* she gave to the child.
Moussaka you ordered, and *moussaka* you've been given.

28.8.2   Finite clauses expressing lack of knowledge

What she expected from me I can't imagine.
How we're going to get there in time I don't really know.

28.8.3   Pronouns which refer to persons or things, events or situations just mentioned

Lea asked me to bring her some tea from London. *This* I did.
He's all right, but *her* I found rather a bore.

28.9   Discourse Themes

In addition to the clausal Themes, the point of departure of the message may consist of items such as Conjuncts, Disjuncts and vocatives, which express various meanings related to the clausal message. In this book such items will be referred to as **discourse Themes**.

28.9.1   Conjunctive Themes

These are items which connect the clause to the previous part of the text. Many different types of connection can be made, according to the semantic nature of the link:

Meaning	Example
additive	also, in addition, besides
adversative	however, on the other hand, yet, conversely
alternative	alternatively, either . . . or, instead
appositive	that is, for instance
causal	because of this, for this reason, so
comparative	in the same way, likewise
concessive	nevertheless, anyway, still
conditional	in that case, under the circumstances
consequential	therefore, consequently, hence
continuative	in this respect, as far as that's concerned
temporal	first, then, next, presently

28.9.2   Modal Themes

By means of these the speaker comments on his attitude to what he is saying.

Meaning	Example
admission	admittedly, to tell the truth
assertion	honestly, really, surely, clearly, of course
conviction	undoubtedly, indeed, undeniably
diffidence	initially, tentatively
doubt	arguably, perhaps, the chances are . . ., very likely
evaluation	wisely, sensibly, predictably, quite rightly
generality	generally/objectively speaking, on the whole
hope	hopefully, let's hope that . . .
opinion	to my mind, in my opinion, personally
probability	possibly, probably, certainly
regret	alas, unfortunately, regrettably
surprise	amazingly, to my surprise

28.9.3   Conjunctions and relatives

Conjunctions of both the coordinating type (*and, or, either, neither, but, yet, so, then*) and of the subordinating type (*after, although, because, before, since, unless, when, while, whether, even if, in spite of the fact that*, etc.) are inherently thematic in that they are placed at the beginning of the clause. This feature is shared by relative items (*who, which, whose, that, when, where, whatever, whichever, however*, etc.). These function as Subject, Object, Complement or Adjunct, either alone or as part of a group (*for whom, in whose house, on whatever occasion*) and generally function as the Theme of the clause in which they occur.

The fact that these items always occupy initial position does not mean that they have no thematic value. The choice is open to speakers and writers to connect their stretches of discourse as they please; it is therefore the meaning chosen (causal, adversative, conditional or whatever), rather than the item that realises this meaning, that is to be interpreted as thematic. They do not, however, exhaust the total thematic potential of a clause and for this reason the Theme can extend to other items, as is explained below.

28.9.4   Relational Themes

These are initial items that present the clausal message from the point of view of something else related to it. They include adverbs such as *morally, ethically, politically, medically, saleswise, status-wise*, and PrepGs such as *from the point of view of ethics, from a medical point of view, as far as politics is concerned*:

> *Legally*, his position is untenable.

Consumerwise, the innovation has not had much impact.
As far as sales are concerned, no company can beat them.

The importance of modal and relational Themes lies in the fact that their scope extends to cover the whole of the following clause.

28.9.5 Continuative Themes

These are a small group of items, such as *Yes, No, Well, Ah*, which serve to indicate that one speaker is taking over from another in a dialogue, or that the same speaker is moving to a different point.

28.10   Multiple Themes

We have now included as possible Themes items which represent some function in the semantic structure and others which are not representational. In this way it is possible to talk of **multiple Themes**. Only a representational element is necessary as Theme; the others, the conjunctive, relational, vocative and continuative elements do not exhaust the thematic potential, but contribute something to the point of departure chosen for the clause. Here are some examples of multiple Themes:

Well	now	Mrs. Jones	what	can I do for you?
continuative	conjunctive	vocative	representational	
Theme				**Rheme**

Much to our surprise	though	the show	was a flop
modal	conjunctive	representational	
Theme			**Rheme**

Technologically	then	it	is admirable
relational	conjunctive	representational	
Theme			**Rheme**

Some instances of single Themes and multiple Themes in main clauses are illustrated in the following text (Themes in subordinate and embedded clauses are not indicated):

> *Towards the end of his life*, [1] Freud concluded that he was not a great man but he had discovered great things. *Arguably*, [2] *the reverse* [3]

might be true. *Judging him with scientific severity*, [4] *many* [5] would say that one can be sure of nothing he claimed to have discovered. *Others* [6] would argue that he made the immense discovery that man is a poetic creature, his dreams a forest of symbols. *Ironically* [7] *he* [8] believed that he followed Darwin in diminishing man's stature; *in reality*, [9] *he* [10] increased it.

[1] adjunctive; [2] modal; [3] unmarked (Subject); [4] relational; [5] unmarked (Subject); [6] unmarked (Subject); [7] modal; [8] unmarked (Subject); [9] modal; [10] unmarked (Subject).

28.11   Preposed and postposed Themes

Preposed and postposed Themes are items which are represented twice in the clause, once in their normal position as clause constituents and again, either at the beginning ('preposed') or at the end ('postposed') of the clause:

> *All these red roses*, who can have sent *them*?
> They're all bad, *these apples*.

Preposing and postposing differ from fronting in that the pre- or postposed element is repeated pronominally. This repetition allows speakers to process their information as they go along; it is for this reason characteristic of unplanned speech.

28.12   Clauses as Themes

Two or more clauses make up a clause complex (see Chapter 7). The importance of the initial element is such that the clause which is chosen to be placed first can be considered thematic in relation to the whole clause complex. This is true whether the clauses are joined paratactically, by coordination or apposition, or hypotactically, by subordination, as in the respective examples below:

I looked everywhere, *Whatever you do,*	but no bag was to be seen. don't forget the plane tickets.
Theme	**Rheme**

The communicative function of the initiating clause as Theme will, however, be different according to the type of clause that is chosen.

28.12.1   Themes in clauses related by coordination

Paratactically related clauses typically reflect the chronological order of the events described. The Theme is, therefore, the natural temporal and factual starting-point of the sequence. Compare:

He bought an oil-tanker and made a fortune.
He made a fortune and bought an oil-tanker.

Even when no chronological order can be discerned, the choice of which clause to thematise is important since it allows what the speaker considers to be the most important information, within the current context, to be placed towards the end of the sentence, such as *foolish to ignore* in the following:

The evidence needs further testing, but it'll be foolish to ignore it.
My mother was fair, but I am exceptionally dark.

28.12.2   Themes in clauses related by subordination

With hypotactically related clauses, the speaker is under no obligation to maintain chronological order. It has been suggested that in most cases the unmarked order is main + subordinate as in *I saw the fire when I turned the corner*. But the reverse is also possible as in *When I turned the corner I saw the fire*, and it would seem that in many cases the tendency to place new and important information towards the end probably conditions the choice of initial clause in the complex. In the case of conditional clauses, however, subordinate + main appears to be the unmarked order, reflecting iconically the logical relationship involved, as in the following short extract from a play:

'I haven't got time, mother, to start putting things in tins. If I want a nail, there's a nail. I bang it in and that's that. If I can't find a nail I use a screw. And if I can't find a screw, I don't bother.

Alan Ayckbourn, *Just Between Ourselves*.

Finite subordinate clauses express meanings of condition, concession, reason, time and degree among others. When such clauses are thematised, they provide a circumstantial framework within which the rest of the sentence develops, or until a new framework is set up. The conditional clause *If I want a nail* sets up a framework which lasts for two sentences, until the new framework *If I can't find a nail* is set up, which introduces the information *I use a screw*. The last conditional framework *And if I can't find a screw* leads to the final conclusion – of not bothering.

Other types of situational frameworks are illustrated in the following examples:

As he approached, he could hear the sound of firing.
As long as the price is right, the colour doesn't matter.
When everyone had gone home, we sat around on the floor.

If a main clause is chosen as Theme, it may be because a personal framework has been preferred, with the current Topic as starting-point:

We were on holiday in Devon when war was declared in September 1939.
He crawled on until he reached a first-aid post.

The three types of non-finite clause, *to*-infinitive, participial *-ing* and participial *-en* clauses, can be thematised and are then sometimes followed by a comma. The communicative function is different for each type.

Initial *to*-infinitive clauses not only set up a circumstantial framework of purpose, but they also name the goal to be achieved:

> *To cure stress*, try a Jacuzzi whirlpool bath.

The goal in this case is *to cure stress*, while the means to attain the goal is expressed in the main clause. An initial purpose clause takes the goal as the point of departure, and creates expectations in the hearer about how this goal is to be achieved. No expectations are created if the purpose clause is final as in *Try a Jacuzzi whirlpool bath to cure stress*.

The information contained in the purpose clause may not be so important or interesting, within the context, as to warrant setting up expectations. In such cases, it is the action performed in the main clause which carries the narrative one step further and this is placed in initial position:

> She went into the kitchen to make a cup of tea.
> He arrived early to pick up Rose.
> I'm going to the pool, to fritter away the day.

Participial *-ing* and *-en* clauses are closely tied to a main participant in the discourse. The *-ing* type is active in meaning and can express economically an action or state which is dependent on the main situation in which the participant is directly involved:

> *Taking advantage of his present popularity*, the Prime Minister called
> a general election.

If the Topic is new or reintroduced, it is probably placed first with the *-ing* clause in post-Subject position:

> The guerilla leader, *receiving no reply to his peace offer*, decided to
> launch an attack.

In sentence-final position, *-ing* clauses add New information:

> The capital was the last to fall, leading to a period of famine and
> privation which was to last for several years.

Participial *-en* clauses are inherently passive and, when initial, focus on some action or state which affects a main participant. At the same time, they are retrospective, summing up what has gone before:

> *Thwarted in the West*, Stalin turned East.

In medial and sentence-final positions, *-en* clauses are less likely to be retrospective and, like *-ing* clauses, are more likely to contain important New information:

> The cotton-growing south, *irritated by the growing threat of the*

Abolitionist movement, and *fearing this predominance in Congress*, began to talk of secession from the Union.

H. G. Wells, *A Short History of the World*.

As the above examples suggest, thematised *-ing* and *-en* clauses are in English rather formal and are characteristic of written rather than spoken language.

MODULE 29
Information focus

Summary

1   In order to be understood, messages are divided into chunks called **information units**, which are realised in speech by **tone units**. These do not correspond to any one grammatical category, since the speaker is free to break up the message as he wishes into units which are smaller or larger than a clause.

2   Each tone unit contains an **intonation nucleus**, which represents the highest point of the **focus of information**. Information focus extends to the syntactic unit in which the nucleus occurs.

3   Each information unit contains an obligatory New element and, optionally, a Given element, the unmarked order being Given–New. The Given is the information that the speaker presents as recoverable by the hearer; the New is the information that is presented as not recoverable by the hearer. The whole tone unit may contain New information, for instance at the start of a conversational exchange.

4   The devices of **ellipsis** and **substitution** are used to avoid repeating information that is known to the hearer.

5   Unmarked focus falls on the last lexical item of the information unit. This leaves the options open as to the amount of information that is New. If the intonation nucleus is made to fall on some other item it is marked and unequivocally represents New information.

6   Focus can coincide with marked Theme and is a cohesive device in texts.

7   Focus can also be used for emotive purposes.

29.1 The information unit

Speakers divide their messages into one or more chunks which are **information units**. Each information unit is realised, not directly by a grammatical unit, but by a phonological unit called a **tone unit**. Information units are therefore defined in terms of the spoken language and how speakers organise it; readers of the written language, however, interpret what they read by mentally assigning information units to the text.

A tone unit consists potentially of a series of stressed and unstressed syllables and always contains one syllable which is marked by a jump in pitch ('pitch prominence') which is accompanied by increased duration and tonic stress. This is the **intonation nucleus**. The syllable on which the nucleus falls is the **focus of information**. Or rather, it represents the peak, or highest point, of the unit which is informationally in focus. The correct placement of the nucleus is of great importance in English, since it is the principal means of communicating contrast and emphasis in the spoken language.

The whole of the clause constituent of which the nucleus is the peak comes within the scope of the focus, as is indicated in the example below:

> It is *absolutely inCREdible*

The syllable which is the nucleus of a tone group will be printed in capitals. The end of the tone unit is indicated by a thick vertical line. The first prominent syllable in a tone unit is the 'onset', which can be indicated, if desired, by a thin vertical line:

> (a) I'm|going to the ŞWIMming-pool.|
> (b) Is he|likely to WIN? |

Pitch prominence is also usually associated with **pitch movement**, corresponding to the different **tones** of intonation. A falling tone (Tone 1), marked by ˋ over the appropriate syllable, accompanies a statement, and a rising tone (Tone 2), marked by ˊ, accompanies a *yes/no* question as in examples (a) and (b) respectively above. The nucleus can also stay level (–) (Tone 3), indicating indecision, tentativeness, etc.; it can fall and then rise (ˇ), indicating reservation (Tone 4); or rise and then fall (ˆ) (Tone 5), the latter being used for strong, and especially contradictory assertions.

There is no one-to-one correspondence between the tone unit and any grammatical unit. A tone unit can be smaller or larger than a clause. If a speaker wishes to make his message highly informative and emphatic, he can even make each word become an information unit, with as many intonation nuclei as there are words as in:

> PÚT| |ȚHAT||KNȈFE| |DȎWN!|

and in short answers or questions a tone unit can consist of a single prominent syllable, as in YES! WHY? DON'T!

Tone units tend to coincide, however, with grammatical units such as the following:

an independent clause:	Have you|watered the PLANTS?|
a dependent clause:	Although it|wasn't your FAULT|
a main clause with an embedded clause:	I|thought it was time to GO|
coordinated Predicators and predications, especially with the same Subject:	He's|seen the pictures and LIKES them|
Nominal Group as Subject:	The |school-children outSIDE|are asking for a doNAtion |
Prepositional Group as Adjunct:	In the|late nineteen THIRties he went to HOLlywood |
Adverbial or Prepositional Group as Disjunct:	|HOPEfully|all will be WELL| At a | rough GUESS|I would say two WEEKS |
Group or clause as Conjunct:	|Better STILL |send a TELEgram| |What is MORE|it was a FAKE|

It must be emphasised, however, that speakers shorten or lengthen tone units in response to their communicative needs. This response is emotive rather than deliberate, and is therefore less likely to be controlled than, for instance, the choice of a lexical item. Variation in the length of tone units also depends on such factors as speed of utterance, familiarity with the content of the message and the consequent relative need to plan ahead, the syntactic structures and lexical items chosen, and even situational factors such as acoustic conditions, or personal factors such as self-confidence or embarrassment.

By treating embedded clauses as separate units the speaker divides the message up into smaller chunks, with the result that more items are emphasised. Speaker A in the following dialogue keeps her tone units rather short:

A ... I'm\|just exPLAINing\| \|how I acquired a SEWing-machine\|by \| foul MEANS\|by\|writing an inSTRUCTion booklet for one\|and saying I\|must HAVE this \|if I'm going to\|write the BOOKlet\| \|When I'd WRITten the booklet\|and it was all OVER\|I\|rang UP\|to the manager's SECretary\|and\|said 'Oh, I've FINished \|'NOW\|... would you come and get the maCHINE\|...

B mm

A and \| they said YES\|And a\|bout three months LATer \|I\|rang up aGAIN\|and\|this time spoke to the manager's WIFE\|who was sort of CO-MAnager and\|she said oh YES\|I'll I'll

B mm

A \|get somebody to come over and GET it\|And a\|THIRD time I \| phoned UP\|and I\|thought well to hell with THIS \|you KNOW\|and they didn't ever come and GET it\|so I've got this fabulous maCHINE\|which I ... in fact ...

B how nice

A in | order to ÙSE it|I 'have to read my inSTRÙCTion booklet|cos it's
   'sọ CÔMPlicated |

B MÂRvellous|

Adapted from Svartvik & Quirk, A Corpus of English Conversation.

29.2   Given and New information

The distribution of 'Given' and 'New' information is to a great extent the motivation for the information unit. Each information unit contains an obligatory 'New' element, which is associated with the nucleus of the tone unit, the focus of information. There can also be optional 'Given' elements of information, which are associated with the rest of the tone unit. Rather than a clear-cut distinction between 'Given' and 'New', however, there is a gradation or cline of givenness and newness. This is compatible with the notion of communicative dynamism, by which the message typically progresses from low to high information value (see 29.7).

The **Given element** is concerned with information that the speaker presents as recoverable by the hearer, either from what has been said before, the linguistic co-text, or because it can be taken as 'known' from the context of situation or the context of culture. The **New element** is concerned with whatever information the speaker presents as not recoverable by the hearer.

The following exchange illustrates the possible relationship of Given and New to information focus:

> A. What's new then?
> B. Well, Jim's bought *a new CAR*, Norma's getting *a diVORCE* and
> Jamie's got *CHICKen-pox*, but apart from that . . .

In each tone unit, the syllable in capitals represents the intonation nucleus; the syntactic unit in which the nucleus occurs (*a new CAR, a diVORCE, CHICKen-pox*) is in each case the focus of information; but in this discourse context, the whole of each tone unit represents the New element, with no Given.

The grammatical devices which enable us to identify information which is given in the previous discourse come under the headings of **ellipsis** and **substitution**.

29.3   Identifying Given information by ellipsis

By means of ellipsis we can leave out that part of the message which is known and in this way concentrate on the New information. As a result of ellipsis, the text is more cohesive.

Information may be known because it has already been said or because it is obvious from the social context. Ellipsis of the first type is textual, and of the second situational. In both types the elliptical part of the structure is recoverable.

29.3.1 Textual ellipsis

This occurs in different classes of unit, principally the Nominal Group and the clause.

Nominal ellipsis involves the replacement of the head element by a deictic such as *these, any, each, all, both, either, neither, none*, possessives such as *John's*, and numeratives such as *the first, the next three*. These are discussed in Modules 46 and 47, and are illustrated briefly here as follows:

> Ask Jane to bring some large envelopes, if there are *any*
> (envelopes).
> He was offered two rather boring jobs and accepted *neither* (job).
> I was unable to answer the first two questions, but *the last two*
> (questions) were easy enough.

In clausal ellipsis some part of the clause is not repeated. Frequently, an auxiliary replaces a whole Predicator, together with the remaining predication:

> I don't know if you*'re looking forward to the trip*; I know I *am* (looking
> forward to the trip).

The operator is not weak, even if, as in this case, it does not receive the tonic stress (which falls on *I*), and therefore contracted forms such as *I'm, we'll, she's*, etc., are not possible.

A change of tense or modality is indicated by a change of auxiliary, the Subject remaining the same. There may in addition be a change in polarity:

> I'm sure he *would help* you, if he *could*.
> I*'ve learned* quite a lot, though perhaps not as much as I *might have*
> */ should have*.
> Peter and James *are likely to vote in favour*, but John certainly *won't*.
> The porter *should have checked the parcels*, but he *didn't*.

In embedded and subordinate clauses, the non-finite part following a *WH*-element can be ellipted:

> He would build an aquarium if only he knew *how*.

Verbs which take *to*-infinitive clauses can retain the *to*, with the rest of the clause ellipted:

> He can *stay longer* if he likes. – No, he *doesn't want to*.
> Would you like to *join us for lunch*? – I'd *love to*.
> It seems that Japanese women drink more wine than they *used to*.

In all the examples seen so far, the ellipted part refers to what comes before; it is anaphoric. It is also possible to ellipt a part of the clause which is taken up later; this is cataphoric ellipsis, as in:

> Those who would like to (join us for lunch) can join us for lunch.

Subject and operator may be ellipted, with replacement of the Predicator and Complement as in:

> Are you writing up your diary? – No, composing a poem.

Whole clauses are ellipted in responses as in:

> I'm going to the supermarket. – When?

29.3.2   Situational ellipsis

In conversation and writing that imitates conversation other elements are ellipted, presumably because they can be recovered from the extra-linguistic context. In casual speech some of these are now institutionalised:

Can't hear a word.	(ellipsis of Subject *I*)
Sorry!	(ellipsis of Subject and *am*)
Back soon.	(ellipsis of Subject, modal and *be*)
Got the tickets?	(ellipsis of Subject and *have*)
See anything interesting?	(ellipsis of Subject and *do/did*)
Anyone at home?	(ellipsis of *Is there*)
You don't like it, you go home.	(ellipsis of *if*) (AmE)
Chances are he'll never find out.	(ellipsis of determiner *the*)

Situational ellipsis is also the organising factor in what is sometimes called 'block language', including notices, newspaper headlines, telegrams and other announcements:

> House to let.   To let.   For hire.   For sale.
> Vacancies.   Bed & Breakfast.   Assistant wanted.

29.4   Substitution

Substitution likewise avoids repetition of known information, with the difference that, while ellipsis leaves a structural slot empty, substitution replaces it by a 'filler' word. Consequently, with substitution the exact words which have been ellipted are not recoverable.

Nominal substitution makes use of *one/ones, this, that*, the pronoun *other*, and the item *the same* (see 45.6.2):

> She gobbled up first one cake, then *another (one)*, and put the *last one* in her pocket to eat later.
> 'I'll have a really cold Coke.' 'I'll have *the same*.'

Clausal substitution makes use of *do so* to replace predications which contain the feature of agency. *Do so* does not commonly substitute for verbs which are not agentive:

> I warned you that I would call the police, and I've *done so*. (= call the police)

*You can hire a self-drive car, but I wouldn't advise you to *do so*. (=
hire a self-drive car)
*Some people like mangoes, others don't *do so*. (= like mangoes)

Some speakers admit a form of *do* as a less formal substitute than *do so*,
especially after modals or perfect forms:

Will these letters reach Britain before Christmas? They *should do*.
I warned you that I would call the police and I *have done*.

Consequently, when the predication refers to a process of 'doing', speakers
often have the choice of three possible forms of ellipsis and substitution:

I warned you that I *would call the police* and I *have*.
                                    and I *have done*.
                                    and I've *done so*.

So substitutes for embedded *that*-clauses which express reports after such
verbs as *say, hope, expect, be afraid, suppose, think* and *believe*.

Is it going to rain tomorrow? The weather man says *so*.
Do you think we'll get there in time? I expect/hope *so*.

So can also be used as an alternative to an auxiliary + *too* to substitute
positively, just as *neither* alternates with auxiliary + *either* to substitute
negatively:

This hair-dryer makes an awful noise. *So does* mine. Mine *does too*.

I wouldn't like to live in this climate. *Neither/Nor* would we. We
wouldn't either.

It substitutes for a fact:

Peter is always late for dinner, and Ann hates *it*.
He says he is optimistic by nature; he certainly looks *it*.

29.5 Identifying Given information by definite deictics

Information may be 'Given' or 'known' because the person or thing is present
in the immediate social context or because it is so well known that it forms
part of the culture shared by speaker and hearer. In both cases the context is
said to be extra-linguistic, as illustrated by the following examples:

The girl over there is WÁVing to us.
Your car needs new TÝRES.
These plants need WÁTERing.
The King made a speech on the TÉLEvision last night.
The sun rises at FIVE TWÉNty a.m. tomorrow.
The bus service is a bit BÉTter these days.

Here, Given information is signalled by the following categories, which represent different types of deictics:

(a) The **definite determiner** indicates a referent identified in the situational context (*the girl over there*), or a referent that is definite and unique in the context of culture (*the King, the sun, the bus service*).

(b) **Personal pronouns** and **determinatives** refer to a person or thing actually present (*us, these plants*) or so well known that it can be taken as 'Given' (*your* car).

(c) **Temporal deictics** such as *these days, tomorrow, a.m., last night* can only be interpreted with reference to speech time.

29.6 Calling attention to something by means of focus

It may happen that a speaker calls attention by means of focus to something which is, strictly speaking, Given in the context such as *my nose, your glasses, the light*:

> My|NOSE is bleeding. |
> Your|HANDbag is open.|
> The |LIGHT has gone out.|

In languages with flexible word order, this type of message might be conveyed by Subject–Predicator inversion. In English, inversion is not possible in such cases and phonological means are used. It comes under the heading of 'marked focus', which is discussed in the following section.

29.7 Unmarked focus and marked focus

In normal, unemphatic discourse, it is customary to start our message from what we think our hearer knows and progress to what he does not know. In other words, the unmarked distribution, which follows the principle of communicative dynamism, starts with the Given and progresses towards the New. This is often called the principle of **end-focus**.

The neutral position for information focus is therefore towards the end of the information unit. In grammatical terms, this usually means that unmarked end-focus falls on the last lexical item in the clause, a clause being understood as an independent clause containing any embedded clauses. Items which occur after the nucleus can be taken as Given and are always unstressed, such as *these days* in *The bus service is a bit BETter these days*.

When the nucleus is placed on the last lexical item in the tone unit it keeps the options open as to how much of the preceding part contains New information. The whole clause may be New or just one part of it. In an example such as *They're building a flyover*, the New information could be as follows:

'a flyover'
'building a flyover'
'they're building a flyover'

The sentence *They're building a flyover* could therefore provide an answer to three different questions:

What are they building?	(They're building) a flyover. New
What are they doing?	(They're) building a flyover New
What's happening?	They're building a flyover. New

If the nucleus is placed on any other syllable than the tonic syllable of the last lexical item, the options are not kept open, and the New information is unequivocally identified. This is called **marked focus**. The purpose of marked focus is often that of contrasting or correcting something which had been said or implied in the previous discourse, or even in the situational context. The first of the following examples has unmarked focus, the rest contain marked focus on non-final items, for contrastive purposes:

My brother has sold his motorbike to the VÈT.
My brother has sold his MÒTORbike to the vet. (not his car)
My brother has SÒLD his motorbike to the vet. (not given it)
My BRÒTHer has sold his motorbike to the vet. (not my cousin)

Focus can fall on other, non-lexical items such as pronouns, determinatives, prepositions and auxiliaries, again with an implied contrast. The following examples illustrate some of the possibilities of marked focus:

|MY brother has sold his motorbike to the vet.|(not someone else's brother)
|What has YOUR brother done with HIS? |
|Put the dog's bowl UNder the table.|(not ON the table)
You'd|better take THIS umbrella| |not that BROKen one.|

When auxiliaries receive focus it is meanings such as those of polarity, tense or modality which are presented as New or important information:

(Wait for me!) I|AM waiting for you. |
(Don't forget to change the video!) I|HAVE changed it.|
(Why didn't you tell the truth?|I |DID tell the truth.|
|Pete promised to bring the CAmera,|but he|HAS'nt.|
He |MAY win the election|(but, personally, I doubt it).
I|MIGHT be able to get away by five|(but I'm not sure).
|That young man COULD be our next Prime MInister.|

29.8 Focus for emotive purposes

Apart from highlighting New information, contrasting and correcting, marked focus is used by speakers for a different purpose: that of conferring emotive stress on what is said. This is not contrastive. If we compare the unmarked focus of the examples on the left below with the marked focus of those on the right, we find in the latter an emotive emphasis, rather than simply emphasis on tense, polarity or modal meanings:

unmarked focus	marked focus
It's|HOT.| I'm|glad you've COME.| It'll be|nice to SEE you. | It |looks DIFficult.|	It|IS hot! | I|AM glad you've come.| It|WILL be nice to see you.| It|DOES look difficult. |

Some speakers convert a statement or a question into an exclamation by focusing the determiners *such* or *so*:

There's\|SUCH a lot to do! \|
It's\|SO hard to talk to him! \|

Lexical words which are already emotive can be heightened by giving them emotive stress:

I\|WISH he would leave her aLONE.\|
\|Don't you just LOVE the way she walks?\|
I\|aDORE raspberry icecream. \|
\|Isn't it just a DARling car!\|

Whether for emotive reasons or for the purpose of emphasising or contrasting, it can happen that a single tone group contains more than one nucleus. The fall–plus–rise or the rise–plus–fall tones often accompany focusing of this kind.

It was \| QUITE exciting REALLY.\|
I\|WISH you would asSERT yourself more.\|
You\|don't know how to REACT at FIRST.\|
I\|read the *GUARdian* in the WAITing-room.\|
She \| DID eventually turn UP.\|

Marked Theme often coincides with marked focus, and this combination provides a strong cohesive device in a text. In the passage on the Greek islands (page 230), the marked Themes *As a holiday destination* and *Thus far* also receive focus, and each sets up a strong point of departure for its clause.

MODULE 30
Syntactic strategies in assigning focus

Summary

1   From the point of view of communicative effect, the important positions in the
    clause are initial position and final position. We have seen that English has
    devices for reordering the clause so as to bring an element to initial position
    ('thematic fronting'). We shall now examine the device of **clefting**, which places
    the element to be focused near the front. Both of these devices provide **thematic
    prominence**.

2   Equally, the language provides resources for shifting information towards the end
    of the clause, where it acquires **tonic prominence**. The function of the *WH*-cleft is,
    in part, just this. Other postponing devices include the active–passive alternative,
    existential sentences and extraposition.

30.1   Clefting

By clefting a clause we divide it into a structure of two components, for the
purpose of identifying a particular element as New information. For instance,
from the basic clause *Mary phoned me last night* we can obtain *It was Mary
who phoned me last night; It was me that Mary phoned last night; It was last
night that Mary phoned me*. As can be seen from these examples, a cleft
sentence starts with the Subject pronoun *it*, which is an 'empty Theme',
followed by some form of *be* (*was*) and the 'real' Theme (*Mary, me, last
night*), also called the 'Predicated Theme'. There is no number or person
concord between *be* and the Predicated Theme, as there is in some languages, since in English the concord is with *it*:

> It is *your eyes* that you should be worrying about.
> It was *the children* who brought the snake into the house.

Of the two parts of the cleft sentence, one provides the New information,
the other the known or Given. Typically, the item following *be* receives the
main focus and so represents the New, as in B's reply to A in the example
below:

A. We flew to Paris on a Jumbo JET.	
B. No, it was to *ROME* that we main focus New Predicated Theme	'flew on a Jumbo. secondary focus Given

But the New information may fall in the second part, the relative construction, as in the following alternative reply to A's remark:

B. No, it was 'on a Jumbo secondary focus Given Predicated Theme	that we flew to *ROME*. main focus New

Choice between one or the other depends on the content of the previous discourse. For this exchange to be cohesive, the Given information will not receive main focus. If B's response had been *No. It was on a JUMBO that we flew to Rome*, cohesion would be broken and the response would be difficult to interpret.

Although they are complex as regards grammatical structure, cleft sentences are easy to understand, because they provide a natural way of emphasising the person, thing or circumstance that is being talked about. In the spoken language they provide an alternative to a clause containing marked focus. Compare below, for instance, B's first (marked focus) replies with his second (cleft):

A. I believe Tom gave you a LIFT this morning.
B. No, BILL gave me a lift this morning. (or No, BILL did)

B. No, it was BILL who gave me a lift this morning.

The saliency of BILL in the latter utterance would be doubly marked, both by position in the cleft and by tonic stress.

In the written language, the cleft sentence is especially useful since it helps the reader to identify correctly where the main focus lies, without the need for graphic aids such as underlining, italics or capitals.

The clause elements which are most usually given saliency by clefting are Subject, Direct Object and Prepositional Object, to emphasise persons or things, and Adjunct, to emphasise a circumstance. Attributes, represented by Subject and Object Complements, are not given saliency by this type of clefting; there are likewise restrictions on clefting Predicator and Indirect Object. The basic clause *Ann bought a jacket for me in Oslo* admits the following clefted items:

Subject: It was *Ann* who bought a jacket for me in Oslo.
Direct Object: It was *a jacket* that Ann bought for me in Oslo.

Prep. Object: It was *for me* that Ann bought a jacket in Oslo.
Adjunct: It was *in Oslo* that Ann bought a jacket for me.

In informal speech, the preposition of the Prepositional Object can be placed after the Direct Object, as in *It was me that Ann bought a jacket for in Oslo*. The Indirect Object cannot be clefted *It was me Ann bought a jacket in Oslo*.

Subordinate clauses of time, purpose, reason, means and condition (with *only if*) can also be given saliency after introductory *it + be*. Other types, such as those of concession and comparison, do not occur clefted:

Time: It's *when he's on guard duty* (that) she feels most
            anxious.
Purpose: It was *in order to pay for her son's training* (that)
            she took a job as a secretary.
Reason: Was it *on account of the rain* (that) the match was
            cancelled?
Means: It's *only by staying up all night* that we'll manage
            to fill in our income tax returns.
Condition: It's *only if John drives* that I'll go by car.

As can be seen from the above examples, the second part of the cleft is introduced by *who* or *that*, but not *which*. Relative adverbs such as *where*, *how*, and *when* can also be used to introduce the second clause in cleft sentences, as in *It was in London where Ann bought the jacket*. *Why* would not be used to introduce a cleft; we would not say *It was because he was hungry why he stole it*.

That is also commonly used instead of *who* even after a proper name as in *It was Mary that told me the news*. *That* or zero is always used instead of *whom* as in *It was Mary (that) I saw*. These differences mark off the clauses in cleft sentences from ordinary restrictive relative clauses. An example of clefting with zero relative pronoun is provided by the following extract from Somerset Maugham's short story *The Happy Couple*:

I don't know if I very much liked Landon. He was a member of a club I belonged to, and I had often sat next to him at lunch. He was a judge at the Old Bailey, and *it was through him* I was able to get a privileged seat in court when there was an interesting trial that I wanted to attend.

Somerset Maugham, in *The World Over, The Collected Stories*, vol. 2.

30.2   WH-cleft sentences

Another type of clefting is illustrated by the following examples, all of which contain a *WH*-word:

What he said was that the machine had broken down.
What he turned out to be was a scoundrel.
What we're all hoping for is a rise in salary.
Where we hope to live is in Padua.

Where we hope to live is in Padua.
When the rains come is in November.
How he got the contract was by bluffing.
Why he left was that he had a better offer.

These *WH*-cleft sentences, which are also called **pseudo-clefts** and **thematic equatives**, constitute a special type of identifying SPCs clause, in which one clause is identified by another clause. The Identifier is typically the one which receives the greater pitch prominence and so carries the focus of information, no matter in which order the clauses occur.

What he 'really likes	is SÙRFING.
Identified	Identifier

The order of the clauses can be reversed:

SÙRFING	is what he 'really likes.
Identifier	Identified

Both clauses of a *WH*-cleft can be *WH*-clauses:

What she always wants is what she can't have.
What I can't imagine is why he did it.

When the Identified is a person, a *WH*-word is hardly ever used, being replaced by *the one(s) who / that*:

*Who likes surfing is my brother.
The one who likes surfing is my brother.

Unlike clefts introduced by *it*, a *WH*-cleft can emphasise an action or event:

What he *did* was *rent a car*.
What we *should* all *do* is *hurry off home*.

The *WH*-cleft identifies a particular element exclusively. In this it differs from the basic clause structure and from the ordinary cleft. Compare:

We all need a holiday.   (neutral: no doubt we need other things too)
It's a holiday we all need.   (implied contrast with something else)
What we all need is a holiday.   (the only thing focused on)

This component of exclusiveness enables the *WH*-cleft to carry out three major functions in discourse, which are:

(a) to introduce a new Topic (by means of the non-*WH*-part) as in:

What we shall consider today is bilingual education.

(b) to refer retrospectively to a previous part of the discourse (the *WH*-part) as in:

We arrived home to find the place flooded; what had happened was that a pipe had burst.

(c) to correct a previous statement as in:

Do you mean that we should buy a caravan? – No, what I meant was that we should hire one.

WH-cleft clauses are always reversible, and this property distinguishes them from other *WH*-embedded clauses which are not cleft:

(a) *What he asked* is not clear. (ˑnot clear is what he asked)
(b) *What he asked* was very reasonable. (ˑvery reasonable was what he asked)
(c) His performance was *what the critics described as masterly.* (what the critics described as masterly was his performance)

In (a) the Subject is an interrogative clause, not a relative. In (b) *What he asked* is a nominal relative clause as Subject, but it is not the identified in an identifying clause. In (c), although the *WH*-clause is reversible, it is not a cleft since the meaning of the reversed clause is not the same as the meaning of the basic clause. Here, the *WH*-clause describes rather than identifies.

Finally, in cleft sentences of all types, it is important that the highlighted element should be pragmatically acceptable in the situational context. For instance, in reply to A's remark *I believe you came with Tom this morning*, it would be communicatively unreasonable to reply *Yes, it was a lift that he gave me* or *Yes, what he gave me was a lift*. This is because a clefted form involves the presupposition that, in this case, Tom gave me something; the ordinary cleft implies a contrast with something else, the *WH*-cleft identifies the new item explicitly. Cleft forms and the simple form are not, therefore, merely stylistic variants.

30.3 The active–passive alternative

Most situations which involve two or more participants can take one or other participant as the point of departure of the message. This is done in English by means of the active–passive choice:

The three Heads of State signed the treaty. (active voice)
The treaty was signed by the three Heads of State. (passive)

In the active construction, the point of departure, the Theme, coincides with Agent as Subject, while the Affected is in final position and receives end-focus:

The three Heads of State Agent Subject Theme	signed	the treaty Affected Direct Object ———— Rheme ———— Focused element

In the passive construction these correspondences are reversed. The Affected now provides the point of departure, coinciding with Subject, while the Agent takes up final position and receives end-focus:

The treaty Affected Subject Theme	was signed by the three	Heads of State Agent Adjunct ————————Rheme ———— ———— Focused element

A Recipient can become Subject in a passive clause with a ditransitive verb as in *The boy was given a beating by the older ones; The astronauts were sent a telegram by the President.*

As can be seen from these examples, the active–passive alternative permits the speaker to arrange his message so that the part presented as New information is placed in end-position, while the element considered to be Given is placed in initial position. He thus exploits to advantage the two main positions in the clause, the beginning and the end.

From the point of view of the textual organisation of what the speaker wants to say, it follows that any of three possibilities may condition the choice between active and passive:

1 The Agent is New information, so will be placed last.
2 The Agent is not New and is silenced. Some other element is New and is placed last.
3 An element which is not Agent is desired as Theme.

We shall now briefly describe the textual and pragmatic motivation for each of these possibilities.

30.3.1 Passives which focus on the Agent

If the Agent (or Instrument or Force participant) provides the New information, this is focused by using a passive clause with a *by*-phrase as in B's response below:

A. Where did you get that silver bangle?
B. It was given to me *by my BOY-friend.*
   Given   New

In speech, as we have seen, New information can be signalled by change of pitch and stress ('tonicity') on an element which is not in end-position, as in B's alternative response below:

> A. Where did you get that silver bangle?
> B. *My BOY-friend gave it to me.*
> New Given

Since tonicity is not available in writing to signal marked focus, end-focus – the unmarked pattern – tends to be sought in written English, since it unequivocally guides the reader towards the most informative part of the message. For this reason, the passive is particularly useful in writing when the Agent represents New information, as occurs at the end of this short extract:

> A chill had come to the pride and confidence of Rome. In 270–275 Rome, which had been an open and secure city, was fortified *by the Emperor Aurelian*.
>
> H. G. Wells, *A Short History of the World*.

or in an invented example:

> Besides having poor eyesight, he was afflicted *by gout.*

An additional motivation for the use of a passive with an Agent *by*-phrase occurs when the Agent is long. By putting it at the end we follow the principle of **end-weight** ('shortest first, longest last') as in the following examples, in which the Agent is 'weightier' than the passive Subject:

> The front seats were filled *by members of the families of the victims.*
> The goal was scored *by Barry Lee, the player with most goals to his credit this season.*

It is clear that **end-focus** and **end-weight** are closely linked. New participants introduced onto the scene of discourse need to be described and defined more fully than known ones. For this reason the Subject in a passive clause is often a short NG or a pronoun.

The Agent need not be a participant; it may be a fact, expressed by an extraposed *that*-clause (see 30.5.1), as in the following active and passive versions:

> *That he should be taken in by such a simple trick* amazed me.
> I was amazed *that he should be taken in by such a simple trick.*

30.3.2 Passives without an Agent

Using the passive without an Agent gives us the choice of *not* stating who carried out the action. This is an important factor, since in the active this information cannot be omitted. In many cases, however, an Agent is understood or implied. This is what distinguishes *he was killed* from *he died* or *he lost his life*, where there is no Agent implied.

There are several reasons for silencing the Agent:

(a) It is unknown although implied:

> He was killed in the Second World War.
> My car has been stolen.

(b) It has already been referred to, directly or indirectly:

> I've finished compiling *the catalogue* and *it* has been sent to the printers.
> When he read his thesis he gave a huge party. Everyone was invited.

(c) It may be understood from the context, but is considered irrelevant:

> Prisoners are allowed visitors only once a month.
> Well, in the end, I was awarded a full travel grant.

(d) The implied Agent is 'people' or 'one', the passive expressing a general statement:

> The national economy is believed to be improving.
> That solution has never been proposed.
> It is hoped that war can be avoided.

(e) The speaker wishes to highlight the Predicator:

> The documents have been thrown away.

(f) Either out of politeness, to avoid blaming someone else, or conversely, to avoid taking the blame oneself, the speaker wishes to mask the origin of the action:

> I'm afraid the Fax hasn't been sent.
> The students were not informed in time.

30.3.3   Focusing on some other element

When the Agent *by*-phrase is omitted in a passive clause, some other element necessarily receives end-focus. This may be a verb, an Adjunct, or a Complement.

For a verb to be focused, it must contain the main New information and the Agent must be dispensable.

> This *must be seen to be believed.*
> No details *were revealed.*
> Don't sit on that bench; it *has* just *been painted.*

The passive is a useful device for focusing on a verb, since in cleft sentences the verb cannot be focused.

A great number of passive clauses, however, have an Adjunct, a Complement or a Prepositional Object in the important end-position:

He was taken *to jail.*
Nothing has been heard of him *for months.*
The letters had been sent *unstamped.*
He was appointed *head of the research laboratory.*
Membership is limited *to the over 65s.*
The retiring chairman was presented *with a gold watch.*

Such instances as these are extremely common, yet the end-focus would have fallen on the same element if the verb had been active. Motivation for the passive in such cases does not lie, therefore, in the placing of end-focus, but rather in the choice of element to be Theme. The Theme may be Affected and Given information (*he, she, the letters*), a nuclear negative (*nothing*), a nominalisation (*membership*) or a Recipient (*the retiring chairman*).

30.3.4   Thematic progression and the active–passive choice

A number of reasons may exist for wanting to have Affected or Recipient as unmarked Theme instead of Agent. We have seen that, when no special emphasis or contrast is aimed at, there is a general tendency for Given information to coincide with the Theme and New information with some part of the Rheme.

Going beyond the clause, a consistent progression from Given to New information will help the reader's understanding of the text, and no doubt contribute to one's pleasure in reading as well. In this respect, the choice of Themes which are also Topics is important. Three basic types of thematic progression can be identified – simple, continuous and derived – and the active–passive choice is relevant to these.

(a) Simple linear progression
In this type a Topic introduced into the Rheme of one clause becomes the Theme of the following clause:

You can see the marks on the wall where *our pictures* used to hang.
These pictures have now all been sold.

This simple linear progression is achieved in the above example by passivising the second clause. The active form *We have now sold all these pictures* would have the Given part of the message *these pictures* in end-position which, in writing at least, might be undesirable.

(b) Continuous progression (topic continuity)
In this type, the same Theme, which is also Topic, is Subject of a series of clauses, and the New part of the message is placed at the end of each clause:

This castle is in a good state of preservation because *it* has been
taken over by the Fine Arts Council and (*it* has been) preserved as a
national monument of historic interest.

Here, the use of the passive (*it has been taken over*) rather than the active (*the Fine Arts Council has taken it over*), together with ellipsis of *it has been*, contributes to topic continuity. A change of Topic as Subject (*the Fine Arts Council*) is avoided, while at the same time the New material in the second and third clauses receives end-focus.

It is not necessarily the passive which maintains topic continuity. Compare the versions (b) and (c) in each of the following sets of clauses. In each case (c) rather than (b) preserves the continuity better with (a), whether by means of the passive (1 and 2) or the active (3):

1a) The Prime Minister stepped off the plane.
1b) Journalists immediately surrounded her.
1c) She was immediately surrounded by journalists.

2a) The Prime Minister stepped off the plane.
2b) The wind immediately buffeted her.
2c) She was immediately buffeted by the wind.

3a) The Prime Minister stepped off the plane.
3b) All the journalists were immediately greeted by her.
3c) She immediately greeted all the journalists.

(c) Derived Themes
A third type of progression has already been mentioned under the concept of **superordinate Topic**. According to this, the different Themes of a number of consecutive clauses all relate to some superordinate Topic or 'hypertheme', as is the case in the following extract about St. Vincent. Of the six independent clauses which make up this text, five start with a different Subject–Topic–Theme, all of which refer to different aspects of the island:

> *St. Vincent* is small; 18 miles long and 11 wide, mountainous and
> lush. [1] *Banana plantations* cling to steep volcanic hills [2] and *coconut
> palms* sway in the brisk trade winds which lash the Atlantic coast[3],
> stirring up its black sand. *The people* are warm, friendly and poor[4].
> *Unemployment* is somewhere between 30 and 40 per cent [5] but *few* go
> hungry in such lush surroundings[6].

> *Observer*, 25 November 1990.

In this instance of textual organisation the active was chosen for all clauses. Needless to say, speakers and writers rarely use any type consistently, but combine and mix them in what may become complex combinations. The following extract from a sports report on a cricket match illustrates derived Themes in which the use of the passive simultaneously achieves several ends: (a) it maintains continuity; (b) different elements receive end-focus; (c) the Agent is known and therefore silenced; (d) additional New information is placed at the end:

> Hanley *was* regularly *subjected to hits that would have stopped a
> locomotive* [1] and, though his spirit *was* never *subdued*[2], his influence

was curbed to an extent that will make his seventeenth appearance as captain of the national side one of his least satisfying memories[3].

Hugh McIllvanney in *Observer* Sport, 25 November 1990.

[1] focus on verb and Prepositional Object; [2] focus on verb; [3] focus on long Adjunct of extent.

30.4   Existential clauses

30.4.1   Types of existential clauses

Existential clauses are introduced by unstressed *there* followed by a verb and a Nominal Group, with *be* as the most common verb. The NG may contain a wide variety of qualifiers and/or be followed by an Adjunct of time or place:

> There are no fairies. (no qualifier)
> There was a storm last night. (Adjunct of time)
> There's a man *at the door*. (Adjunct of place)
> There are several pages *blank*. (AdjG)
> There are machines *which can extract cholesterol from the blood.*
> (finite clause qualifier)
> There's a dog *barking outside*. (non-finite *-ing* clause)
> There's plenty *to eat*. (non-finite infinitive clause)
> There was another plane *hijacked yesterday*. (non-finite *-en* clause)

Syntactically, the NG is the notional Subject which has been transferred to the position after the verb, a position usually occupied by a Complement. Unstressed *there* is brought in to fill Subject position, which must be filled in English. *There* fulfils most of the syntactic requirements for Subject (see 5.1.1), although it cannot be replaced by a pronoun, as normal Subjects can, nor does it exhibit the same concord relations as normal Subjects.

Semantically, an existential clause predicates the existence of something, or that something happened. This aspect of existentials is described in 18.2.

30.4.2   The textual function of existential clauses

In all these types of existential clauses the NG, which is the notional Subject, represents New information, and for this reason is usually indefinite. An indefinite Subject in initial position will violate the hearer's expectations regarding the development of the message, especially when followed by a verb low in communicative dynamism like *be*. The result is an unacceptable, or at least awkward, clause as in:

> *Fairies are not.
> ?A man is at the door.
> *Machines which can extract cholesterol from the blood are.
> *A storm was last night.
> *Plenty to eat is.

For these there is no acceptable alternative to the existential clause. These are 'basic' existentials.

For 'Existents' which have an *-ing* clause qualifier or an *-en* clause qualifier, there is an alternative structure without introductory *there*, based on the 'weightier' verb which figures in the non-finite clause. The existential is therefore derived from this:

> A dog is barking outside.
> Another plane was hijacked yesterday.

Similarly, with 'weightier' verbs of existing such as *remain, exist*, or of position such as *stand*, alternatives without *there* are also possible:

> Fairies don't exist.
> Many problems remain.
> A man stood at the door.

Unstressed *there* is, therefore, a presentative device whose function is to move the indefinite Subject to a position following the verb, where it also carries end-weight and end-focus.

Without a presentative device English does not admit Subject–verb inversion such as *Is a man at the door*, since such an inversion would lead the hearer to expect an interrogative structure. Unstressed *there*, therefore, also functions as a mood marker at Subject, indicating to the hearer that the clause is declarative.

In this respect, unstressed *there* is similar to those locative and directional Complements which, when fronted, bring about S–v inversion as in *Up went the umbrellas; down came the rain* (see 28.5.1)

Relational clauses of the circumstantial type (17.2) such as *A new hotel is at the end of the road* are reversible, and when the Carrier (see 17.1) is indefinite and specific and represents New information they are most frequently reversed, leaving the locative Complement to act as a presentative device:

> At the end of the road is a new hotel.

Because of their similarity to existential clauses, *there* can be added, if wished, to the reversed relational clause:

> At the end of the road there is a new hotel.

Indefinite mass or generic plural Carriers are not common, whether reversed or not, and such entities are presented by means of existential clauses with obligatory presentative *there*. Compare:

> *In the back of the car is room for more.
> In the back of the car there's room for more.

> *Little good football was in last night's match.
> There was little good football in last night's match.

> *In India are tigers.
> In India there are tigers.

As a presentative device, unstressed *there* is only minimally referential, in contrast with the stressed deictic adverb *there* which has the meaning 'in that place'. This difference is shown by the possibility of their both occurring in the same clause as in *There's a telephone kiosk over there*. Both types of *there* occur in the following extract from a story, which relates how the shipwrecked sailors in an open boat try to attract the attention of a man on the shore:

'Oh, say, *there* [1] isn't any life-saving station *there*. [2] That's just a winter-resort hotel omnibus that has brought over some of the boarders to see us drown.'
'What's that idiot with the coat mean? What's he signaling, anyhow?'
'It looks as if he were trying to tell us to go north. *There* [3] must be a life-saving station up *there*.' [4]
'Well, if he'd just signal us to try the surf again, or to go to sea and wait, or go north or go south or go to hell, *there* [5] would be some reason to it. But look at him! He just stands *there* [6] and keeps his coat revolving like a wheel. The ass!'
'*There* [7] come more people.'
'Now *there*'s [8] quite a mob. Look! Isn't that a boat?'
'Where? Oh, I see where you mean. No, that's no boat.'

Stephen Crane, *The open boat* in *Cuentos americanos*.

[1] unstressed; [2] stressed; [3] unstressed; [4] stressed; [5] unstressed; [6] stressed; [7] stressed; [8] unstressed.

30.4.3   The verb in existential structures

With *be* as the existential verb all tense, aspect and modality combinations are common, with the exception of the progressive, since the dynamic quality of the progressive is incompatible with the stative meaning of *be*:

There *have been* heavy snowfalls in the north.
There *is bound to be* another opportunity.
Are there *likely to be* many people at the meeting?
There *can't have been* more than two or three hundred spectators in the stadium.
*There *is being* a lot of work lately.

A few other verbs such as *seem*, *appear*, *arise*, *rise*, *emerge* and *loom* regularly occur with presentative *there*, and with the dynamic verbs of direction such as *emerge* even the progressive is possible:

There *is emerging* in Parliament a movement of protest against the Prime Minister's attitude to Europe.
There *rose* into the sky a plume of smoke.

In formal and literary English, verbs of appearing and emerging lend themselves naturally to the presentation of New information. However, existence or appearance should not be taken in a literal sense, but rather in relation to the discourse: it is appearance on the scene of discourse that counts. Because of this, many intransitive verbs of movement such as *run* can be used with presentative *there* as in the example *There ran across the lawn a large black dog*. Even a verb like *disappear* may, in an appropriate context, function as a presentative, as in the first sentence of the novel by H. P. Lovecraft, *The Strange Case of Charles Dexter Ward*:

> From an asylum for the insane near Providence, Rhode Island, *there* recently *disappeared* an exceedingly singular person.

From this it becomes clear that the notion 'presenting on the scene' as the discourse function of *there*-structures is more appropriate than that of expressing 'existence'.

30.4.4 *There*-structures as states of affairs

A *there*-structure is commonly used in English to express events, happenings and states of affairs which are brought on to the scene of discourse. Frequently, the noun is a nominalisation of a process of any kind (see 18.2):

> There was *a fight*.
> There was *a strange whistling sound*.
> There has been *unprecedented industrial expansion*.
> There was *a sudden feeling of panic*.
> There is still *bribery*, there is still *corruption*. No doubt there always will be.

An *-en* clause as qualifier has a passive meaning:

> There were hundreds of people *killed*.
> There is much *to be said* on both sides.

Both this type and the *there*-constructions with nominalisations have the effect of silencing the Agent of the action. We do not know who panicked, who bribes whom, who fought whom. The nominalised process is the only important part of the message.

An *-ing* clause as qualifier in a *there*-clause can present an entity in action, or even a state:

> There are hundreds of people *clamouring for food*.
> There is a box *containing dynamite* in the corner.

Adjectives which express a temporary state of the Existent can occur:

> There was plenty of food *available*.
> There were several passengers *ill*.
> There are not many shops *open* at this hour.

Since the important factor is that of presentation on the scene of discourse, even definite NGs which represent referents that are in a sense 'known' can be introduced into the discourse by a *there*-construction:

There's *your mother* to be considered.
There's still *the washing* to be done.

This is how a woman described her portable sauna bath acquired from a mail-order company:

> There's *an oval mat you put down on the floor*, [1] then *there's the box which holds the heating element*, [2] with a wooden seat on it – I put a towel on top, otherwise it gets too hot – then *there are the sides which are soft and which you zip up*. [3] It all packs away neatly afterwards.

> *The Independent Magazine*, 24 November 1990.

[1] indefinite NG; [2] definite NG; [3] definite NG.

30.5   Extraposition

When a long Subject clause is shifted to the end of the superordinate clause and is replaced by *it* in initial Subject position, this is called **extraposition**. Both finite and non-finite Subject clauses can be extraposed and, in fact, are in many cases more common in English than the canonical form, since they satisfy the principles of end-weight and end-focus.

30.5.1   Extraposed finite Subject clauses

The most typical kind of extraposed clause is the finite *that*-clause:

> It's a nuisance *that banks here are closed on Saturdays.*
> It surprises no-one *that people demonstrate against war.*

Initial Subject *that*-clauses sound marked in English unless preceded by *the fact* (5.1.3(b)), and lead the hearer to expect an emphatic contrast, as in:

> *That hijacking should continue* is lamentable; *that hostages should be taken and even killed* is to be condemned by all.

Finite *WH*-clauses are also commonly extraposed:

> It's unbelievable *how much that child eats.*
> It's horrifying *what they are proposing to do.*

30.5.2   Extraposed non-finite Subject clauses

To-infinitive clauses are more regularly extraposed than *-ing* clauses. With *to*-infinitive clauses, the focus typically occurs in the postponed clause:

> It would be unwise *to interFERE.*
> It's difficult *to think of a convincing exCUSE.*

There is no constraint on *-ing* clauses occurring in initial Subject position. When they are postponed they are usually short and do not necessarily carry

the main focus. For this reason they give the impression of being additions to
the main clause, rather than extraposed Subjects:

> It's been a PLEAsure, *having you with us.*
> It was NÌCE *seeing all the family again.*

Unlike some languages, English does not normally allow extraposed NGs:
It was amazing, his insolence is not possible. (As a postposed Theme, with
the appropriate intonation, it is possible to have *it was amazing, his
insolence.*) A few extraposed NGs occur and these contain expressions of
quantity, manner or extent:

> It's unbelievable *the lengths some people are prepared to go.*
> It wearied us *the way the flight kept being delayed.*
> It surprises me *the amount of work he can get through.*

Obligatory extraposition after *seem, appear, happen, chance, look as if,*
after the expressions *it's high time, it's a pity, it's no use,* and the passive of
say, hope and *intend* is illustrated in 5.1.3d.

Certain constructions do not admit extraposition. One of these is the *WH*-
cleft with a clause as Subject, as in *What we should do next is the main
problem.* (*It is the main problem what we should do next.*) Another is
multiple embedding, as in *That he failed his driving test the seventh time
demonstrates that he lacks confidence.* Here the first *that*-clause cannot be
extraposed over the second (*It demonstrates that he lacks confidence that
he failed his driving test for the seventh time*).

30.5.3   Extraposition of Object clauses

Occasionally anticipatory *it* stands for an extraposed Direct Object (6.1.3d).
This is usually obligatory with finite clauses and *to*-infinitive non-finite
clauses:

> We find *it* strange *that the lawyers have not appealed.*
> I consider *it* essential *to know the conditions of payment.*

30.5.4   Type 'Bill is difficult to live with'

A person or thing mentioned in the extraposed clause, as Direct Object or
even as part of the Adjunct, can sometimes be brought forward to stand as
Theme:

> To cook rice is easy – It is easy to cook rice – Rice is easy to cook.
>
> To live with Bill is difficult – It is difficult to live with Bill – Bill is
> difficult to live with.
>
> To teach her is a pleasure – It is a pleasure to teach her – She is a
> pleasure to teach.

The possibility appears to be fairly restricted, however, and cannot be freely extended to other nouns and adjectives.

30.6 Postponement

30.6 Postponement by discontinuous units

Qualifiers in NGs and AdjGs can be postponed. This enables us to avoid the awkwardness of having long heavy units to the left of the main verb. Finite and non-finite clauses, PrepGs and appositive reflexive pronouns all occur:

> *The time* will come *when no-one will write by hand any more.*
> *A man* appeared *carrying the puppy.*
> *You* did it *yourself.*
> *How willing* is he *to undergo a major operation*?
> *Everyone* arrived on time *except the prima donna.*

Clauses of comparison and result can also be made discontinuous:

> *More people* are buying a second car *than used to twenty years ago.*
> She was *so thankful* when her wallet was found *that she almost cried.*

30.6.2 Postponement with ditransitive verbs

We saw in 10.2 that certain ditransitive verbs such as *give, deny, grant, lend, owe, show* among others allow two alternative structures:

> We've given the children bicycles. (SPOiOd)
> We've given bicycles to the children. (SPOdOprep)

This alternative allows us to place end-focus either on the Recipient ('the children') or on the other participant, without using the passive. This way of adjusting the clause to get the end-focus where we want it is especially useful when one of the participants is Given information, often realised by a pronoun; this will normally be placed in medial position:

> We've given *them* bicycles.
> We've given *them* to the children.

These structures must be distinguished from SPOdCp structures in which the Predicator Complement is realised by a *to*-PrepG. Compare:

> I've sent the telegram to the club's treasurer. (SPOdOprep)
> I've sent the telegram to his home. (SPOdCp)

If we wish to combine destination and Recipient in the same clause, we replace the preposition *to* of the Adjunct by *at*:

> I've sent the telegram to the club's treasurer at his home.

No other alternative is possible.

Two-complement verbs which do not admit postponement of a Recipient are explained in 10.3.

TASKS ON CHAPTER 6
Organising the message: Thematic and information structures of the clause

Module 28

1 *Discussion:*

   1) Which is the semantic choice associated with the Theme–Rheme structure? How is Theme realised in English?

   2) To what different kinds of category do Subject, Theme and Topic each belong? Can they coincide in one realisation? Can they be realised by different elements?

   3) Discuss the possible hierarchisation of Topics suggested in 28.2. Name some of the devices for introducing new Topics. Can 'old' Topics be reactivated?

   4) Discuss the notion of 'marked Theme'. Which types of marked Themes produce Subject–Predicator inversion? Which do not produce inversion?

   5) How many different types of Theme could, in principle, together make up an instance of 'multiple Theme'. Which of these types do not exhaust the thematic potential of a clause, and why?

2 †*Underline the Theme in each of the following examples and say whether it is marked or unmarked. If marked, say which clause constituent has been thematised (fronted) in each case*:

   1) Paul telephoned an antique dealer in Brussels.

   2) Abruptly they were cut off.

   3) Is he a friend of yours?

   4) High quality consumer goods they specialise in.

   5) One of the most popular artists of this century David Hockney must be.

   6) Meet me at eight at the Café de Paris.

   7) In the American soft-drink industry, plastic bottles are extensively used.

   8) Celebrating her victory today is downhill ski champion Marina Kiehl of West Germany.

   9) For months, all had been quiet in the Holy Wars.

   10) Absolutely dumbfounded he left me.

   11) Another thing you're likely to come across there, and that's a certain lack of humour.

12) How did the police find out?
13) Never again will I fly with that airline.
14) Ludicrous his expression was.
15) Crazy I call it.

3 †*Say which clause constituent could appropriately be thematised in the second clause of each pair*:
1) He asked me for paper, glue, sellotape and clips. I bought him all of these.
2) I swim thirty lengths a day for fun. You call it fun!
3) He told us the history of the place. We already knew most of it.
4) I can't remember what post Biggins occupies in the Government. He is Government spokesman.
5) You'll never guess how I met Jones. No. He was riding on a donkey at the seaside.

4 †*Turn to the extract from* **The Boarding House** *on page 225 and carry out the following tasks*:
1) Of the syntactic devices listed in 28.2 as possible introducers of new Topics, which is used by the author to introduce Mrs Mooney's husband as a new Topic?
2) If you have a copy of Joyce's story, read it, then close the book and, from memory, make a summary of what Mr and Mrs Mooney each did immediately after they separated. Check for topic continuity.
3) Now introduce as new Topics (a) the young men at the boarding house, and (b) Mrs Mooney's daughter Polly, in any way you feel is appropriate.
4) If you haven't a copy of the story, carry out Tasks (2) and (3) as free composition exercises.

5 †*Read again the extract from* **Miguel Street** *on page 226 and try to work out possible answers to the following questions*:
1) What clause constituent coincides with each numbered Topic?
2) Does Topic coincide with Theme?
3) The title *Miguel Street* could be considered to be the superordinate Topic of the whole book. What superordinate Topic would you suggest for this extract?
4) Would you consider the numbered Topics to be basic-level Topics or subordinate Topics?
5) Which Topic or Topics are maintained by topic continuity?

6 †*Read the travel advertisement again on page 230 and continue as follows*:
1) Identify the clausal Topic and the Subject of each clause and see how far they coincide with the italicised clausal Theme.
2) Discuss the notion of 'old Topic' and 'new Topic' in relation to this text.
3) Note the dexterity with which Antipaxos is introduced. The Theme includes the means of getting there, with the implication that Gaios, which has not been previously mentioned, must be on Paxos.

Imagine that the travel agency now wants to include a third island in its offer. You have to write a few lines in continuation of the present advertisement. Compare your version with those of your friends.

7   *Each of the clauses below contains a representational element as Theme. Add as many discourse Themes as you can from the selections given in 28.9 (conjunctions, vocatives, conjunctive, relational, modal and continuative Themes), to make up suitable multiple Themes:*

e.g. Those flowers are quite dead.
But honestly, Mary, judging by the look of them, those flowers are quite dead.

1)   Violence in schools is an issue requiring urgent attention.
2)   The current state of the National Health Service makes me shudder.
3)   Bad manners among motorists mean danger to others.
4)   The recent deal between the two companies is a marriage of mutual interests.
5)   What would you like for your birthday?

8   [†]*Read the passage below and then answer the questions that follow:*

Little 'green' enzymes take the sheen out of new jeans

For even the only remotely fashionable, there is nothing so naff as wearing a pair of brand new jeans, bright blue, pressed and pristine[1].
Indeed, so heinous is this crime of fashion that manufacturers spend millions of pounds pre-washing their denim with pumice to produce a faded, worn look worthy of any aspiring James Dean[2].
But stone-washing is expensive and energy-consuming [3] – which is why a newly-developed enzyme, which replaces pumice, is transforming denim manufacture[4]. Developed by Nova Nordisk, the Danish chemical giant, the enzyme – cellulase – produces a pair of jeans that looks as if the wearer had been on the road for months and had not, in reality, bought them that morning in the high street[5].
A cupful of cellulase produces the same effect as pumice 100 times its weight[6]. As a result, Levi, Wrangler and other denim-makers are turning to cellulase to 'bio-stonewash' their jeans[7].

Observer Sunday, 25 November 1990.

1)   Underline the single Theme element or the multiple Theme elements of each numbered clause.
2)   Identify the syntactic category of each thematic element.
3)   Which of the thematic elements has a connective function?
4)   Discuss the function within the text that each thematic element fulfils. Make your commentary as full as possible.

Module 29

1 *Discussion:*

1) How is information broken up and presented by the speaker so that the hearer is guided to a proper understanding of the message?

2) In what way are ellipsis and substitution associated with Given information? In what respects does ellipsis differ from substitution?

3) What is the neutral or 'unmarked' position for information focus? In what way is this related to the principles of 'communicative dynamism' and 'end-focus'? What is 'marked focus' and what does it unequivocally identify?

2 In the extract from a conversation below, B tells how Susie looks for the money left by fairies under her pillow in exchange for her tooth, but the parents have forgotten to leave the money. The following symbols used for the main prosodic features are as follows:

| | tone unit boundary
| first prominent syllable of the tone unit ('onset')
\ falling tone
/ rising tone
— level tone
^ rising–falling tone
˅ falling–rising tone
\./ fall–plus–rise (on separate syllables)
ı the next syllable is stressed
↑ the next syllable is stressed and also steps up in pitch
" extra strong stress

. ⎫
– ⎬ pauses, from brief to long
–– ⎪
––– ⎭

Capitals are used to indicate the nucleus

B |ÀNYway|–|Susie SĀID|– that . there were|no such 'things as FÁIRies|ÉLVES|this 'that and the ↑ Other|– WÈLL|. the|night she ↑ PÙT|her 'tooth 'under the PÍLlow|we for|got to 'put the ↑ MÒney there|and take it a↑WAỲ|we for|got all a↑BOÙT it|(A laughs) so she got |ÙP in the MÓRning|– my|TOÒTH'S all 'gone|and there's|no MÓney||Dave said well 'there you ↑ ÀRE you SÉE||YÓÙ said|you didn't be|LIÈVE in FÁIRies|so|how can you ex'pect the ↑ fairies to come and ↑ SÈE you if|– –|ÔH|but I |DO believe in FÁIRies| (D laughs) you|KNÓW|I|really DÒ|(A laughs) so|Dave said well – ↑ try ágain toNÌGHT|– –

Adapted from D. Crystal and D. Davy, *Advanced Conversational English*.

Practise reading this text aloud two or three times. Then tape your own reading of it and compare it with the reading of a native speaker.

3   †*Read the following exchange aloud, trying to identify the intonation nucleus of each tone unit:*

    A. What did she say?
    B. I don't know. I didn't hear her.
    A. Didn't you hear anything?
    B. No, I've told you, I was in the other room.
    A. I don't think you care about Leslie.
    B. I do care.
    A. Why don't you talk to her then?
    B. I'm always talking to her.

1)   Write in capitals the syllable which contains the nucleus of each tone unit.
2)   Which of the units have unmarked focus and which have marked focus? Justify your identification of each in terms of Given and New information, including emphasis and contrastive polarity.

4   †*The following extract is from the play by Giles Cooper, **Everything in the Garden**. In pairs, reproduce it from memory and then act it out, marking the intonation nuclei clearly. Next, look at the discussion question below:*

Jenny:	Do you want an egg?
Bernard:	Are you having one?
Jenny:	Do you want one?
Bernard:	If you're having one, I will, otherwise no.
Jenny:	You are a lazy devil!
Bernard:	No. It's just that I don't want an egg enough to start everything going towards cooking it, but if you were going to do one for yourself, well, I'd want it enough for that.
Jenny:	I don't think I'll have one.
Bernard:	I'll do you one if you like.
Jenny:	You do want one?
Bernard:	No, I don't. I'll just do you one. You ought to eat.

What do you consider to be the principal communicative purposes of the marked focuses in this text?

5   †*In pairs, read the following text aloud while your friend marks the intonation nuclei. Then change over.*

Well, I was one of those lucky people who didn't inherit his place at Harvard. I'm certainly not a child of the American aristocracy, I'm the child of immigrants, so ... of the second generation, and I was lucky enough to do well in high school and Harvard looks for unknown talents to bring to the fore because your being chosen by Harvard is a kind of anointment, an initiation, it's almost a passport to success, it really is, and so the very moment of my selection at Harvard meant I was very likely to become a success at something. This is not bragging, this is just saying I was very blessed by being touched by the finger of Harvard.

Erich Segal in the magazine, *Speak up.*

6   †*Complete each of the sentences below using elliptical or substitution forms. Some have more than one possible form*:
   1)   If you can't do it, I very much doubt whether I . . . .
   2)   I told you I'd given it back and I . . . .
   3)   They arranged to come and put in a new water-heater, but they
        . . . . yet.
   4)   Peter asked the girls if they would like to go for a sail and they said
        Yes, they . . . .
   5)   Ed has the ambition to do some script-writing, but he really doesn't
        know . . . . . .
   6)   You look rather tired. – Yes, and I feel . . . . .
   7)   He told me to turn down the next side-street and I . . . . . .
   8)   And it was a one-way street? – Yes, I'm afraid . . . .
   9)   Does it matter what colour it is? – No, I suppose . . . .
                                    – No, I don't suppose . . . .
10 10)   Were you at the farewell dinner yesterday? – Who . . . . !

Module 30
1   *Discussion*:
   1)   What are the structural differences between a cleft sentence ('Predicated Theme') and a *WH*-cleft ('pseudo-cleft' or 'thematic equative')? In what way is the information they presuppose different?
   2)   What communicative purpose is common to the active–passive choice, *there*-clauses, extraposition and postponement?
   3)   What communicative purpose is common to fronting and clefting? To which of these purposes does the *WH*-cleft conform?

2   †*Change the information structure of each of the following clauses into one cleft and, when acceptable, two WH-cleft structures*:
   1)   Experts are working on the recycling of plastic.
   2)   Smoking can cause fatal diseases.
   3)   This kind of garment is best reserved for the evening.
   4)   She bought the children some icecream.
   5)   We are counting on your help to put up the tents.
   6)   John was not on the train that crashed, because he didn't reach the station in time.
   7)   Last thing at night I unwind by reading and listening to the radio.
   8)   The computer industry is fighting against viruses.
   9)   At 12.30 p.m. I nip down to Marks and Spencer's in Oxford Street for a sandwich.
   10)   Shortly after I got home I realised I had lost my purse.

3   †*The following extract is the opening paragraph of a short story, **Lord Mountdrago, by Somerset Maugham**:*

> *Dr. Audlin was a psycho-analyst.* [1] *He had adopted the profession by accident and practised it with misgiving.* [2] *When the war broke out he had not been long qualified and was getting experience at various hospitals;* [3] *he offered his services to the authorities and after a time was sent out to France.* [4] *It was then he discovered his singular gift.* [5]

> *The World Over, The Collected Stories, vol. 2.*

1)   Identify the single cleft sentence contained in the paragraph and say which element is focused.
2)   Try rewriting each sentence of the original paragraph as a cleft and as a *WH*-cleft. Which sound pragmatically possible, and which do not? Why?

4   †*Decide whether option (b) or option (c) provides better topic continuity with (a). Combine your choices by means of a conjunction to produce a sentence.*
1   (a)   They stepped out of the coach.
(b)   The owner of the hotel greeted them.
(c)   They were greeted by the owner of the hotel.
2   (a)   Edith chose a piece of chocolate gateau.
(b)   Someone took it to her table together with an iced drink.
(c)   It was taken to her table together with an iced drink.
3   (a)   James had planned to take the plane to Vancouver.
(b)   An air-controllers' strike delayed it.
(c)   It was delayed by an air-controllers' strike.
4   (a)   She stood on the solitary beach.
(b)   She let the wind ruffle her hair.
(c)   The wind was allowed to ruffle her hair.
5   (a)   My flat-mate wanted to trace an old friend.
(b)   He had changed his address.
(c)   His address had been changed.

5   †(i)   *Write below each of the following sentences the corresponding passive form, if passivisation is possible:*
1)   They founded the first kindergarten in the United States in 1856 in Watertown, Wisconsin.

   ....

2)   That legacy has traditionally benefitted Milwaukee residents.

   ....

3)   People have taken four-year-old kindergarten as much for granted as summer breezes off Lake Michigan.

   ....

   ....

4) Now there is a severe budget crunch. Milwaukee Public School officials have proposed the unthinkable: eliminating four-year-old kindergarten.

....
....
....

5) 'Are we to raise property taxes or are we to keep four-year-old kindergarten? These are the choices we may have to make,' said a school board member.

....
....
....

6) Gov. O'Keefe's new budget has produced the dilemma. The budget reduces the proportion of the state's share of education costs and imposes cost controls on local district spending.

....
....
....
....

(ii) *You now have a number of active–passive alternatives. Note that (2) does not passivise, but that the verb 'benefit' allows different postponed alternatives.*

Now make the sentences into a text, choosing the active or passive alternative in each case, according to which you find more cohesive. Add conjunctions and conjunctive expressions wherever these help to clarify the logical connections.

6   *Read the extract below from Raymond Chandler's* **The Long Goodbye**, *noting the use of presentative* there:

There are blondes and blondes and it is almost a joke nowadays. All blondes have their points, except perhaps the metallic ones who are as blonde as a Zulu under the bleach and as to disposition as soft as a sidewalk. There is the small cute blonde who cheeps and twitters, and the big statuesque blonde who straight-arms you with an ice-blue glare. There is the blonde who gives you the up-from-under look and smells lovely and shimmers and hangs on your arm and is always very, very tired when you take her home. She makes that helpless gesture and has that god-damned headache and you would like to slug her except that you are glad you found out about the headache before you invested too much time and money and hope in her. Because the headache will always be there, a weapon that never wears out and is as deadly as the bravo's rapier or Lucrezia's poison vial.

   There is the soft and willing and alcoholic blonde who doesn't care what she wears as long as it's mink or where she goes as long as it is the Starlight Roof and there is plenty of dry champagne. There is the small perky blonde who is a little pale and wants to pay her own way and is full of sunshine and common sense and knows judo from the ground up and can toss a truck driver over her shoulder without missing more than one sentence out of the editorial in the 'Saturday Review'. There is the pale, pale blonde with anaemia of some non-fatal but incurable type. She is very languid and very shadowy and she speaks softly out of nowhere and you can't lay a finger on her because in the first place you don't want to and in the second place she is reading 'The Waste Land' or Dante in the original, or Kafka or Kierkegaard or studying Provençal. She adores music and when the New York Philharmonic is playing she can tell you which one of the six bass viols came in a quarter of a beat too late. I hear Toscanini can also. That makes two of them.

And lastly there is the gorgeous show piece who will outlast three kingpin racketeers and then marry a couple of millionaires at a million a head and end up with a pale rose villa at Cap d'Antibes, an Alfa Romeo town car complete with pilot and co-pilot, and a stable of shop-worn aristocrats, all of whom she will treat with the affectionate absentmindedness of an elderly duke saying goodnight to his butler.

The dream across the way was none of these, not even of that kind of world. She was unclassifiable.

1) The blondes described by Chandler are obviously stereotypes, seen from an ironical male perspective, of the early days of Hollywood, made familiar by American films even more than by novels.

Analyse Chandler's use of existential clauses for the presentation of these types. Use this check-list to help you:
(a) Basic existentials or derived existentials?
(b) Indefinite NGs or definite NGs? If definite, what meaning is conveyed here? (see also generic NGs 46.8)
(c) Does the NG which denotes the Existent have a qualifier, or a following expression of place or time, an -*ing* clause, a participial clause or no extension at all? Which type of extension does the author use most? What kind of information is contained in these long qualifiers? (see also Module 49)
(d) Is topic continuity maintained between one blonde and the next?

2) Write up your own account of certain other stereotypes; for instance, men as Chandler might see them; or the jet-set stereotypes of the present decade; or the current stereotypes among your own age group, etc. . . .

Use unstressed *there* to introduce each type, and make use of relative clause or PrepG extensions of the NG, and any others that you consider appropriate. Check that you maintain topic continuity before going on to a further type.

7

Expanding and projecting the message:

The clause complex

MODULE 31
Clause combining

Summary

1 The term 'sentence' is widely used to refer to quite different types of unit: grammatically, it is the highest unit and consists of one independent clause or two or more related clauses; orthographically and rhetorically, it is that unit which starts with a capital letter and comes between full stops.

2 'Clause complex' is the term we shall use to refer to a unit consisting of two or more clauses related either paratactically or hypotactically, but not by embedding. An embedded clause functions as a constituent of another, superordinate clause. A conjoined clause or a dependent clause do not function as a constituent of another clause.

3 A dependent clause may relate to a combination of clauses, rather than to one single clause.

4 Clause complexes are the linguistic expressions of complex situations, and reflect the cognitive organisation of our experience into what is more salient and what is less salient.

31.1   Clause complex and sentence

If the single independent clause can be thought of as the linguistic expression of a situation, the combination of several clauses together to form a larger unit can be thought of as the linguistic expression of a complex situation.

This larger unit, the highest grammatical unit on the scale of rank, is traditionally called the **sentence**. Three possible types of sentence are usually distinguished:

(a) the simple sentence, consisting of one independent clause, as in *John bought the tickets*.

(b) the compound sentence, consisting of two independent clauses, linked in a relationship of coordination, as in *John bought the tickets and Mary parked the car*.

(c) the complex sentence, consisting of one independent clause and one dependent clause, linked in a relationship of subordination, as in *While John bought the tickets, Mary parked the car*.

This simple structural outline is accompanied in traditional grammar by an equally simple semantic labelling, consisting mainly in the characterisation of main clauses as 'complete thoughts' and subordinate clauses as nominal or adverbial clauses, the latter of time, condition, manner, concession, etc.

Such a view may be sufficient for the analysis of uncontextualised examples which contain few clauses. But in natural discourse the combinations may be both more syntactically complex and less semantically explicit; the result is that such a simplified analysis tells us very little about how the grammatical structures are functioning in a larger stretch of language and what their semantic contribution is to the whole. There is an even more serious objection to the structural outline expressed above. It can happen that a dependent clause relates, not to a single main clause, but to a whole combination of clauses. This can be shown by expanding our original example:

> While Mary was parking the car, John bought the tickets, then started
> back across the road without looking to right or left and, just as he
> was reaching the other side, he was knocked down by a bus and
> badly injured.

Here the subordinate clause *while Mary was parking the car* relates not simply to *John bought the tickets* but to the whole clause complex which constitutes the sentence.

We shall say, then, that a **clause complex** can constitute a sentence, and that any number of clauses may be involved.

Without rejecting the use of the term 'sentence', since this would involve practical difficulties, given its long-standing use in English grammar, we shall usually prefer the term 'clause complex'. There is yet another reason for this.

31.2   The sentence as an orthographical or rhetorical unit

The structural criteria outlined in the preceding section are not the only criteria which have intervened in the traditional and widely accepted concept (or concepts) of 'sentence'. For most native speakers of English a sentence is something that starts with a capital letter and comes between full stops. It is, therefore, a category associated primarily with the written language and can be described as an orthographical and rhetorical unit. The following recollection of childhood, taken from the radio script *Holiday Memory* by Dylan Thomas, will serve to illustrate the wide variety of units that from a rhetorical–orthographical point of view constitute a sentence:

> August Bank Holiday. A tune on an ice-cream cornet. A slap of sea and a tickle of sand. A fanfare of sunshades opening. A wince and whinny of bathers dancing into deceptive water. A tuck of dresses. A rolling of trousers. A compromise of paddlers. A sunburn of girls and a lark of boys. A silent hullaballoo of balloons.
>
> I remember the sea telling lies in a shell held to my ear for a whole harmonious, hollow minute by a small wet girl in an enormous bathing-suit marked 'Corporation Property'.
>
> I remember sharing the last of my moist buns with a boy and a lion. Tawny and savage, with cruel nails and capacious mouth, the little boy tore and devoured. Wild as seed-cake, ferocious as a hearth-rug, the depressed and verminous lion nibbled like a mouse at his half a bun, and hiccupped in the sad dusk of his cage.
>
> Dylan Thomas, *Quite Early One Morning*.

If we take the clause complex as the highest structural unit, we shall be able to say that, structurally, the sentence is composed of clauses, but that rhetorically and orthographically it need not be. This will enable us to handle many present-day texts such as the following advertisement for facsimile copying:

> With Fax the possibilities are endless.[1]
>
> It can send a document anywhere in the States within minutes.[2]
>
> Including drawings, diagrams – even musical notes.[3]
>
> Exactly as it's written.[4]
>
> Fax.[5] Worth making a song and dance about.[6]
>
> *Newsweek*, 8 May 1989.

[1]independent clause; [2] independent clause; [3] PrepG or non-finite clause; [4] dependent finite clause; [5] NG; [6] AdjG.

The graphic devices used in this text reinforce the presentation of each rhetorical unit as if it were independent, as would be done equally clearly if the text were read aloud.

In spontaneous speech it is often difficult to determine where one sentence ends and another begins. As a structural unit the clause is easier to identify, because of its own internal structure, as finite, non-finite or abbreviated. When a spontaneous conversation is transcribed into writing, there could be disagreement as to where the sentence divisions lie. The following dialogue on the subject of American English, adapted from *A Corpus of English Conversation*, will serve to illustrate this problem. Pauses, from brief to long, are indicated by a dot (.), a dash and dot (–.) and one to three dashes (–), (––), (–––). The tone-unit boundaries are marked by |.

> b I mean American you know really has different tenses and different prepositions it's getting to that point if you look at it at all close .
> A m .
> b things like in back of matching in front of . Yes | That's right | and do you have | instead of have you got | – – that sort of thing |. Gilbert and I are going to write an oeuvre one of these days when we get down to it – –
> A m |
> b there's a lot more in grammar than people notice people always notice the lexis .
> A Yes | – – –
> b lots has been done about that – – but I mean you can only get so far and so much fun out of pavement sidewalk etcetera –
> A m |
> b it's the grammar where the fun is
> A Yes it's the | grammar which is interesting| – – – one finds one I I I find myself| adopting phrases| having this kind of chameleon approach to
> b oh yes . so do I

Jan Svartvik & Randolph Quirk (eds), *A Corpus of English Conversation*.

31.3 Embedding and dependency

In previous chapters (see Chapters 1, 2 and 3) we have encountered the phenomenon of **embedding**, by which one clause functions as the constituent of another clause. In clause structure this occurs at Subject, Object or Complement functions as in:

> *Why he resigned* was never discovered. (clause embedded at S)
> She explained *that the machine was out of order.* (clause embedded at Od)
> The watchman asked *what we were doing inside the grounds.* (clause embedded at Od)
> He has become *what he always wanted to be.* (clause embedded at Cs)
> I left the documents *where you told me to.* (clause embedded at Co)

These embedded clauses function as immediate constituents of what is sometimes called the **superordinate clause** (the clause of which a constituent is realised by another clause). Semantically, we can think of embedded clauses as representing situations which are participants in a superordinate situation.

There are other situations, however, which are ancillary to, rather than participative in, a larger situation. Returning to our example in 31.1 above, we can see that *while Mary was parking the car* is syntactically and semantically ancillary to the series of clauses which express the main events. There is no single superordinate clause in which it could be considered as embedded. This is an argument against considering such clauses as Adjuncts in sentences. Instead, we shall prefer to say that clauses such as *while Mary was parking the car* are dependent (in this case upon the rest of the clause complex) but not embedded.

This dependent but non-embedded status is even more clear in the case of many finite and non-finite dependent clauses as in:

He has a summer job with a travel agency, *guiding parties of tourists.*
It's my new timetable – *to help me finish my thesis.*
They advised me to emigrate – *which is the last thing I'd do.*

By postulating the **clause complex** as the grammatical unit above the clause, we may be able to describe both the structural relations holding between the clauses and the logico-semantic relations which unite them. The latter are essential if we are to say anything of interest about the grammatical structure of a text, since a mere enumeration of main and dependent elements reveals at best only the degree of complexity at sentence level in a text, but not the semantic relations holding between the component clauses. We shall also find, in both spoken and written texts, a great deal of **dependency** between clauses of a rather inexplicit kind, which cannot always be satisfactorily accounted for by **constituency**. We feel that the clause complex as a grammatical category applicable to discourse can be defined and delimited more specifically than can the sentence, enabling us to determine in each case the degree of correspondence between this and the rhetorical–orthographic sentence of written English. Lastly, as the linguistic expression of a situation, the clause complex reflects the ways in which the mind organises experience in order to present certain parts as more salient and other parts as less salient.

MODULE 32
Types of relationship between clauses

Summary

1 The clauses which comprise a clause complex are related in two different ways: syntactically and logico-semantically.

2 Syntactic relationships are either paratactic, holding between clauses of equal status, or hypotactic, holding between clauses of unequal status.

3 The logico-semantic relations are grouped into two main types: expansion, by which one clause expands the meaning of another in some way; and projection, by which one clause is projected through another via a verb of saying or thinking.

32.1 Syntactic relationships and logico-semantic relationships

There are two kinds of relationship between clauses in a clause complex:

(a) the syntactic relationship of interdependency. Clauses are related to each other basically in one of two ways: either the relationship is one of **equivalence**, both or all clauses having the same syntactic status, or the relationship is one of **non-equivalence**, the clauses having a different status. A relationship of equivalence is called a **paratactic** relationship. A relationship of non-equivalence is called a **hypotactic** relationship.

(b) the logico-semantic relations, which are very varied, since they represent the way the speaker or writer sees the connections to be made between one clause and another. Such connections do not simply link clauses within a clause complex, however, but also clauses within a paragraph and paragraphs within a text. Connection is, therefore, very much a discourse phenomenon. Here, our principal aim is to describe the logico-semantic relations that can be expressed between clauses, together with the various connectors used for this purpose.

These logico-semantic relations can be grouped together under the two main headings of **expansion**, by which a nuclear situation is expanded by means of other situations, and **projection**, by which a situation is 'projected' through a verb of saying or thinking.

Both types of relationship, the syntactic and the logico-semantic, are present in all clause complexes. We shall expect to find, therefore, such combinations as paratactic / hypotactic expansion and paratact / hypotactic projection.

We shall briefly summarise these two types of relationship, and then proceed to examine them in greater detail.

32.2   Syntactic relationships between clauses

32.2.1   Equality relationships: parataxis

When clauses are linked in a relationship of equality, we say that the relationship is paratactic. **Parataxis** is the relationship between units of equal status. We explain in other chapters of this book that all classes of units can be joined paratactically (e.g. *milk and sugar*, *black and white*, *take it or leave it*). Here we shall be concerned with the linking of clauses. Paratactic linking is often treated as equivalent to coordination, as in the examples above; more exactly, coordination is one type of parataxis, others being juxtaposition and linking by conjunctions such as *so* and *yet*.

Semantically, as paratactically linked clauses have equal status, the information presented in one clause is as important as that presented in the other or others. If we say, for instance, *Tom is an astrophysicist and works at the CERN in Geneva* or *Tom is an astrophysicist; he works at the CERN in Geneva* there is no hierarchisation of the information. One part is not presented as being dependent upon the other. This does not mean that paratactic clauses (whether coordinated or juxtaposed) are necessarily reversible, as is sometimes maintained. Syntactic and pragmatic factors frequently intervene to make reversibility impossible. Three such factors are the following:

(a) if the second clause contains a term which refers anaphorically to an antecedent in the first clause, as does *it* and *them* in the following examples:

> Hundreds of Parisians have seen the exhibition and many hundreds of visitors are expected to see *it* in the next few weeks.

> I have bought some beautiful tapestries and I think you will like *them*.

(b) if the second clause contains an item which makes it cohesive with the first, as does *as a result* in the following example:

> There was no moon that night and, *as a result*, they took the wrong turning.

(c) if the order of the clauses is of pragmatic significance. For instance, the following two combinations suggest different pragmatic interpretations:

> He made a fortune and bought an oil-tanker.
> He bought an oil-tanker and made a fortune.

It must be remembered, also, that the second or last of a series of paratactically related clauses will be the most prominent in terms of information focus, while the first represents the point of departure of the message. These also are pragmatic considerations, which belong to the information-processing strategies described in Chapter 6.

Syntactically, we shall call the primary clause in a paratactic sequence the **initiating** clause, and the secondary or further clauses the **continuing** clause(s).

32.2.2   Dependency relationships: hypotaxis

When units of unequal status are related, we say that the relationship is one of **hypotaxis**. In hypotactically related clauses, one clause is syntactically and semantically subordinated to another or to a series of clauses. Semantically, the information contained in the subordinate clause is often presented as backgrounded or presupposed in relation to the information contained in the superordinate clause. In the following example, *since you have come after all* is presented as Given or known information (and this, incidentally, is part of the meaning of *since*, but not of *for* as a Conjunct):

> *Since you have come after all*, why don't you sit down?
> **For you have come after all*, why don't you sit down?

Syntactically, the clearest cases of hypotaxis are those signalled by subordinating conjunctions such as *because*, *although*, if; but just as with parataxis, the nature of the relationship is not always marked explicitly. We shall keep the usual term **main** for the independent (primary) clause in a hypotactic clause complex and call the subordinate (secondary) clause the **dependent**.

32.3   The logico-semantic relationships of expansion and projection

Traditional grammar has no terms for the overall logico-semantic relationships holding between clauses, although as we shall see, the individual types are traditionally established. Following the classification proposed by M. A. K. Halliday we shall say that:

(i) the secondary clause **expands** the primary clause by (a) **elaborating**, (b) **extending**, (c) **enhancing** it, either paratactically or hypotactically. These combinations are shown below:

Expansion	(i) Paratactic	(ii) Hypotactic
(a) elaboration	Tom kept quiet; he said nothing.	Tom kept quiet, which was unusual.
(b) extension	Tom kept quiet, but Ed spoke out.	Tom kept quiet, whereas Ed spoke out.
(c) enhancement	Tom was afraid, so he kept quiet.	Tom kept quiet, because he was afraid.

In clause combining by elaboration, one clause expands another by elaborating on it in greater detail, by exemplifying it or by clarifying it in other words. In clause combining by extension one clause expands another by adding something new, giving an alternative or an exception. In clause combining by enhancement, clauses of time, place, condition, purpose, cause or concession expand the primary clause by contributing these circumstantial features.

(ii) the secondary clause is **projected** through the primary clause as (a) a locution, via a verb of saying, or (b) an idea, via a verb of thinking, as is shown below:

Projection	(i) Paratactic	(ii) Hypotactic
(a) locution	Tom said: 'I'll say nothing.'	Tom said he would say nothing.
(b) idea	Tom thought: 'I'll say nothing.'	Tom thought he would say nothing.

In the following sections we shall explain and exemplify further the syntactic and semantic characteristics which result from the combination of these two systems.

MODULE 33
Elaborating the message

Summary

1 Elaborating clauses are clauses which clarify or comment on a primary clause. They can be finite or non-finite and in a paratactic or hypotactic relationship with the primary clause. Conjunctive expressions can be used to connect the clauses.

2 Parataxis combining with elaboration gives clauses in apposition, the second clause specifying, exemplifying or clarifying the first. Hypotaxis combining with elaboration gives non-defining relative clauses which add further information to the whole previous clause or to part of it.

3 As in all clause combining, the semantic relationships are typically much less explicit when realised by non-finite clauses.

33.1   Apposition (paratactic elaboration)

The 'clarifying' meaning of elaboration together with the 'equality' relation-ship of parataxis yields two clauses of equal status in apposition. The second elaborates the first as a whole, or one or more of its constituents. The symmetry of this type of clause complex is reflected in punctuation by the use of the semi-colon, colon or dash:

> It's like going out with a child; she stops dead and refuses to go any further.
> You must make up a better excuse: no-one will believe that.
> He had been drinking very hard – only I knew how hard.

When clauses are simply juxtaposed in this way, a strictly syntactic view would interpret them as separate, independent units. Viewing them as a possible complex is to give priority to discourse and semantic criteria. We feel that the punctuation conventions illustrated above reinforce this in-terpretation. It may be difficult in the spoken language, however, to decide whether such combinations of clauses can be considered to constitute a clause complex, that is to say a single unit, or whether they are to be interpreted as two separate clauses. Two factors can be taken as criterial: first, if intonation and rhythm are maintained, and second, if the semantic link of elaboration is present, then the clauses can be treated as a complex. Ultimately, it is the choice of the speaker or writer to present the relationships as he sees them. The choice of juxtaposed clauses serves to highlight what is felt to be their semantic connection.

33.1.1   Elaborating connectors

Instead of relying on an implicit semantic connection between the juxta-posed clauses, the connection can be made explicit by the use of Conjuncts which provide cohesive, not structural linking. The meanings and the con-nectors which express them are as follows:

(a) **expositive**: the second clause restates the content of the first from another point of view, often making it more specific. Conjunctive expressions include:

> *in other words*;   *or rather*;   *that is (to say)*;
> *specifically*;   *namely*;   *as follows*;   *i.e.* (in writing)

> This picture is not an original; in other words, it's a forgery.
> We became tourists; or rather, we became tramps.
> There is still another topic to be discussed; namely, the re-allocation of space in this building.
> We need someone to fix this machine, that is to say, we need a mechanic.
> Alcoholic drinks are sold only to adults, i.e. people over 18.
> Several countries have signed the agreement; specifically, all the EC countries have done so.

(b) **exemplifying**: the second clause develops the content of the first by means of an example. Conjuncts include:

for example; *for instance*

There are lots of things you might do – for example, you might learn to play a musical instrument.
You can't count on the trains being punctual here; for instance, the 10.55 left at 11.15 yesterday.

(c) **clarifying**: the second clause clarifies the meaning of the first by explanatory comment. The cohesive Conjuncts are:

in fact; indeed; actually

I was completely ignorant of women; in fact, I knew none except my own sisters.
I didn't mind their questions – indeed, I was glad to be able to answer them.
We should get through this job fairly soon; actually, there is very little left to do.

33.2   Non-restrictive relative clauses (hypotactic elaboration)

The combination of dependency and elaboration gives the category known in traditional grammar as **non-defining** or **non-restrictive relative clauses**. The dependent clause can be either finite or non-finite.

33.2.1   Finite clauses

In both spoken and written English, non-restrictive relative clauses differ from the restrictive or defining type in both meaning and expression.

With regard to meaning, non-restrictive relative clauses do not define subsets, as does the restrictive type. Their function is to add a further specification of something that is already presented as specific. Compare the restrictive relative clause of (a) below with the non-restrictive one of (b):

(a) I met his brother who lives in New York. (= one of his brothers, the one who lives in New York)
(b) I met his only brother, who lives in New York. ('his only brother' is already fully specific.)

A further difference is that in the non-restrictive type the specific antecedent is not necessarily a noun, but may be the whole clause, or any one or more of its constituents. These may be illustrated as follows:

(a) **whole clause as antecedent**. The relative pronoun is *which*:

They decided not to go, *which turned out to be a mistake*.

(b) **nominal group as antecedent**. The relative pronoun is *who, whose,* preposition + *whom* or *which* (rarely *that*):

> She had been to the hairdresser, *who had done a remarkable job.*
> Glasses of champagne were poured by Mr. Blake, *whose birthday it was.*
> And the captain, *for whom everyone had the greatest respect,* made a speech.
> She made a pot of very strong tea, *which revived them considerably.*

When the Nominal Group is in non-final position in the main clause, the dependent clause is often enclosed:

> Plans for the new airport, *which will cope with ten times the present air traffic,* are now under way.

(c) **an expression of time or place as antecedent**. The relative adverbs *where* and *when* are used:

> It should be ready by July, *when the holidays start.*
> We drove down to Valencia, *where some of the best oranges come from.*

In some cases, the non-restrictive relative clause introduces a completely new element, rather than characterising the noun which is its antecedent:

> We drove down to Valencia, *where Nadine and Margaret were waiting for us.*
> I gave the ticket to my son, *who promptly lost it.*
> The door may be locked, *in which case go round to the back.*
> His chief absorptions were social work and philosophy, *where he found himself at variance with the prevailing fashion.*

With regard to expression, non-restrictive relative clauses are clearly distinguished from the restrictive type in both speech and writing. In spoken English, a restrictive relative clause belongs, with its antecedent, to one tone group (see 29.1); this in turn is reflected in written English by the lack of punctuation between the antecedent and the relative clause:

> The children ran across *the field which / that had just been sown.*

A non-restrictive relative clause, on the other hand, forms a separate tone group which is linked to the main clause by tone concord; that is to say, they are spoken on the same tone. This tone concord is a signal of apposition between units. In the written language it is reflected by punctuation signals, usually commas, but sometimes a dash, especially when the antecedent is a whole clause:

> The children ran across the newly-sown field – *which displeased the farmer.*

33.2.2　Non-finite and abbreviated clauses

The non-finite verb forms *-ing*, *to*-infinitive and *-en* participle are used non-restrictively to express the same meanings as the finite forms:

> At that moment Charles appeared in the hall, *propelling himself in a wheelchair.*
> I've brought down the table from upstairs, *to put the television set on.*
> The mountains were invisible, *enveloped in a thick mist.*

The non-finite form may have its own explicit Subject:

> That was the last time I saw him, *his face all covered in bandages.*
> The soldiers filled the coaches, *the younger ones eating sandwiches and chocolate.*

Abbreviated clauses can also be used with an elaborating function:

> *Anxious but hopeful*, relatives awaited news of their loved ones.
> *Full of magic and imagination*, his new film is sure to be a box-office success.

Some of the elaborating types of clause combining occur in the following extract from an anthropologist's account of life with the Dowayos, a people of Cameroon:

> Faced with the impossibility of eating off the land[1], I decided to keep my own chickens. This, also, was not a success. Some I bought, some were given to me[2]. Dowayo chickens, on the whole, are scrawny, wretched things; eating them is rather like eating an Airfix model of a Tiger Moth[3]. They responded to treatment, however. I fed them on rice and oatmeal, which Dowayos who never feed them at all found a huge extravagance[4]. One day, they began to lay. I had fantasies of being able to eat an egg every day. As I sat in my hut, gloating over my first day's haul, my assistant appeared in the doorway, an expression of bland self-satisfaction on his face[5]. 'Patron,' he exclaimed, 'I just noticed the chickens were laying eggs so I killed them before they lost all their strength!'
>
> Nigel Barley, *The Innocent Anthropologist.*

[1] non-finite *-en* clause used non-restrictively in hypotactic elaboration; [2] two finite clauses in paratactic elaboration; [3] finite SPCs clause (with non-finite *-ing* clause embedded at Subject) in apposition to finite initiating clause; [4] hypotactic elaborating clause (non-restrictive relative clause) whose antecedent is the whole primary clause; a further hypotactic elaborating clause introduced by *who* has 'Dowayos' as antecedent; [5] abbreviated clause in hypotactic elaborating relationship to the previous finite clause.

MODULE 34
Extending the message

Summary

1 Extension has an additive meaning. The secondary clause extends the meaning of the primary clause by such meanings as addition, variation, alternation, explanation and exception. Cohesive connectors can be used to reinforce these meanings.

2 Coordination is paratactic extension.

3 Hypotactic extension expresses the same meanings, but in a dependency relationship. Non-finite clauses can be introduced by the conjunctive prepositions *besides*, *without* and *instead of*.

34.1 Coordination between clauses (paratactic extension)

The combination of parataxis and extension gives **coordination** between clauses. It is expressed by the coordinating conjunctions *and*, *or*, *nor* and *but*. These are often accompanied by cohesive expressions such as *too*, *in addition*, *moreover*, *also*, *on the other hand*. The meanings expressed by coordination and reinforced by the appropriate Conjuncts are illustrated in the following sections.

34.1.1 Addition

Two situations are represented as adjoined in a relationship of equality that is positive, negative or adversative:

> He doesn't like bacon, *and also* he's better without it. (positive)
> I have no intention of going, *nor in fact* did I ever promise to. (negative)
> It's an extremely simple device, *but actually* it's very effective. (adversative)

Additive Conjuncts include *also*, *furthermore*, *in addition*, *besides*. **Adversative Conjuncts** include *in fact*, *actually*, *as a matter of fact*.

34.1.2   Variation

This is replacive coordination. The secondary clause is presented as replacing the primary clause:

> He didn't stay even an hour, *but instead* returned to London on the next train.
> Peaches are marvellous just now, *only* they are very expensive.

Variation Conjuncts include *instead* and *only*.

34.1.3   Alternation

Alternative coordination is expressed by *or*, the second clause presenting an alternative to the first. The meaning can be reinforced by adding *else* (*or else*) and by preceding the first unit by *either* (*either . . . or*):

> You should (*either*) accept his offer *or* (*else*) never see him again.
> *Either* we give the tickets back *or* (*else*) we drop everything and go.

Cohesive conjuncts associated with this meaning include *alternatively*, *conversely*, *on the other hand*:

> There are several medium-priced hotels: *alternatively*, self-catering facilities are available.
> You can add the wine to the water; *conversely*, you can add the water to the wine.

34.1.4   Explanation

The secondary clause comments on or explains the primary clause:

> There's one thing you must realise *and that is that I'm leaving*.

The following passage shows the use that can be made of apposition and coordination to present a situation as being composed of a number of related, though independent situations. It is noticeable that the author makes no use of explicit Conjuncts to establish connections; the semantic connection between the clauses is conveyed by means of punctuation signals:

> There were few left in the mess now of the batch of volunteers who trained together at the outbreak of war; one way or another they were nearly all gone[1] – some had been invalided out[1a], some promoted to other battalions[1b], some had volunteered for special service[1c], one had got himself killed on the field firing range[1d], one had been court-martialled[1e] – and their places were taken by conscripts[2]; the wireless played incessantly in the ante-room nowadays[3] and much beer was drunk before dinner[4]; it was not as it had been[5].
>
> Evelyn Waugh, *Brideshead Revisited*.

[1]elaboration (clarifying apposition); [1a–e] elaboration (exemplifying apposition); [2] extension (adversative coordination); [3] elaboration (expository apposition); [4] extension (additive coordination); [5] elaboration (expositive apposition).

34.2   Contrastive dependency

Meanings similar to those of addition, replacement and alternation can also be expressed by the combination of hypotaxis and extension, but with the secondary clauses dependent, either finite or non-finite.

34.2.1   Finite clauses

The conjunctions *whereas* and *while* introduce finite dependent clauses which **contrast** in some way with the primary clause, especially when there is also some point of similarity between the two, as in:

> Jane already speaks two foreign languages, *whereas her brother hasn't yet learned any.*
> *While most people enjoy an occasional holiday,* not many are able to indulge to the extent that my neighbour does.

Whereas is more formal than *while*. For the temporal meaning of *while*, see 35.2.2).

Except that, *but that* and *but for the fact that* have a **subtractive** meaning:

> I'd take you to the station, *except that the car is being repaired.*
> It would have been a disaster, *but for the fact that everyone helped to save the situation.*

The forms containing Subject–Predicator inversion (*were it not for the fact that . . ., had it not been for the fact that . . .*) can also be used, but are more formal and are stylistically marked forms to express hypothetical situations.

The hypotactic form which expresses the meaning of **alternation** is *if . . . not*, and corresponds to *either . . . or* in paratactic combinations:

> If your purse isn't here, you must have left it somewhere.
> (= Either your purse is here, or you must have left it somewhere)

34.2.2   Non-finite clauses

Non-finite dependent clauses which extend the meaning of the primary clause by contributing additive, replacive, adversative and subtractive meanings are usually *-ing* clauses, often introduced by such prepositions as *besides*, *instead of*, *without*, *other than*, functioning conjunctively:

> *Besides breaking her leg,* she caught a bad throat infection.
> (additive)

Instead of turning down that side road, you should have kept straight
on. (replacive)
He has embarked on a huge project, *without realising what is
involved.* (adversative)
You won't get any information from him *other than by paying him.*
(subtractive)

Without a conjunctive preposition, the form is the same as that of the
elaborating non-finite *-ing* clauses (see 33.2.2). Since non-finite dependent
clauses are by nature less explicit than finite ones, it may be difficult in some
cases to determine the exact semantic nuance expressed. Conversion to the
corresponding finite form may prove helpful in identifying hypotactic types:

They drove on, *wondering how long their petrol would last.* (additive)
(= and wondered)
He barely stayed to express his condolences, *returning to London on
the next train.* (replacive) (= instead, he returned . . .)
Hardly realising the danger, she stumbled towards the exit.
(adversative) (= she stumbled . . . but she didn't realise the danger)

Non-finite *-ing* forms also frequently express enhancing, that is circumstantial meanings, especially when they are not introduced by a conjunctive
preposition, as in the following example:

Hardly feeling the cold, she removed her coat and gloves.

This means 'because she hardly felt the cold, she removed her coat and
gloves', and is causal in meaning. (See section 35.2.2 b for further examples
of circumstantial meanings expressed by non-finite *-ing* clauses.)

MODULE 35
Enhancing the message

Summary

1   An enhancing clause is a secondary clause which adds to the meaning of the
primary clause by reference to some circumstantial feature: time, place, manner,
condition, purpose, cause, concession, etc.

2   Enhancing clauses can be in a paratactic or a hypotactic relationship to the
primary clause.

> 3 A great variety of conjunctions and conjunctive expressions are available to express circumstantial meanings. Non-finite verb forms are also used, of which the *to*-infinitive is the most explicit.

35.1 Associated circumstantials (paratactic enhancement)

The combination of parataxis and circumstantial meaning gives a kind of coordination or juxtaposition reinforced by a circumstantial element. The secondary clause is introduced by one of the following:

(a) the conjunctions *then*, *so*, *for*, *but*, *yet*, *still*;
(b) a conjunctive combination formed by *and* followed by another item: *and then*, *and here*, *and this*, *and so*, *and yet*;
(c) *and* together with a cohesive, not structural, conjunction such as *at that time*, *soon afterwards*, *till then*, *in that case*.

Some of the circumstantial meanings expressed by these combinations are listed below:

time: *now*; *then*

> The lights have gone out; *now we won't be able to do any more today*.
> They spread the cloth on the grass *and then began unpacking the picnic things*.

place: *and there*

> She turned the corner, *and there stood Robin waiting for her*.

manner: (a) **means** *(and) (in) that way*

> Put labels on everything, *and (in) that way you'll know what you've got in the freezer*.

(b) **comparison**:   *(and) similarly*; *in the same way*; *likewise*;
                      and so ...

> The Secretary of the Association should be informed of any change of address; *similarly*, the Treasurer should be notified of changes regarding the payment of subscriptions.

> The face of a small baby is different from that of every other baby; *in the same way*, the development of each child is different.

> He likes music, *and so does she*.

cause / effect: *and so*

> We had left the tickets at home, *and so there was nothing to do but go back for them*.

effect / cause: *for* (rather formal)

> We left in silence, *for there was little we could say*.

condition (positive): *and then*; *(and) in that case*

> You might have an accident, *and in that case* who would rescue you?

condition (negative): *otherwise*; *or else*

> Replace everything carefully in the drawers; *otherwise something will get mislaid.*

concession: *still*; *yet*; *though*

> My age is against me; *still, there's no harm in trying.*
> He criticises his colleagues, *yet relies on them for support.*
> He'll probably say no, *though it's worth trying.*

consequence: *consequently*; *as a result*

> He had not taken the precaution of being vaccinated; *consequently, he got malaria*

35.2 Dependent circumstantials (hypotactic enhancement)

Dependency combined with the circumstantial meanings associated with enhancement gives the 'adverbial clauses' of time, place, condition, purpose, concession, reason and manner of traditional grammar. They are either finite or non-finite.

35.2.1 Finite clauses

Finite dependent clauses are introduced by subordinating conjunctions which serve to indicate the dependent status of the clause together with its circumstantial meaning. Formally, subordinating conjunctions can be grouped as follows:

(a) **simple conjunctions**: *when, whenever, where, wherever, because, if, unless, until, while, as*

(b) **conjunctive groups**: *as if, as though, even if, even though, even when, soon after, no sooner*

(c) **complex conjunctions**: there are three subclasses:

(i) derived from verbs, usually from present or past participles, but occasionally from imperatives. All have optional *that*: *provided (that), granted (that), considering (that), seeing (that), suppose (that), supposing (that), say*

(ii) containing a noun: *in case, in the event that, to the extent that, in spite of the fact that, the day, the way*

(iii) adverbial   *so/as long as, as soon as, so/as far as,*
                                much as, now (that)

Some of these conjunctions and the meanings they convey in finite
dependent clauses are illustrated below:

As (time)	The crowd roared *as* the ball went into the net.
As (manner)	*As* I said in my last letter, I'll be away in August.
As (reason)	*As* he is an only child, he gets a great deal of attention.
As (comparison)	Sylvia treated him, *as* she treated everyone, with a certain disdain.
Because	We came back, *because* the car broke down.
Before (time)	He got away *before* they could stop him. (implied condition) Get out *before* I call the police.
Since (time)	I haven't seen him *since* we were at school together.
Since (reason)	*Since* he won't answer the telephone, we'd better leave a note.
While (time)	The burglar broke into the house *while* they were asleep.
While (concession)	*While* I admire his tenacity, I deplore his ruthlessness.
When	*When* he saw me, he waved.
Now that	*Now that* the days are longer, it's worth driving up to the Lakes.
Soon after	*Soon after* the war ended, the men returned.
The day	I met him for the first time *the day* we went on the staff excursion.
The way	*The way* things are going, there'll be more tourists than residents here.
Until	Stay in bed *until* the pain goes away.
As far as	*As far as* I know, no date has been fixed for the wedding.
In so far as	*In so far as* their marketing policy is a policy at all, it may reach its targets.
As long as (time)	He won't come into this house *as long as* I'm alive.
As long as (condition)	Go wherever you like, *as long as* you don't get lost.
Provided that	*Provided (that)* you give me the order, I will deliver the goods in ten days' time.
Much as	*Much as* I dislike driving in heavy traffic, I've got to put up with it or live somewhere else.
So that (purpose)	Fasten the sunshade securely, *so that* it won't blow away.

| *So that* (result) | The oil tanker ran aground, *so that* the whole coastline was polluted. |
| *In order that* | *In order that* no mistakes should be made, everyone was informed by letter. |

35.2.2   Non-finite clauses

Non-finite dependent clauses of enhancement express many of the meanings conveyed by the finite type in addition to some others. The semantic relationships may be made clear by means of a conjunction or a conjunctive preposition, or they may be left inexplicit. The syntactic status of dependency is always clear, since non-finite clauses are always dependent. (The rhetorical use of dependent clauses as if they were independent should be noted, however; examples of this use occur in the advertisement in 31.2.)

(a) Explicit markers of circumstantial meanings

Not all conjunctions and prepositions are able to function as introducers of non-finite dependent clauses. Those that can do so form a subset of the total class of each. We shall summarise them as follows:

subset of conjunctions

when	Take extra care *when* driving at night.
while (time)	*While* talking, he jotted everything down in a pad.
while (concession)	*While* agreeing basically with your proposal, we would nevertheless suggest certain amendments.
though	*Though* feeling unwell, he made an effort to appear cheerful.
if	*If* travelling abroad, watch out for pickpockets.

subset of conjunctive prepositions

before	Look both ways *before* crossing the road.
after	*After* applying one coat of paint, leave to dry.
since	I have thought about it a great deal *since* receiving your letter.
from	*From* being a junior clerk, he rose to become General Manager.
by	*By* turning this handle, you can make ice-cubes come out.
in	*In* learning a foreign language, several skills are involved.
on	*On* entering the mosque, we were impressed by its spaciousness.
with	*With* redecorating the house, our funds are pretty low.
without (concession)	*Without* wishing to offend our hostess, I should like to leave now.
without (reason)	*Without* having read the book, I can't give an opinion.

Without has also an extending use, as in:

> They left *without* saying a word. (= and didn't say a word)

Besides and *as well as* appear to be additive, rather than enhancing:

> *Besides / as well as* caring for her own family, Mary runs a kindergarten.

(b) Verb forms as circumstantial markers

Certain circumstantial meanings of enhancement are frequently expressed by the *to*-infinitive, the *-ing* and the *-en* participle forms alone. Of these, the *to*-infinitive form is the most explicit, since it usually signals purpose.

The meanings expressed by the *-ing* and *-en* forms may sometimes be clarified by adding one of the conjunctions or conjunctive prepositions listed in the previous section. It is worth remembering, however, that non-finite forms are in themselves less explicit than finite forms, and the speaker is free to exploit this inexplicitness, which is not to be considered as some sort of deficiency but rather as an economical means of expressing relationships which are not required to be further specified. When greater specification is required, the finite forms, preceded by specific conjunctions, are available.

Some examples follow of verb forms used in this way:

> *to*-infinitive   *To relieve backache*, apply liniment twice daily.
> clauses: Don't do it just *to please me*.
> *-ing* clauses: *Living abroad*, he rarely sees his relatives. (= because he lives abroad)
> *-en* clauses: *Raised in Texas* he had no knowledge of other parts of the United States.

There is one use of the *to*-infinitive in dependent clauses which is extending rather than enhancing in meaning; that is, it seems to replace coordination, as in:

> She arrived home *to find the house empty*. (= and found the house empty)

Conventions of good English require that the implicit Subject of a non-finite clause should be identical with the explicit Subject of the primary clause. Compare the acceptable (a) with the less acceptable (b):

> (a) Bathing in the sea, I got stung by a jellyfish.
> (b) Bathing in the sea, a jellyfish stung me.

That this norm is not always adhered to is illustrated by the following 'editor's comment' from the BBC series *Yes, Prime Minister*:

> [Working funerals are the best sort of summit meeting. *Ostensibly arranged for another purpose, statesmen and diplomats* can mingle informally at receptions, churches and gravesides, and achieve more

than at ten 'official' summits for which expectations have been aroused. This is presumably why Hacker immediately agreed to a state funeral for his late and unlamented predecessor – Ed.]

Jonathan Lynn & Anthony Jay, *The Complete Yes Prime Minister.*

MODULE 36
Projecting the message

Summary

1   Projection is the relationship which exists between a clause containing a verb of saying or thinking and a clause which expresses what is said or thought.

2   Between clauses of equal status (paratactic projection), the result is quoted speech or thought. This is traditionally known as 'direct speech'.

3   Between clauses of unequal status (hypotactic projection) the result is reported speech or thought, traditionally known as 'indirect speech'. A number of formal adjustments are made in indirect speech, which shift deictic elements away from the speech situation.

4   Writers of present-day fiction use a wide variety of verbs, many not strictly verbs of speaking, to introduce both quoted and reported speech.

5   In addition, and in order to give the reader the illusion of entering a character's mind, writers of fiction combine features of quoted and reported speech to produce the varieties known as 'free direct speech' and 'free indirect speech'.

36.1   Projection as dependency

In Chapter 3 we have described the types of complementation governed by verbs, among them verbs of saying and thinking. In that chapter, clauses which follow such verbs had been implicitly analysed as embedded, as in *She said she might be late*; *I thought no-one would know*; *Paul told the children to be quiet*. According to this analysis, which is based on the concept of constituency, each of the subordinate clauses in these examples would be considered to be a constituent, in this case a Direct Object, of the superordinate clause. As a realisation of Direct Object function, these clauses would not be prototypical, since they cannot become Subject in the passive clause, even though the verbs in question passivise.

Alternatively, the relationships holding between clauses such as those illustrated above can be analysed in terms of dependency. The category of clause complex is based on the notion of dependency; as explained earlier in this chapter, two or more clauses are considered to be related in some form of interdependency, without one clause being a constituent of the other. Now, in terms of the logico-semantic notion of projection and its combination with parataxis and hypotaxis, we shall examine within the integration of the clause complex what are traditionally called 'direct' speech and 'indirect' speech.

36.2   Locutions and ideas

In projection, one clause is projected through another, either as a **locution**, after a verb of saying, or as an **idea**, after a verb of thinking. Their combination with parataxis and hypotaxis is illustrated below.

Types of projection		
	Parataxis	**Hypotaxis**
locution	She said, 'I'll go.' 'Go!' she told him.	She said she would go. She told him to go.
idea	She thought, 'I'll go.' 'Go!' she willed him.	She thought she would go. She wanted him to go.

Locutions and ideas, when projected paratactically, give 'direct speech', that is, direct statements such as *'I'll go'* and direct directives such as *'Go!'* in which the exact words of the Sayer are quoted.

Locutions and ideas, when projected hypotactically, give 'indirect speech', that is, reported statements such as *She said she would go*; *She thought she would go* and reported directives such as *She told him to go*; *She wanted him to go*. In these, the meaning is reported, but the exact words of the Sayer are not repeated.

Projection differs from expansion in that the projected clause reflects, not the representation of an extra-linguistic reality, as is reflected in elaborating, extending and enhancing clauses, but the representation of a representation, that is, of something that someone said or thought. So, for instance, in another example, such as *'I don't know'*, *she answered*, the issue is not whether she knew but whether in fact she said those words.

Between quoted and reported speech, there is a difference of immediacy. In quoting, the projected clause has independent status; its effect, therefore, is more dramatic and life-like. Deictic elements are oriented towards the speech situation, while in reported speech they shift away from it. The formal modifications of this shift are explained in 36.4.1.

There is also a difference in referring back to something which has been quoted and something which has been reported. To refer to the actual words quoted, a reference word such as *that* is typically used, whereas to refer to a report, a substitute form such as *so* or *not* is used:

He said, 'I'll pay this time.'	Did he really say that?
He said he would pay that time.	Did he really say so?

This is because the quoted words refer to a real event that can be referred back to, whereas the reported version is merely a version, a representation of what someone said.

36.3 Quoted speech and quoted thought

36.3.1 Quoted speech (paratactic locutions)

In quoted speech the projecting clause contains a verb of saying. The projected clause contains that which is said. The order of the two clauses is free, as is illustrated below:

(a) 'Two notable successes have marked this trip,' he said.
(b) He said, 'Two notable successes have marked this trip.'
(c) 'Two notable successes', he said, 'have marked this trip.'

In (a) the projected clause comes before the projecting one. In (b) the reverse happens, and the projecting clause is first. In (c) that which is said, the projected clause, is made discontinuous by the projecting one.

In spoken English, the projecting clause receives less prominence than the projected one, in whatever position it occurs. This reflects the fact that what is said is more important than the introductory verb of saying. In written English the quoted clause is marked by inverted commas, and if the quotation extends to a new paragraph, the quotation marks are normally repeated.

Verbs used to introduce direct speech include:

(a) *say* (and, less frequently, *tell*).

(b) verbs introducing statements: *announce, observe, point out, remark* and *report*.
    verbs introducing questions: *ask, demand, inquire, query*.

(c) other verbs of communication which contain some reference to the circumstances of the speech act: *affirm, answer, argue, beg, boast, declare, interrupt, object, protest, repeat, urge, warn*.

(d) verbs of uttering which have other, connotative meanings: *bark, bleat, blurt, chirp, complain, croak, cry, drawl, exclaim, grumble, hiss, holler, mumble, murmur, mutter, scream, shout, shriek, snap, snarl, snort, stammer, stutter, twitter, whine, whisper, yell.*

To this last group can be added many other verbs which are not, strictly speaking, verbs of uttering but rather behavioural verbs which express some emotive state which accompanies the act of speaking. Such verbs can be classified according to the emotive state they reflect:

laughter:	*chuckle, laugh, smile, grin, giggle, smirk, simper, twinkle*
weeping:	*sob, wail*
excitement, concern:	*breathe, pant*
incredulity:	*gasp*
pain, anger:	*bellow, choke, flash*

These groups of verbs are used, with varying degrees of frequency, by some authors of popular narrative as more stimulating substitutes for basic verbs of saying. The following examples are taken from Gordon Parker's *Lightning in May*:

'I'll take the cases,' he whispered.
'Don't be a fool,' Tilmouth snarled.
'What's happened? What's wrong?' he pleaded.
'Come on, lads,' Tommy yelled.
'Mr Cox,' John snapped, matter-of-factly.
'I said come in, Mrs. Friar!' John barked at her.

Also from *Lightning in May* is the following passage in which John suspects for the first time that his wife may have tuberculosis. His reaction is expressed partly in quoted speech and partly in free indirect thought (see below). The projecting verbs are italicised:

'Ruth,' he *breathed*, 'how long have you had this cough?' He stood up and she followed. He opened the handkerchief again. There was no mistake. Silently he cursed himself. He saw her now in a completely different light. 'How long?' he *demanded*.
    He looked at her then held her to him. It became bluntly clear to him now. The pale, tired face that was thinner; the droop of her body. All the symptoms that he had put down to her mental state had matured into a physical one. And now a cough. How could he have been so stupid? Yet he had to make sure.
    'Ruthy,' he *whispered*. 'Let's get back to the surgery. I want Dr. Jenkins to see you.'
'What is it, John?' she *queried*.

Gordon Parker, *Lightning in May*.

36.3.2 Quoted thought (paratactic ideas)

Not only words may be quoted, but also thoughts, as in:

> 'I'll have to get a new bulb for this lamp,' thought Peter.

Mental process verbs which occur in the projecting clause include:

(a) *think*, the basic verb.
(b) other verbs of cognition which express some additional, often aspectual meaning: *muse, ponder, reflect, wonder.*

These are relatively few in number in English, in comparison with the wide variety of verbs used in quoted speech, and also in comparison with the considerable number of cognitive verbs which can occur in reported speech (see section 36.4.2).

In representing their characters' thought, writers of fictional narrative often omit the prosodic signals of quoting (inverted commas or dashes), and make the projecting clause parenthetical. The following example will illustrate this technique:

> He's very well dressed, thought Clarissa, yet he always criticises me.
> Here she is mending her dress; mending her dress as usual, he thought; here she's been sitting all the time I've been in India; mending her dress; running to the House and back and all that, he thought, growing more and more irritated, more and more agitated, for there's nothing in the world so bad for some women as marriage, he thought; and politics; and having a Conservative husband, like the admirable Richard. So it is, so it is, he thought, shutting his knife with a snap.
>
> Virginia Woolf, *Mrs Dalloway.*

36.4 Reported speech and reported thought

36.4.1 Reported speech (hypotactic locutions)

Reported speech (traditionally called 'indirect speech') is characterised by a series of formal features which distinguish it from quoted ('direct') speech. They have the effect of shifting all deictic elements away from direct reference to the speech situation, as can be seen by comparing the following versions:

'I want you to drink this juice.'	She said she wanted him/me to drink that juice.
'Can you leave it here?'	She asked if I could leave it there.
'Do it yourselves!'	He told us/them to do it ourselves/ themselves.
'Must you go tomorrow?'	He asked whether I/he had to go the next day.

The shifts involved are as follows:

(a) First person pronouns, which refer to the speaker, are shifted to third.

The second person pronoun, which refers to the listener, is shifted to first or third, according to the identity of the listener.

(b) Demonstratives and deictic adverbs which refer to the here and now (*this*, *these*, *here*, *now*) are replaced by more remote forms (*that*, *those*, *there*, *then*).

(c) Verb tenses are 'back-shifted', that is, present forms are replaced by past forms.

> 'I *won't* be long,' she said. She said she *wouldn't* be long.
> '*Can* you wait?' he asked. He asked if I *could* wait

Tense back-shift is not obligatory if the situation is still valid:

> 'Ed *is* a bore.'   She said that Ed *was/is* a bore.

(d) Mood type is also affected. An interrogative in quoted speech is replaced by a declarative in reported speech. Imperatives and moodless abbreviated clauses have less clear correspondences, and are discussed later in this and other sections.

In the reported representation of an utterance, the speaker or writer may keep close to the original wording, except for the necessary temporal, spatial and pronominal shifts:

> 'It's raining,' Peter said.   Peter said that it *was* raining.

More often, however, reported speech involves paraphrase or summary of the original utterance. For instance, a clause complex involving quoted speech such as *'Dammit, man,' he shouted, and slammed his fist hard on the desk top* might be reported as *He cursed as he slammed his fist hard on the desk top*. As the formal correspondence between the reported form and a possible original becomes more and more tenuous, grammarians differ as to how far they can be considered grammatical versions of the same meaning. Those who give the semantics priority are willing to allow greater latitude, while those who require formal correspondences to be explicit would discount such reported versions from consideration in a grammar.

It is not only with regard to grammatical considerations that differences of opinion may occur regarding the fidelity of a reported version to an original. In real life, any version involving paraphrase or summary is bound to be subjective, and one speaker's interpretation of the original need not coincide with another's. For instance, some speakers might consider *curse* or *swear* too strong as possible paraphrases of *'Dammit, man'* and avoid such verbs in a reported version. In another dimension, present-day journalism, particularly of the more 'popular' type, makes use of supposedly faithful quoted and reported speech which, on closer reading, sometimes turns out to be unsupported by evidence that such words were actually spoken. Readers may disagree as to how far this practice is to be condoned in the interest of dramatic liveliness.

Verbs used in reporting statements and questions are essentially the same as those used in quoting. The main exceptions are the following:

(a) Semantically complex verbs which express rhetorical processes are used only in reporting, not in quoting. These include: *claim, deny, hypothesize, imply, insinuate, maintain, make out, pretend.*

> She claims her mother was related to a Polish aristocrat.
> He denies being involved in the incident.
> Are you insinuating that he knows something about it?
> Paul is trying to make out that he is really hard up.

(b) Conversely, verbs which are not intrinsically verbs of saying are not normally used to report. These include behavioural verbs such as those exemplified in 36.3.1 as verbs of laughing, weeping, etc. Thus, a quoted locution such as '*So what?*', *he sneered* would be difficult to report in a similar form, and even perhaps with a similar meaning. A paraphrase such as *He asked with a sneer what it mattered* may be considered acceptable within a certain context.

36.4.2 Reported thought (hypotactic ideas)

Verbs which represent mental processes are used to report ideas, beliefs, fears and speculations. These include *believe, feel, hold, imagine, maintain, understand, fear, suspect, think.*

There is some overlap between these cognitive verbs and verbs of saying, since processes expressed by verbs such as *hold* and *wonder* may be exteriorised in speech or writing or may remain exclusively cognitive.

The combination of mental processes with a dependent 'reporting' clause is the normal way of representing what people say, think and believe.

36.5 Reported offers, suggestions and commands

The projected clauses we have considered so far have been quoted or reported statements and questions. We now turn to the projection of directives: reported offers, suggestions and commands, sometimes grouped together under the label 'goods and services' as opposed to that of 'information' related to statements and questions. They may be projected either paratactically or hypotactically.

There is, however, no strong correspondence between the paratactic and the hypotactic forms of expressing offers, suggestions and commands, since the reporting of directives involves summary and paraphrase. Certain verbs are used in quoted directives which are not used for reporting. Conversely, there are many verbs used in reported directives that are not used in quoting. There is some overlap, however, as may be seen from the following table:

Quoted directives	Reported directives
(a) the general verb *say*	the general verb *tell* (for uses of *say* see 36.5.1(b))
(b) verbs specific to offers, suggestions and commands: *call, suggest, offer, order, request, tell*	some, but not all of (b): *suggest, order, command, request, tell*
(c) verbs embodying some circumstantial or other semantic feature: *threaten, vow, promise, agree, beg, insist, plead, urge, warn*	the same as (c)
(d) verbs with a connotative meaning: *blare, thunder, fuss*	not available
(e) not available	verbs expressing a wide range of complex rhetorical processes: *encourage, forbid, persuade, recommend*

36.5.1   Clause type in the projected clause

(a) When we quote an offer, order or suggestion directly, there is typically an imperative in the quoted clause:

> '*Hurry* up!', she said (to us).
> 'Do *eat* more slowly', she begged the child.
> '*Come* in and *sit* down', I suggested (to her).

(b) In reported directives the imperative of the quoted type is replaced by the following structures:

   (i) an Object + *to*-infinitive after verbs such as *tell, order, command, urge, beg* (see 10.3.5).

   (ii) a *that*-clause after verbs of recommending, insisting, proposing and suggesting (see 9.3.3).

The examples in (a) above of quoted directives would be reported as follows:

> She told/urged us to hurry up.
> She begged the child to eat more slowly.
> I suggested that she (should) come in and sit down.

   (iii) *Say* takes a *that*-clause containing an embedded directive expressed, either by the semi-auxiliary *be to*, or by a modal of obligation (*should, must, have to*):

> She said that we were to hurry up.
> She said that we should/must hurry up.

Say can also project a *to*-infinitive clause with no Subject:

> She said to hurry.

In AmE a Subject of the reported clause is here preceded by *for*:

> She said for us to hurry.

(iv) Of the connotative verbs listed in section 36.3.1 d used in fictional narrative to introduce quoted speech, only a few can be used in reporting, and require a Prepositional Object. They are usually verbal processes with an emotive element predominating:

> ('Turn off the gas!', he yelled.)
> He yelled to me to turn off the gas.
>
> ('Stay a little longer', he whispered.)
> He whispered to her to stay a little longer.

Abbreviated clauses are quite common in quoted speech, especially in fictional narrative:

> 'Not a word!', he whispered (to us).
> 'This way, please', the usher said.

Such clauses present a problem in reporting, since they contain no verb. Frequently a verb can be provided, although again, this involves an interpretation on the part of the person who utters the reported version:

> He whispered to us not to say/breathe a word.

Inevitably, therefore, more than one reported version is possible, some differing considerably from the quoted version:

> ('This way, please', the usher said.)
> The usher asked/invited (us?) to accompany him.
> The usher showed (us) the way.

As can be seen from these examples, an additional problem in reporting abbreviated clauses is that not only a verb but also a Complement must be provided. Presumably, the context or the co-text would enable the Recipient of the offer, order or suggestion to be identified. The abbreviated clause, itself, however, does not provide this information. In effect, the two versions are different messages.

36.5.2 Projected affectivity processes

Parallel to offers, suggestions and commands, which are projected by verbs of saying, asking and telling, there are affectivity processes which are projected mentally by such verbs as *hope*, *fear*, *wish*, *want* and *like*. These typically occur as reported states of wishing, wanting, etc., since such mental states are rarely quoted; even the possible form with *let* as in '*Let me be the first to speak to him'*, *Janet wished* is relatively infrequent. Here are some examples of reported affective processes:

I hope	that no damage has been done,
They fear	that many lives have been lost.
She doesn't want	people coming in and out all day.
I wish	I had never met him.
I wish	he would stop telling those awful jokes.
We would like	you to come with us to the Spanish ballet.

Again, the analysis of the secondary clause as reported presents an alternative view to the constituency analysis, according to which such clauses would be embedded.

36.6   Free direct speech and free indirect speech

We have seen so far in this chapter that speakers and writers make use of quoted ('direct') speech and reported ('indirect') speech to reflect the statements, questions and directives of others.

In their attempts to portray the stream of thought of their characters, writers have modified the paradigm of projection as outlined in the preceding sections in certain ways.

What we might call 'free direct speech or thought' consists in simply omitting the inverted commas or dashes which conventionally signal quoting, and has been illustrated in 36.3.2 in the extract from *Mrs Dalloway*.

More drastically, the projecting clause is omitted altogether. This is called 'free indirect speech' and also covers cognitive processes. In addition, certain structures of direct speech are retained, such as direct questions and exclamations, vocatives, utterance-time adverbs such as *now* and tag questions. Other features may belong to indirect speech, however: tense back-shift, and the temporal and spatial shifts of deictic words towards remoteness.

Some of these features are present in the following extract, which describes a girl's journey home from the airport with her mother and her mother's new husband:

> They stopped for dinner at a Polynesian restaurant ten miles up the Turnpike, her mother explaining *that there wasn't anything decent to eat at home*,[1] *also it was getting late, wasn't it, tomorrow she'd be making a big dinner*,[2] *That's okay honey isn't it?*[3] She and her new husband quarrelled about getting on the Turnpike then exiting right away, but at dinner they were in high spirits again, laughing a good deal, holding hands between courses, sipping from each other's tall frosted bright-colored tropical drinks. *Jesus I'm crazy about that woman*,[4] her mother's new husband told the girl when her mother was in the powder room, *Your mother is a high-class lady*, he said[5]. He shifted his cane chair closer, leaned moist and warm, meaty, against

her, an arm across her shoulders. *There's nobody in the world precious to me as that lady, I want you to know that*, he said,[6] and the girl said *Yes I know it*,[7] and her mother's new husband said in a fierce voice close to tears, *Damn right, sweetheart, you know it*[8].

> Joyce Carol Oates, *Happy*, in *Sudden Fiction: American Short-Short Stories*.

[1] indirect speech; [2] free indirect speech; [3] direct speech without a projecting clause; [4–8] free direct speech.

A variant of free indirect speech, illustrated in [2] above, is to retain the projecting clause, together with the features enumerated above. Here is an instance from *Mrs. Dalloway*:

And she opened her scissors, and said, *did*[1] *he*[2] mind *her*[3] just finishing what *she*[4] *was* doing[5] to her dress, for *they*[6] *had*[7] a party *that night?*[8]

[1] direct interrogative + past form;[2–4, 6], pronominal shifts;[5–7] tense shifts;[8] temporal deictic shift.

TASKS ON CHAPTER 7
Expanding and projecting the message: The clause complex

Module 31

1   †*Read again Dylan Thomas's* **Holiday Memory** *in 31.2. Each of the three paragraphs is organised differently as regards the kinds of units which are placed between full stops, as orthographical–rhetorical sentences. Try to identify these units. Write beside each the class of unit to which each belongs (Nominal Group, finite clause, word, etc.).*

Would you agree that the first paragraph gives the reader quick glimpses, as it were, of people and things on the beach, whereas the second paragraph develops an event within an event, and the third paragraph contrasts two incidents within a larger one?

How do the structures chosen by the author contribute to these effects? (Paragraph 3 may be better analysed after working through this chapter.)

2   *State the argument for analysing circumstantial clauses as dependents in a clause complex rather than as Adjuncts. Apply the criteria to the following news item:*

> After hundreds of shrimps came gushing out of taps in Warrington, Cheshire, yesterday, householders collected teapots full of the creatures and were forced to filter the water before they could drink it.

Module 32

Discussion:
1)   What is the meaning of 'parataxis'? Which syntactic relationships does it cover?
2)   What factors prevent coordinated clauses from being reversible?
3)   What is the meaning of 'hypotaxis'?
4)   Name the two main types of logico-semantic relationship holding between clauses and the subtypes of each.

Module 33

1   *Explain the syntactic and logico-semantic relationships involved in apposition.*

2   *Using (i) prosodic signals alone, and (ii) the conjunctive expressions listed in 33.1, add further clauses to the following examples so as to make clause complexes which stand in an appositive relationship to each other:*
1)   **with expositive meanings** (*or rather, that is to say, in other words, namely, i.e.*)
   (a) For ten days she ate nothing but yoghurt
   (b) At three in the morning the party was over
   (c) The bar is open only to members of the club

2)   **with exemplifying meanings** (*for example, for instance*)
   (a) It's not clear how much she understands
   (b) There are a hundred things you could do to get fit
   (c) He's no good at mending things

3)   **with clarifying meanings** (*in fact, indeed, actually*)
   (a) The week started badly
   (b) She looks marvellous in a sari
   (c) I was beginning to feel most embarrassed

3   *Taking all possible units as antecedents, add (i) finite and (ii) non-finite non-restrictive relative clauses to each of the following primary clauses so as to form clause complexes:*
1)   She blamed herself for the accident
2)   Most party members were disheartened by the congress
3)   In the spring of last year we were in Buenos Aires
4)   The Prime Minister has carried out a reshuffle of his cabinet
5)   Among the passengers released by hijackers today are the two eldest sons of the president

4   *Now write a paragraph starting: 'These are exciting times':*

Module 34

1   *Explain the meanings covered by 'extension' and describe the combinations resulting from the combination of extension with parataxis and hypotaxis.*

2   *Which are the conjunctions and cohesive expressions associated with coordination?*

3   *Using the conjunctions and Conjuncts you have listed, add a conjoined clause to the following examples:*
1)   A man carrying a new strain of AIDS virus has left the country
2)   The job was quite attractive
3)   I don't like sleeping in caravans
4)   Either you take travellers' cheques
5)   The dress suits you very well

4   [†]We have in this chapter seen three meanings of *but*. One is adversative, in

which case it can be replaced by *yet* as in *It's a very simple device but /
yet it's very effective.* Another is replacive, with the meaning *except for* or
instead as in *He didn't stay even an hour, but returned to London on the
next train.* The third meaning is concessive, corresponding to hypotactic
although as in *The story is certainly strange, but it's not entirely
unbelievable.*

Decide which of these three meanings correspond to **but** *in each of the
clause complexes below, and replace it by an appropriate Conjunct*:
1) The city may be prosperous, but to claim that it is a tourist attraction is
   ridiculous.
2) Zoo officials are trying to find new homes for the animals, but it is
   difficult to re-house orang-utangs.
3) A degree in engineering should open many doors, but without business
   expertise many graduate engineers have difficulty in finding a job.
4) Lorne originally thought of doing social biology and chemistry, but has
   changed to the new BSc in Industrial and Business Systems.
5) He almost decided to work on an oil-rig, but turned down the offer at the
   last minute.

5 *Which are the conjunctions and conjunctive prepositions associated with
   contrastive dependency?*

6 *Using the connectors you have listed in 5, make clause complexes from the
   following examples by adding finite and non-finite clauses*:
   1) The singer has filed a lawsuit against her video company
   2) Gillian buys all her clothes in boutiques
   3) It might have been a good idea to wait a little while
   4) It would have been most enjoyable
   5) We sat there in silence

Module 35
1 *Explain the kinds of meanings which come under the heading of
   'enhancement'.*
2 *List the conjunctive items which can be used to introduce the secondary
   clause in paratactic enhancement.*
3 *Using these items, add further clauses to the following examples*:
   1) I opened the door
   2) The new law came into force a year later
   3) The milk is sure to have turned sour by now

4 *Enumerate the conjunctive items used in hypotactic enhancement.*

5 *Using as many of these items as possible, make clause complexes based
   on the following clauses*:
   1) He is fascinated by Morocco
   2) It's too early for dinner
   3) Weather reports are good

4)   The film is certainly watchable
5)   We were not allowed to see each other

6   †*Analyse the following paragraph from the point of view of enhancement:*

You can blow up a balloon so far, and then it bursts[1]; you can stretch a rubber band so far, and then it snaps[2]; you can bend a stick so far, and then it breaks[3]. How much longer can the human population go on damaging the world's natural systems before they break down altogether?[4]

Newsweek, 24 June 1991.

7   *Try writing a paragraph on, for instance, **Why people need friends**, using a series of hypotactic clauses of reason and another series using **to**-infinitive clauses of purpose.*

Module 36

1   *Describe the concept of projection and its combination with parataxis and hypotaxis.*

2   †*Read again the passage from **Lightning in May** in 36.3.1. Which parts do you think can be analysed as free indirect thought? Give reasons for your answer.*

3   †*Give one or more possible reported forms for each of the following statements and questions taken from **The Complete Yes Prime Minister**. Replace **say** and **ask** by verbs with connotative meanings:*
1)   'I'm sorry to interrupt you in this vital discussion,' said Annie.
2)   'What exactly is your job?' I said to the EEC official.
3)   'Minister! You realise the press will be printing something that isn't true?'
   'Really?' I smiled at him. 'How frightful!'
4)   'But what about Duncan?' Annie asked. 'You'd recommend him?'
   'No.' Desmond was unequivocal.
5)   'I mean, Prime Minister ... you ... you ... lied,' said Humphrey.

4   †*Give a possible reported form for each of the following quoted directives, taken from the same script:*
1)   'Won't you sit down for a minute?' Annie said to the official.
2)   'Why don't you wear a sports jacket?' Fiona said to Godfrey.
3)   'Suppose I sort of put on my glasses and take them off while I give my speech,' said the Prime Minister.
4)   'My God,' croaked Luke, a broken man, 'You can't send me to Israel. What about my career?'
5)   'Don't be silly,' I replied briskly, 'It's an honour. Promotion.'

5   †*In the following news item each paragraph consists of one clause complex realised by a primary clause and a secondary clause. Read the text and then answer the questions below:*

i) Toxic algae is poisoning our drinking water, health experts warned yesterday.

ii) The blue-green algae, discovered in 21 reservoirs, can kill animals and cause nausea, diarrhoea, skin rashes and minor liver damage in humans.

iii) Notices have already been posted at most of the reservoirs and 78 other lakes and rivers, warning water-sports enthusiasts of the dangers.

iv) Water companies claim there is no threat to public health once drinking supplies have been filtered.

Daily Express, 18 June 1990.

1) Identify the type of clause complex which occurs in each of the paragraphs above.

2) Collect some further news items from different newspapers (both 'popular press' and 'quality press') and compare them for features such as the following:
   (a) the number of clauses in each clause complex;
   (b) the presence or absence of embedded clauses;
   (c) the number of clause complexes consisting only of coordinated clauses (paratactic extension);
   (d) the number of clause complexes containing non-restrictive relative clauses (hypotactic extension);
   (e) the number of clause complexes containing circumstantial clauses (paratactic and hypotactic enhancement), and the type of circumstance involved;
   (f) the number of clause complexes of the projection type;
   (g) whether the projected clause is quoted or reported;
   (h) the type of verb used to introduce the projected clause (verbs of saying, mental process verbs, connotative verbs, etc.).

3) Collect a corpus of newspaper headlines which contain direct speech or indirect speech, for instance, *"The chance of freedom was wasted"*, *says hostage's wife* and *Hostage's wife claims chance of freedom was wasted*, respectively. Then check in the report itself whether it seems clear that the actual words were indeed spoken by the person quoted.

4) Turn to the text in 18.1 in which one newspaper, *The Sunday Times*, reports on the report of another newspaper, *The Mail on Sunday*. Does it appear to aim at fidelity to the original report?

5) Try writing a news item under one of the following headings:
   (a) Students defy army in new protest
   (b) Death of the LP as cassettes and compact discs win
   (c) Air controllers' strike leaves thousands of tourists stranded

6   †*Using information you have learned throughout this chapter, analyse the following extract from Pat Rushin's story **Speed of Light** from the point of*

*view of orthographic–rhetorical sentence, of clause complex as expansion
and clause complex as projection:*

Things go wrong.

Take Constantine Muzhikovsky. He had everything going for him.
Good law practice. Nice secluded house on the outskirts. Sweet little
vegetable garden out back that brought him no end of pleasure come
springtime. Handsome, devoted wife. Kids grown and gone. The way
Muzhikovsky saw things, it was time to ease off and enjoy a tranquil,
orderly life.

Then zap.

One night while they lay in bed watching Johhny Carson,
Muzhikovsky's wife told him it was over. Johnny's last guest, a religious
nut plugging a book, ranted on.

'Did you hear me?' Muzhikovsky's wife said.

'Yes,' Muzhikovsky said. He stared at the glowing TV. 'What' he said.

A blind man could see it, Johnny's guest assured him. The signs, the
portents: all heralding the impending arrival of the blazing glory of our
Lord and Saviour, you bet. Johnny nodded sagely; then, when his guest
wasn't looking, dropped his jaw, mugged dopey credulity.

The audience roared.

'I said I want a divorce.'

In *Sudden Fiction: American Short-Short Stories*.

8

Talking about events:
The Verbal Group

MODULE 37
Expressing our experience of events

Summary

1 Verbal Groups refer to actions, events and states.

2 The experiential structure of the VG consists of Finite + Event + optional auxiliaries. The Finite expresses tense, modality, person and number, which relate the verbal process to the 'speaker-now' and establish the Verbal Group in relation to the speech exchange. The Event expresses lexical meaning which provides the representational content. Finite and Event are fused in e.g. *runs*, *asked*. The optional auxiliaries contribute to the meanings expressed by the progressive, the perfect and the passive.

3 The Finite is realised by primary auxiliaries, modal auxiliaries and lexical auxiliaries. The Event is realised by lexical verbs (*run*, *ask*, etc.)

4 The first auxiliary, the operator, is distinguished by certain syntactic features.

37.1   Experiential structure of the Verbal Group

The Verbal Group is the grammatical unit by means of which we most typically express our perception of events. 'Event' will be used in this chapter to cover all types of process, whether events, actions, states or acts of consciousness. These are described from the point of view of their place in the semantics of the clause in Chapter 4.

The experiential structure of the Verbal Group is Finite + Event. In one-word VGs such as *took*, the Finite and the Event are fused and are realised by one lexical item. In longer sequences the Finite is realised by an operator and may be followed by one or more auxiliaries:

took
Finite/Event

should	have	been	being	taken
Finite	aux	aux	aux	Event

There is a parallelism between the Nominal Group and the Verbal Group as regards their respective experiential structures. Both begin with an element which relates them to the 'speaker-now'; the NG does this by means of the deictic element, the VG by means of the auxiliary which carries tense, modality and person. The Verbal Group ends with the Event, which corresponds to the Thing in the Nominal Group, and provides the representational content. Both Event and Thing represent the nucleus of the lexical meaning. The auxiliaries contribute to the meanings expressed by the perfect, progressive and passive combinations, operating not in isolation but each overlapping with the next, as is explained in Module 38.

37.2   Syntactic elements of structure of the Verbal Group

Like most other classes of group, the Prepositional Group excepted, the VG consists of a main element (**v**) and one or more optional elements (**x**) which precede it. All these elements are realised by verbs, the main element by a finite or non-finite form of a lexical verb, and the optional ones by auxiliaries. The first auxiliary is usually called the 'operator' (**o**), for reasons which are explained in 37.4. The constituent elements of the English VG can therefore be represented and exemplified as follows:

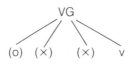

v	waited	I *waited* an hour
o v	is waiting	Everyone *is waiting*
o × v	have been waiting	He *has been waiting* an hour
o × × v	will have been waiting	He *will have been waiting* an hour

37.3   Realisations of the elements

The elements of the VG are realised by the following classes and forms of verbs:

lexical verbs:	wait, come, rain, bring, etc.
primary auxiliaries:	be, am, is, are, was, were, being, been, have, has, had, having; do, does, did
modal auxiliaries:	shall, should, will, would, can, could, may, might, must, ought

semi-modals:	need, dare (modals in certain uses)
lexical auxiliaries:	(i) be able to, be about to, be apt to, be bound to, be due to, be going to, be liable to, be likely to, be certain to, be sure to, be meant to, be to, be unlikely to, be supposed to
	(ii) have to, have got to
	(iii) had better, would rather, would sooner

The primary and modal auxiliary verbs are limited in number, as this list shows, and constitute closed sets. Lexical verbs, the **v** or main element, constitute an open set; new ones can be coined and added to the lexicon.

The term 'lexical auxiliary' is used to cover a set of verbs of modal or aspectual meaning which form concatenated or chain-like structures with the main verb of the VG. The majority are followed by a **V-*to*-inf** form, but a few take the infinitive without *to*. They can be divided into three groups according to whether their first word is (i) *be*; (ii) *have*; (iii) a modal idiom:

(i) *Be* + lexical item + V-*to*-inf

be able to	I *am* not *able to* guarantee the results.
be about to	The plane *is about to* take off.
be apt to	He'*s apt to* ask awkward questions.
be bound to	Prices *are bound to* go up this autumn.
be certain to	The match *is certain to* start on time.
be due to	He'*s due to* arrive at any moment.
be going to	We'*re going to* need more staff here.
be liable to	This machine *is liable to* break down.
be sure to	He'*s sure to* be waiting outside.
be to	We *are to* meet the President tomorrow.
be likely to	They'*re likely to* win by several goals.
be meant to	*Are* you *meant to* work overtime?
be supposed to	We'*re not supposed to* smoke in here.

It may sometimes be difficult to distinguish a VG containing a lexical auxiliary of this type from the use of *be* + adjective as in *I was sorry to see him leave*, or *be* + participle as in *He was forced to stay behind*. One test is the ability of the part that follows *be* to stand at the beginning of a minor clause (see 2.4.1):

Sorry to see him leave, I accompanied him to the door.
Forced to stay behind, he went into the garden.
*Bound to go up this autumn, prices are alarming shoppers.

According to this criterion, adjectives and participles following *be* are more easily separable than lexical auxiliaries. This distinction is one of degree rather than absolute, however.

(ii) *Have/have got* + V-*to*-inf

have to	There *has* to be a solution.
have got to	I've *got* to finish these letters.

(iii) **Modal idioms with *had* and *would* + V-inf**

had better	You *had better* come back tomorrow.
would rather	I *would rather* stay here with you.
would sooner	I *would sooner* pay in advance.

A further group of verbs which also enter into chain-like structures with non-finite forms of lexical verbs (*appear to, fail to, get to,* etc.) do not fulfil all the criteria for operators (see 37.4); in particular, they resemble lexical verbs in needing *do*-support to form interrogative and negative structures (*Did you get to know him well?* not **Got you to know him well?*). For this reason they are treated as part of VG complexes, in section 39.4.

The primary and modal auxiliaries carry grammatical meaning (tense, aspect, modality, person, number) rather than lexical meaning. On the other hand, the main verbal element of the VG expresses both lexical and grammatical meaning.

The primary auxiliaries *be, have, do* can function both as auxiliary and main elements of the VG (with the exception of *doing* and *done*, which function only as main elements). The syntactic function determines the type of meaning expressed, whether grammatical or lexical:

Auxiliary element	Main element
Elections *are* to take place.	Elections *are* imminent.
We *did*n't do anything about it.	Mary *did* everything.
We *have* had nothing to eat.	We *had* nothing to eat.

The lexical auxiliary *have to* can also function both as auxiliary (*Have you to work on Saturdays?*) and as main verb taking *do*-support (*Do you have to work on Saturdays?*), the latter now increasingly frequent. *Have got + to-*infinitive functions only as an auxiliary (*Have you got to work on Saturday?* not **Do you have got to work on Saturday?*). However, *have got + to-*infinitive has no non-finite forms and does not combine with modals. None of the following structures are possible, therefore:

> **To have got to* live there must be dreadful.
> **I don't like *having got to get up early*.
> **We have *had got to* repaint the kitchen.
> **You will *have got to* watch out for mosquitoes there.

37.4 Syntactic features of the operator element

Any of the primary or modal auxiliaries can stand in initial position and so function as operator in a VG.

The operator element has a number of syntactic features which distinguish it from the other elements of a complex VG:

(i)   It can be marked for negation, often enclitically joined to the negative particle *not*: *I don't eat meat.* Not **I eatn't* ...

(ii) It is placed before the Subject in the interrogative and certain marked thematic structures (see 28.5): *Would all parents present at today's meeting* please sign here.

(iii) It can substitute for the Predicator and part or all of the predicate in a clause (cf. 29.4): *John drives a car but his wife doesn't.*

(iv) It can receive tonic stress to emphasise polarity (see 29.7):
      Do you think he was caught? Yes, he WAS caught.

(v)   Frequency Adjuncts typically follow operators, whereas they precede lexical verbs. Compare: *You can't often have seen a blue heron. No, in fact, I never saw one before.*

(vi) The quantifiers *all* and *both* can follow operators: *They have all / both vanished.*

(vii) The operator is the verbal element which appears in a tag question: *You will come, won't you?* (see 27.3)

(viii) The operator is also the verbal element which appears with *so* or *too* and *neither* or *not* ... *either* in positive and negative substitution, respectively, as in *Ann went home and so did Jill*, *Ann went home and Jill did too*; *Pete can't play golf today and neither can we / and we can't either*.

(ix) When a predicate is fronted as in the second clause of *He was sure he would pass, and pass he did*, or when the predicate is replaced in the second clause by a relative pronoun as in *He was sure he would pass, which he did*, the operator occurs in final position, taking end-focus and polarity emphasis.

(x)   In comparison with main verbs, the operator is semantically independent of the Subject. This is shown with verbs that admit the active/passive contrast; operators usually show no change of meaning, whereas with some finite lexical verbs there is a change of meaning. Compare: *Peter will teach the beginners*, *The beginners will be taught by Peter*; *Peter expects to teach the beginners*, *The beginners expect to be taught by Peter*.

MODULE 38
Basic structures of the Verbal Group

Summary

1   Verbal Group structures can be **simple**, consisting of one element only (*runs,
    asked*), or **extended**, consisting of one or more auxiliaries + a main verb (*may
    have been running*).

2   Up to four auxiliaries can occur, or five if a lexical auxiliary is included.

3   The meanings expressed by the auxiliaries are: **modal**, **perfect**, **progressive**,
    passive, in this order. The structures which realise these meanings overlap
    successively in the VG.

4   The longer combinations are more frequent in spoken than in written English.

5   Non-finite VGs (*having been seen*) can express perfect, progressive and passive
    meanings, but not tense or modality.

38.1   Simple structures of the Verbal Group

A simple Verbal Group structure consists of a single element, usually the
lexical element, realised by a finite or non-finite form of a lexical verb, for
example *drive*:

Finite forms

drive (pres. indic.)   They *drive* on the left in the U.K.
drives (pres. indic.)   He *drives* to work every day.
drove (past indic.)   He *drove* out of the garage.

Non-finite forms

drive (imperative)   *Drive* slowly!
(to) drive (infin.)   It's important *to drive* with care.
                     They won't let you *drive* without a licence.
driving (pres. part.)   *Driving* to work this morning, I heard the
                       9 o'clock news.
driven (past part.)   *Driven* away by night, the car was then
                     abandoned.

Simple VG structures are illustrated in the passage below:

Rivers perhaps *are* the only physical feature of the world that *appear* at their best from the air. Mountain ranges, no longer *seen* in profile, *dwarf* to anthills; seas *lose* their horizons; lakes *have* no longer depth but *look* like bright pennies on the earth's surface; forests *become* a thin impermanent film, a mass on the top of a wet stone, easily *rubbed* off. But rivers, which from the ground one usually *sees* in cross sections, like a small sample of ribbon – rivers *stretch* out serenely ahead as far as the eye *reaches*.

A. M. Lindbergh, *North to the Orient*.

38.2   Extended structures of the Verbal Group

An 'extended' Verbal Group structure consists of a lexical verb at the head, preceded by up to four auxiliaries, or five if we include the lexical auxiliaries. The order in which the auxiliaries occur is fixed and depends upon the grammatical meanings they convey. The features of grammatical meaning which can be expressed in an extended VG include the following:

tense	present, past
finiteness	finite, non-finite
anteriority	perfect
aspect	progressive, non-progressive
modality	prediction, possibility, probability, volition, obligation, necessity, advisability, ability, permission
polarity	positive, negative
emphasis	contrastive, non-contrastive

These major features of grammatical meaning represent sets of options between which speakers choose every time they combine elements to form a Verbal Group. The meanings are described in this and other chapters. In the following examples, we let *has* and *is* stand for any form of **have** and **be**, *must* for any of the modal auxiliaries and *be about to* for the set of lexical auxiliaries.

38.3   Structures with one auxiliary: o v

In the finite VG with only one auxiliary, this auxiliary is necessarily the operator and, according to its type, selects a corresponding form of the lexical verb. The ov structure can express the following features of grammatical meaning, in addition to the obligatory choices of tense, finiteness, polarity and contrastiveness:

		Features	**Realisations**		**Example**
A	1.	modal	modal aux.	+ V-inf	must drive
B	2.	perfect	have	+ V-*en*	has driven
C	3.	progressive	be	+ V-*ing*	is driving
D	4.	passive	be	+ V-*en*	is driven
E	5.	lexico-modal	lexical aux.	+ V-inf	is about to drive

The four basic combinations also combine with each other to make up more complex Verbal Groups, all of which function as one Verbal Group at Predicator in clause structure. The features **modal, perfect, progressive, passive** occur in ordered combinations like the letters of the alphabet ABCD. Thus, for instance, B can follow A or E follow D, but not vice versa. A certain feature may be omitted, as in ACD, BDE. Lexical auxiliaries can occur with any combination, as will be illustrated in the following section.

The choices among the grammatical meanings listed above which are realised by one auxiliary (the operator) + the lexical verb are illustrated in the following passage. Forms of *be* occur as main verb, there is one main verb *fell* and also one 'phased' VG: (see 39.4)

> One day, as you *are washing*[1] your hands, you *happen to glance*[2] into the mirror over the basin and a sudden doubt *will flash*[3] across your mind: '*Is*[4] that really me?' 'What *am* I *doing* [5] here?' 'Who *am*[6] I?'
>
> Each one of us *is* so completely *cut off*[7] from everyone else. How *do* you *know*[8] you *are reading*[9] a book? The whole thing *may be*[10] an illusion. How *do* you *know*[11] that red *is*[12] red? The colour *could appear*[13] blue in everyone else's eyes. A similar doubt, differently expressed, *is*[14] inherent in the well-known question: 'A tree that *has fallen*[15] in the forest, far from the nearest man – when it *fell*,[16] *did* it *make*[17] any noise?'

Magnus Pike, The Boundaries of Science.

This text illustrates the options listed as ABCD choices. It must be remembered, however, that *all finite Verbal Groups* also select obligatorily for tense, polarity and contrastiveness. This means that a full description of any one VG realisation would have to specify all these choices, as can be exemplified by [1] *are washing*:

> *are washing*: finite, present, positive, non-contrastive, non−modal, +progressive, non−perfect, non−passive.

38.4   Structures with two auxiliaries: o×v

6.	modal + perfect	must have driven
7.	modal + lexical–modal	must be about to drive
8.	modal + progressive	must be driving
9.	modal + passive	must be driven
10.	perfect + lexical–modal	has been about to drive
11.	perfect + progressive	has been driving
12.	perfect + passive	has been driven
13.	lexico–modal + progressive	is about to be driving
14.	lexico–modal + passive	is about to be driven

Structures with two auxiliaries occur widely in both spoken and written English. The following extract is adapted from a report about problems facing language-school students when they come to Britain to study English. Positive choices only are indicated:

> It *must be realised*[1] that many students *will be going*[2] abroad for the first time and *may* well *be likely to feel*[3] anxious about the kind of reception they *will be given*,[4] about the kind of work they *are about to have to do*[5] or about the host family to which they *happen to have been assigned*.[6] Many of these worries *can* easily *be allayed*[7] by giving them as much information as possible beforehand. In the past, some students *have been apt to complain*[8] that they *have had to face*[9] certain difficulties in the first weeks owing to lack of sufficient information.
>
> [1]modal + passive; [2]modal + progressive; [3]modal + lexico-modal; [4]modal + passive; [5]lexico-modal + lexico-modal; [6]catenative (*happen to*) + perfect + passive; [7]modal + passive; [8]perfect + lexico-modal; [9]perfect + lexico-modal.

38.5   Structures with three auxiliaries: o××v

15.	modal + perfect + lexical–modal	must have been about to drive
16.	modal + perfect + progressive	must have been driving
17.	modal + perfect + passive	must have been driven
18.	modal + progessive + passive	must be being driven
19.	modal + lex.–mod. + progressive	must be about to be driving
20.	modal + lex.–mod. + passive	must be about to be driven
21.	perfect + progressive + passive	has been being driven
22.	perfect + lex.–mod. + progressive	has been about to be driving
23.	perfect + lex.–mod. + passive	has been about to be driven
24.	lex.–mod. + progressive + passive	is about to be being driven

38.6   Structures with four auxiliaries: o×××v

25.	modal + perfect + lex.–mod. + progressive	must have been about to be driving
26.	modal + perfect + lex.–mod. + passive	must have been about to be driven
27.	perfect + lex.–mod. + progressive + passive	has been about to be being driven
28.	modal + perfect + progressive + passive	must have been being driven

38.7   Structures with five auxiliaries: o× × × ×v

Only one meaningful structure is possible with this combination of grammatical elements and semantic features:

29. modal + perfect + lex.–mod. +   must have been about to
progressive + passive   be being driven

38.8   Overlapping order of elements of the Verbal Group

It is important to note that each semantico–syntactic feature of a complex VG (tense and modality, perfect, progressive and passive) is expressed, not by one element only, but by each element overlapping with the following one:

modality:	must + V-inf			
perfect:		have + V-en		
progressive:			been + V-ing	
passive:				being + V-en
main verb:				driven
= Verbal Group:	must	have	been	being driven

With respect to the other auxiliaries, lexical auxiliaries have a relatively free ordering, the basic requirement being that they are followed by an infinitive. This precludes such combinations as *is likely to must drive*. However the meaning of *must* can be expressed by the lexical auxiliary *have* + *to*-infintive, giving the acceptable combination *is likely to have to drive*.

38.9 Relative frequency of complex Verbal Groups

It is obvious that, in practice, some of the longer combinations, those with four or five auxiliaries before the lexical verb, are fairly uncommon, simply because the contexts which require them are likewise uncommon. The language's resources, nevertheless, can generate them so that they are always there, at the user's disposal when they are needed. They occur more frequently in speech than in written texts, where it is rare to find passages containing more than an occasional example of VG structures with several auxiliaries. When speaking, we string our structures together one after the other, following the thread of our spontaneous thoughts; this does not mean that spontaneous expression is less complex than written expression. Both may be equally complex, but in different ways. Whereas carefully written English tends to have high lexical density with relatively low grammatical complexity, the opposite occurs in spontaneous spoken English. Here, lexical density tends to be low, but grammatical complexity is often high, particularly in the Verbal Groups. The reason for this lies in the nature of the meanings conveyed by the Verbal Group, meanings related not simply to an objective point of time at which an event occurred, but also related, more subjectively, to others such as the hypothetical speculations and predictions made by the speaker as to what might happen in the future or what might have happened in the past. All of these meanings are subtle, but are handled intuitively with great skill by native speakers. The following examples of long Verbal Groups occurring in spontaneous conversations are attested by M.A.K. Halliday:

> will have been going to be tested
> must have been going to have finished
> is going to have been being discussed

The first could have occurred in an exchange such as the following:

> A: Can I use that machine when I come in tomorrow?
> B: No, it's going to be being tested then.
> A: (irritated) It'll have been going to have been being tested every day for a fortnight.

38.10   Extended non-finite structures

Non-finite VGs do not possess the full set of sequences displayed by finite groups because they do not express the grammatical meanings of tense, mood or modality.

The perfect, progressive and passive meanings can, however, be expressed in the non-finite VG, giving the following possible combinations:

Infinitive structures	Participle structures
30. to have driven	having driven
31. to have been about to drive	having been about to drive
32. to have been driving	having been driving
33. to have been driven	having been driven
34. to be about to drive	being about to drive
35. to be about to be driving	being about to be driving
36. to be about to be driven	being about to be driven
37. to be driving	(being driving)
38. to be being driven	(being being driven)
39. to be driven	being driven
40. to have been about to be driving	having been about to be driving

41. to be about to be being driven   (being about to be being driven)
42. to have been about to be being driven   having been about to be being driven

38.11   Sequence of two V-*ing* forms

The bracketed participial forms do not generally occur, not because they are ungrammatical, but because they have not yet attained full currency and acceptability. They are all sequences in which the first auxiliary is *being*, and in practice this element is generally omitted:

He died while (being) being taken to hospital.

Given an appropriate lexical verb and an appropriate context, the participial sequence of *being* + V-*ing* is acceptable, as in the following attested example:

You might get an extension on the grounds of being teaching.

or the following imaginary conversation between speakers A and B:

A. You didn't come to hear our guest speaker yesterday.
B. I was interviewing the new candidates then.
A. What, at six in the evening?
B. I can't help *being interviewing* all day if it's absolutely necessary.

The sequence *being being* + V -*en* is more difficult to contextualise and does not appear to have been attested.

MODULE 39
Organising our experience of events

Summary

1 Verbal Groups are **discontinuous** when the sequence of elements is interrupted by other clause elements or by intensifiers.

2 As with other types of group, VG elements can be realised recursively, by coordination or by subordination.

3 Not only elements of structure, but whole VGs can also be realised recursively.

4 VGs in a dependency relationship are **phased**. They form chain-like sequences, the first VG being finite, the second non-finite (*end up winning*, *appears to be improving*, *started to rain*).

5 The first VG in a phased structure can express such meanings as initiation, termination, attempt, manner and modality.

39.1 Discontinuous Verbal Groups

The sequence of elements in VGs is often interrupted by other clause elements, such as Subject, Adjunct and intensifiers, as can be seen in the following exchange, in which A asks B about her father, who is a wine dealer:

> A. *Did* he *import*[1] from any particular place in France, or all over?
> B. Well, he *used to* sort of *be*[2] forever *going*[3] to Bordeaux, so I
>   assumed from that that that was his main connection.

Adapted from J. Svartvik & R. Quirk, *A Corpus of English Conversation*.

[1]interrupted by Subject; [2] interrupted by intensifier; [3] interrupted by Adjunct.

As well as in interrogative structures, separation of the VG by the Subject is produced in certain types of thematisation (Little *did* he *realise* the harm he had done; *Had* we *known* your address, we would have got in touch with you). This is explained in 28.5.

Discontinuity of the VG is also produced by the negative or semi-negative items (I *would* never *have believed* that of him; You *can* hardly *expect* them to wait all day).

39.2   Recursive elements of the Verbal Group

Just as with other types of groups, elements of the VG can be realised recursively by two or more units of the same class, related to each other by coordination or by dependency.

39.2.1   Elements related by coordination

modal aux.	The Government *can and must* reduce public expenditure.
primary aux.	We *are or* at least *were* thinking of buying a new car.
lexical aux.	I *had better and*, in fact, *would rather* come back some other time.
main verb + predication	You should *stay and find out*. Need we *hang around here and waste the afternoon*?

In spoken English coordinated auxiliaries frequently occur in elliptic structures, since the event expressed by the main verb is already known (29.3.1), as in this imaginary dialogue:

A. Do you think he *will*?
B. I think he *can*, if he wants to, *but* perhaps he *won't*.
C. Of course, all his colleagues *have*, *but* perhaps he thinks he *needn't*.

39.2.2   Elements related by dependency

These are the structures described in Module 37. They consist of an initial finite auxiliary followed by a succession of non-finite auxiliary forms in an overlapping relation of dependency, making up one complex VG.

He *would have to have driven* very fast to get to the airport in time.
Surely that poster *wasn't meant to have been printed* in those colours?
The Minister *will be bound to be taking* precautions after the latest terrorist attack.
The plane *was due to have taken off* an hour ago.
She *is supposed to be being operated on* for appendicitis immediately, but the ambulance *can't have been able to reach* the hospital yet.

39.3   Verbal Groups related by coordination (conjoined VGs)

Whole VGs can be linked by coordination, making what is referred to as **conjoined VGs** or a **VG complex**. The process expressed is made up of two events or happenings which are semantically related (*washed and dressed* but hardly *washed and scolded*). Just as with the conjoining of other types of grammatical unit, the VGs may be joined by a linking word such as *and*, *or* and *but*; asyndetically, without a linking item; or by a combination of both:

> She *washed and dressed* the child.
> Our last typist just *left, disappeared* without saying a word.
> He *was born, lived and died* in Bristol.
> He started his first business after *having saved or* possibly *having borrowed* a sizeable sum of money.

39.4   Verbal Groups related by dependency (phased VGs)

Verbal Groups in a dependency relationship, e.g. *happened to see*, can in many cases be interpreted semantically as one complex or phased process, realised by two VGs, the second dependent on the first. The first verb differs from the lexical auxiliaries described in previous sections in that verbs such as *happen*, *seem*, *keep*, etc., are lexical verbs which cannot themselves be operators; they can combine with modals (*may happen to see*) and take *do*-support (*Did you happen to see it?*).

The primary group is a catenative VG, which may be finite or non-finite, such as *may have appeared to*, *will keep on*, *having failed to*. It is this group which carries the mood of the clause and which is picked up in tag questions as in *She will keep on doing it, won't she?* The secondary group is always non-finite, the form of the verb being selected by the primary group. The infinitive form, with or without *to*, e.g. *tried to relax*, tends to draw attention to the perfective or completed aspect of the second verb, and the participial *-ing* form, e.g. *tried relaxing*, to the imperfective or incompleted aspect (40.2).

Verbs which can function as the primary group in a VG complex include the following:

   (i) appear to, chance to, come to, fail to, get to, happen to, help to, hesitate to, manage to, prove to, regret to, seem to, tend to, try to, turn out to, venture to
   (ii) keep (on), go on, carry on
  (iii) begin, start, cease, stop
  (iv) get

Type (i) is followed by a *to*-infinitive and type (ii) by a V-*ing*; type (iii) can be followed by either the infinitive or-*ing*. Type (iv) is the so-called *get*-passive, as in *he got run over by a bus*. The non-finite forms are illustrated as follows:

to-infinitive	He *tried to kill* the snakes.
-ing form	He *went on killing* the snakes.
to-inf/ *-ing*	He *began to kill* the snakes.
	He *began killing* the snakes.
-en	He *got killed* by a snake.

These verbs have in common with the lexical auxiliaries the ability to form concatenated sequences of non-finite constructions as in *Those pears don't seem to be getting eaten* and *He always seems to be about to pass his driving test, but in the end he keeps on managing to fail.* They are not to be confused with fully lexical verbs which enter into monotransitive constructions with Direct Objects or Prepositional Object (see 9.2). Although they require *do*-support, in common with lexical verbs, many of them satisfy the 'independence of the Subject' criterion which is characteristic of auxiliaries:

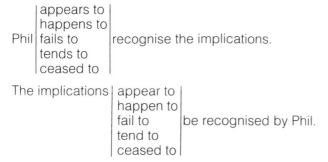

Phil | appears to / happens to / fails to / tends to / ceased to | recognise the implications.

The implications | appear to / happen to / fail to / tend to / ceased to | be recognised by Phil.

39.5 Types of phase

Verbal Group complexes of this kind are said to be 'phased', because the process expressed by the VGs is interpreted as being realised by a single Subject in two phases. The types of phase can be classified notionally as follows, some verbs admitting the perfective–imperfective contrast:

(a) **the phase of initiation**

perfective	**imperfective**
It began *to rain*.	It began *raining*.
She started *to cry*.	She started *crying*.
I got *to know* him well.	Come on, get *moving*!

(b) **the phase of continuation**

———	Why do you keep on *complaining*?
He went on *to talk* about his future plans.	He went on *talking* for hours.
It continued *to snow* for a week.	It continued *snowing* for a week.
———	I'll never stop *loving* you.
———	Carry on *working*, please!

(c) **the phase of termination**

I have ceased *to mind* the harsh climate. —— —— —— ——	I have ceased *minding* the constant noise. He will end up *resigning*. Have the children finished *eating*? Can't you stop *making* such a noise? The horse ended up *winning* the Grand National.

The use of *stop* with a following *to*-infinitive indicates the end of one process and the beginning of another, rather than one phased process. Syntactically, the *to*-infinitive form is a separate VG, analysed as an Adjunct. Compare:

> He stopped *to think*.   He stopped *thinking*.

(d) **the phase of appearing or becoming real**

> The sky *seemed to get* darker.
> The job *proved to be* quite unsuitable.
> The stranger *turned out to be* a neighbour after all.
> The patient *appears to be improving*.

(e) **the phase of attempting or not attempting, succeeding, failing**

The verbs used with these meanings include *try, attempt, manage, be able, fail, neglect, omit, learn*, which are followed by the *to*-infinitive form of the subordinate verb. Again, this form often draws attention to the perfective aspect of the process:

> He *tried to learn* Arabic.
> We *managed to find* the key.
> Don't *fail to write* when you arrive.
> You must *learn to relax*.
> I *attempted to explain* but they wouldn't listen.
> She *neglected to turn off* the gas and there was an explosion.

(f) **the phase of manner or attitude**

Some catenative verbs express the manner in which a person performs an action or an attitude of mind towards performing it. These are verbs such as *regret, venture, hesitate, hasten, pretend, decline, bother*. All are followed by the *to*–infinitive form only, except *bother*, which can reflect the perfective–imperfective contrast.

I *regret to inform* you . . .	= inform with regret
We *ventured to question* the decision.	= question tentatively
I *hesitate to ask* you this favour.	= ask reluctantly
They *hastened to reassure* her.	= reassure immediately
He's only *pretending to be* deaf.	= acting as if deaf
He *declined to answer* the question.	= was not willing to answer
I never *bother to iron* sheets.	= trouble myself to iron

Why *bother trying to remember* useless facts?	= trouble to remember

(g) **the phase of modality**

Certain lexical catenative verbs express an element of chance or usualness in the performance of the action denoted by the second verb. The process is then described as 'modalised'. Semantically, these verbs are similar to the lexical auxiliaries described in section 37.3, such as *be apt to*, *be liable to*, which express usualness, *be supposed to*, which expresses obligation, and *be bound to*, *be certain / sure to*, which express certainty.

She *happened to see* the accident.	= saw by chance
I *chanced to overhear* their conversation.	= heard by chance
You *tend to be* nervous, don't you?	= usually are

An illustration of the occurrence of complex and phased VGs (together with phrasal verbs) in spoken English is provided by the following short extract from a recorded conversation:

Rachel: We *got locked out*[1] of the flat yesterday.
Harry: How did you *get back*[2] in?
Rachel: We *had to borrow*[3] a long ladder and *climb up*[4] to the first floor balcony.
Harry: I thought that with the kind of security lock you've got, you're *not supposed to be able to lock* yourself *out*[5].
Rachel: That's true. But if you *happen to bang*[6] the door a bit too hard, it locks itself.
Harry: It's better *to have to lock*[7] it from the outside.

[1] *get*-passive, phrasal verb; [2] phrasal verb; [3] lexico-modal; [4] phrasal verb; [5] lexico-modal + lexico-modal + phrasal verb; [6] phased VG; [7] lexico-modal.

MODULE 40
Multi-word verbs

Summary

1   **Phrasal verbs** consist of a lexical verb + an adverb (*He rang off*); **prepositional verbs** consist of a lexical verb + a preposition (*He came into a fortune*); **phrasal–prepositional verbs** consist of a lexical verb + an adverb + preposition (*We look forward to seeing you*). These three types are distinguished by their syntactic behaviour.

2   Other multi-word combinations include prepositional verbs with two complements, some idiomatic (*I caught sight of the whale*), others not (*remind someone of something*).

3   The more idiomatic multi-word verbs are functionally equivalent to one lexical item. Other, more transparent combinations, combine the meaning of the verb and the particle, and these can be permuted (*walk out/run out/hurry out; walk away/run away/hurry away*, etc.). Idiomaticity is not clear-cut, but on a cline.

4   In some cases the particle adds an end-point to the verbal meaning (*hammer it in*), or suggests indefinite duration or iteration (*hammer away*).

40.1   Classification of multi-word verbs

Some lexical verbs are followed by one or two particles which seem on intuitive semantic grounds to be part of the verb (*give in, look after, make up, take off, run out of, look forward to*, etc.). Idiomatic sequences such as these can be considered as multi-word verbs and are often equivalent to one lexical item. They can be grouped into three main classes: (a) phrasal verbs, (b) prepositional verbs, (c) phrasal–prepositional verbs. We shall also refer to (d) prepositional verbs with two Complements. The characteristics of these four groups are as follows:

40.2   Phrasal verbs

Phrasal verbs are combinations of a lexical verb and an adverbial particle (*come to, go off, die away, get by, break down, take back, mess about, get on*). They may be intransitive:

The injured man *came to.*   The bomb failed to *go off.*
The music *died away.*   We'll *get by* somehow.
Stop *messing about.*   How did you *get on* at the interview?

or transitive. With a transitive phrasal verb, the particle in most cases may precede or follow the Object, if this is realised by a NG with a noun as head:

They *broke down* the door.   They *broke* the door *down.*
Let's *take back* the glasses.   Let's *take* the glasses *back.*

With some combinations, however, one sequence is more common than the other: compare *We can count John out* (? *We can count out John*); *He told the child off* (**He told off the child*).

If the Object is a pronoun, the particle is placed after it:

They *broke* it *down.*   We *took* them *back.*

With a noun as Object, this discontinuous structure permits the speaker to place either the Object or the particle in final position, where it receives end-focus (29.7); in other words, to emphasise either the Object or the verbal process. This choice is not possible with a synonymous one-word verb. Compare:

They *cancelled* the meeting.   (end-focus on *meeting*)
They *called off* the meeting.   (end-focus on *meeting*)
They *called* the meeting *off.*   (end-focus on *off*)

A pronoun does not normally receive end-focus, since it represents Given information (29.2), and so does not occupy final position, except for contrastive purposes:

They *ruled* us *out.*   They ruled out *me*, but not Tom.

If the Direct Object is long, it is placed at the end, where the heavy NG receives end-focus, and also avoids a gap between verb and particle:

He *rang up* all the friends he had made on the Mediterranean cruise the previous summer.

and not

*He *rang* all the friends he had made on the Mediterranean cruise the previous summer *up.*

Some verb + particle combinations can be used both transitively and intransitively, e.g. *blow up, pull up, break down, give out.* In some cases the transitive and intransitive clauses form an ergative pair (see 14.7) with a causative meaning in the transitive:

Terrorists have *blown up* the power station. (transitive)
The power station has *blown up.* (intransitive)

The traffic policeman *pulled* him *up* for speeding. (transitive)
The cyclist *pulled up* at the traffic lights. (intransitive)

while in others the meaning is related by metaphorical extension or is even entirely different:

> They *broke down* the door to rescue the child. (transitive)
> Her health *broke down* under the strain. (intransitive)

> The radio transmitter *gave out* signals. (= emit) (transitive)
> Our petrol supply has *given out.* (= be used up) (intransitive)

40.3   Prepositional verbs

Prepositional verbs are combinations of a lexical verb and a preposition with which it is semantically associated: *look into, call for, set about, come by, make for, touch on, run across, leap at, see to, deal with, scrape through,* etc.

> The police are *looking into* the matter.
> This job *calls for* a person of considerable initiative.
> He *set about* filing the documents in quite the wrong way.
> How did you *come by* such a valuable picture?
> This kind of get-together *makes for* good social relations.
> He *touched on* many interesting points in his lecture.
> I *ran across* your brother at the airport the other day.
> Most people I know would *leap at* such an opportunity.
> Will you *see to* the children's lunch?
> A special commission will *deal with* donations for the refugees.
> I just managed to *scrape through* the final exam.

In these cases, the NG together with the preposition constitute the Prepositional Object (Oprep) of the single verb, e.g. *look + into the matter.* This suggests a parallel with a Direct Object, and it is the analysis adopted for those verbs which can passivise (see 6.3). Arguments which support this analysis include the following:

(a) Many such combinations can be replaced by a verb used transitively: *The police are studying the matter* (= *look into*).

(b) Questions can be formed with prepositional verbs eliciting the Oprep by means of *who(m)* or *what*: *Who did you run across? What are the police looking into?*

(c) Many clauses containing prepositional verbs can be passivised: *The matter is being looked into*; *Many interesting points were touched on in his lecture*. The preposition is then said to be *stranded*.

(d) Prepositional Objects can be conjoined: *He looked into the fraud and also into the murder case.*

Unlike Direct Objects, however, many Prepositional Objects admit an adverb between the verb and the Oprep: *The police are looking carefully into the matter*; *He touched briefly on many interesting points in his lecture*. Such instances suggest that the cut-off point is between the verb and the prep-osition. Others do not easily admit insertion of an adverb: *?I ran by chance across your brother at the bus station*. The more cohesive and idiomatic the prepositional verb is, the less likely it is to admit discontinuity by an adverb.

40.4   Differences between phrasal verbs and prepositional verbs

The differences are reflected both syntactically and phonologically. We illus-trate them here with the prepositional verb *break with* and the phrasal verb *break up*:

(a) A preposition cannot be placed after the Object, unless it is stranded, whereas the adverbial particles of phrasal verbs can generally precede or follow the Object:

He *broke with* his girl-friend.   He *broke up* the party.
*He *broke* his girl-friend *with*.   He *broke* the party *up*.

(b) A pronoun follows a preposition but precedes the adverbial particle of a phrasal verb:

He broke with *her*.   He broke *it* up.
*He broke *her* with.   *He broke up *it*.

(c) As was seen in 40.3, an adverb can potentially be placed between a verb and its following preposition. Phrasal verbs do not admit an adverb between the verb and the particle:

He broke *completely* with his   *He broke *completely* up
girl-friend.   the party.

(d) A *WH*-interrogative or relative can often be preceded by the preposition of a prepositional verb (although there may be a clash of register) but not by the particle of a phrasal verb:

With whom did he break?   **Up what* did he break?
The girl *with whom* he broke.   *The party *up which* he broke.

(e) The particle in a phrasal verb is stressed and in final position receives the main focus. The preposition of a prepositional verb is typically unstressed and in final position receives the 'tail' of the nuclear stress belonging to the lexical item. Compare:

Which girl did he BREAK with?   Which party did he break UP?

Some verb + particle combinations can function as both phrasal and prepositional verbs, e.g. *turn on*, *get over*, *come across* although the mean-ings are different in the two cases:

Prepositional verb	Phrasal verb
His former allies *turned on* him. She'll never *get over* the shock. I *came across* some old letters.	Let's *turn on* the light. I want to *get* my operation *over*. Her voice *comes across* well.

40.5   Phrasal–prepositional verbs

Phrasal–prepositional verbs consist of a lexical verb followed by two particles, the first adverbial and the second prepositional: *go in for*, *run up against*, *do away with*, *cut down on*, *look forward to*, etc. They are particularly characteristic of informal English:

> He *goes in for* wind-surfing.
> We *ran up against* difficulties.
> They have *done away with* free school meals.
> You'd better *cut down on* fatty foods, cakes and alcohol.
> The waiter says they have *run out of* doggy-bags.
> I don't think I can *go through with* this ordeal.
> Don't *monkey about with* the computer.
> It all *boils down to* money in the end.
> She *is* always *on at* him to buy a bigger car.

Phrasal–prepositional verbs function like prepositional verbs, taking a prepositional complement after the preposition. There are a few transitive combinations such as *do out of*, *put down to*:

> Some people *put* success *down to* sheer luck.
> He was *done out of* the first prize by a knee injury.
> They've *let* me *in for* a great deal of trouble.
> The other boys *have* it *in for* him, he says.

40.6   Prepositional verbs with two Objects

These are verbs followed by two Nominal Groups, the first being the Object of the verb, the second the Object of the preposition. They are treated as one type of 'two-complement pattern' in 10.3.

> I *reminded* him *of* the appointment.
> He *talked* me *into* accepting the job.
> He *frightened* them *into* signing the paper.
> I'll *keep* you *to* your word.
> They were unable to *make* anything *of* the scrawled message.

With certain verbs of this type, the first Nominal Group forms an idiomatic unit with the verb and the preposition:

> I have *lost touch with* most of my old school friends.
> Phil can *turn his hand to* any job in the house or garden.

Someone may have *set fire to* the forest deliberately.
I *lost track of* Bill when he changed his job.
We suddenly *caught sight of* her among the crowd.

40.7 Semantic cohesiveness and idiomaticity

The multi-word verbs examined so far display a high degree of semantic cohesiveness and idiomaticity. It is for this reason that we have considered them as a single lexical item functioning as Predicator in clause structure.

Other verb + particle combinations, however, present varying degrees of cohesiveness and little or no idiomaticity. For practical purposes, the following three degrees will be recognised: non-idiomatic, semi-idiomatic and fully idiomatic.

40.7.1 Non-idiomatic free combinations

The lexical verb and the adverbial particle each keeps its own meaning, the sum of the meanings being one of movement + direction. The particle indicates the direction of the movement, while the lexical verb indicates the manner:

go down: Temperatures *went down* last night.
get in: Water *gets in* through the cracks in the roof.
put up: *Put up* your umbrella; it's starting to rain.

Many of the lexical verbs in such combinations are among the most frequently used English verbs, denoting in their basic sense a physical or directional movement (*go, carry, come, get, bring, take, put, walk,* etc.). They combine with a wide variety of adverbs in both transitive and intransitive uses. Since they can be permuted it is possible to list them starting from one particular lexical verb such as those below:

	up		up		up
	down		down		down
	out		out		out
go	in	get	in	carry	in
	over		over		over
	off		off		off
	away		away		away

Alternatively, they can be listed by replacing the basic lexical verb by a more specific verb of movement, while retaining the same adverbial particle. Instead of the basic *go out*, for instance, we may specify the manner of movement more exactly: *walk out, run out, hurry out, rush out, sidle out, creep out,* etc. In this way a situation or event may be expressed either in a basic analytical way or by means of lexical verbs with emotive, physical or other connotations. Compare:

I'll *take down* those posters and *put up* some new ones.
I'll *pull down* those posters and *stick up* some new ones.
I'll *tear down* those posters and *paste up* some new ones.

40.7.2 Semi-idiomatic verb + adverb combinations

In these combinations the lexical verb, generally speaking, keeps its meaning while the particle is used as an intensifier or as an aspectual marker of perfectivity in the sense of completion. In phrasal verbs the notion of completion is most clear in those cases in which there is a contrast with a single verb, as in *use* v. *use up*, *eat* v. *eat up*, etc. Compare *I've used this detergent* (i.e. some of this detergent) with *I've used up this detergent* (= there is none left). In other cases perfectivity is interpreted in various ways, according to the situation represented by the clause. Some of the many shades of meaning are illustrated below:

I'll *cut up* the meat for the child. (cut into pieces)
She always keeps old letters, never *tears* them *up* (tear into pieces)
or *throws* them *away*. (discard)
Don't forget to *lock up* (the house) before going on holiday.
(lock all the doors and windows.)
Our water supply was *cut off* while repairs were carried out. (be discontinued)
These stains won't *wash out*. (disappear by washing)
He *spoke out* in favour of the disabled. (speak forcefully)
We never *found out* who sent the anonymous letter. (discover)
The sound of thunder *died away*. (gradually disappear)
The clamour finally *died down*. (come to an end)

The adverb *away* can add an imperfective meaning, frequently iterative:

I could hear him *hammering away*.

40.7.3 Fully idiomatic combinations

Fully idiomatic combinations are those in which the meaning of the whole cannot be deduced from the parts, as in many of our examples in previous sections.

She can *run up* a dress in an hour on that machine. (make)
Many smaller firms have been *taken over* by larger ones. (gain control of)
That child *catches on* quickly. (understand)
Schools *broke up* last week for the summer holidays. (disperse)
It's difficult to *get out of* a bad habit. (lose, drop)

A brief review of the examples given above of the classes of multi-word verbs shows that it is by no means easy to establish boundaries between what is idiomatic and what is not. Many verbs, both one-word and multi-word, have a number of related meanings according to their collocation with different nouns and to the contexts in which they are used. Particularly characteristic of multi-word verbs are their metaphorical extensions of meaning, from concrete to abstract or abstract to concrete; and from one context to another less congruent one. Phrasal verbs in particular lend themselves to metaphorical extension. They consist mostly of common verbs (*go*, *come*, *get*) of very general reference, and so easily adaptable to different contexts, and a small number of adverbial particles (*off*, *up*, *out*, *down*, *away*), also of very general reference, so that they can be made to mean almost anything. On the other hand, a few others, such as *peter out*, *tamper with*, only occur as multi-word verbs; there is no single-word verb *peter* or *tamper*. The degree of semantic cohesion between verb and particle varies considerably from one use to another, and it is difficult to measure the idiomaticity accurately. A simple phrasal verb such as *put up* yields the following examples:

> The boys have *put up* the tent. (erect)
> They're *putting up* a new block of flats. (build)
> They've *put* the bus fares *up*. (raise)
> I can *put* two of you *up* for a couple of nights. (provide a bed for)
> The others will have to *put up* at a hotel. (lodge)
> The project has been approved, but someone will have to *put up* the necessary funds. (provide)
> Our neighbours have *put* their house *up* for sale. (announce, offer)

Finally, it is important to realise that any verb, whether single- or multi-word, can be followed by a Prepositional Group functioning as a completely separate structural element, Adjunct or Predicator Complement, in the clause:

Multi-word verb		Single-/multi-word verb	+ A/Cp
She ran up	large bills.	She ran	up the stairs.
I'll call on	Dr. Jones.	I'll call	on Friday.
They looked into	the matter.	They looked	into the cave.
We ran out of	petrol.	We ran	out of the pub.
The car ran over	the cat.	The car ran	over the field.
She came by	a fortune.	She came	by bus.
We put up with	the noise.	We put up	at a hotel.
They played on	our sympathy.	They played	on their home ground.

The following syntactic tests help to distinguish multi-word verbs from verbs followed by PrepGs as Adjunct or Predicator Complement:

(a) The Nominal Group Object of a phrasal or prepositional verb can in many cases become Subject in a passive clause, whereas the Nominal Group which is part of an Adjunct or Predicator Complement cannot:

> The matter was looked into.   *The cave was looked into.

The cat was run over by a car.   *The field was run over by a car.
How was the fortune come by?   *The bus was come by.

The NG of an Adjunct can become Subject in a passive, however, if it can be interpreted as in some way an Affected participant in the semantic structure (see 14.3):

The fields of this historic school must have been played *on* by thousands of boys.

(b) Whereas a phrasal or Prepositional Object is elicited by *what* or *who(m)*, an Adjunct is elicited by *when*, *where*, or *how*:

What did she run up?   *Where* did she run?
Who will you call on?   *When* will you call?
What did he come by?   *How* did he come?

(c) Fronting of the particle + complement is not possible with idiomatic multi-word verbs, whereas it is usually possible with Adjuncts and Predicator Complements:

*Up large bills she ran.   *Up the stairs* she ran.
*On Dr. Jones I'll call.   *On Friday* I'll call.

The adverb (and following PrepG) may be fronted in intransitive phrasal verbs of the type we have called 'non-idiomatic free combinations' (*go off*, *get up*, etc.) and this fact supports the analysis often made of such adverbial particles as Adjuncts:

Off they go!   *Up* you get!
Away to the east they flew.   *Down to the bottom* it fell.

There is a parallel, therefore, between intransitive phrasals of the 'free combination' type and single verbs of movement followed by a PrepG as Adjunct or Predicator Complement. In many cases, it is possible to analyse the former as the ellipted version of the latter, when the complement of the preposition represents known information. Compare *He walked past the entrance* with *He walked past*.

In the following extract, multi-word verbs provide much of the liveliness and informality in the situations described:

When George *drew out*[1] a tin of pineapple from the bottom of the hamper and rolled it into the middle of the boat, we felt that life was worth living after all.

We are very fond of pineapple, all three of us. We *looked at*[2] the picture on the tin; we *thought of*[3] the juice. We *smiled at*[4] one another, and Harris got a spoon ready.

Then we *looked for*[5] something to open the tin with. We *turned out*[6] everything in the hamper. We *turned out*[7] the bags. We *pulled up*[8] the boards at the bottom of the boat. We *took* everything *out*[9] on to the bank and shook it. There was no tin-opener to be found.

Then Harris tried to open the tin with a pocket-knife, and broke the knife and cut himself badly; and George tried a pair of scissors, and the scissors *flew up*[10] and nearly *put* his eye *out*.[11] While they were dressing their wounds, I tried to make a hole in the tin with the spiky end of the boat pole, and the pole slipped and *jerked* me *out*[12] between the boat and the bank into two feet of muddy water, and the tin *rolled over*[13] and broke a tea-cup.

Jerome K. Jerome, *Three Men in a Boat*.

[1] transitive phrasal; [2–5] preposition; [6–9] transitive phrasal; [10] intransitive phrasal; [11] transitive phrasal; [12] causative transitive phrasal; [13] intransitive phrasal.

TASKS ON CHAPTER 8
Talking about events: The Verbal Group

Module 37

1 *Discussion:*

   1) In what way does the first element of the VG relate the content of the VG to the 'here and now'?

   2) Discuss the importance of the operator in English by examining its various syntactic features. Taking your own or another language as a basis of comparison, discuss how in that language each of the functions of the English operator would be realised.

   3) *Have* + *to*-infinitive and *have got* + *to*-infinitive seem at first glance to be very similar both syntactically and semantically. Make a syntactic comparison by drawing up a list for each of the syntactic features of each of these verbs. Consider past and present forms, non-finite forms and possible combinations with modals and lexical auxiliaries. For example:

   will + *have to* = *will have to.*   *will* + *have got to* = ?
   be going to + *have to* = *be going*   *be going to* + *have got to* = ?
   to have to.

   Test these combinations by inserting them into sentences. Then try the possible combinations with other lexical auxiliaries.
       Semantically, is it equally possible, with the two verbs *have to* and *have got to*, to express modal meanings such as possibility, and to refer to future time?

2 †*Underline the Verbal Groups in the sentences below and then answer the questions*:

   (a) A bicycle whizzed past me as I was crossing the road.
   (b) It startled me.
   (c) It also startled the elderly woman just ahead of me. She was clutching a bag or bundle or something, and almost fell.
   (d) 'Can't you be more careful?' I shouted after the cyclist.
   (e) He just turned his head a little, but said nothing.
   (f) He was pedalling fast and was soon lost in the traffic.
   (g) He could have injured us both.

(h) The elderly woman's bundle had fallen open into the middle of the road. A strange collection of objects was rolling everywhere.

(i) 'Are you all right?' I asked, as we scrambled to pick up the things before the lights changed.

    1) List the Verbal Groups of one element (v).

    2) List the Verbal Groups of two elements (ov)

    3) Are there any Verbal Groups of three elements (oxv)?

    4) Draw a diagram to illustrate the experiential structure (Finite + Event) of (a) *whizzed* and (b) *was pedalling*.

    5) Draw a structural tree to illustrate the syntactic structure of *could have injured*.

    6) What is the experiential and syntactic status of *are* in (i)?

    7) Write the elderly woman's answer to the question in (i).

    8) Continue with another sentence starting: *We might have* ...

    9) Now give the speaker's opinion of the cyclist, starting *He was*

    10) Conclude with a general comment starting *People should* ...

3 †*Using the lexical auxiliaries listed in 37.3, fill in the blanks in the sentences below with a form of **be** or **have** and the lexical auxiliary you consider most appropriate in each case*:

    1) Wheat-germ .... good for you, isn't it?

    2) We .... have finished exams by the second week in July.

    3) At what time .... the concert ...... start?

    4) Don't you think we .... inquire at the information desk?

    5) This kind of cotton .... shrink in the wash.

    6) I .... say something tactless, but I stopped myself in time.

    7) The storms are so severe in this part of the world that basements .... flooded after ten minutes' rain.

    8) Do you feel you really .... work in the library on a day like this?

    9) What .... we .... do if all the trains are cancelled?

    10) ..... what he said to be taken seriously?

Module 38

1 *Discussion*:

    1) Which are the four meanings expressed by the auxiliaries together with their non-finite forms and in what order do they combine?

    2) Try to reproduce from memory the diagram illustrating how the formal expression of these meanings overlaps in a structure with four auxiliaries.

2 †*Give the syntactic structure of the Verbal Groups in the sentences below, and analyse them for the tense and ABCD features they contain*:

    1) Someone *should be telling* the present administration about Kenya.

    2) Kenya *was about to take off* economically.

    3) Our population *has been* greatly *increased*.

4) That increase *should have been expected*.
5) It *was realised* that modern medicine *was cutting back* the death rate dramatically.
6) But numerous mistakes *were being made* in the allocation of scarce national resources.
7) Our exports *were earning* less in real terms than *they had been earning* a decade ago.
8) Many developing nations *are* gradually *shifting* their economic policies towards free enterprise.
9) We feel that the country *has* not yet *been able to achieve* its potential.
10) But that potential *should* at least *be receiving* recognition.

3 †*Complete the sentences below (which make up a text) with Verbal Groups containing two, three or four auxiliaries, using the verbs indicated:*
   1) The last photograph . . . . (*take* + prog. + pass.) when I arrived.
   2) Pete . . . . (*instruct* + past + perf. + prog. + pass.) on how to use a wide-angle lens.
   3) He . . . . (*use* + *must* + perf. + prog.) a filter.
   4) He . . . . (*use* + *can't* + perf. + prog.) a filter.
   5) She . . . . (*move* + *must* + perf.) when the photograph . . . . (*take* + prog. + pass.)
   6) The film . . . . (*develop* + *will* + prog. + pass.) by my brother.
   7) More colour films . . . . (sell + *be likely* + pass.) than ever this year.
   8) And more cameras . . . . (*buy* + *be sure* + perf. + pass.) in the holiday period.
   9) Look! Some kind of television film . . . . (*shoot* + prog. + pass.) over there.
   10) I should say it . . . . (*shoot* + *must* + perf. + prog. + pass.), rather. They seem to have finished.

4 †*You have decided to put your house up for sale. Unfortunately, two other houses in your neighbourhood have also been put on the market. You are debating what attention the house needs in order to give the best possible impression to prospective buyers. Complete each section, using the suggested verbs in any combination of modal, perfect, progressive, passive that seems appropriate.*
   1) The outside of the house hasn't been painted for several years, and the paint is peeling off in places. I think it . . . . (repaint).
   2) The garden is in rather a mess, too. First impressions are important, so it seems to me that the hedges and the grass . . . . (trim) and the flower-beds . . . . (tidy up). One or two pots of geraniums in the windows . . . . (brighten up) . . . .
   3) Inside the house, there's too much clutter everywhere. Just look at the hall. Hats and coats, fishing tackle, school-bags and the dog's basket.

The whole place . . . . (look) a good deal more spacious if
we even just put away all this stuff.

4) And you can't even open a cupboard without everything . . . .
(fall out). The cupboards would look a lot larger if everything
. . . . (hang) or (stack away) out of sight.

5) Prospective buyers always go to the sitting-room first and look at the
view. . . . . we . . . . (had better, clean) the windows, for a start?
And it . . . . (be) a good idea to have got new curtains; but its
too late for that now.

6) The view . . . . (improve) if we were to remove those unsightly
dustbins to some place around the corner where they . . . . (not/
see).

7) The bedrooms are not too bad, although they . . . . (not/decorate)
in years either. At least they . . . . (not use) as a dumping
ground for cast-off clothes and hobbies.

8) I can't say the same for the garage. It . . . . (clear out) years ago.
As it is, it . . . . (take) days to get rid of all this stuff. That is, if we
. . . . (allow) to do so. You know how children refuse to let you throw
any of their possessions away.

9) What . . . . (worry) me for some time is the kitchen. It has no
sparkle. Not surprising, really, considering the number of meals that
. . . . (have to, prepare) there over the years.

10) Never mind. The most we can do is give the whole place a coat of
paint. We . . . . (can, involve) in refurnishing the kitchen. We
would lose more than we'd gain.

5   †*Underline the Verbal Groups in the following passage and then answer the
questions below:*

A car with a trailer coming our way is passing and having trouble
getting back into his lane. I flash my headlight to make sure he sees us.
He sees us but he can't get back in. The shoulder is narrow and bumpy.
It'll spill us if we take it. I'm braking, honking, flashing. Christ Almighty,
he panics and heads for our shoulder! I hold steady to the edge of the
road. Here he COMES! At the last moment he goes back and misses us
by inches.

Robert M. Pirsig, *Zen and the Art of Motorcycle Maintenance.*

1) Which are more important to this text – actions or states?
2) Identify the finite VGs in the text. List separately the VGs in which the
Finite is fused with the Event, and those in which the Finite is realised
by an operator.
3) Are there any non-finite Verbal Groups in this extract?
4) What tense choice has been made in this text?
5) What aspectual (progressive) choices have been made?
6) What modality choices have been made?

7) What polarity choices have been made?

8) What choices of contrastiveness have been made?

9) Can you explain how the sum of these choices helps to give the impression of movement and excitement and danger in this text?

6   *Write a short paragraph using VGs in the present tense to portray a series of actions or events on one of the following topics*:
(a) an escape from a burning building;
(b) running to catch the train;
(c) chasing a bag-snatcher (handbag thief).

Module 39

1   *Discussion*:

1) What do you understand by 'discontinuity' in the Verbal Group. Which clause constituents can produce discontinuity? Does this occur, to a similar extent, in other languages you know?

2) Discuss the notion of 'phase' to account for combinations such as *appears to be improving, tend to buy too much*. (See 6.1.3(c) for the syntactic criteria which preclude analysing the second VG as an embedded clause.) In what way can we say that the action denoted by the non-finite verb is 'phased in' or 'phased out' by the finite VG?

3) The types of 'phase' described in 39.5 are notional categories and do not pretend to be exhaustive. Discuss the types exemplified in this section and consider whether other verbs might also be included, for instance *rush to do something* and *trouble to do something*. Test first for the ability of the verb to take an Object (see 6.1.1 and 6.1.3), which would exclude it from 'phasing'.

2   †*Using the VGs listed in 39.4 and 39.5, complete the phased Verbal Groups in the sentences below. The first one is done for you*:

1) The supposedly quiet fishing village **turned out to be / proved to be** quite different from what the travel agency had led us to expect.

2) Did you go all the way to the other side of town to take part in the demonstration against the visit? – No, I just .... there.

3) Some years ago we .... to inquire whether a visa was necessary and were held up at the frontier for two days.

4) After .... unsuccessfully on several occasions .... the seamanship test, he eventually .... so at the fourth attempt.

5) Isn't there any washing-up liquid anywhere? – Well, there .... a little left at the bottom of the container.

6) The shop assistant .... reassure the child that her mother would come soon.

7) Even old black-and-white films .... coloured these days.

8) He .... convince the Customs official that he was not smuggling anything, but it .... impossible.

9)   I . . . . ask you this, but perhaps you could . . . .
helping Peter with his statistics course.

10)   You can't afford to . . . . working at this point, or you'll find that you
won't be able to . . . . started again.

3   *Read the following letter, taking note of the variety of Verbal Group
structures used. Then write a reply to it, telling your own experiences in any
environment you like*:

Dear Angela,

Sorry I've taken so long to answer your very welcome letter. I meant to
do so ages ago but then it got left to the half-term break. I must say,
holidays do suit me much better.

School is insane because of the new exam. No-one knows what rules
we're supposed to be following for criteria assessment. Someone high-
up issues a decree and then disappears while the opposite is decreed. If
parents really knew what a mess it was, they'd be frantic. I've stopped
worrying about my 'O' level candidates as I feel it's out of my control.
We're also secretly planning another reorganisation in Liverpool. I
haven't been hit or sworn at yet.

Philip is doing teaching practice in a hilarious school in Leicester
where there is no 'confrontational discipline', i.e. some were arm-
wrestling, some talking, some listening to walkmans and some working.
I hesitate to think about exam results. They've a 90% attendance record,
which implies that our arm-wrestlers are just shop-lifting somewhere, so
perhaps they've hit on the right idea. They're all on individual
programmes. Here am I intending to try *Romeo and Juliet* on my low
ability fourth year. I've told them it's not fair to deprive them.

Claire's brother seems to have worked out a good arrangement. He
lectures in Manchester, has three months on sabbatical leave and goes
digging in Turkey or Greece. Funding doesn't seem to be a problem
because the relevant countries or international groups give him grants,
because his wife, who's a botanist, also comes up with information
about plant types and soil, etc., that have succeeded or failed in the
past. They have three children and all go camping, the baby being two
weeks old on the last trip.

I have talked about my family all the time. How are all of you? Keep
me in the picture.

Much love,

Jean

Module 40

1   †*Tasks on **Three Men in a Boat*** (in 40.7.3)

1)   Identify in the text all Adjuncts/Predicator Complements realised by
Prepositional Groups. Notice particularly those which follow multi-word
verbs.

2)   Try to replace the multi-word verbs in the text by single-word verbs.
Have the single-word verbs the same force and the colloquial flavour of
the original?

3)   Here is the continuation of the passage: identify and classify the multi-
word verbs it contains. Are there any of doubtful analysis?

Then we all got mad. We took the tin out on the bank, and Harris went up into a field and got a big, sharp stone, and I went back into the boat and brought out the mast, and George held the tin and Harris held the sharp end of the stone against the top of it, and I took the mast and poised it high in the air, and gathered up all my strength and brought it down.

It was George's straw hat that saved his life that day, while Harris got off with merely a flesh wound.

After that I took the tin off by myself, and hammered at it with the mast till I was worn out and sick at heart, whereupon Harris took it in hand.

We beat it out flat; we beat it back square; we battered it into every form known to geometry, but we could not make a hole in it. Then George went at it, and knocked it into a shape, so strange, so unearthly in its wild hideousness, that he got frightened and threw away the mast. Then we all sat round it on the grass and looked at it.

There was one great dent across the top that had the appearance of a mocking grin, and that drove us furious, so that Harris rushed at the thing, and caught it up, and flung it far into the middle of the river, and as it sank we hurled our curses at it, and we got into the boat and rowed away from the spot, and never paused till we reached Maidenhead.

Jerome K. Jerome, *Three Men in a Boat.*

2   *Decide on a problematic situation like that of opening a tin without a tin-opener. For instance:*
1) Trying to get into the house if you have left your keys inside.
2) Trying to get the coins out of a money-box.
3) Trying to get the cat into the cat-basket.

Each student relates one incident in the situation, using multi-word verbs wherever possible. Write up the full narrative at the end.

3   †*Classify the verbs in the sentences listed below as follows:*
(a) transitive phrasal; (b) intransitive phrasal; (c) prepositional; (d) phrasal–prepositional; (e) one-word verb + PrepG at Adjunct/Predicator Complement. (Remember that all combinations may be followed by Adjuncts).

1)   He was rushed off to hospital.
2)   A lot of this scrap metal can be melted down and used again.
3)   We'll drive over some time tomorrow.
4)   Fill up the tank, please.
5)   His vocation urged him on.
6)   She accidentally knocked a book off the bedside table.
7)   He was kept on by his firm.
8)   He got on his bike and rode off.
9)   He blew the crumbs off his desk and shook them off his collar.
10)   The new job hasn't come up to her expectations.

11)   The orders were sent out yesterday.
12)   He gulped down his beer.
13)   The cracks in the wall have been plastered over.
14)   He cycled back home.
15)   He raced back home.
16)   He was sent out to get some stamps.
17)   Several trees were blown down.
18)   Some weird specimens have slipped through the net.
19)   He dragged his bike up the path.
20)   Watch out for snakes.

4   English phrasal and prepositional verbs often require to be translated into
    other languages by a verb which expresses the meaning of the particle and
    an adverb which expresses the sense of the English verb, e.g. *He rowed
    across the lake* can be translated into Spanish as *cruzó el lago remando* or
    cruzó el lago en barca. This process is called **cross transposition**. In this
    case the transposition was complete, since both verb and adverb were
    translated. In other cases, either the verb or the particle is better not
    expressed, being taken for granted, as in: *A bird flew in*: *Entró un pájaro*.
    The transposition is then 'incomplete'.

    *Translate the sentences in Task 3 into your own or another language and
    indicate whether the transposition is complete or incomplete.*

9

Viewpoints on events:
Tense, aspect and modality

Introduction

1   The choices represented by the systems of tense, aspect and modality are among the most fundamental in the grammar. Tense and aspect are obligatory categories: every time we encode an event of our experience through a finite clause we select one or other tense, one or other aspectual distinction. With modality the choice is to modalise or not to modalise: that is, to express our statements and questions by means of a plain declarative or interrogative, or instead, to add by means of a modal auxiliary a subjective meaning such as possibility, probability, necessity, obligation or prediction.

2   The influence of these categories extends to three different levels of linguistic expression. On the level of lexis, the meaning-structure of the lexical verb contains built-in features of an aspectual kind, such as duration versus punctuality, completion versus incompletion. As regards the semantics of the proposition expressed by the clause, tense, aspect and modality express various features of the state, event or action. And in connected discourse, these categories play a vital role in the sequencing of events, in foregrounding some and backgrounding others, and in indicating the attitude of the speaker towards the content of the message.

3   Each in a different way, **tense, aspect** and **modality** represent three different angles of vision on our experience of events in time. Tense primarily involves visualising events as points in a sequence, preceding or following a central point which is usually the present moment. Aspect involves the notion of boundedness: whether the action is visualised as having limits or not, whether it is seen as an on-going process or as completed. Different aspects will centre on the expression of the beginning, middle or end-points of the event or action. Finally, modality reflects our view of an event as in some way potential, as having a potential existence in time rather than the factual existence which is expressed by the indicative.

For the purpose of description we treat these three categories as if they were separate functional areas. In reality, they are interconnected, both conceptually and syntactically, and no doubt it is for this reason that the important meanings which they convey are realised primarily in one single unit, the Verbal Group. Time, aspect and modality relations can be expressed by other linguistic units in addition to the VG, and reference will be made to these in the course of the description.

MODULE 41
Expressing time relations through the verb: tense

Summary

1   Tense is the expression of time relations by means of the verb. It refers to events situated at points along the linear flow of time in reference to the 'now', or speech time. In narrative, a point in past time is the reference point.

2   English has two tenses, the Present and the Past, the Past being the marked form. Both Past and Present tenses combine with Progressive aspect as in *It is raining, It was raining*, respectively. This Module deals with the non-progressive tenses, leaving the progressive to be treated in a later section.

3   The non-progressive Present can refer to an event coincident with speech time (*Off they go!*) but more typically refers to events that are recurrent or belong to all time.

4   The Past refers to a definite event or state that is seen as remote, in time or as unreality or for reasons of politeness.

5   Future events and states can be referred to in a number of ways, interacting with modality.

41.1   The meaning of tense

Tense can be defined as the linguistic expression of time relations when these are realised by verb forms. Time is independent of language and is common to all human beings. It is conceptualised by many peoples, though not necessarily by all, as being divided into past time, present time and future time. Tense systems are language specific and vary from one language to another, both in the number of tenses they distinguish and in the ways in which these tenses reflect temporal reference. In English, for instance, it would be erroneous to imagine that the Past tense refers exclusively to events in past time, that there is a Present tense to refer exclusively to events in present time and a Future tense to refer exclusively to events in future time. In the following examples, the forms often thought to correspond to past and future time reference, respectively, in fact refer to the moment of speaking:

> I thought you *were* on the beach.
> *Will* you *sign* here, please?
> I *was wondering* whether you *needed* any help.

Conversely, the 'Present tense' forms used in the following examples do not refer exclusively to the moment of speaking:

> These trees *look* beautiful in autumn.
> We *leave* for Paris tomorrow.
> Temperatures *drop* to below zero.
> In *walks* an Irishman, *sits down* and *orders* a pint. . . .

Besides tense forms of verbs, other linguistic forms, particularly adverbs of time such as *now, then, tomorrow* and Prepositional Groups such as *in 1066* can make reference to time; English, in fact, relies to a considerable extent on such units to make the temporal reference clear.

41.2   Points in time and points of reference

Tense is a way of expressing events as occurring at points situated along the linear flow of time. Within the linear flow, a point of reference must be established, with respect to which past events precede and future events follow. The normal, universal and therefore unmarked point of reference is the moment of speaking – speech time. This is the 'now', which is implicitly understood in everyday interaction. It can be diagrammed as follows:

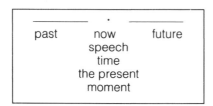

Further distinctions such as 'remote past' and 'immediate future' can then be additionally made.

41.3   The Present and Past tenses in English

Even in our everyday use, 'at present' and 'at the present time' have a wider application than simply to the present moment of speech time. Thus, the example *Birds have wings* includes in its time reference the present moment but also past and future time. It can be diagrammed in the following way:

Present time in this sense can therefore mean (a) at all times, or (b) at no particular time.

The grammatical tense which is used in examples such as this is the unmarked form, having no modification, consisting of the lexical verb alone with no grammatical meaning beyond that of 'verb'. It can consequently cover a wide range of temporal references. If we retain the traditional term **Present** or **non-progressive Present** for convenience, rather than the term **Non-past** preferred by some grammarians, it is with the recognition that as a tense it only rarely has a direct relation to speech time.

The **Non-past** as an alternative term to **Present** tense is based on the following reasoning: while the Present tense can refer to future time as in *We leave for Paris tomorrow. When do we arrive?* it can not normally be used with a time expression which refers specifically to an event in the past: *ˣI see that film last week* instead of *I saw that film last week* (but see 41.4.4 below). The unmarked form therefore can be used to make specific reference to a future event but not normally to a past event.

The Past tense in English is the morphologically and semantically marked form; morphologically in that the vast majority of verbs have a distinctive past form, and semantically in that the Past tense refers to an action that is visualised as remote, either in time (*I saw that film last week*) or as unreality (*I wish we **were** on the beach*). We have, consequently, in English an unmarked tense, which we shall call the Present and a marked tense which is the Past.

In accordance with the criterion that tense is a category realised by inflection on the verb, English, strictly speaking, has no Future tense. Against this view it might be argued that, in spoken English at least, the enclitic form *'ll* corresponding to *shall* and *will* is very similar to an inflection. More important, however, are the form-meaning relationships: first, *shall* and *will* belong to a set of modal auxiliaries and can express meanings other than reference to future time, such as willingness in *Will you sign here?* and request for instructions as in *Shall I carry your case?*; furthermore, *will* has its own past form *would*; and finally, future time can be referred to by a number of grammatical and lexical forms.

We shall examine in the following sections the meanings expressed by the Present and the Past tenses, the various ways of referring to future events, and the status of the Present Perfect.

41.4   Meanings expressed by the non-progressive Present

The meaning expressed by a verb in the non-progressive Present tense depends to a great extent on whether the verb is stative, such as *be, seem, belong*, or dynamic, such as *kick, eat, write*. More exactly, we should say that the meaning depends on whether the verb is being used statively or dynamically, since many verbs lend themselves to both interpretations. *Stand* in *the house stands on a hill*, for instance, expresses a state, whereas the phrasal verb *stand up* is used dynamically in *All the children stood up*.

In general, dynamic but not stative meanings occur after *do* in pseudo-cleft sentences:

> What the children did was stand up.
> *What the house does is stand on a hill.

41.4.1   Present and timeless states

With stative verb meanings the Present can express timeless statements, that is, statements which apply to all time, including speech time. These include scientific, mathematical and descriptive statements, as in the following examples:

> Steel *is* a strong metal.
> Gold *has* a relatively low melting-point.
> Two and two *make* four.
> Silk *feels* smooth to the touch.

Human affairs often involve states whose time span is not endless, e.g. *know, seem, belong*. They are nevertheless states, in which no change or limitation into the past or future is implied:

> He *knows* Morocco quite well.
> This land *belongs* to the National Trust.
> Those exercises *look* difficult.

Here, too, the temporal reference includes speech time.

41.4.2   Repeated events in the present

With dynamic verbs the Present expresses a series of events which cover an unspecified time. Speech time is not necessarily or even usually included; such statements are, however, valid at speech time:

> He *works* in an insurance company.
> Many trees *lose* their leaves in autumn.
> They *spend* most of their holidays abroad.

Adjuncts of time, frequency, place, destination, etc., often accompany statements in the Present which express repeated or recurrent events. Indeed, many such statements as *They spend most of their holidays* are incomplete without a circumstantial specification.

41.4.3   Instantaneous events in the present

In certain situations the event coincides, or is presented as coinciding, with the moment of speaking, and without having any duration beyond speech time. The Present is used in such situations, which are classified as specific types:

Performatives: I *warn* you that this gun is loaded.

Exclamations with initial directional adverb: Off they *go*!
Commentaries: Jones *passes* and Lineker *heads* the ball into the net!
Demonstrations: I *place* the fruit in the blender, *press* gently, and then *pour* out the liquid.

41.4.4   Reference to past events

The Present can be used to refer to past events in certain limited ways:

(a) **In newspaper headlines**

> Hard Cash *sends* back a blank Czech. (Pat Cash beats Ivan Lendl at Wimbledon)
> Thousands *flee* persecution.

The effect of the Present in such cases is to dramatise the event, making it appear before the reader's eyes as if it were in fact an instance of the instantaneous Present.

(b) **In relating incidents**

> He was only an average athlete, and then suddenly he *wins* two Olympic medals.
> I was just about to go to bed when all of a sudden there's a knock at the door and Sam *rushes in*.

This use, called the 'historic present' is also motivated by a desire to achieve dramatic effect, in this case in order to highlight the main point in a narrative or anecdote by bringing it into the moment of speaking. Instances of the historic present in casual conversation tend to be inserted into discourse containing Past tenses and are often preceded by an Adjunct signalling immediacy such as *suddenly, all of a sudden*.

In written English the historic present can occur in stage directions (*He sits on the bed and takes off his shoes*) and captions to photographs (*Demonstrators clash with armed police as violence increases*), but is rarely employed throughout a whole fictional work except for autobiographical effects.

Perhaps a variant of the historic present is the predominant use of the Present in recounting the plots of books and films. The following extract from a conversation about the power of the press contains a brief summary of Evelyn Waugh's *Scoop*, a fictional account of the inventiveness of press reporters:

> It's one of Evelyn Waugh's best, I think, because he's got this—er—situation where a man is going off to report on some trouble somewhere in America. I've forgotten the details now but he *gets* on the wrong train and *ends up* in the wrong place – and *finds* that he's in a place that's perfectly quiet and perfectly innocent and there's no story – and so he

just *writes* one – and within a week he's managed to create riots, you know, the whole place *is* in a furore.

Adapted from D. Crystal & D. Davy, *Advanced Conversational English*.

(c) **In reporting information**: with verbs of communicating (*say, tell*) and of perception (*see, hear, understand*) the use of the Present implies that the reported information is still operative, even though the communicative process took place in the past. If a past verb is used, e.g. *said, announced*, the present validity of the information is not stressed:

> The weatherman *forecasts* heavy showers in the north.
> Peter *tells* me he has changed his job.
> I *understand* that you would like to move to London.

The novel from which the following extract is taken makes great use of the Present, both progressive and non-progressive, to convey the autobiographical sequence of events, as well as the author's thought. Here, various meanings are also illustrated:

> Chris and I *are traveling* [1] to Montana with some friends riding up ahead, and maybe headed farther than that. Plans *are* [2] deliberately indefinite, more to travel than to arrive anywhere. We *are* just *vacationing*. [3] Secondary roads *are preferred*. [4] Paved country roads *are* [5] the best, state highways *are* [6] next. Freeways *are* [7] the worst. We *want* [8] to make good time, but for us now this *is measured* [9] with emphasis on 'good' rather than 'time' and when you *make* [10] that shift in emphasis the whole approach *changes*. [11] Twisting hilly roads *are* [12] long in terms of seconds but *are* [13] much more enjoyable on a cycle where you *bank* [14] into turns and *don't get swung* [15] from side to side in any compartment. Roads with little traffic *are* [16] more enjoyable, as well as safer. Roads free of drive-ins and billboards *are* [17] better, roads where groves and meadows and orchards and lawns *come*[18] almost to the shoulder, where kids *wave* [19] to you when you *ride* [20] by, where people *look* [21] from their porches to see who it *is* [22] where when you *stop* [23] to ask directions or information the answer *tends to be* [24] longer than you *want* [25] rather than short, where people *ask* [26] where you're [27] from and how long you've been riding.

> Robert M. Pirsig, *Zen and the Art of Motorcycle Maintenance*.

[1] historic Pres. Prog.; [2] copular; [3] historic Pres. Prog.; [4] state (affective); [5–7] state (copular); [8] state (affective); [9] instantaneous; [10, 11] habitual event; [12, 13] copular; [14, 15] habitual event; [16, 17] copular; [18] habitual state; [19–21] habitual event; [22] copular; [23] habitual event; [24] copular; [25] state (affective); [26] habitual event; [27] copular.

41.5   Meanings expressed by the non-progressive Past tense

We have seen that the global meaning of the Past tense in English may be said to be 'remoteness' or distancing from the moment of speaking, whether in time, towards the past, or with regard to potential or hypothetical events which have not yet occurred in the present or the future.

41.5.1 Definite events in the past

When used to refer to a past event or state, the Past in English contains two semantic features:

(a) The speaker visualises the event as having occurred at some specific time in the past.
(b) The event was completed in the past, and a gap in time separates its completion from the present.

These features are illustrated in the following examples:

> I bought some biscuits yesterday.
> James Joyce was born in Dublin in 1882.
> He lived in Ireland until 1904 and spent the rest of his life abroad.

They are also nicely reflected in the following anecdote, in which the writer Lytton Strachey puts down a gushing admirer:

> Gushing admirer: Oh, Mr. Strachey, we *met* four years ago.
> Lytton Strachey: Quite a nice interval, I think.

These requirements mean that there is a fairly rigid distinction in English between what can be expressed by the Past and what can be expressed by the Present Perfect. (For the meanings expressed by the Present Perfect see section 43.1) The meanings of specific occurrence, completed event and disconnectedness from present time are *not* normally expressed by the Present Perfect; the above examples, for instance, are ungrammatical with the verb in the Perfect:

> *I have bought some biscuits yesterday.
> *He has been born in Dublin.
> *We have met four years ago.

Adjuncts of specific past time such as *yesterday* and *in 1882* naturally combine well with the Past, but not with the Perfect, since their function is to signal the past moment in time explicitly.

Speakers do not need to specify a past occurrence by means of an Adjunct, however. As long as the speaker has a specific time in mind and can assume that the hearer understands this, from inference or from the situational context, the Past tense can be used alone, as in:

> *Did* you *see* that parachute coming down?
> You *didn't tell* me you *met* Mary at the supermarket.
> *Did* Phil *remember* to post my letters?

The situations referred to in these examples are situationally definite, the definiteness of the event being in many cases confirmed by the definiteness of the participants (*that parachute, my letters*) or the circumstance (*at the supermarket*).

The definiteness of the event expressed by the Past does not require that the time in question be specified, only that it is specifiable. For this reason even unspecific adverbs such as *once, when* and conjunctions such as *while* and *as soon as* can introduce Past tense verbs:

> I *once knew* a dancer from the Bolshoi ballet.
> *When did* you *learn* Swedish?
> *While* we *drove* along, he *told* me about his latest film.
> *As soon as* they *saw* us, they *disappeared* into a doorway.

The use of the Past tense to express a sequence of events and activities is illustrated in this extract from J. G. Ballard's short story *Memories of the Space Age*:

> Mallory *began to re-start* the engine, when the machine-guns over the pilot's wind-shield *opened* fire on him. He *assumed* that the pilot was shooting blank ammunition left over from some air display. Then the first bullets *struck* the metalled road a hundred feet ahead. The second burst *threw* the car onto its flattened front tyres, *severed* the door pillar by the passenger seat and *filled* the cabin with exploding glass. As the plane *climbed* steeply, about to make its second pass at him, Mallory *brushed* the blood-flecked glass from his chest and thighs. He *leapt* from the car and *vaulted* over the metal railing into the shallow culvert beside the bridge, as his blood *ran* away through the water towards the waiting forest of the space grounds.
>
> In M. Bradbury (ed.), *Modern British Short Stories*.

41.5.2   The Past tense with present and future reference

The Past tense can refer to time spheres other than the past in the following three ways:

(a) **In reported speech or thought**: after a reporting verb in the Past tense, the reported verbs in the dependent clauses are also in the Past. This phenomenon is known as 'backshift' (see 36.4.1). Present tense forms are optional as in *She said she would/will be glad to see us*, as long as the situation is still valid, and are sometimes preferred when a resulting temporal contrast would be undesirable, as in: *I didn't realise that you were/are the president of the tennis club*.

(b) **In polite requests and enquiries** the Past form 'distances' the proposed action, so making the imposition on the hearer less direct:

> *Would* you just sign here, please.
> *Did* you want to speak to me now?
> I *wondered* whether you needed anything.

(c) **In hypothetical subordinate clauses** which express a counterfactual belief or expectation on the part of the speaker. The Past in such expressions was originally a subjunctive whose only relic remains in the form *were* for all persons of *be*.

> He talks as if he *owned* the place.
> If only we *had* more time!
> I often wish I *were* somewhere else.

41.6   Referring to future events

We cannot refer to future events as facts, as we can to past and present situations, since events in the future have not yet happened. We can predict with more or less confidence what will happen, we can plan for events to take place, express our intentions and promises with regard to future events. These are modalised rather than factual predications, and are treated in 44.3. Here we simply outline the main syntactic means of referring to future events as seen from the standpoint of present time.

41.6.1   'Safe' predictions

These are predictions which do not involve the Subject's volition, and include cyclical events and general truths. *Will* + infinitive is used, *shall* by some speakers for 'I' and 'we':

> Janice *will be* nineteen tomorrow.
> The twenty-first century *will* soon *be* with us.
> We *shall be* free for most of August.
> You'*ll find* petrol more expensive in France.

Prediction of generalities can include speech time:

> If people have the opportunity, they'*ll take* it.

Will/shall + Progressive (see 42.5) combine the meaning of futurity with that of limited duration, at the same time avoiding the implication of promise associated with these modals when the subject is 'I' or 'we':

> I'*ll be seeing* him tomorrow at about ten.
> We *shall be studying* your application shortly.

41.6.2   Programmed events

Future events seen as certain because they have been programmed can be expressed by the Present + time Adjunct or by *be due to* + infinitive:

> Our holidays *start* next Saturday.
> The sun *sets* at 20.15 hours tomorrow.
> He *is due to retire* in two months' time.

41.6.3   Intended events

Intended events can be expressed by *be + going to* + infinitive, or simply by the Present Progressive + time Adjunct:

> I am *going to try to get* more information about this.
> Pete says he'*s changing* his job next month.

41.6.4   Imminent events

An event which is seen as occurring in the immediate future is expressed by *be + going to* or by *be about to* + infinitive:

> It looks as if there'*s going to be* a storm.
> This company *is about to be taken over* by a multinational.

A prediction or expectation oriented to past time is expressed by these same forms in the past:

> It's not what I *thought* it *was going to be*.
> She *looked* as if she *was about to collapse*.

41.6.5   Future anterior events

A future event anterior to another event is expressed by the **Future Perfect**:

> The programme *will have ended* long before we get back.
> By the time he is twenty-two, he'*ll have taken* his degree.

Otherwise, the Future Perfect expresses the duration or repetition of an event in the future. The addition of the Progressive emphasises the 'stretching out' of the sequence (see 42.5):

> We'*ll have lived* here for ten years by next July.
> We'*ll have been living* here for ten years by next July.

MODULE 42
Stretching out the event: Progressive aspect

Summary

1   Aspect refers to such contrasts as durative/punctual and perfective/imperfective.

2   English has only one obligatory aspectual contrast: progressive/non-progressive. Progressiveness is one type of imperfectivity. Another, that of discontinued habit or state, is expressed by *used to* + inf.

3   Progressiveness, realised by *be* + *-ing*, combines with the inherent verbal meaning to produce such effects as the 'stretching' of the event, repetition of the event, etc.

4   These effects are exploited in discourse.

5   Perfectivity is not realised unambiguously in English by verbal forms, but must be interpreted from the whole clause.

42.1   The meaning of aspect

While tense primarily relates the event to speech time, or to a reference point in the past, aspect is concerned with the internal character of the event as it is presented by the speaker; it focuses on such contrasts as durative (extending in time) or non-durative, whether the event is seen in its initial stage or its final stage, whether it is completed or uncompleted. We have already had occasion to refer to the stative / dynamic contrast in describing the meanings of the tenses in English and to the perfective / imperfective contrast expressed to some extent in some complex VGs. Having fewer aspectual inflections, English has fewer aspectual choices than some languages. The one obligatory choice is that of the progressive (*is/was going*) versus the non-progressive forms (*goes, went*). We shall treat progressiveness as a type of imperfectivity, or incompletion. Perfectivity is not to be confused with the Present Perfect, whose meanings are examined in 43.1.

42.2   Perfectivity and imperfectivity

Perfective aspect is a term used to indicate that the situation expressed by the predication is viewed as a single whole, without attention being drawn to the separate phases that make up that situation. Certain uses of the Present (Jones *passes* the ball; We *start* tomorrow) can be considered perfective. The problem is that habitual meanings, which are a form of imperfectivity (He *works* at night; He *works* on and off), are expressed in English by the same base form of the verb, the imperfectivity being conveyed by circumstantial expressions (*at night, on and off*) or deduced from the co-text (*On Saturdays he works on the night-shift. He gets home at 8 a.m., has breakfast and goes to bed*).

With past time reference, a perfective interpretation is equally dependent on outside information. The verb *spoke*, for instance, in the sentence *He knew he spoke too fast* can have a perfective interpretation if it is understood to refer to one specific occasion, but an imperfective interpretation if it is understood as repeated, that is that he habitually spoke too fast. In many languages, these distinctions would be signalled morphologically.

Imperfectivity draws attention to the internal structure of the event or situation. It is a wide category, which can include such aspects as habituality, discontinued habit, iterativity and progressiveness. While habituality is signalled by adverbs or the co-text, and iterativity partly by lexical items in VG complexes (*kept on shouting*) and by phrasal verb particles (*he hammered away*), English does have a specific form to express discontinued habit or state. This is the lexical auxiliary *used to* + infinitive as in *He knew he used to speak too fast*.

42.3   Expressing discontinued habit or state

Used to + **infinitive** is illustrated in the following examples:

> Fred *used to be* a friend of mine.
> There *used to be* trees all round this square.
> This ring *used to belong* to my mother.
> A monastery *used to stand* on this hill.
> He *used to speak* several languages.
> We *used to visit* each other quite often.

This structure has the following features:

(a) It can be used with both stative verbs (*be, belong, stand*) and dynamic verbs (*speak, visit*) to express either a state or a series of events which were discontinued before speech time.

(b) It is particularly useful in being able to express, without an accompanying time Adjunct, the fact that the state or habit no longer occurs. The time expression can be added; for instance, *many years ago* could be added to all the above examples, but the implicit meaning of *not any longer* is so strong that an additional expression is unnecessary.

(c) It makes an event into a sequence of events, that is a habit. In other words, it makes a potentially perfective expression into an imperfective one. Compare:

He visited me.	He used to visit me.
We went to the theatre.	We used to go to the theatre.

(d) It is not to be confused with *be used to* + *-ing* (= 'be accustomed to' + *-ing*) as in *He is not used to working late hours*.

The following extracts illustrate the meaning of *used to* + infinitive, the first as an elliptical response:

'You're the ball player,' Danny said. 'The big-leaguer. You played with the Washington Senators.'
'*Used to*. Don't play anymore.'

William Kennedy, *Billy Phelan's Greatest Game*.

Josias *used to* turn out regularly to political meetings and he took part in a few protests before everything went underground, but he had never been more than one of the crowd.

Nadine Gordimer, *No Place Like*.

42.4   Duration, boundedness and agency

In order to understand the meanings expressed by the Progressive in English, and the restrictions on its use, it is necessary to elaborate on the stative / dynamic distinction already made in treating the verb. The following classification overlaps in many details with the transitivity categories examined in Chapter 4. Here, however, we are concerned primarily with the duration or non-duration (punctuality) of the verbal situation, whether or not it is agentive (see section 42.4.2) and finally, whether or not it is bounded by an end-point.

42.4.1   Stative verbs

States are durative, in that they last throughout time; they are unbounded in that no end-point is implied in the verb itself, and they do not have agentive Subjects.

Stative verbs can be grouped into the following classes:

relational verbs: *be, belong, consist, cost, depend, own, possess, seem, sound*, etc.
verbs of involuntary perception: *see, hear, smell, taste, feel*
verbs of cognition: *know, think, understand, recognise*, etc.
verbs of affectivity: *like, dislike, hate, detest, love*.

Verbs such as *stand, lie, live* are intermediate between stative and dynamic. With inanimate Subjects a stative interpretation is common (*The farm lies in a valley, The monastery stands on a hill*); with animate Subjects a stative interpretation would be normal in *They were lying on the beach, They were standing in the rain, He lived till the age of eighty-five*. When an end-point is established, expressed by a directional adverb, the situation is evidently dynamic, as in *Lie down on the ground!*, *Stand up!*, *He'll never live down the disgrace*.

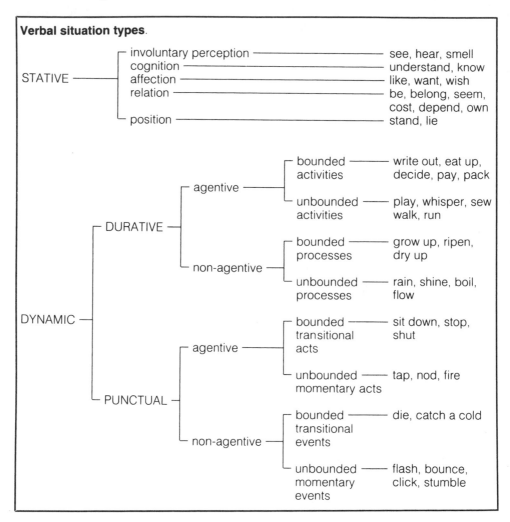

Verbal situation types.

STATIVE
- involuntary perception —— see, hear, smell
- cognition —— understand, know
- affection —— like, want, wish
- relation —— be, belong, seem, cost, depend, own
- position —— stand, lie

DYNAMIC
- DURATIVE
  - agentive
    - bounded activities —— write out, eat up, decide, pay, pack
    - unbounded activities —— play, whisper, sew walk, run
  - non-agentive
    - bounded processes —— grow up, ripen, dry up
    - unbounded processes —— rain, shine, boil, flow
- PUNCTUAL
  - agentive
    - bounded transitional acts —— sit down, stop, shut
    - unbounded momentary acts —— tap, nod, fire
  - non-agentive
    - bounded transitional events —— die, catch a cold
    - unbounded momentary events —— flash, bounce, click, stumble

42.4.2 Dynamic verbs

Dynamic verbs can be classified as either durative or punctual. Durative verbs represent dynamic situations which extend through time such as *rain, read, sleep, ripen*. Punctual verbs do not extend through time: *kick, blink, jump, drop*.

Durative verbs can be either agentive (*play, sing, whisper*) or non-agentive (*ripen, grow, rain, snow*):

    The children have gone off to *play*.   (agentive)

Doesn't she *sing* beautifully?	(agentive)
Weeds *grow* even faster in this climate.	(non-agentive)
Grapes won't *ripen* without some sun.	(non-agentive)

Punctual verbs can likewise be either agentive (*kick, hit, swat, jump*) or non-agentive (*drop, blink, sneeze, explode*):

I *swatted* the mosquito with a newspaper.	(agentive)
The cat *jumped* out of the window.	(agentive)
The dust made me *sneeze*.	(non-agentive)
The bomb *exploded* outside a Government office.	(non-agentive)

The action of swatting an insect is always agentive, whereas that of hitting something need not be, as in *The truck hit a wall*. Similarly, it is not only animate beings that jump, but also inanimates such as profits, temperatures, prices and populations. In this very general outline of verb types, it must be remembered that a great many verbs can be associated with many different types of Subject and express a wide variety of situations. Only the most prototypical associations are presented for our current purpose.

Both durative and punctual verbs can either have an end-point or have no end-point, that is, be bounded or unbounded. Here, again, certain verbs, such as *boil*, can be either bounded (= 'come to the boil') or unbounded (= 'boil continuously'). Unbounded verbs can become bounded by means of an adverbial particle (*boil away*) or a resulting Attribute (*boil dry*). Rather than the verb, it is, of course, the situation as it is expressed linguistically that is bounded (*The water has boiled away*) or unbounded (*The water is boiling*), and a number of devices, including the adverbial particles of phrasal verbs, expounded or unexpounded Objects (see 9.1.2), Progressive aspect, etc., are exploited to establish the differences.

I don't mind which we have; I'll let you *decide*. (durative + bounded)
He *runs* every morning to keep fit. (durative, unbounded)
The traffic lights *changed* to red. (punctual, bounded)
The ambulance light *flashed*, warning motorists to give way.
(punctual, unbounded)

Durative verbs which have an end-point are either agentive such as *write out, eat up, decide* (bounded activities), or non-agentive such as *grow up, improve, ripen* (bounded processes).

Durative verbs without an end-point are either agentive such as *sew, whisper* and *play* (unbounded activities), or non-agentive such as *rain, shine, boil* (unbounded processes).

Eat up your cornflakes! (agentive, durative, bounded)
You'll find the children *have grown up* in your absence. (non-agentive, durative, bounded)
It's not polite to *whisper* during a speech or a lecture. (agentive, durative, unbounded)
She brushed her hair till it *shone*. (non-agentive, durative, unbounded)

Punctual verbs which have an end-point are transitions; the agentive type includes *sit down*, *stop* (bounded transitional acts); the non-agentive type includes *die, catch a cold* (bounded transitional events).

Unbounded punctual events are momentary, either agentive such as *tap, nod, pat* (unbounded momentary acts), or non-agentive such as *flash, bounce, flap* (unbounded momentary events). Both types will frequently be interpreted in context as iterative.

> I *sat down* nervously on the edge of the chair. (agentive, punctual, bounded)
> The country's foremost humourist *died* unexpectedly in his home last night. (non-agentive, punctual, bounded)
> The child *patted* the dog. (agentive, punctual, unbounded, probably iterative)
> A tattered flag *flapped* in the wind. (non-agentive, punctual, unbounded, iterative)

The **Verbal situation types** table summarises these contrasts.

42.5   The meaning of the Progressive

English has a Progressive aspect realised by verbal periphrasis: some form of *be* and the *-ing* participle. It combines with both Present and Past tenses, and also with the Perfect, with modals, with lexico-modals and with the passive:

> He *is* writ*ing*   Present + Progressive
> He *was* writ*ing*   Past + Progressive
> He *has been* writ*ing*   Perfect + Progressive
> He *will be* writ*ing*   Modal + Progressive
> He *is bound to be* writ*ing*   Lexico-modal + Progressive
> It *is being* writt*en*   Present + Progressive + Passive

The full range of such combinations in the Verbal Group has been treated in sections 38.3 to 38.7.

The basic function of the English Progressive aspect is to indicate a dynamic action in the process of happening. Attention is focused on the middle of the process, which is seen as essentially dynamic.

Unlike some languages which also have a Progressive, English makes a grammatical contrast with the non-progressive, as in *What are you doing?* as opposed to *What do you do?* That is to say, there is an obligatory choice between viewing the action as in the process of happening (*What are you doing?*) and not viewing it in this way.

42.6   Inherent verbal meanings and the Progressive

As the Progressive is essentially dynamic in character, it lends a dynamic interpretation to whatever verbal action it is applied to. For this reason, not all types of verbal situation admit the Progressive, and those that do admit it are affected in different ways.

42.6.1 States and the Progressive

Many stative situations are incompatible with the Progressive. Permanent qualities such as *Peter is tall*, states of the weather such as *It's quite hot today* and relations expressed by such verbs as *own, belong, seem, sound* are visualised in English as invariable and therefore non-dynamic. We would not find instances such as:

<blockquote>
*Peter is being tall.
*It's being quite hot today.
*He is owning / possessing land in the south.
*Your hay-fever is seeming a bit less severe lately.
*That music is sounding too loud.
</blockquote>

Be and *look* as copular verbs linking the Subject with a temporary Attribute are more versatile and can take on dynamic meanings, often indicating an attitude on the part of the speaker:

<blockquote>
Peter is being unusually patient with the children.
You are looking a little depressed.
</blockquote>

Verbs of involuntary perception (*see, hear, smell, taste*) are incompatible with the Progressive, whether the Subject is the one who perceives (the Experiencer in semantic terms (see 16.1) such as *I* in *I saw the match on television, we* in *We heard the radio commentary*), or the thing perceived (the Carrier/Phenomenon, such as *this fish* in *This fish doesn't smell too good*, and *it* in *It tastes even worse*).

When the Senser is Subject, an imperfective interpretation is made possible by means of *can / could* with the verb of perception:

<blockquote>
I can smell something burning. (not *I am smelling...)
We could see the flamingoes wheel overhead and (could) hear the noise of their wings. (not *we were seeing ... hearing)
</blockquote>

See, smell, feel and *taste* have regular dynamic, agentive uses which combine easily with the Progressive. In such uses these verbs refer to a deliberate action rather than involuntary perception:

<blockquote>
I'm seeing the doctor tomorrow. (= visiting)
Who will be seeing to the sandwiches? (= attending to)
Janet must be seeing her friends off. (= taking leave of)
We have been tasting the pudding.
Experts were smelling the fungi in order to identify them.
I am feeling the child's foot to see if any bones are broken.
</blockquote>

Verbs of cognition (*know, believe, understand, wonder, suppose, realise*) do not normally admit the Progressive:

<blockquote>
I believe you are right.   *I am believing you are right.
He knows the answer.   *He is knowing the answer.
</blockquote>

However, with *wonder, suppose* and *understand* the Progressive can 'stretch' the state, while verbs such as *understand* and *realise* can combine with the Progressive of *begin* to express the stretched-out initiation of the mental state:

> I'*m wondering* whether it was a good idea after all.
> I'*m supposing* that the money will be returnable without interest.
> I'*m understanding* Arabic a little better now.
> We *are beginning to understand* the intricacies of the plan.
> He *is beginning to realise* the implications of all this.

Affective verbs (*like, dislike, love, hate*) do not combine easily with the Progressive, with the exception of *enjoy*, which is dynamic. They sometimes occur with the Progressive, however; the question *How are you liking X* seems to be more indirect and therefore more polite than the non-progressive *How do you like X*:

> How are you liking your visit to Disneyland?
> Oh, I'*m just loving* it.
> Frankly, I'*m hating* it.

42.6.2   Durative situations and the Progressive

Durative 'process' verbs are already inherently dynamic (*dance, write, sew, whisper, rain, ripen, ache*, etc.).

The use of the Progressive with durative verbs which have an end-point (*decide, write out, grow up, ripen*) is to stretch out the durative phase of the process before the end-point:

> He *is deciding* about his future.
> We *are writing out* the invitations.
> She *is growing up* into a beautiful girl.
> The apricots *are ripening* well.

This effect is illustrated in the following invented passage:

> Autumn has come early in the north. The leaves *are turning,* [1] the nights *are drawing in* [2] and the lustre has faded from the lakeside boathouses. On the playing-fields, smallish boys in red shirts *are bending and hooking* [3] in a scrum, before straightening up again to run, pass and tackle, try and kick, urged on by men with large knees and piercing whistles. Rain *is starting to fall* [4] as the last whistle of the day shrills out over the darkening field.
>
> [1] stretching out the process before the end-point; [2] as in [1];
> [3] stretching out the processes; [4] stretching the phase of initiation.

With those durative verbs which have no end-point (*sew, whisper, play, rain*), including verbs of bodily sensation (*ache, hurt, itch, feel cold*), the Progressive has the effect of **limiting** the duration of the process, so that it includes speech time (or orientation time if this is in the past):

Who *is whispering* over there?
It *was raining* hard when I left.
Where's Ken? He*'s playing* golf.

With this type of verb, unlimited duration is expressed by the simple Past. Compare:

Lamps *were glowing* in the dark.	Lamps *glowed* in the dark.
Snow *was falling* gently.	Snow *fell* gently.
My back *is aching.*	My back *aches.*

42.6.3 Acts, events and the Progressive

With act and event verbs the use of the Progressive results in a stretching out of the verbal action; it becomes a sequence.

With transitional events (those which have an end-point, such as *arrive, die, catch a cold*) and agentive transitional acts (*sit down, catch a ball*) the Progressive has the effect of stretching out the stage before the end-point:

Just as I *was sitting down*, the doorbell rang.
Hurry! The taxi *is arriving*.
I think I *am catching a cold*.
The old king *is dying*.

With momentary verbs (those which have no end-point, whether agentive such as *tap, kick, fire*, or non-agentive such as *sneeze, bounce, flash*), the use of the Progressive must be interpreted as a repetition of the act or event. The sequence is an iterative sequence:

Someone *is tapping* on the wall next door.
The soldiers *are firing* on the rifle range nearby.
Why *is* that light *flashing*?
He*'s kicking* the ball all over the field.

These categories are approximate, rather than absolute. Some actions appear to be more punctual than others. Some end-points appear to be more final than others. It would, for instance, be unusual to hear *He's slamming the door* for it is not possible to keep on slamming a door unless you keep on opening it.

Moreover, the type of Subject and/or Direct Object can also lead to a different interpretation. *Arrive*, with a singular Subject, will be interpreted as a transitional event, the Progressive stretching the stage previous to the end-point, as in *Hurry! The taxi is arriving*. With a plural Subject and the Progressive, *arrive* will be interpreted as an iterative sequence: *Hurry! The guests are arriving*.

42.7 The discourse functions of the Progressive

Since the Progressive does not establish time boundaries, it has the effect of providing a temporal frame around some point of time.

With the Present Progressive the point of time is typically the 'now' (*What are you doing? I'm switching off the answer-phone*); but it may be interpreted as repeated as in *When he gets out of bed at seven o'clock, she's already doing aerobics*, or as a historic present as in *We finally reach the supermarket and they are just closing the doors*.

Similarly, the Past Progressive provides a temporal frame without time boundaries around some point of time or some bounded act or event:

> *At half-past five* crowds *were pouring* into the subways. (point of time)
> *When we stopped at the door,* Pat *was shouting* to us. (bounded act)

Within the flow of discourse, especially narrative, the Progressive frequently has the effect of 'backgrounding' certain information in order to highlight or 'foreground' events expressed in the non-progressive Past tense. A series of Past tenses, by contrast, will be interpreted as a sequence of events:

> When we stopped at the door, Pat *shouted* to us.

The Progressive may be used alone in a situation made bounded by a time expression (an on-going process within a situation seen as perfective):

> I *was working* in the garden *all afternoon.*

Be can be replaced by forms of *come* and *go* + *-ing*. The resulting combination can be both perfective and imperfective:

> The soldiers *came running* across the fields.

For uses of the Progressive to refer to future events, see 41.6.3.

The following text shows how Past and Past Progressive forms express different inherent verbal meanings according to the different ways in which the whole situation is conceptualised and expressed linguistically by the writer:

> When Henry *tired* [1] of his play and *wandered off* [2] along the beach, Roger *followed* [3] him, keeping beneath the palms and drifting casually in the same direction. Henry *walked* [4] at a distance from the palms and the shade because he *was* [5] too young to keep himself out of the sun. He *went down* [6] to the beach and *busied* [7] himself at the water's edge. The great Pacific tide *was coming in* [8] and every few seconds the relatively still water of the lagoon *heaved* [9] forward an inch. There *were* [10] creatures that *lived* [11] in this last fling of the sea, tiny transparencies that *came questing in* [12] with the water over the hot, dry sand. With impalpable organs of sense they *examined* [13] this new field. Perhaps food had appeared where the last incursion there had been none; bird droppings, insects perhaps, any of the strewn detritus of landward life. Like a myriad of tiny teeth in a saw, the transparencies *came scavenging* [14] over the beach.
>
> William Golding, *Lord of the Flies.*

[1] bounded process; [2] unbounded process; [3] unbounded process; [4] unbounded process; [5] relational state; [6] transitional process; [7] unbounded process; [8] stretching out the process before the end-point; [9] iterative event; [10] state of existence; [11] positional state; [12] sequence of bounded actions; [13] implicitly unbounded sequence of actions; [14] sequence of bounded actions.

MODULE 43
Past events and present time connected: the Present Perfect

Summary

1   The Present Perfect in English differs from the Past tense in that the event is seen as occurring in a period of time which extends up to and includes speech time.

2   The event is simply anterior to speech time and indefinite.

3   Whereas the event expressed by the Past tense is seen as disconnected from the present, when expressed by the Present Perfect the event is psychologically related to the present.

4   These differences are reinforced by collocation with adverbs.

5   The Past Perfect is used in English to refer to all degrees of pastness more remote than the Present Perfect and the Past tense.

43.1   Meanings expressed by the Present Perfect

We have already seen (see 41.5.1) that in English the Present Perfect, expressed by some form of *have* + past participle, is not normally interchangeable with the Past tense. This is because the two forms reflect different ways of looking at an event. The Present Perfect places the event in a period of time which extends up to and includes speech time, sometimes called the 'extended now'. There is, therefore, no disconnectedness from present time such as is implied when using the Past. This inclusiveness is often reinforced by a time Adjunct which refers to a period of time not yet over. Compare:

> *Have* you *seen* any good films *this month*?
> *Did* you *see* any good films *last month*?

It would not be normal in English to say *Have you seen any good films last month*? since 'last month' represents a period of time in which speech time is not included.

A period of time expressed by an Adjunct such as *in July, in the summer of 1990* may be either open or closed from the viewpoint of speech time. If the period is still open, the Perfect is used; if closed, the Past tense is used. Compare:

> Temperatures *have reached* an all-time high in July / in the summer of 1990. (July / the summer of 1990 are not yet over.)

> Temperatures *reached* an all-time high in July / in the summer of 1990. (July / the summer of 1990 have ended.)

43.1.1 Anteriority

Within this 'extended now', the Present Perfect is used in English when the speaker does not wish to refer to a definite moment of occurrence of the event, but simply to the **anteriority** of the event in relation to speech time. The action is viewed as occurring at an **indefinite** or **unspecified time** in the past. This represents a marked contrast with the simple Past, which is used when the speaker does view the event as occurring at a definite and specific time in the past. Compare:

> They *have left* for New York.
> They *left* for New York an hour ago.

As a consequence of its indefiniteness, the Present Perfect is incompatible with Adjuncts which express definite time, such as the following:

> *yesterday*
> *last week, last year, last month*, etc.
> *an hour ago, two years ago*, etc.
> *on Monday, last June, in 1066*, etc.
> *at 4 o'clock, at Christmas, at Easter*, etc.

Adjuncts which can be used with the Perfect include the following:

> adverbs of frequency, which are themselves indefinite as regards time specification: *sometimes, often, always, never, at times, twice, three times*, etc.
> *already, yet, ever*
> *in the last ten years*, etc.
> *lately, recently, now*

Similarly, the Present Perfect is not used after interrogative conjunctions such as *when* and *at what time*, which imply definite time. We cannot say *When have you met my brother?* or *At what time have the students finished?* Such interrogatives must be expressed with the Past *When did you meet my brother?* and *At what time did the students finish?*

In a declarative clause, with future reference, the Present Perfect can follow *when*, since this use refers to an unspecified time: *When I have finished, I'll call you.*

It is important to realise that the Present Perfect is used when the meanings of anteriority and indefiniteness are present in the speaker's mind even though no Adjunct accompanies the verb. In accordance with this, the following are normal:

> *Has* John *brought* the books back?
> I *haven't read* anything on that subject.

whereas these others are not, since they imply definite events which occurred at a definite point of time and require the verb to be in simple Past:

> *What *have* you *said* just now?
> *I *haven't noticed* what time he came in.
> *Have* you *heard* what he answered?
> *Have* you *seen* that flash of lightning?

Utterances such as these would be based on shared knowledge between speaker and hearer that past time is in the focus of reference. When the Present Perfect is used there is no such understanding. For this reason the Perfect often occurs at the start of an exchange, and serves to establish past time focus, subsequent references to events being made by means of the Past tense:

> — *Has* John *brought* the books back?
> — No, he *hasn't*. His car *broke down* on the way home, and he *had to walk* most of the way. After that, he *was* too tired to go out again.

43.1.2   Current relevance

By 'current relevance' it is meant that the event referred to by means of the Present Perfect is psychologically connected to speech time. This meaning is quoted in all accounts of the Present Perfect and is considered by some to be the main one. We prefer to consider current relevance as a pragmatic inference deriving from the basic meaning of 'anteriority'; we consider that current relevance in its various forms is a consequence of the combination of the Present Perfect with the inherent meaning of the verb or even of the situation. We shall therefore examine the Present Perfect in combination with the verb types displayed on page 366. At this point we simply illustrate the notion of current relevance as follows: *The children have come back* implies and will be interpreted by the hearer as meaning that the children are still back, whereas *The children came back* has no such implication. English differs from some languages in not being able to combine in one expression the notions of current relevance and definite past. It is not normal to say *The children have come back a moment ago*. Occasional occurrences of utterances in spoken English which appear to combine the two can be explained as mental switches from indefinite to definite past produced when the speaker constructs his message as he goes along.

The following letter addressed to the editor of a newspaper illustrates the meanings of anteriority and current relevance of the Present Perfect:

> Sir, Agreed that the media have the democratic right, and the duty, to inform and be informed. But it is undeniable that this right *has been grossly abused* of late. In recent months, *we have seen* the growth of a new and lamentable style of reporting which consists of detailed revelations of the intimate life of some of our politicians, either with a view to hounding them out of office or at least discrediting them in the eyes of their electors. Sex *has always been* a potent sales technique, but what has it to do with politics? Our members of Parliament *have been elected* to govern. I am only interested in how they do that and not what they do in bed.

43.2   Inherent verbal meanings and the Perfect

43.2.1   States and the Perfect

With most verbs expressing states (*be, belong, know, like, stand*, etc, but not *see* and *hear*) the Perfect is anomalous without an Adjunct of duration or frequency: **That ring has belonged to my mother; *I have known Bill; *He has liked Mary; *I have wanted to visit Italy; *The monastery has stood on the hill*. By adding an Adjunct of extent or frequency the state is visualised as lasting up to and including speech time as in:

> That ring *has always belonged* to my mother.
> I *have known* Bill *since we were at school together.*
> He *has never liked* Mary.
> I *have wanted* to visit Italy *for years.*
> The monastery *has stood* on the hill *for centuries.*

For + a unit of time (*for an hour, for two years, for centuries*) expresses extent of the state viewed from the point of view of speech time, and is therefore retrospective. *Since* + a point of time expresses extent viewed from the beginning of the state, and is prospective. With *since* the time expression can be omitted when this information is known from the co-text: *Phil was here this morning but I haven't seen him since.*

Be followed by an Attribute can express an anterior state:

> I*'ve been* ill.
> She *has been* lonely without you.

The Perfect of *be* followed by a directional Complement expresses the notion of having gone to or been at a place and then returned. The preposition is *to*:

> *Have* you ever *been to Venice*?
> I*'ve been to the National Theatre* to try to get tickets.

The Perfect is also used in English with *be* as follows:

> It's the first time I*'ve been* here.

With relational verbs such as *cost, weigh* an Adjunct is required:

> It *has cost* a hundred pounds *since it came on sale.*
> He *has weighed* over a hundred kilos *for years.*

Tonic stress on *have* permits the use of the Perfect without an Adjunct, since the focus is on the notion of anteriority:

> He *HAS weighed* over a hundred kilos, but now he's slimmer.

43.2.2 Acts, events and the Perfect

Momentary acts and events (*knock, wink, break*, etc.) and transitions (*sit down, arrive, die*, etc.) + the Perfect are presented as 'hot news'. The recency of the event can be reinforced by *just*:

> Someone *has* (just) *knocked* at the door.
> The strike *has ended.*
> The lights *have changed.* Let's go!
> *Has* a relative of his (just) *died*?
> The car *has broken down.*
> A Picasso *has been stolen* from the exhibition.

This meaning is expressed in AmE by *just* + Past. Compare:

> We *just ate.* (AmE) We've *just eaten/had lunch.* (BrE)

The happening or series of happenings may be seen as less recent but occurring within a period of time leading up to the present:

> Several pictures *have been stolen* over the years.
> People *have settled* here from many different parts.
> We *have* all *been vaccinated* against cholera.

Transitive and intransitive acts and events with the Perfect can sometimes be interpreted as having a visible result as in *I've baked a cake, The car has broken down*, but this depends on the type of verb used and is not inherent in the meaning of the Perfect itself.

43.2.3 Durative processes and the Perfect

Processes with an end-point + the Perfect (*grow up, ripen, type out*, etc.) are interpreted as being completed:

> His brothers *have grown up* and have left home.
> The apricots *have ripened.*
> The secretary *has typed out* the report.

With the Perfect, processes without an end-point (*walk, work, rain*, etc.) typically require a circumstantial Adjunct:

> We *have walked* for miles.
> He *has worked* in the same firm for years.
> It *has rained* all night.

> He *has driven* a taxi since he was a young man.
> They *have lived* in caravans, houseboats and tents.
> The sun *has shone*, on and off, all this month.

As can be seen from the last three examples, the process must in some cases be interpreted as iterative, rather than one continuous situation.

The following extract from a novel, written in autobiographical form, illustrates the different time focus of the Present Perfect and the Past, in conjunction with various types of verbs:

> I've *grown old* with the century; there's not much left of either of us. The century of war. All history, of course, is the history of wars, but this hundred years *has excelled itself*. How many million shot, maimed, burned, frozen, starved, drowned? God only knows. I trust He does; He should have kept a record, if only for His own purposes. *I've been on the fringes of two wars*; I shan't see the next. The first *preoccupied* me not at all; this thing called War *summoned* Father and *took* him *away* for ever. I *saw* it as some inevitable climactic effect: thunderstorm or blizzard. The second *lapped* me *up* but *spat* me *out* intact. Technically intact. I *have seen* war; in that sense I *have been present* at wars, I *have heard* bombs and guns and *observed* their effects.

Penelope Lively, Moon Tiger.

43.3   Meanings expressed by Perfect and Progressive aspects

The Perfect Progressive combines the meaning of unboundedness, characteristic of the Progressive, with the indefiniteness that is characteristic of the Perfect. The verbal situation is visualised as continuing from some indefinite time in the past up to the present, frequently up to speech time as in:

> I *have been looking forward to* meeting you.
> Buses *have been running* rather more punctually lately.

Again, the inherent meaning of the verb interacts with the Perfect and Progressive meanings.

43.3.1   State predications

Most states are incompatible with the Perfect Progressive, as they are with the Present Progressive, even with the addition of an extent Adjunct: *It has been belonging to my mother for years*. Some verbs of perception (*hear, feel, see*) and affection (*want*), however, admit the Perfect Progressive:

> He *has been hearing* better since he got the hearing-aid.
> I *have been feeling* rather down lately.
> If you *have been seeing* double, that's a bad symptom.
> I *have been wanting* to meet him for ages.

Behavioural verbs (*cough, sneeze, laugh*, etc.) and verbs of bodily sensation (*ache, hurt, itch*, etc.) easily admit the Perfect Progressive:

My back *has been aching* a lot recently.
You *have been coughing* since you got up.

43.3.2 Event and activity predications

Event and activity predications in the Perfect Progressive are visualised as being stretched out from an indefinite time in the past up to the moment of speaking. According to the semantics of the predication, the following interpretations are possible:

(a) **incompletion**

I *have been fixing* the lamp. Compare: I *have fixed* the lamp.

(b) **iteration**

He *has been killing* ants.
The light *has been flashing* all night.
The door *has been banging*; perhaps it doesn't shut properly.

With an intransitive event verb (*arrive, blink*, etc.) the Perfect Progressive may be incompatible unless it can be interpreted as iterative. This may be achieved by a suitable Adjunct or by a plural Subject. Compare:

*He *has been arriving*.
He *has been arriving* late recently.
Guests *have been arriving* all afternoon.

43.3.3 Durative predications

(a) Normally bounded durative situations (i.e. those which have an endpoint such as *write a letter, choose a tie*) are made unbounded with the Perfect Progressive:

I *have been writing* a letter.
Peter *has been choosing* a tie.

This does not mean that the event or activity was necessarily not completed; simply that the Perfect Progressive concentrates on the middle part of the process, which is situated at an indefinite, probably recent, time in the past:

He *has been driving* John to the station.
I *have been persuading* your parents to stay.

The non-progressive Perfect would, in such predications, be interpreted as completed:

He *has driven* John to the station.
I *have persuaded* your parents to stay.

(b) Normally unbounded predications (without an end-point, such as *snow, wait, rain*) are 'stretched' but still seen as unbounded by specific limits. With an Adjunct of extent, the process is seen to continue up to speech time:

> Look! It *has been snowing*.
> You look tired. – I*'ve been painting* the bathroom.
> We *have been living here* for ten years now.
> I *have been waiting* for you for over an hour.

43.4   Expressing more remote events: the Past Perfect

To refer to an event that is previous to another in past time, the Past Perfect is used (*had* + past participle):

> We *had heard* nothing from Tony before he returned.
> She didn't mention that she *had seen* you at the match.

In these examples the Past Perfect represents the past of the Past tense. When the time relation is unambiguous, the Past often replaces the Past Perfect in English:

> We *heard* nothing from Tony before he returned.
> She didn't mention that she *saw* you at the match.

The Past Perfect also refers to the past of the Present Perfect:

> He *has made three good films* since he left Hollywood.
> He *had made three good films* before he left Hollywood.

The Past Perfect Progressive combines the remoteness and anteriority of the Past Perfect with the features of the Progressive:

> I *had been seeing* her quite a lot at that time. (iterative)
> We *had been living* in the north before we came here. (unbounded duration)

As English has only one tense more remote than the Past, the Past Perfect is used to express a series of events each preceding another. In the following extract from William Boyd's *The New Confessions*, several degrees of remoteness are expressed, beyond past time:

> Duric Ludokian *was* [1] a huge wealthy Armenian who *had fled* [2] from his native country to Russia in 1896 shortly after the first Turkish massacres and pogroms against the Armenian people *had begun*. [3] He *had fled* [4] again in 1918 after the Russian Revolution and was among the first of the thousands of Russian émigrés who *found* [5] sanctuary in Berlin. Ludokian *had made* [6] his fortune in nuts. He described himself as a 'nut-importer'.
>
> William Boyd, *The New Confessions*.

The sequence of events in time would be as follows, reading from right to left:

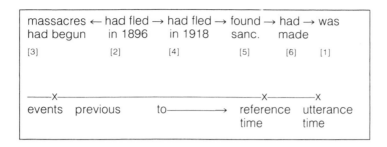

43.5   Non-finite Perfect forms

Anteriority is expressed in the non-finite Perfect forms *to have* + participle and *having* + participle:

> *To have made such a declaration in public* was rather unwise.
> *Having satisfied himself that everything was in order*, he locked the safe.

The Perfect can also combine with the Progressive, the Passive and lexical auxiliaries to form complex non-finite Verbal Groups (see 38.10):

> *To have been forced to resign for medical reasons is no slur on his reputation.*
> *Having been driving throughout the night*, he needs a rest.
> *Having been pursued by photographers for most of her childhood*, she hardly knows what privacy is.
> She stopped herself in time, *having been about to make a terrible mistake.*

MODULE 44
Expressing attitudes towards the event: modality

Summary

1   Modality is the category by which speakers express attitudes towards the event contained in the proposition.

2   The attitude may be that of assessing the probability that the proposition is true in terms of modal certainty, probability or possibility. This is epistemic (or extrinsic) modality.

3   All modal expressions are less categorical than a plain declarative. For this reason modality is said to express a **relation** to reality, whereas an unmodalised declarative treats the process **as** reality.

4   By means of modality speakers can intervene in the speech event, by laying obligations or giving permission. This is intrinsic or deontic modality. Closely related to these meanings are those of ability and intrinsic possibility.

5   The modal auxiliaries in English express both types of modal meanings, which have in common the fact that they express the speaker's attitude to a potential event. In addition, a number of other forms are available for the expression of particular modal meanings.

44.1   The meaning of modality

From a semantic point of view, in making an assertion such as *It's raining*, speakers express a proposition and at the same time commit themselves to the truth of that proposition. In ordinary subjective terms, we should say that speakers **know** the truth of their own assertion. For this reason, an utterance such as *It's raining but I don't believe it* is semantically unacceptable since the second part contradicts the categorical assertion expressed in the first.

If, on the other hand, speakers say *It may be raining, It can't be raining, It must be raining* they are not committing themselves wholeheartedly to the truth of the proposition. They are not making a categorical assertion, but are rather modifying their commitment to some degree by expressing a judgement or assessment of the truth of the situation. This is an important choice which faces speakers every time they formulate a declarative clause: to make a categorical statement or to express less than total commitment by modalising.

A different kind of modification is made when the speaker intervenes directly in the speech event itself, by saying, for example, *I must leave now, You'd better come too, The rest of you can stay*. Here the speaker makes use of modal expressions to impose an obligation, to prohibit, to express permission or consent to the action in question.

From these considerations, modality is to be understood as a semantic category which covers such notions as possibility, probability, necessity, volition, obligation and permission. These are the basic modalities; recently the concept of modality has been extended to cover other notions such as doubt, wish, regret and desire, and temporal notions such as usuality. The projection of any of these notions onto the content of the proposition indicates that the speaker is presenting this content not as a simple assertion of fact, but coloured rather by personal attitude or intervention. In very general terms, modality may be taken to express a **relation** with reality, whereas a non-modal utterance treats the process **as** reality. Contrast:

That man over there *is* the President's bodyguard. (categorical assertion)
That man over there *may be/can't possibly be/could perhaps be* the President's bodyguard. (modalised assertion)

These two main types of modal meaning are here called, respectively, 'epistemic', in which the speaker comments on the content of the clause, and 'non-epistemic', in which the speaker intervenes in the speech event. Other terms are 'extrinsic' and 'intrinsic'. 'Epistemic' refers to knowledge; it is, however, the lack of knowledge that is characteristic of this kind of modality. Within non-epistemic modality the term 'deontic' is used to refer to obligation and permission. By means of these two main kinds of modality speakers are enabled to carry out two important communicative functions:

(a) to comment on and evaluate an interpretation of reality;

(b) to intervene in, and bring about changes in events.

Certain other types of modality are recognised and will be mentioned in the following sections.

44.2   The realisations of modal meanings

Since the semantic field of modality has, for some linguists, been widened to cover the attitudinal notions specified in the previous paragraph, so consequently have the number and type of forms which realise these concepts. They may be divided into two main groups: the verbal and the non-verbal exponents.

44.2.1   Verbs expressing modal meanings

These include the following:

(a) Lexical verbs such as *allow, beg, command, forbid, guarantee, guess, promise, suggest, warn*, discussed in 22.5 as performatives.

(b) The verbs *wonder* and *wish*, which express doubt and wish, respectively.

(c) The lexico-modal auxiliaries listed in 37.3 composed of *be* or *have*, usually another element + infinitive (*have got to, be bound to*, etc.).

(d) The modal auxiliaries *can, could, will, would, must, shall, should, may, might, ought*, and the semi-modals *need* and *dare*.

44.2.2   Other means of expressing modality

It is suggested that the following also express modalities:

(a) Modal Disjuncts such as *probably, possibly, surely, hopefully, thankfully, obviously*.

(b) Modal adjectives such as *possible, probable, likely* used in impersonal constructions such as *It's possible he may come* or as part of a Nominal Group, as in *a likely winner of this afternoon's race* or *the most probable outcome of this trial*.

(c) Modal nouns such as *possibility, probability, chance, likelihood* as in *There's just a chance that he may come*.

(d) Certain uses of *if*-clauses as in *if you know what I mean; if you don't mind my saying so; what if he's had an accident?*

(e) The use of the remote past as in *I thought I'd go along with you, if you don't mind*.

(f) The use of non-assertive items such as *any* as in *He'll eat any kind of vegetable*.

(g) Certain types of intonation, such as the fall–rise.

(h) The use of hesitation phenomena in speech.

It is clear from the diversity of these categories that there is a danger that modality may become indistinguishable from tentativeness. In the sections which follow we shall adopt a somewhat more limited scope, taking modality to be basically the expression of possibilities, probabilities, certainty, obligations and permission. Even so, it is clear that modality can be expressed not simply at one point in an utterance, by a modal auxiliary, but at different points right throughout the clause. If we choose to discuss modality in the chapter devoted to the Verbal Group, it is because the verb, and particularly the modal and lexico-modal auxiliaries, are the most basic exponents of modality in English. The other modal elements tend to reinforce the modal meaning expressed by the verb, modal auxiliary or lexico-modal, as in the example: *Do you think it could by any chance be the winning number?*

Some of the various suggested realisations of modality are exemplified in this short extract, in which George expresses his doubts about his future as a doctor:

> 'Dad – ' [1] George shifted his feet. 'I *wonder* [2] *if I'm really suited for medicine.'* [3]
> 'Of course you are,' his father told him briefly. 'We've had medical men in this family since the days of Gladstone bags and leeches. I *wish* you'd [4] follow the example of your sister. She *will* [5] certainly be studying upstairs with her usual diligence. And what, *might I ask*, [6] *would* [7] you *intend* [8] to do instead?'
> 'I've thought of the – er, [9] drama.'
>
> Richard Gordon, *Doctor on the Boil*.

[1] hesitation; [2] lexical modal verb; [3] conditional clause expressing doubt; [4] lexical modal verb + hypothetical *would*; [5] *will* of prediction; [6] ironical use of *might* = requesting permission; [7] hypothetical *would*; [8] lexical verb of intention; [9] hesitation.

44.3 Modal certainty, probability and possibility

These three options represent the three degrees of confidence, or lack of it, that the speaker feels towards the truth of the proposition formulated.

44.3.1 Modal certainty: *will, must, be bound to*

What we call modal certainty is not the hundred per cent certainty of a categorical assertion. An unmodalised declarative constitutes a far stronger statement of fact than any additional expression of certainty can. If, for instance, I know for a fact that Pat forgot your birthday, I simply say 'Pat forgot your birthday'. If instead I say 'Pat must have forgotten your birthday' or 'Pat may have forgotten' I am admitting an element of doubt. Modal certainty is, therefore, diminished certainty, chosen either because the speaker's state of knowledge has not permitted a plain assertion or because the speaker does not want to exteriorise commitment at any given moment in a particular interpersonal interaction. In many cases, reasons of politeness or the desire to avoid commitment provide the motivation for a modalised rather than a categorical assertion.

There are two kinds of modal certainty, illustrated as follows:

> The concert *will be* over by now.
> The concert *must be* over.

The first, which forms part of the wider notion of 'prediction', is a certainty based on repeated experience or common sense. It is realised by *will*. It can refer not only to future occurrences as in *She will be twenty tomorrow* (see 41.6) but to the three types of present reference: coinciding with speech time, timeless and habitual as in the following examples:

> (The doorbell rings). That *will* be Peter. (speech time)
> Ice *will* melt at room temperature. (timeless)
> They'*ll* gossip for hours. (habitual)

When the orientation frame is past time, as in a narrative, *would* is used:

> He *would* be about sixty when I first met him.
> They *would* gossip for hours, sitting in the park.

Predictive *would* in narrative is illustrated in the following extract:

> When Grandpa got to his office, he *would* put his hat on his desk. .... It was a device of his to get away from bores or talkative friends. As the door opened, he *would* automatically reach for his derby, and if it was somebody he didn't want to see, he *would* rise and say, 'I'm sorry, but I was just about to leave.' He *would* then walk to the street with his visitor, find out which way the man was going, and set off in the opposite direction, walking around the block and entering the store by the back door.
>
> James Thurber, 'Photographic Album: Man with a Rose'.

With the lexico-modal *be apt to*, prediction shades into usuality, since it is based on the natural habits or tendency of the Subject. It refers to repeated states or happenings:

> Their parties *are apt to be* boring.
> He'*s apt to turn up* for dinner without warning.

The second type of modal certainty is usually called 'logical necessity', and is based on a process of deduction; *The concert must be over* might be said, for instance, if the speaker sees that the lights are off, the concert hall is closed, etc. This meaning is realised in English by *must*, which is subjective, and also now with some speakers by *have to* which is more objective.

> The key *must* be in your pocket.
> The key *has to* be in your pocket.

Be bound to and *be sure to* are alternative realisations to *must*, and equally subjective:

> The key *is bound to be / is sure to be* in your pocket.

44.3.2 Probability, or 'reasonable inference': *should, ought*

When the speaker's deduction leads to a provisional conclusion, less firm than that expressed by *must*, we have the notion of probability, or what is reasonable to expect, expressed by *should* and *ought*.

The main semantic feature distinguishing these modals from *must* is that they implicitly admit non-fulfilment of the predicated activity, whereas *must* does not. We can say *We should have enough petrol to get there, but of course we may not*, but not *We must have enough petrol to get there, but of course we may not*. *Should* and *ought* are said to be 'non-factive', that is not binding, as opposed to *will* and *must* which are 'factive' or binding. They can be illustrated as follows:

> Supper *should* be ready. Let's go into the dining-room.
> You *must* be hungry.

With past time reference, *should* and *ought*, but not *will* and *must*, have an implication of probability, but can be 'counter-factive', leaving open the interpretation that the expected action did not occur. Contrast:

> He *should have reached* the office by now (and he probably has / but it seems he hasn't).
> He *will have reached* the office by now.
> He *must have reached* the office by now.

The expression of inference by *should* and *ought* is often merged with that of obligation (see 44.7.2), as in *For this price the hotel should be much better*, i.e. one would expect it to be better/it has the obligation to be better. *Likely* and *likelihood*, with the corresponding negative forms *unlikely* and *unlikelihood*, unambiguously express probability:

Rain is *likely* in the west later today.
All flights *are likely to be* delayed.
The most *likely* outcome of Saturday's match is a draw.
There's no *likelihood* of frost tonight.

Probable and *probability* can also be used, except with a 'raised' Subject such as *he* in *He's likely to be late.* There is no *He's probable to be late.*

44.3.3   Epistemic possibility: *may, might, could*

In order to assess the possibility of something being true, English speakers make use of the modal auxiliaries *may* and *might*; in addition, stressed *could* is increasingly used, particularly in the media. These can be paraphrased as 'it is possible that x':

They *may* be real pearls, you know.
They *might* be real pearls, you know.
They *could* be real pearls, you know.

All three expressions mean 'It is possible that they are real pearls'. It is clear from this paraphrase that *might* and *could*, although historically past forms, do not in such cases refer to past time, but to present states of affairs. They can also be used to refer to future events:

It *may / might / could* snow tomorrow. (= it is possible that it will snow tomorrow)

Can is not used in positive declarative clauses which express epistemic possibility. We do not say *They can be real pearls *It can snow tomorrow.*

Can replaces the other modals, however, in the negation of possibility (= it is not possible that x) as in *They can't possibly be real pearls, you know.* It is also used in the interrogative, although it is less common to question extrinsic possibilities (*Can they be real pearls?*).

When the lexical meaning is negated, *not* is used (*It may not snow; They might not be real*). *Could* is even less used in interrogative clauses meaning *is it possible that x?*, presumably because its prototypical meaning is that of intrinsic possibility, *is it possible for x?*, as is explained in 44.8.

It is not easy to claim with certainty that *may, might* and *could* represent points on a scale of confidence or, in other words, that one or other of these modals expresses a stronger or a more remote possibility. They can all be intensified by *(very) well*, which heightens the possibility, and by *just*, which lowers it:

They *may / might / could very well* be real pearls.
They *may / might / could just* be real pearls.

The following examples, one from spoken English, the other written, illustrate how the three can be used in one utterance:

I *may* be a few minutes late; it *might* be seven o'clock before I can get away; it *could* even be half-past.

The provision *might* be deleted altogether; it *may* remain as it stands; or it *could* emerge considerably strengthened and broadened.

The Observer, 19 January 1975.

In these examples the three modals are interchangeable, with little difference to the message. Other factors such as speakers' age, social dialect and the degree of formality or informality of the situation undoubtedly influence the choice of modal. It is suggested that *may* is more formal and indicates reserve, *might* being now the more neutral form, especially with younger speakers, and *could* perhaps express a more assertive attitude.

It is clear that the various options outlined above permit the speaker to make fine distinctions in English with regard to judgement about the truth or likelihood of the proposition:

He'll be there by now.	(prediction based on common sense)
He must be there by now.	(almost certainty, based on deduction)
He's bound to be there.	(almost certainty + inevitability)
He has to be there by now.	(almost certainty, objective)
He's likely to be there.	(probability)
He should be there by now.	(reasonable inference)
He could be there by now.	(strong possibility (?))
He might be there by now.	(neutral possibility)
He may be there by now.	(reserve as to possibility)

44.4   Syntactic features of epistemic modality

The modal meanings we have examined so far, when realised by modal auxiliaries in English, can co-occur with certain syntactic features. Taking *might* as representative of the modals, we have the following co-occurrences:

(a)	existential Subject:	*There might* be enough.
(b)	*be + ing*	He *might be waiting*.
(c)	stative verbs	He *might be* twenty.
(d)	dynamic verbs	I *might* leave early.
(e)	passive voice	It *might be* rebuilt later.
(f)	lexical auxiliary	It *might have to* be abandoned.
(g)	past reference by *have + -en*	He *might have left* by now.

When reference is made to events in past time by the epistemic modals, the modal meaning of prediction, certainty, possibility or probability is not itself past; the speaker carries out the act of predicting, etc., in present time. Pastness is realised by the *have + -en* Perfect form attached to the main verb (*They will have arrived by now, I may have made a mistake, It must have got lost in the post, Things might have been a lot worse*).

For past time reference with modalities of obligation see 44.5, for past with modals of intrinsic possibility see 44.8. For backshifted modals in reported speech see 36.4.1.

44.5   Features of intrinsic modality: volition, obligation, necessity, ability, permission

These modal meanings have as a group a number of features in common. Functionally, they are instrumental in the establishing and maintaining of social relations and interaction. Through them, speakers influence and control others, and commit themselves to certain courses of action. They may bring about changes in their surroundings, by obligations which are met, permissions given, promises kept and so on.

Semantically, the modal part of the utterance is not, as is the case with extrinsic modality, a comment on the possibility that the action expressed in the clause may occur. With intrinsic modality, the modality forms part of the linguistic event, and the speaker intervenes in the action.

Syntactically, these modal meanings are associated with certain features such as the following:

(a) Past time reference is not realised by *have* + *-en*, but frequently by forms of other verbs:

> I *must* leave.   I *had to* leave.
> We *may* leave.   We *were allowed* to leave.

(b) There is an agentive relationship between the Subject and the verb when the verb is active; that is, the Subject carries out the action by his or her own energy (*You must finish writing; Will you wait here for a moment?*).

(c) The existential Subject which is a common co-occurrence with extrinsic modality is virtually excluded.

(d) Stative verbs are equally uncommon.

44.6   Volition

The concept of volition covers the meanings of **willingness** as in *Will you sign this for me?* and **intention** as in *I'll bring it back tomorrow*.

44.6.1   Willingness: *will, (shall)*

Willingness can be paraphrased by *be willing to*. The action predicated by the main verb can coincide with speech time, or refer to repeated or future events:

> *Will* you give a donation to the Wildlife Society? – Yes, I will.
> Our cat *won't* eat anything but the best brands of cat-food.
> *Will* you marry me?

> The key *won't* go in the lock.
> The car *won't* start.

In the last two examples, the speakers unload their frustration by attributing unwillingness to cooperate to an inanimate object.

Heavily stressed *will* is interpreted as 'insistence' as in:

> He *will* ring me up late at night asking silly questions.

As in the examples seen above, the meaning of 'volition' is realised by *will* for all persons; the reduced form *'ll* occurs in the affirmative, except when stressed as in the meaning of insistence, which requires the full form.

In interrogatives *shall* is used with a first person Subject to make an offer or a suggestion. This is the most widespread use of *shall* in present-day English.

> *Shall* I carry those bags for you? (= Do you want me to . . . ?)
> *Shall* we go back home now?

The meaning of willingness, realised by *will*, readily lends itself to various pragmatic uses. For instance, *will* would be interpreted as a directive in *Will you listen to me and stop interrupting*? and as a polite offer in *Will you have another slice of melon?*

44.6.2   Intention: will, *(shall)*

Intention is the second type of volition and can be paraphrased by *intend to*. When a speaker expresses an intention, the intention is, naturally, coincident with speech time, but the intended action is in the future:

> I'*ll* ring you sometime next week.
> We'*ll* take the night train to the coast.
> I think I'*ll* just tape this bit of opera.

Will is used for all persons, *shall* by some speakers for the first person singular and plural. Both are reduced to *'ll* in affirmative clauses.

The speaker's commitment in using these modals is as strong as in the epistemic meanings. For this reason the *will* of intention can have the illocutionary force of either a promise or a threat, according to whether the intended action is beneficial to the addressee or otherwise. The co-occurrence with such verbs as *promise* and *warn* reinforces the interpretation:

> I'*ll* bring you something back from Paris, I promise.
> I warn you that if you keep talking this way I'*ll* hang up.

On a higher level of abstraction than that which has been adopted here, it is possible to postulate a core meaning for each of the modals. Each particular meaning would then derive naturally from the semantic and pragmatic factors with which it is related. A core meaning such as 'inescapable constraint' for *must*, for instance, would explain such constants as the binding nature of *must* in both its meanings as opposed to the non-binding nature of *should* and *ought* in their meanings. It also helps to explain the overlap of meanings in certain contexts; such is the case with *will* when it refers to a future event and the Subject is first person, as in *I'll take the early train to London tomorrow*, in which prediction seems to overlap with intention. A brief outline of the core meaning of *can* is given in 44.8, with the derived meanings.

44.7   Obligation and necessity

In English, obligation and necessity can be conceived as an inescapable duty or requirement, realised by *must, have (got) to* and, in a lesser degree, by *shall*; or else, simply as an advisable course of action, realised by *should* and *ought*.

44.7.1   Inescapable obligation: *must, have to, have got to*

Inescapable obligation when realised by *must* can have the force of a direct command, as in:

> You *must* try harder.
> You *must* copy this out again.

The strength and directness of the illocutionary force in these examples is a result of the following factors:

(a) The Subject is 'you'.

(b) The authority resides in the speaker, who takes responsibility for the action; the obligation is subjective.

(c) Within the cultural context of the exchange, as in school, family, the Armed Forces, the speaker has authority over the addressee.

(d) The verb is agentive and in active voice.

The force of *must* is diminished if one or more of these factors is modified, as in the following examples:

> *I must* catch the last bus without fail. (Subject is *I*)
> *Drug-traffickers must be punished.* (3rd person Subject; authority does not reside in the speaker; passive voice)
> *You must tell* me how to get to your house. (speaker has no authority over addressee)
> Applications *must be* in by June 30. (non-agentive verb; 3rd person Subject; passive voice)

It seems that the more subjective the expression of obligation, the more strongly it is perceived by the addressee, especially in face-to-face interaction. Since *must* is subjective in the imposition of an obligation, the use of a third person Subject and the passive voice are useful strategies to mitigate the directness, although not the inescapability of the obligation.

When no human control is implied, the meaning is that of intrinsic necessity, as in:

> Lizards *must* hibernate if they are to survive the winter.

Of all the modal expressions of obligation *shall* is the most imperious, direct and subjective, and for this reason is little used in the spoken language. It occurs in legal language and other formal contexts, as in the regulations of the Olympic Games:

> All competitors in the Games *shall wear* a number.

Of the lexico-modals, *have to* is objective and *have got to* subjective. Compare:

> I'*ve got to* go now. (the obligation is internal)
> I *have to* go to see the Dean. (the obligation is external)

There are further differences between the modals of obligation:

(a) Syntactically, *have to*, unlike *must* and *have got to*, has non-finite forms *having to, to have to*.

(b) Both *have to* and *have got to*, unlike *must*, have a past form *had (got) to*, but only *have to* can combine with the modal auxiliaries (*may have to*, **may have got to*). Forms of *have to* are therefore used as suppletives for *must*:

> We *had to* pay in advance. We'*ll have to* pay in advance.

(c) *Have got to* and *must* tend to be used, rather than *have to*, to actualise an event that coincides with speech time:

> We *must / have got to / *have to* call a doctor straight away.

Conversely, *have to* is preferred for a repeated action:

> The child *has to have* an injection every other day.

Have to and its negative forms (*don't/doesn't/didn't have to*) have for many speakers supplanted *need* as the interrogative and negative of *must*. Compare:

> *Need* you leave so soon?   *Do* you *have to* leave so soon?
> You *needn't* wait.   You *don't have to* wait.

In such cases it is the modal concept that is questioned or negated. When the lexical concept is negated, this is achieved by *not*, which can be attached enclitically as *n't* to *must*:

> We *mustn't* forget to ask Mary to water the plants.

44.7.2   Unfulfilled obligation, advisability: *should, ought*

With *should* and *ought* an obligation is expressed as not binding, as it is with *must*; it may be unfulfilled:

People *should* drive more carefully.
You really *ought to* cut down on smoking.

Motivations for using these modals instead of *must* include the lack of authority on the part of the speaker to impose the obligation, tact, politeness or a lack of conviction of the absolute necessity of the predicated action. The following invented advertisement clearly distinguishes the necessary from the merely desirable:

Candidates *must* be university graduates.
Candidates *must* be between 21 and 35.
Candidates *should* have a knowledge of two foreign languages.
Candidates *should* have at least three years' experience.

With *should* and *ought* + *have* + *-en*, the speaker implies that the obligation was not fulfilled:

He *should have driven* more carefully.
The Government *should have taken* a decision earlier.

Be supposed to is similar to *should* and *ought* in being contrary to fact:

We *are supposed to* be on holiday. We shouldn't be working.
They *were supposed to* be here by eight, but most people turned up at a quarter past.

44.8   Intrinsic possibility, ability, permission: *can*, *could*, *may*, *might*

These three related meanings are expressed by *can*, negative *can't*:

This paint *can* be applied with a spray. (= It is possible to apply this paint ... / for this paint to be applied ...)
Can you reach the top shelf? (= Are you able to reach ... ?)
You *can't* park here. (= you are not allowed to park here)

It is important to distinguish intrinsic possibility, which is expressed by *can* and is paraphrased by 'It is possible *to* ...' or 'It is possible *for* ... *to* ...), from epistemic (extrinsic) possibility, which is expressed by *may*, *might* and *could* and is paraphrased by 'It is possible *that* ...' Compare:

I can be there by 10 o'clock. (= It is possible *for* me *to* be there by ten o'clock.)
I may / might be there by 10 o'clock. (= It is possible *that* I'll be there by 10 o'clock.)

The meanings expressed by *can* all correspond to a basic pattern, which in its positive form can be expressed as 'nothing prevents x from occurring' and in its negative form as 'something prevents x from occurring'. That 'something' in each case represents a set of laws, whether natural laws, moral laws, laws of physics, of good manners, and perhaps many more. For this reason, an utterance such as *You can't do that* will be interpreted in different ways according to the context in which it occurs, and depending on which set of laws applies in a particular case:

> You can't do that = It's not possible for you to do that. (e.g. walk from the mainland to Mallorca)
> You can't do that = You are not able to do that. (e.g. lift such a heavy box)
> You can't do that = You are not allowed to do that. (e.g. park your car in the Dean's garden)
> You can't do that = social norms prevail against doing that. (e.g. infringe local customs)

Since the possibility and ability to carry out an action is a necessary requirement for a person to perform that action, *can* lends itself to various pragmatic interpretations by inference, such as willingness (*I can get the copies for you, if you like*), command (*If you can't keep quiet you can get out*), request (*Can you help me lift this sofa?*) and potential usuality (*It can be very cold in Madrid in winter*).

May (negative *may not*) is a more formal alternative to *can* in the meanings of permission and intrinsic possibility, and is extended to such meanings as polite offer.

> *May* I come in? Yes, you *may*. (request for permission)
> In spring, wild orchids *may* be found in the woods. (possibility = it is possible to find . . .)
> *May* I help you with the luggage? (polite offer)

Might is sometimes used for an indirect request:

> You *might* fetch me a coke and a bag of crisps.

The past of *can* is *could* or *was/were able to* + infinitive, depending on whether an imperfective or perfective meaning is intended. With *be able* the predicated action is achieved, that is to say, it is seen as perfective; with *could*, the action is viewed as extended in the past, that is, as imperfective:

> From the top of the hill we *could* see for miles.
> *Was* he *able to* escape?   not *Could* he escape?

This distinction is obligatory only in the affirmative and the interrogative. In the negative, *could* and *be able to* are interpreted as having the same result and are therefore interchangeable:

> He *wasn't able* to escape. He *couldn't* escape.

44.9   Hypothetical uses of the modals

Apart from their other meanings, the past tense modals *could, might, would* can be used in a 'remote' or hypothetical sense in both main and subordinate clauses. Compare:

> I *will* help you if I can.   I *would* help you if I *could*.
> She *may* pass if she tries.   She *might* pass if she *tried*.

To refer to a past event *have + -en* is used. The event is understood to be contrary to fact:

> I *would have helped* you if I had been able.
> She *would / might have passed* if she had tried.
> If anyone had seen you, you *might have got* into trouble.

Should is used by some speakers with a first person Subject:

> I *should have thought* he might have written before now.

Should is also used, especially in BrEng, as the replacement of a subjunctive in referring to states of affairs that may exist or come into existence:

> It is only natural that they *should* want a holiday.
> I am amazed that he *should* think it's worth trying.

The following extract illustrates some of the realisations of modal meanings in English. It is noticeable that the dialogue, in which members of a family debate possible courses of action, contains more modals than the narrative part:

> Their Dad *would be coming* [1] home the next day and they *would* [2] have to [3] look after him until he was too ill to stay out of hospital. The question was, *should* [4] he be told?
> 'How long . . . ?' somebody *wondered*[5]. The doctor hadn't been specific. A matter of months rather than weeks. One *could* [6] never be sure. 'Who *would* [7] tell him?' 'I *couldn't*. I just *couldn't*,' [8] said their mother and wept. 'I *would*,' [9] said Angela, 'if we agreed that was the right thing to do.' 'Why tell him?' said the youngest sister. 'It *would* [10] just be cruel.' 'But if he asks . . .,' said another. '*Are* you *going to* [11] lie to your own Dad?'
> Tom lit a cigarette and blew smoke from his nostrils. A grey haze from previous cigarettes hung in the air. All the men in the family were heavy smokers, perhaps because cigarettes had always been readily available. No reference was made by anyone to this as the *likely* [12] cause of their father's disease.
> 'I see no reason to tell Dad yet,' Tom said at length. 'We *should* [13] try to keep him as cheerful as possible.'
> Their mother looked at Tom gratefully, but fearfully. 'But he *must* [14] have time to . . . receive the last . . . sacraments and everything,' she faltered.
> 'Of course, Mum, but there's *no need* [15] to rush these things. Let's make him as happy as we can for the rest of his days.'
>
> David Lodge, *How Far Can You Go.*

[1] past time prediction; [2] past time prediction; [3] obligation; [4] advisability; [5] doubt; [6] intrinsic possibility; [7] willingness; [8] incapability; [9] willingness; [10] hypothetical; [11] intention; [12] probability; [13] advisability; [14] inescapable obligation; [15] lack of necessity/obligation.

TASKS ON CHAPTER 9
Viewpoints on events: Tense, aspect and modality

Module 41

1   *Discussion:*
  1) To what extent do the Present and Past tenses of English correspond to present and past time?
  2) Discuss the global meaning of the Past tense in English. Which are the two semantic features that distinguish the Past from the Perfect in English?
  3) What grammatical devices are used in English to refer to future events, and how is the choice between these conditioned by the way the speaker visualises the future event?

2   †*Say whether the Present tense verb in each sentence below represents a state or an event. If an event, is it repeated, instantaneous, past or future?*
  1) They cycle to work on a tandem most days.
  2) Ignorance is bliss.
  3) Animals face slaughter as London Zoo decides to close.
  4) Black coffee without sugar tastes rather bitter.
  5) Rose suddenly leaps to her feet, goes to table, grabs her purse, slings it on her shoulder and makes for right door.
  6) I had just got on the bus when up comes this guy and asks me for a light. . . .
  7) She looks just like a little kid.
  8) Do you drink wine or only beer?
  9) The villages nestle in deep valleys between the mountains.
  10) Finally, I plug in and the machine is ready for use.
  11) Wounded tell of terror march.
  12) Many people believe that violence on television is partly the cause of violence in real life.
  13) Clinical tests prove conclusively that untreated gum disease leads to tooth loss.
  14) He earns a good salary in a secure job.
  15) *Queen Elizabeth II* sails from Southampton on May 24.

3   *Write a summary of a play or film that you have seen recently, using the Present tense.*

4　*Write a description, in the form of statements, of some piece of equipment that you find useful, for instance an answer-phone, an all-purpose mixer, a walkman, a personal computer. Use the Present tense.*

5　†*Decide which is more meaningful, the Past or the Perfect, in the sentences below. Give reasons for your choice:*
　　1)　We .... (set off) early and .... (leave) the car by the bridge.
　　2)　'I .... (get) it,' he shouted, 'I think I .... really (get) it.'
　　3)　During his short lifetime, he .... (compose) some of the most beautiful organ music of his time.
　　4)　How many plays .... Shakespeare (write)?
　　5)　I .... (wake up) late this morning and .... (have) any breakfast yet.
　　6)　What .... you (say) your name .... (be)?
　　7)　........ you (come) for a work permit, or for something else?
　　8)　When .... your son (qualify) as a doctor?
　　9)　.......... the children (like) the circus?
　　10)　I'm afraid there .... (be) a mistake. You .... (put, passive) in the wrong group.

6　*Write an account of a hazard-filled journey, from the point of view of the afflicted tourist or from that of the harassed tour operator. Use the Past tense mainly; you may need to use the Perfect and Past Perfect too.*

Module 42
1　*Discussion:*
　　1)　How is the notion of 'discontinued habit or state' expressed in English? What are the advantages of this construction?
　　2)　What is the basic meaning of the English Progressive aspect? With which category of verbs does the Progressive not easily combine? Can you explain the occasional uses of the Progressive with verbs such as *be, understand* and *like*?

2　†*Decide whether the verb as it is used in each sentence below is (a) durative or punctual, and (b) agentive or non-agentive:*
　　1)　They dumped their bags on the floor.
　　2)　He holds a professorship at Oxford.
　　3)　The West wind blows constantly across the beaches of Almería.
　　4)　The door banged, the telephone rang and the light went out.
　　5)　The cat pounced on the unwary mouse.
　　6)　Snow fell throughout the day.
　　7)　A shudder ran through the crowd as the glider plunged down.
　　8)　I've made some oatcakes for tea.
　　9)　Cattle graze in the mountains in the summer months; then, in early autumn they come down to the pastures.
　　10)　He blinked in the sudden blaze of light.

3   †*Decide whether the process expressed by the verb and predication in each of the following sentences is bounded (has an end-point) or is unbounded (has no end-point):*
1)   Temperatures dropped sharply during the night.
2)   The dog whimpered to be let out.
3)   He dragged himself along the road.
4)   She doesn't sleep well.
5)   He gazed long and deeply into her eyes.
6)   She handed me the paper bag containing the mushrooms.
7)   His rubber-soled shoes squeaked on the vinyl floor.
8)   A man in a pin-striped suit stepped off the curb.
9)   He slipped the pen into his pocket.
10)   The sofa cast a shadow on the wall.
11)   Soon the path petered out.
12)   His wallet dropped from his pocket; he didn't pick it up.
13)   They are negotiating with the Chinese to buy a panda.
14)   We know them both and feel sympathy for them both.
15)   His memoirs were published after his death.

4   †*Put the verb in each of the sentences below into the Progressive, and say what kind of meaning ensues:*
1)   Paul drove us home.
2)   Something sizzled in the oven.
3)   The children jumped up and down with excitement.
4)   I tried to trace an old friend who lived in an unfamiliar town.
5)   Peter sees the Health Officer tomorrow.
6)   A big fire crackled in the grate.
7)   They photographed the trail of footprints around the pool.
8)   I shiver and cough.
9)   The police car pulled up in front of the hotel.
10)   The doctor stooped over the man who lay on the ground.

5   *The following extract from Vera Brittain's* **Testament of Experience** *contains many occurrences of the non-progressive Past and one instance of the Progressive. Discuss the discourse functions of each in this text. Could any of the Past forms be replaced by Progressive forms? If so, how would the meaning be changed?*

On the nineteenth anniversary of August 4th, 1914, we travelled to the Somme battlefields. At Louvencourt, now a peaceful Somme village, I looked down upon the carefully tended, flower-adorned grave to which my twenty-year-old lover had been carried in the second December of the war. Amid the African marigolds on the grave a rambler was growing; I picked a spray for his mother, and laid two withered roses – pink from the Leightons' garden, red from my own – against the words 'Never Goodbye' on the white stone.

'Never Goodbye.' Yet though I could still weep for Edward, my childhood companion, I had now no tears to shed for Roland. As I stood beside his grave I could feel only a deep impersonal sorrow for brilliant youth thrown remorselessly away, and a profound thankfulness that he never knew – as we who were left realised already – that the sacrifice had been in vain.

Module 43

1   *Discussion*:
  1)   Which are the main features of the meaning expressed by the Perfect in English? How do they fit the expression 'the extended now'?
  2)   What meanings are produced from the following combinations:
      (a) State verbs + Perfect (e.g. *like, belong*)
      (b) Event and activity verbs + Perfect (e.g. *break, rob*)
      (c) Durative processes + Perfect (e.g. *rain, live*)
      With which types is an Adjunct necessary?
  3)   Can the Progressive be added to these combinations? If so, what is the result?

2   †*Discuss the difference in meaning between the use of the Past and the Perfect in the following sentences. What pragmatic inferences would be made to establish the psychological link between past and present time in the case of the Perfect uses?*
  1)   (a) His last film set a new standard in horror and violence.
       (b) His latest film has set a new standard in horror and violence.
  2)   (a) I was a colleague of hers, working in the same Department, for several years.
       (b) I have been a colleague of hers, working in thc same Department, for several years.
  3)   (a) How far did you get?
       (b) How far have you got?
  4)   (a) Where did you go?
       (b) Where have you been?
  5)   (a) What did you do?
       (b) What have you done?
  6)   (a) She made a fool of herself in public.
       (b) She has made a fool of herself in public.
  7)   (a) Mobile phones suddenly became popular with executives.
       (b) Mobile phones have suddenly become popular with executives.
  8)   (a) That report that I gave you has a couple of serious errors.
       (b) That report that I've just given you has a couple of serious errors.
  9)   (a) Did anyone go ahead with the project?
       (b) Has anyone gone ahead with the project?
  10) (a) She was explaining to me about the plan they have.
       (b) She has been explaining to me about the plan they have.

3   *Turn to the William Boyd text in 43.4. You will see that the dates make explicit the exact relationships in some cases of the Pluperfect. Change the first **was** to **is** and examine carefully the effect on the rest of the verb forms. Justify your decision to make or not to make changes in the verb forms.*

Module 44

1   †*Supply the modal which corresponds to the paraphrase in each case. In some cases more than one form is acceptable:*

1) I . . . . let you know as soon as I have any news. (willingness, promise)
2) We . . . . get away until the end of August. (It will not be possible for us to get away.)
3) If she . . . . (is not able to) do it by herself, she . . . . . . (it is possible that . . .) have to ask you for help.
4) There . . . . be a fire somewhere (it is necessarily the case that . . .); I . . . . smell burning. (I smell it right now.)
5) This . . . . . be enough for three. (prediction)
6) Five bars of chocolate . . . . . . be enough for five children, don't you think? – Well, it depends on the children. (probability, reasonable inference)
7) Prices . . . . to go up while everyone is on holiday. (It is certain that . . .)
8) Surely that . . . . be the President's wife. (It is not possible that . . .)
9) You . . . . not feed the animals at the zoo. (You are under the obligation not to . . . .)
10) You . . . . not tip the waiter. (It is not necessary that you tip the waiter.)

2   †*Give the appropriate form of the past for each of the Verbal Groups containing modals in the sentences below:*

1) They *will not wait* for us more than ten minutes.
They . . . . for us more than ten minutes yesterday.
2) He *must be mistaken* about his daughter's age.
He . . . . about his daughter's age.
3) You *can't be listening* to what I'*m saying*.
You . . . . to what I . . . .
4) Ben *should take* two tablets every day.
Ben . . . . two tablets yesterday.
5) Lying in our tent, we *can hear* the wind howling down from the heights.
Lying in our tent, we . . . . the wind howling down from the heights.
6) With their fast patrol-boats, the police *can capture* drug- traffickers operating in the Strait.
With their fast patrol-boats, the police . . . . drug-traffickers operating in the Strait yesterday.
7) There *may be* a hold-up on the motorway this afternoon.
There . . . . a hold-up on the motorway this morning.

8) I *must have* the baby *vaccinated* today.
I . . . . the baby . . . . yesterday.

9) He *will telephone* us immediately if he *can*.
He . . . . us immediately if he . . . .

10) They *oughtn't to be talking* while the pianist is playing.
They . . . . while the pianist was playing.

3 †*The following text is part of an article in* **The Times Higher Education Supplement** *(27 December 1985) criticising the proposed cuts in student grants. The occurrences of modal verbs have been deleted. Suggest possible replacements, and discuss the differences in meaning produced when more than one modal verb is possible:*

The first aspect is clear enough. Students . . . . . [1] experience real hardship because their grants in many cases . . . . [2] be well below the level necessary to maintain them. A point has now been reached where it is no longer honest to pretend that the grant . . . . [3] to be sufficient to cover the living expenses of students; it is now simply a contribution to those expenses, one element in a student's income that . . . . [4] be supplemented from other sources, parental handouts, bank overdrafts, weekend work.

The second aspect is equally significant. The penury of students . . . . . . [5] have a marked impact not only on the management of universities, polytechnics and colleges but also on the character of the higher education they provide. The character of British higher education – the intensive teaching of students, their close supervision, the brevity of the honours degree – rests on the assumption that students . . . . [6] study for most of the time rather than serve in bars, and that they . . . . [7] afford accommodation that is conducive to study.

The third aspect . . . . . [8] worry the Government most. Despite Sir Keith Joseph's well-signalled support for a thorough reform of student support and especially for the introduction of loans, nothing has been done. And nothing is . . . . [9] be done. The political will simply does not exist. That being so, the Government has an obligation to maintain the present system of student grants in reasonable order. That it has also failed – and is failing – to do.

4 *Write an essay describing the system of higher education in your own country. What improvements do you think could be made? What modifications should be given priority?*

5 *Study the following extract from an article by Angela Carter about her memories of her parents. The occasion is a visit to her father's new home, after her mother's death:*

My father had lined the walls of his new home with pictures of my mother when she was young and beautiful; and beautiful she certainly was, with a broad, Slavonic jaw and high cheekbones like Anna Karenina, she took a striking photograph and had the talent for histrionics her pictures imply. They used to row dreadfully and pelt one another with household utensils, whilst shrieking with rage. Then my mother would finally break down and cry, possibly tears of sheer frustration that he was bigger than she, and my father, in an ecstasy of remorse – we've always been very good at remorse and its manifestations in action, emotional blackmail and irrational guilt – my father would go out and buy her chocolates.

Angela Carter, Nothing Sacred.

1) Which tense-aspect does the author use to describe her father's activity in his new house, before her visit?
2) Which tense does the author use to describe her mother? Do the verbs in this part of the article refer to states, repeated actions or events in the past?
3) The description of her parents' life together is very lively, and this liveliness is in part achieved by the combination of dynamic verbs and constructions which express discontinued habit and past prediction. Identify these forms.
4) In which part of the text does the author establish a psychological link between past and present time, with regard to certain family characteristics? Which tense-aspect form is used to make this link?
5) Try writing a paragraph about your own parents.

6 *Read the following extract from a newspaper article:*

I love birds and watching them has coloured the tedium of many a long car-drive, bringing bare mountains to life and turning raw plains into enchanted places.

One group of birds has come to fascinate me more than most – vultures. Now vultures, by and large, have not enjoyed a good press. Call someone a 'vulture' and you lose a friend. In biblical times they were regarded as unclean. To the ancient Greeks they were birds of ill-fortune; they followed armies, and Homer attributed to them the power of predicting slaughter.

What, then, is their appeal? Not their looks: vultures are hideous. Not their song, for they have none. Nor their habits – though in truth vultures eat only dead flesh, just as we do, and are less cruel than magpies, cuckoos, or the garden thrush smashing open a snail. No, it is something else. Vultures have the power to fascinate because they are awe-inspiring in flight and they are majestic, patrolling vast areas without the slightest movement of their wings. Furthermore, their eyesight is at least seven times sharper than our own, capable of detecting a carcass the size of a rabbit from 11,000 feet.

A Carrion Call by Edwin Mullins in *The Sunday Times*, 7 April 1991.

List the uses of the Present, Past and Perfect in this text and discuss the meaning that is conveyed in each case.

10

Talking about 'things':
The Nominal Group

MODULE 45
Expressing our experience of 'things'

Summary

1 **Nouns refer to classes of 'things'**
   Persons, objects, places, institutions, actions, abstract ideas, qualities, relationships, phenomena, emotions, etc.

2 **How we experience 'things'**
   Experiential features: definiticity, deixis, quantity, intrinsic and extrinsic features.

3 **Structural elements that realise experiential features**
   The head, the determiner, the modifier, the qualifier.

4 **Pronominal heads**
   Personal pronouns: *it, this, that*.
   Substitute words: *one/ones, same, such*.
   Discourse function of pronouns.

45.1   Classes of 'things'

Nominal Groups refer semantically to those aspects of our experience which we perceive as 'things' or 'entities'. The term 'thing' refers here not only to concrete entities such as persons, objects, places, institutions and other 'collectives', but also to the names of actions (*reading, laughter*), abstractions (*thought, experience*), relationships (*friendship, obedience*), qualities (*beauty, speed*), emotions (*anger, excitement*), phenomena (*thunder, success*) and many other classes of entities. The semantic classification of

NGs varies from language to language. The following description of a town, which is made up almost entirely of NGs, contains examples of several classes of 'things':

> *Lagos* assaults you with its *squalor* and *vitality*. The narrow *streets*, the *houses* – which are *hovels* mainly – made of *mud* or old *tin* and packed as close as playing *cards*, the stinking open *drains*, the *noise*, the *traffic*, the jostling *throngs* – *Lagos* is Eastern in its *feeling* that sheer, naked, human *life*, mere *existence*, bubbles and pullulates with the frightening *fecundity* of *bacteria*. The *town* is on an *island* surrounded by a *lagoon* into which all the *drains* empty, and a sour and sulphurous *smell* frequently envelops the *Marina*.

> Elspeth Huxley, *Four Guineas*.

45.2   What a Nominal Group looks like

When we name a 'thing', we usually add some information about it which shows how we 'experience' or perceive the 'thing'. It is important to remember that language is not reality itself, but only the way we see reality, the way we experience it. In expressing this 'experiential' information about an entity or 'referent' some of it is placed before the noun and some after it, as we can see in the groups contained in the example text:

Pre-head	Head	Post-head
1 its	*squalor and vitality*	
2 the narrow	streets	
3 the	houses	– which are *hovels* mainly – made of *mud* or old *tin* and packed as close as playing *cards*
4 the stinking open	*drains*	
5 the	*noise*	
6 the	*traffic*	
7 the jostling	*throngs*	
8 its	*feeling*	that sheer, naked, human *life*, mere *existence*, bubbles and pullulates with the frightening *fecundity* of *bacteria*.
9 The	*town*	
10 an	*island*	surrounded by a *lagoon* into which all the *drains* empty
11 a sour and sulphurous	*smell*	
12 the	*Marina*.	

In this text, we see that the post-head information, given on the right about the head nouns in the middle column, also contains nouns with their own pre-head and post-head information.

45.3   Types of experiential information

The mere position of items before and after the head noun tells us little about the meaning of a NG. For this we need to know the experiential types of elements of which it is composed, the semantic and grammatical functions which they realise, and the logical relations existing between them. The following are the main primary and secondary experiential elements of English NGs:

45.3.1   The head element (see also 46.1–3)

This is the central element of a NG structure which refers, as mentioned before, to a substantive entity experienced as a 'thing', and which is realised typically by a noun or a pronoun. Sometimes the entity is not named, and the head element is realised by a word expressing one of its Attributes, as in *the poor*, or a determinative feature such as *those* or *each*, or its quantity: *many, twenty*. Some writers consider these items as pronouns when they stand alone as head element. It is useful, however, to distinguish between pronominal heads, which cannot be combined with a noun (e.g. *I like white roses but I prefer red ones*: *red ones roses), and heads which can be combined if necessary with the presupposed noun (e.g. *I like white roses, but I prefer red* = *red roses*). The word *red*, which is an adjective, we shall call an **elliptical head** since it conflates the functions of epithet and the unexpounded head element (see 48.5.1).

45.3.2   The articles (see also 46.4–7)

In a very large number of NGs, the first element is realised by one of two items which merely present the noun referent as a definite or indefinite entity. These are the definite and indefinite articles *the* and *a/an*. *The* does not identify the referent, but tells us that it can be identified somewhere, either in the text or in the situation or in our common knowledge of the world at large; for example, *the streets, the houses, the traffic, the fecundity (of bacteria)* in the extract describing the town of Lagos. In the same extract, the article *a/an*, as in *a lagoon, an island, a … smell* indicates that the referent cannot yet be identified as something known to the reader or listener, from anything that has been said previously in the text or from general knowledge. Once it has been presented by *a/an* (or *some*), it is then known and can on the next occasion be referred to as *the lagoon, the island* and *the smell*.

When the head noun is used alone, without any pre-head element, this also is significant. It indicates that the noun, for example the singular noun *chocolate* in *I like chocolate*, or the plural noun *oranges* in *I like oranges*, is used in a general, global sense. For the purpose of grammatical description, this significant absence of a pre-head item is called the 'zero article'; *the* and *a/an* (and sometimes *some*) are called **definite** and **indefinite**. It is important to understand the terms definite and indefinite in the grammatical sense we have explained above and not in a 'common sense' way: obviously 'a lagoon' refers here to a lagoon which definitely exists, but textually we do not consider it as a 'definite' noun until it has been presented in the text or is already known outside the text and can then be referred to as '*the* lagoon'. Until this happens, we describe *a lagoon* in this text as 'indefinite but specific'.

45.3.3   The determining element (see also 47.1–11)

The first element of a NG is sometimes realised, not by an article, but by a word which relates the head noun to the situation in which it exists. This is known as deictic reference, which points to an entity as being near or not near the speaker in space or time (*this book, that reason*) or to a person or thing to which it belongs or is related (*my* book, *the Minister's* reasons). Other particularising words of less specific reference are *WH*-items as in *which book?, whatever reasons*, and distributives: *each, all, either, neither*. Since deictic reference includes the concepts of 'definite' and 'indefinite', these words are usually grouped with the articles as a single class of unit realising the function known as determination of the head noun referent. This element is called the **determiner**, and the lexical items which expound the determiner we shall call 'determinatives'.

In many grammars, the function of 'determination' also includes that of 'quantification', which may be exact (*six, a hundred, the first, the next*) or inexact (*many, a lot, a few, some*). Certain particularising adjectives such as *same, whole, customary, original, certain, own*, etc., are sometimes used with a deictic meaning. Both the quantifiers and these items are called 'post-deictic determiners'.

45.3.4   The modifying element (see also 48.1–5)

After the defining, determining and quantifying items of information, which particularise or select the noun referent from others in the surrounding context, we find those which describe the inherent, more permanent qualities of the entity itself. Examples contained in the description of Lagos were: *narrow* (streets), *stinking, open* (drains), *sheer, naked, human* (life), etc. Some of these words describe objective qualities (e.g. *narrow*) while others are subjective and represent the personal attitude of the writer (e.g. *stinking*); others do not describe the entity qualitatively, but indicate a particular subclass of the referent in question (e.g. *human* life as distinct from *animal, organic, social, family life*) (see 48.3). The difference between 'subjective' and 'objective' is sometimes not clear, but depends on interpretation.

The items that describe subjective and objective qualities of an entity we will regard for the moment as a single element termed the **epithet** (**e**). The item which indicates a subclass of the entity will be called the **classifier** (**cf**).

At a more general level of analysis, they can all be subsumed under the broad function of 'modification', just as definers, deictics and quantifiers are subsumed under the general function of 'determination'. Whereas the classifier restricts the head noun to a subclass of its referent, the epithet may refer to an individual member or members of the class of referent.

45.3.5   The qualifying element (see also 49.1–6)

This refers to all the experiential items which are placed after the head noun and which, like the pre-head items, help to define, describe and identify the referent of the head noun still further. In English, they do this typically by adding information of a temporary, extrinsic kind, in contrast to the modifying pre-head elements which describe its inherent, relatively permanent Attributes; e.g.

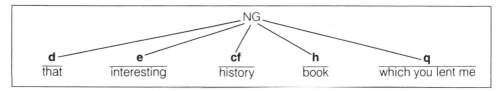

The qualifier is potentially, and in practice nearly always is, much longer than the pre-head elements, because the kind of information it adds is usually more extensive, and is realised not by individual words, but by embedded groups and clauses which themselves may have other groups and clauses embedded within them, as we saw in the 'Lagos' text.

Because the forms and types of 'experiential' or 'ideational' information given by the post-head items are different from that expressed by the pre-head ones, we consider it appropriate, in accord with certain other modern linguists, to use, instead of the well-known terms 'pre-modifier' and 'post-modifier', the two distinctive terms **modifier** (for the pre-head items) and **qualifier** (for the post-head ones). This is purely a question of terminology, and is used to reflect a semantic difference as well as the positional one. Obviously, both types do, in fact, 'modify' the head noun, in the general sense of the word. Qualifiers express three broad types of experiential information about an entity: nominal, circumstantial and attributive. When these are realised by clauses, they may also be characterised as 'situational'.

45.3.6   Summary of NG elements

We have now established four primary elements of NG structure which are used in English to describe a speaker's or writer's experience of 'things'. In addition each functional element can express various kinds of 'experience' so that we have several semantic and formal options from which to choose at each place in the structure. These two aspects of Nominal Groups are shown in the following diagram:

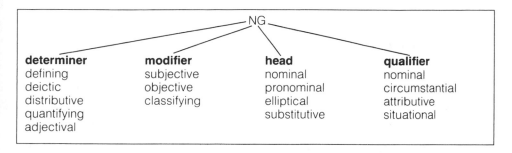

The terms used for these choices are explained and illustrated in Modules 47, 48 and 49.

45.4 Examples of NG structures

The paragraph on page 412, taken from a popular scientific journal, contains examples of NGs with two, three or four elements; the structure of each group is shown below:

	determiner (d)	modifier (m)	head (h)	qualifier (q)
dh	a number of		children and young people	
mh		mild	depression	
hq			something	exciting
h			This	
dmhq	a	pop	concert	with music at pain-producing intensity
h			it	
hq			authority	at home or at school
h			it	
h			stealing	
dmh	other	law-breaking	activities	
dh	the		challenge	
dh	their		depression	

Nowadays *a number of/children and young people* [1] have found that *mild/depression* [2] may be overcome by doing *something/exciting*[3]. *This* [4] may be going to *a/pop/concert/with music at pain-producing intensity*[5], *it* [6] may be challenging *authority/at home or at school*[7], or *it* [8] may involve *stealing* [9] or *other/law-breaking/activities*[10]. The more depressed they are, the more exciting *the challenge* [11] has to be to mask *their/depression*[12].

New Scientist, October 1982.

Even in a straightforward style of writing such as this, we find a moderate amount of recursion and embedding:

[1] recursive head: *children and young people*;
[7] recursive qualifier: *at home or at school*;
[7] embedded PrepG: *at home or at school*;
[5] embedded PrepG: *with music at pain-producing intensity*.

Nominal Groups vary greatly not only in the types of 'things' they refer to, but also in the experiential information encoded in their elements, in the number of these elements, the classes of formal items that realise them and the vast range of lexical items that expound them. These linguistic resources make the NG a powerful unit of expression for 'talking about 'things''.

45.5   Pronominal heads

Whereas nouns refer directly to entities in the 'real' world outside language, personal pronouns refer indirectly to entities mentioned by other NGs in the text. We can only interpret the meaning of a personal pronoun by first identifying in the text the noun or NG for which it substitutes. (Exceptions are *I, you, we, us*, because they refer to participants present in the speech situation.) For example:

Technology has solved many age-old problems for *us*, but *it* [1] has also created many new *ones*[2]: for example the problem of waste material. The best method *we* have nowadays of dealing with waste is not to burn *it* [3] or bury *it* [4] but to recycle *it*[5]. The procedure is *this*[6]: people return their cans, containers, bottles, paper and plastic objects to depots in their local community, where *they* [7] are sold to firms *that* [8] convert *them* [9] into new articles. In this way *everybody* contributes to solving the problem.

Speak Up, no. 66

In this paragraph, we can identify the textual references of the numbered items as follows:

	Pronoun	Reference
[1]	*it*	'Technology'
[2]	*ones*	'problems'
[3, 4, 5]	*it*	'waste'
[6]	*this*	the following clauses
[7]	*they*	'cans, containers, bottles, paper and plastic objects'
[8]	*that*	'firms'
[9]	*them*	'cans, containers, bottles, paper and plastic objects'

These references are not identified solely by their nominal form, but by their proximity to the pronoun, by the predication (animate *they return* and inanimate *they are sold*), and by our experience of the world.

The pronouns compounded with *some-, any-, no-, every-* (e.g. *everybody*) differ from those mentioned above, in that they refer directly to a broad class of things or people, not to a NG elsewhere in the text. In this respect, they behave more like nouns than pronouns, often being qualified, for example, as in *nothing new, everybody that I know, anyone you like*.

We assume the reader to be familiar with the grammar of the possessive, reflexive, reciprocal, interrogative negative and relative pronouns, and limit ourselves to the following remarks on the personal pronouns and on *it, this, that*.

45.5.1 Personal pronouns

When a personal pronoun functions alone as Cs, the objective form is usually preferred, because it bears the phonological stress of end-focus more easily than the subjective form: *It was me, it was him, it was us, it was them*. In this structure, the subjective forms, *It was I, it was he, it is we, it is they*, are considered over-correct.

If the personal pronoun at Cs is followed by a relative pronoun functioning as Subject of its clause, both the subjective and the objective forms can be used; if the relative pronoun is Object of its clause, only the objective forms are used:

> It was *he/him* who needed us. It's *they/them* who want to go.
> It was *him* that we needed. It's *them* that I suspect.

The plural pronouns *we/us* may include or exclude the addressee(s), though the reference is sometimes ambiguous:

inclusive *we*:	Shall we sit together?
	As we saw in the previous class, ...
exclusive *we*:	We both sat down.
	We hope you enjoyed the show.
ambiguous *we*:	We really must see that film next week.

We/us can have generalised reference to include 'everybody', and also certain colloquial uses in informal speech:

generalised *we*:   We don't seem to be near world peace yet.
we = you: How are we getting on?
us = me: Give us a chance! I've hardly started yet.

45.5.2   The pronoun *it*

The pronoun *it*, besides referring to specific objects, can refer to a situation, a process, a fact, a report or extraposed Subject:

They were all shouting and fighting; *it* was terrible.
She was very scared, but she tried not to show *it*.
It has been very nice talking to you.

It is often non-referring, and its presence is due to the need, in English, for an overt syntactic Subject or a syntactic Direct Object with a transitive verb such as *like*:

It's too early to start worrying.
I like *it* here.
If *it* hadn't been for your help, we would have lost the train.

The reference is even less explicit (though conventional) in idiomatic uses such as:

If you speak to the boss like that, you're asking for *it*. (= trouble)
How goes *it*? (= life in general)
You're not *with it*. (= informed, up-to-date)

For the syntactic use of *it* as dummy Subject or dummy Object, see 5.1.3(d) and 6.1.3(d).

45.5.3   The pronouns *this* and *that*

The items *this, that, these, those* function mainly as determiners (47.2) or as elliptical head elements (47.9). The singular forms *this, that* can, in addition, refer to a whole proposition or situation or something inferred from it, a use which we classify here as pronominal. (For the difference between a pronominal head and an elliptical head, see 47.9) These pronominal references may be anaphoric (to a previous part of the text), cataphoric (to a later part of the text) or exophoric (to something outside the text), and some are idiomatic:

anaphoric: You are working too long and too hard, and *this/that* is bound to affect your health in the long run.
cataphoric: The plan is *this*: plane to Cairo, night train to Luxor and then up the Nile by boat as far as Aswan.
   That makes sense, what you've just said.
exophoric: I hate working *like this*! (= in this way)
   I never thought things would come to *this*!
idiomatic: I won't allow you to go, and *that's that*! (= that is decisive)

> We spend hours chatting about *this* and *that*.
> I wrote them an apology – and a very humble one *at that*. (= in fact)
> *At that*, he got up and walked out. (= when he heard that)

It can be seen that all the referents in these examples are inanimate and general, and some of them refer to pieces of extended text.

It is well known that *this* indicates proximity to the speaker and *that* indicates distance. However, these terms are often interpreted subjectively, and the distinction is blurred. For example, an event distant in time may be referred to by *this* if it has just been mentioned:

> Columbus discovered the Bahamas in 1492 and *this* changed the course of history.

Conversely, events near in time may be referred to by *that* when an effect of psychological distancing is required:

> If the Opposition wins the motion of 'No Confidence' today, *that* will be the end of the present government.

In many cases, either of the pronouns is psychologically appropriate, and the choice depends on the attitude of the speaker:

> The two countries have been exhausted by eight years of war, but it is the leaders who refuse to put an end to it – and *this/that* is precisely the problem.

45.5.4   The discourse function of pronouns

The major function of the third person pronouns is to refer to NGs or other classes of units mentioned elsewhere in a text. Since English clauses require the Subject to be stated, except in some cases of ellipsis, pronouns perform this and other clause functions economically, by avoiding long repetitions of parts of the previous discourse. The connections are short and usually clear, so that the flow of conversation or reading is well maintained. The following snatch of conversation shows how frequently pronouns are needed in English, even in such a short piece of discourse.

In the conversation, Dennis is telling his friend Neil about the bad relations that exist between his mother and his wife, Vera:

Neil: Vera's looking better.
Dennis: Oh, *she* is. *She*'s a lot better. *She*'s getting better every day.
            Once *she* and mother can bury the hatchet, *we*'ll be laughing.
Neil: Are *they* still ... ?
Dennis: Not talking at all.
Neil: Really.
Dennis: Well, actually, it's Vera *who*'s not talking to mother. Mother
            comes in one door, Vera goes out the other. Ridiculous. Been

going on for weeks. *I* said to *them* – look, girls, just sit down
and have a laugh about *it*. There's only one life, *you* know.
That's all *you*'ve got. One life. Laugh and enjoy *it* while *you*
can. *We*'ll probably *all* be dead tomorrow so *what*'s the
difference? Do *they* listen to *me*? Do *they* hell!

Alan Ayckbourn, *Just Between Ourselves*.

In interpersonal communication of this kind both speakers share the same
knowledge of the situation and the participants involved in it, so that the
pronominal references of the speaker are easily interpreted by the addressee,
even when they are not explicit but only inferred, as in the case of *it* in *have a
laugh about it*, and *you* in *while you can*. The meaning of *all* in *We'll
probably all be dead* is indeterminate, but so slightly that communication
would not be affected.

In written communication, where there is often less shared knowledge
between writer and reader, correct interpretation of a pronoun's reference
depends on factors related to the text, such as proximity of the pronoun to its
antecedent, general preference for the Subject rather than the Object as
antecedent and the amount of inference the reader is required to make. On
the whole, common sense and the reader's general understanding of the text
seems to be the decisive factor:

Tom jumped in the river to save Bill *though he* couldn't swim. (*he* =
Tom)
Tom jumped in the river to save Bill *because he* couldn't swim. (*he* =
Bill)

If the references of the pronouns in a text are not transparently clear, the text
will be difficult to understand.

In the flow of spontaneous conversation, personal Subject pronouns and
other structural items are sometimes omitted or subvocalised if they are self-
understood:

(I):   Was she angry?   – ∧ Don't honestly know. ∧ Hope not.
(it): Sorry I'm late.   – ∧ Doesn't matter, you're the first.
(he): Why isn't Tom here?   – ∧ Couldn't come today.

45.6 Substitute heads

Each of the different classes of pronouns used in English has its characteristic meaning, referring to persons or objects, statements, facts or events,
which may be near or distant, reflexive, reciprocal, indefinite, relative or
interrogative. They all refer to participants in the situations mentioned in the
discourse or otherwise known to the speaker and the addressee.

Sometimes, a previously mentioned noun is referred to, not by a pronoun
of this kind, but by a word which has no semantic identity of its own, but only
the grammatical function of substituting for a presupposed noun or NG. This

function is carried out mainly by the word *one* and its plural form *ones*; it is also realised by the items *same* and *such*, which have the additional semantic feature of 'comparison'. When used in this way, these items are classed as 'substitute heads', to distinguish them from the classes of 'pronominal heads' of NGs.

45.6.1   Substitution by *one*/*ones*

It is important to note that *one*/*ones* does not replace a whole antecedent NG, but only part of it:

> I knew Mavis wanted a blue scarf, so I bought her a lovely *one* this morning. (*one* = blue scarf)
> I couldn't find a blue scarf for Mavis, but I bought her a lovely green *one*. (*one*= scarf)

The substitute item *one*/*ones* is always accompanied by a determiner, a modifier or a qualifier, thus producing NGs of varying structures:

> **dh**:   this one, each one, either one, which ones, any ones.
> **dmh**:   that big one, a small red one, a few ripe ones.
> **dhq**:   that one over there, any one you like.
> **dmhq**: some fresh ones from the country.

Possessive determinatives are rarely used before *one*/*ones*:

> ? my one, Peter's one, my friend's ones.

The word *one* can also be used elliptically as the elliptical form of the article *a*/*an*, in which case its plural form is *some*.

> We need a carpet. – OK, let's buy *one*. (= *a* carpet)
> We need carpets. – OK, let's buy *some*. (= carpets)

For other comments on substitution and ellipsis in the NG, see also 48.5.

45.6.2   Substitution by *the same*

(a) Whereas *one*/*ones* replace only part of an antecedent NG, *the same* can substitute for a whole NG:

> Alice bought a red dress and Monica a blue *one*. (= dress)
> Alice bought a red dress and Monica *the same*. (= a red dress)

(b) The scope of substitution by *the same* extends beyond NGs to parts of a clause or to a whole clause:

> A. The journey was too long.   B. I think *the same*.
> A. Thanks for helping.   B. You'd do *the same* for me.

In this function, *the same* is a NG treating the clause or part of the clause as a nominal unit.

The above functions of *the same* as a substitute form are different from its use as an elliptical adjectival head, as in:

> A. What make of car are you going to buy?
> B. *The same* as I always buy. (= the same make of car)

When *the same* expresses identity with the presupposed noun, it is often followed by substitute *one/ones*:

> B. *The same one* as I always buy.

The broad scope of reference of this item leads to its use in a number of fixed colloquial expressions such as:

> A. You're a twit! B. *Same* to you!
> *Same* again, please. (customer to barman)
> It's all *the same* (= It doesn't matter)
> Just *the same* . . . (= Nevertheless . . .)
> A. Television adverts annoy me! B. *Same* here! (= They annoy me, too)
> A. Can I give you a lift? B. No, but thanks all *the same*.

In most of these expressions, *the same* does not substitute for a clearly identifiable nominal unit. In the following sentence, its reference seems to be clearly circumstantial:

> He works *the same* as he always did. (= in the same way)

45.6.3   Substitution by *such*

A third item which can function as a substitute for a presupposed NG is *such*. In the following sentences, *such* refers anaphorically or cataphorically to a NG, a clause or extended text.

> (a) We spent our *summer holiday* in England, if rain every day can be called *such*. (= can be called *a summer holiday*)
> (b) Is India *a peaceful country*? I wouldn't consider it as *such*. (= as *a peaceful country*)
> (c) Holidays are always too short. *Such* is life! (= that is life)
> (d) After a summary trial, *he was shot*; *such* was the price he paid for disloyalty. (= that was the price)

In other cases it expresses similarity, and so substitutes for a noun similar in meaning implied by the context:

> (e) He went on a safari and got killed by *a lion*, or *an elephant*, or *some such*.
> (f) *Drugs, AIDS* and *such* are matters of great concern nowadays.

In (a) and (b), *such* substitutes for a previous NG with a meaning similar to pronominal *that*. In (c) and (d) it substitutes for a previous clause, also equivalent to *that*. In (e) and (f) it refers to an implied hyperonym of the preceding nouns, such as 'animal' (e) and 'topics' (f). Since it can be followed by these words, it is better analysed as an elliptic determinative head: *some such (animal)* and *such (topics)*.

In the following sentence (g), *such* substitutes exophorically for a referent which might be represented by a NG or a clause, but to which there is no clue in the text:

(g) My boss is always telling me not to forget *such and such*, and to take *such and such* into account.

As an elliptical or substitute head element, *such* can be determined or quantified, as in (e) (*some such*) and as in (h) and (i).

(h) We have been asked to consider radical alternatives. *Many such* have been proposed in the last few years.
(i) Some people always seem to win large sums of money on the football pools, but *none such* ever come my way.

MODULE 46
Presenting 'things' as mass, countable, indefinite and definite

Summary

1 **The system of countability**
   The mass and count references of nouns.
   Grammatical markers of mass and count reference.
   Degrees of countability.

2 **Observations on the countability scale**

3 **The system of definiteness**
   Obligatory choice of definite/indefinite NG.
   Distribution of the three articles.

4 **Indefinite NGs**
   Indefinite specific/non-specific; indefinite proper nouns.

5 **Definite NGs**
   Endophoric/exophoric reference of *the*.
   Identification of referent by inference.
   The + proper noun.

6 **Generic statements** with *a*, *the*, *zero* + noun. Constraints.

7 **Discourse function of articles**; Given/New information.

46.1   The system of countability

46.1.1   The notions of 'mass' and 'count'

In English, when we use a NG, the language obliges us to make it clear whether the referent is perceived as a discrete, countable entity, either one or more than one, or as an indivisible, non-countable 'mass' entity. This is a contrast between two semantic categories which is made on the perceptive, cognitive plane, and which constitutes a feature that for English speakers is salient in their experience of 'things'. If it is salient, obviously this is only because it is considered necessary for successful communication.

When semantic contrasts are actualised in language, they are usually matched by linguistic contrasts, which may be lexical, morphological, syntactic or intonational. The count/mass distinction is expressed in English by morphological and syntactic means. In languages which do not grammaticalise the distinction, we may presume that either it is not perceived because it is not needed for successful communication, or that it is not expressed because the language does not have the resources for doing so.

One process involved in lexicalising semantic categories consists in denoting a mass entity by a given word such as *travel* or *rain* or *food*, and an associated count entity or phenomenon by a different word, e.g. *journey*, *shower*, *meal*, respectively. The mass or count feature, which is an inherent component of its meaning, is at the same time reinforced by the fact that each of the two classes of noun is used in different sets of syntactic or morphological patterns, which are mutually exclusive.

> We made *a journey*; but not: *We made *a travel*.
> We liked *every meal*; but not: *We liked *every food*.

Similarly, we can say:

> *Travel* broadens the mind; but not: *Journey* broadens the mind.
> *Health is* more important than *wealth*; but not: *Healths are* more important than *wealths*.

A second way of marking the mass/count contrast is purely grammatical, that is, to use a single noun in both types of syntactical patterning, mass and count. This is not possible with all nouns, but the number is very large, as we explain in 46.2. Grammatical marking of the mass/count contrast is clearly more economical than lexicalisation, which would tend to overload the lexicon.

In 46.2 we outline the grammatical markers of prototype mass and count nouns, that is fully mass and fully count nouns, in English; and in 46.3 we comment on their distribution in various sections of the lexicon. Before doing so, we invite our readers to identify, from the knowledge they already have of this matter, the countability features they observe in the following paragraph, and to try to formulate the grounds on which each interpretation is based.

Work [1] in *cooperation* [2] is *a frequent aspect* [3] of *primitive economic life*[4]. *The stimuli* [5] which keep *the working group* [6] together may be different from those we use. *The responsibility* [7] of *employed* [8] to *employer* [9] and *the fear* [10] of *loss* [11] of *pay* [12] or *job* [13] are not *the prime forces* [14] which keep them at *work*[15]. More important are *the conventions* [16] about *industry*[17], *the reproof* [18] which *laziness* [19] is likely to draw from *a man's fellows*[20], and *the stimulus* [21] given by *work* [22] in *company* [23] with *songs* [24] and *jokes*[25] which lightens *drudgery* [26] and gives it *some tinge* [27] of *recreation*[28].

R. W. Firth, *Human Types*.

46.2   Grammatical markers of countability

By definition, the semantic notion of countability correlates with the grammatical category of number. Count nouns refer to 'things' which are perceived as 'one' or 'more than one', and are represented linguistically by the formal singular/plural contrast.

However, the perception of a 'thing' as 'mass' does not involve the 'one/more than one' contrast, so that semantically, mass nouns do not correlate with the singular/plural opposition in grammar; and we should not, strictly speaking, say that they are represented by 'the singular form of the noun', but only by 'the base form', which is not marked for number. Nevertheless, in a grammatical description of the language, all NGs and finite VGs must be described morphologically as singular or plural. We are therefore obliged to say that *music* has singular form, even though it does not contrast with a plural form *musics; and that *athletics* has plural form even though it does not contrast with a singular form *an athletic*. Syntactically both are singular since both take singular verbs and are referred to by the singular pronoun *it*.

To understand and to use English NGs correctly, one must know which grammatical forms and structures realise each of the semantic features 'mass' and 'count'. These are as follows:

(a)   Grammatical markers of mass NGs
The following grammatical forms and structures mark a NG typically as 'mass':

(i) The singular form of the noun with zero determiner:

Beauty is in the eye of the beholder.
I always take *coffee* with *milk*.

(ii) The singular form of the noun preceded by *all*:

I say this in *all sincerity*.

(iii) The singular form of the noun, quantified by *much, little, a little*:

There isn*'t much room* in our apartment so we have *little furniture*.

(b) **Grammatical markers of count NGs**

(iv) The singular form of the noun determined by *a(n)*:

I'm looking for *a new job.*

(v) The singular form of the noun determined by *each, every*:

Each day is different. We go there *every year.*

(vi) With number contrast marked on the noun:

lion/lions; child/children; mouse/mice; stimulus/stimuli.

(vii) Invariable or plural form of the noun preceded by a plural determiner:

many choices, few opportunities; these aircraft, those sheep, several series.

(viii) Plural number concord with verb or pronoun:

People *like* to be happy, don't *they?*

(c) **Nominal Groups that are not marked for countability**

The determiners *the, this, that, my, your, his, her, its, our, their* are neutral to the mass/count distinction and can be used with both types of reference: *this house, this bread; our friend, our friendship*. When these determinatives are used with nouns that can have either mass or count reference, e.g. *the hope, the fear, this work, that kindness*, the interpretation can only be clarified by inference from the context.

46.3   Degrees of countability

When these markers are applied to a representative number of nouns, as they are used in texts, it is found that countability is not a neat binary system of mass nouns and count nouns, but a scale of varying degrees of potentiality for countness and massness. The table on page 423 shows six small sample sets of nouns, each sharing a different degree of potentiality for use with the grammatical forms mentioned above. The plus sign '+' indicates that most nouns in the set admit the given mass or count marker, and the bracketed sign (+) indicates that some do not admit it. The six degrees of countability (A to F) refer to nouns which may be described as:

(A) fully mass; some occasionally with *a(n)*;
(B) fully mass; some occasionally with *a(n)* or pluralised;
(C) fully mass; fully count;
(D) never mass; partially count;
(E) never mass; fully count except number contrast on the noun;
(F) rarely mass; fully count.

The presence of variation in all of the small samples given in the table on page 423 shows that many more than six sets would be required in order fully

Distribution of countability markers of English nouns

Type	MASS				COUNT				Example
	1	2	3	4	5	6	7	8	
	0 + N.sing.	all + N.sing.	much little + N.sing.	a(n) + N.sing.	each every either + N.sing.	Number contrast on noun	many (a) few + N.plur.	number concord with verb, pron.	
A FULLY MASS (some occasionally with a(n))	+	+	+	(+)					drinking, running, eating; weather, luck, thunder, advice, courage; furniture, information, news, sincerity, music.
B FULLY MASS (some occasionally with a(n) or pluralised)	+	+	+	(+)		(+)			rain, sand, snow; bitterness, happiness; help, sleep; literature, education, patience, pride, progress, thirst.
C FULLY MASS FULLY COUNT	+	+	+	+	+	+	+	+	oil, ink, cake, metal; building, painting; ambition, truth, doubt, mood; kindness, friendship, love, need, fever.
D Never mass Partially count							+	+	(the) Alps, riches, goods, morals, belongings, surroundings; scissors, trousers; cattle, people, police, vermin.
E Never mass FULLY COUNT (except number contrast on noun)					+		+	+	sheep, deer, aircraft, offspring, insignia, barracks, gallows, means, links, series, crossroads.
F Rarely mass FULLY COUNT	(+)	(+)	(+)	+	+	+	+	+	car, house, table, library; deed, fault, detail, mood, advantage; way, wrap, look, go, turn.

to describe the countability potential of all English nouns. This fuzziness is characteristic of many of the categories and rules which have to be established for the description of any language, and is a natural consequence of the fact that there are always more contrasts in the meanings we express (the semantics), than there are in our forms of expression (the syntax). The countability potential of a NG depends greatly on lexical considerations which cannot be dealt with adequately in a grammar of the present dimension, and which, in any case, could not be learnt simply from a grammar book presentation. All good monolingual dictionaries of English include information about the mass and count features of individual nouns, to which we add the following observations.

46.3.1   Type A: Fully mass; some occasionally with *a(n)*

e.g. *drinking, running, eating; weather, thunder; luck; economics; furniture, information; courage, sincerity; music.*

This pattern applies to a large number of fully mass nouns with a virtually nil degree of the count feature. We do not say **a weather, *each information, *every furniture, *many sincerities*. Individuated specimens of the referents are expressed by the well-known partitive items such as *piece of advice, item of information, stroke of luck, drop of water, clap of thunder*, etc., or the general word *kind* as in *a kind of sincerity*. Some mass nouns admit *a(n)* with the sense of 'a kind of': *You don't meet a courage like hers every day*. In this example, the use of *a* is motivated by the defining qualifier *like hers* referring to a specific person on a specific occasion. The use of *courage like that* or *courage like hers* (without individuation by *a*) is equally suitable but refers to a less specific instance of courage. Pluralisation of Type A words is exceptional but may occur in set expressions such as: *Fishermen go out in all weathers*.

46.3.2   Type B: Fully mass; some occasionally with *a(n)* or plural

e.g. *water, rain, fog, frost; butter, cheese, sugar; knowledge, happiness; help, sleep, pride; money, literature, education.*

Another very large set of fully mass nouns, which includes concrete as well as abstract nouns admitting more easily than those of Type A, individuation by *a(n)* (*a butter, a cheese, a knowledge, a happiness*) in the sense of 'a kind of' or 'an instance of', especially when they are modified:

> We had to drive through *a thick fog*.
> He fell into *a deep sleep*.
> You'll need *a good knowledge* of English for that job.

The singular determiners *one, another*, are admitted by some of this group: *One sand is never exactly the same as another.*
Some of these nouns admit pluralisation in the sense of 'instances of' as in

the different literatures of the world or as a mass collective rather than a count sense:

constant rains	some moneys were owed
in Atlantic waters	the morning frosts

These nouns do not admit numeratives: *six rains*, *four snows*, etc., though some admit indefinite quantifiers, as in *a few mists, many frosts*.

Writers sometimes produce non-standard forms which most people would not use and which we recommend should not be imitated. There is a certain tendency to pluralise mass nouns in AmE, less so in BrE. The following were recently attested:

It would seem, then, that *our formal educations* should equip us with at least *reading knowledges* of those major European languages that do not find their way into the curriculum for specialist treatment.

New York Herald Tribune

Eudora Welty presents a particularly interesting case, because she has published a number of comments which reveal *the relative importances* she attaches to poetic qualities in fiction.

W. R. Patrick, *Poetic Style in the Contemporary Short Story*.

46.3.3   Type C: Fully mass and fully count

e.g. *painting, killing, writing, meaning; kindness, friendship; business, success, failure; need, doubt, hope, truth; wood, oil, metal, fever; hake, plaice, grouse; darts, bowls, skittles, draughts*.

This large group of both abstract and concrete nouns referring to actions, relationships, states, emotions, concepts, materials, is potentially usable with all the eight mass and count markers we have used as tests. However, the nouns vary in the ease and frequency with which they are used with the different markers.

The basic reference of most nouns in this set is best considered as mass. Many of their count references denote individual manifestations of a process (*killings*), an emotion (*hopes*), a quality (*kindnesses*), a relationship (*friend-ships*), a phenomenon (*fevers*), etc., denoted by the mass reference. These meanings constitute a transfer from the 'mass' referent to an associated 'count' referent, e.g. *a business* (act of business or commercial firm), *paint-ings* (acts of paintings or the resulting pictures), *failures* (acts of failing or persons who fail). As we have mentioned, these are lexicological phenomena having grammatical consequences. Most of the words having the potential for full mass and count references maintain closely associated meanings in both cases: *mashed potato – a new potato; a lot of noise – many strange noises*. With some words there can be a shift of meaning:

chance (mass) = the phenomenon of things happening without cause.
chance (count) = opportunity: *a good chance; many chances*.

As count nouns, most of these words can be individuated by *a(n), one, each, every*, and pluralised. Some may be pluralised (his writings, his many writings) but not counted (*six *writings*). Although such constraints are conventional rather than ungrammatical, we recommend caution and observance of conventional usage in the application of all countability markers.

The fish and bird names mentioned above do not admit the plural affix, but are otherwise fully countable: *four salmon, those hake*. The mass forms (e.g. *Salmon is nice*) refer to the flesh.

Although most animal names admit the plural affix, a few can take either -*s* or *zero* when used as count nouns: *many fish* or *many fishes*.

The small number of nouns denoting certain games have mass reference, despite their invariable plural form:

> Do you play *much darts? Draughts is* an interesting game.

The same nouns also denote the countable objects used in the games:

> Give me *another dart*. Each player throws *three darts*.

46.3.4   Type D: Partially count, never mass

e.g. *the young, the Dutch, the living; cattle, police, people, vermin; riches, goods, morals, surroundings, remains, earnings, dregs, belongings; trousers, scissors, glasses, pyjamas, shorts*.

This type consists of four small sets of nouns denoting collections of things. Some have invariable singular form, and others have invariable plural form, but they all have plural reference and show plural concord with verbs, pronouns and determinatives. For this reason, they are never conceived as denoting a mass entity but, at the same time, their count markers are strictly limited, in the ways mentioned below. These lexical idiosyncrasies reflect the tension or conflict sometimes occurring in language between the morphological and syntactic aspects of form.

(a) None of them admit a singular determiner; we do not say: *a Dutch*, *each cattle*, *every belongings*, *either remains*.

(b) Some of the invariable singular forms can be individuated by a partitive counter: *a head of cattle, a member of the police*; or a different lexical item, e.g. *policeman*.

(c) None can be enumerated: we cannot say *I caught *three vermin*, or *we received *six goods*.

(d) Some admit indefinite plural quantifiers: *many people, many goods, several police, few remains*. Others that are more 'collective' and less divisible in concept do not do so. No one is likely to say *many morals or *a few riches*.

(e) Plural nouns denoting objects composed of two identical parts can be individuated and pluralised by the partitive expression *a pair of: a pair of scissors, three pairs of glasses*, etc.

(f) De-adjectival nouns such as *the young, the Dutch, the British* have plural reference to a group and can only be individuated and pluralised lexically: *a young person, many Dutchmen, a Britisher* (colloq: *a Brit, the Brits*), not *a young, *three British.

46.3.5   Type E: Never mass; fully count, except number contrast on the noun

e.g. *sheep, deer, aircraft, offspring, insignia;*
gallows, means, links, series, crossroads, barracks.

These two small sets of words are invariable in form but admit all other countable markers for singular and plural reference:

> *a sheep, those sheep; every sheep, many sheep, ten sheep*, etc.
> *a barracks, those barracks, each barracks, several barracks*, etc.

46.3.6   Type F: Rarely mass and fully count

e.g. *car, house, table, library, guitar, plate; deed, detail, fault, mood, advantage, way, wrap, look, turn, find, go*.

This is a very large set of English nouns which have the greatest preference for count references of all nouns in the language. Their uses in all countable syntactic frames are well known and do not need exemplification here. For the advanced student, it is perhaps more interesting to note less frequent patterns such as the following:

(a) Examples of mass reference being ascribed to nouns which are typically count, such as the following:

> My brother plays *guitar* in a pop group.
> Your problem is *too much office*.

While this usage is common in some languages, it is exceptional in English. On the other hand measurement expressions such as the following are easily accepted: *six square feet of window, three feet of shelf*.

(b) Certain fully countable nouns may have mass reference when used as part of a manner or locative circumstance, e.g. *by plane, by letter, by chance, by accident; in detail; in class, in prison, in hospital, at breakfast, at church*. Such nouns admit only the zero marker of mass reference, and rarely the other two (*all* and *much, little*, etc.)

(c) We have mentioned the occasional deviant pluralisation of mass nouns such as *our formal educations*. Similarly it may happen that an entity that typically has count reference (e.g. *tomato, cat*) is used in a mass sense:

You've got tomato on your tie! This room smells of cat! Such uses are felt to be more deviant and idiosyncratic than some others. They nearly always have affective value and occur in informal spoken registers rather than written ones. For this reason the non-native is recommended to avoid using them in normal conversation. In written English this pattern is being used increasingly by journalists, especially in AmE.

(d) An aggregate of countable objects is sometimes treated as a 'mass' referent, though usually in restricted contexts such as hunting, shooting, fishing, agriculture, etc.:

> They went to Africa to hunt *lion*.
> I've been collecting *worm* for fish bait.
> England was once covered with large forests of *elm*.

(e) The nominalised processes included in Type F (*find, look, go*, etc.) are different from those mentioned in Type C (*doubt, need, taste, hope, abuse, fear*), in that whereas the latter can be used with both mass and count reference, the process nouns are very rarely perceived as mass. The following are examples of these and similar de-verbal nouns used with various count markers:

> At the fair, they charge 25p for *each go* on the roundabouts, and 50p for *a try* on the rifle range. There's a prize for *every hit* you score.
>
> These clothes need quite *a few more washes* to get them absolutely clean.

De-verbal count nouns of this kind may refer to several types of entity, such as an action (*a try*), the result of the action ('*a try*' in rugby), the agent of the action (*a cheat*), the instrument of an action (*a cover*), the place of an action (*a rise* = slope of a hill). A single item may have varied references: a *turn* in the road, a *turn* of the wheel, to take *turns*, a new *turn* of events, he did me a good *turn*, etc.

In the foregoing paragraphs we have not included other nouns which can have two or more completely different semantic references, and which should therefore be treated as homonyms, e.g. *toast* (= toasted bread, a fully mass noun) and *a toast* (act of drinking to someone's health or success).

46.4   The system of definiteness

In English, the grammar obliges NGs to be presented as indefinite, definite or generic. This is done syntactically by the use of specific and non-specific determiners, and among these, in particular, by the definite, indefinite and zero articles, which are traditionally treated separately as a subsystem of the system of determination.

Definiteness is marked by *the* or a deictic determinative (see Module 47) and indefiniteness by *a(n)*, *some*/sm/, *any* or the absence of a marker, which, since its absence is grammatically significant, is called the 'zero article'.

'Zero' does not mean that an article has been omitted, as might occur in a newspaper headline: *Plane crashes on village.*

The three articles are distributed as follows with mass and count nouns:

	Mass	Singular count	Plural count
definite:	the butter	the man	the men
indefinite:	– butter some/sm/butter	a man –	– men some/sm/men

Each of the articles can also be used when we wish to make a generic statement about a whole class of entities:

the:	The dog is a faithful animal.
a:	A dog is a faithful animal.
zero:	Dogs are faithful animals. Exercise keeps you healthy.

An entity is considered as 'indefinite' if there is nothing in the discourse or the situation or our general knowledge of the world which identifies it for us: *She bought a blue dress; Some letters have arrived.* It can be considered as 'definite' once the entity has already been mentioned (*Did you answer the letters?*) or if there is sufficient information to identify it, either in the text (*The tickets for the concert were expensive*) or in the non-linguistic situation (*Put the flowers in a vase*) or in general knowledge (*The Olympic Games . . .*). It is important to understand the terms 'definite' and 'indefinite' in a grammatical or textual sense, rather than a 'common-sense' way. When we say, *Lagos is surrounded by a lagoon*, obviously we are referring to a lagoon which definitely exists, but textually it remains an unidentified member of a class of entities called 'lagoon', until it is mentioned again and is then marked as 'known' by *the*, as in *We crossed the lagoon.*

46.5 Indefinite NGs

46.5.1 Indefinite common nouns

Although the term 'indefinite' might appear to be synonymous with 'non-specific', it can in fact be applied to both non-specific and specific entities, whether these are count or mass:

singular:	I've bought *a new car.*	(indef. specific)
	I need *a new car.*	(indef. non-specific)

plural:	I've got *some friends* in the United Kingdom.	(indef. specific)
	I've got *friends* in the United Kingdom.	(indef. non-specific)
mass:	I managed to find *some work*.	(indef. specific)
	I managed to find *work*.	(indef. non-specific)

The examples show that with singular count nouns (*a car*), the article *a* refers to both specific and non-specific entities, the different interpretations being deduced from the different predications. When we need a car, it is obviously not yet specific, but potentially any car. When we have bought a car, it is obviously a specific one.

An indefinite noun can occur in generic statements when it is modified or qualified, provided it is non-specific and not a specific member of the class. Contrast the following meanings:

generic:	*A stockbroker* who studies the market carefully becomes an expert at buying and selling shares.
indefinite specific:	*A stockbroker* whom I know is an expert in the buying and selling of shares.

As indefinite article, *some* (pronounced /sm/) is used mainly with mass and plural count nouns, but the stressed form /s ^ m/ is sometimes used with mass or count nouns with the meaning of indefinite specific as in: *There is still some hope of recovery*.

mass:	There is still *some hope* of recovery.
singular:	Let's meet *some day* next week.
plural:	*Some days* are more convenient than others.

46.5.2   Indefinite proper nouns

Since proper nouns refer to unique entities, they are already definite and cannot logically be conceived as indefinite. Nevertheless, since it is possible for several entities to be denoted by the same name, such as persons or days of the week, they can be treated sometimes as classes composed of individual members. This allows expressions such as the following:

Is there *a John Smith* in this class?	(indef. specific)
I was born on *a Monday*.	(indef. non-specific)
We had *a very hot June* last year.	(indef. specific)

A unique entity, such as a continent, country or city, may be presented sometimes as indefinite, when something abstract or imaginary is predicated about it:

A politically united Europe will not be easy to achieve.
I can't imagine *a Greece without an Athens*.

Proper nouns can be presented as indefinite when used as metonyms:

I've got *a Goya* at home, but it's only a reproduction.

46.6 Definite NGs

46.6.1 Definite common nouns

The definiteness of a common NG is indicated by the article *the*. As we said in 45.2, this does not by itself identify the referent, but indicates that it can be identified endophorically (within the text) or exophorically (outside the text, in the situation or from general knowledge). Within the text, the reference may be anaphoric (backwards)or cataphoric (forwards). The anaphor often expresses the antecedent differently:

> Ten lionesses at the city zoo are to be put on a contraceptive pill to prevent a population explosion. For 20 years *the lions* [1] have prided themselves on their breeding capabilities. Now, *the treatment* [2] will make them infertile for 3 years and so stop *the increase*[3].
>
> [1] = ten lionesses; [2] = a contraceptive pill; [3] = a population explosion.

The referent of a definite head noun can be identified cataphorically by the information contained in a qualifying element, as in: *the bus coming now, the journey home, the Ministry of Health*; or by a determiner or modifier: *this bus, the first bus, the blue bus*. The identity of a definite noun is often found, not in a previous mention of the referent, but only by inference from something that has been said in the context as, for example the word 'businessmen' in the following:

> For businessmen on trips abroad getting messages from *the office* can be a problem. When *the job* requires travelling by land over long distances, *keeping in touch* with base becomes even more difficult.
>
> *Financial Times*

Exophoric reference to shared knowledge of the non-linguistic world immediately identifies the referent of NGs such as *the sun, the sky, the rain, the government, the seaside, the flu, the television*, etc.

When a personal noun, such as *secretary, queen, director, head*, functions as Subject Complement in a clause and refers to a unique social role, definiteness can be marked either by *the* or by *zero*, with certain lexico-grammatical constraints:

> He soon became *director/the director* of the firm.

When the noun functions as Complement in a minor clause introduced by *when, while, if, although*, definiteness can be marked by zero:

> *While Minister*, he introduced many reforms.
> *Although not party leader*, he greatly influenced the party's policies.

46.6.2   Definite proper nouns

Proper nouns (*Disneyland, Big Ben, Coca Cola, William Shakespeare*) denote unique entities and so are definite in themselves, without needing the article *the*. Since, however, there may exist several entities with the same proper name, any one of them may be individualised by a restrictive modifier or qualifier, in which case the article is needed:

> I shall never forget *the Christmas of last year.*
> *The swinging London* they used to talk about no longer exists.

When a proper noun is presented in this way, it is behaving grammatically like a common noun, and as such may show number contrast:

> *The Hitler who ruled Germany* came to a sticky end.
> Not *all the Hitlers* of this world are brought to justice.

Proper nouns are occasionally modified non-restrictively by attitudinal or emotive epithets as in *poor Elizabeth, little Johnnie*. In certain cases, *the* is added to emphasise the uniqueness of the noun:

> Several films have been made about *the world-famous Don Quixote.*
> Mark Anthony was crazy about *the beautiful Cleopatra.*

46.7   Discourse functions of the system of definiteness

As we said in 46.4, the semantic function of the articles is to present the referents of NGs as definite, indefinite or generic.

The first two meanings are basically textual functions, associated with the organisation of the information content of a clause or sentence or extended text, from two points of view: information which has already been **Given**, that is, mentioned in the discourse or otherwise known to the interlocutors, and information that is **New**, that is, not known to the addressee (see 29.2). The following paragraph containing the stage directions for a play illustrates these functions. 'New' is marked by *a/an* or *zero*, and 'Given' by *the*:

> February. *A* garage attached to *a* medium price executive house on *a* private estate belonging to DENNIS and VERA. Down one wall of *the* garage *a* workbench littered untidily with tools, etc. In fact *the* whole place is filled with *the* usual garage junk, boxes, coils of rope, garden chairs, etc. In *the* midst of this, *a* small popular car, at least seven years old, stands neglected. Over *the* work bench *a* grimy window which looks out over *a* small paved 'sitting area'. On *the* other wall *a* door, leading across *a* small dustbin yard to *the* backdoor of *the* house. There is also *a* paved walkway round *the* side of *the* garage, nearest us, leading to *the* 'sitting area'.
>
> Alan Ayckbourn, *Just Between Ourselves.*

The text begins naturally with New items (*a garage, a house* and *a private estate*); followed by a second mention of *the garage*, which is now known or 'Given', then a 'New' item, *a workbench*, with indefinite 'New' *tools*, and a second mention, by inference, to *the whole place*. The text continues to build up a description of the stage cohesively, bit by bit, in a straightforward, coherent way. This is a normal way of introducing Given and New information in a text of this kind.

Sometimes, a writer will create a special literary effect by introducing a New item as yet unknown to the reader, but marking it by *the* as if it was already known. For example, one short story begins:

> *The dog* was called Thompson, a name without significance, except that *Timmy's* nephew, aged ten, had named him so.
>
> Fay Weldon, *Polaris*.

Here we do not know which dog it is, or who it belonged to or who Timmy is; we are kept in suspense and have to read on until we can find it out from what else the author tells us. Another story by the same writer begins:

> Towards *the end* as Christmas approached . . .
>
> Fay Weldon, *Christmas Lists*.

The end of what? Obviously a lot has happened before the story begins but we have to read twelve more lines before the writer gives a long list of twenty-six activities that the main character has been carrying out in the previous four months. This 'marked' use of the articles is clearly a tactic designed to puzzle the reader and stimulate his interest in the narrative.

46.8   Generic statements about 'things'

Whereas definite and indefinite NGs refer to entities as they participate in real-world situations, generic NGs refer to them as representatives of their whole class, in abstract statements about their typical characteristics or habitual activities. Genericity can be realised by any of the three articles: definite, indefinite or zero, in the following structures:

(a) *a(n)* + singular count noun: They say *an elephant* never forgets.
(b) *the* + singular count noun: They say *the elephant* never forgets.
(c) *zero* + plural count noun: They say *elephants* never forget.
(d) *zero* + mass noun: They say *charity* begins at home.

The three articles express genericity from different points of view, which we will gloss as follows:

(a) *a(n)* represents any individual member of a class of entity as typical of the whole class;

(b) *the* represents the referent of the noun as a single undifferentiated whole class of entities;
(c) *zero* implies that all or most members of the class of entity possess the characteristic that is predicated of it.

The four structures mentioned above are not freely interchangeable in all generic statements. The generic use of *the* and *a(n)* is formal in style, and each may be incompatible with certain predications. For example, *the* but not *a(n)* is acceptable in the following:

The kangaroo is common in Australia.
˙*A* kangaroo is common in Australia.

Both are acceptable with a characterising predication such as:

The female kangaroo carries its babies in its pouch.
A female kangaroo carries its babies in its pouch.

By contrast *a(n)* but not *the* is likely in the following:

A dog chases cats.
˙*The* dog chases cats.

The article *the* tends to generalise more readily than *a(n)*, which refers essentially to a singular indefinite member as representative of its class. ***The*** + **singular count noun** may have a generalising value, even when not used in a generic statement:

Do you play *the piano*?
Some people sit for hours in front of *the television*.

It is also used with adjectival heads of NGs referring to abstract qualities or to groups of people named by a common Attribute, but having plural concord with the verb:

Science proceeds from *the known* to *the unknown*.
Braille was invented to enable *the blind* to read.

Not all adjectives can function in these ways and the non-native speaker should be cautious in choosing them.

The support of a modifier or a qualifier, or a clausal Adjunct such as *usually* can strengthen the generic or generalising interpretation of both *the* and *a(n)*.

An unhappy child usually cries a lot.
The unhappy child usually cries a lot.

A driver who drinks is sometimes dangerous.
The driver who drinks is sometimes dangerous.

The loosest and therefore most frequent type of genericity is that expressed by the zero article with plural nouns:

Kangaroos are common in Australia.
Dogs chase cats.
Unhappy children cry a lot.
Drivers who drink a lot are dangerous.

Zero article with plural count nouns may have generic or indefinite reference according to the predication:

Frogs have long hind legs.   (generic)
He catches *frogs*.   (indefinite)

A mass noun with zero article can be considered generic even if it is modified or qualified: *Columbian coffee is said to be the best. I don't like tea without sugar.* It is definite, however, if preceded by *the*. Contrast for example:

generic: *Nitrogen* forms 78% of the earth's atmosphere.
definite: *The nitrogen* in the earth's atmosphere is circulated by
                living organisms.

Singular count nouns are not normally presented as generic with the zero article. The following, however, are sometimes used with zero to denote common activities or phenomena associated with the count noun:

places: It's time for *bed*. He's in *hospital*.
times: I usually get up at *sunset*. I like driving at *night*.
meals: *Breakfast* is my favourite meal.
transport: Let's go by *plane*; We came on *foot*.
set phrases: *arm*-in-*arm*, *side*-by-*side*, *face*-to-*face*.

This structure occurs frequently in PrepGs.

MODULE 47
Selecting and particularising 'things'

Summary

1   **Determination**
    The need to particularise referent things in discourse.
    The first element of the NG, the determiner, particularises by 'selection'.
    Two types of selection: deixis and quantification.

2 **Deictic determinatives**
   Demonstrative: *this, that, these, those.*
   Possessive: *my coat, her money, Tom's house*, etc.
   Relational: *my university, our bus, the moon's orbit*, etc.
   Distributive: *all, both, each, every, either, neither.*
   Relative: *which, what, whose, whichever*, etc., *such.*
   Adjectival: *famous, other, usual, original, tallest*, etc.

3 **Quantifying determinatives**
   Exact: cardinal and ordinal numerals.
   Non-exact: *much, many, little, few*, etc., *the next, the last*, etc.

4 **Determinatives as elliptical head elements**.

5 **Discourse function of determination**.

47.1   The system of determination

Common nouns in the dictionary refer to classes of things, but when used in discourse they need to be particularised. This is done by the first element of the NG, called the **determiner**. The basic function of this element is to particularise and so help to identify the noun referent in the context of the speech situation.

As in other areas of the grammar, we distinguish between an element of structure, in this case the determiner, and the classes of units, here called **determinatives**, that realise the element. The determiner is an element in the 'logical structure' of the NG (see Module 50); the various classes of determinatives contribute to the 'experiential structure' of the NG; that is, their functions are semantic, and express the different features the speaker chooses in order to select and particularise the noun referent within the context of discourse.

In this module, we assume the reader has a knowledge of the forms and grammatical behaviour of English determinatives, and so comment only on the two main types of determination, deictic and quantifying, as well as the syntactic use of determinatives as elliptic head elements.

Determiners identify a nominal entity by telling us which or what or whose it is, how much, how many, what part or degree of it we are referring to, how big or frequent it is, how it is distributed in space or time. In the following short passage about the problem of waste disposal, the writer refers to the entities: *rubbish, day, year, goods, amount, plants, factories, fuel, snags, risk, damage, degrees centigrade*, and specifies them in respect to the questions given below:

> *Three quarters* [1] of the rubbish we generate *every* [2] *day* could be recycled, and *more* [3] could be, if the production of biodegradable goods were encouraged. At present *the same* [4] *amount* is wasted *every* [5] day because of *the notorious* [6] lack of incineration plants. *Such* [7] plants could be installed in *all* [8] factories so that *each* [9] company

could burn *its own* [10] rubbish and save *a great deal of* [11] fuel. *The only* [12] snag about waste burners is that they emit *certain* [13] kinds of highly contaminating gases, but it is calculated that in *a few* [14] years rubbish will be burned *without* causing *any* [15] damage to the environment. A *further* [16] argument is that, although nuclear fusion has *none* [17] of the risk of fission, so far, *no* [18] scientist has yet found a system which can function at temperatures lower than *millions* [19] of degrees centigrade.

Speak Up, no. 66.

[1] how much? [2] how often? [3] how much? [4] which amount? [5] how often? [6] which kind? [7] which ones? [8] how many? or which? [9] which? [10] whose? [11] how much? [12] which? [13] which? [14] how many? [15] how much? [16] which? [17] what part? [18] how many? [19] how many?

47.2 Specific deictic determinatives

47.2.1 Demonstratives: *this, that, these, those*

These items particularise the noun referent by indicating whether it is near or not near the speaker, in space or time or psychologically. They can refer to both human and non-human entities (*this girl, this century*), but are restricted in their human reference when used as elliptical heads or as pronominal heads, e.g. *That girl married a friend of mine*, but not *'That married a friend of mine* (see 47.9.1).

47.2.2 Genitive determinatives

The inflected genitive determinative must be understood in a broader sense than that of the traditional term 'possessive'. The semantic function of the genitive determinative can be shown by paraphrase, as in the following examples:

Example	Paraphrase	Function
Napoleon's army	N. commanded the army.	subjective
Napoleon's mistake	N. made a mistake.	subjective
Napoleon's defeat	N. defeated X.	subjective
Napoleon's defeat	N. was defeated by X.	objective
Europe's chief cities	The chief cities in Europe.	locative
A month's holiday	The holiday lasted a month.	extent
The dog's tail	The dog has a tail.	possession
The sun's rays	The rays come from the sun.	source

These varied functional relationships also exist between a noun head and the determinatives *my, your, his, her, its, our, their, someone's, everyone's, nobody's*, etc.:

His mistake	He made a mistake.	subjective
Our friendship	We became friends.	reciprocal
Their love	They love each other.	reciprocal
Its collapse	It collapsed.	subjective
Everyone's opinion	Everyone thinks . . .	subjective

It is possible to describe a semantic relation of this kind in more than one way, but the grammatical significance of the 'genitive determinative + head noun' structure is that it constitutes an economical way of expressing by nominalisation, a variety of implied or presupposed relationships and processes occurring between two entities. This type of NG is particularly useful in the production of texts, for referring back to previous mentions of such processes and relationships between nouns. It contributes to the coherence of texts and ensures a natural flow of description or narrative or the logical exposition of ideas.

The genitive determinative is formally a NG plus an inflected genitive morpheme. The inflection is added not merely to the head noun but to the group as a whole:

> *My supervisor's* advice; *my mother and father's* wishes.
> I liked *those other children's* paintings very much.
> *That young Japanese pianist's* performance was wonderful.
> I need *someone competent's* advice.

Longer modifiers and qualifiers are grammatically possible, though less frequent:

> *That shop you recommended to me's* prices were very high.

However, such determiners are generally avoided and can easily be replaced by the use of *of* or some other structure. Examples occur mostly in conversation when a speaker begins a spontaneous unplanned utterance and then finds it necessary to genitivise the determiner or else stop and begin the sentence again.

Some genitive NGs may function as determiners or classifiers, and so have two interpretations. The NG *a lady's bicycle* may refer to the bicycle of a particular lady, or to the class of bicycle designed for ladies, not for men. The context of discourse normally clarifies the interpretation.

47.3 Non-specific deictic determinatives

These select entities by referring to:

(a) **their indefiniteness**: *a(n), some, any, no.*
(b) **their distribution**: *all, both, either, neither, each, every, another, other.*

The word *some* is pronounced /sm/ or /səm/ without stress, when used as an indefinite article (see 46.5), and /s ⋅△ m/, with stress, when it has a selective value:

> **non-selective** /sm/:   We're spending some days by the sea.
> **selective** /s ∧ m/:   Some days it's hot, other days it's cold.

Stressed *some*/s ∧ m/ can also be used with various types of evaluative forces:

> **quantifying**:   I haven't seen you for *some time*. (= a long time)
> **appreciative**:   That really was *some meal!* (= a wonderful meal)

Similarly *any* is pronounced with reduced vowel /ə/ when unstressed and full vowel /e/ when stressed:

> **unstressed**:   Have you *any* money? I haven't *any* money.
> **stressed**:   Have you *ANY* money at all? I haven't *ANY* money at all.

The determiner *no* has mass, singular and plural references: *no time, no change, no changes*, and is also used in familiar expressions such as:

> It's a short flight. We shall get there in *no time*. (= a short time).
> He's *no youngster*. (= no longer young).

Of the distributive determinatives, *all* can refer to mass nouns (*all power corrupts*), plural nouns in a generic sense (*all men are mortal*) and certain temporal and locative nouns (*all day, all night, all America*).

Both refers to two entities together. *Either* and *neither* refer to two entities as alternatives. *Each* refers to any number of entities considered individually; *every* refers to any number of entities considered individually, with the additional feature *all of them*.

47.4   WH-deictic determinatives; *such*

Which, whose express specific selection. *What, whatever, whichever, whoever's* express non-specific selection.

WH-determinatives are used in the following three types of structures:

> **interrogative**:   *Which play* would you like to see?
> *What ideas* have you got about this problem?
> *Whose car* did you come in?
> **relative**:   I may be late, in *which case* don't wait for me.
> You'll find plenty of traffic *whichever road* you take.
> *What hopes* we had have been lost.
> I shall vote for *whoever's plan* I consider best.
> **exclamatory**   (requires *a(n)* before singular nouns):
> *What a pity! What nonsense! What lovely rooms!*

The forms which we describe here as 'relative' are determinative in the sense that they can be paraphrased as equivalent to the demonstratives *this, that, these, those*:

in which case   = and in that case
whichever road   = whether this road or that road
what hopes   = those hopes (that we had)
whoever's plan   = (the plan) of that person who

The word *such* identifies an entity by relating it or comparing it to another entity of a similar kind or a similar degree of its Attribute which has been mentioned in the discourse. Like exclamatory *what!*, *such* also requires *a(n)* before a singular noun:

I've never heard of *such an animal*. (= of that kind)
Don't be *such a fool*! (= of that degree)
Such men are dangerous. *Such cruelty* is incomprehensible.

Such can be preceded by quantifiers with or without *of* according to the meaning intended:

You will not have many *such* opportunities again.

47.5   Adjectival determinatives

Nominal entities are sometimes determined by a small group of adjectives which have a selective function, not the attitudinal or qualitative functions which are realised by the epithet element. The following are among the most typical features and exponents:

similarity: same, identical
difference: other, different
totality: complete, whole, entire, total
familiarity: familiar, well-known, famous, notorious
usuality: usual, normal, customary, regular, odd
particularity: particular, certain, original, chief, main
uniqueness: (a) sole, solitary, only, (the) precise
                     (b) superlative adjectives: (the) best, smallest

The identifying function of these adjectives is usually reinforced by a preceding article or other determiner:

He always asks *the same* two questions.
The lecture was given by *the famous* Professor Jackson.
There is *a certain* opposition to the government's proposals.
Our meeting ended in *the usual* confusion.
Their only reason for coming was to spy on us.
The original idea has now been abandoned.
This is one of *his best* books.
He received us with *his normal* cordiality.

When one of these adjectives is used as an epithet it has a different meaning: *His behaviour was not quite normal. That is a very original suggestion. Opposition to the government's proposals is quite certain.* In some expressions the function of the adjective is ambiguous, as in *Three different proposals were made*, where the adjective *different* may be considered as selective and determinative (= three proposals different from three others), or as a qualitative epithet (= three proposals which are different one from another).

Superlative adjectives, like the ordinal quantifiers, presuppose a plurality of entities from which the head referent has been selected. The comparative forms are also sometimes semantically superlative and defining:

> The *newer* parabolic TV dishes are smaller than the previous ones.
> We always stay at the *cheaper* hotels.

It must also be remembered that even the base form of an adjective can have a selective, defining feature when preceded by *the*, as well as its basic qualitative feature:

> I'll carry *the large* case; you take *the small* one.

Superlative adjectives usually precede other adjectives:

> These were *the best cheap* shoes I could find.

This places them in the position typically occupied by determiners and indicates their defining value. We cannot, however, classify them as determinatives, since they also have predicative functions in clauses, as for example in:

> The weather *is hottest* in July and August.

47.6   Selection by quantity

In addition to representing an entity as definite/indefinite or as specific/non-specific, a speaker may select or particularise it by referring to its quantity, which may be exact (*three friends*) or non-exact (*many friends*) or ordinal (*the first friend*).

We assume here a knowledge of the English forms of numeration and quantification, and comment only on the partitive structures.

47.7   Partitive selection

All the determinatives mentioned so far have preceded the head noun directly, representing implicitly the selection of one or more entities from the whole class of entities; for example, *that student* refers to a specific student selected from the whole class of entities called 'student'. Other times, the selection may be from an already selected set of class members, as in *some of our students*, or from two previously selected sets, such as *some of the best of our students*. In expanded structures of this kind, the selections are marked explicitly by the preposition *of*. Partitive selection occurs with both types of determination: deictic and quantifying.

The following are examples of partitive quantifiers:

cardinal: three of my friends; one of these days;
ordinal: the first of her children; the last of their requests;
nominal: a great deal of trouble; a large number of people;
(colloq.):   tons of energy; pots of money.

The selector *of* is obligatory when the noun referent is definite (*my friends, these days*), except after *all, both* and *half* where it is optional: *all (of) the rules, on both (of) those occasions, half (of) the time. Of* is not used after multipliers such as: *double that amount, twice the work, three times this price*.

Some nominal quantifiers refer to containers of the head referent:

a small bottle of wine   a whole library of books
three cans of beer   a roomful of people
a packet of cigarettes   a pound box of chocolates

In these cases, items such as *library, bottle*, etc., function as the logical heads of their own NGs, modified by *whole, small* and qualified by *of books, of wine*, etc. The structure of these NGs, and so their meaning, may have two interpretations:

1) **Experiential structure**

d	h
a whole library of a small bottle of	books wine

2) **Logical structure**

d	m	h	q
a a	whole small	library bottle	of books of wine

The choice of meaning is sometimes marked by number concord in the predication:

(a) A whole library of *books were* destroyed in the fire.
(b) A whole *library* of books *was* destroyed in the fire.

If this 'container' type of quantifier is pluralised as, for example, in *six small bottles of wine*, number concord always follows *bottle* not *wine*.

(c) Six small bottles of wine *were* drunk.

This syntactic feature does not, however, rule out the possibility of interpreting the expression as a reference primarily to the quantity of wine that was drunk, and of regarding *six small bottles of* as a quantifying determiner.

The following types of nominal quantifiers are also usually included among the partitive determinatives:

Expressions of measurement
Two metres of cloth is not enough (cloth) for a suit.
Small quantities of mass entities (= a little)
a bit of cheese; an item of news; not an atom of truth; a speck of dust; a piece of advice; a drop of whisky.
Certain singular and plural collective nouns (= many)
a pack of lies; a gang of thieves; a swarm of photographers; herds of tourists; crowds of people; loads of ideas.

Deictic determinatives are mutually exclusive: *those my books, *some that cake, *each your friends; but they can occur together in a partitive relationship, joined by *of*:

those of my books; some of that cake; each of your friends.

On the logical order of determinatives, see 50.6.1–2.

47.8   Modification of determiners

Quantifying determinatives are sometimes modified by adverbs of degree expressing notions such as the following:

intensification: *fully ten* weeks, *all of six* months, *many more* people, the *very first* opportunity, a *good half-* hour, *over forty* miles, *quite half* the work;

approximation: *roughly a hundred* people, *about a million* pounds, *some ten* thousand years, *virtually the whole* village;

comparison: *more than fifty* messages, *as many as a hundred* votes, *less than five* dollars, *fewer than ten* members;

restriction: *only four* survivors.

Deictic determinatives are also sometimes modified:

only those students, *virtually no* reason, *almost every* match, the *very same* day, *how much* time we've wasted! *how few* people care! *so much* trouble, *so little* help, *so few* times.

47.9   Determinatives used as elliptical heads

In some NGs, the head element is not realised by a noun or pronoun, but by a determinative item. This does not change the class of the item from determinative to pronoun, but simply its function from determiner element to head element. In the experiential structure of the NG, it continues to express a determinative feature of the presupposed noun which has been ellipted; in the logical structure, this feature functions as the syntactical head of a NG.

We shall consider this as a type of ellipsis, because a determiner can always be followed by a noun, whereas a pronoun cannot:

elliptical head: I'll go this way and you go *that*. (= that way)
pronominal head: I'll go my way and you go *yours*. (*yours way)

In these structures, we shall describe the determinative as an elliptical head and the unit as an elliptical NG. The following are examples of the main classes of determinative heads:

47.9.1 Demonstrative heads: *this, that, these, those*

The singular demonstratives *this, that* can refer to specific persons, as Subject of a copular structure, but not if the copula has a compound tense form or is a verb other than *be*. We can say *This is my friend Julia*, but not *This used to be my friend Julia*.

The singular forms can have personal reference as Complement if the subject is *Who?*, but not otherwise. We can say *Who is that?* but not *My friend is that*. These constraints are probably due to the danger of *this/that* being interpreted as pronouns with non-personal reference meaning 'this thing', 'that thing'.

The plural forms *these/those* can presuppose personal referents more easily than *this/that*, provided that their mention is recent enough to be obviously presupposed:

A. I don't like talking to *policemen*.
B. Oh, I don't mind. Let's ask *these*. (= these policeman)

In this case, B. could not say *Let's ask this*.

47.9.2 Locative heads

e.g. *the former, the latter, the above-mentioned, the following.*

We have received strong protests about the food, and strong protests about the prices, at this hotel. We have passed *the former* on to the manager, and *the latter* to the Ministry of Tourism. (= former/latter protests)
My argument is *the following*. (= the following argument)
How can ideas like *the foregoing* be taken seriously. (= the foregoing ideas)

47.9.3 Genitive NGs

Bernini's sculptures are wonderful, but *Michelangelo's* are sublime. (= Michelangelo's sculptures).

Longer genitive NGs are avoided when they end in an unstressed item such as a personal pronoun or a preposition and are replaced by alternative structures:

    A. Whose are these gloves?
    B. ˚They must be that lady (whom) we spoke to's.
       They must be that lady's (whom) we spoke to.
       They must belong to that lady (whom) we spoke to.

Such long forms are infrequent and occur mainly in conversation where it is easy for the hearer to supply the ellipted noun.

47.9.4 *WH*-heads: *Which? Whose?*

Of these bilingual dictionaries, *which* would you recommend?
One of our friends has got a birthday tomorrow, but I can't remember *whose* it is.

Even if the presupposed noun is not mentioned in the text, it can always be supplied by the situation:

Which came first, the chicken or the egg? (= which thing?)
Whose won the prize? (whose novel? whose song?, etc.)

47.9.5 Distributive and non-specific heads

e.g. *all, both, either, neither, each, some, any*.
Elliptical *all* presupposes only plural NGs:

We sent out the questionnaires, but not *all* were returned.

It cannot presuppose a specific singular NG or a mass NG. The following sentences are not possible:

The plane crashed and ˚*all* was destroyed.
This meat is uneatable; ˚*all* is bad.

When used without an accompanying noun, singular *all* refers to a global totality equivalent to a non-specific entity such as *everything*, as in *All is well* or *That is all for today*. With this meaning, it is better classified as a pronominal head rather than as an elliptical one.

When the items *both, either, neither, each* are used as elliptical heads, they refer sometimes to hyperonyms of the antecedent nouns or NGs:

Adults and children are welcome; the film is suitable for *both*.
(= both kinds of person)
There's tea or coffee; you can have *either*. (= either kind of drink)
A film star should have intelligence as well as talent, and he has *neither*. (= neither quality)
They sat there, *each* lost in his own thoughts.

The indefinite article *a/an* is not used elliptically; as head element it is represented by *one*:

> If you need *a stamp*, I can give you *one*.

Plural and mass nouns are presupposed by elliptical *some*:

> If you need *stamps*, I'll get you *some*.
> If you need *writing paper*, I'll get you *some*.

In non-assertive structures, *any* is used instead of *some*:

> I need stamps. Have you got *any*?
> I need writing paper. Have you got *any*?

The determinative *any* can also refer elliptically to singular, plural or mass nouns with the meaning of 'it doesn't matter which' or 'any kind of':

> **mass**:   Bring me some cheese; *any* will do. (= any cheese)
> **plural**:   Bring me some flowers, *any* will do. (= any flowers)
> **singular**: Bring me a newspaper, *any* will do. (= any newspaper)

The negative determinative *no* is not used elliptically; as head element it is represented by *none*, which may have count or mass reference:

> Did you have any *problem* in parking?   No, *none*. (no problem)
> Haven't you any *friends*   No, *none*. (no friends)
> Did you have any *luck*?   No, *none*. (= no luck)

(For a fuller treatment of 'assertion' and 'non-assertion', see Module 23.1–5.)

47.9.6   Indefinite and definite determinative heads

The specific and non-specific determinatives do not combine with the articles with the exception of the genitive noun forms. The following types admit *a(n)* or *the* in both determiner and head functions:

> **genitives**:   I need a specialist's opinion, not a *journalist's*.
> **cardinals**:   Is there room for *the six* of us in your car?
> **ordinals**:   After her first marriage, there was a *second* and a *third*.
> **non-exact**
> **quantifiers**: I haven't given you much help, but I hope *the little* I
>   have given has proved useful.

47.9.7   Elliptical quantitative heads

When used as elliptical heads, quantifiers may themselves be determined, modified or qualified:

> **dh**   Which are our seats? – *These two*.
> **dh**   We missed our train and had to wait for *the next*.
> **dhq**   What weeks will you be away? – *The first three in July*.
> **dhq**   Is this your first visit to London? – Yes, *my first ever*.

mhq   I was lucky to get tickets; there were *very few left*.
mhq   They haven't got a lot of money but *quite enough to live on*.

47.10   Summary of experiential features of determination

The following table summarises the four broad experiential types of determination by which referent things can be particularised in English, together with their subtypes and principal exponent. The logical relations between them, within the overall organisation of nominal structure, are discussed in Module 50.

47.11   Use of determiners in texts

Texts do not normally contain a large number of different kinds of determinatives, but the repetition of one type of item can be effective. The following paragraph describes how a scientist, who has been knocked unconscious by two friends that prove to be criminals, wakes up in total darkness and gradually discovers his surroundings through sensations in parts of his body. The repetition of the possessive determiner *his*, together with other deictic items, serves to concentrate our attention on the scientist's experience as he gradually realises his situation. Key words and phrases are marked:

> When *he* came to *his* senses, *he* seemed to be in bed in a dark room. *His* head ached pretty severely and the room seemed to *him* remarkably warm. Moving *his* arms to fling off the bed clothes, *he* touched a wall at *the right side* of the bed: it was not only warm, but hot. *He* moved *his* *left hand* to and fro in the emptiness on *the other side* and noticed that *there* the air was cooler – apparently the heat was not coming from *that* part of the room. He felt *his* face and found a bruise over *the left* eye. *This* recalled to *his* mind the struggle with the two men, and *he* instantly concluded that *they* had put *him* in an outhouse behind *their* furnace.

> C. S. Lewis, *Out of the Silent Planet*.

Summary of determinative features

1 Partition	2 Deixis	3 Quality	4 Quantity
Fractional (± of) half, (a) quarter, two-thirds, four-fifths, etc. **Multiplying** (* of) double, treble, twice, three times, etc. **Non-specific** All of, both of, some of, any of, none of, each of, several of, either of, enough of. **Other quantifiers** Cardinal + of the + ordinal + of non-exact + of (See column 4)	**Definite** the **Indefinite** a(n), some /sm/ **Specific** this, that, these, those; my, your, his, her, its, our, their; John's, my friend's; which, what, whose; whichever; etc; such; some (s∧m). **Non-specific** some, any, no; each, every; either, neither; all, both. **Exclamatory** what (a) ….! such (a) ….!	**Adjectival** same different, usual, customary, regular, typical, certain, famous, well-known, given, complete, entire, whole, original, other, chief, possible, probable, following, further, principal, previous, particular, former, latter, etc. **Superlative** best, biggest, most intelligent.	**Cardinal** ten, two hundred, three thousand, a dozen, a score, hundreds, etc. **Ordinal** first, second, etc; last, next, etc. *****Non-exact** much, little, a little, many, few, a few, less, more, most, least, fewer, fewest, several, enough, some.

MODULE 48
Expressing intrinsic features of 'things'

Summary

1 After deictics and quantifiers that select and particularise the head noun with reference to the contextual situation, we find items that describe and classify its more permanent characteristics.

2 Epithets, realised mostly by adjectives whose reference may be:
   objective: *a popular disco, a sunny day*;
   subjective: *a princely meal, a vile crime*;
   either: *absolute zero, absolute rubbish*;
   non-inherent: *a good lecturer, a poor speaker*;
   impressionistic: *a shabby overcoat, a taciturn person*.

3 Classifiers limit the entity to a subclass by referring to:
   another entity: *army officers, a football club*;
   a quality: *a poisonous snake, electric light*;
   a process: *the rising tide, a growing population*;
   a circumstance: *a round-the-world trip*;
   a situation: *a devil-may-care attitude*.

4 Some words can function as epithets or classifiers:
   civil: *a civil manner* (epithet); *civil rights* (classifier).

5 Some epithets and classifiers may function as NG heads:
   elliptical epithets: young people and *old* alike . . .
   elliptical classifiers: the public sector of industry and the *private*.

48.1 Intrinsic features of 'things'

After the defining, determining and quantifying items of information which particularise or select the noun referent from others in the surrounding context, we find those which describe the inherent, more permanent qualities of the entity itself. Examples contained in the description of Lagos were: *narrow* (streets), *stinking, open* (drains), *sheer, naked, human* (life), etc. Some of these words describe objective qualities (e.g. *narrow*) while others are subjective and represent the personal attitude of the writer (e.g. *stinking*); others do not describe the entity qualitatively, but indicate a particular subclass of the referent in question (e.g. *human* life as distinct from *animal, organic, social, family* life).

The items that describe subjective and objective qualities of an entity are considered in this grammar as two types of epithet ($\mathbf{e}^{\text{subj}}$ and $\mathbf{e}^{\text{obj}}$). The item which indicates a subclass of the entity will be called the **classifier** (**cf**). At a more general level of analysis they can all be subsumed under the broad function of 'modification', just as definers, deictics and quantifiers were subsumed under the general function of 'determination'. Both the epithet and the classifier refer to semantic features which are permanent and intrinsic in the referent 'thing' named by the head noun, and which contrast with most of the extrinsic temporary features expressed by the qualifier.

If we divide the determinative features of a referent 'thing' into the two broad types: deictic ($\mathbf{d}^{\text{d}}$) and quantifying ($\mathbf{d}^{\text{q}}$) we can now give some idea, in the following tree, of the experiential structure of the NG as we have described it so far, and without including the qualifier described in Module 49:

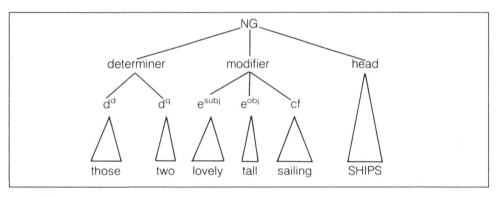

This Module describes the formal, syntactic and semantic functions of epithets and classifiers.

48.2   The epithet

The epithet element is realised typically by AdjGs in which very often only the adjectival head is expounded (see 51.2). In the previous example, the adjective *lovely* indicates what the speaker thinks about the ships subjectively; on the other hand the adjective *tall* refers to a quality which is inherent and permanent in the ships, independently of what anyone may think about them.

48.2.1   Objective references of the epithet

Adjectival epithets expressing objective qualities may simply 'describe' an entity (*I bought a small bottle*) or 'define' it (*I bought the small bottle*). The meaning of the epithet *small* remains the same in both expressions (relative to a common norm) and is clearly 'experiential' in origin: that is, it refers to a quality experienced by everyone and denoted in English by the term *small*. The two semantic functions of describing and defining are reflected in the grammar by the *a/the* contrast. That is to say, the terms 'descriptive' and 'defining' do not refer to **subclasses** of adjectives but to two potential **functions** of most objective adjectives. The 'defining' function of an epithet is different from the classifying function and this may be appreciated in the following short extracts:

> The car carrying the two *escaped* [1] killers, Rickman and Hoser, nosed carefully into the *unidentified* [2] desert town. It was that *darkest* [3] hour before dawn of a *moonless*, [4] *starlit* [5] night. Rickman, the more *vicious* [6] man, driving, with *cold*, [7] *snake-like* [8] eyes and *bloodless* [9] mouth.

> <div align="right">Paul Gallico, <i>The Silent Hostages</i>.</div>

[1–3] defining; [4–5] descriptive; [6] defining; [7–9] descriptive.

> Since they had murdered their three hostages, they had been attempting to find their way towards the *Mexican* [1] border, driving without lights on *back* [2] roads and *wagon* [3] trails.

> <div align="right"><i>Idem</i>.</div>

[1–3] classifying.

48.2.2 Subjective references of the epithet

This type of epithet expresses the speaker's or writer's subjective experience or attitude to the referent of the head noun, in contrast to the objective qualities of other epithets. There are two broad kinds of attitude:

appreciative: wonderful, heavenly, huge, rapturous.
pejorative: appalling, ghastly, idiotic, monstrous.

Subjective epithets are usually placed before objective ones:

a marvellous sunny day; a horrible brown colour.

Attitudinal epithets are sometimes preceded or followed by others which express similar or related meanings and so reinforce or intensify the attitude or emotion in question:

There was a *mighty great* explosion.
He's a *nasty slimy* toad.
She's a *sweet little* girl.
Thank you for that *lovely, gorgeous* meal.

These reinforcing adjectives replace the normal intensifiers and grading words such as *very, most, extremely*, which are not often used with attitudinal epithets: *a very horrible cough* or *an extremely terrible experience*. They are more common in colloquial speech than in written texts, and include strongly emotive words like *bloody* and other less socially acceptable expressions.

48.2.3   Words having both types of reference

Many Attributes can be used subjectively or objectively by the same adjective:

objective	subjective
a *mediaeval* castle a *sheer* cliff a *provincial* city *pure* wool	a *mediaeval* state of sanitation *sheer* nonsense a *provincial* attitude *pure* chance

48.2.4   Non-inherent reference of the epithet

Although most epithets express intrinsic, inherent characteristics of an entity, sometimes they are used to refer not to the thing itself but to an entity or to the manner of performing an action associated with the entity. This type of reference is called non-inherent.

the epithet	non-inherent reference
a *light* eater a *sound* sleeper a *dying* wish *good* friends a *beautiful* singer	person who eats light food or doesn't eat much who has sound sleep or sleeps soundly the wish of a dying person whose friendship is good person who sings beautifully

If such NGs are transposed to an SPC clause structure, *the eater is light, the friends are good*, the Attribute becomes inherent and the meaning is changed. In some NGs, the reference may be ambiguous, e.g. *a beautiful singer*.

48.2.5   Impressionistic reference of the epithet

It is usually said that 'subjective' or 'attitudinal' adjectives always precede 'objective' ones. However, epithets are not divided into two rigid sets called 'objective' and 'subjective', although their semantic reference does affect the order in which they tend to occur (see Module 50). Between strongly subjective adjectives such as *stupid, nauseous, absurd*, and neutral, objective ones like *short, bright, thin*, there are numerous Attributes which are objectively inherent in the entity, but to which a writer or speaker may attach a certain emotive or descriptive value. We suggest they may be called 'impressionistic' or 'evocative' epithets, always bearing in mind that it is not the adjective itself, but the way it is experienced by the writer, that determines its contextual meaning. Some of the epithets in the following paragraph may be interpreted in this way:

The Tramway

There is in the Midlands a single-line tramway system which boldly leaves the county town and plunges off into the *black, industrial* countryside, up hill and down dale, through the *long, ugly* villages of workmen's houses, over canals and railways, past churches perched high and nobly over the smoke and shadows, through *stark, grimy cold little* market-places, tilting away in a rush past cinemas and shops down to the hollow where the collieries are; then up again, past a *little rural* church, under the ash trees, on in a rush to the terminus, the *last little ugly* place of industry, the *cold little* town that shivers on the edge of the *wild, gloomy* country beyond. There the *green and creamy coloured* tram-car seems to pause and purr with *curious* satisfaction. But in a few minutes away it starts once more on the adventure. Again there are the *reckless* swoops downhill, bouncing the loops: again the *chilly* wait in the hill-top market-place: again the *breathless* slithering round the *precipitous* drop under the church: again the *patient* halts at the loops, waiting for the *outcoming* car.

D. H. Lawrence, *England, my England*.

48.3   The classifier

48.3.1   Classification by nouns

The classifier element restricts the class of entity named by the head noun to a subclass, and so it is natural that the great majority of classifiers are also realised by nouns. These may be simple (*orange* blossom), genitive (a *girls'* school), de-verbal (*fishing* rod), compound (*farmyard* animals) or short NGs (*Social Security* contributions). The classifying function of a genitive noun or NG, as in *The Minister gave a typical Minister of Labour's reply*, must be distinguished from its deictic determiner function as in *the Minister of Labour's reply*.

Nominal classifiers are not usually pluralised: *trouser belt, shoe shop, eye shade, car production*; but plural forms are used when the referent of the classifier has come to be regarded as a collective noun, as in *the arms race, sports field, Olympic Games medal*. Present-day English shows a tendency towards such pluralisation.

When the semantic relation between a classifier and a noun is very cohesive, they are sometimes fused as a compound denoting a single referent. Some such combinations are written as separate words (*head waiter*), some are joined by a hyphen (*record-player*) and others written as a single word (*software*), depending on the degree to which they have become institutionalised in public usage as denoting single class referents rather than as subclasses of larger class referents. We will not enter here into details of certain formal features of compounds which are interesting but far from constituting reliable criteria for setting up clearly differentiated grammatical categories of 'compound' and 'classifier + head noun' structures.

Secondly, knowledge of the field is often required in order to interpret correctly the meaningful relationship between the classifier and the head noun. In many cases the meaning is opaque to the uninitiated:

air traffic: movement of vehicles which fly in the air; passengers, cargo or mail carried.
air speed: speed of vehicle in air (not speed of the air).
air strip: strip of land cleared for planes to land and take off (not a strip of the atmosphere).
air rifle: rifle operated by air pressure.
air bed: plastic or rubber mattress which can be folded flat or filled with air for sleeping (not a bed suspended in air).

48.3.2   Classification by adjectives and participles

Classifiers are also realised by adjectives, especially de-nominal ones, and also by present and past participles expressing processes. The subclasses may refer to:

places: African politics
periods: prehistoric remains
styles: classical music
institutions: municipal authorities
professions: medical student
processes: coming events, leading article, fallen leaves
science: atomic energy
scales: main road
activities: social worker
qualities: heavy water
qualities: soft ware

The *-ing* classifiers mentioned here are different from de-verbal nouns such as *boxing, cycling, reading*, etc., and are to be classed as participial peripheral adjectives (see 51.3.2).

48.3.3   Classification by other classes of units

Certain institutionalised word, group and clausal expressions are sometimes used:

Adverbs: after effects, a home match, an away match;
PrepGs: a round-the-town trip;
NGs: an end-of-course party;
VGs: a stop-and-go policy, a live-and-let-live philosophy;
AdjGs: a bored-with-life attitude;
Clauses: a couldn't-care-less attitude.

Phrasal classifiers are not found as often as the simpler forms, but tend to be generated spontaneously when a speaker or writer feels the need to characterise a noun referent by a slightly more complex experiential concept than that expressed by single words. For example:

> ... and years later I wrote a poem about and for this *never, by me, to be forgotten* hunchback of the park.
>
> Dylan Thomas, Quite Early One Morning.

Examples like this one express a personal subjective way of experiencing the referent (*hunchback*), and are therefore better regarded as epithets than classifiers. We cannot reasonably say that there is a subclass of hunchbacks characterised as being 'never-to-be-forgotten'.

It can be seen that there is a great variety of simple and complex word and group forms available in English for the pre-head modification of nouns. It is natural that some writers take a delight in creating original expressions, such as:

> So he went out nodding politely to various *walnut-skinned, early-morning coffee-suckers*.

> She wore *church-going* clothes of *sensible-district-nurse-type hat and costume* in a kind of *under-done-pie-crust* colour.

> An official with a peaked-cap did a *caged-tiger* walk up and down.
>
> Anthony Burgess, Enderby Outside.

Phrasal modifiers are not used only for literary effect. They are used daily in many practical registers of English. The following short example occurred in the report of a meeting called to prepare an English language examination of the Royal Society of Arts:

> It was decided that section 1 of the examination would involve *no-choice short-answer* questions, and section 2 an *essay-style* question on language systems. The group felt that the candidates should also be required to submit six *non-exam-type* pieces of work done at home.

Classifiers are normal and comprehensible in many fields of applied science and technology:

architecture:	town planning, landscaping techniques, safety regulations, high-rise blocks, air flow, fire-retardant fibre-glass panel, lift shaft.
chemistry:	corrosion prevention, fluid dynamics, textile printer, paint chemistry, printing inks.
mining:	mining geology, exploration geophysics, concrete product manufacture, dust extraction.
medicine:	eye disorders, heart surgery, speech therapy, cell components, virus diseases.
electronics:	data processing, text instruments, laboratory equipment, radio transmitter systems.

48.4   Words that have dual function

The differences between the experiential functions of determination, description and classification are not absolute. All the pre-head elements of a NG contribute to the identification of the head in different ways. The determiner is mainly selective, the epithet qualitative and often gradable, while the classifier is taxonomic. However, the functions often overlap. Many words can have more than one function. The following are examples of words which can expound both the epithet and the classifier elements:

Epithet	Classifier
coloured birds	the *coloured* vote
a *criminal* act	the *criminal* court
a *legal* separation	a *legal* adviser
a *sick* person	*sick* pay, *sick* leave
a *blind* person	*blind* flying
a *cutting* remark	a *cutting* instrument
a *fast* train (= goes fast)	a *fast* train (= classed as 'express')
a *sleeping* child	a *sleeping* compartment
industrial areas	*industrial* unrest
an *iron* will	an *iron* bridge
a *plastic* smile	*plastic* bombs

The examples show that most dual function words are adjectives: only two of them (*iron* and *plastic*) are nouns. As epithets some of them are gradable:

> multi-coloured birds   a perfectly legal separation
> a really plastic smile   an absolutely iron will

As classifiers, they cannot be graded. We cannot say:

> *the very coloured vote   *a perfectly legal adviser
> *an absolutely iron bridge   *a really plastic bomb

As epithets, they have intrinsic reference, even when it is metaphorical. As classifiers, their reference may be inherent or non-inherent.

48.5   Epithets and classifiers as elliptical heads

Like determiners, the epithet and classifier elements can conflate their function with that of head element when the latter is not expounded. The NG is then described as 'elliptical', and can always be filled out if necessary by the presupposed noun or a synonym.

48.5.1   Elliptical epithets

The head of a NG is not often realised by an elliptical adjective, the commonest being adjectives of colour, and superlatives usually preceded by *the*. We say:

(a) Which shoes shall I wear: *the black* or *the brown*?
(b) He writes good novels, but this is *the best* so far.

but not:

Which shoes shall I wear: **my new* or **my old*?
He writes good novels, and this is **a very good*, too.

The presupposed noun may also be a mass noun:

(c) I prefer strong coffee to *weak* (coffee).

When the head noun is not expounded in a NG, the adjectival epithet is usually followed by the substitute word *one/ones*.

(d) Our club has two *swimming pools*, a *deep one* for grown-ups and a *shallow one* for children.
(e) Some of our lectures are interesting, but I go to sleep in the *boring ones*.

The substitute item *one/ones* may differ from the presupposed noun in number, as in example (d) above. It substitutes for the head of the presupposed NG, but is used especially when its own modifiers are different from those of the presupposed NG:

(f) Some people lead a busy active life, but I prefer a *quiet one*.

Structurally, substitute *one/ones* functions as head of its own NG, which is therefore not elliptical. At the same time, it replaces a head noun which has not been repeated (e.g. *life* in example (f)). On the other hand, with ellipsis, the presupposed NG has not been replaced by a substitute item. Or, it is substitution by zero. Both substitution and ellipsis constitute economical ways of tying New information and previous information together without having to repeat the previous information. This makes the text more cohesive and easier to follow.

Certain adjectives are used elliptically to refer to entities outside the text which are not expounded because they are self-understood:

a social group: The future is in the hands of *the young*.
The French and the English have not always been good friends.
a fact: Have you heard *the latest*? (= news, rumour)
an event: I did well in *the oral*, but not in *the written*. (= exam)
a phenomenon: *The impossible* sometimes happens.

Not all abstract adjectives can function as elliptical NG heads, **the interesting*, **the strange*, **the unforgiveable*, etc., unlike some languages which have a neuter form of the article or the adjective for this purpose. In English, the meaning can be expressed, not by ellipsis of a noun, but by adding the word *thing*:

The strange thing was that they never answered our letter.

The use of *the* before such adjectives emphasises their status as NG head. Since adjectives are not marked for number in English, expressions such as *the empties* (empty bottles), *two bitters* (glasses of beer), *particulars* (details), *regulars* (regular visitors) must be classified as nouns, although they cannot all be singularised: *a bitter, a regular, one particular*, but not *an empty.

48.5.2   Elliptical classifiers

Adjectival classifiers are sometimes used elliptically, though there is a general preference for the addition of substitute *one/ones*:

Gas cookers are cheaper than electric (ones).

Nominal classifiers are rarely used elliptically, as they can easily be mistaken for a true head noun:

*A stone cottage is prettier than *a brick*.

Ellipsis is more acceptable if the ellipted noun is definite or plural:

The stone cottage is prettier than *the brick*.
Stone cottages are prettier than *brick*.

In general the use of *one/ones* is preferable after a classifier if the head of a NG is not expounded:

A *stone cottage* is prettier than *a brick one*.
Riding boots are more expensive than *walking ones*.
I enjoy *historical novels* more than *psychological ones*.
We won our *home match* but not the *away one*.

If a mass noun is qualified, it can be replaced by *that* (slightly formal):

Pronunciation in the north is different from *that* in the south.

A singular count noun can be replaced by *that* and *the one* if it has non-personal reference:

The flight to Moscow takes the same time as *that/the one* to New York.

Plural count nouns can be replaced by *the ones* or *those*.

The sweetest oranges are *the ones/those* grown in Spain.

Single count nouns with personal reference are not replaced by *that*, owing to the association of *that* primarily with non-personal referents. Plural nouns with personal reference can, however, be replaced by *those*, as well as *the ones*:

The guide we had was better than *the one* you had.
The drivers we had were better than *those/the ones* you had.

If a personal noun (e.g. *fans*) is classified by a noun, it is rarely replaced by *one/ones*:

I'm referring to football *fans* not cricket ˙*ones*.

If the classifiers are adjectival, *one/ones* is more acceptable:

I'm referring to keen *fans*, but not violent *ones*.

The contrast between the two classifiers seems to facilitate the use of *one/ones*. Without it, their use seems problematic:

A. My brother's a scientist.
(?)B. Is he a nuclear one?

As with elliptical epithets, *one/ones* cannot be used after a classifier if the ellipted noun has mass reference:

Modern furniture is generally more practical than *antique*.
Japanese technology seems more advanced than *European*.

Alternatively, the noun can be repeated: *antique furniture, European technology*. Or, in order to avoid repetition, a noun of general reference can be used:

I prefer modern furniture to antique *stuff*.

Substitution is not possible when the semantic relation between a classifier and a head noun is close enough for them to constitute a single compound noun. For example, in the following sentence, the italicised head nouns cannot be replaced by *one/ones*:

Overcoats are more expensive than raincoats. (˙rain ones)

For the treatment of clausal ellipsis and substitution, see pp. 240–3.

MODULE 49
Expressing extrinsic features of 'things'

Summary

1 Extrinsic features, realised by the qualifier, identify an entity by something outside it, or add supplementary information not essential for identifying it. There are three types of information.

2 **Nominal qualification**
   Appositive NGs: Einstein, the famous physicist . . .
   That-clauses: The idea that you are always right . . .
   Nominal *WH*-clauses: The problem (of) who we should invite . . .

3 **Circumstantial qualification**
   AdvGs: The meeting tomorrow . . .
   Rel.adv. clauses: The place where I was born . . .
   PrepGs: The President at that time . . . My interest in meeting him . . .

4 **Attributive qualification**
   AdjG: He's not a person likely to succeed.
   Rel. clauses: The decision (that) you took . . .
   -ing clauses: All the money remaining there . . .
   -en clauses: The poems written when he was young . . .
   inf. clauses: The thing to do in that case . . .
   verbless clauses: I've got a lot of friends, *most of them students like me.*

5 **Overlap with Adjuncts**:
   Qualifier: A fisherman's life *at sea* is often very hard.
   Adjunct: *At sea*, a fisherman's life is often very hard.

49.1 Extrinsic features

By the term 'extrinsic' we mean those features of an entity which are not inherent in the nature of the entity itself but which relate to something outside the entity: another entity, a temporary state, a circumstance, a process or a contingent situation. This type of information tends to be more varied in form than that expressed by determiners, epithets and classifiers. It is hardly ever realised by single words but typically by groups and clauses which sometimes combine into a long chain (see Section 50.7). Whereas in some languages all the required information about a referent entity is given before the noun is mentioned, English prefers to place the shorter, intrinsic features *before* the noun, and the longer units of extrinsic features *after* it, so that the chain can be extended freely and uninterruptedly as far as the speaker or writer wishes. This information constitutes a separate element of NG structure which we call here the **qualifier** (**q**).

49.2 Communicative functions of the qualifier

The qualifier element has two basic communicative functions:

(a) to supply information enabling the hearer/reader to identify the entity in question, as in:

That's the house *where the President lives.*

(b) to add supplementary information about the referent when it has already been identified, as in:

That's the White House, *where the President lives.*

These two roles or functions of the qualifier are called 'restrictive' and 'non-restrictive', or 'defining' and 'non-defining'. To show the difference, non-restrictive units are usually written between commas, dashes or brackets and pronounced between short pauses as separate information units:

The winner, in a blue dress, looked very attractive.

Noun heads and restrictive qualifiers are not separated by commas or pauses:

The girl in the blue dress looks very attractive.

In practice, many qualifiers are neither clearly restrictive nor clearly non-restrictive, and have been classified by some grammarians as 'descriptive', however they are written or spoken:

One newspaper claimed that two British helicopters *firing machine guns and rockets* had carried out the attack.

Restrictive qualification is similar in function to classification. Consequently, because some types of classification, such as place, time, material, process (see 48.3), may refer to extrinsic features of a 'thing', such features are to be found in both positions: before or after the head noun:

	Classifier	Qualifier
place:	the corner house	the house on the corner
profession:	my doctor friend	my friend the doctor
material:	a brick house	a house built of brick
process:	a growing child	a child that is growing up

In each example, the two structures give the same information about the noun. Nevertheless, the pre-head classifier is always felt to express a more intrinsic Attribute than the post-head qualifier, which adds information after the noun. The following lines from a novel about the British Museum in London illustrate restrictive qualification:

Many of them had been there all day: their countenances were fatigued but contented, conveying the satisfaction of *work well done – so many books read, so many notes taken*. Then there were the Night People of the Museum – *those writing books or theses*.

David Lodge, *The British Museum is Falling Down*.

49.3 Realisations of the qualifier

In order to give a clear, though admittedly over-simplified, picture of this complex area of English grammar, we have divided the various classes of units that can qualify NGs into three broad types according to the kind of extrinsic features they express: (a) those that explicate an entity in terms of another entity or fact or situation considered as a 'thing', and which are therefore termed 'nominal'; (b) those that characterise an entity in terms of an attendant circumstance; and (c) those that refer to a temporary quality or state or action of the entity which are therefore of an attributive nature. These three broad types of extrinsic features are realised by the following twelve classes of units:

Nominal (49.4)	**Circumstantial** (49.5)	**Attributive** (49.6)
Nominal Groups	Adverbial Groups	Adjectival Groups
That-clauses	Relative adv. clauses	Relative clauses
Nom. *WH*-clauses	Prepositional Groups	Non-finite clauses

The following excerpt from the novel mentioned above contains six examples of these classes of qualifiers:

> ... the Department did not have the resources *to mount a proper graduate programme*[1], and in any case espoused the traditional belief *that research was a lonely and eremitic occupation* [2] a test *of character rather than learning*[3], *which might be vitiated by excessive human contact*[4]. As if they sensed this, the new postgraduates, *particularly those from overseas*[5], roamed the floor accosting the senior guests. As he left the bar with his first sherry, Adam was snapped up by a cruising Indian:
> 'How do you do', said Mr Alibai.
> 'How do you do', said Adam, *who knew what was expected of him*[6].

> David Lodge, *The British Museum is Falling Down*.

[1] attributive; [2] nominal; [3] circumstantial; [4] attributive; [5] nominal; [6] attributive.

The numbered nouns are qualified by the following classes of units: (1) infinitive clause; (2) *that*-clause; (3) PrepG; (4) non-restrictive relative clause; (5) Nominal Group; (6) non-restrictive relative clause. The NG qualifiers (3) and (4) are embedded in the *that*-clause at (2).

49.4 Nominal qualifiers

The closest relationship of qualification is that between the head of a NG and an appositive unit, that is, a nominal unit that has the same reference. Nominal qualifiers are realised by the three classes of unit mentioned in this section. The relation between them and the head noun may be restrictive (*my friend the doctor ...*) or non-restrictive (*my friend, the doctor I told you about ...*).

49.4.1 Nominal Groups as qualifiers

The following are some of the appositive relationships these may express:

(a) definition: My niece, *a very pretty girl.*
(b) naming: The explorer *Marco Polo.*
(c) role: Marco Polo, *the explorer.*
(d) definition: Chivalry, *the dominant idea of the mediaeval ruling classes*, was symbolised by the Round Table, *nature's perfect shape.*
(e) particularisation: The members voted for a change in the statutes: *the election of the chairman by popular vote.*
(f) synonym: A cowshed, *or cowhouse* . . .
(g) identity: We *Americans*; you *children.*

The semantic relation between nominal appositives is sometimes made explicit by linking expressions such as *for example, in other words, that is to say, namely, mainly, chiefly, such as, including*, etc.

49.4.2 Nominal *that*-clauses as qualifiers

That-clauses represent situations which can participate as Subjects and Objects in other clausal situations and for this reason are classified as 'nominal'. As nominal units, they can also be used as appositives to NGs, which they qualify and endow with an extrinsic feature of meaning. In the following sentence, the two situations *inflation is going down* and *our economy is improving* serve to identify the entities *the fact* and *a sign*:

The fact that inflation is going down is *a sign that* our economy is improving.

The following lines about social systems in the Pacific islands illustrate this type of qualifier:

No culture has failed to seize upon the conspicuous facts of sex and age in some way, whether it be *the convention* of one Philippine tribe *that no man can keep a secret*, the Manus' *assumption that only men enjoy playing with babies*, the Toda *belief that almost all domestic work is too sacred for women*.

The Sunday Times, February 1991.

That-clauses occur frequently as qualifiers of de-verbal and de-adjectival nouns:

de-verbal: His *suggestion that* the meeting be postponed was accepted. (cf. He suggested that . . .)
de-adjectival: There is no *evidence that* he committed the crime. (cf. It is not evident that . . .)

Other nouns in these three categories include the following:

de-verbal: knowledge, doubt, regret, thought, report, hope, agreement, reply, wish, proof, guess, answer.

de-adjectival: anxiety, confidence, probability, eagerness, happiness, possibility, likelihood.
simple: story, idea, news, message, rumour.

49.4.3 Nominal *WH*-clauses as qualifiers

These are finite and non-finite (infinitive) clauses introduced by the words *who(m), which, when, where, what, why, whether, how, how much, how long*, etc. In this structure they have interrogative value and so qualify only certain nouns such as *question, problem, doubt, discussion, decision*. They function as appositives to the noun and in both a restrictive and a non-restrictive sense. The preposition *of*, or another, is usually felt to be necessary for restrictive qualifications:

Finite appositive clauses
(a) The question (of) *how much we should spend on our holidays* ...
(b) The problem (of) *who we have to vote for* ...
(c) I have strong doubts (about) *whether I ought to sign a contract* ...

Infinitive appositive clauses
(a) The question (of) *how much to spend on our holidays* ...
(b) The problem (of) *who to vote for* ...
(c) I have strong doubts (about) *whether to sign a contract* ...

49.5 Circumstantial qualifiers

Referent 'things' are sometimes defined or characterised by circumstantial features expressed grammatically by adverbs and AdvGs, or by Prepositional Groups and clauses.

49.5.1 Adverbial Group qualifiers

The only AdvGs used to qualify nouns are those that express certain notions of space and time:

place: Is this the way *out*?
The food *there* is good.
time: He came, and left the week *after*.
They haven't advertised the concert *tomorrow*.
His success *later* is assured.

Some of these adverbs can also present the feature as intrinsic by being placed as classifiers before the noun:

extrinsic: *The cinemas downtown* are closed on Sundays.
intrinsic: *The downtown cinemas* are closed on Sundays.

Others cannot be used in this way:

extrinsic: *A holiday abroad* will make a nice change.
but not: *An abroad holiday* . . .

Some such adverbs have different meanings in the different positions:

qualifier: One of *my days off* = days when I do not work (extrinsic).
modifier: One of *my off days* = days not as good as usual
(intrinsic).

49.5.2   Relative adverbial clauses as qualifiers

Nouns denoting places, times or reasons can be qualified by relative clauses introduced by the relative adverbs *where, when, why*, respectively. These clauses have circumstantial value:

Restrictive	Non-restrictive
She took her degree at the university *where she was studying.* The week *when the exams take place*, I intend to be ill. The reason *why I ask* is very simple.	She took her degree at Yale University, *where she was studying.* The week after, *when the exams took place*, I was ill. The mystery, *why the numbers were changed*, was never solved.

The word *why* collocates almost exclusively with the noun *reason*, except when it introduces an appositive clause as above. The relative adverbs *when* and *why*, but rarely *where*, can be replaced by *that* or *zero* in restrictive clauses:

In the week (*that*) the exams take place . . .
The reason (*that*) I ask you . . .
*The town that I was born.

49.5.3   Prepositional Group qualifiers

This is by far the commonest class of circumstantial qualifiers used in English NGs. The preposition links the head of the NG to its nominal complementive, which may be realised by:

a noun: The concert *on Monday* will be free.
a NG: The concert *by the municipal orchestra* will be free.
a Clf: The discussion *about what we should do next* led
nowhere.
a Clnf: My apologies *for not writing to you before.*
The confusion *through passengers panicking* made the
situation worse.

49.5.4   The preposition *of*

This is by far the commonest preposition of all. It can in fact be regarded, not as a true preposition having a certain degree of semantic content as other prepositions have, but as a generalised syntactic marker of various semantic relations between two nominals. The relations are to be interpreted in terms of the type of information the nominal completive gives about the nominal head of the group.

In the following text, the completives specify the head noun:

> Adam toyed with the *idea of going* [1] to the cinema. He had a *premonition of the guilt* [2] he would feel at adding a further *act of idleness* [3] to a day already characterised by total non-achievement.

> David Lodge, *The British Museum is Falling Down*.

In the following sentence, they attribute a quality to the head noun:

> A famous Spanish writer described the Spaniard as *the man of passion*, [4] the Frenchman as *the man of thought*[5], and the Englishman as *the man of action*[6].

In the following uncontextualised examples, the completives of *of* give various types of information about the head noun:

content: large crowds *of people*
cause: a loud outburst *of anger*
place: the Battle *of Britain*
whole entity: the wheels *of my bicycle*
whole period: the end *of the century*

Other more varied classes of attributive qualifiers are discussed in section 49.6.

49.6   Attributive qualifiers

This type of qualification is realised by Adjectival Groups, relative clauses and non-finite clauses.

49.6.1   Adjectival Group qualifiers

Single adjectives are rarely used as qualifiers and are limited to the following types:

(a) a small number of fixed expressions, the relic of a French structure:

> the body *politic*, the devil *incarnate*, from time *immemorial*.

(b) after certain pronominal heads:

> those *present*, something *nice*, nobody *interesting.*

(c) adjectives placed after a modified noun head, but which qualify the modifier, not the head: *the worst time possible* = the worst possible, not *the time possible. The close relationship between *worst* and *possible* is shown by the possibility of placing them together as an epithet: *the worst possible time.*

Attributive qualifiers are realised more easily by coordinated adjectives than by single ones. For instance, while it is not possible to say

> (a) *The other candidates, *confident*, all passed the test,

a longer, coordinated structure is quite acceptable:

> (b) The other candidates, *confident and well-prepared*, all passed the test.

If the two coordinated adjectives functioned as a modifier, as in:

> (c) *The confident and well-prepared* candidates all passed the test,

they would be interpreted as intrinsic features of the noun *candidates.*

When functioning as a non-restrictive qualifier, as in (b), written between commas and spoken between pauses, they are interpreted intuitively as causal, equivalent to a clause beginning *who were ...*, or *because they were ..., or being. ...*

Adjectival Group qualifiers usually contain their own modifier or qualifier elements:

> We chose the solution *most likely to succeed.*
> He always wore socks *full of holes*.
> The campaign produced results *much better than were expected.*
> Anybody *so confident that peace is just round the corner* is guilty of wishful thinking.

Qualitative Attributes are sometimes presented as extrinsic by PrepGs introduced by *of* or *with* in NGs such as *a woman of great beauty* or *a man with exceptional talent*. Just as in 49.1 we saw a parallelism between qualification and classification, so here it is clear that qualifiers may express attributive meanings similar to those of the epithets:

Epithet (mh)	Qualifier (hq)
a *very beautiful* woman an *exceptionally talented* man	a woman *of great beauty* a man *with exceptional talent*

In these examples, the **mh** structure focuses on the entity (*woman, man*) that has an inherent quality; the **hq** structure focuses on the quality (*beauty,* *talent*) which it nominalises, as if it were itself a separate entity extrinsic to the person possessing it. The semantic content realised by the two structures is the same; the ways in which it is presented are different.

This slight difference in meaning between an Attribute presented as intrinsic by an adjectival epithet and the same Attribute presented as extrinsic by an AdjG, NG or PrepG qualifier can also be appreciated in the following pair of structures, in which the Attribute is quantified:

Modifier + head	Head + qualifier
such a young child	a child of that age a child that age a child that young

NG structures such as *the subject of archaeology, the state of Virginia* and *the city of New York*, in which the two elements are joined by *of*, may also be considered as instances of restrictive apposition since the preposition *of* expresses a copular relation of identification (*the city is New York*) rather than a circumstantial one.

The following italicised NGs have a superficially similar structure, though in fact they are different.

> *That brute of a dog* bit me.
> They've got *a dream of a garden.*
> He's *a terror of a child.*

Here, the copular paraphrases are not *'That brute is a dog', *'The dream is a garden', *'The terror is a child', but the reverse: 'That dog is a brute', 'Their garden is a dream', 'The child is a terror'. The notional head nouns are therefore *dog, dream, garden*, and for this reason we must analyse the above NGs not as:

* d	h	q
that a a	brute dream terror	of a dog of a garden of a child

but as:

d	e^subj	h
that a a	brute of a dream of a terror of a	dog garden child

The determiner element determines the head nouns (e.g. *dog*), and the expressions *brute of a, dream of a, terror of a*, function as subjective epithets. The essentially qualitative value of the sequences is clear from the possibility of replacing them by adjectives such as *brutish, dreamlike, terrible*. From a lexical point of view it might be said that the nouns are more emotive of the qualities than the corresponding adjectives.

This rather anomalous structure cannot be pluralised. We cannot say: *those brutes of dogs*; and expressions like *dreams of gardens* or *terrors of children* would have a different structural form and meaning.

The style of a writer is sometimes marked by a liking for certain classes of structure. The following types of qualifier are an example:

> She gestured vaguely to a cabinet where reliquaries, statuettes and vials of Lourdes water were ranged on shelves, *dim, dusty, devotional*.
>
> He was in another country: *dark, musty, infernal*.
>
> Voices, *sharp and authoritative*, were raised on the other side of the door.
>
> David Lodge, *The British Museum is Falling Down*.

A different writer exploits this particular structure more fully, at the beginning of a short story:

> We were children together once. There was Alan – and Claire – and me. I think Alan – and Claire by complicity – were the evilest people I've ever known … Alan, *pushy and masterful*, like his father in the courtroom, *impatient, unscrupulous, unforgiving*; Claire – *sensitive and thoughtful and conciliatory* like her decent father, but in the end *fickle and weak*; and me, I don't know what, nothing very much, *careful, hesitating, testing, uncommitted*, and at the mercy of them both.
>
> Ronald Frame, *The Tree House*.

49.6.2   Relative clause qualifiers (situational)

The use of the word *that* to introduce a nominal appositive clause as in:

> The news *that you're coming* cheered me up,

must not be confused with its use as a relative pronoun equivalent to *who* or *which*:

> The news *that you gave me* cheered me up.

Whereas *that*-clause qualifiers represent a proposition or situation as equivalent to the head noun, relative clauses represent it as an Attribute of the head noun. In both cases, the information may be presented as restrictive or non-restrictive:

restrictive :   My friend *who/that* lives in Boston, . . .
non-restrictive: My friend Isobel, who lives in Boston, . . .

The pronoun *that* is rarely used in non-restrictive structures. We assume here a knowledge of the forms and functions of relative clauses in English and limit ourselves to the following remarks:

(a) With some ditransitive verbs (e.g. *give, lend*) the Oi element can be replaced by Oprep, with the preposition *to* or *for* preposed or postposed, thus generating the following options:

 (i) The girl to whom I lent my coat has disappeared.
 (ii) The girl who(m) I lent my coat to has disappeared.
(iii) The girl that I lent my coat to has disappeared.
(iv) The girl I lent my coat to has disappeared.

(b) The relative pronoun cannot be omitted when it functions as Subject, except very occasionally in existential or cleft clauses (see 30.1–2) spoken in colloquial style as in the following sentences:

There's something (   ) really fascinates me about Egypt.
Excuse me, there's a student outside (   ) wants to see you.
It was John (   ) told me about you.

(c) The relative pronoun *whom* is formal in style, and is replaced by *who* or *that* in non-formal style, except after a preposition, as in (i).

(d) The relative pronouns are frequently omitted in informal style when they function as Od or Oi, or as completive of a postposed preposition, as in (iv).

(e) Relative *that* cannot follow prepositions. *Who* is occasionally heard after a preposition in colloquial speech but is best avoided in that position.

The following paragraph illustrates the role that can be played by relative clause qualifiers in a text, where they allow a writer to add subjective comments and reflections of his own to the factual content of the narrative or description:

I became absorbed by my reading and a quietness settled in the room. The tapping of knitting needles and the occasional rustle of the now-glowing fire were sounds *that touched only the outermost edge of my mind*. Occasionally, I would look up as I turned a page and note my grandmother in that repetitive and only half-conscious way *in which a mother will check a sleeping child with a single there-and-back motion of her eyes*.

Philip Smith, *The Wedding Jug.*

For an alternative analysis of non-restrictive relatives, in terms of hypotactic clause elaboration, see pp. 284–5.

49.6.3 *-ing* clauses as attributive qualifiers

This class of qualifier is very common in English:

He wrote a book *containing his reminiscences of five U.S. Presidents.*
The book also described his own life *serving them in the White House.*

'*Libra*' (Journal of Foyle's Ltd).

The attributive value of these *-ing* clauses is similar to that of a relative clause: *a book which contained ..., a press officer who had served them. ...* However, the Present Participle does not express tense or aspect, which must therefore be inferred from the context.

49.6.4 *-en* clauses as attributive qualifiers

This class of 'situational' qualifiers also expresses an extrinsic Attribute of the head noun and is therefore similar in meaning to a finite relative clause. It may focus either on the process affecting the noun or on the state resulting from the process:

process: They travelled in canoes *preserved for generations by a hard, shell-like water-proof plaster.*
state: She wore a white silk wrap *buttoned up to the throat* and a basket *slung over her shoulder.*

Unlike *-ing* clauses, *-en* clauses can show contrast of aspect but not of tense; both are usually indicated in the main clause:

simple: The stories *put out by the press* are/were false.
progressive: The stories *being put out by the press* are/were false.

The attributive value of *-en* clause qualifiers is also, like that of *-ing* clauses, similar to that of a relative clause, as can be seen in all the above examples and the following short paragraph:

Some years ago I lived in that part of the city, *known* [1] *as St Ann's.* It was a sprawling area of industrial and pre-industrial houses *set* [2] *in cobbled hilly streets to the north of the city centre.*

Carol Singh, *Trotsky's Other Son.*

[1] = which was known; [2] = which were set.

49.6.5 Infinitive clauses as qualifiers

Like participial clauses, infinitive clauses can be paraphrased by a corresponding relative clause. However, whereas with participial clause qualifiers the antecedent head noun can only be **Subject** of the relative clause (e.g. a book containing his reminiscences = *A book which contained* his reminiscences), with infinitive clause qualifiers, the antecedent noun can realise any element of the corresponding relative clause:

> **S**:   The next train *to arrive at platform 5* is the express train to Edinburgh. (= the train *which will arrive . . .*)
>
> **Od**: We have no time *to lose*. (= we must not *lose any time*)
>
> **Oi**: He's not a man *to lend money to*. (= a man *to whom* we should lend money)
>
> **Cs**: The commonest kind of worker *to become* nowadays is an unemployed one. (= the commonest kind *which you can become*)
>
> **A**:   Summer is the best time *to go* to the seaside. (= the best time *in which* you should go)

Other features of infinitive clause qualifiers are as follows:

(a) They may contain a Subject introduced by *for*, and if the Subject is a personal pronoun it has objective case form:

> The boss gave permission *for the staff* to take the day off.
> The boss gave permission *for us* to take the day off.

In this structure, the items the *staff* and *us* conflate the two functions of completive of the preposition *for* and Subject of the infinitive *to take*. The structure occurs with only a few nouns such as *permission, agreement, need, sign, movement, campaign, appeal, demand, request, order*, and some others. It must be distinguished from expressions such as the following:

> I've bought two tickets *for us to go to the concert.*

in which the infinitive clause is best interpreted, not as qualifier of *tickets*, but as a clausal Adjunct of purpose.

(b) Unlike *-ing* clauses, infinitive clauses can express time and aspect contrasts:

> *Russian is a useful language to study/to have studied/to be studying/ to have been studying.*

(c) Infinitive clause qualifiers may have either active or passive form, often with little difference in meaning:

> There are a lot of interesting *places to see/to be seen* in Rome.

This applies especially to existential clauses, but also to non-existential ones:

> We have been given a long list of books *to read/to be read* before the course begins.

(d) Like other qualifiers, infinitive clauses can be restrictive or non-restrictive:

> **restrictive** :   *Her wish to own a pony* was never fulfilled.
> **non-restrictive**: *Her greatest wish, to own a pony*, was never fulfilled.

49.6.6 Minor clauses as qualifiers

Group units are sometimes recognised as minor clauses when their elements can be described in clausal terms:

(a) The President, *aware of the gravity of the problem*, decided to consult his team of advisers.
(b) This library is open only to students *currently on research work*.
(c) We all looked at Klaus, *still with his head down*.
(d) After the bombing, many families never returned to their homes in east London, *now a shambles of ruined* buildings.

In (a), the AdjG following the Subject can be analysed as qualifier equivalent to an *-ing* clause (*being aware of* ...) or a non-restrictive relative (*who was aware of* ...). If placed before the Subject (*Aware of the gravity* ... *the President decided* ...), it would be interpreted as a clausal Adjunct of reason or cause (*Because he was aware* ...), marked off from the Subject and predicate by a pause or a comma.

In (b), the adverb *currently* suggests that the PrepG qualifier is equivalent to a restrictive relative clause (*who are currently doing research work*).

In (c) the expression *still with his head down* cannot be adjunctive since it does not relate to *We all looked*, but to *Klaus*. The circumstantial adverbs *still* and *down* also suggest that this expression can be analysed as a verbless non-restrictive relative clause equivalent to: *Who still held his head down* or *Who still sat with his head down*.

In (d) the qualifier is an appositive NG preceded by the circumstantial adverb *now*. This suggests that the adverb and the NG can be interpreted as Adjunct and Complement in the clause *Which was now a shambles of ruined buildings*. The assignment of a qualifying function to these minor clauses may be considered, as in 49.6.2, alternative to that of hypotactic elaboration of a primary clause.

The following short paragraph illustrates this feature of NG qualifiers:

> *The people from the incoming train* [1] crowded through the barrier: *young girls spruce in their chainstore clothes*; [2] *women avidly talking to each other*; [3] *young men with non-committal eyes*. [4]
>
> Dorothy Goulden, *The Girl in the Mad Hat*.

One would tend to avoid using four consecutive relative clauses in such a short text:

> The people (*who arrived*) from the incoming train crowded through the barrier: young girls (*who looked*) spruce in their chainstore clothes; women (*who were*) avidly talking to each other; young men (*who had*) non-committal eyes.

The use of 'reduced' forms calls attention immediately to the extrinsic characteristic of each group of persons, and makes for a shorter and more varied description.

49.6.7 Qualifier or Adjunct?

It is important to distinguish between the use of groups and clauses as qualifiers of a NG and the use of the same groups and clauses as Adjuncts of a clause. For example:

qualifier: Life *a hundred years ago* was different from ours.
Adjunct: Life, *a hundred years ago*, was different from ours.
    A hundred years ago, life was different from ours.
    Life was different from ours *a hundred years ago*.

PrepGs can also have alternative placements and functions:

A capital city *with so many ancient buildings* is bound to attract tourists.
A plague *in the fourteenth century* killed 75 million people.

The same applies to non-finite *-ing* and *-en* clauses:

Nobody *having worked so hard* should be made redundant.
Some drugs *taken in moderation* are not harmful.

In post-head position, these units are usually interpreted as qualifiers, that is as **part** of a clausal constituent (e.g. Subject or Object). When placed at the beginning or end of a clause or when otherwise separated by commas and pauses from all or part of the predication, they become dependent clauses in a clause complex.

non-restrictive   Nobody *having worked so hard* should be
qualifier: made redundant.
dependent clause: *Having worked so hard*, nobody should be made
    redundant.
    Nobody should be made redundant *having
    worked so hard*.

The following introduction to a historical study of banditry defines the social and psychological motives giving rise to banditry and the kinds of men and women who have become bandits in the past. This treatment of the topic naturally obliges the writer to define or describe the abstract and concrete entities he refers to, by using a variety of qualifying units. In this particular case, they all have restrictive reference.

Qualifiers

Man has an insatiable longing *for justice*. [1] In his soul he rebels against a social order *which denies it to him*, [2] and, whatever the world *he lives in*, [3] he accuses either that social order or the entire material universe of injustice. Man is filled with a strange, stubborn urge *to remember, to think things out and to change things*, [4] and in addition he carries within himself the wish *to have what he cannot have*, [5] if only in the form *of a fairy tale*. [6] That is perhaps the basis *for the heroic sagas* [7] *of all ages, all religions, all peoples and all classes, including our own*. [8]

For the law, anyone *belonging to a group of men* [9] *who attack and rob with violence* [10] is a bandit, from those *who snatch payrolls at an urban street corner*, [11] to organised insurgents or guerillas *who happen not to be officially recognised as such*. [12]

E. J. Hobsbaum, Bandits.

[1] PrepG; [2–3] relative clauses; [4–5] infinitive clauses; [6–8] PrepGs; [9] *-ing* clause; [10–12] relative clauses.

MODULE 50
Organising and communicating our experience of 'things'

Summary

1　The elements of a NG are organised in a relation of successive dependency and selection, from the head leftwards to the classifier, the epithet and the determiner, and rightwards to the qualifier:

$$d \longleftarrow e \longleftarrow c \longleftarrow h \longrightarrow q$$
that short summer course we attended

2　When an element is realised by two or more units, the same principle applies. All elements can be realised recursively, by coordination or subordination:

head (coord):　men, women and children; a year or two.
classifier
　(coord):　　army, navy and airforce personnel;
　(subord):　　river pollution control techniques;
　(bracketing):　an African←Olympic Games←world champion.
epithet
　(coord):　　a very informative (and) entertaining talk;
　(subord):　　a disturbing though fascinating novel.

determiner
(subord):   most of←these←customary←first←reactions;
(coord):   for those and other reasons; my or your idea.
qualifier
(coord):   he's a man to be admired but to be feared;
(subord):   those books→on the top shelf→of the bookcase.

3   The qualifier can be realised by words, groups and clauses; these can contain embedded elements, and generate long sequences.

50.1   Summary of experiential structure of the NG

In this chapter, we describe the experiential structure of the English NG in terms of five basic elements: head, determiner, epithet, classifier and qualifier, each of which identifies or describes the head referent in several meaningful senses shown in the following diagram:

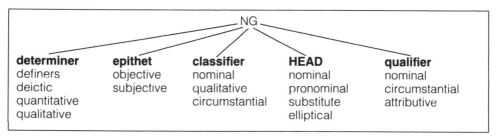

Not all the elements occur in every NG. Each one is realised by a primary class of item chosen from a system of semantic options offered by the language. It is these paradigmatic choices of semantic features which really constitute the experiential structure of any NG and which combine with their syntactic functions to form a complex network of grammatical relationships:

Text:	that	short	summer	course	we attended
Elements	determiner	epithet	classifier	HEAD	qualifier
Primary class	deictic	objective	circumstantial	abstract 'thing'	attributive

The third stage in the construction of a linguistic unit is the choice of a secondary class of item with which to realise the function of each element.

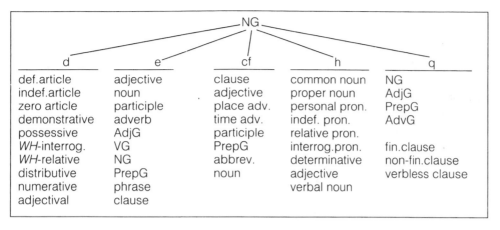

If we now combine these choices with those of the previous analysis, the experiential structure of the above example NG is describable, in abstract, on three separate levels of analysis, though in communication they are realised simultaneously and in combination.

Text:	that	short	summer	course	we attended
Elements	determiner	epithet	classifier	HEAD	qualifier
Primary class	deictic	objective	circumstance	'thing'	attributive
Secondary class	demonstr.	adjective	common noun	common noun	relative clause

The correct expression and understanding of a NG depends not only on the semantic, experiential information conveyed by its elements, but on the syntactic relations between the elements. These are of a logical, not experiential, nature, and refer to relations such as order, dependency, restriction and non-restriction, embedding, discontinuity, scope and the recursive realisation of the elements.

50.2   Logical structure of the NG

Between the head of a NG and the other elements, there is one basic logical relationship: that of successive hypotaxis or subordination. This is left-branching between the head and pre-head elements and right-branching in the case of the qualifier, as indicated by the arrows in the following example:

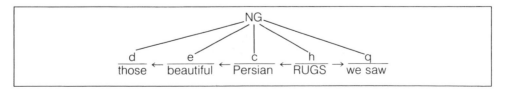

Since the closest intrinsic relationship is that between a class of entity and its subclasses, the classifier is placed immediately before the head as in *Persian rugs, radio programme, park entrance*. The relation is sometimes so close that the classifier can be regarded as fused with the entity, forming a single compound class noun denoting a single referent: *car park* or *car-park* or *carpark*.

There is, in fact, no definable point at which a 'classifier + head noun' structure becomes a compound noun. Compounding is sometimes a kind of subclassification, but constitutes a cline of associations and degrees of semantic cohesiveness. Many compounds were originally subclasses which in the course of time have come to be regarded as a class in their own right at a more specific taxonomic level, and so susceptible of being used as heads of a NG, with their own modifiers and qualifiers. This is sometimes marked by the following formal features:

(a) orthographic hyphenation or fusion, as in the above example of *car-park, carpark*;
(b) phonological primary stress on the first element, as in *train fare, swimming pool, control tower*.

However, these criteria are far from reliable. Orthographic usage varies considerably. Phonological stress is not always so marked as to distinguish compounds from classified heads, since classifiers also tend to carry strong stress, e.g. *football field, trouser belt, main road*.

A clearer distinction can be made in the case of first elements of compounds which do not have a subclassifying value. For example, a *gate-crasher*, a *network* and *daybreak* are not classes of *crasher, work* and *break* respectively, and their two elements have therefore been easily fused to give a joint compound meaning independent of the parts.

The next degree of permanence, subordinate to the classifying one, is that of the inherent, qualitative Attribute. This is placed immediately to the left of the classifier, as in *beautiful Persian rugs, short radio programme, narrow park entrance*. If the NG also contains a determiner this is placed before the epithet. Such is the unmarked order from right to left, from most permanent to least permanent features, which causes us to say:

a large oil tanker	and not *an oil large tanker
a brilliant army officer	and not *an army brilliant officer
a wonderful patriotic speech	and not *a patriotic wonderful speech
a silly conceited person	and not *a conceited silly person

In everyday forms of social communication (informal conversation, private letters, the popular press, much fiction), people tend to use uncomplicated NGs, whose logical order of elements cannot be changed:

Dear Philip,
    I've just had *a dental operation* and am trying to catch up with *my Christmas cards*. Hard, since we're frantically busy with *work at the*

office. I got *the 'Food from Spain' business* by the way, so see you *next year.* I'll be over *the first week in March* for *our next Food Congress in Barcelona.*

Personal letter

Customs officer and suspected thief

'*Logbook*, please. You're *the owner of this car?*'

'*'S right.*'

'But *this* isn't *the name that's on the passport.* Procter. *Who*'s *that?*'

'*He* was *the owner* all right. *We* never bothered changing *the name on the registration.*'

'But it's *your car*, you claim?'

'I do*n't* claim *anything.* 'S *my car.*'

'Then how d'you explain that *Mr Procter* says you have stolen *his auto?*'

'Ah! *I* see how *it* is! *The old bastard*'s mad at me, so *he* thinks up *a tale* to try and drop *me* in *the soup.*'

Nicolas Freeling, *Valparaiso*.

In the dialogue quoted above, expressions such as *'S right* (= That's right) and *'S my car* (= It's my car) show how novelists often represent certain phonological features of authentic very relaxed speech. If a full printed representation were attempted of all such features (even of standard articulation), especially of those due to the very marked neutralisation of unstressed vowels which is perhaps the most characteristic feature of spoken English, the result would prove unreadable. Authors tend to introduce a few examples which serve to indicate the cultural level, and possibly the social attitudes of a speaker.

Pronunciation is also closely linked to choice of language, particularly lexical forms, such as the above expressions *The old bastard's mad at me* and *drop me in the soup*. These constitute a type of non-polite usage which is commonly heard in less educated circles, and which is not presented here as a model of standard English.

In contrast to these examples of simple structures, any element of a NG can be realised recursively, and generate expressions such as:

recursive determiner: all those six other (persons)
recursive epithet: long, uninteresting and very difficult (texts)
recursive classifier: an east European trade department (official)
recursive qualifier: (nothing) very interesting to report.

Sections 3–7 of this module describe certain grammatical features of the recursive realisation of each of these elements.

50.3 Recursive realisation of the head element

The head of a NG can be realised by two or more nouns or pronouns coordinated syndetically or asyndetically:

Syndetic coordination (= with conjunction)

> What are the *advantages and disadvantages* of this plan?
> *You or I or someone* will have to take the final decision.
> *Weeks and weeks* have passed since I wrote to them.

Asyndetic coordination (= without conjunction)

> I've tried *reasoning, promises, gifts, threats, anger, everything,* but
> he refuses to change his attitude.
> All he thinks about is *money, money, money.*

If a recursive head is modified, the scope of the modifier may be ambiguous, though it is usually understood in context.

> Jobs are available for *young men and women* (any women or only
> young women?)

50.4   Recursive realisation of the classifier

50.4.1   Left-branching dependency

The classifier element of an English NG is frequently realised recursively by left-branching hypotaxis. Sequences of two, three, four, five or even more nouns are to be found, especially in technical and scientific description, and in social, institutional contexts. Classification proceeds leftwards from general to specific. In many cases, the subordination is regular as it proceeds towards the left. For instance, the NG *newspaper advertisement agency employees*, refers to *employees* who are classed as *agency employees*, the agency is classed as an *advertisement agency* and the advertisements as *newspaper advertisement(s)*.

Some such expressions are institutionalised and often reduced to an acronym, that is, initial letters which themselves are pronounced as a word.

> AIDS   Acquired Immune Deficiency Syndrome
> VAT   Value Added Tax
> BASIC   Beginners' All-Purpose Symbolic Instruction Code.

The fact that acronyms are pronounced as words means that the combinations of words which they represent are thought of as denoting a single referent. They can therefore be considered as semantic compounds. Structurally, however, they are unpredictable in various ways and therefore differ from normal compounds.

50.4.2   Bracketing

In many other cases, however, as the sequences become long, the chain of subordination is not as regular and uniform as this, and words tend to adhere in small groups and mini-sequences, such as:

    (a) Present government←unemployment pay←policies
    (b) Our←King's Cup←lawn tennis team's←tournament performance

It is obvious that we cannot group the classifiers as follows:

    ˙Present←government unemployment←pay policies
    ˙Our King's←Cup lawn tennis←team's tournament performance

The grouping of mini-sequences of this kind is called 'bracketing', and it may be said that the internal bracketing of modification structures is crucial for the correct understanding of English NGs. There are sometimes two or more ways of interpreting a NG, according to different ways of bracketing the modification structure. For example, the following NG:

    (c) a small business computer assembly operation

might be interpreted and bracketed in the following ways according to the scope or focus of the epithet *small*:

  (i) a small   business computer   assembly operation
 (ii) a small business computer   assembly operation
(iii) a small business   computer assembly   operation

The meanings of these three different bracketings can be paraphrased as follows:

  (i) *a small operation* of assembling a business computer;
 (ii) the operation of assembling *a small computer* in a business firm;
(iii) the operation of assembling a computer in *a small business* firm.

It is interesting to observe that the paraphrasal versions are right-branching, that is to say, the information expressed by the original modifiers has been transferred to a qualifier (except for the epithet *small* in the first paraphrase).

    A knowledge of the situation usually facilitates the correct reference. Other expressions require a knowledge of the subject matter or cultural background, as perhaps with NGs like *National Savings Bank Account*. Initial capital letters sometimes distinguish meanings, as for example between *National Savings bank account* and *national Savings Bank account*.

    Alternatively, hyphens may be used, this being more common in BrE than in AmE; as in *unregistered voting-age blacks*. Hyphenation is often useful, even when there is no ambiguity or vagueness, in order to lead the eye comfortably across the printed page. Compare, for example, the two printings:

    off line meteorological satellite data archive
    off-line meteorological-satellite data-archive

    In speech, different interpretations can be marked by placing strong stress on different classifiers, as in the following:

    (d) A NEWSPAPER crime report.
    (e) A newspaper CRIME report.

Example (d) would refer to a newspaper report, not a government one or private one or any other source. Example (e) contrasts a crime report with other subclasses such as a sports report, political report, financial report, etc. Example (e) could also be interpreted non-contrastively and refer to a crime committed on the premises of a newspaper, or even a crime considered as being committed by the newspaper itself for being the cause of someone's death or misfortune.

The possibility of alternative bracketings may give opportunities to the humourist, such as the radio news reader who ended a bulletin with *That is the end of the world ... news* instead of *That is the end ... of the world news*.

The dependency relationship is usually clearer when the classifier of an embedded group is adjectival, since adjectives usually modify a following noun. So, a *social activities programme* is more likely to be interpreted as 'a programme of social activities' rather than 'a social programme of activities'.

Where doubts arise as to the semantics of structures such as these, they are due to the economy of expression (characteristic of the English language) represented by the mere juxtaposition in ordered sequence of all the pre-head elements of a NG. The order indicates the general hypotactic relationship which binds them together to form a cohesive and coherent unit, but it leaves to the reader the task of interpreting the specific semantic relationship that obtains between the various lexical items of the sequence. In some other languages, these relationships are grammaticalised and made explicit. English, on the other hand, is sometimes ambiguous and other times merely vague.

50.4.3   Coordination of classifiers

Recursive classification may be paratactic, the most frequent syndetic coordination being with *and*, as in *lunch and dinner menus, teacher and pupil interaction, house and flat prices*. If there are several classifying items, the last is linked to the head noun by *and*, while the preceding ones are usually coordinated asyndetically, as in the following sentences from a newspaper article dealing with problems of modern law firms:

> Increasingly, law firms are recruiting managers from areas such as
> *personnel, accounting, information retrieval and systems*
> MANAGEMENT. An average large corporate project will often require in-
> house specialists from *property, pension, tax, litigation, intellectual
> property and company* LAW.

Here, the classifiers of the head nouns MANAGEMENT and LAW are independent of each other and could therefore be placed in any order, unlike those in hypotactic relationships.

Syndetic coordination of classifiers is frequent in many social contexts:

The History and Geography Faculty	Apple and blackberry tart
The Management and Finance Committee	A plane and coach trip

The singular head noun indicates that there is only one faculty, committee, tart and trip, each of a dual kind. Ambiguity may arise if the head noun is plural. For example, *plane and coach trips* could refer to several trips of a *plane + coach* type, or to *plane trips* separate from *coach trips*.

50.5 Recursive realisation of the epithet

Sequences of two epithets are found in many types of speech and writing. However, strings of three, four or five or even more epithets give a text a marked style. The following are chosen from a large number of examples occurring in a single novel:

two items:	the *smooth, foamless* sea
three items:	*old hard stale* cheese
four items:	what an *absurd cruel strange mad* thing to do
five items:	her *tired pale wrinkled soft round* face

Iris Murdoch, *The Sea, the Sea.*

50.5.1 Coordination of epithets

When an epithet is realised by several words or groups, the relation between these is usually paratactic, since Attributes are normally independent of one another and not linked in a relation of dependency. The parataxis may be realised asyndetically as in the above examples or syndetically, with coordinators as in the following:

and	As a speaker, he has a ready *and* fluent delivery.
both . . . and	We have stayed at *both* good *and* bad camping sites.
or	(We serve) hot *or* cold meals.
either . . . or	I usually wear *either* white *or* light-blue shirts.
but	A long *but* interesting trip.
but not	A complicated *but not* difficult calculation.
yet	She's a strange *yet* friendly person.

As with recursive classifiers, ambiguity may arise when a recursive epithet modifies a plural head noun, e.g. *black and white* cats: some black and some white? or all black-and-white?

Independently of recursion, it may be mentioned that any of the adjectives in a sequence may be modified or compounded, so expanding the epithet element still further, as in the following attested literary examples:

the long *quite pretty* face;
that *well-meaning, almost parental* stiffness;
the ordinary, average, *completely selfish* person;
various *far from reassuring* masks;

into the *thickly darkly sunny* garden;
those great *wide open, light brown* eyes;
a *remarkably long*, reddish, *faintly bristly* seaworm;
a sort of painful humorous grimace;
the *already dewy* grass;
the *now-somehow-central* question.

and the following journalistic one from a popular American weekly:

The Vietnamese war was an *anguishingly and distinctly lonely* one for
both protagonists. For the Americans it was a *more than dismal* failure.

Time Magazine, 1991

Compound adjectives and nouns may also occur in sequence, though this constitutes a very marked style as in the following examples of commercial publicity:

Feather-light, hand-tossed, golden pancakes stuffed with *creamy apple-and-blackberry* mousse and served with *luscious maple* syrup.

Sun-kissed, summer-fresh tropical fruits grown, gathered and packed on the *dew-drenched, olive-studded* hills of *Southern* California.

It can be noticed that sometimes it is the qualitative epithet which is realised recursively; other times it is the attitudinal one, and in other expressions, both are recursive:

qualitative: old hard stale cheese;
attitudinal: what an absurd cruel strange mad thing to do!
mixed: a loathsome, spineless, idle, ill-mannered man.

50.5.2   Subordination of epithets

Epithets can be related hypotactically by conjunctions such as:

if   an enlightening *if* heated discussion;
though   a disappointing *though* not unexpected result;
because   rebellious *because* maltreated children;
and therefore a well-educated *and therefore* polite person.

The subjective + objective order of epithets customary in asyndetic recursion is often inverted when the structure is syndetic:

Asyndetic	Syndetic
an enchanting old church those hideous modern buildings	an old and enchanting church those modern but hideous buildings

Syndetic structuring, both paratactic and hypotactic, is favoured especially when the epithets are modified and submodified. Its use may give a text a somewhat inflated tone, perhaps appropriate to a public occasion, such as the meeting of shareholders when one of them said the following:

> Mr. Chairman: I do not understand this *deeply disappointing and frankly quite unjustifiable* drop in the company's earnings this year. It seems to me that the Board has been guilty of *the most dangerous if not criminally short-sighted* complacency.

50.5.3   The order of epithets

We have already mentioned that subjective, attitudinal adjectives tend to precede objective, qualitative ones, but that, apart from this, they are not necessarily linked in a relation of left-branching dependency in the same way as classifiers are. Nevertheless, their order of occurrence is not totally free, and different grammarians have suggested certain tendencies to preferred orders. These include the following:

(a) de-verbal adjectives tend to precede denominal ones, as in: *an attractive, ambitious woman.*

(b) attributes of size, age, shape and colour usually occur in that order: *a large, modern, rectangular, black box.*

(c) short adjectives tend to precede long ones, as in: *a small, pretty, well-kept garden.*

(d) Well-known words are usually placed before less common ones: *a peculiar antediluvian monster.*

(e) The most forceful or 'dynamic' adjective tends to be placed at the end: *a sudden, loud, ear-splitting crash*; such sequences are also felt to be more satisfying rhythmically, compared with *an ear-splitting, loud, sudden crash.*

It is easy to find examples of each of these general tendencies in English sentences, and fairly easy to find others which refute them. In any case, they are no more than common preferences. Even the general tendency for subjective adjectives to precede objective ones, as in *He made a magnificent well-prepared speech*, may well be reversed, especially if the subjective adjective is graded or intensified, as in *He made a well-prepared and really magnificent speech*. This order is motivated by the principle of end-focus (see 29.7), and by the speaker's desire to emphasise his attitude to the quality rather than the quality itself.

It may also be mentioned that these general tendencies or constraints on the order of pre-head epithets do not apply to adjectives used predicatively as Complements of the Subject or Object, where greater freedom and variety of sequence is admitted.

50.5.4 Punctuation

When multiple modifiers are coordinated asyndetically, commas are usually placed between the items to indicate that they are independent of one another:

> those hideous, modern buildings (= hideous and modern)

If, however, they are felt to be in a hypotactic relationship commas are not used:

> those hideous modern buildings (= hideous because modern)

It can be seen that punctuation corresponds here to the attitude of the writer. In speech, the difference is indicated by the presence or absence of a short pause.

50.6 Recursive realisation of the determiner

50.6.1 Logical order of determinatives

The governing principle of placement of items in a recursively realised determiner is the same as that of a whole NG, that is, a gradual process of hypotactic selection from right to left, as in the following example:

$\leftarrow$ \qquad $\leftarrow$ \qquad $\leftarrow$ \qquad $\leftarrow$

Partitive	Deixis	Quality	Quantity	HEAD
half	the	usual	six	dollars

Here, from all *dollars*, we first select *six*; these are particularised as *the usual six dollars* and of these we select *half* and say: 'I paid only *half the usual six dollars* for my seat'.

The following are further examples of this unmarked sequence of the four basic types of determinatives, set out in 47.9.

	Partition	Deixis	Quality	Quantity	HEAD
2 determinatives	1) half 2) all (of) 3) – 4) –	an my the your	– – following –	– – – one	HOUR TIME STATEMENT CHANCE
3 determinatives	5) double 6) twice 7) – 8) –	their the that no	original usual entire other	– – first two	ESTIMATE NUMBER WEEK PERSONS
4 determinatives	9) a few of 10) most of	our these	former customary	many first	FRIENDS REACTIONS

When the determiner element is expounded by more than one determinative, normally only one exponent of each class is chosen. The above examples show, however, that non-specific deictics (*all, both, some, each, either*) can be linked to the specific deictics (*the, this*, etc., *my*, etc.), by the partitive selector *of*.

Although the above sequential order of determinatives can be considered the norm, it is sometimes broken. In particular, deictic adjectives may be found *after* the quantifiers instead of *before* them, when they are felt to be descriptive rather than determinative. This could apply to examples (8) and (10) above, where a given context might prefer the following order:

8)   no *two other* persons
10)   *most of these first customary* reactions

50.6.2   Coordination of determinatives

Syndetic coordination by *and, or, but (not)* permits the collocation of determinatives of the same class (e.g. *his and her* friends), which cannot be collocated asyndetically (*his, her friends). Other examples are:

partitive:	twice or three times the amount;
genitive:	with the chairman's and the vice-chairman's compliments;
possessive:	in both your and everybody else's interest;
demonstrative:	for this or that reason;
superlative:	the biggest and best opportunity;
ordinal:	for the third and last time;
quantity:	some but not enough effort.

50.7   Recursive realisation of the qualifier

In general, more information is expressed by the qualifier of a NG than by the pre-head elements. This is due to (a) its realisation by groups and clauses more than by words and (b) its greater facility for expansion by coordinated and embedded units. As explained in Module 49, the qualifier can be realised by single nouns, adjectives, adverbs and non-finite verbs, by Nominal, Adjectival, Verbal, Adverbial and Prepositional Groups, and by finite, non-finite and verbless clauses. When the element is realised recursively, the logical relations between the multiple realisations may be paratactic, hypotactic or mixed.

50.7.1   Coordination of qualifiers

Each of the following NGs is qualified by two syndetically coordinated units of the same class:

1	NGs:	my grandfather,/*a rich man/but a miser/*
2	AdjGs:	a person/*easy to approach/and generous with her time/*

3	PrepGs:	The road/*up to the pass/and down into the valley* ...
4	VGs:	A man/*to fear/but to admire/* ...
5	*that*-Cls:	the view//*that work is unpleasant//but that it's inevitable//* ...
6	*WH*-Cls:	the reason//*why I rang//and why I complained//* ...
7	Rel Cls:	my grandfather,//*whose wife died//and who married again//* ...
8	Clnf:	any applicant//*already married//or expecting to marry//* ...

Each of the following NGs is qualified by two asyndetically coordinated units of different classes:

9	Clnf + Rel Cl:	(I have) something//*to tell you//that you won't like//*
10	Rel Cl + Clnf:	the decision//*(which) they took//to organise a demo//* ...
11	AdjG + Rel Cl:	something/*very odd//that may surprise you//* ...
12	PrepG + Rel Cl:	the woman/*in hospital//whose life you saved//* ...
13	AdjG + AdvG:	Nobody/*intelligent/there* (would believe that) ...
14	AdvG + Rel Cl:	the journey/*back//which was quite short//* ...
15	Rel Cl + Clnf:	the officer//*that came,//sent by the general//* ...

50.7.2   Order of coordination

The right-branching sequence of qualifying units is not motivated by the one main factor of successive semantic dependency, as is the left-branching order of the modifiers. It is also determined by other factors, such as:

(a) Appositive qualifiers are usually placed immediately after the nominal head.
(b) Restrictive qualifiers are placed next.
(c) The longer units are placed last.
(d) The emphasised units are placed last or near last.
(e) Position is affected by the logical relation between the qualifiers.
(f) Position may be affected by the need to avoid ambiguity.

The validity of these criteria can be tested by reversing the order of the qualifier in the above fifteen examples and observing the effect produced by the change. The effect is more marked in asyndetic coordination (examples 9–15), where the results may be graded as:

(a) possibly acceptable, with phonological support in speech;
(b) possibly acceptable, but not the natural order;
(c) unacceptable, because ...

The following extract describes how dozens of farmers and their families are evicted from their homes and land in midwestern USA, by an army of tractors sent by the bankers to whom they owe money. We can notice how the *-ing* clause qualifiers describing the movement and noise of the tractors emphasise the implacability of the whole operation:

> *The tractors* came over the roads and into the fields, *great crawlers* moving like insects, having the incredible strength of insects. . . . *Diesel tractors*, puttering while they stood idle . . . *Snub-nosed monsters* raising the dust and sticking their snouts into it straight down the country, across the country, through fences, through door-yards, in and out of gullies in straight lines.
>
> John Steinbeck, *The Grapes of Wrath*.

We can observe that the *-ing* clauses qualify three NGs – *great crawlers, Diesel tractors, snub-nosed monsters* – which are related paratactically to the head noun *tractors*, although they are separated orthographically by full-stops. Their order is cinematographic: first their movement of approach, then their noise when stopped and finally, in the third and longest qualifying clause, their animal-like behaviour as they pursue their way across country. In this way, the lexico-grammatical resources of the language are used to convey a powerful impression of the scene.

50.7.3 Subordination of qualifiers

In hypotactic recursion, each unit is embedded in the preceding one. The units may be of the same class, like the PrepGs in the following NGs:

> Those books [on the top shelf [of the bookcase [in my bedroom]]].

Note the stylistic defect inherent in a string of PrepGs all introduced by *of*:

> Today's newspapers are full of the news [of the cancellation [of the government's prohibition [of the report [of details [of attacks [of terrorists yesterday]]]]]].

Alternatively the embedded units may be of different classes. The following represents a normal style of institutional, public speaking at an international Fisheries congress:

> Recently I have been engaged in an EFFORT [to interpret and apply the provisions [of the resolution [adopted at the 38th Meeting [concerning whaling [under special scientific permits]]]]].

In terms of unit classes or functional types, the structure of this sentence may be shown as follows:

Unit classes: NG [Cl inf [PrepG [Cl -*en* [PrepG [PrepG]]]]]
Functions: NG [Process [Circumstance [Process [Circumstance [Circumstance]]]]]

50.7.4 Mixed recursion of the qualifier element

The following is an example of a pronominal head (something) which is qualified hypotactically by a single finite relative clause, some of whose elements are realised recursively. Embedding is indicated here by a bracket, and coordination by '+':

> The other night, on television, I saw SOMETHING [which reminded me of the Spaniards [going into South America + and advancing over the mountains + and terrifying the population with terrible new weapons, + cannon + and the horse [which nobody [in their world] had ever seen]]].

A different organisation of recursive qualification is used in the following sentence, where each of the two NGs, at S and Oprep, is qualified by three coordinated units: AdjG + PrepG + relative clause in the case of the Subject, and PrepG + two relative clauses in the case of the Object. Three of these six qualifiers contain embedded units of their own:

Virtually every STUDENT
[normally resident in England or Wales],
[with specified minimum qualifications],
[who is admitted to a full-time degree,
[at a university [in the UK]]]
is entitled to a GRANT
[from his Local Education Authority],
[which is intended to cover his TUITION FEES AND
MAINTENANCE [for the duration
[of the course]]]
[and which also includes AN ELEMENT
[towards his vacation maintenance.]]

50.7.5 Ambiguity

The relation between two qualifying units may be potentially ambiguous in NGs such as *Those books on the table which you bought*:

> **paratactic**: Those books on the table
> Those books which you bought.
> **hypotactic**: Those books on the table (which you bought).

If the order is reversed – *Those books which you bought on the table* – it becomes nonsensical. Two possible solutions are:

> (a) **Non-restric. relative**: Those books on the table, which you
> bought, . . .
> (b) **Paratactic relative**: Those books which are on the table and
> which you bought.

50.8 Functions of the Nominal Group

In previous modules we have described: (a) the grammatical resources offered by the English language for expressing our experience of 'things', and (b) the ways in which the experiential information is organised in the form of interrelated elements of a NG. In this study, we have been dealing with the **internal structure** of the NG, its elements and the functions of its elements. We now consider the group as a whole, to describe (a) its **external functions** as an element of clauses and other units, and (b) some aspects of its use in communication.

In clauses, NGs can realise any structural element except the Predicator. At group rank they can be embedded in PrepGs as completives of the preposition and in NGs as modifiers or qualifiers of the head element. Here are examples of the functions that can be realised by a simple NG such as *the best player available*:

NGs as clause elements

S	*The best player available* was a Spaniard.
Od	The committee engaged *the best player available*.
Oi	They offered *the best player available* a high salary.
Cs	Tom Smith seemed to be *the best player available*.
Co	Everybody considered him *the best player available*.
Cp	He weighs *eighty kilos*.
A	He signed the contract *last week*.

NGs as group elements

c	They paid a high price for *the best player available*.
m	*The best-player-available* topic was not discussed at the meeting.
q	Jack Wilkins, *the best player available*, earns a high salary.

Some of these functions are obviously more likely to occur than others. The following short paragraph from a widely-read periodical exemplifies some of the syntactic potential of English NGs.

> It has been known for *nearly a century* [1] that *starvation for about two weeks* [2] increases *the speed and accuracy of mental processes, especially mental arithmetic.* [3] This is probably *the explanation of the huge increase in self-starvation among young women doing academic work.* [4] *An extreme form of this condition known as 'anorexia nervosa'* [5] is now common and *our studies* [6] have shown that in *75% of cases* [7] they start *crash-dieting* [8] in *the year in which they are working for a major examination.* [9]
>
> *New Scientist*, October 1982.

[1] c; [2] S; [3] Od; [4] Cs; [5] S; [6] S; [7] c; [8] Od; [9] c.

Of the nine major NGs numbered in the text, three of them contain other shorter NGs embedded within them. If we add to these the nominals realised by a pronoun head alone (*it, this, they*), we have twenty nominal structures in a text made up of three sentences containing nine verbal forms and eight adjectives.

It is hardly necessary to point out that the potential complexity of NG structure, combined with its functional flexibility and frequency of occurrence, make this class of unit the most important class of structure at group rank.

50.9   Nominal Group complexes

Recursion occurs at all ranks of unit structure. So just as the elements of a group can be realised by word complexes, so the elements of a clause, and sometimes of a group, can be realised by a 'group complex'. Thus any of the clause and group elements mentioned in 50.8 may be realised by a NG complex, the most frequent ones being the clausal participants (Subject, Object and Complement) and prepositional completives. The constituent units of a complex may be related paratactically or hypotactically.

The most obvious types are lists, that is, of paratactically related NGs.

> [1]Recursive Subject.
> On the flight the following articles when retained in your custody can be carried free: *a lady's handbag, an overcoat, wrap or blanket, an umbrella or walking stick, a small camera, a pair of binoculars, a reasonable amount of reading matter for the flight, an infant's carrying basket or carry cot*[1].
>
> > *Hand Baggage Regulations of the International Air Transport Association.*

> [1]Recursive Complement.
> Primary health care is *the central function and main focus of a country's health system, the principal vehicle for the delivery of health care, the most peripheral level in a health system stretching from the periphery to the centre, and an integral part of the social and economic development of a country.*[1]
>
> > Glossary of Terms, World Health Organisation.

[1]Recursive completive and complement

NG complexes are often used for literary effect, as in the following lines, where they realise the completive of the preposition *to* and the Complement of the Subject *all I ask*:

> I must go down to the seas again, to *the lonely sea and the sky*,[1]
> And all I ask is *a tall ship* and *a star to steer her by*;
> And *the wheel's kick* and the *wind's song* and *the white sail's shaking*,
> And *a grey mist on the sea's face*, and *a grey dawn breaking*.[2]
>
> > John Masefield, *Sea Fever.*

50.10 Verbal style and nominal style

In Module 21, we have described how processes, circumstances, Attributes and dependent situations are often realised linguistically as 'things'. It was pointed out that such 'nominalisations' are normal in all types and fields of expression, and do not necessarily constitute a marked style. The following extract from a talk by a police chief to new recruits, about race relations in Britain, illustrates this:

> *Anti-police prejudice* is just as destructive as any other prejudice. During your twenty weeks of basic training, you'll constantly return to *the theme* of cultural *differences* and barriers and *the elimination* of prejudice. Your own as well.
>
> The training will tell you how to overcome *many of your anxieties*, and will give you *suggestions* for coping with any situations that may arise. The special *knowledge* that police officers from ethnic minorities have of *people, language and customs* will often be of *great value* to your colleagues.
>
> We won't pretend that unpleasant situations will not *prove a challenge* from time to time, but until *racism* has been eradicated from *within society*, there will inevitably be *echoes* of it inside the *police service*. However, you will find that *distrust* turns to *trust* when people get to know you.
>
> *The Sunday Times Magazine*, 29 April 1982.

It is clear that 'social English', even when it is spoken as in this example, makes frequent use of abstract nouns and of nominalisations, though these features are hardly noticeable to the hearer or reader when they are used in appropriate situational contexts.

By contrast, in specialised fields, such as the natural sciences, the social sciences, politics and administration, business, finance, technology, etc., there is a stronger tendency towards abstraction and nominalisation. This tendency is reflected to some extent in the more serious press, which informs its readers on matters related to these fields. For example, instead of:

> The government *spent much more* in the last quarter than was planned, whereas *it spent considerably less* in the previous one.

we are likely to read:

> Government spending showed *positive growth* in the last quarter, in contrast to its *sharp fall* in the previous one.

The 'verbal' style is simple and could easily be spoken. The 'nominal' style is abstract, more formal or technical, and would only be spoken by economists.

Nominalised structures are not necessarily either longer or shorter than their clausal 'equivalents'. They may be longer:

> When we arrive . . . . At the time of our arrival

or they may be shorter:

> People in all countries are ...... Foreign travel is everywhere
> now travelling abroad much   on the increase.
> more than they used to.

It is hardly necessary to add that writers and speakers do not consciously and deliberately transform one type of unit structure into another, but simply choose the type that best suits their intentions, their subject matter and the speech situation.

TASKS ON CHAPTER 10
Talking about 'things': The Nominal Group

Module 45

1   *Read the following extract about two six-year-old boys, Lionel and Ulysses, who visit the public library. Observe the Nominal Groups marked in the text, and write each one out in three parts as for the description of Lagos in 45.1. Discuss any problems with your neighbour.*

When *the two boys* [1] entered *this humble but impressive building*, [2] they entered *an area of profound and almost frightening silence.* [3] There were *old men reading newspapers.* [4] There were *town philosophers.* [5] There were *high school boys and girls doing research,* [6] but *everyone* [7] was hushed, because they were seeking *wisdom.* [8] They were near *books.* [9] They were trying to find out. Lionel not only whispered, he moved on tiptoe. Lionel whispered because he was under *the impression that it was out of respect for books,* [10] not *consideration for readers.* [11] Lionel didn't read books and he had not come to *the public library* [12] to get any for himself. He just liked to see them – *the thousands of them.* [13] He pointed out *a whole row of shelved books* [14] to *his friend* [15] and then he whispered, '*All of these – and these.* [16] Here's *a red one.* [17] *All these.* [18] There's *a green one.* [19] All these.'

The two friends moved off into *still greater realms of mystery and adventure.* [20] Lionel pointed out *more books* [21] to Ulysses. 'These' he said. 'And *those over there.*' [22] 'I wonder what they say in all these books.'

William Saroyan, *The Human Comedy*.

2   *Imagine that the student next to you in class is Lionel and you are his older brother or sister. Answer Lionel's last question, giving him some examples of interesting books. Use simple language but try to introduce some Nominal Groups, not single nouns, into your descriptions, e.g.*

Here's *an interesting book that you would like.* It's about *the continent of Africa.* The author describes *the lives of lions and elephants and apes and other wild animals – their organisation in families, the different ways of communicating with each other, the kinds of things they eat*, and *many other things*.

3   *Read the following short description of a city on the coast of California, which was published in a newspaper. Then answer the questions and do the task given below:*

> Monterey fully repays an overnight stay. Apart from *the attractions of its streets and monuments* [1] and *a stunningly-designed aquarium,* [2] which is undoubtedly *one of the biggest and best in the world,* [3] you will need to be up early in the morning to enjoy *its echoes,* [4] *the sounds that drift in from the 31-kilometre wide bay* [5] – *the crash of breakers on rocks,* [6] *the barking of seals and sea-lions basking almost within touching distance.* [7]

1) What do you think is the purpose of this paragraph?
2) Consider the 'things' described in the NGs. In what way are they appropriate to the purpose?
3) Write a similar paragraph for the same purpose about a place which you like very much. Prepare it in this way: first, decide the 'things' you wish to mention; then add some modifying information where it is appropriate; finally, add qualifying information where appropriate.

4   †*Read the following advertisement. Then say, (a) which element of NG structure is realised by each numbered item, and (b) the type of experiential information it expresses:*

> English explorer *planning trip to Tibet* [1] needs *male* [2] secretary with *adventurous* [3] spirit and experience in handling *pack* [4] mules. *Applicants* [5] who should be under 35, should be in *first-class* [6] *physical* [7] condition, [8] with *some* [9] knowledge *of mountain-climbing.* [10]

e.g.

Item	Element	Type of experiential information
2 (*male*)	classifier	gender (inherent quality)

5   *Complete the following advertisement for an 'au pair' in the country where you live, using NGs different from those in task (4):*

> Young married couple need _____ with _____ and _____.
> Applicant must have _____ as well as _____.The family consists of _____.

6   *Write an advertisement for your college notice board beginning as follows:*

> Penniless student offers the following articles for urgent sale: ...

Describe each article in the form of a full NG.

7   *Look at the conversation between Neil and Dennis in 45.5.4 and identify the referent of each personal pronoun.*

8   †*In the following conversation, Neil is telling his friend Dennis about the bad relations existing between him and his wife Pamela. After reading it, answer the questions on the numbered pronouns:*

> NEIL: ... You see, my trouble – Pam's trouble – is *this*[1]. I think *we* [2] both expect things *from each other*[3]. Things that *the other one* [4] is not prepared to give – *to the other one*[4]. Do you get me?
> DENNIS: Uh – huh.
> NEIL: I suppose *it's* [5] nature really, isn't *it*? [5]
> DENNIS: Ah.
> NEIL: *You* [6] have your opposites – like *this* [7] (he holds up his hands). *This* [8] is *me* [9] – *that's* [10] *her*[11]. And *they* [12] attract – like a magnet. Only with people, as opposed to magnets, the trouble is with people – *they* [13] get demagnetised after a bit. I honestly think Pam and *me* [14] have reached the end of the road.

> Alan Ayckbourn, *Just Between Ourselves*.

1)   Explain the reference of each of the numbered pronouns.
2)   Comment on the use of the objective pronouns *me*, [9] and *her*. [11] Comment also on the use of *me*. [14]
3)   Which pronouns have anaphoric, cataphoric or exophoric reference?

9   †*Read the following news item and then answer the questions:*

> Health workers in two Birmingham hospitals went on strike yesterday after one of their members had been dismissed. About 300 laundry staff and kitchen staff walked out, and within a few hours, their colleagues at the city's main maternity and children's units had stopped work in sympathy. *This* has caused disruption to all areas of health care and forced the cancellation of operations.

1)   If somebody asked you: *This what?*, what would you answer?
2)   Would you, in this particular text, analyse *This* as a pronoun or as an elliptical determinative?

10   †*The following expressions with **it** and **that** are idiomatic. Can you express each one in a clearer way? How would you define the reference of **it** in these phrases? Consult a dictionary if necessary.*
1)   You've had *it*.
2)   I don't get *it*.
3)   Damn *it*!
4)   You really think you're *it*, don't you?
5)   He knows a lot about building *and that*.
6)   He gave me the answer *just like that*.
7)   That's more like *it*!

Module 46
1   *Apply the eight mass/count markers mentioned in the table on page 423, to*

the following ten nouns and describe their degree of countability. In which of the sets A–F would you place each noun? A good dictionary with plenty of examples may help you.

intelligence   perfume   spacecraft   equipment   piano   bacteria
linguistics   error   headquarters sugar   effect   the living

	Noun	Mass markers	Count markers	Degree of countability
e.g.	intelligence	1, 2, 3	4	A. Fully mass, rarely count

2   †*Are the italicised units in the following sentences grammatically acceptable? If not, say why and suggest an acceptable form:*
1)   He has *many brains* but doesn't use them properly.
2)   When we go abroad, we usually travel by *the car* and stay at *campings*.
3)   You seem to have made *a great progress* in speaking *the English*.
4)   *Every information* they gave me proved correct.
5)   She always buys *expensive perfume*, so I bought her *a very expensive one* for her birthday.
6)   We live in *a quiet outskirt* of the city.
7)   Your report lacks *detail*, I'm afraid.
8)   My girl friend has been reported by *a police* for dangerous driving.

3   †*If you read or heard the following, what would you say about the grammatical forms?*
1)   That's *a lot of hat* you're wearing!
2)   You're getting a bit fat. *Too much knife and fork*, if you ask me.
3)   'Get *more car* for your money'! (*Sales slogan*)
4)   We love the open air and go out in *all weathers*.
5)   His was *a treason* not to be pardoned.
6)   'The *snows* of Kilimanjaro'; the *mists* of history.
7)   At the seaside we usually have *two swims* a day.
8)   Do you mind giving my car *a push*?
9)   *Several* important *finds* were made in the course of the excavations.
10) He broke the world record with *his third throw* of the javelin.

4   †*Although many English nouns can have mass or count reference in different degrees, their reference in a given text can only be one of the two types. Read the following extract from this point of view, and then do the tasks:*

It is deep in *one's nature* to expect or not to expect *material comfort* and it starts as a *habit* in *childhood*. That is why I did not find *the cosmonaut's denial* of *terrestrial comforts* difficult.

The space flight was like being born again – not only the *satisfaction* of *the scientific achievement*, but also *the impact* of seeing how fragile *our planet* looks from *outer space*. It is so beautiful. I wish I could be *a painter*. *The sight* convinced me that we must treat it kindly and that *humanity* must have *the common sense* never to let *atomic flames* engulf it. *All cosmonauts* feel like *members* of *one family* but *my space experience* inspired me to see *the people who live on our planet* also as one family.

Valentina Tereshkova, the first woman in space,
in *The Sunday Times Magazine*, 23 June 1991.

1)   Say whether you interpret each NG as mass or count.
2)   Say which nouns could be used in the other sense.

5   †*The article* **the** *indicates that the referent of a noun is being presented as definite, and can be identified either somewhere in the text or from our general knowledge. Read the following short paragraph and then do the task given below:*

The Don was a real man at the age of twelve. Short, dark, slender, living in the strange Moorish-looking village of Corleone in Sicily, he had been born Vito Andolini, but when strange men came to kill the son of the man they had murdered, his mother sent the young boy to America to stay with friends. And in the new land he changed his name to Corleone to preserve some tie with his native village. It was one of the few gestures of sentiment he was ever to make.

Mario Puzo, *The Godfather*.

1)   Write out the definite nouns in the text and say how each one is identified, within the text or outside it.
2)   Write out the indefinite nouns in the text, and say how their indefiniteness is marked, e.g.

The Don: The article forms part of a proper noun and proper nouns are inherently definite.
the age: Identified by the qualifying information *of twelve*.
a real man: Marked by *a* as an indefinite–specific count noun.

6   †*The following is the first paragraph of a short story, and in it all the 'things' mentioned are presented as definite. How does the reader identify them?*

I stood at *the* backdoor and looked up at *the* moon. Its brightness from over *the* dark hump of *the* hillside made clear *the* pale drifting smoke from somebody's garden. *The* woodsmoke and *the* moon made me restless, eager to be moving in *the* sharp October night.

Philip Smith, *The Wedding Jug*.

Read the paragraph aloud, replacing **the** *and* **its** *by* **a**. *Is it possible to do so? If so, how does it change our interpretation of the scene?*

7   †*The following are generic statements in which the first noun is preceded by a definite or indefinite or zero article. Test each noun for its use with the other two articles, and say whether either of them can also be used to express generic reference.*

1) *A liquid* has no shape.
2) *Gases* have no mass.
3) *A human being* needs the company of others.
4) *War* is politics carried out by violent means.
5) *Animals* that live in captivity play with their food as if it were a living animal.
6) *Television* is a mixed blessing.
7) *The bicycle* is a cheap form of private transport.
8) *The computer* has revolutionised business methods.

8 †*Which of the following statements do you interpret as indefinite and which as generic, according to the definition of genericity given in 46.8?*
1) *Bicycles* are very useful during a holiday.
2) We always hire *bicycles* during our holidays.
3) I have *official information* for you.
4) *Official information* is usually difficult to obtain.

9 (a) †*Some of the following sentences are grammatically unacceptable. Which ones would you want to correct?*
1) The money makes the world go round.
2) A drug addiction is difficult to cure.
3) Weather can be seen but climate not.
4) The poor King Charles had his head cut off.
5) Lions are dangerous. The lions are dangerous.
(b) *What are the two possible interpretations of the final noun in the following sentence?*
My sister wants to marry *a Frenchman*.

Module 47

1 †*What type of semantic function is realised by the genitive determiner in each of the following expressions (see 47.2.2)?*
1) the firm's success
2) our team's defeat (by our rivals)
3) America's film industry
4) today's news
5) a stone's throw
6) the BBC's director
7) the director's orders
8) nobody's responsibility
9) my bus
10) cow's milk

2 †*Express the following sentences differently, using genitive determiners, if you think this structure is acceptable:*
1) I should like the opinion of another doctor.
2) Have you read the report of the chairman of the examination committee?
3) The failure of the Regional Training Scheme was inevitable.
4) The dog belonging to my next-door neighbour barks all night.

5) The grandmother of one of the girls in my class has died.
6) Here's the address of the only person I know in London.

3 †*Complete each sentence with a suitable determinative of the class indicated on the left:*
1) Non-specific: _____ member of our family has a car.
2) Non-exact cardinal: My young brother has collected _____ of butterflies.
3) Non-specific: I had _____ very good news today.
4) Specific (indef) _____ people wouldn't agree with that opinion.
5) Partitive: _____ of their energy is devoted to sport.
6) Negative: _____ of this work will be wasted.
7) Specific comparative: You will never have _____ _____ opportunity again.
8) Fractional: _____ my friends have given up smoking.

4 †*Complete the following sentences with one, two, three or four determinatives, using some of the items from the table given at the end of Module 47. Modify them if you wish:*
1) We had to pay the _____ _____ dollars entrance fee.
2) I've lost my briefcase, but a new one now costs _____ _____ price.
3) _____ _____ _____ friends came to our wedding.
4) Have you read _____ of _____ books I recommended to you?
5) _____ Europeans have abandoned _____ _____ political beliefs.
6) You can sleep in _____ bedroom you like.
7) That's _____ of _____ _____ remarks.
8) I can only stay for _____ _____ hour.

5 †*Insert the determiners, articles and substitutive items that you think were used by the writer of this paragraph. Articles are indicated by . . .*

... decision ... computer is told to make is, by itself, ... simple _____; for example: Is _____ number greater than _____ number? _____ operation is small; for example: multiplying ... _____ figure number by ... _____ figure number, producing _____ print on ... word processor or changing ... position of letters in _____ data in _____ memory. . . . computer goes through ... lengthy series of small steps as _____ programmer instructed it to do, perhaps repeating _____ steps _____ times with very _____ changes. . . . medium-sized computer can execute ... _____ instructions in _____ seconds, at ... cost of about _____ cents. It will normally make _____ errors in _____ execution. . . . result it obtains is better than _____ human can obtain, because _____ person has ... patience or time to perform _____ ... operation.

Module 48

1   †(a) *Read the following passage and discuss with another student which NG heads are modified by epithets and which by classifiers. Is any of the post-head information of a classifying type? Test this by the effect on the meaning when the information is omitted.*

> MORE THAN 200 young *Europeans* will assemble in Lisbon's national assembly *building* this weekend to debate *issues* ranging from the need for a common defence *policy* to nuclear *power* and pollution.
>   The *students*, aged between 17 and 19 and chosen after competitions between *schools* throughout the Community, make up the European Youth *Parliament*. How they vote over the coming *week* of activities will reveal much about young people's *attitudes* to major European *questions*.
>
> Nigel Dudley, *The Sunday Times*, March 1991.

(b) *Now discuss the following passage in the same way:*

> From a distance, these mountains look like a herd of driven *animals*, lean, diseased and beaten to the bone. Near at hand they revealed a shuttered, oppressed *world*, particularly so this stormy *day*, under its heavy *sky*. There was *something* about the streaming *rocks* and wet, lead-coloured *trees* that gave one a sense of a desolate secret *life*.
>
> Laurie Lee, *A Rose for Winter*.

(c) *Which of the above two texts has a preponderance of classifying modifiers and which a preponderance of epithets? What, do you think, is the reason for this tendency?*

2   †*The following newspaper advertisement of a job vacancy consists of twelve NGs, in which each head noun is modified by an epithet or a classifier. Identify these and comment on their distribution between the 'essential qualifications' and the 'outstanding benefits'. Can you explain the difference which you will observe?*

Essential qualifications
1) A good examination record at school
2) Effective self-presentation
3) Persuasive rapport with others
4) An optimistic commitment to hard work
5) Sound judgement
6) Mental agility

Outstanding benefits offered
7) A competitive salary
8) Excellent leave entitlement
9) Non-contributory pension scheme
10) Personal home loans

11)   A company car
12)   Career development and training

3   *Write a letter to a business firm or a public organisation in which you would like to work. Present it in two parts, describing, in the form of Nominal Groups, (a) your qualifications for the job and (b) the working conditions and benefits you would like to receive. Do not use the phrases contained in the example.*

4   *Choose some of the following nouns and mention three or four subclasses of each general class. Use any form of classifier you wish:*

train	machine	department	officer	tree
club	shop	commander	engine	life
house	affairs	production	problems	work

e.g. passenger train, goods train, express train, etc.

5   †*In this list of astrological predictions for the following year you will notice that all the modifiers of the noun 'month' are 'non-inherent'; that is, they do not refer to features of the month itself, but to the characteristic situation and activities of persons born under each of the twelve signs of the zodiac. After reading the forecasts, do the following:*
1) Paraphrase the first six NGs to show you understand them.
2) Express the others as NGs.
3) Invent some others, using adjectival or phrasal epithets.

NGs	**Paraphrases**
Aries: a soft-pedal month	....
Taurus: a go-ahead month	....
Gemini: a surprising month	....
Cancer: a static month	....
Leo: a tricky month	....
Virgo: a moving month	....
Libra: ....You	will have a lot of good luck
Scorpio: ....Many	problems will baffle you
Sagittarius: ....You	will get rich very quickly
Capricorn: ....You	will spend little and be thrifty
Aquarius: ....You	must watch your actions carefully
Pisces: ....You	will spend money extravagantly

6   †*Do the classifiers in the following NGs have inherent or non-inherent reference? How would you paraphrase them?*

a nuclear explosion	a nuclear physicist
a technological expert	a technological error
industrial areas	industrial unrest
travelling salesmen	travelling permission
abnormal psychology	abnormal behaviour

7   †*Correct the following sentences if you think they are grammatically incomplete or wrong:*

1) I prefer cotton shirts to woollen.
2) The trip was too short; the next will have to be a longer.
3) A cargo boat is not as comfortable as a passenger.
4) I think a round boxing ring would be better than a square.
5) He has made some good films but this is the best.
6) I'm referring to sea-fishing, not river.
7) My father runs a sports club and also a youth one.
8) She wore a crimson sari and her sister a golden one. The golden was stunning.

8   *Paraphrase the following elliptical NGs to show that they are fully nominalised:*
1) The famous are soon forgotten and the notorious long remembered.
2) The impossible sometimes happens.
3) Suddenly the unexpected occurred.
4) Most people are fascinated by the supernatural.
5) It's hard to believe in the invisible.
6) Why do you always say the obvious?

9   *In the following PrepGs, the adjectives are also nominalised, but with very specific contextual references. Can you explain their meanings? Consult a dictionary if necessary:*

in the open   in the red   on the quiet
in the dark   all for the best   out of the blue

10 *A small number of circumstantial adverbs are sometimes used to modify nouns, but with a figurative sense. Can you paraphrase the following?*

the in set   inside information   on the off chance
an off day   an outside chance   further details

11 †*Which of the adjectives in the following NGs function as epithets, and which as classifiers? Remember that classifiers are non-gradable:*

cultural activities   popular activities
a professional attitude   a professional opinion
medical treatment   a medical student
a mechanical engineer   a clever engineer
quick agreement   international agreement
efficient workers   mining workers
electric light   bright light

Module 49

1   †*In the following sentences, which NG qualifiers are restrictive and which are non-restrictive?*
1) The morning *we were supposed to leave* my car broke down.
2) I didn't like certain strange noises *coming from the engine.*
3) These noises, *which I had never heard before,* worried me.
4) We went to Greece, *a country which I didn't know.*
5) An archaeologist, *an American from Yale,* was in the party.

6) Excursions *with a well-informed guide* are more interesting.
7) I finally achieved my ambition *to see the Parthenon.*
8) It was the main reason *why we went to Greece.*
9) The narrow streets, *full of chaotic traffic,* made progress slow.
10) We gazed up at the night sky, *studded with bright stars.*

2   †*Some semantic features of a nominal entity can be expressed either by a modifier before the noun or by a longer and different class of unit placed after the noun, where attention is focused on the feature rather than on the entity itself. You can show this by changing the structural order of the following sentences:*
1) I couldn't climb *such a high mountain.* (*a mountain of such height*)
2) I find *such long journeys* terribly tiring.
3) You seem to be *quite an enterprising person.*
4) February is *the rainiest month* here.
5) It was *his most creative period.*

3   *Sometimes, the modifier and the qualifier can have the same form, but a qualifier can more easily be expanded by additional extrinsic information. Show this with the following examples, and insert the* **dhq** *structure in a sentence:*

dmh structure   **dhq structure**

e.g.
1) the *intervening* years   ....
I hardly recognised the town after all *the years intervening* between my childhood and adulthood.
2) the *expected result*   ....
3) the *suggested* solution   ....
4) the three *absent* members   ....
5) the *available* money   ....
6) the *required* resources   ....

4   †*Read the following sentences and texts, looking especially at the qualifying information given after each numbered noun; then do the task given below:*

The new Youth Training *Scheme*[1], a failure by any standard, has been abandoned.

His *daughter*[2], the most naive of girls, believes that everyone is honest.

Inflation[3], the curse of twentieth century democracy, is once again out of control.

It was a warm night. Far above him he saw *rows* [4] of elbows upon windowsills and shadowy *heads* [5] staring down, and above the heads a rocky *outline* [6] of roofs and steep, black, gable *walls* [7] blocking the night sky. Sometimes, he turned back for a closer *look* [8] at the scrolls or archways or to search for some, small stone *head* [9] over a door.

Elspeth Davie, *The Time Keeper.*

We are meeting at *a time* [10] of dramatic international changes. *Relations* [11] between East and West are improving; *the countries* [12] of Eastern Europe are one by one casting off *the dead hand* [13] of *communism* [14] imposed on them from outside, reasserting *their right* [15] to run their own affairs as they see best; further afield, *cooperation* [16] between *the countries* [17] of the Pacific Rim and the West continues to develop at great speed, particularly in the commercial and economic fields. All this at *a time* [18] when the members of the European Community are redoubling *their efforts* [19] to achieve an economic and perhaps a political *union* [20] of a new kind.

H.R.H. The Prince of Wales,
Foreign Languages for the New Europe,
Address to the Royal Society of Arts, 23 May 1990.

Write a list indicating for each of the twenty nouns (a) the class of unit realising the qualifier element, and (b) the type of extrinsic information it gives about the nominal head of the NG, e.g.
   1)   (a) Realisation by an appositive NG.
        (b) Expressing an attributive feature of the head noun.

5 *Complete the following sentences with the classes of NG qualifier given on the left:*
   1) **PrepG**:   There should be a law . . . .
   2) **PrepG**:   The countryside . . . . is lovely.
   3) **PrepG**:   A book . . . . would be a best-seller.
   4) *That*-**clause**: The discovery . . . . was fundamental for
                         scientific advance.
   5) **WH-adv clause**: The day . . . . has not arrived yet.
   6) **Rel. clause**:   She had a raucous voice . . . .
   7) **V-*ing* clause**: We went up a rickety old staircase . . . .
   8) **V-*en* clause**:   All my postcards . . . . got lost in the post.
   9) **V.inf clause**:   Have you got a licence . . . . ?
   10) **AdjG**:   I would like something . . . .
   11) **NG**:   I've just read a book about Martin Luther
                          King, ...
   12) **PrepG**:   Have you any experience . . . . ?

Module 50
1 *Mark the boundaries between the functional elements of these NGs and then analyse them as follows:*
   (a) Indicate by symbols the structure of each NG, repeating the symbol if an element is realised more than once.
   (b) Say what class of experiential information is expressed by each element.
   1)   university students
   2)   nice bright classrooms

3) my new English programme and timetable
4) our first day in class
5) that new colour magazine about photography that I bought
6) six beautiful old Chinese Ming vases
7) somebody more knowledgeable with teaching experience
e.g. 2) **eeh**: subjective adj. + objective adj. + common noun of place.

2 *Give a right-branching paraphrase of the following NGs:*
1) television aerial repair service
2) Manchester University Research Fellowship Appointments
3) daytime telephone calls price reduction
4) adult education reform proposals alarm
5) Bird Conservation Organisation Investigation Department

3 (a) *Bracket the pre-head units in the following NGs, and then paraphrase each group:*
1) the present government's unemployment benefit policy
2) European regional banks central control council report
3) the hard line Middle East crude oil exporting countries
4) university athletics team gold medal awards

(b) †*Express the following as single NGs:*
1) missiles based on land and carrying multiple warheads
2) weapons of a nuclear type having an intermediate range
3) an exhibition of robots designed for use in the home and now available all over Europe
4) a lady's suit for wearing in the evening made of velvet and having the blue colour of the night in a classic style
5) a farmhouse made of stone having the colour of honey and built two years ago in Malta.

4 †*Complete the following sentences, by reorganising, in the form of a single NG, the information given under each one. This is based on NGs which have been found in newspapers. They may however be structured in more than one way. Indicate the structures of the ones you compose, but try to place all the information before the head noun shown in brackets.*
1) *First I have to say that I'm* (a cyclist) . . . .
I'm a professional one; that is to say, my profession is racing. I have been classed in the first category and am specialised in races that have massed starts.
2) *When we were in Italy, we saw* (a statue) . . . .
a tiny statue; it was Greek; it belonged to an early period. However, it was slightly damaged; it was really exquisite; my sister said she would like to steal it.
3) *At the meeting, emphasis was laid on* (a need) . . . . .
teachers need courses; the courses should be fairly concentrated; the courses would deal with the methodology of teaching foreign

languages; they should be programmed from the point of view of other disciplines.

4)   *In the film there was* (a character) . . . .
the film was about Star Wars; the character was typical of that kind of film; he was frightening; he was grotesque.

5   †*Consider the order of the epithets and classifiers in the following sentences. Change the order if you think it is necessary, and say why. Insert a coordinator or subordinator where you think it is required; and insert commas where needed (see 50.5.4).*
1)   It was an *unforgettable, heart-breaking sad* sight.
2)   We heard a *tinkling mysterious faint* sound.
3)   Her *artistic slender long* hands fluttered in the air.
4)   She had *absolutely bewitching, black, penetrating, deep, round* eyes.
5)   The toilet was a *wooden brown smallish* box inserted in the floor.
6)   We drove through the *granite wooded threatening dark* mountains.

6   †*Revise section 50.7.2 referring to the order of qualifying units in NGs, and describe the effect of reversing their order in the examples given in 50.7.1.*

7   †*In the following sentence from a novel we have changed the positions of four qualifying units. Can you say why these positions are not appropriate and how they should be rearranged?*

A clear fire burned in a tall fireplace and an elderly MAN with a chain round his neck in evening dress and standing with his back to it, glanced up from the NEWSPAPER he was holding before his calm and severe face spread out in both hands.

8   *Read the following sentence and notice the long qualifier of the Od (**a scarf**) which continues to the end of the sentence.*

She was knitting a scarf, (the only thing I had ever known her to knit, (a long strip of red, brown, green, yellow, black (divided into sections of random sizes (according to the amount of wool she could find or unravel (from some previous scarf (that none of us could bring ourselves to wear.

Philip Smith, *The Wedding Jug.*

Can you write a sentence with a similarly long qualifier, composed of five or six units, and beginning with one of the following expressions?
(a)   She was making a dress . . .
(b)   She was preparing a meal . . .
(c)   She was writing a letter . . .
Try to use varied classes of units arranged in successive right-branching dependency.

9   *Write a short description of one of the following groups of persons or things. Include a sufficient number of epithets, classifiers and qualifiers to make the description interesting. Write it in the form of a letter to a friend:*
   1)   the members of your family
   2)   persons that you met when you were on holiday
   3)   columns of people you have seen on television, fleeing from a war zone
   4)   people and things at the scene of an earthquake (seen on TV)
   5)   some new clothes that you need to buy for yourself and some that you have seen in shops.

10   *The following extract from a savings society brochure addressed to students illustrates the coordination of infinitive qualifiers and of qualified NGs forming a group complex:*

> *Why should I save?*
> Developing the saving habit gives you more independence. Without some money behind you, you will always have to depend on someone else. Savings can give *the confidence to switch to a more challenging job, to move to a better place to live, to buy a new car, or to enjoy a more exciting holiday*. Savings give you *the power to choose* for yourself and *the freedom to run your own life*. They can make a difference for you which is well worth having.
>
> *Nationwide Building Society*

Write a similar paragraph for a travel agency under the heading: 'Why should I travel?' Change the content of the qualifiers and use other head nouns if you wish: **the chance to, the opportunity to, the possibility to,** *etc.*

11   †*Read the following short paragraph and identify the extent of each numbered NG; then indicate the syntactic function of each one in a clause or group:*

> In describing his taste in women[1], the famous baby doctor[2], Benjamin Spock [3] said: 'I have always been fascinated by rather severe women[4], women I then could charm despite their severity'[5]. The model for these women [6] – as Dr. Spock is well aware – was his own mother[7]. And if, in his early eighties[8], he is indeed a most exceptionally charming man[9], the wish to win over his mother [10] may help explain why.

12   †*Read the following extract from a travel brochure describing a tour of Scotland, and identify the extent of each numbered NG. Then write out a table of the groups indicating their syntactic functions and the class of matrix unit of which they are elements:*

This tour [1] has been devised to reveal within the space of nine days [2] much of the glory of the Highlands[3]. An added attraction [4] is a visit to the incomparable 'Winged Isle' of Skye[5], the most fascinating and perhaps most beautiful island in Great Britain[6]. Long days [7] are spent exploring the wonderful scenery of Scotland [8] with each day full of new and stimulating sights[9]. By loch side and mountain pass[10], through glens [11] and dipping into enchanting wooded valleys[12], across heather-clad moors where the red deer roam[13], the coach [14] seeks out places of outstanding natural beauty and memorable interest[15].

e.g.

Nominal Group	Class of matrix unit	Syntactic function
1) This tour	Clf	S
2) the space of nine days	PrepG	c

13   *Write a similar description of a tour you are organising with a group of students in your year. Use the following framework for an information sheet you are preparing:*

This tour has been devised to reveal within _____ much of _____. One of the highlights of the tour will be _____ _____ which is _____. We shall spend three days exploring _____, and each day we shall see _____. We shall travel through _____, along _____ and over _____. You will be able to take photos of _____ so take _____ and _____. We shall sleep in _____ _____. (*Add other information about meals, clothes, purchases*, etc.)

14   *Rewrite the following sentence in simpler, less abstract terms. Instead of de-verbal nouns like **training, supervision, replacement, recommendations, recognition,** use the corresponding verbs: **train, supervise,** etc. Avoid other abstractions such as those in the last two lines:*

Good training will come from good supervision. Mass training in research techniques cannot serve as a replacement for high quality dialogue between student and supervisor, and recommendations for improved research training should give full recognition to the problems being created in the present context by the ratio of student numbers to availability of staff.

15   *Rewrite the following sentence in a more abstract way, by nominalising some of the verbal predications:*

Most archaeologists think that men and women began to become civilised in the Middle East, where natural conditions helped them to change the way they lived from constantly moving around and hunting animals to settling down in one place and cultivating the land.

Begin: It is the opinion of most archaeologists that. . . .

11

Talking about Attributes:
The Adjectival Group

MODULE 51
Characteristics of the Adjectival Group

Summary

1   Attributes are expressed mainly by AdjGs.

2   Three structural elements: head (adj: *difficult*), modifier (adv: *extremely difficult*), qualifier (groups and clauses: *difficult to solve this problem*).

3   Many AdjGs are realised only by the head element.

4   Formally, adjectives may be simple (*tall*, *brilliant*), prefixed (*un-, im-, dis-, ab-*), suffixed (*-ful, -able, -ous, -ive*), participial (*-ing, -en*), compound (*home-made, duty-free, sunburnt*).

5   Syntactically, AdjGs function typically as **m** (in NGs) and **Cs** in clauses; less often as **d** or **h** or **q** (in NGs), **c** (in PrepGs), **m** (in AdjGs), **Co** or **A** or **D** (in clauses).

6   Semantically, AdjGs can express a state (*lonely*), a quality (*lovely*), a process (*increasing*), space (*northern*), time (*modern*), activity (*creative*), emotion (*odious*), evaluation (*true*), specification (*main*), etc.

7   Recursive realisation of adjectives (*bright and eager*) and of AdjGs: *quite easy to understand, but rather hard to remember*.

51.1   Characteristics of the AdjG

English AdjGs vary considerably in their **form**, their syntactic **functions** and in the types of lexical and grammatical **meanings** they express; and it is only on the basis of different combinations of these three types of features that it is possible to make a loose definition of the adjective as a word class.

51.2   Structure of the AdjG

The AdjG is composed of three structural elements: a head (**h**), a modifier (**m**) and a qualifier (**q**), which combine to form the following four basic structures:

```
                              AdjG
                 _____|_____
                /                |                \
               m                 h                 q

1  h:                          good
2  hq:                         good            at chess
3  mh:          very           good
4  mhq:         very           good            at chess
```

Other examples of full AdjG structure are:

extremely	hot	indeed
very	glad	that you won the match
quite	fond	of music
rather	difficult	to solve

The head of an AdjG is always realised by an adjective, which may function alone in representation of a whole AdjG. The following sentence contains four coordinated AdjGs forming an AdjG complex:

> You couldn't call it a bang or a roar or a smash; it was a *fearful, tearing, shattering, enormous* sound like the end of the world.

G. B. Shaw, *The Emperor and the Little Girl*.

In the following paragraph, only two of the AdjGs are modified ([14] and [16]) and only two qualified ([5] and [20]). Of the other groups, seven consist of single adjectives and nine of AdjG complexes:

> The Reverend James Mavor Morell is a *Christian Socialist*[1] clergyman of the Church of England, and an active member of the Guild of St. Matthew and the *Christian Social*[2] Union. A *vigorous, genial, popular*[3] man of forty, *robust and good-looking*[4], *full*[5] of energy, with *pleasant, hearty, considerate*[6] manners and a *sound, unaffected*[7] voice which he uses with the *clean, athletic*[8] articulation of a *practised*[9] orator and with a *wide*[10] range and *perfect*[11] command of expression. He has a *healthy*[12] complexion: *good*[13] forehead, with the brows somewhat *blunt*[14], and the eyes *bright and eager*[15], mouth *resolute but not particularly well-cut*[16], and a *substantial*[17] nose, with the *noble spreading*[18] nostrils of the *dramatic* [19]orator, *void*[20], like all his features, *of subtlety*.

51.3   Formal features of the adjectival head

51.3.1   Simple and derived forms

We assume here a familiarity with the morphology of English adjectives and limit ourselves to the following brief summary:

(a) The most frequently used adjectives in English are monosyllabic or bisyllabic words of native origin such as *good, tall, low, foul, dumb, narrow, early, earnest*, which have no distinctive form to mark them as adjectives.

(b) Many adjectives are derived from nouns, adjectives and verbs by the addition of certain characteristic suffixes, about half of them being of native origin, as in green*ish*, hope*ful*, hand*some*, handy, fore*most*; and others from Latin or French, as in read*able*, second*ary*, appar*ent*, civ*ic*, creat*ive*, dub*ious*, and very many others. The variety is so great that a complete list does not help to identify a word as an adjective.

(c) Most adjectival prefixes are added to words which are already adjectives: *unhappy, discourteous, subnormal, irrelevant*. Some adjectives are formed by adding the prefix *a-* to a verb (*asleep, awake, ablaze*).

(d) Many adjectives have compound forms composed of various classes of words, e.g.

noun + adjective:	duty-free goods	= free of duty
adjective + noun:	long-distance calls	= made over long distances
adverb + adjective:	evergreen tree	= it is always green
adverb + adverb:	well-off persons	= (idiomatic)

Once again, there is no morphological characteristic of compound words that by itself classes them as adjectives. Consequently, additional criteria must be sought.

51.3.2   Participles and participial adjectives

Many present and past participles of verbs realise grammatical functions which are typical of those realised by adjectives, and for this reason are recognised as adjectival homomorphs. We indicate them here by the symbols *-ing* and *-en*, and recognise the following classes:

(a) A small set of forms which are never or very rarely used as part of a Verbal Group, but only as modifiers in NGs or as attributive Complements in a clause:

> *-ing*: interesting, amazing, charming, disappointing, pleasing, etc.
> *-en*: indebted, ashamed, concerted, assorted, sophisticated, etc.

(b) An increasing number of adjectives functioning both as modifiers and Complements, and coined by adding *-ing* or *-ed* not to verbs but to nouns:

> *-ing*: enterprising, neighbouring, appetising.
> *-en*: talented, skilled, gifted, wooded, detailed.

We shall call these 'pseudo-participial' adjectives.

(c) A large number of participial forms derived from transitive verbs, which can be used as modifiers and Complements, and also as part of the Predicator in a clause:

A *confusing* remark. That is *confusing*. You are *confusing* me.

Other common examples:

-ing:	annoying	bewildering	frightening	surprising
	amusing	convincing	satisfying	boring
-en:	annoyed	bewildered	frightened	surprised
	amused	convinced	satisfied	bored

In their attributive functions (as modifiers or Complements), these participial adjectives can be graded:

-ing: *very* bewildering news; the news is *most* bewildering.
-en: *rather* bewildered tourists; the tourists seemed *extremely* bewildered.

(d) Certain participles which modify a referent noun can focus on the process as a temporary, non-intrinsic feature of the referent, and not as an intrinsic or permanent quality. In this case, the participle cannot be graded nor be classed as an adjective:

*a very approaching train; *an extremely dying custom;
*a rather furnished apartment; *a slightly setting sun.

It can, however, be modified by adverbs referring to the speed or extent of the process:

the slowly setting sun;   a fast approaching train;
a fully furnished apartment;   a well polished table.

The semantic difference between focusing on a state and focusing on a process is sometimes reflected in the choice of *very* or *much* as modifier:

a *very* polished speech   (*state*: well presented, elegant)
a *much* polished speech   (*process*: carefully revised)

When used predicatively, *-ing* participles of this type have verbal not adjectival value: *A train was approaching*; *The custom is dying*. Past participles may often have either interpretation: in *The flat was furnished*, the participle may be understood either as part of a passive verb form or as the Complement of the copula *was*.

When used as modifiers, participles of this kind often denote a subclass of the noun referent, by indicating a process associated with it:

running water, writing paper, a washing machine, trained workers,
fried eggs, furnished flats.

Most participial adjectives are related to verbs; a few are derived from nouns: appetite – *appetising* (food); enterprise – an *enterprising* person; neighbour – *neighbouring* villages.

Some have a figurative meaning in certain collocations:

-ing: driving rain; a promising student; a running commentary.
-en: a tried method; a guarded remark; a drawn face.

(e) Many participial forms are compounded with a noun, an adjective or an adverbial prefix, whose syntactic relationship with the verbal participle may be Subject, Object or Adjunct:

> heart-breaking news; good-looking girl; incoming mail.

Pseudo-participial adjectives can also be compounded:

> a fair-haired child; a four-footed animal.

In these cases, the pseudo-participle cannot be used alone:

> *a haired child, *a footed animal.

Compound forms are extremely common in English where new ones are freely coined every day, many of them being nonce formations, such as *ankle-twisting* and *toil-broken* coined by Bernard Shaw in the following paragraph. They are found especially in registers such as journalism, advertising, fast-moving narrative or poetic style, where complexity of thought is combined with economy of expression.

The relative absence of morphological markers in English adjectives can be observed in the following text, where some are marked (e.g. poison*ous*), others are not (e.g. *dull*), and two are compounds:

> As I am not a *born*[1] cockney I have no illusions on the subject of the country. The *uneven*[2], *ankle-twisting*[3] roads; the *dusty*[4] hedges; the ditch with its *dead*[5] dogs, *rank*[6] weeds and swarms of *poisonous*[7] flies; the groups of children torturing something; the *dull*[8] *toil-broken*[9], prematurely *old*[10], *agricultural*[11] labourer; the savage[12] tramp; the manure heaps with their *horrible*[13] odour; the chain of mile-stones, from inn to inn, from cemetery to cemetery: all these I pass heavily by until a *distant*[14] telegraph pole or signal post tells me that the *blessed*[15], *rescuing*[16] train is at hand.
>
> G. B. Shaw, *A Sunday on the Surrey Hills*.

[1]participial; [2]prefixed; [3]compound; [4]suffixed; [5]participial; [6]unmarked; [7]suffixed; [8]unmarked; [9]compound; [10]unmarked; [11]suffixed; [12]unmarked; [13]suffixed; [14]unmarked; [15]participial; [16]participial.

51.4 Semantic types of Attributes expressed by AdjGs

Adjectives express the following major types of Attributes:

(i) an inherent quality:

> *tall trees*; *a beautiful dress*; *a reliable person*.

(ii) an emotion or evaluation of the speaker:

> *outrageous behaviour*; *encouraging results*; an entrancing smile.

(iii) an active or passive process ('participial adjectives'):

> *a frightening experience; a surprising result; a soothing sound; a frightened child; a surprised winner; frozen foods.*

(iv) a temporary state:

> *The baby is asleep; I felt lonely; He left the door ajar;* You look pretty; *He turned white; They became silent.*

(v) a spatial feature:

> *Greek* sculpture; the *Western* powers; *parliamentary* debates.

(vi) a temporal feature:

> *mediaeval history; occasional* visitors; the *future* king.

(vii) an Attribute related to a field of activity:

> an *atomic* explosion; a *medical* analysis; a *mechanical* process.

(viii) emphatic evaluation:

> *sheer* nonsense; *mere* repetition; **utter* rubbish; a *real* mess; a *true* genius; *absolute* folly; a *perfect* fool; *pure* ignorance.

(ix) restriction or specification:

> an *only* child; the *previous* page; a *certain* person; the *main* road; the *sole* survivor; the *chief* reason.

(x) Some adjectives denote a subclass, not an Attribute, of the noun referent (see also 48.3.2):

> *electric* light, *annual* meeting, *cultural* activities.

In types (viii) and (ix), the words *sheer, mere, utter, only, previous, main, chief, sole* cannot function as predicative Complements. The words *real, true, absolute, perfect, pure, certain* are used predicatively when they have qualitative (not emphatic or restrictive) meaning.

The following short extract illustrates some of the major types of Attributes expressed by English adjectives, all used as modifiers in NGs:

> There was someone or something in the house. What was I to do? I could now hear the *soft*[1] *grating*[2] sound of the waves, like a *gentle*[3] scratching of fingers upon a *soft*[4] surface. And I felt upon the *empty*[5] *darkening*[6] road a *shuddering*[7] sense of my *utter*[8] solitude, my vulnerability, among these *silent*[9] rocks, beside this *self-absorbed*[10] and *alien*[11] sea.
>
> I. Murdoch, The Sea, The Sea.

[1]inherent quality; [2]process (auditory); [3]inherent quality; [4]inherent quality; [5]state (physical); [6]process (visual); [7]process (mental); [8]emphasis (totality); [9]inherent quality; [10]process (mental); [11]emotive.

Although it is mainly the semantic feature of attribution that induces us to classify a word as an adjective, as we have tacitly done in the above text, this is not an infallible criterion for classification, any more than the morphological one. For example, in the expressions *the then president*, *the iron curtain*, *rising prices*, the words *then*, *iron*, *rising* are normally classed as an adverb, a noun and a verb, and it would be confusing to reclassify them as adjectives simply because the temporal circumstance, the material entity and the active process which they denote function semantically as Attributes of nouns. There is no grammatical problem in saying that an adverb or noun or verb functions as an epithet or a classifier in a NG or as Subject Complement in a clause; but word classification is, in fact, affected by syntactic function and therefore calls for a brief consideration.

51.5   Syntactic functions of AdjGs

AdjGs can realise the following syntactic functions in group and clause structures:

In groups:

1	modifier in a NG:	a *very good* actor, *rather heavy* rain
2	qualifier in a NG:	something *cheap*, the person *responsible*
3	head of a NG:	the *poorest*, the *sick*, the *most expensive*
4	completive of a PrepG:	at *last*, for *good*, in *short*
5	modifier in an AdjG:	*bright* red, *pale* blue, *red* hot

In clauses:

6	Complement of the Subject:	The acting was *brilliant*.
7	Complement of the Object:	I consider that *offensive*.
8	Adjunct:	I'm receiving you *loud and clear*.
9	Disjunct:	*Strange*, I never suspected him.

Since all of the syntactic functions mentioned above can be realised by other classes of words besides adjectives, no single function can identify a word as an adjective. At the same time no single word in the language can realise all the functions mentioned above. It is normal to classify as 'central' adjectives those many words which function both as 'descriptive' modifiers of nouns (see 48.2) and as Complements of the Subject (see 7.1.3). Those which realise other functions or only one or neither of these 'central' functions are classified as 'peripheral' or 'non-central'. The following have only one of the two central functions and are classed as peripheral adjectives:

(a) not used as modifiers: *afraid, asleep, ablaze, afloat, alive, alone, alike, aware, averse, well*.

(b) not used as Subject Complement: *utter, outright, chief, main, sole, only, principal, former, latter, etc.*

The items of set (b) have a further restriction in that they cannot be graded or intensified: **very principal*, **extremely chief*, **fairly utter*. This also applies to adjectives functioning as classifiers: **a very atomic bomb*, **a rather Egyptian mummy*, **fairly prehistorical remains* (see 48.4). Others, such as *legal*, *blind*, *agricultural* can denote an Attribute or a subclass; they are gradable as Attributes, but not gradable as classifiers.

The following description illustrates the relative frequency of some of the grammatical functions which can be realised by adjectives and AdjGs. In this particular example of elaborate description, the function of NG epithet is by far the most frequent.

Arriving in Spain

A *brilliant*[1] November morning with a sky of diamond *blue*[2] above the bay and the *red*[3] flowers of a *long*[4] summer still glowing darkly on the Rock. The *intense*[5] blackness of the *lampless*[6] night had rolled away to reveal, *incandescent on the northern horizon*[7], the country we had come to seek. It crouched before us in a great ring of *lion-coloured*[8] mountains, *raw, sleeping and savage*[9]. There were the *scarred and crumpled*[10] valleys. The *sharp*[11] peaks *wreathed in their dusty fires*[12] and below them the *white*[13] towns *piled high on their little hills*[14] and the *empty*[15] roads running *crimson*[16] along the faces of the cliffs. Already, across the water, one heard or fancied one heard the sobbing of asses, the cries and *salty*[17] voices cutting through the *thin gold*[18] air. And from a *steep*[19] hillside rose a column of smoke, *cool as marble, pungent as pine*[20], which hung like a signal over the landscape, *obscure, imperative and motionless*[21].

Laurie Lee, *A Rose for Winter*.

[1]**m** in NG; [2]**h** in NG; [3–6)]**m** in NG; [7]**Co** in Clnf; [8]**m** in NG; [9]**q** in NG; [10–11]**m** in NG;[12]**q** in NG;[13]**m** in NG; [14]**q** in NG; [15]**m** in NG; [16]**Cs** in Clnf; [17–19]**m** in NG; [20–21]**q** in NG.

The non-central syntactic functions that can be realised by adjectives are not criterial for classification, since they can also be realised by nouns, verbs, adverbs or PrepGs. Among these functions must be included classifying modifiers, which are typically realised not by adjectives but by nouns (e.g. *leather* jacket) or non-attributive participles (e.g. the *coming* year, a *growing* tendency, an *unposted* letter). It must be recognised, however, that the distinction between attribution and non-attribution is not always clear, and may depend on our interpretation.

MODULE 52
Modification of the Attribute

Summary

1   Five systems of modification: grading, intensification, attenuation, quantification, description.

2   **Grading**: knowledge of basic forms is assumed; comment only on the meaning of certain items: *further*, *elder*, etc. Structures of sufficiency (*enough*) and excess (*too*).

3   **Intensification**: high: *very*, *much*, *most*, *extremely*; *raving* (mad); medium: *quite*, *rather*, *pretty*, *fairly*.

4   **Attenuation**: *slightly* (soiled), *somewhat* (different), *not very* (good), *not fully* (aware), *hardly* (likely).

5   **Quantification**: exact: *a mile* (long); *2-feet* thick; *10 years* old; non-exact: *not that* long; *not so* long.

6   **Description**: by adjs: *pale* green, *dark* blue, *deep* red; by advs: *strangely* silent, *cheerfully* confident.

7   **Submodification**: *much too* easy, *really quite* angry; *not very academically* inclined.

8   **Recursive modification**: *really and truly* grateful; *more and more* certain.

52.1   Grading the Attribute

We assume here a knowledge of the basic forms of grading adjectives summarised in the following six levels, and comment only on certain semantic and syntactic features of individual items:

		Morphological	Syntactic
1	**Absolute superiority**:	the easiest	the most difficult
2	**Comparative superiority**:	easier	more difficult
3	**Equality**:		as easy, as difficult
4	**Comparative inferiority**:		less easy, less difficult
5	**Absolute inferiority**:		the least easy, the least difficult
6	**Sufficiency**:		easy enough, difficult enough, adequately furnished

The following adjectives have irregular forms for grades 1 and 2:

good, better, best   far, farther, farthest
bad, worse, worst   far, further, furthest

The word *further* can also be used with the sense of 'other', 'later', 'additional':

There will be a further meeting next week.
The theatre is closed until further notice.

The adjective *elder, eldest* (alternative to *older, oldest*) refer only to persons and function only as modifiers not as Complements:

my elder son; our eldest daughter; an elder brother or sister;
*My brother is elder than me. *He is the eldest of the children.

The adjective *elderly* is not comparative, but refers euphemistically to a person approaching old age.

The words *upper, inner, outer*, are used in a positive, not a comparative, sense:

the upper classes; my inner life; the outer walls.

The following formations of superior degree may be noticed:

uppermost, innermost, outermost, foremost, hindmost, topmost.

The following adjectives have comparative form but, when modifying nouns, they do not always imply comparison:

higher: higher education   (= university level)
lower: lower classes   (= working class)
earlier: his earlier novels (= first or previous)
later: his later years   (= last)
prior: a prior occasion   (= previous)

The comparative degree of certain other adjectives is also sometimes only implicit and almost equivalent to a positive degree:

junior rank (= low)   inferior quality (= bad)   major error (= great)
senior rank (= high) superior quality (= good) minor error (= small)

Some of these features of grade 2 forms can be observed in texts such as the following, referring to matters of status and dimension:

Both the basic rate of income tax charged on *lower* levels of income,
and the *higher* rate of income tax charged on *higher* incomes, have
been increased ... A revised personal allowance for *elderly* taxpayers
has now been introduced and any *earlier* provisions have been
abolished.

The grade of 'sufficiency' (grade 6) may be considered as a small subsystem in itself, consisting of three terms: 'excess', 'sufficiency', 'insufficiency', expounded by the adverbs *too, enough, not enough*, respectively. When functioning predicatively, that is at **Cs**, the AdjG structure is as follows:

excess: This knife is *too sharp.*
sufficiency: Is this knife *sharp enough*?
insufficiency: This knife is *not sharp enough.*

When the AdjG modifies a noun, the NG structures are as follows:

excess: This is *too sharp a knife.*
sufficiency: This is *a sharp enough knife.*
insufficiency: This is *not a sharp enough knife.*

If the noun is uncountable or plural (e.g. *weather, knives*), only the predicative structure is used for the expression of 'excess':

excess: The weather was *too wet.*   *It was *too wet weather.*
             These knives are *too sharp.* *These are *too sharp knives.*

The degree of excess is sometimes expounded by the lexical item *over* (AmE *overly*) used as the first element of a compound adjective, or by other lexical adverbs in *-ly*:

Don't be *over-anxious* about the future.
Perhaps you are being *overly cautious* in your proposals.
I think you are *exaggeratedly pessimistic* about your chances.

52.2   Intensifying the Attribute

Intensification is a kind of grading and will be described here in terms of three degrees: 'high', 'medium' and 'attenuated'. They constitute a cline rather than a scale of fixed points, since they are realised exclusively by lexical items rather than varied structures. In spoken language, the intended degree of intensification can be reinforced by stress and intonation patterns. The following lists of lexical exponents and representative collocations illustrate the three broad degrees of intensification.

52.2.1   High intensification

This is expressed by 'grammatical' adverbs, 'lexical' adverbs, adjectives and, exceptionally, nouns. The following examples show them in AdjGs in both of the central adjectival functions:

most:	a *most* beautiful woman;	His ideas are *most* odd.
very:	A *very* fortunate event;	The lecture proved *very* boring.
all:	An *all*-powerful leader;	She seemed *all* upset.
quite:	*Quite* a different matter;	You are *quite* right.
how:	*How* strange!	*How* sincere do you think he is?

more than: A *more than* stupid remark; Rain is *more than* likely.
litotes: *Not a little* worried (= very); I'm *not unaware* (= I'm
Less than brilliant (= not at quite aware).
all).

Some intensifiers, such as *very* and *extremely*, have a wide range of use. Others are more limited to specific types of adjectives or to individual ones. The following are common collocations:

raving mad;   dripping wet;   boiling hot;   freezing cold;   blind
drunk;   dead straight;   wide awake;   fast asleep.

highly controversial;   radically opposed;   loudly
proclaimed;   eminently suitable;   acutely aware;   deeply
moving;   deadly serious;   desperately busy;   supremely important.

Emotive intensification occurs in both colloquial and non-colloquial style:

hellishly hot;   stinkingly rich;   fiendishly cruel;   desperately
busy;   maddeningly forgetful;   deadly serious.

Notice the emotive use of *too* in expressions such as:

The film was *too* awful for words!

and its meaning of *very* in:

I shall be *only too pleased* to help you (= very pleased)

Adjectives of colour and nationality, which are typically non-gradable, can be graded and intensified when they refer not to the colour or nationality itself but to a temporary state or characteristic of the entity which has the Attribute:

His face went very red.
That's a very American way of thinking.

The adverb *quite* which normally expresses a medium degree of intensification (see 52.2.2) as in *quite good*, *quite interesting*, takes on a high degree when it modifies an emotive adjective as in *quite amazing*, *quite incredible*, *quite disastrous*. The intensifying value of this word varies according to the Attribute it modifies.

52.2.2   Medium intensification

A medium degree of intensification is expressed by the four adverbs *quite*, *pretty*, *rather*, *fairly*. Within the degree of 'medium', we can recognise four subdegrees in order of descending intensification:

It's *quite* cold here in the winter.
It's *pretty* cold here in the winter. (informal, spoken style).
It's *rather* cold here in the winter.
It's *fairly* cold here in the winter.

We may gloss the meanings of these words in broad terms as follows:

(a) *Quite* denotes moderate but unequivocal intensification of the Attribute, whether this is appreciative as in *quite pleased, quite satisfactory, quite nice*, or pejorative as in *quite dangerous, quite pessimistic, quite nasty*, or neutral as in *quite tall, quite cheap/expensive, quite short/long*.

(b) *Pretty* expresses the same degree of intensification as *quite*, with all types of gradable Attributes, but has an approximative, less categorical value characteristic especially of informal speech; e.g. *She's pretty good-looking, I feel pretty tired after that long walk, It's pretty hot here in summer, When I twisted my ankle, the pain was pretty awful*.

(c) *Rather* intensifies less strongly than *quite* and *pretty*, and implies on the part of the speaker a subjective attitude oscillating between approval of favourable Attributes such as *rather good, rather easy, rather clever*, and reserve or disapproval of unfavourable ones: *rather ill, rather poor, rather difficult*. With Attributes such as *warm, easy, slow* which may be interpreted either as favourable or unfavourable, *rather* implies a negative attitude meaning *too warm, too easy, too slow*. In the case of antonymous pairs of Attributes such as *clean/dirty, happy/unhappy, satisfactory/unsatisfactory*, one of the two terms is semantically unmarked, that is, the norm. In these examples it is the first of each pair; and the other is the marked term. In these cases *rather* is not used with the unmarked term; we do not usually say **rather clean, *rather happy, *rather satisfactory*, though we may certainly do so if that is the attitude we wish to express: for example, of polite, tentative appreciation, in reply to a pejorative attitude:

    A. That was a foolish thing to do!
    B. Oh, really? I thought it was *rather clever*.

(d) *Fairly* can oscillate between moderate intensification and slight attenuation. It collocates more frequently with favourable Attributes than with unfavourable ones, e.g. *fairly honest, fairly intelligent, fairly reasonable*, but not **fairly dishonest, *fairly foolish, *fairly unreasonable*.

We may add that *rather* can, in addition, modify a noun as a predeterminer: *rather a bore, rather an angel, rather a devil*, where the noun is affective and has a corresponding adjective (*boring, angelic, devilish*). *Fairly* does not have this possibility: **fairly a bore/angel/devil*.

The above glosses represent only the typical semantic orientation of these four intensifiers. At the same time, their references are all slightly indeterminate, rather than fixed points on the scale. The attitudes they express can be varied in speech, but not in writing, by intonation. A strong falling tone on the adjective (not the intensifier) marks an increase of the intensification, and a fall–rise indicates a reduction of the normal degree of intensification, implying doubt or hesitation.

The following ironical report from the economics section of a newspaper may be cited as a normal everyday use of intensified Attributes in English:

> A remarkable *entirely new* economic cure-all has just emerged from *widely extensive* tests. The miracle drug, called taxcuts, is the *most versatile* drug since penicillin. The manufacturers say that if applied in *sufficiently liberal* doses, it will make people *more hardworking* and *less preoccupied* with their own financial problems.

52.3 Attenuating the Attribute

Attenuation refers to a slight degree of the Attribute or its entire absence, and is expounded by the following items:

slightly:	This soup is *slightly salty*.
somewhat:	I am *somewhat worried* about your health.
mildly:	Export figures have been *mildly encouraging* recently.
to some extent:	What you say is *to some extent true*.
a little:	My rheumatism has been *a little troublesome* lately.
a bit (colloq.):	I thought his smile was *a bit ironic*.
kind of (colloq.):	The atmosphere was *kind of weird and threatening*.
sort of (colloq.):	I don't trust him very far; he's *sort of shifty*.

The non-assertiveness of polar interrogative and conditional clauses is sometimes attenuated slightly by inserting *at all* before or after the adjective:

Are you *at all* worried? Are you worried *at all*?
We'd like to stay another week, if it's *at all* possible (*or* if it's possible *at all*).

Slight attenuation or reservation can be expressed by negating a high degree.

not very:	Forest fires are *not very likely* in winter.
not quite:	I'm *not quite sure* what you mean.
not entirely:	I'm sorry, but that's *not entirely true*.
not particularly:	Most people are *not particularly fond* of washing up.
not fully:	Your arguments are *not fully convincing*.
not too:	I'm *not too familiar* with the technical details.
not altogether:	David is *not altogether satisfied* in his new job.
not nearly:	He's *not nearly clever enough* to study at a university.

The following modifiers express a minimal degree of attribution and often imply a certain degree of the opposite Attribute; they are sometimes called 'semi-negatives':

none too:	His marriage is *none too happy* and his future *none too bright.*
(not) any too:	Efforts to reduce unemployment haven*'t* been *any too successful* so far.
hardly:	It is *hardly likely* that the problem will be solved soon.
scarcely:	The amount of poverty in the world is *scarcely believable.*
barely:	Light summer dresses are *barely necessary* in Britain.
. . . at all:	Hardly likely *at all*; scarcely believable *at all*; barely necessary *at all.*

Absence or denial of the Attribute is expressed as follows:

not at all:	I'm *not at all surprised* at the result.
not in the least:	It's *not in the least necessary* to drive so fast.
not in the slightest:	Their reasons are *not in the slightest difficult* to understand.

These three modification structures may be discontinuous:

I'm *not* surprised *at all* at the result.

52.4 Quantifying the Attribute

52.4.1 Exact quantification

If we ask the questions *How deep is the ocean? How long was the queue? How high is Everest? How old are you?*, the depth, length, height and age can be measured or quantified by saying:

The ocean is *a mile deep.*   The queue was *100 yards long.*
Everest is *8,708 metres high.*   I am *20 years old.*

These AdjGs can be lexicalised as compound adjectives to modify nouns:

a *mile-deep* ocean   a *hundred-yards-long* queue
an *8,708-metres-high* mountain a *twenty-year-old* girl

The noun of measurement is sometimes singularised in this structure: *a twenty-years-old girl* or *a twenty-year-old girl*. Sometimes, the quantifier is just a number:

The cars were *four* deep on the motorway.

52.4.2 Non-exact quantification

Non-measurable quantification is expressed by the deictic adverbs *that* and *so*, their reference being either anaphoric (back to something mentioned previously in the text) or exophoric (to some standard generally understood outside the text):

anaphoric reference: A. My grandfather is over ninety years old.
                           B. Really? I didn't think he was *that old/so old.*

exophoric reference: A. Did you enjoy the trip?
                           B. No, it wasn't *that/so interesting* after all.

The same AdjG structure can be used to modify a singular noun:

B. It wasn't *that/so interesting a trip* after all.

It cannot be used, however, to modify a plural or a non-countable noun:

The trips were not that/so long.   **They were not that/so long trips.
The thunder was not that/so loud.   *It was not that/so loud thunder.

When the quantified head is a singular indefinite count noun, the determiner *a* is placed immediately before it.

These patterns are the same as those used with the intensifying adverb *too*. They should be contrasted with those of the determiner *such* which can also express intensification and, in addition, be used with mass and plural nouns:

It wasn't such an interesting trip after all.
I have never known such kindness before.
I have never seen such interesting places before.

Questions with *How*? can also be asked about non-measurable Attributes:

How important is this matter?   How serious are you?
How intelligent is he?   How hungry are you?

52.5   Describing the Attribute

If adjectives serve to describe nouns, they themselves can also be described, by reference to (a) a quality or (b) a specific context:

(a) Qualitative modification of adjectives is realised by the following classes of units:

-ly adverbs: strangely attractive; deathly pale; wretchedly poor; happily married.
adjectives: light brown; deep red; soft pink; dark blue; vivid green; bright yellow.
nouns: pitch black; emerald green; blood red; rose pink; pearl grey; paper-thin; feather-light; day-long; world-wide.

The following comments are necessary regarding these structures. An expression like *a strangely attractive city* does not mean '*a strange and attractive city*' but '*a city which is attractive in a strange way*'; it is the adjective (*attractive*) which is modified, not the noun (*city*). The structure 'adj + adj' (e.g. *light brown*) is used specially with colour adjectives. When it modifies a noun, ambiguity may occur: *The deep blue sea* (a sea of *deep blue*? or a *deep sea* which is blue?)

(b) Relational (or contextual) modification indicates the sense in which the adjective is to be understood. It is realised by:

-ly adverbs:	socially acceptable; economically difficult; technologically impressive; financially independent; mentally retarded; physically handicapped.
nouns:	music mad; girl crazy; foot weary; duty free.

The 'noun + adj' structure is frequently lexicalised as a compound adjective: *music-mad*, *duty-free*, etc. The structure is extremely productive owing to its economy of expression. For this very reason, however, its meaning is not always clear:

trigger-happy:	ready to shoot on any pretext.
air-tight:	hermetically closed (so tight that air cannot enter).
fool-proof:	infallible; proof against human misuse.
house-proud:	excessively devoted to, and proud of, maintaining the appearance, cleanliness, etc., of one's house.

The following short paragraph exemplifies the use of modified AdjGs characteristic of a reputable newspaper:

He is one of *the most compellingly*[1] *watchable* comic talents I have seen for a long time; a *slightly*[2] *comic* nose, a *retiringly*[3] *unassertive* chin and a wide *loosely*[4] *shaped* mouth contribute a *totally convincing*[5] performance as the court jester. He obviously has a *cheerfully perceptive*[6] gift for comedy.

[1]intensification; [2]attenuation; [3]description; [4]description; [5]intensification; [6]description.

Modification of adjectives is particularly frequent in advertising texts, which are designed to convince the public of the exceptional attributes of commercial products:

BECAUSE we offer you a choice of over 200 of the *very* finest destinations in 12 countries throughout Europe.
BECAUSE each and every one of our camp-sites is *carefully* hand-picked for their wonderful facilities.
BECAUSE our *ready* erected tents and mobile-homes are *the most* luxurious, spacious and comprehensively equipped you will find.
BECAUSE of our *fully* trained, *ever*-helpful, *completely* bilingual couriers.
BECAUSE of our *widely* comprehensive guides, travel documentation and children's fun packs – *quite simply* the best in the holiday business.
. . . . . etc.
Anything else is just camping.

Eurocamp

52.6   Submodification of the Attribute

Modifiers of degree (e.g. *less* in *less interesting*) are often themselves graded or intensified by a submodifier (**sm**) placed before them, e.g. *rather less interesting*. The following are examples of this **smhq** structure which occur in both spoken and written discourse.

sm	m	h	sm	m	h
far	too	servile	quite	seriously	wounded
much	more	productive	very	deeply	grieved
much	the less	remarkable	most	unusually	late
quite	the most	useful	so	oddly	aggressive
not	all that	attractive	sort of	mysteriously	silent
all	the more	intriguing	kind of	threateningly	dark
none	the more	justifiable	rather	sentimentally	inclined
none	the less	enjoyable	somewhat	strangely	preoccupied
just	as	complicated	really	soaking	wet
not nearly	as	nice	absolutely	stark	naked

Descriptive modifiers in *-ly* can be submodified by degree adverbs in *-ly*, though this combination tends to be avoided in writing more than in speech:

sm	m	h
absolutely	completely	mad
extremely	badly	written
extraordinarily	attractively	presented
really	absurdly	long

Submodifiers in AdjGs can be further modified by subsubmodifiers (**ssm**), the following being attested examples:

	ssm	sm	m	h	noun
The report is not	all	that	tremendously	convincing.	
Aren't you being	just	the least	tiny bit	presumptuous?	
The concert was	quite	unusually	deeply	moving.	
She always					
stays at a	far	too	absurdly	expensive	hotel.
Those are	much	too	easily	forgotten	truths.

The following examples have also been attested, in which the first word of the AdjG may be described as a subsubsubmodifier, a structure which may be considered as over-elaborated and emotive:

	sssm	ssm	sm	m	h
She divorced her	at that time	still	very	sadly	impecunious husband.

	sssm	ssm	sm	m	h
She was	really	quite	the most	stunningly	handsome woman.

This type of AdjG structure reflects two converse types of intensification which are characteristic of many English speakers:

(a) That of attenuating the negative value of an Attribute:

His work is *really not quite* accurate enough.

(b) That of reinforcing a positive value:

She wore *the most absolutely* gorgeous dress.

The submodifier of the modifier *enough* is placed immediately before the adjective:

hardly good *enough*;   *not nearly* clever *enough*;   *quite* old *enough*.

52.7   Recursive modification of the Attribute

We refer here not to progressive modification and sub- or subsubmodification of an adjective as in *quite absurdly long,* but to the use of two or more paratactically or hypotactically related adverbial modifiers, as in the following attested examples:

. . *absurdly, incomprehensibly and untypically* long.

. . the most stylish, *the most gorgeously, adorably,* artificial, slightly patronising jokey tone.

His latest novel has been *unusually, in fact surprisingly, though quite deservedly* successful.

(Book review).

It can be appreciated that this type of structure would prove excessively ornate if used too much in a single text. Examples, however, can be found in certain florid styles of writing.

Finally, as in other languages, we may notice the repetition, in familiar speech, of certain short adverbs to modify or submodify adjectival heads:

very very good;   more and more difficult;   much much better;   far far longer;   less and less interesting.

MODULE 53
Qualification of the Attribute

Summary

1   When an Attribute (e.g. *happy*) functions in a clause, as Complement of the Subject (e.g. *I am happy*) or the Object, it is often followed by a qualifying unit relating it either to a fact (e.g. *... that you are here*) or a process or situation (e.g. *... to see you*), or to a circumstance (e.g. *about your success*). This information explains the different ways in which the Attribute is to be understood and is expressed by different grammatical structures, mainly finite and non-finite clauses and PrepGs.

2   When the Attribute is not modified, the structures are as above. When the qualifier is a PrepG the preposition is determined by the adjective and the context: *dependent on*, *clever at/with/in*, etc.

3   When the Attribute is modified (graded, intensified, etc.), the modifier partly determines the type of qualifier: *too cold for us*, *too cold to swim*, *too cold for us to swim*, *too cold for swimming in the sea*.

4   When the Attribute modifies a noun, it is separated from its qualifier: *so difficult* a problem *that I couldn't solve it*.

5   The qualifier may be realised recursively, when the AdjG functions as Cs or Co: *Such behaviour is difficult to forgive and even to explain.*

53.1   Qualification of unmodified adjectives

When adjectival heads are not modified, they are often qualified by finite clauses, non-finite clauses or Prepositional Groups, which relate the Attribute to a fact, a situation, a process or a circumstance and so tell us how the Attribute is to be understood.

53.1.1   Qualification by finite clauses

This structure relates the adjectival Attribute to a factual qualifier and is realised by a finite clause introduced optionally by *that*:

We are sure (that) he is innocent.
We are proud (that) you are so successful.

After some adjectives of emotive or modal meaning such as *anxious, willing, eager, insistent, agreed, glad, sorry, determined, resolved*, the putative auxiliary *should* is sometimes used in a *that*-clause, especially in BrE (see 44.9).

> We are proud (that) you *should be so successful.*
> The public is anxious that the truth *should be known.*
> We are not willing that justice *should be forgotten.*

The putative or hypothetical meaning of *should* must be distinguished from its use as an auxiliary denoting obligation, as in: *You should always tell the truth*.

After a very small number of adjectives (e.g. *anxious, insistent, willing, determined, resolved*, but not common ones such as *glad, sorry, happy*, etc.) the subjunctive mood is occasionally found:

> Bill's wife is *insistent that he give* up smoking.

This form is used more frequently in AmE. In BrE, the subjunctive is moribund and used only in formal style.

The qualifier can also be realised by a *WH*-clause:

> I am not quite *clear what you mean.*

If both clauses refer to the same Subject, the qualifier may be non-finite:

> Many people are *doubtful how to vote.*

In the following type of sentence, the second clause does not function as qualifier of the preceding adjective, but as extraposed Subject, replaced by *it* in the main clause (see 30.5.1).

Postposed S	
It is not clear *why he left.*	= *Why he left* is not clear.
It's possible *that he's ill.*	= *That he's ill* is possible.
It was crazy *to drive like that.*	= *To drive like that* was crazy.

53.1.2   Qualification by non-finite clauses or VGs

This AdjG structure is used to describe the relation between an Attribute and a process or situation. In the following examples (i–ix), both refer to the same Subject:

(i) The adjective evaluates the process performed by the Subject:

> You are *kind to visit me.*
> She must be *clever to have won the first prize.*

(ii) The adjective describes the manner of performing the process:

> The Minister was *quick to reject the accusation.*
> You are *very slow to give your opinion*, aren't you?

(iii) The adjective expresses an emotion caused by the process:

> Everyone was *indignant to hear about the scandal.*
> We were all *delighted to receive your invitation.*

(iv) The adjective expresses an attitude or state concerning the process:

> I am not *willing to believe that story.*
> The police are *powerless to take action in this matter.*

(v) The adjective expresses a state of the Subject:

> Mountain water is not always *safe to drink.*
> Are these pamphlets *free to take away* (or *to be taken away*)?

(vi) The adjective forms part of a lexical auxiliary (*be sure to*, *be likely to*, *be bound to*, etc., in a VG (see 37.3). It has modal value denoting the tendency of the process to occur:

> He is *sure to arrive late.*   It is *bound to rain.*
> She is *likely to get angry.*   I am *apt to forget details.*

(vii) The adjective evaluates the process, realised by an *-ing* clause:

> You were *foolish going out without an overcoat.*
> He must have been *crazy driving as fast as that.*

(viii) The adjective denotes an Attribute simultaneous with the process:

> Mrs. Smith was *busy getting the lunch ready.*
> I was *surprised suddenly getting a letter from you.*

(ix) After some adjectives, but not others, either V-*to*-inf or V-*ing* can be used:

> You are *foolish going out.*   She was *busy getting lunch.*
> You are *foolish to go out.*   *She was busy to get lunch.

After certain adjectives both forms can be used, but with different meanings:

> Be *careful crossing the road.*   (= Be careful while crossing . . .)
> Be *careful to cross the road.*   (= Do not forget to cross . . .)

The above examples refer to processes performed by the Subject of the clause, that is, the Carrier of the Attribute. The following ones refer to processes not performed by the Subject:

(x) The adjective does not refer to the Subject:

> Smoking is *difficult to give up.*

This sentence does not mean that smoking is difficult, but that to give up smoking is difficult.

(xi) In other cases, the Subject may possess the Attribute and at the same time be the Object of the qualifying process:

> This paper is *thin to write on.*   The Atlantic is *cold to swim in.*
> Her skin is *soft to touch.*   This cloth is *rough to wear.*

In these examples, the process has a conditional value: *if you write on it,*
when you touch it, etc.

53.1.3   Qualification by PrepGs

In this type of realisation, the completive (**c**) of the preposition may be a
noun, pronoun or NG, or a finite *WH*-clause, a non-finite *WH*- clause or non-
finite *-ing* clause.

The following examples are grouped according to types of meaning
expressed by the adjective and the type of completive:

  (i) an emotion related to a clause:

about:	*angry about* what I said;	*annoyed about* the delay;
at:	*happy at* the prospect;	*alarmed at* the news.

  (ii) a personal quality related to any activity or state:

at:	*clever at* getting what he wants;	*terrible at* letter-writing;
	brilliant at mathematics;	*hopeless at* remembering names;
of:	*slow of* speech;	*hard of* hearing;
in:	*quick in* thought;	*slow in* reacting;
to:	*prone to* headaches;	*quick to* anger.

  (iii) mental state or attitude related to a phenomenon:

of:	*conscious of* the need;	*convinced of* the fact;
with:	*satisfied with* the results;	*bored with* life;
to:	*opposed to* innovation;	*kind to* old people;
for:	*anxious for* success;	*hopeful for* the future.

  (iv) physical or emotional state due to a cause:

with:	*trembling with* fear;	*black with* the smoke;
from:	*sleepless from* anxiety;	*tired from* overworking.

  (v) a state related to location:

about:	*heavy about* the eyes;	*sick about* the stomach;
in:	*strong in* the legs;	*weak in* the arms;
at:	*weak at* the knees;	*generous at* heart.

  (vi) the value the Attribute has for something or someone:

for:	*surprising for* all of us;	*good for* the health.

  (vii) dependence or aim:

on:	*contingent on* his state of health;	*intent on* divorce;
	dependent on other people;	*set on* studying abroad.

  (viii) intensified state:

beyond:	*cruel beyond* endurance;	*injured beyond* recovery;

to:	*virtuous to* a degree;	*fed up to* the eyebrows;
past:	*ill past* all hope;	
as:	*alike as* two peas;	*right as* rain

(ix) the Attribute is attributed to the completive of the preposition:

of: It is very *kind of you*;   that was *foolish of John*.

The fact that a PrepG occurs after an adjective does not necessarily mean that it qualifies the adjective; it may be functioning as a clausal Adjunct:

Qualifier: He is *brilliant in all respects.*
Adjunct: He is *brilliant, in my opinion.*

Many adjectives are always followed by the same preposition, and this is the clearest indication of the qualifier role of a PrepG:

dependent on	ignorant of	compatible with
contingent on	certain of	bored with
based on	sure of	content with

e.g. Theories must be *compatible with* the facts.
That argument seems *based on* pure supposition.

53.2   Qualification of modified adjectives

When the adjectival head is graded the qualifier is realised by words, groups and clauses introduced by *than*, *of*, *in*, *as*, *for*, or *that*, according to the structure and type of the pre-head modifier. The following are examples serving as a brief summary of this area of English grammar.

53.2.1   Comparative degree

PrepG: cooler *than in Russia*;
Clf: less complicated *than any of us expected at that time*;
Clnf: more comfortable *than travelling by air.*

53.2.2   Superlative degree

PrepG (of):   the most famous *of all his plays*;
PrepG (in):   the longest *in the world*;
Clf: the least interesting *I have ever read.*

53.2.3   Degree of equality

AdvG: as lovely *as ever*;
Clf: not as easy *as most of us expected on that occasion*;
Clnf: nothing like as humiliating *as being sent to prison.*

If the comparison is between two adjectives, the qualifier of equality is realised by a finite clause:

She is as good-looking *as she is intelligent.*
*She is as good-looking as intelligent.

If the comparison is negative, the modifier *not as* may be replaced by *not so*, though *so* suggests intensification besides equality:

In winter, London is *not as/so cold as* New York.
None are *so deaf as* those that will not hear.

The **mhq** structure of equality has generated many institutionalised comparisons and lends itself easily to the creation of new ones:

as bold as brass (= impudent);   as flat as a pancake;   as good as gold (= well behaved);   as hard as nails.

The modifier *as* is sometimes omitted:

The terrain was *flat as a pancake.*

53.2.4   Degree of sufficiency

Heads modified by postposed *enough* are qualified by similar units to the above:

PrepG: Is the water *hot enough for you?*
CInf: Is the water *hot enough to take a bath?*
   Is the water *hot enough for you to take a bath?*

The verb in the qualifying unit may be passive:

Some kings have not been important enough *to be remembered.*

The verb may also be phrasal or prepositional:

It is not dark *enough to put* the lights *on.*
That light is not good *enough* for you *to read by.*

53.2.5   Degree of excess

PrepG: This coffee is *too hot for me.*
CInf: This coffee is *too hot to drink* (not *to drink it).
   This coffee is *too hot for me to drink* (not *for me to drink it).

If the verb of the qualifying unit is prepositional (e.g. *think about*), the Subject of the main clause functions as its Object:

CInf: Your project is too expensive to think about (*about *it*).
   This knife is too blunt to cut with. (*with *it*).

53.2.6   Qualification of quantified Attributes

Heads modified by the adverbs *so* and *that* are qualified by finite clauses, introduced optionally by the conjunction *that*:

Clf: The explanation was *so clear (that) everybody understood it.*
The interference was *that bad I couldn't catch a word.*

or by infinitive clauses introduced by *as*:

Clnf: The explanation was *so clear as to admit (of) no misunderstanding.*

In this group structure, it is the adverbial modifier, or better, the modifier + head together, which are qualified, not simply the adjectival head.

The following alternative sequence of clauses is often used orally:

Everybody understood the explanation, *it was so clear.*
I couldn't catch a word, *the interference was that bad.*

In this case, the AdjGs *so clear*, *that bad* remain unqualified, and we have two independent clauses, one main clause and another, which has been called a 'comment clause'.

It is important not to confuse the use of the above finite clauses as qualifiers in AdjGs with similarly worded clauses functioning as a 'continuing clause' in a clause complex (see 32.2.1) such as:

The explanation was clear, *so everybody understood it.* (= result)
The whole village was evacuated *so (that) a reservoir could be built.*
(= purpose)

Here, *so* does not modify the adjective *clear*: it is a conjunction introducing a subordinate clause of result or purpose.

53.3 Discontinuous qualification

If a qualified AdjG functions as pre-head modifier of a noun, the qualifier is placed after the noun, thus being separated from its adjectival head in a discontinuous AdjG structure:

Theirs is *so ambitious* a project *as to be unrealisable.*
What is the reason for the *much more resounding* success the orchestra has met with this year *than that which it achieved* last year?

This is a normal ordering of the elements and does not constitute a marked style.

53.4 Recursive qualification of the adjectival head

This occurs chiefly in AdjGs functioning as Complements (Cs or Co). The units realising it may be related paratactically or hypotactically:

paratactic
What is needed is a system where students are provided with the necessary finance REPAYABLE *in the future*, + *on reasonable terms*, + *out of their taxable income*.

The Robbins Report.

hypotactic
The committee is not SURE (that you are experienced (enough to take on a post (as important as this one))).

A. J. Cronin, *The Citadel.*

Two qualifying exponents can be closely related to each other logically, without the relation being clearly paratactic or clearly hypotactic:

How STRANGE/*of them/not to write to us*!

Here, each of the qualifiers could function alone:

How strange of them! (= they were strange)
How strange not to write to us! (= not to write to us was strange)

This is sometimes explained as an example of reductionism, so typical of the English language, which often prefers not fully to express grammatical meanings which can be logically understood in reduced form. It seems true, however, that the structure chosen above (*strange of them not to write to us*) is semantically slightly different from the fully finite form (*strange that they did not write to us*), in that it emphasises the strangeness of the people themselves (*of them*) rather than the strangeness of what they did not do. Such a difference is small but it does suggest that different structures of the same propositional content usually entail slight semantic differences – a view not held by all linguists.

When an adjective is graded by a modifier, e.g. *more convinced*, one qualifier may relate to the modifier as in *more (convinced) than I was*, and a second one to the head, as in *(more) convinced of the man's guilt*. They may be placed in either order, the emphasis normally being on the second one:

The judge seemed more convinced than I was *of the man's guilt.*
The judge seemed more convinced of the man's guilt *than I was.*

If one qualifier is notably longer than the other(s), it is usually placed at the end:

The judge seemed more convinced than I was *of the evidence that had been given by one of the witnesses.*
*The judge seemed more convinced of the man's guilt after listening to the evidence given by one of the witnesses than I was.

When qualifiers or qualified adjectives are coordinated by *and*, *but*, *or*, the qualifiers are often of the same class form:

PrepG: She's fond *of teaching* and good *with children.*
ClInf: The programme was delightful *to watch* and *to listen to.*

53.5.   Use of AdjGs in texts

Because AdjGs serve mainly to denote the Attributes of the numerous noun referents occurring in all types of texts, there is clearly plenty of scope for their use. AdjG complexes realised only by the adjectival heads or modified heads are quite common, whereas the modifier and qualifier elements are not exploited to the same extent. The following description by a modern novelist illustrates this.

> It was *equally true of her* now, at thirty, that she gave the impression of someone who is still going to be, perhaps just about to be, '*beautiful*': the same *tilted* nose, the *small* ears, the *warm brown* eyes, *clouded now and hurt-looking*, the same *wide*, *full-lipped* mouth, *warm too and generous*, the *slightly weak* chin. Yvonne's was the same *fresh bright* face, that could collapse, as Hugh would say, like a heap of ashes, and be *grey*.
>
> Malcom Lowry, *Under the Volcano*.

Here we find AdjGs functioning as Subject Complements and as modifiers of nouns; they include simple, derived and compound forms of the adjectival head; the group structures contain a discreet amount of recursion, appropriate to the purpose of describing a person. A more marked poetic style characterises the following description of a small Welsh seaside town at night, in which the writer uses no less than eighteen adjectives – simple, derived, participial and compound – to describe the town, the streets, the sky, the wood, the houses, the square and the sea.

> It is spring, *moonless* night in the *small* town, *starless and bible-black*, the cobble-streets *silent* and the *hunched*, courters'-and-rabbits' wood limping *invisible* down to the *sloeblack*, *slow*, *black*, *crowblack*, *fishing-boat-bobbing* sea. The houses are *blind as moles* (though moles see fine tonight in the *snouting*, *velvet* dingles) or *blind* as Captain Cat there in the *muffled* middle by the pump and the town clock, the shops in mourning, the Welfare Hall in widow's weeds. And all the people of the *lulled* and *dumbfound* town are sleeping now.
>
> Dylan Thomas, *Under Milk Wood*.

Writing of this kind, charged with overtones and associations, stimulates the imagination and creates an appropriate atmosphere for the radio 'Play for Voices'.

For AdjGs to be effective, they need to be chosen and used with care. It is for this reason that they are not greatly exploited in unplanned spoken discourse such as informal conversation, where there simply is not the time for an elaborate description of Attributes. They may well occur, however, in speech situations – politics, lectures, debates, conferences and public addresses of all kinds – which have been prepared or semi-prepared beforehand.

TASKS ON CHAPTER 11:
Talking about Attributes: The Adjectival Group

Module 51

1   *After reading G. B. Shaw's description of a clergyman in his play* Candida *(page 513), use some of the structures he uses to write a description of any person you know or have seen, man or woman, public or private, e.g.*

> *X is a _____. A _____, _____. _____ man/woman of _____, _____ and _____, full of _____, with _____, _____, _____ manners, and a _____, _____ voice. He/She has a _____ complexion, _____ forehead, with the eyes _____ and _____, a mouth _____ but not particularly _____.*

   Add any other information you like.

2   †*Express the following sentences differently using a pseudo-participial adjective formed from the noun shown in italics:*
   1) His face was framed in a great *beard*.
   2) You have shown great *enterprise* in setting up this firm.
   3) The newspapers reported all the *details* of the case.
   4) Conflicts often arise between countries that are *neighbours*.
   5) We live in an ancient town with a great *wall* round it.
   6) Dresses with designs of *flowers* on them are no longer in fashion.

3   *Some participial adjectives can be used with a figurative meaning. What do the following expressions refer to?*

   a commanding view;   a punishing climb;   a blazing row;   a resounding victory;   a scalding remark;   a taxing problem;   a drawn face;   a guarded remark;   canned music.

4   *Form participial adjectives from the following transitive and intransitive verbs and collocate each one with an appropriate noun. Use both -**en** and -**ing** participles:*

   transitive: surprise, alarm, frighten, worry, relax.
   intransitive: rise, fall, die, live, fade, grow.

5   *Write very short sentences using the following formal types of compound*
    adjectives. If you are not sure of the meaning, consult a good dictionary:
    1)   **Adj + V-*ing*:** nice-looking, good-looking, easy-going, hard-wearing,
         slow-moving.
    2)   **Adj + V-*en*:** quick-frozen, wide-spread, clean-shaven, big-headed,
         sharp-eyed, loud-mouthed.
    3)   **Noun + Adj:** water-tight, self-confident, duty-free, baby-soft,
         fool-proof, war-weary.

6   *Suggest appropriate nouns or adjectives to form compounds with the*
    following adjectives, e.g. sea-green.

    -blue, -green, -grey, -pink, -red, -cold, -hot, -black, -sweet, -white.

7   †*Express the following NGs differently, using a compound adjective as*
    modifier of the head noun:
    1)   a story so scarifying that it raises the hair on your head
    2)   an activity that consumes too much of your time
    3)   cakes that have been made at home
    4)   a speed that takes your breath away
    5)   troops that are borne (= transported) by air
    6)   a plain that has been swept by the wind
    7)   the performance that won an award
    8)   a device that saves a great deal of labour.

8   *The following compound adjectives are composed of a past particle and*
    an adverbial particle. Look up their meanings in a good modern dictionary
    and use them in sentences in their figurative sense.
    1) laid-back.   2) stuck-up.   3) run-down.   4) worn-out.
    5) burnt-out.   6) broken-down.   7) made-up.

9   *Imagine that you wish to teach a class of students the various syntactic*
    functions that adjectives and Adjectival Groups can realise in English
    clauses and groups. Base your explanation on the list of nine functions
    given in section 51.5, and find different examples for each function. Look
    for examples in English books and magazines or newspapers to which you
    have access. If you do not find all the examples you need, compose some
    yourself.

10   †*Consider the list of semantic types of Attributes given in section 51.4,*
     which express, basically, the following features:

a quality	space	emphasis
an evaluation	time	restriction
a process	a field of activity	a subclass
a state		

1) Now read the following passage, and assign each adjective to one of the above types.
2) Which of the adjectives are simple, affixed and compound?
3) The writer is describing his impressions of the outside world, as he explored it when he was still only a baby. What impressions does he give, especially through his choice of adjectives.?

A memory of childhood

Radiating from that house, with its *crumbling* walls, its thumps and shadows, its *fancied* foxes under the floor, I moved along paths that lengthened inch by inch with my *mounting* strength of days. From stone to stone in the *trackless* yard I sent forth my acorn shell of senses, moving through *unfathomable* oceans like a South Sea savage island-hopping across the Pacific. Antennae of eyes and nose and *grubbing* fingers captured a few tufts of grass, a fern, a slug, the skull of a bird, a grotto of *bright* snails. Through the *long* summer ages of those first few days I enlarged my world and mapped it in my mind, its *secure* havens, its dust-deserts and puddles, its peaks of dirt and *flag-flying* bushes. Returning, too, *dry-throated*, over and over again, to its several *well-prodded* horrors: the bird's *gaping* bones in its cage of *old* sticks; the *black* flies in the corner, *slimy dead*; *dry* rags of snakes; and the *crowded*, *rotting*, *silent-roaring* city of a cat's *grub-captured* carcass.

Laurie Lee, *Cider with Rosie.*

Module 52

1 *In the course of a conversation, a friend makes the following remarks to you. Disagree with your friend emphatically using highly intensified adjectives and, where possible, an emotive adjective. Use a different intensifier each time, chosen from the following:*
very, extremely, absolutely, really, thoroughly, extraordinarily, most, exceedingly, completely, highly, utterly, perfectly.
  1) I don't think much of Picasso's painting, do you?
  2) The food in the students' canteen is pretty awful.
  3) Have you met the Dean's wife? She's a real beauty!
  4) I've heard they may be getting divorced.
  5) You don't seem to know what's going on.
  6) I find the new lecturer's classes rather boring.
  7) Did you see that lousy film on the telly last night?
  8) It wasn't fair to make the exam so difficult.
  9) You're looking very energetic and happy today.
  10) We think the idea of a demo is a good one.

2 *On this occasion, your friend will ask you for your opinion, and you will answer using adjectives that are moderately intensified by **quite**, **pretty**, **rather**, **fairly**, **reasonably** or attenuated by expressions such as:*
a bit, a little, slightly, somewhat, hardly, scarcely, not particularly, not

altogether, not very, not really, to some extent, in some respects, kind of,
sort of, not at all.
1) Did you have an interesting time in Egypt?
2) Was it very hot there at that time of the year?
3) Were you in a very large group?
4) What were the hotels like?
5) Did you find it difficult to communicate with people?
6) Were the guides well informed?
7) Was the trip expensive?
8) Didn't you find it tiring all that travelling?
9) I expect you were glad to get home, weren't you?

3 (a) *What is the difference in meaning between the following four*
sentences? Place them in order of intensification.
1) We had quite a rough flight.
2) We had a fairly rough flight.
3) We had a pretty rough flight.
4) We had rather a rough flight.

(b) *Would the order of intensification be the same or different if the*
adjective was **interesting** *instead of* **rough**?

4 (a) *Working in pairs, ask and answer questions using* **how**? *and the*
following measurable adjectives:
How long is ...?   How old ...?   How deep ...?   How thick ...?
How high is/are ...?   How tall ...?   How wide ...?

(b) *Ask each other questions with* **How**? *and non-measurable adjectives,*
and use any types of intensifier you wish in the answers:
How important ...?   How clever ...?   How tired ...?
How serious ...?   How hungry ...?   How difficult ...?

5 *Add qualitative modifiers to the adjectives in these sentences, choosing*
them from the following list:
beautifully, essentially, ideally, imaginatively, pleasantly, ferociously,
peacefully, cruelly.
1) The new cultural centre is an _____international project.
2) It will be in a style _____different from the usual urban architecture.
3) It will be _____placed outside the city, and ...
4) _____surrounded by fields and trees.
5) Some traditionalists have been _____critical of the design.
6) The architect has said: 'We have tried to combine the _____old with the
_____new'.

6 *Express these sentences differently by using a 'relational modifier +*
adjective' unit, as in the following example:
From a human point of view I cannot accept that opinion.
That opinion is humanly unacceptable.

1)   Drugs are necessary for medical purposes, but if abused they may be dangerous from a social point of view.
2)   The new oral examinations are very good in theory but have proved somewhat time-consuming to administer.
3)   Countries which are advanced in technological matters should help those in which science is under-developed.

7   *We have said in 52.5 that some adjectives and participles modified by nouns form compounds whose meaning is not always transparent. Could you paraphrase the following examples and use them to modify a noun? Consult a dictionary if you are not sure:*

   top-heavy, punch-drunk, face-saving, tongue-tied, head-strong, word-perfect, mouth-watering.

Module 53

1   *Qualify the adjectives in the following clauses with a finite or non-finite clause expressing the types of information shown on the left, e.g.*
   1)   a fact: We are sure *that he is innocent.*
   2)   a fact: I am *proud* . . .
   3)   a wish: My girl-friend is *insistent* . . .
   4)   a reason: You are very *kind* . . .
   5)   a process: French perfume is *expensive* . . .
   6)   a process: Jasmine and Nick are *certain* . . .
   7)   a fact: Jasmine and Nick are *certain* . . .
   8)   a process: You must be *crazy* . . .
   9)   a fact: I am *happy* . . .
   10) a process: I am *glad* . . .

2   †*Qualify the following adjectives with PrepGs expressing the types of information mentioned on the left, e.g.*
   1)   a cause: I'm angry *about what you did.*
   2)   a cause: I was *delighted* . . .
   3)   a process: Not all the students are *satisfied* . . .
   4)   a phenomenon: Many of them are *opposed* . . .
   5)   an emotion: He went *white* . . .
   6)   an activity: He is really *expert* . . .
   7)   an activity: I'm *tired* . . .
   8)   a subject: I'm very *keen* . . .
   9)   a cause: He got *ill* . . .
   10) an activity: Our teacher is *good* . . .

3   *The following table illustrates discontinuous Adjectival Groups in which the adjectival modifier in a NG is separated from its qualifier by the head noun. Can you complete the examples with appropriate qualifiers?*

	h (adj)		q
I have a	HOPELESS	memory	FOR NAMES
It was a	TERRIFYING	experience	FOR ...
He is a	CLEVER	fellow	AT ...
She proved an	EXCELLENT	teacher	WITH ...
I never met a	BRAVER	man	THAN ...
They have	SIMILAR	plans	. . . .
The President isn't	AS GOOD	a speaker	. . . .
This is	TOO DIFFICULT	a problem	. . . .

4   *When AdjGs or simply their qualifiers are coordinated by* **and**, **but**, **or**, *they often have the same class form. Working in pairs (A and B), A makes a statement, and B adds an appropriate conjoin of similar form, as in a conversation, e.g.*

A

1) You seem to be good *at making money.*
2) I'm anxious *to pass the exam.*
3) I'm crazy *about Swedish girls*!
4) Are you willing *to pay for the cinema*?
5) I'm sure *that Bob will arrive late.*
6) He is *quick to offend* people.
7) He says he's busy *studying* these days.
8) He's very fond of *borrowing money.*

B

– Yes, and *at spending it.*
– But not to ...
– Yes, and about ...
– Yes, but not ...
– Yes, and that ...
– Yes, but ...
– Yes, and ...
– Yes, but not ...

12

How, where and when:
The Adverbial Group

MODULE 54
Forms and meanings of the Adverbial Group

Summary

1   AdvGs have certain general characteristics similar to those of AdjGs:
    (a) Four potential structural forms: **h**, **mh**, **hq**, **mhq**.
    (b) They are frequently represented by the head element alone.
    (c) Morphologically, the adverbial head may be simple, derived or compound.
    (d) Semantically, many adverbs express qualities of processes and situations,
    just as adjectives express qualities of 'things'.

2   In other respects, AdvGs are different from AdjGs.
    Adverbs are a more heterogeneous word class, and consist of three major sets,
    each divided into subclasses, and these into subsubclasses:
    circumstantial: space, time
    expressive: manner, modality, degree, focus
    conjunctive: addition, reinforcement, result, concession, etc.

3   As a result of these characteristics, AdvGs:
    (a) express very many meanings;
    (b) realise many syntactic functions;
    (c) are used in many different types of communication.

54.1   Structure of the AdvG

The structure of the AdvG is similar to that of the AdjG; that is, it is composed of three elements: the head (**h**), the modifier (**m**) and the qualifier (**q**). These elements combine to form the following four basic structures:

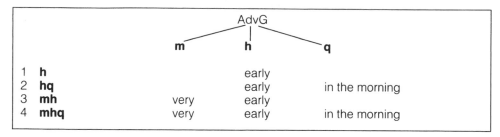

		m	h	q
1	**h**		early	
2	**hq**		early	in the morning
3	**mh**	very	early	
4	**mhq**	very	early	in the morning

Other examples of full AdvG structures are:

more	slowly	than necessary
far	away	from civilisation
so	fast	(that) I couldn't catch him
quite	clearly	enough

The head element is always realised by an adverb (54.3.1–3). The modifier (56.1) is realised typically by grading and intensifying adverbs, as in these examples. It is also, less frequently, modified by descriptive adverbs (*delightfully clearly*) or by quantifiers (*ten miles across*). The qualifier (56.3) expresses a different type of meaning from that of the modifier, as it does in AdjGs. It expresses the scope or context of the meaning expressed by the head (e.g. early *in the morning*); alternatively, it can serve to define the modifier more explicitly (e.g. *more* correctly *than before*). It is for this reason that qualifiers of adjectives and adverbs are mostly realised by embedded groups and clauses, whereas modifiers are usually realised by words.

54.2   General characteristics of AdvGs

AdvGs have a number of general characteristics which distinguish them from other classes of groups. These are as follows:

(a) They express a wide variety of types and subtypes of meaning (54.4).

(b) They perform a wide variety of syntactic functions (55.1).

(c) They can occupy many different positions in clause structure, when functioning as Adjuncts and Disjuncts (55.2).

(d) They are very frequently optional in the sense that they can be omitted without the clause becoming ungrammatical. For this reason we say that, when they function as Adjuncts or Disjuncts of a clause, AdvGs typically play a 'non-inherent' role in clause structure, as distinct from the roles of 'process' and 'participant' which are 'inherent' in any situation.

(e) Both AdjGs and AdvGs share the characteristic of being realised frequently by the head alone, as 'simple' group structures.

The adverb is an extremely heterogeneous word class. Practically any word that is not easily classed as a noun, an adjective, a verb, a determiner, a preposition or a conjunction, tends to be classified as an adverb. In order to describe the grammatical features of adverbs, it is useful to establish a certain number of classes and subclasses among them, from either a functional or a semantic point of view. Whichever of these two criteria is chosen, reference has to be made constantly to the alternative one. Section 54.3 deals with the formal features of English adverbs.

The following short passage gives an idea of the average frequency of adverbs occurring in informal styles of English. The adverbs occur naturally without any special literary effect, as the narrator needs them. It will be noticed that in each case there is only a head element, without modifier or qualifier:

> I could see my studio from *where* I stood, an old boathouse *down* by the water-wall. A bit rotten in places, but I had been glad to get it . . . When I had my canvas *up* it was two feet off the ground, which *just* suited me. I like to keep my pictures above dog level.
> "*Well*", I thought, "the walls and roof are *there*. They haven't got blown *away*, *yet*. No-one has leaned *up* against them." I was pleased, but I didn't go *along* in a hurry. One thing at a time. Last time I was locked *up*, I left a regular establishment *behind*. Nice little wife, two kids, flat and a studio with a tin roof. Water-tight *all round*. . . . When I came *back*, there was nothing. Wife and kids had gone *back* to her mama. Flat let to people who didn't *even* know my name. My cartoons, drawings, ladders, they'd *just* melted. I hadn't expected to see the frying-pan and kettle *again*. You can't leave things like that *about* for a month in a friendly neighbourhood and expect to find them in the same place. When I came *back* from gaol, *even* the smell had gone.

> Adapted from: Joyce Cary, *The Horse's Mouth*.

54.3 Formal features of the adverbial head

Morphologically, English adverbs are either simple, compound or derived.

54.3.1 Simple forms

These are one-syllable or two-syllable words of native origin not marked for class:

> down, up, out, over, in, below, above, often, always, ever, never, once, twice, also, back, away, off, soon, else, now, then, there, here, far, where, when, why, how . . .

54.3.2   Derived forms

Those formed from adjectives by the addition of the suffix *-ly* include:

> happily, freely, slowly, proudly, honestly, cheerfully, etc.

Those formed from nouns by the addition of *-wise*, *-ways*, *-wards*, include:

> clockwise, moneywise, profitwise, businesswise; sideways,
> lengthways, crossways; seawards, backwards, frontwards,
> homewards, inwards.

A small group of adverbs beginning *a-* indicate mainly position or direction:

> aback, aboard, about, above, abreast, abroad, across, adrift, again,
> aground, ahead, along, alongside, aloof, aloud, amiss, apart,
> apiece, around, ashore, aside, askance, askew, astern, astride,
> away.

Another small set of adverbs has *be-* as first syllable, also indicating position or direction:

> before, behind, below, beneath, besides, between, beyond.

54.3.3   Compound forms

Some of these are shortened forms of PrepGs:

> downhill, downstairs, downstream, downtown, downwind, downriver;
> indoors, inland, inshore, inside, instead; offside, off-limits, off-centre;
> up-country, up-state, upriver; overboard, overhead, overseas,
> overnight, over-all, overland, overleaf, overmuch.

Others are combinations of other classes of words:

> however, moreover, nevertheless, somewhere, anywhere, nowhere,
> everywhere, anyway, anyhow, elsewhere, herewith, thereof,
> whereabouts, hereby.

54.3.4   Correlative forms

The comparative degree adverbs *more* and *less* can be used correlatively when introduced by *the* in the structures: *the more ... the more, the less ... the less, the more ... the less, the less ... the more*. They may realise the functions of Adjunct in clauses, modifier in AdjGs and AdvGs, and head or determiner in NGs:

A (Cl):   The *more* I meet other people, the *more* I love my dog.
                The *sooner* you forget the whole incident, the *better*.
m (AdjG):   The *more technical* you make your explanations, the
                less easy it is for me to understand them.
m (AdvG):   The *more closely* I look at the problem, the *less clearly*
                I see a solution.

d (NG):   The *less time* you devote to study, the *less progress* you'll make.

h (NG):   *The more* you spend, *the less* you can save.

In each of these sentences, the adverbs *the more*, *the less* have parallel syntactic functions in the two clauses. They may, however, modify words of different classes, thus having different functions:

The more powerful one's car is, *the more dangerously* one tends to drive.

Here, the degree adverb *the more* modifies first an adjective (*powerful*) and secondly an adverb (*dangerously*).

54.4   Types of meanings expressed by AdvGs

Adverbs express six broad types of meaning in clauses and groups: circumstantial, process, modal, degree, focusing, conjunctive. Each of the six main types is made up of several subtypes, which are exemplified by lexical exponents in the following subsections.

54.4.1   Circumstantial adverbs: where and when things happen

Space
Position: Put the chairs *here/outside/upstairs*. An *away* match.
Direction: Push it *inwards/down/through/out/away*. The trip *back*
Distance: Don't go too *far/near/close*.

Time
Moment: They will be coming *tomorrow/sometime/then/soon/later*.
Frequency: The doctor came *once/daily/frequently/now and again*.
Duration: We didn't stay *long*. We spoke *briefly*.
Relation: The train will arrive *soon*. It hasn't arrived *yet*.
Sequence: *first*, *secondly*, *next*, *then*, *lastly*, *finally*.

54.4.2   Process adverbs: how things happen

Manner: She spoke *hesitantly*. The policeman looked round *suspiciously*.
Respect: The concert was a success *artistically* but not *financially*.

54.4.3   Modal adverbs

Possibility: You are *certainly* right. *Perhaps* I'm wrong.
Restriction: That is *hardly* true. It is *only* a half-truth.
Necessity: The houses were *necessarily/compulsorily* pulled down.
Volition: The boss has *reluctantly/unwillingly* raised my wages.
Viewpoint: We are in good shape *financially*, and *healthwise*, too.
Emphasis: He is *plainly/obviously just* a miser. *Indeed* he is.

Judgement: The Minister has *wisely/rightly/understandably* resigned.
Attitude: *Thankfully* it didn't rain. *Hopefully* it will be fine tomorrow.

In this last type of modalising adverbs, we must also include the idiomatic use of the degree adverbs *rather, sooner, better, best* combined with the modal auxiliaries *would* and *had*:

I *would rather* live here than anywhere else. (= *I'd prefer* to.)
Personally, *I'd much sooner* live in the city. (= *I'd much prefer* to.)
It's getting late, you *had better* leave.
There are no buses, you'd *best* order a taxi. (= It's advisable to.)

54.4.4   Degree adverbs

Comparison: Sheila is *more/the most/less/the least* industrious as a student.
Intensification: She lives *all* alone but seems *quite* happy.
Attenuation: That is *somewhat/slightly/a little* surprising.
Approximation: There were *about/roughly/more or less* 20 people there.

54.4.5   Focusing adverbs

Restriction: That is *merely* a detail. He is *solely* interested in money.
Reinforcement: *Even* a child knows that. It's obvious, *as well*.

54.4.6   Conjunctive adverbs

Logical connection
Sequence: *First* it's important to get a job and *secondly* to save.
Equation: You must take plenty of food, and *likewise* warm clothes.
Reinforcement: The house is small and *furthermore* has no garden.
Conclusion: It was a tiring trip, but *altogether* very interesting.
Apposition: We've got two pets, *namely* a rabbit and a canary.
Result: I've lost my job and *so/consequently* have no money.
Alternation: Take an umbrella, *otherwise* you'll get wet.
Contrast: He wants to live abroad, *or rather* anywhere away from home.
Opposition: The theatre is expensive; let's go to the cinema *instead*.
Concession: What you said was true; *however/nevertheless* it was unkind.
Transition: *Now*, you listen to me! *Now then*, what do you propose?

54.5 Use of adverbs in texts

54.5.1 Literary description

All writers instinctively use adverbs, such as those of manner, frequency, direction, degree, etc., to heighten the dramatic effect of a description such as the following in George Orwell's account of an Indian being led to his execution. In it we may observe the use of process adverbs of manner.

> It was *about*[1] forty yards to the gallows. I watched the bare brown back of the prisoner marching in front of me. He walked *clumsily*[2] with his bound arms, but quite *steadily*[3] with that bobbing gait of the Indian who *never*[4] straightens his knees. At each step, his muscles slid *neatly*[5] into place, the lock of hair on his scalp danced *up and down*[6], his feet printed themselves *cleanly*[7] on the wet gravel. And *once*[8], in spite of the men who gripped him by each shoulder, he stepped *slightly*[9] aside to avoid a puddle on the path.
>
> G. Orwell, *A Hanging*.

[1] degree (approximate); [2,3] manner; [4] frequency; [5] manner; [6] movement; [7] manner; [8] frequency; [9] degree.

The following extract from Freya Stark's personal narrative *A Winter in Arabia* describes a plane flight up the east coast of Africa. In it, one can notice that the different semantic classes of spatial adverbs are used (together with other words and structures) to convey, unobtrusively, a sensation of vastness, height, the smallness of objects on the earth, slow motion, as well as isolation and suspension in the air.

> In the first week of November, we flew *eastward*[1] from Aden . . . with the Indian Ocean on our right. Seen from *so high*[2], the triple, lazy lacelike edge of waves crept *slowly*[3], they did not turn all at once, but unrolled from end to end in a spiral motion as if it were the heart of a shell unwinding . . . We moved *eastwards*[4] *even*[5] as the great globe below *imperceptibly*[6] moved, and were gaining on its circular horizon. Sharks *far down*[7] were *dimly*[8] visible, *so*[9] limpid was the water; small black boats, pointed at either end, were *out*[10] with their fishermen near the shore; a village or two, earth-coloured huts unnoticeable but for the fields *around*[11], took shelter *here and there*[12] from wind and sand. On our right, the unfurrowed ocean . . .; on our left, the gaunt leopard-coloured lands, *equally*[13] lonely.
>
> Freya Stark, *A Winter in Arabia*.

[1] direction; [2] extent; [3] manner; [4] direction; [5] focus; [6] manner; [7] extent; [8] description; [9] intensification; [10–12] position; [13] degree.

54.5.2 Technical description

Technical description often makes use of adverbs of degree and quantity as in the following extracts from an elementary text book on 'Metals'.

> Of the ninety or *so*[11] *naturally*[2] occurring elements, *about*[3] seventy are metals. Of these, *over*[4] half are put to practical use, although many of them *only*[5] in small amounts. In every household there are dozens of metal implements – from water-tanks to tea-spoons. Industrial machinery is made *almost entirely*[6] of metals. If man had not learnt to use metals, we would *still*[7] be living in the Stone Age. Some metals are used in a *relatively*[8] pure state, for example aluminium, whose lightness and corrosion-resistance make it *especially*[9] useful. But meals are used *mostly*[10] with other elements to form alloys and *so*[11] in this way their properties can be improved and their range of uses *widely*[12] extended.

> H. Moore, *Metals and Alloys*.

[11] quantity; [2] classification; [3, 4], quantity; [5] restriction; [6] degree; [7] duration; [8] degree; [9] intensification; [10] degree; [11] consequence (Conjunct); [12] degree.

54.5.3 Interpersonal communication

Many English speakers are diffident in the expression of their opinions, and tend to insert in their conversations what may be called adverbs of 'modality', such as *just, rather, quite, probably, almost, never, always, not at all, generally, usually*. These adverbs are then not used in their normal, positive sense but, instead, to attenuate the force of what the speaker is saying. The following light-hearted conversation about camels, recorded among four university lecturers, illustrates this (together with other linguistic modalising devices):

> J.W. What in fact do we think of when we think of a camel?
> A.R. *Well,*[1] . . .
> J.W. Is it a pleasant animal or . . .
> A.R. An unpleasant animal? . . . Obtuseness I should say *generally,*[2] the whole attitude of a camel seems to be, er, obtuse. It has this, er, *rather*[3] supercilious look on its face . . . for example . . . and they have, I'm told, I've *never*[4] experienced this I'm happy to say, but they have this magnificent facility for spitting *quite*[5] a considerable distance with great accuracy, er . . .
> J.W. I don't know that spitting shows obtuseness. I should have thought it *probably*[6] shows perspicacity . . .
> G.T. I think he's *slightly*[7] ridiculous, the camel, isn't he? The, er, weird expression he has on his face is *rather*[8] like the ostrich, but the ostrich carries it off. The ostrich looks marvellous, where, whereas the camel *just*[9] doesn't bring it off at all.

K.B. Camels *always*[10] strike me as *rather*[11] mean, they're ready to do
you down at the slightest opportunity.

L. Dickinson and R. Mackin, *Varieties of Spoken English*.

[1] hesitation; [2,3] attenuation; [4] self-denial; [5] intensification;
[6] modality; [7] attenuation; [8] medium intensification; [9] emphasis;
[10] self-justification; [11] intensification.

The following is an interesting example of the combined use of process
manner adverbs and stative adjectives for practical purposes in an interpersonal situation. It represents one of the common present-day techniques
used by hypnotists for the induction of a hypnotic state in their patients. It is
based on the slow reiteration of a small number of appropriate classes of
adverbs and adjectives. The suspension dots marked on this text represent
points at which the hypnotist repeated previously-used expressions several
times accumulatively. The procedure continues for several minutes until at
the end it consists almost entirely of adjectives and adverbs, as the voice of
the hypnotist dies away into silence.

I want you to listen very *carefully* to what I say, I want you to listen
carefully to what I say; your eyes are *closed*, your eyes are *closed* . . . you
are feeling *comfortable*, *relaxed*, thinking of nothing, nothing but what I
say, your eyes are *closed*, *comfortably closed* . . . your arms and legs feel
heavy . . . your whole body feels *relaxed* . . . your face, *legs* and *arms* . . .
it feels as though you are going *backward* into the darkness, you are
listening *only* to my voice . . . thinking of nothing, *absolutely* nothing . . .
listening *only* to what I say . . . and you begin to feel *drowsy*, breathing
regularly and *deeply*, *regularly* and *deeply* . . . and you are going into a
sleep, a *deep*, *sound*, *comfortable*, sleep . . . breathing *deeply* and
regularly . . . *you are now sleeping deeply* . . . more *deeply* . . . as you go
gently *backward* into the darkness, your sleep is getting deeper and
deeper, deeper and deeper . . .

F. L. Marcuse, *Hypnosis*.

The previous text examples have illustrated the use of adverbs and AdvGs
almost entirely in their modifying, complementing and adjunctive functions,
within clauses. Those listed as conjunctives express the logical semantic
relationships that exist between clauses (see Modules 33, 34, 35).

MODULE 55
Syntactic functions of the Adverbial Group

Summary

1   The fact that there are so many semantic classes of adverbs causes them to realise many kinds of syntactic functions:
    (a) as modifiers, qualifiers and completives in AdjGs, AdvGs, NGs, VGs and PrepGs;
    (b) as Adjuncts, Complements and even Subjects and Objects in clauses:
    (c) as Disjuncts associated with whole clauses;
    (d) as Conjuncts between clauses.

2   Some adverbs have fixed position; others are mobile.

3   Some adverbs vary their aspectual meaning according to their functional role: *altogether* (Adjunct, Conjunct, modifier); *naturally* (Adjunct, Disjunct).

4   Adverbs that realise functions typical of other word classes, without changing their form (e.g. *fast*) are sometimes considered as separate class words, called homomorphs.

55.1   Syntactic functions of AdvGs

Adverbial Groups, whether simple (head element only) or complex (with **m** and **q** elements), realise the following syntactic functions as elements of group and clause structures. In this section, AdvGs will be exemplified by the head element alone; that is to say, by adverbs.

In group structures	Examples of exponents
1 Modifier in AdjGs:	*all* wet; *quite* happy; *fairly* good; *too* long; *completely* new.
2 Modifier in AdvGs:	*nearly* there; *more* easily; *very* often.
3 Modifier in NGs:	the *then* President; a *nearby* hotel; *quite* a success.
4 Modifier of determiners:	*about* double; *roughly* half; *almost* all.
5 Modifier in PrepGs:	*right* out of sight; *just* down the road. She should behave *more* like a real nurse and *less* like a film star.
6 Submodifier in AdjGs:	*much* too short; *rather* more interesting.

7	Submodifier in AdvGs:	*(not) all* that easily; *far* too often.
8	Qualifier in AdjGs:	quick *enough*; very beautiful *indeed*.
9	Qualifier in AdvGs:	quickly *enough*; beautifully *indeed*; never *again*.
10	Qualifier in NGs:	the President *then*; the journey *back*; the castle *there*.
11	Qualifier of determiner:	any (interest) *at all*; no (doubt) *whatever*.
12	Completive in PrepGs:	over *here*; through *there*; from *inside*; till *now*.
13	Particle in VGs:	pick *up*; put *on*; take *out*; pull *off*; go *in*.

In clause structures

14	Adjunct:	I *much* regret this incident. You *little* realise the consequences it may have. He studies *hard*. I *completely* forgot it.
15	Disjunct:	*Fortunately*, it didn't rain.
16	Conjunct:	*So* you don't want to come, *then*.
17	Predicator Complement:	He strode *off*.
18	Subject Complement:	They're *off*! I'm *through* with you!
19	Object Complement:	I helped the old man *across*.
20	Direct Object:	I don't know *when*. They didn't tell me *why*.
21	Subject:	*Tomorrow* will be too late. *Slowly* does it!

Since clause Adjuncts, Disjuncts and Conjuncts are syntactic elements that can be realised not only by AdvGs but also by PrepGs, and finite or non-finite clauses, some grammarians group all of these classes of realisations under the general name of 'Adverbials'. In this book, for the purposes of terminological clarity, we reserve the term 'Adverbial' strictly for a class of unit, the Adverbial Group, not to be confused with a type of function.

The different functional roles in group structures played by the different classes of AdvGs are mentioned in Chapters 10, 11, 12, 13, relating to the groups. Their functions in and between clauses are illustrated mainly in Chapters 2 and 7.

55.2 Distribution of adverbs in the clause

55.2.1 The mobility of adverbs

In all of the above syntactic functions, except those of clause Adjunct and Disjunct, adverbs occupy fixed positions, these varying with their function. As Adjuncts or Disjuncts they are more mobile, as the following examples show:

> *Legally*, the man couldn't have been sent to prison.
> The man *legally* couldn't have been sent to prison.
> The man couldn't *legally* have been sent to prison.
> The man couldn't have *legally* been sent to prison.
> The man couldn't have been *legally* sent to prison.
> The man couldn't have been sent *legally* to prison.
> The man couldn't have been sent to prison *legally*.

Not all adjunctive or disjunctive adverbs are equally mobile. The choice of position is determined by its type (circumstantial, modal, degree, etc.), the scope of its meaning (whole clause or part of a clause), the degree of emphasis the speaker wishes to give to it, and the general information structure of the clause (see chapter 6).

55.2.2 Circumstantial adverbs

Adverbs referring to the place and time in which a material process occurs are most frequently placed after the verb or at the end of the clause, as in the examples given in 54.4.1.

Indefinite time adverbs such as *sometimes*, *originally*, *eventually*, *immediately*, *finally*, *recently*, *previously* can be placed in end, middle or initial position:

> (a) We take a long holiday *sometimes*.
> (b) We *sometimes* take a long holiday.
> (c) *Sometimes* we take a long holiday.

(a) is the normal unmarked position, (b) focuses on the process *take*, and (c) on the whole of the clause.

Certain adverbs of frequency: *always*, *never*, *seldom*, *hardly ever*, *often*, *rarely*, *sometimes*, *usually*, tend to occur in mid-position, between Subject and Predicator or between operator and main verb. The word *often* may also focus on the whole clause, in initial position:

> (d) We *always* spend our holidays abroad. (*Always we spend . . .)
> (e) We have *never* been to Africa. (*Never, we have . . .)
> (f) Women are *often* successful in business. (Often women are . . .)

The adverbs of negative import *never*, *seldom*, *rarely*, *hardly ever* are occasionally fronted and followed by Subject–operator inversion for purposes of emphasis, though this structure is formal in style:

> *Rarely does one* find such kindness nowadays.
> *Never in my life have I* heard such crazy ideas!

Frequency adverbs are rarely found in cleft clauses, but we may note the following:

> It *is not often (that)* you get a chance like that.

The adverbs *still*, *yet*, *already* express certain time relationships which are described briefly and illustrated in the table on page 560 in question-and-answer structures which show their contrasting meanings. Naturally, their use is not confined to such a context. In other structures, their position may vary:

> She is *still* beautiful. She is beautiful *still*.
> *As yet* we have received no answer.
> We have *as yet* received no answer.
> We have received no answer *as yet*.
> I've *already* been there. I've been there *already*.

The examples given of these three adverbs show that their scope of meaning extends to the process or the whole predicate, and for this reason they normally occur in mid- or end-position. Exceptionally, *still* and *already* are placed in initial position as 'sentence Adjuncts', where the scope includes the Subject as well:

> I've spoken to him many times, but *still* I can't convince him!
> You're very careless! *Already* you've made three mistakes!

Here the adverbs have emphatic modal value and are spoken with strong stress. Nevertheless, we recommend caution in the use of this structure.

Finally we may observe the similarity of meaning of *still* and *yet* in a *be* + *to*-infinitive structure:

> A cure for cancer is $\begin{pmatrix} (still) \\ (yet) \end{pmatrix}$ to be found.

We ignore, here, the use of *still* and *yet* as Conjuncts of concession. Spatial adverbs such as *abroad*, *across*, *back*, *everywhere*, *downstairs*, *inside*, *uphill*, *forwards*, *sideways*, etc., expressing position and direction, are normally placed after the Predicator or in end-position.

55.2.3 Adverbs of manner

Adverbs referring to the manner in which a process occurs are placed most frequently at the end of the clause, as in *He speaks English fluently*, not **He speaks fluently English*. If the Object is long, and the adverb is a single word, the Object is placed at the end, as in *He speaks fluently several European and oriental languages*. If the adverb is modified or qualified as a group, it may still occupy end-position, according to the principles of end-focus and end-weight, even if the Object, too, is long:

> He speaks English *fluently*.
> He speaks several European and oriental languages as well as
> Arabic *very fluently indeed*.

Manner adverbs include many -*ly* items: *carefully*, *easily*, *correctly*, *nicely*, *cheaply*, *politely*, *peacefully*, *urgently*, etc., as well as those expressing

The adverbs *still, yet, already*

These three adverbs express, in broad terms, the following time relationships:
Still refers to processes or states which continue to occur or not occur up to the present.
Yet refers to processes or states which may occur in the future or have not occurred up to the present moment.
Already refers to processes or states which occurred before the present moment.
The following table shows their interrelated uses in questions and answers, as in interpersonal communication. In negative replies, there is sometimes an equivalence between the *not yet* and the *still not* structures. When used in monologues or continuous prose, these adverbs may be found in other syntactic frames, but mostly in the same basic placements as those shown in the table.

Question	Affirmative answer	Negative answer
1 Does Tom *still* visit you?	Yes, he *still* visits us. Yes, he *still* does.	No, he doesn't visit us *any more*. No, he doesn't visit us *any longer*. No, he *no longer* visits us.
2 Is Tom *still* working?	Yes, he is *still* working. Yes, he *still* is.	No, he *isn't* working *any more*. No, he *isn't any more*. No, he *isn't* working *any longer*. No, he is *no longer* working.
3 Is Tom working *yet*?	Yes, he is *already* working. Yes, he *already* is.	No, he *isn't* working *yet*. No, he *still isn't* working.
4 Has Tom arrived *yet*?	Yes, he has arrived *already*. Yes, he has *already* arrived. Yes, he *already* has.	No, he hasn't arrived *yet*. No, he *still* hasn't arrived. No, he hasn't *yet*.
5 Has Tom *already* gone? Has Tom gone *already*?	Yes, he has *already* gone. Yes, he has gone *already*. Yes, he *already* has.	No, he hasn't gone *yet*. No, he is *still* here.
6 Does Tom know *yet*?	Yes, he *already* knows. Yes, he knows *already*. Yes, he *already* does.	No, he doesn't know *yet*. No, he *still* doesn't know. No, he doesn't *yet*.

human feelings, such as *angrily*, *happily*, *desperately*, *passionately*, *sincerely*, *eagerly*, *proudly*, etc.

Manner adverbs occur not only at the end of a clause as in *I need you urgently*, or immediately after the Predicator as in *They lived happily ever after*, but also in mid-position:

> We *sincerely* hope you enjoyed your stay with us.
> I have been *seriously* thinking of changing my job.
> I will *gladly* help you if you need me.

55.2.4 Modal adverbs

The examples given in 54.4.3 show that, as clause Adjuncts, modal adverbs are typically placed in mid-position or after *be*, since they tend to focus on the process expressed by the verb. Other examples are:

> They will *probably* get married next month.
> She is *supposedly* a rich woman.
> The independence movement is *allegedly* gaining strength.

The tendency to occupy mid-position extends also to adverbs of degree and intensification:

> I *completely* forgot to tell you.
> He *positively* shouted at me!
> I *totally* disagree with you.

55.2.5 Adverbs in initial position

When an adverb is placed at the beginning of a clause, its meaning extends to the whole clause and not simply to the predication or to an element of the predication. In this position, the meaning may be of two broad kinds:

(a) It may function as an element within the clause and have the same status as the other elements, though referring to all of them together, as in:

> *Slowly*, the rising sun appeared over the distant horizon.
> *Suddenly*, a fresh breeze began to ruffle the surface of the sea.

In this way, the scope of the adverb ranges more widely over the clause than it would do in mid- or end-position:

> The rising sun *slowly* appeared over the distant horizon.
> The rising sun appeared *slowly* over the distant horizon.

Adverbs share this syntactic role, usually termed 'sentential Adjunct', with other classes of unit.

(b) Other adverbs occur in initial position but are considered, both syntactically and semantically, to be outside the clause, and are usually called 'Disjuncts' (see 8.2). Semantically, Disjuncts express either the speaker's attitude to what he is saying:

> *Frankly*, I don't believe you.
> *Hopefully*, the new plan will lead to some improvements.

or a comment on the truth or the value of what is said:

> *Undoubtedly*, the success is due to your efforts.
> *Very sensibly*, they are going to buy a smaller car.

Many adverbs can be used as both Disjuncts and Adjuncts; the following are used as Adjuncts of manner:

> I spoke *frankly* to him.
> He behaved *very sensibly*.

It is therefore important to distinguish the two meanings of the two functions.

55.3   Function and class

Since there is rarely a one-to-one relationship between function and class, many words can realise more than one syntactic function, e.g.

altogether:	He owes me a hundred dollars *altogether*. (adjunct)
	I think you are *altogether* wrong. (mod. of adj.)
	There were a lot of interesting people at the party, so *altogether* we had a very good time. (conjunct)
later:	There will be another performance *later*. (adjunct)
	The *later* performance will be at midnight. (mod. of noun)
	The performance *later* will be a better one. (qualifier of noun)

This chameleon-like quality of some English words, due partly to the relative lack of class markers in the language, makes it difficult to assign them exclusively to one class. In this book, rather than saying that a word is, for example 'an adverb functioning like or as an adjective', we shall consider it as two words belonging to two different classes. We shall refer to *the adjective 'long'* in *a long street* and to *the adverb 'long'* in *Don't stay long*. The following lexical items can be treated in this way, as is shown in the examples that follow them:

> clean, clear, close, dear, direct, early, fast, first, fine, flat, hard, high, late, light, long, loud, quick, sharp, tight, daily, weekly, etc., aloof, alone, alike, adrift, afoot, aground.

Adverb	Adjective
She works *hard*.	She's a *hard* worker.
We flew *direct* to Paris.	We had a *direct* flight to Paris.
The plane arrived *late*.	We took a *late* plane.
I *clean* forgot to tell you.	I need a *clean* handkerchief.

In these four pairs of clauses, the italicised words realise a syntactical function which is typical of the class to which we have assigned it. In the case of *fast* and *direct*, the meaning is the same, whether it refers to a process or a person, but in the case of *late* and *clean*, the semantic references differ: *A late plane* is not a plane which arrives late, but one which leaves at a later hour. *Clean* as an adverb in *I clean forgot* intensifies the process of 'forgetting' (= *I completely forgot*), whereas *clean* as an adjective denotes an attribute antonymous to *dirty*.

In clauses such as *She works hard* and *We flew direct to Paris*, the words *hard* and *direct* tell us how the material processes were carried out. They must therefore be classed as adverbs of manner, functioning as Adjuncts. By contrast, in clauses such as *He sat still/kept quiet/stood aloof/looked well/came close/jumped clear/feels fine/lives alone*, the words *still*, *quiet*, *aloof*, etc., refer to Attributes of the Subject (*He*), and must be classed as attributive or circumstantial Subject Complements after the copular verbs *sit*, *keep*, *stand*, *look*, etc.

55.4 Homomorphy

Word categories cannot be defined by one single criterion in English. From the practical point of view, the function and the semantic reference of a word are, in fact, more relevant to its interpretation than its supposed class or 'part of speech'. For the purposes of grammatical description, the notion of homomorphy is perhaps the simplest and most useful. With it we can say, for example, that some words function most typically like words of a given class (for example that of adverbs), but that occasionally they realise syntactic functions which are normally realised by words of a different class (for example, adjectives). Such an item can therefore be regarded as two different 'words' having the same form, both written and spoken. The two words are called 'homomorphs'. Some homomorphs have not only different functions, but also different semantic references in the different functions, as in *sharp at 8 o'clock* (Adjunct = *punctually, exactly*) and *a sharp knife* (modifier = *cutting*). Sometimes such a word may have more than two functions and meanings, as in the case of *back*, which can be classed as a noun, a verb, an adverb or an adjective. Some of the simple-form adverbs mentioned in this section have alternative forms ending in *-ly* which, with certain verbs, can be used interchangeably with them; e.g.

loud(ly): Don't speak so *loud/loudly*.
tight(ly): He held her *tight/tightly*.
dear(ly): The government will pay *dear/dearly* for its errors.

In some cases the two different meanings allow the two words to be juxtaposed in a clause:

Jane has been arriving *late, lately*. (= unpunctually, recently)

In other cases their use depends on the context or collocation:

Stay *close*! (place)   Watch *closely*! (manner)

It must be pointed out that adjective/adverb homomorphs are restricted mainly to fixed expressions, some of which are idiomatic:

Look *sharp*!	(= Hurry up!)
Go *slow*!	(= Traffic sign, to drive slowly)
Take it *easy*!	(= Be calm; Be relaxed)
Still going *strong*.	(= Thing or person still active after a period or when old)
They're going *steady*.	(= Boy and girl who spend much time together)
He didn't play *fair*.	(= According to the rules)

The phenomenon of homomorphy occurs in all English word classes, and is more frequent between adverbs and prepositions than between adverbs and adjectives. It is in some cases difficult to say whether the following are adverbs having prepositional homomorphs or prepositions with adverbial homomorphs:

above, across, aboard, along, alongside, before, behind, below, besides, between, beneath, beyond, by, near, in, over, on, down, up, round, past, since, through(out).

Adverb	Preposition
Have you seen this film *before*?	Yes, I saw it *before* the Flood! (= long ago)
Days went *past* without any news.	His condition is now *past* hope.
Hundreds of planes flew *over*.	They flew right *over* our heads.
He disappeared and I haven't seen him *since*.	I haven't seen him *since* his disappearance.
I love watching the trains go *by*.	That's why I live *by* the station.

55.5 Function and meaning

Despite the multi-functional character of adverbs; it remains a fact that different groups of functions tend to be realised by the different subclasses of adverbs mentioned in 54.4. The determining factor is the lexical meaning of each one. Some adverbs beginning with *a-* have adjectival homomorphs while others do not. Adverbs of place and time do not have the same syntactic functions as those of degree. Conjunctive adverbs have a completely different function from those that realise clause Adjuncts. Adverbs which can be used equally as Adjuncts, Disjuncts or Conjuncts usually belong to different semantic subcategories in these different syntactic functions, e.g.

Function		Semantic subcategory
Adjunct:	She answered me *frankly*.	(manner)
Disjunct:	*Frankly*, I didn't believe her.	(attitude)
Adjunct:	It's *still* raining, I'm afraid.	(duration)
Conjunct:	So we can't go. *Still*, it's not really important.	(concession)
Adjunct:	Let's discuss this *again* later.	(frequency)
Conjunct:	The news might be true, (or) *again*, it might not.	(contrast)

MODULE 56
Modification, qualification and expansion of the Adverbial Group

Summary

1   Many circumstantial and expressive adverbs can be modified and qualified in the same way as adjectives.

2   For semantic reasons, different classes of adverbs and different individual exponents admit certain modifiers but not others. These differences cannot be easily systematised, but can be explained *ad hoc*.

3   Many adverbs (e.g. *slowly*) can be modified by items expressing:
    superiority   excess   quantification
    inferiority   intensification   description
    equality   attenuation   modality

4   Modified adverbs are sometimes followed by a qualifier which is correlative with the modifier: (more) . . . *than*; (least) . . . *of*; (so) . . . *that*; (as) . . . *as*; (too) . . . *to/for*; etc.

5   Modifiers are sometimes themselves modified, e.g. *far too slowly*.

6   Unmodified adverbs can be qualified by PrepGs, NGs, AdjGs and clauses.

7   The recursive realisation of AdvG elements is not frequent in normal social communication, but can be found in formal and some literary styles.

56.1   Modification of the adverbial head

Most of the circumstantial and other adverbs, but not the conjunctive ones, can be modified and qualified in the same way as adjectives, and often by the same lexical items. We therefore limit ourselves to the following brief summary:

Grading

Adverbs are graded by the same words as adjectives:

> *more often, most often, less often, least often, as often, often enough, too often.*

Although the adverb *enough* is placed after the head adverb, we shall consider it as a modifier as we do with adjectives, since it can itself be submodified by an adverb placed before the head:

> *not quite often enough*   (`*not quite enough often*`).

The following forms are adverbial homomorphs of the corresponding adjectives:

> *better, best, worse, worst, further, furthest:*
>
> Tomorrow morning would suit me *best*, for the meeting.
> It was the driver who came off *worst* in the accident.

The adverbial and adjectival homomorphs *early*, *late*, *quick*, *fast*, *long*, *soon* take *-est* and *-er* in grades 1 and 2. *Soonest* is rare and restricted to telegraphic style.

> His speech was long*er* than mine. He spoke long*er* than I did.
> I arrived lat*er* than Monica, because I came by a lat*er* train.
> Please come *the earliest* you possibly can. Take the *earliest* train.

Intensification

As with adjectives, intensification may be (a) high, or (b) medium.

(a) *very* soon	*quite* recently	*right* now	*all* through
just then	*extremely* naturally	*soon* after	*close* by
far back	*utterly* sincerely	*high* up	*near* by

(b) *quite* softly	*fairly* well	*reasonably* sucessfully
pretty easily	*rather* badly	*averagely* fast

Attenuation

a bit harshly	*kind of* hesitantly	*almost* never
somewhat casually	*sort of* sarcastically	*hardly* ever

Attenuation can be expressed by negating a high degree:

> *not particularly* beautifully   *not altogether* happily
> You did*n't* behave *too* sensibly. I'm *not* feeling *too* well today.

Absence or denial of the adverbial Attribute is expressed as with adjectival ones:

> *not at all* surprisingly   *not* surprisingly *at all*
> *not in the least* satisfactorily   *not* satisfactorily *in the least*

Quantification

As with adjectives, this refers mainly to circumstantial adverbs of space and time and may be (a) exact, (b) non-measurable:

(a)   Our houses are *only two streets* apart.
       The airport is *at least ten miles* away.
       He fell ill and died *a month* later.

(b) As with adjectives, non-measurable quantity is expressed by the deictic items *so* and *that*:

      A. The fool must have been driving at 100 m.p.h.!
      B. Surely he couldn't have been driving *so* crazily!
         Surely he couldn't have been driving *that* crazily!

Under this type of quantifier, we may also include modifiers such as:

    soon after, *long* before, *quite* soon, *shortly* afterwards.

The adverb *how* is used to ask or to exclaim about the degree or quantity of an adverbial circumstance or quality:

Degree: *How* beautifully she dresses!
           How highly do you rate her as an actress?
Quantity: *How* long have you been waiting? – Half an hour.
           How far is it to the railway station? – Half a mile.

Description

Adverbs of space or time are often preceded by modifiers which reinforce or describe them more explicitly; such modifiers are often themselves more descriptive adverbs of space and time:

    straight ahead   *back* home   *up* above   *early* today
    out there   *late* yesterday *down* below *in* here

Adverbs of manner are not usually modified by other adverbs of manner:

    (?) He imitated the professor *comically–seriously*. (= pretending to be serious but in a comic manner)

Modifiers in *-ly* are, however, more acceptable when they express modal attitudes:

    The actors spoke *admirably* clearly for once.
    For amateurs they also acted *surprisingly* naturally.

The adverb *so*, when used as substitute for a clause, can be similarly modified:

    She complained about the poor service, and *rightly* so.
    Do you think she was right in complaining? – *Definitely* so.

As with adjectives, we may note the emotive modification of adverbial heads by swear words such as *damn(ed)*, as in *You behaved damn foolishly*, and other less polite ones.

56.2   Submodification of the adverbial head

Because modifiers and submodifiers are usually also adverbial, it is not usual to find long modification structures in AdvGs. Nevertheless, examples can be found of adverbial heads, usually of manner, preceded by modifiers of degree which are themselves modified by grading or intensifying adverbs. These latter we refer to as submodifiers, symbolised as *sm*. Subsubmodifiers (*ssm*) may also occur:

	AdvG		
ssm	**sm**	**m**	**h**
	rather	less	fluently
	all	the more	inevitably
	just	as	usefully
	most	unusually	carelessly
	a good deal	more	interestingly
	by far	the most	reliably
very	much	more	profitably
not	quite	so	pleasantly
nothing	like	as	simply

56.3   Qualification of unmodified heads

Some circumstantial adverbs of space and time can be qualified by the following classes of items:

PrepGs:	He's a missionary *somewhere in China.*
	A nurse stood *close at hand*, in case of emergency.
NGs:	*Once a week*; *twice this year.*
Clf:	Please sit down *anywhere you like.*
Clnf:	Book a hotel or you'll have *nowhere to sleep.*
else:	*Where else* did you go besides Istanbul?
otherwise:	*How otherwise* can we get there except on foot?
AdjG:	Why don't we go *somewhere slightly more exotic* for a change?

The *WH*-items *when, where, why, how* and their compounds (*somewhere, whenever*, etc.) have nominal as well as circumstantial value, as is shown in their qualification by AdjGs (*somewhere more exotic**), PrepGs (*everywhere in the world*), Clnf (*nowhere to sleep*) and the adverb *else/otherwise*:

    where else? = in what other place?
    when else?   = at what other time?
    how else?   = in what other way?
    why else?   = for what other reason?

The forms *somewhere, anywhere, nowhere* are often replaced in informal AmE by *someplace, anyplace, no place*, though not in WH-questions, e.g.

someplace else, anyplace else, no place else.
  Circumstantial adverbs can also be qualified by the intensifying use of *ever*:

> *Where ever* did you get that awful hat?
> *When ever* are you going to grow up?
> I'll *never ever* speak to him again!

and also by the non-assertive use of the phrase *at all* (see 23.1):

> Do you know *anywhere at all* where we can get a good meal?
> Our former friends *seldom* visit us *at all* these days.
> Our former friends *seldom ever* visit us these days.

Circumstantial adverbs are sometimes qualified by others of a similar type, so that it is not always clear which is the head and which the modifier or qualifier:

> Pip and her boyfriend are getting married *sometime soon.*
> Where shall I put those letters? – Leave them *anywhere there.*
> I need a drink – there must be a pub *somewhere about.*
> I saw a policeman *about somewhere,* let's ask him.
> Let's go outside; there's too much noise *inside here/here inside.*

  In clauses like the following, the AdvG realising the Adjunct is composed of two apposed adverbs:

> We'll meet *tomorrow Sunday.*

  In informal speech, intensification and reinforcement of circumstantial adverbs may be expressed by qualifiers such as the following:

> The train will be arriving *now any minute/any minute now.*
> It always arrives *punctually on the dot* (= on time).
> *Where the blazes* have you been all this time?
> *Why the devil* didn't you tell me you weren't coming?

  Expressive adverbs are sometimes qualified by *enough*, in the sense of intensification rather than sufficiency:

> *Strangely enough*, he doesn't seem to mind criticism.
> The police never found out, *oddly enough*, who stole the jewels.

56.4   Qualification of modified heads

Adverbs modified by *more* and *less* can be qualified by the following classes of units introduced by *than*:

NGs:	Bill speaks Spanish *much more* fluently *than his sister.*
AdvGs:	But he speaks *more* fluently *than accurately.*
PrepGs:	People work *less* hard here *than in some other countries.*
Clf:	Our coach left earli*er than it should have done.*
Clnf:	Working at night I study *less* efficiently *than getting up early in the morning.*

Such structures may be considered (as with AdjGs) as discontinuous modification, though the two parts of the structure, before and after the head, differ in position and content. The modifiers *more* (*-er*) and *less* do not require overt qualification necessarily; on the other hand, qualifiers introduced by *than* cannot be used without a previous modifier. Despite this close relation between modifier and qualifier, the concept of two semantically different elements and two distinctive terms for them is useful for descriptive grammar.

Qualification of equality is expressed by *as* and the following unit classes:

NG: I do not translate *as* accurately *as a professional.*
AdjG: You must translate *as* accurately *as possible.*
AdvG: She still plays the piano *as* beautifully *as ever.*
PrepG: You haven't translated *as* well *as on the previous occasion.*
Clf: People don't work *as* hard *as they do in some other countries.*

If a comparison of equality (*as ... as ...*) is established between two adverbs of manner (e.g. *elegantly, amusingly*) the second *as* must be followed by a finite clause with a form of *be*, *do*, or *have* substituting for the Predicator:

Jane Austen wrote as elegantly as *she did* amusingly. (and not *as elegantly as amusingly*)

The grades of excess and sufficiency realised by the modifiers *too* and *enough* are qualified in the same way as in AdjGs:

PrepG: Sheila married *too* hastily *for a girl of her age.*
Clnf: She didn't take long *enough to get to know her boyfriend.*

Adverbs modified quantitatively by *so* and *that* are also qualified in the same way as adjectives:

Clf: He explained the problem *so clearly* (*that*) everybody understood.
Clf: He interrupted me *that rudely* (*that*) I completely lost my patience.

The sequence of the clauses can be inverted, the second one then becoming an explanatory comment on the first:

Clf: Everybody understood the problem, he explained it *so clearly.*
Clf: I completely lost my patience, he interrupted *that rudely.*

It is important to distinguish the functions and meanings of *so* as modifier, as Conjunct and as subordinating conjunction:

Modifier: He explained it *so* clearly *that* everybody understood.
Conjunct: He explained it clearly, *so* everybody understood. (*result*)
Conjunction: He explained it clearly, *so* (*that*) everybody could understand. (*purpose*)

56.5   Recursive realisation of AdvG elements

56.5.1   Recursive heads

Any of the three elements of AdvGs, but especially the head, can be realised recursively. Many recursive heads are fixed expressions used commonly in everyday speech and writing. Some are coordinated syndetically by *and*, *but*, *or*:

and:	now and again	when and where	up and down
	far and wide	here and there	to and fro
	backwards and forwards	on and off (= occasionally)	
	up and about (= active after an illness)		
but:	slowly but surely	quietly but confidently	last but not least
or:	rightly or wrongly	somewhere or other	more or less
	now or never	sooner or later	once or twice

Others are reduplicative, joined either syndetically:

more and more	through and through	by and by (= later)
less and less	over and over	up and up
better and better	again and again	down and down
worse and worse	round and round	by and large (= in general)

or asyndetically:

very very	never never	so so

Syndetic recursion requires that the component items should belong to the same semantic class or subclass:

round and about	(direction)
first and lastly	(sequence)
cruelly but calculatingly	(manner)
*round and often	(direction + frequency)
*first and quickly	(sequence + manner)

Recursive items belonging to different semantic classes or subclasses are considered as separate heads, that is, separate AdvGs, which are not coordinated, and which may be separated in the clause:

Have you seen John *anywhere*, *recently*? (place + relative time)
I *often* have to work *overtime* to keep my job. (frequency + duration)
I suppose we'll meet again *sometime somewhere*. (time + place)
I think he will *probably* answer *truthfully*. (modality + manner)

56.5.2   Recursive modifiers

Recursive modification is realised in two main forms:

(a) Degree adverbs, which may be related paratactically, as in:

They lived *more or less* amicably for more than twenty years.
His paintings are selling *more and more* successfully every day.

or hypotactically, as in:

> His refurbished apartment turned out to be *by far the most* elegantly appointed chambers in the whole of Chelsea.

(b) Adverbs of manner, also related paratactically, as in:

> My secretary is getting *progressively and annoyingly* behind with her work.
> The men and women prisoners were kept *strictly and ruthlessly* apart from each other.

or hypotactically, as in:

> We have a departmental meeting *fairly, though perhaps not sufficiently, often.*

Such a structure is somewhat heavy and formal in style; in ordinary conversation, one would probably say:

> ... *fairly often, though perhaps not often enough.*

56.5.3   Recursive qualification

This can be realised by combinations such as the following:

Clf + Clf: As regards hotels, you may stay *anywhere you like that's not too expensive.*
PrepG + PrepG: I have to be on duty *sharply at eight in the morning.*

56.6   Conclusion

In section 54.4 we presented several families of adverbs:

(a) the hardworking circumstantials, ranging over all types of situations in the space–time dimension, a relatively closed, largely grammatical body of words, without which there can be no communication about *where and when* things happen in our lives;

(b) various sets of process, modal, degree and focusing adverbs, some grammatical and others lexical, that say *how* processes take place and *how* we experience them.

The difference between these two broad fields of adverbial reference is reflected textually in the following ways:

(i) Circumstantial adverbs, together with those of degree and focus, are needed, to different extents, in nearly all oral and written modes of communication.

(ii) The other adverbs, especially when modified or qualified, are characteristic of prepared texts, oral or written. They are used frequently, for example, by book reviewers, art critics, writers on films, music, the theatre and other cultural fields, where there is also room for the expression of personal opinions, interpretations and attitudes. A single article in a reputable newspaper attested frequent examples such as: *fairly temperamentally suited*; *this apparently quite dispassionate criticism*; *his characters are convincingly quirky, edgily at odds with their surroundings*; *he writes sensuously, fluently, wittily, compassionately, about her*; *cunningly and consistently entertaining*. The constant use of these structures tends to tire the reader, rather than stimulate him.

(iii) Despite the ease with which adverbs can be modified and qualified in the ways we have exemplified in this module, full AdvGs are rare, and recursive realisation of the elements even rarer.

(iv) Informal conversation employs looser structures and fewer lexical items per utterance than written texts. Although it may occasionally produce an expression such as:

Things were settled *finally fairly quietly*,

we more often use a style such as:

A grown man who calls his father 'Daddy' is *really out*!

Or as in the following exchange:

A. Where do the knives go?
B. In the drawer of the table. *Here.*
A. Any special order?
B. *Any old how.*

The following recorded conversation is an example of how we often talk to each other, without saying very much. It is characterised by the repetitious use of a small number of very common modal and other adverbs in a variety of syntactic functions, which we invite the reader to identify:

A. So what's new Ann?
C. Well I don't know if anything's *terribly*[1] new *at all*[2] – *really*[3] – or is it all *much*[4] the same?
B. You *still*[5] living with Deb?
. . . . .
C. No, she moved *out*[6] at the end of April.
B. Oh.
A. *So,*[7] you know, *well,*[8] we'd been *scarcely*[9] speaking for almost a year *really,*[10] *so*[11] it was *a bit of* a[12] heavy atmosphere – it didn't *really*[13] bother me – in fact . . .
B. m
C. In fact we *just*[14] *sort of*[15] lived *entirely*[16] separate lives. I used *only*[17] to see her when she came through the kitchen – her nose in the air sort of thing. *Anyway,*[18] *really,*[19] I think, the kitchen
. . . . . .

B. A bit[20] awkward, that, I should think – you would think a door could be pushed *through*,[21] through where you've got that little room with the cupboard in it.

C. I suppose *so*,[22] you see, I mean, *even*[23] if it were a couple living *together*,[24] it would be – *just*[25] ideal, that sort of thing wouldn't matter, but it isn't *really*[26] suited to people who are living separate lives *really*.[27] *So*,[28] at any rate, she moved *out*.[29] I *never*[30] heard from her *since*.[31]

B. You haven't, not a word?

C. No, I have*n't* heard from her *at all*[32] – and I haven't contacted her, and she hasn't contacted me. I haven't *really*[33] felt I wanted to, cos it was *a little*[34] *sort of*[35] *rather*[36] unpleasant in the end.

Adapted from Jan Svartvik and Randolph Quirk (eds.), *A Corpus of English Conversation*.

TASKS ON CHAPTER 12
How, where and when: The Adverbial Group

Module 54

1 †*Read again the passage quoted in 54.2 and identify the type of meaning expressed by each adverb or AdvG printed in italics. Are any types preponderant over others? Do you think there is any reason for this?*

2 †*Do the same with the following passage, and say whether the relative preponderance of the types of meanings is the same as in the previous text:*

> Is there life *elsewhere* in the cosmos? One view is that life on earth, *especially* intelligent life, is the result of an *incredibly* unlikely set of circumstances, and that there is no intelligent life *anywhere* else in our Galaxy, *perhaps* none in the entire Universe. The opposing argument is that there are *so* many stars and planets in the Galaxy that, provided there is *even* a small chance of intelligence developing on one planet, it has *probably* happened on many others, *too*. Observations show that *about* 10% of all bright stars are *roughly* similar to the sun. In our Milky Way Galaxy *alone* that means *approximately* 40 billion stars of the right type. This number is great *enough* to suggest that the odds are *quite* high.

3 *Insert in the following sets of sentences, in appropriate places, suitable adverbs chosen from the list of examples suggested for each set. All the sentences have been attested in periodicals and books, but each contained one of the listed adverbs which we have omitted from the sentence:*

(a) **Attitudinal adverbs**
certainly, reportedly, obviously, allegedly, admittedly, undeniably, actually, clearly, undoubtedly, eminently.
1) This novel is well suited to the cinema.
2) The film is brilliant and moving, though it might have been even more so.
3) A visit to the National Theatre is an educational experience for anyone interested in twentieth-century architecture.
4) The President has not decided yet on seeking a second term.
5) The collection includes a poem written by Hitler.
6) It was not a well-planned 'coup', because it failed so quickly.

7) He became a star during the revolt, which allowed him to turn it into a political asset.
8) Their popularity is rising judging by the number of fans at their concerts here.

(b) **Viewpoint adverbs**
   historically, stylistically, politically, socially, racially, ideologically, morally, constitutionally, clinically, formally.
   1) Though not 'true enemies', they are unyielding.
   2) He is well connected.
   3) The sentences are too long and complex.
   4) Bad socialism isn't, for all that, better than capitalism.
   5) The British are mixed.
   6) The war was the culmination of the nineteenth century.
   7) Most of the new towns are still villages.

(c) **Restriction and reinforcement**
   merely, hardly, solely, alone, exclusively, simply, just; also, too, again, as well, besides, similarly.
   1) The doctor who begins by searching for a heart-beat on the right-hand side will convince the patient that he will be able to help him.
   2) Very often a language is taught in a formal guise.
   3) This indicates how wrong ideas of what a language is can be ingrained in a whole generation of teachers.
   4) To put it in a few words, we do not know the answer.
   5) The emphasis in language study, was for a while on grammar.
   6) Harry said that the river would suit him perfectly, and I said so.
   7) What has happened explains many problems of the past and will help us avoid future ones.
   8) Grammar is important, but it's important to practise.

(d) **Process adverbs of manner**
   cautiously, quietly, surreptitiously, heavily, momentarily, secretly, endlessly, rigorously, slowly, mechanically.
   1) Yusuf was sleeping on his back.
   2) There was a message that the man was suspected of carrying diamonds and should be searched.
   3) Behind the barrier, Wilson worked at his code books.
   4) He went on speaking, choosing his words.
   5) It was said that he drank.
   6) The sky wept around him.
   7) 'Yes' he said, as if accepting a penance.
   8) The rain had stopped.

Module 55

1 *Revise briefly the list given in 55.1 of the syntactic functions which can be realised by AdvGs in groups and clauses. Then make a list of the functions*

realised by all of those used in the texts of sections 54.5.1,2,3. Write out the list and comment on the relative frequency of each function.

2 †*Revise the table of uses of **still**, **yet**, **already** given in section 55.2.2. Then answer the following questions, (a) affirmatively, and (b) negatively. Give two or three answers to each question:*
1) Is it time to go yet? ....
2) Have you had your lunch yet? ....
3) Do you still love me? ....
4) Are you still studying Russian? ....
5) Is it 10 o'clock already? ....
6) Have you already been to Venice?

3 †*In the following sentences, insert the adverb given on the left in its appropriate position. Indicate alternative positions where they are acceptable, and say whether this affects the meaning in any way:*

1) *sometimes*: We take long holidays abroad.
2) *often*: Women are successful in business.
3) *abroad*: He works hard.
4) *yesterday*: They gave a concert.
5) *longingly*: I gazed at the brightly coloured fish in the aquarium.
6) *perhaps*: You'd better take an overcoat with you.
7) *probably*: We shall leave tomorrow.
8) *hopefully*: They have arrived at their destination.

Module 56
1 *Modify the adverbs marked in the following sentences, in the senses indicated on the left:*
1) **Intensification**: She answered *automatically*, without thinking.
2) **Intensification**: He recovered *quickly* after the operation.
3) **Description**: They treat prisoners *harshly*.
4) **Attenuation**: The critics have spoken *highly* of the book.
5) **Attenuation**: The book is selling *well*.
6) **Quantification**: He had a few drinks and *later* was involved in an accident.
7) **Description**: The winner of the car rally drove *fast*.
8) **Intensification**: Our team didn't play *well* on that occasion.

2 *Add a qualifying expression to the AdvG in the following sentences:*
1) It's hotter in the Sahara than *anywhere*.
2) *Why* don't you buy yourself some decent shoes for a change?
3) When we came out of the Pyramids, I said to myself: '*Never*'.
4) I can't find my glasses. They must be *somewhere*.
5) *Curiously*, he used exactly the same word as I did.
6) *How* can we buy a new car just at this moment?
7) Our plane arrived two hours *later*.

8) She doesn't dance as *beautifully*.
9) Do your friends live *far*?
10) If all the hotels are full, *where* can we spend the night?

3   *Read the examples of submodified AdvGs given in 56.2 and include them in expressions which serve to complete the following sentences. Use them in the order in which they are printed on the page:*
1) You have a good command of English, but I'm afraid that . . . . .
2) The accumulation of stocks of armaments seems inevitable these days, and . . .
3) Some politicians spend all their time talking. I think they could . . .
4) Janet normally writes very good essays, but . . .
5) I used to find his classes very dull, but . . .
6) I always read this paper. In my opinion it is . . .
7) Industrialists say that . . . if . . .
8) When I got my exam results, I . . .
9) We live quite simply, though . . .

4   *Read the examples of fixed adverbial expressions mentioned in 56.5.1 and compose short sentences to illustrate the use of the following ones:*
1) now and again; far and wide.
2) slowly but surely; last but not least.
3) sooner or later; rightly or wrongly.
4) over and over; through and through.

5   †*Read the conversation quoted at the end of the module, and identify the syntactic function of each numbered adverb and the semantic type to which it belongs (see 54.4).*

13

Spatial, temporal and other relationships:

The Prepositional Group

MODULE 57
Formal features of the Prepositional Group

Summary

1   The sequence **preposition + nominal completive**, with optional modifier, functions as a clause element and so is classified as a 'group', although it is exocentric. The preposition is recognised as 'head' element.

2   Prepositions may consist of one word (*from*) or two (*because of*) or three (*in contact with*). All are single prepositions.

3   The completive may be realised by a noun (in *town*), a pronoun (after *me*), a NG (for *a long time*), an adjective (in *short*), an adverb (for *now*), a PrepG (except *in here*), a WH-Clf (because of *what happened*), a Clnf (by *studying hard*).

4   When modified, the PrepG may be graded (*more* like this), intensified (*right* through the wall), quantified (*a mile* down the road) or described (*wonderfully* on form).

Introduction

A notable feature of the English language is the extremely wide lexico-grammatical use it makes of prepositions. And where there is a preposition there is a PrepG, since prepositions cannot stand alone. Here is a recorded conversation between three students and a teacher (T):

    T: *What*'s this *about?* [1]
    B: Oh, animals.

T: Oh, yes. People are obsessed *in this country* [2] *with being kind* [3] *to animals,* [4] aren't they?

A: Alison and her cat ... !

B: Don't talk *to us* [5] *about Alison's cat!* [6]

C: That cat is definitely not popular *in our house!* [7]

B: That cat moults constantly *all over our carpet and sofa!* [8]

T: But is it true, though? See what I mean? She hates cats!

A: Just *for that silly reason?* [9]

T: No, but there seems to be more cases *of animal cruelty* [10] going on here *than anywhere else.* [11]

A: Yeah. I get the impression *from the little I know* [12] they're just as crazy *about dogs* [13] *in Belgium and Holland and France and Italy* [14] as they are *over here.* [15]

T: Is it just one *of those myths that we perpetuate* [16] *regarding the British character?* [17] Is it true?

A: I think it probably is a myth.

Private recording.

As can be seen, this frequency of PrepGs is quite normal. It has grammatical, but not stylistic significance.

57.1   Status of the PrepG

In order to accommodate syntactic structures such as *precisely for that reason, right into the water, straight along this street, only because of you,* to the scale of unit ranks adopted for this course, they are assigned to the rank of 'group'. We base this analysis on three of its grammatical features:

(a) There is a close semantic relationship between the three parts of their structure which binds them together and obliges us to treat them as a single unit.

(b) This class of unit normally functions as (i) an element of clause structure, for example as Adjunct (e.g. I decided to become a writer *precisely for that reason*); or (ii) as a unit embedded in other classes of groups, for example as qualifier of a noun (e.g. the man *in the moon*) or an adjective (e.g. delighted *at your success*).

(c) When the preposition is stranded to the end of a clause and is separated from the nominal, the concept of 'group' helps to affirm the grammatical relation existing between them as elements of the same unit:

> *That writer* nobody in our class had ever heard *of* before. (= of that writer)
> *What book* did you say the lecturer who gave us the talk yesterday referred *to*? (= to what book ... ?)

Although there are good reasons for classifying this structure as a 'group', its internal structure differs from that of other groups, as we explain in 57.2.

57.2   **Internal structure of the PrepG**

In AdjGs, AdvGs and NGs, there is one main element called the 'head', to which the other elements (modifier, qualifier, determiner) are subordinate. For this reason, the head element – a noun, an adjective or an adverb – can be used alone, without other elements, in representation of the whole group. Structures of this kind centred on the 'head', are termed **endocentric**. In a PrepG, the relation between the preposition and the nominal unit that follows it (e.g. *into bed, from Britain*) is not endocentric. A preposition cannot occur without a nominal unit, and a nominal unit is not part of a PrepG if there is no preposition. Both are equally necessary to form the group; both have equal grammatical status. Such a structure is called **exocentric**.

Having classified the sequence somewhat anomalously as an 'exocentric group' structure able to realise clausal elements, we shall name its elements as follows: the first element (such as *straight* in *straight to bed*) which is optional and usually realised by an adverb, will be called the 'modifier' (**m**). The main element is the preposition which gives its name to the group and will, for simplicity, be called the 'head' (**h**). This is followed by a nominal unit which is needed to complete the structure, and is called here the completive (**c**). We reserve the term 'Complement' for the three clausal elements 'Complement of the Subject' (Cs), 'Complement of the Object' (Co), 'Complement of the Predicator' (Cp), and use 'completive' in the PrepG. This does not mean a difference in function, but is simply a different term for a somewhat similar function at a different rank of unit structure.

Just as with many transitive verbs the 'Complement' has to be there, so in a PrepG both the preposition and the completive (or Complement) are also obligatory. Just as a transitive verb 'governs' its Complements, so a preposition governs its completives. However, we consider that the difference in rank between a clausal 'Complement' and a group 'completive' should be indicated by different terms.

The internal structure of PrepGs can be represented as follows:

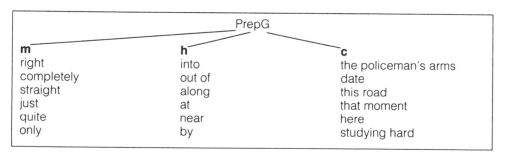

Not all PrepGs contain a modifier but all of them contain a preposition and a completive. The fact that the relationship between a preposition and its completive is an exocentric one affects the status and the scope of the modifier. Whereas in an endocentric structure the pre-head and post-head elements are centred on the head, the PrepG has no endocentric head, and the modifier normally relates to the **preposition + completive** taken together as a single item. In the groups cited above, sequences such as *only by*, etc., cannot stand alone as **mh** structures in the way that *good news, very sincere, rather slowly* can. The structure is therefore *only + by studying hard*.

57.3   **Realisation of the head element**

(a) As we have said, the head of a PrepG is realised only by prepositions. These may be 'simple' (consisting of a single word) or 'complex' (consisting of two words or three). The 'simple' forms are by far the commonest:

> as, at, by, down, for, from, in, like, near, of, off; given, granted;
> above, across, beneath, besides, during, inside, throughout;
> considering, regarding, opposite, underneath, notwithstanding.

(b) Two-word prepositions consist of a preposition (e.g. *except*), an adjective (e.g. *contrary*), an adverb (e.g. *instead*), or a conjunction (e.g. *because*) followed by one of the prepositions *for, from, of, to, with, against*:

> along with, except for, but for, near to;
> contrary to, due to, inclusive of, prior to;
> apart from, together with, regardless of, instead of;
> as for, as from, because of.

In most two-word prepositions, the meaning is expressed by the first word, the second serving to link it to the completive:

> *according* to my information; *because* of what I said.

(c) Three-word prepositions have the form **prep + noun + prep** (e.g. *in conflict with*), with the noun sometimes being determined by *the* (e.g. *in the hands of*). The first preposition is virtually limited to *in, on, by, at, for, with*, and the second to *of, with, for* and *to*. Such complex heads are then followed by the completive:

> *in aid of* the blind; *in contact with* you; *in return for* this;
> *by way of* a change; *by dint of* force; *by means of* signs;
> *on (the) ground(s) of* cruelty; *on top of* that; *on the part of* everyone;
> *at the expense of* your health; *at the hands of* a tyrant;
> *with regard to* your first question; *with the exception of* Tom.

Sometimes the noun of a complex preposition may be modified by an adjective, as in *with the surprising exception of Tom* or *in close contact with you*.

A small number of PrepGs containing complex prepositions ending in *of* have an alternative structure:

> for the sake of the children;   on behalf of the committee;
> for the children's sake;   on the committee's behalf.

However, the genitive form is used primarily with completives having personal reference: *for peace and quiet's sake.

The sequence **prep + noun + prep + completive** can represent not only a complex prepositional head + completive structure but also the following two structures which express different meanings:

(a) A simple prepositional head + qualified completive:

near + the bar on the corner.

(b) Two independent PrepGs which might be reversed in order:

near the bar + on the corner
on the corner + near the bar

57.4   Realisation of the completive element

The completive element of a PrepG may be realised by the classes of groups and clauses shown below. Simple nouns and pronouns, adjectives and adverbs are treated as 'groups' represented by the head:

NGs:	in *command*	after *which*	on account of *his age*
AdjGs:	in *private*	at *last*	through *thick and thin*
AdvGs:	for *ever*	since *when*	until *quite recently*
PrepGs:	except *in here*		from *out of the forest*
Clf (WH-):		Have you decided about *when you're leaving*?	
Clnf (WH + V-inf):		Have you any problems apart from *where to stay*?	
Clnf (V-ing):		The miners charge the employers with *ignoring their claims*.	

The following restrictions exist on the realisation of completives:

(a) The use of AdjGs and AdvGs as completives is infrequent and limited to certain set expressions such as those given above. The reason for this is that completives have nominal reference rather than circumstantial or attributive meaning.

(b) English prepositions are not followed by *that*-clauses or finite clauses; the following structure is not acceptable:

*I was pleased about (that) Monica won the prize.

(c) English prepositions are not followed by *to*-infinitive clauses, other than those introduced by a *WH*-item; the following is not acceptable:

*We were annoyed at not to get any news from you.

The following continuation of the student–teacher conversation shows that the largest number of completives are realised by nouns, pronouns and NGs, with a sprinkling of finite and non-finite clauses, and the occasional adjective or adverb.

The 'Green' Party
A: It's really making a come back all of *a sudden*. [1]
B: Seems to come in and out of *fashion*. [2]

A: Yeah.

B: We had elections at *school* [3] and the 'Green' party did win, actually.

A: So did we. It was a big surprise to *everyone*, [4] so many anti-establishment adherents amongst *us*. [5]

T: I get the impression that it's a non-vote, just a comfortable way of *not having to take a decision*. [6]

B: Yeah, a pressure vote, so that you don't have to vote either for *the Conservatives* [7] or for *the Labour Party*. [8] People just can't be bothered with *comparing programmes and thinking about who to vote for*. [9]

T: And you think this has a significant impact on *the way the other parties have formed their policies*? [10]

B: Yeah, but it's . . . it's just waffle, just an excuse for *getting votes*. [11]

T: Do you feel very cynical about *them*, [12] then?

B: Suppose I do, a bit.

T: One of *the things people say* [13] about, well, at least some of the *younger generation*, [14] not all of *them*, [15] but on *the whole* [16] is, there's no radicalism among *people today* [17] *who are in their late teens and twenties*. [18] It's what the forty-year-olds say about *the twenty-year-olds*. [19] They think back to *when they were young* [20] and *what they were like then* [21] and say that the younger generation don't have any radical or controversial views any more.

A: I don't think radicalism has disappeared. Maybe it has been channelled into *that 'green' area*. [22]

B: Yeah. A lot of former ideas have been ditched in favour of *moving towards a position much closer to the centre than before*. [23]

idem.

57.5   Realisation of the modifier element

Like nouns, adjectives and adverbs, prepositions can also be modified, though, as we have mentioned, it would be truer to say that what is modified is not simply the preposition but the relationship expressed by the *preposition + completive* group unit. The modification usually takes the form of grading, intensification, or attenuation, quantification, description (as with adjectives and adverbs), or simply of focusing and reinforcement. These rhetorical purposes are more characteristic of interpersonal communication than of straightforward narrative or informational types of written discourse. The following are attested examples:

Grading modifiers

more, less, far more, much less, the most, the least:

They are *far more* behind the times than us.
You are *the least* in need of help.

Intensifying modifiers

completely, directly, right, well, all, absolutely, greatly, straight, badly, much:

I'm *greatly* in favour of reducing working hours.
Today I'm feeling *absolutely* on top of the world.
It rains *all* through the year there.
The parachutists landed *almost* within enemy lines.

Attenuating modifiers

somewhat, partly, scarcely, not fully, to some extent, slightly, a little, hardly, not at all, not altogether:

It's *somewhat* against my principles to go absent.
I think you're *slightly* out of touch with reality.
I'm afraid this is *hardly* up to your usual standard.

Quantifying modifiers

a mile, six feet, a long time, not that much, miles, two hours, way back, light years, streets:

She was *streets* ahead of her rivals.
All that was *way back* in history.
That's *miles* from the truth. (colloq.)

Descriptive or attitudinal modifiers

surprisingly, hopelessly, dangerously, unexpectedly, perilously:

We were *dangerously* close to having an accident.
After ten hours in the water, I was *perilously* near to exhaustion.

Focusing or reinforcing modifiers

precisely, mainly, solely, just, principally, chiefly, merely, only:

I failed *precisely* because of not feeling well that day.
You say that *just* for the sake of arguing.

With prepositions that have adverbial homomorphs, such as *near, after, before, in, above*, one may feel it is the preposition rather than the **prep + completive** which is being modified:

We live *quite near* the main square.
We arrived *just before* midnight.

On the other hand, certain modifiers seem to relate more closely to the completive, as is sometimes seen in the possibility of using an alternative structure:

I obtained my first job *purely by accident*.	I obtained my first job *by pure accident*.
We worked *almost until midnight*.	We worked *until almost midnight*.
The firm is *badly in debt*.	The firm has some *bad debts*.

MODULE 58
Syntactic features of the Prepositional Group

Summary

1   The basic grammatical role of a preposition is to establish a functional
    relationship between its completive and another syntactic element of a clause or
    a group, such as the Predicator, or the Subject Complement of a clause, or the
    head of a Nominal Group.

2   In doing this, the whole PrepG itself functions as an element of the clause (e.g.
    as Predicator Complement in: *He sat by the fire*) or group (e.g. qualifier in: angry
    at his refusal).

3   PrepGs can realise up to five syntactic functions in groups and eight in clauses.
    Some of these are frequent and others infrequent.

4   Some words can be used not only as prepositions but also as adverbs (e.g.
    about) or conjunctions (e.g. *until*) or verbs (*considering*). These words are called
    'homomorphs'. It is important to recognise their different class and functions.

5   The two-word and three-word prepositions tend to have a 'core' or 'prototype'
    meaning. The one-word items cover a more varied range of case meanings.

58.1   The grammatical role of prepositions

The grammatical role of prepositions is to express a variety of syntactic and
semantic relationships between nominal entities and (a) other nominals (*the
bridge over the river*), (b) verbs (*he ran into the room*), (c) clauses (*support
for raising the subscription*), adjectives (*angry at his refusal*), adverbs (*up to
the top*).

When a preposition links its completive to another element of a clause or a
group, the whole Prepositional Group itself becomes a functional element of
the clause or group.

58.2   Syntactic functions of PrepGs

PrepGs can realise up to fourteen syntactic functions as constituents of other
groups, of clauses or outside clauses. They share the functions with other
classes of unit and are therefore mentioned again in the sections below.

58.2.1 PrepGs embedded as elements of groups

1	Qualifier in AdjG:	My son is *brilliant at mathematics*.
2	Qualifier in AdvG:	They do not live *far from here*.
3	Qualifier in NG:	Have you any *books on astronomy*?
4	Modifier in NG:	*Off-the-record* comments should not be printed in a newspaper.
5	Completive in PrepG:	I'm free all day *except on Mondays*.

58.2.2 PrepGs as elements of clauses

6	Adjunct:	All this happened *long before the war*.

Occasionally a circumstance realised by a PrepG can realise a Subject or Direct Object.

7	Subject:	A. When can we discuss this matter?
		B. *After supper* would suit me best.
8	Direct Object:	I don't consider *next to a railway line* as a good place to live.

Some verbs are related to their Object by a specific preposition. The verb is called a prepositional verb and the Object a prepositional Object (see also 6.3.1).

9	Prepositional Object:	I don't believe *in wasting money*.
		Her parents paid *for the wedding*.
		She decided *on the detailed arrangements* herself.
10	Subject Complement:	Monica must be *out of her mind* to reject such an interesting offer.
11	Object Complement:	His illness left him *without a job*.
12	Predicator Complement:	The procession came *to a halt*.

Here the PrepGs are expressing certain circumstantial states as temporary characteristics or Attributes of the Subject and Object nouns. The attributive nature of the relationship could equally well be expressed by an adjective of similar meaning: Monica must be *mad*.

58.2.3 Other functions of PrepGs

Like other classes of units, certain PrepGs can function syntactically as Disjuncts, that is to say outside clause structures, to express a comment on or an attitude to the form or content of a whole clause:

13:	Disjuncts:	*In all honesty*, I don't believe a word he said.
		From my point of view, all his fine promises don't mean a thing.

Although we regard Disjuncts here as syntactically outside clause structure, from a semantic and psychological point of view they are part of the thematic organisation of the discourse surrounding the clause. For this reason, we include Disjuncts in Chapter 6 as a type of 'thematisation' termed 'discourse themes'.

PrepGs can also be used as Conjuncts to link clauses, or groups and words within clauses:

14 Conjuncts: A. I'm leaving now. B. *In that case*, I'll go too.
                I'm very fond of music, *in particular*, the piano.

Of these syntactic functions, by far the commonest are Adjuncts, Subject Complements and Predicator Complements in clauses, and qualifiers in group structures, especially Nominal Groups. The following incident from the autobiography of Shirley MacLaine, the actress, contains nineteen numbered examples whose functions we invite the reader to identify as one of the tasks in this module:

Late one evening *on our way home* [1] *from the studio*, [2] we pulled up
at a red light. [3] As we chatted quietly *about the day's work*, [4]
something suddenly kicked us *in the rear* [5] and my feet went *over my
head.* [6] I reached out *for Steve*, [7] screaming. I didn't know where
down was, and my head wouldn't move *on my neck.* [8] The car came *to
a halt.* [9] We had been knocked sixty feet *to the opposite side* [10] *of the
highway* [11] *into the path* [12] *of oncoming traffic.* [13] Our trunk was *in
the front seat* [14] and Steve was pinned *under it.* [15] 'Are you all right?'
he called *to me.* [16] He was twisted *out of shape* [17] *on the floor*, [18]
with one arm tangled *in the steering wheel.* [19]

Shirley MacLaine, *Don't Fall off the Mountain*.

58.3   Homomorphs of prepositions

Some of the words included in 57.3 can also realise functions characteristic of verbs, conjunctions, adverbs and adjectives. Such items are considered here as homomorphs, not as being converted from one class to another.

58.3.1   Prepositions and verbs

The following participial forms can function both as head elements of a PrepG, and as Predicator (or part of the Predicator) of a clause; as such they can be classed both as prepositions and as verbs: *barring, considering, excepting, excluding, following, including, regarding, given, granted*:

prep: No-one *barring* a lunatic would start a nuclear war.
verb: There are restrictions *barring* the employment of
            children under sixteen.

prep:	There are always problems *regarding* punctuality.
verb:	Up to now I have been *regarding* you as a friend.
prep:	We open seven days a week *excluding* Christmas Day.
verb:	I'm not *excluding* the possibility of an agreement.
prep:	*Granted* his long experience, (but) it doesn't mean he's always right.
verb:	They have *granted* me a tourist visa for three months.

58.3.2   Prepositions and conjunctions

It was mentioned in 57.4 that prepositions may be followed by finite *WH*-clauses and by non-finite clauses in *-ing*, since these have nominal reference. A small number of items referring to moments of time can, however, be used to introduce declarative finite clauses, and are then considered as having conjunctive function:

prep:	*after* his accident; *after* having an accident.
conj:	*after* he had his accident.
prep:	*before* your arrival; *before* arriving.
conj:	*before* you arrived.
prep:	*since* our meeting; *since* meeting you.
conj:	*since* we met.
prep:	*until* my visit to Paris; *until* going to Paris.
conj:	*until* I went to Paris.

Three of the participial items mentioned in 57.3 – *considering, given, granted* – also enter into construction with finite *that*-clauses and so can be classified as conjunctional homomorphs of the corresponding prepositions:

prep:	*Considering* his age, he did very well in the competition.
conj:	*Considering* that he is so young, he did very well . . .
prep:	*Given* your interest in painting, you'll enjoy living in Florence.
conj:	*Given* that you are so interested in painting, you'll . . .
prep:	*Granted* the changes nuclear energy will bring about, it will still need to be carefully controlled.
conj:	*Granted* (that) nuclear energy will bring about many changes, it will still need to be carefully controlled.

58.3.3   Prepositions and adverbs

Both prepositions and adverbs express, typically, circumstantial meanings, especially those of space and time. It is not surprising, therefore, that some words can realise functions of both classes. The following are examples:

aboard, about, above, across, after, along, around, behind, below, beneath, between, beyond, down, in, inside, near, off, on, opposite, outside, through, throughout, under, underneath, up.

In the following examples, both the adverb and the PrepG are functioning as Adjuncts or Predicator Complements:

> There are always two pilots *aboard/aboard the plane*.
> All the children were running *around/around the playground*.
> The last time I met Monica was at her wedding in September, but I'm afraid I haven't seen her *since/since then*.
> The workmen must go *outside/outside the factory* if they want to smoke during the morning break.

In the following examples, the homomorphs function as head of a PrepG (left) and as modifier of a NG head (right):

near the town centre;	*near* neighbours of mine.
outside the gates;	an *outside* broadcast.
inside the museum;	some *inside* information.
tears rolled *down* her cheeks;	a *down* payment.

Prepositions are identified by the obligatory presence of a completive. Adverbs do not enter into construction with a following nominal unit.

MODULE 59
Semantic features of the Prepositional Group

Summary

1   The choice of preposition in a PrepG may be (a) governed by the particular noun, verb or adjective that precedes it (*a threat to, depend on, bored with*), or (b) chosen from a set of prepositions expressing different relationships: look *at/ for/out of/into/after/around/behind/up/down*.

2   We propose 55 broad relationships expounded by some 140 prepositions, each of which may denote two or more relationships (e.g. *for*) or different aspects of a single relationship (e.g. *with*).

3   It is difficult to define the semantic boundaries of prepositional meanings.

59.1   Two types of prepositional meanings

Prepositional meanings can be divided into two broad types: (a) those in which the choice of preposition is determined by the verb, noun or adjective preceding it and the meaning of its completive; and (b) those in which the choice of preposition can be varied independently in accordance with the speaker's intentions:

dependent: I *agree with* you; *confidence in* you; *good for* you.
variable: We flew */ in / into / out of / through / above / below / close to / near / a long way from* the clouds.

We assume here that the reader is already reasonably familiar with those prepositions which are dependent on and determined by nouns, verbs and adjectives, e.g.

nouns: damage *to*, a liking *for*, an attack *on*, a quarrel *with*.
adjs: compatible *with*, opposed *to*, free *of/from*, lacking *in*.
verbs: to insist *on*, to pay *for*, to amount *to*, to hope *for*.

The following list shows the very large number of meanings expressed by English prepositions, especially if we take into consideration that most of them can be used in different contexts, and therefore different senses.

Spatial reference

1	interiority	9	di rection	16	indeterminacy
2	exteriority	10	separation	17	continuity
3	superiority	11	oppositeness	18	extent
4	inferiority	12	transversality	19	accompaniment
5	anteriority	13	verticality	20	parallelism
6	posteriority	14	horizontality	21	origin
7	proximity	15	circularity	22	partition
8	contiguity				

Time reference

23	point in time	26	relative to a period	29	frequency
24	relative to a point	27	anteriority		
25	period of time	28	posteriority		

Abstract reference

30	cause	39	reaction	48	replacement
31	reason	40	attribution	49	reference
32	purpose	41	existence	50	contingency
33	source	42	support	51	concession
34	manner	43	opposition	52	result
35	comparison	44	exception	53	process
36	role	45	condition	54	state
37	means	46	addition	55	approximation
38	agency	47	exchange		

The following comments on this list are necessary:

(a) The spatial terms cover both position and movement according to context.

(b) Many spatial prepositions are used in abstract or metaphorical expressions where the case meaning cannot be described by a concrete 'literal' term. For example, *about* in *walk about the house* expresses 'indeterminate spatial movement', whereas in *talk about the house* it expresses the notion of 'reference'.

(c) We have not included the Recipient and Beneficiary roles realised by the prepositions *to* and *for*, since these functions are treated fully in 14.5. Possession and related meanings expounded by *of* are mentioned in 59.2.2. 'Agent' is broadened to cover a non-animate Agent or 'Force'. These, and other grammatical roles not realised by PrepGs, are introduced in Chapter 4 as participant functions in the clause.

(d) A list of this dimension is large enough to permit a practical interpretation of prepositional meanings, but not necessarily a full description, which is affected by lexical and situational context in every individual utterance. For example, in the following expressions, the different contextual uses of the preposition *under* may be subsumed under the broad term 'inferiority', but they clearly refer to different types of 'inferiority', which we shall call here 'contextual' differences.

(1) He slept *under the bridge.*
(2) He walked *under the bridge.*
(3) He crawled *under the table.*
(4) The ferry from Calais to Dover takes *under an hour.*
(5) *Under the influence* of drugs; *under his leadership; under the threat* of expulsion; *under control; under the circumstances; under contract* for a year.

Such contextual meanings of a given broad relationship are not easy to formulate and may sometimes appear as vague as the broad terms themselves. It is not possible to systematise them adequately, and consequently even less possible to systematise their exponents. The selection of one rather than another depends on the semantics of prepositional relations and on lexical collocation. Some prepositions can express not merely different aspects of a single 'meaning', but entirely different meanings. For this reason we may describe them as 'polysemous'.

The following paragraphs illustrate the variety of 'case' meanings that can be expressed by PrepGs in any short passage of uncomplicated written English:

Wilson stood gloomily *by his bed* [1] *in the Bedford Hotel* [2] and contemplated his sash, which lay uncoiled and ruffled *like an angry snake*[3]; the small hotel room was hot *with the conflict* [4] *between them*[5]. *Through the wall* [6] he could hear Harris cleaning his teeth *for the fifth time* [7] that day. Harris believed *in dental hygiene*[8]. 'It's cleaning my teeth *before and after every meal* [9] that's kept me so well *in this climate,* [10] he would say, raising his pale exhausted face *over an orange squash*[11]. Now he was gargling: it sounded *like a noise* [12] *in the pipes*[13].

Wilson sat down *on the edge* [14] of his bed [15] and rested. He had left his door open *for coolness*[16], and *across the passage* [17] he could see *into the bathroom*[18]. The Indian *with the turban* [19] was sitting *on the side* [20] *of the bath* [21] fully dressed: he stared inscrutably back *at Wilson* [22] and bowed. 'Just a moment, sir,' he called. 'If you would care to step *in here* [23] . . .' Wilson angrily shut the door.

Graham Greene, *The Heart of the Matter.*

[11] proximity; [2] interiority; [3] comparison; [4] cause; [5] reciprocity; [6] transversality; [7] frequency; [8] process; [9] time relative to point; [10] state; [11] superiority; [12] comparison; [13] interiority; [14] contiguity; [15] partition; [16] purpose; [17] transversality; [18] direction; [19] accompaniment; [20] superiority; [21] partition; [22] direction; [23] direction.

59.2 Polysemy

59.2.1 One form, several meanings

The following six functions can be expounded by the preposition *by*:

(1) position near: I sat *by* my secretary.
(2) movement near: I walked *by* the Post Office.
(3) agency: The letters will be typed *by* the secretary.
(4) relative to a
      point in time: She will finish them *by* tomorrow.
(5) means: They will be sent *by* registered mail.
(6) extent: The envelopes measure 9 cms *by* 6 cms.

It is clear that these relationships depend greatly on the semantic references of one or both of the constituents which are linked by the preposition. For example: in (1), the relationship of 'proximity' is governed by the verb *sit*; if the verb were passive (e.g. *was abandoned*), the relationship with *my secretary* would be 'agentive'. In (2), if the verb were *stood* instead of *walked*, the meaning of *by* would be 'position near', not 'movement near'. In (3), if the completive were inanimate (e.g. *computer*) instead of animate (*my secretary*), its case relationship would be that of 'Instrument' or 'means', not 'agency'.

At the same time, the individual preposition does have a certain autonomy of reference. For instance, in (1) and (2) it contributes the case feature of 'proximity' to the more general dimensions of 'position' and 'movement'.

Because we are dealing here with three semantically variable items, 'first item + preposition + second item', the relationships between them can only be given broad names such as 'position', 'period', 'extent', 'goal', 'movement', 'agency', 'means', etc. Any attempt to refine the description of relations brings us into the area of contextual features. For example, the prepositions *round/around* express circular movement along a path in *She danced around me*, but circular position on a path in *The children sat round the teacher* (though probably the circle was not a full one). In the sentence *They drove furiously round the race track*, the track was probably irregularly curved, not circular. Sometimes the meaning is indeterminate movement in different directions within an area, as in *We walked for hours round the streets looking for a cheap hotel*. Other times, the movement may be neither circular nor along a clear path, but varied and indeterminate in a volume of space (e.g. *The bees swarmed around us*.) These differences may be regarded as different senses of the general meaning of 'circularity'.

Some of the common prepositions may express not only various senses of a broad meaning, but also quite different meanings. For example, the preposition *for* in *I've bought a ticket for the theatre, I've bought a ticket for you, I've bought a ticket for ten dollars*, may be said to express the meanings 'goal', 'support' and 'exchange' respectively. Grammarians vary in the number of prepositional meanings (sometimes called 'cases') that they recognise, as well as in the names they give to them. The two examples *for the theatre* and *for you* might both be regarded as expressing 'destination' or 'benefaction' and 'purpose' respectively; and *for ten dollars* could be described as 'price' or 'quantity' instead of 'exchange'. Semantic boundaries are difficult to define.

59.2.2   Meanings expounded by *of*

One of the most polysemous prepositions is *of*, which can cover the following and other functions:

subjective:	the fall *of* an empire; the rise *of* capitalism.
objective:	the study *of* English; the writing *of* novels.
partitive:	six *of* the students; the door *of* the house.
content:	the waters *of* the Nile; a photo *of* us all.
quantity:	a population *of* forty million; a family *of* six.
extent:	in an area *of* ten square miles.
source:	the heat *of* the sun; a man *of* the people.
attributive:	a work *of* great beauty; an act *of* stupidity.
temporal:	as *of* yesterday; at the height *of* the season.
cause:	die *of* hunger; tired *of* studying.

To these we must add the function of *of* when used in complex PrepGs:

because *of* that, out *of* spite, for lack *of* money, in the capacity *of*, on the grounds *of*, with the exception *of*.

Many languages have an all-purpose preposition of this kind.

59.3   Prototype meaning

The phenomenon of polysemy, even if it is only contextual, invites the natural question: 'What feature of the meaning of a preposition is it that permits it to express various case relations and that is presumably present in all its uses?' Prepositions do seem to have a 'core sense' or 'prototype meaning', but it is often extraordinarily difficult to formulate it clearly, and we do not claim to have proposed in 59.1 a particularly transparent set of terms. For instance, in the five uses of *around* cited in 59.2.1 the only semantic component common to them all is the very general one of 'movement in space', a feature which does not distinguish it from any other preposition of spatial movement, such as *from, into, out of*.

Similarly, to say that the relationship expressed by *in* is prototypically that of 'interiority' (i.e. its 'in-ness'), is tautological, that is, defining a concept in terms of itself. Moreover, the term 'interiority' can hardly be expected to cover expressions such as *in contact, in front, in a line*, and certainly not most of its uses in abstract contexts: *in love, in French, in such a manner, in exchange for, in a rush, in demand*, etc. The commonest and most polysemous prepositions, that is to say, some 40 of the one-word items, cannot be reduced to 'core' meanings, and may almost be regarded as mere signals pointing in different directions.

On the other hand, contextualised expressions are usually fairly easy to interpret even when the only variable is the completive. For example, the following PrepGs may be rightly understood in terms of the states and activities they imply, provided the reader/hearer is familiar with the socio-cultural context; for example, that *be at Oxford* refers to the activity of studying at the university which is in Oxford, and not to the mere state of being in that town.

	Implication
He is *in the library*.	He is reading or studying.
He is *in politics*.	He is a politician.
It is *in italics*.	It is printed in italic type.
It is *in marble*.	It is made of marble.
She was *at Oxford*.	She was a student at Oxford University.
She was *at the wheel*.	She was driving the car.
She was *at church*.	She was attending a service.
He's always *on the go*.	He's always busy and active.
He's *on a pension*.	He's retired, he lives on a pension.
He's *on his own*.	He is/lives alone.

Another feature of Prepositional Group usage is their occurrence in periphrastic SPCs structures such as the following, which are similar, though not identical, in meaning to the structures shown on the right:

Don't get *in a panic*!	Don't panic!
My car went *into a skid*.	My car skidded.
She went *into hysterics*.	She became hysterical.
Please get *in touch with me*.	Please contact me.
They made *a search of the whole area*.	They searched the whole area.

We have the situation *under control*.	We control the situation.
They made an investment *of £100*.	They invested £100.
I put my trust *in you*.	I trust you.

The reverse phenomenon also exists in which the relations of manner or means or Instrument, which are normally expressed by a PrepG, are incorporated in the meaning of the verb:

to milk a cow = take milk from a cow
to paper a wall = put paper on a wall
to knife a person = stab a person with a knife

From all the above examples, we can observe a certain parallelism between the preposition + completive and the verb + Object relationships. Both can be regarded as types of transitivity.

The plasticity and vagueness of some one-word prepositions is seen especially in certain fixed phrases which border on the idiomatic and whose meanings are difficult to identify in the terms proposed in 57.2, e.g.

in: *in* fact, all *in* all, (be) *in* the know.
on: *on* the whole, *on* line, *on* the cheap, *on* the sly.
for: (know) *for* a fact, *for* good, *for* certain.
off: *off* the cuff.
at: (be) *at* a loss, *at* sight, *at* a pinch.

Such expressions are best analysed as semantic wholes, rather than two-element group structures.

59.4   One meaning, several forms

A preposition can not only have several meanings; it can also share some of its meanings with other prepositions. That is to sy there can be several prepositions referring to a given type of general case relationship but differing in the details of their reference. Sometimes there is little difference in meaning between two prepositions:

I felt sick *in* the stomach.	I felt sick *at* the stomach.
I dreamt *of* you last night.	I dreamt *about* you last night.
He died *of* a heart attack.	He died *from* a heart attack.
In consequence of this, . . .	*As a consequence of* this, . . .
In reference to your letter, . . .	*With reference* to your letter, . . .
She was thrilled *with* the idea of a holiday.	She was thrilled *at* the idea of a holiday.

Whereas the members of a grammatical paradigm (e.g. *this, that, these, those*; or *work, works, worked, working*) are in complementary distribution, that is, are mutually exclusive, so that only one member of the paradigm can be used in any given syntactic frame, this is not always true of prepositional sets, in which alternative choices are sometimes possible, because the differences between them are semantic rather than syntactic.

For example, some verbs can be used fairly freely with several different prepositions without any great difference in meaning. The verb *belong* is always followed by *to* when it refers to possession (*This book belongs to me*); but when it is used with the meaning of 'have a certain connexion indicated or implied by the context' (O.E.D.), or 'be in the right place; be suitable or advantageous' (L.D.C.E.), the following prepositional uses have been observed:

with:	Cheese belongs *with* salad.
in:	This chair belongs *in* the other room.
among:	He belongs *among* the radicals.
around:	He looks as if he belonged *around* a racetrack.
on:	The story belongs *on* a low level of literature.
under:	The theories of Science belong *under* a different heading.
(zero):	I don't belong *here*.

Similarly with the verb *to centre*, we find the following prepositions:

on:	Our thoughts centred *on* the young girl about to be married.
in:	The whole centred *in* man, *in* each individual.
about:	The real interest of the story centres *about* the lives of four personages.
around:	The group of gifted men and women who centred *around* Henry Adams.

On the other hand, in some three-word prepositions, the meaning changes when the verb or the preposition changes:

He was *held in the hands of* terrorists.	He *suffered at the hands of* terrorists.
In need of money.	*For need of* money.

If the noun item of a three-word preposition is defined by *the*, this also may change the meaning, even if the rest of the PrepG remains unchanged:

in view of (= *because of*)	in *the* view of (= *in the opinion of*)
in search of (= *looking for*)	in *the* search for (= *during* the search for)
in contact with (= *touching* or *in touch with*)	in *the* contact with (= *during* the contact)

59.5 Prepositional sets

The following are the most frequent exponents of the prepositional relationships proposed in 59.1.

59.5.1 Spatial reference

Case		Exponents
1	Interiority:	in, inside, within, into, among, amid(st), in the midst of, between, in the middle of.
2	Exteriority:	out, outside, out of.
3	Superiority:	on, upon, on top of, atop, above, over, onto.
4	Inferiority:	under, underneath, beneath, below.
5	Anteriority:	before, in front of, ahead of, preceding.
6	Posteriority:	behind, at the back of, in back of (AmE), following.
7	Proximity:	by, near (to), close to, with, beside, alongside, approaching.
8	Contiguity:	at, against, in contact with, at the end/beginning of, in the middle of, on.
9	Direction:	to, for, towards, up to, after, at, on, in, about, around.
10	Separation:	from, away from, apart from, off.
11	Oppositeness:	opposite, facing.
12	Transversality:	through, across, past, over, by.
13	Verticality:	up, down.
14	Horizontality:	along.
15	Circularity:	round, around, about.
16	Indeterminacy:	about, around, round.
17	Continuity:	past, by, beyond.
18	Extent:	for, throughout, over, all over, as far as, from ... to.
19	Accompaniment:	with, without, along with, together with, in company with, in the company of.
20	Parallelism:	parallel to, in parallel with, in line with.
21	Origin:	from, at.
22	Partition:	of, per.

59.5.2 Time reference

23	Point in time:	at, on, (close) on, (just) on, as of.
24	Relative to a point:	by, until, (up) to, (as) from, since, pending, for, in.
25	Period of time:	for, over, during, through, throughout, from ... to ..., in the course of.
26	Relative to a period:	in, at, outside, inside, within, in the course of, between ... and ....
27	Anteriority:	before, prior to, previous to, preliminary to, preparatory to.
28	Posteriority:	after, following, subsequent to.
29	Frequency:	per, at intervals of.

59.5.3   **Abstract reference**

30	Cause:	because of, on account of, due to, owing to, for, through, of, from, thanks to.
31	Reason:	for, from, out of, for love of, for want of, by reason of, for need of, for lack of, for the sake of, in view of, in the light of, on the grounds of, by virtue of.
32	Purpose:	for, to, at, with a view to.
33	Source:	from, of.
34	Manner:	like, in, with, in the manner of, à la, after.
35	Comparison:	like, unlike, than, as, such as, with, in comparison with, as against, over, above, under.
36	Role:	as, in the capacity of, by way of.
37	Means:	in, by, by means of, by dint of, with, without.
38	Agency:	by.
39	Reaction:	to, at, by, with, for.
40	Attribution:	of, in, with, without.
41	Existence:	with, without.
42	Support:	for, on behalf of, in aid of, in favour of, in support of, for the sake of.
43	Opposition:	against, up against, contrary to, at variance with, at the expense of.
44	Exception:	except (for), excepting, with the exception of, excluding, bar, barring, apart from, aside from, but, other than, save, beyond.
45	Condition:	in case of, but for.
46	Addition:	besides, as well as, in addition to, with, together with, along with.
47	Exchange:	for, in exchange for, in return for.
48	Replacement:	instead of, in place of, in lieu of.
49	Reference:	regarding, respecting, concerning, with regard to, with respect to, in regard to, as regards, as to, as for, on, of, at, about, ref., re, with reference to, regardless of, irrespective of, for.
50	Contingency:	with, without.
51	Concession:	for, despite, in spite of, for all, with all, notwithstanding.
52	Result:	in consequence of, as a consequence of, consequent on, as a result of, (resulting) from.
53	Process:	at, in, in the process of, in search of, into.
54	State:	in, out of, on, under, beneath, through, over, beyond.
55	Approximation:	about, around, approaching.

59.6   **General remarks**

(a) In the semantic domains covered by these sets of prepositions we are not suggesting that the members of each set are synonymous but only that the meanings overlap. For example, the following share a common ground of meaning, but suggest slightly different inferences:

	Inference
There were quarrels *among them.*	(several persons)
There were quarrels *between them.*	(several small groups or pairs)

(b) In most instances the specific meaning is greatly inferred from the lexical environment, that is, the preceding verb, noun or adjective and the following completive:

	Inference
We swim *in the summer.*	(whole period)
We married *in the summer.*	(point in period)

Different lexical environments often involve different case meanings:

I'm staying here *for your sake.*	(31	Reason)
I'm staying here *for two months.*	(25	Period)

It is interesting to note the large number of abstract notions that can be expressed by English PrepGs (see 59.1) and the many simple and complex prepositions involved in doing so. Many are in common use: *be out of work* (unemployed), *be out of date* (obsolete), *be up against it* (face difficulties), *be past caring* (not worry any more). New extensions of basic prepositional meanings are frequent, especially in informal speech, e.g. *I'm into yoga these days* (I'm practising yoga), *He's off alcohol now* (He no longer takes alcoholic drinks). Others are more idiomatic, though widely used: *run or work like mad* (perform the action intensively), *do something on the spot* (do it immediately), *be off colour* (slightly ill), *it's up to you* (depends on you). This feature of PrepG meanings is of a lexical rather than a grammatical nature, and will not be elaborated further here.

MODULE 60
Expanded and discontinuous Prepositional Groups

Summary

1   PrepGs can be expanded by multiple realisations of any one of their elements: the prepositional head (*into and out of, before and after*), the modifier (*fairly and squarely, two or three feet*), and especially the completive (any two or more Nominal Groups or clauses). Normally only one element is recursive, occasionally two, rarely three.

2   There are five clause structures in which the preposition is normally or optionally separated from its completive and placed after the verb. Inversion permits different constituents to be fronted as marked theme and so emphasised (see 28.4). In some fixed expressions discontinuity is not possible.

60.1   Expansion of the PrepG

Each of the three elements can be realised recursively, either by coordination (parataxis) or by subordination (hypotaxis).

60.1.1   Recursive head element

Coordination: There are other expenses *over and above* books.
Are you *for or against* this proposal?
I go by bus *to and from* the university.
Democracy means government *of, for and by* the people.
This offer is valid *up to and including* the last day of the month.

Subordination: Most of the club members are *under, though not much under*, 25 years of age.

60.1.2   Recursive modifier

Coordination: We borrowed the money *purely and simply* because of the urgent need for it.

Subordination: The club is now *practically, if not entirely*, without funds.

60.1.3   Recursive completive

The greatest amount of expansion occurs in this element, since it is realised by embedded groups and clauses, e.g.

Coordination: Kindest regards TO *your wife and all the children.*
It appears that the Unions are not fully unanimous AS TO [*whether to accept the latest offer made by the employers or whether to go on strike again*].
Opinions are divided AS REGARDS [*how much they should claim in higher wages and what reduction in working hours they can reasonably demand.*]
Many of the workers themselves are AGAINST [*declaring so many strikes and risking the loss of their jobs.*]

Subordination: Six months into the American Civil War, Lincoln came UP WITH [*what seemed to him a fair, sensible, humane solution* [*to the divisive issue* [*of black slavery* [*in the U.S.*]]]].
One of the Nobel prizes was awarded TO [*an Indian doctor* [*still only a young man* [*at the time*]]].
We do not agree WITH [*the verdict* [*that the accident was due to dangerous driving* [*while under the influence of drink*]]].'

60.2   Discontinuous PrepGs

Discontinuity occurs in the PrepG when the normal order of the elements, **preposition + completive**, is inverted, so that the nominal completive is fronted to initial position in the clause, and the preposition is placed at the end. This occurs frequently in English, particularly in the five types of sequence illustrated below. Although grammatically it is a marked form, it is perfectly normal for the purpose it serves, which is principally to give prominence to certain parts of the message. The following examples illustrate its use contrasted with the normal unmarked order placed on the left:

(a) **In cleft clauses**:

I am worried *about your health.*   It is *your health* I am worried about.
Your health is *what* I am worried *about.*
What I am worried *about* is your health.

(b) **In clauses with restrictive meaning**:

He only thinks *about his work.*   *The only thing* he thinks *about* is his work.
His work is the only thing he thinks *about.*
All he thinks *about* is his work.

(c) **In passive clauses, with completives as Prepositional Objects**:

Nobody ever asks *for my opinion.*	*My opinion* is never asked *for.*
They should have gone *into the matter* more thoroughly.	*The matter* should have been gone *into* more thoroughly.
They will take care *of our dog* while we are away.	*Our dog* will be taken care *of* while we are away.
I don't like people shouting *at me.*	I don't like being shouted *at.*
No-one has yet paid *for these books.*	*These books* have not yet been paid *for.* (completive implicit)

Normally, passivisation of this kind is possible only if the completive is a visibly affected Object. In this sense, we may contrast the following passive structures:

Acceptable:	The house has been lived in for years.
Unacceptable:	*Spain has been lived in for years.

(d) **In active clauses equivalent to sequences that are introduced by anticipatory *it***:

It is wonderful to work *for that firm.*	*That firm* is wonderful to work *for.*
It is easy to get on *with my boss.*	*My boss* is easy to get on *with.*
It is interesting to listen *to her* as a lecturer.	*She* is an interesting lecturer to listen *to.*

In each of these examples, the two different forms of predication have different 'theme' and 'focus'. For instance, in the last example, one structure tells us that *to listen to her* is interesting, and the other that *she* is interesting. Furthermore, pronominal completives have objective case form (*her*) after the preposition, but subjective case form (*she*) when inverted to Subject position.

(e) **With *WH*-completives in interrogative and relative clauses**: When the completive of a preposition is realised by a relative pronoun, the discontinuous structure is normal in familiar styles of expression, while the continuous (preposition + completive) order is distinctly more formal:

Formal style	**Familiar style**
On whom can we rely?	*Who* can we rely *on?*
Of what was the man accused?	*What* was the man accused *of?*

(f) **Some *WH*-questions admit only the discontinuous structure**:

What's the weather *like?*	**Like what* is the weather?
What have you come *for?*	**For what* have you come?
Where do we leave *from?*	**From where* do we leave?

(g) **On the other hand, certain PrepGs which constitute fixed phrases are very rarely discontinuous**:

To what extent do they disagree?	**What extent* do they disagree *to?*
In which respect do you think I am wrong?	**Which respect* do you think I am wrong *in?*

In (f) the preposition is more cohesive with the verb than with its completive; in (g) the preposition is more cohesive with its completive than with the verb.

The same applies to completives containing a *WH*-determiner:

On what grounds did the jury base their verdict?	*What grounds* did the jury base their verdict *on*?
At which hotel will you be staying?	*Which hotel* will you be staying *at*?
Under whose direction did you say this project was carried out?	*Whose direction* did you say this project was carried out *under*?

Finally it may be mentioned that PrepGs containing complex (two-word or three-word) prepositions can also be discontinuous, though perhaps less often than those based on simple prepositions:

His death was *due to natural causes.*	*What* was his death *due to*?
There are certain regulations which are *in conflict with* these proposals.	There are *certain regulations* that these proposals are *in conflict with.*

In some cases, a three-word preposition can be split, so that the second of the two prepositions precedes the completive and the rest is separated from it:

> There are certain regulations *with* which these proposals are *in conflict.*

The following paragraph from a personal letter written by the actor Dirk Bogarde to a friend, shows that the use of slightly expanded PrepGs and of PrepG complexes is quite a normal feature of this type of communication. We include the analysis of the five examples among the tasks proposed for this module:

> Got back here *just before dusk after a superb day on a three-mile long beach at Piera* [1] ... nothing *but miles of silver sand and mangrove,* [2] no people, *apart from one old shepherd mounted on a rangy horse,* [3] and, late in the afternoon, a big fat negress swarmed about with children, who sauntered *along the beach with a huge basket on her head filled with every kind of fruit you could imagine.* [4] It was a day *of unbelievable beauty and solitude.* [5] I have never felt so happy and relaxed, lost to the world.
>
> Dirk Bogarde, *A Particular Friendship.*

TASKS ON CHAPTER 13
Spatial, temporal and other relationships: The Prepositional Group

Module 57

1   *Complete the PrepGs in these sentences with units of the classes indicated on the left:*

   1)   NG: We were woken up by a sound like _____.
   2)   AdjG: I didn't understand much at _____ but I do now.
   3)   AdvG: I was sitting in the back row and couldn't hear the speaker from _____.
   4)   PrepG: The shops are open every day except _____.
   5)   Clf (*WH-*):   Can you see the sea from _____?
   6)   Clnf (*WH-inf*): Have the judges decided on _____?
   7)   Clnf (*V-ing*): Are you worried about _____?

2   †*Read again the conversation on 'The Green Party' included in 57.4. Write a list of the completives of all the PrepGs used, and say what classes of unit they belong to. Compare the relative frequency of the classes. Which classes are not represented in this text?*

3   *Insert appropriate modifiers of the types indicated, before the PrepGs used in the following sentences. Refresh your memory first by re-reading the examples in section 57.5:*

Grading
   1)   His proposals for changes in the public transport system are _____ in line with the opposition party _____.
   2)   However, they also go _____ against public opinion.

Intensification
   3)   Many villages isolated by the snow were left _____ without electricity for several days.
   4)   Our plane flew _____ over the North Pole.

Attenuation
   5)   I am _____ in agreement with you.
   6)   We moved to this area for financial reasons, but also _____ on account of my health.

Quantification

7) Archaeologists found prehistoric remains _____ below the surface.
8) You would have to travel _____ into space to find another planet like the earth.

Description or viewpoint

9) As a journalist, he is _____ out of touch with what's going on in the Third World countries.
10) Industries that have not been modernised are now finding themselves _____ in a difficult situation.

Focus or reinforcement

11) She was unmarried and _____ for that reason could devote all her time to charity work.
12) She got the job _____ because of her knowledge of Arabic.

Module 58

1 *To illustrate the syntactic potential of PrepGs in English, re-read the three extracts quoted in Modules 57 and 58, and:*
   1) identify the syntactic function of each PrepG.
   2) say whether the preposition is a free choice or whether it is governed by a preceding VG, NG or AdjG.

2 *Many verbs and adjectives govern only one or two specific prepositions. We assume you are familiar with most of these, but suggest you test your knowledge of the following items:*

Verbs		Adjectives		Nouns
ask	plot	bored	aware	answer
agree	hope	tired	averse	damage
amount	pay	delighted	prone	desire
appeal	suffer	anxious	related	search
boast	derive	eager	heedless	control
comment	dabble	liable	mindful	crime
depend	complain	rich	fraught	anger
grieve	insist	suspicious	conversant	effect
operate	invest	surprised	lacking	interest
point	flirt	sorry	rooted	escape

3 *Words related in meaning though of different class usually occur with the same preposition, though not always. Illustrate this by composing sentences with the following related words:*

to rely	reliant	reliance
to care	careful	care
to boast	boastful	boast
	grateful	gratitude
	furious	fury

4   †*The meanings of certain PrepGs expressing manner or instrumentality are sometimes included covertly in a verb. Compose sentences to illustrate this, e.g.*
1)   draw *milk* from a cow. They milk cows mechanically.
2)   put milk *in a bottle*. . . . . . .
3)   press clothes *with an iron*. . . . . . .
4)   take the *bones* from a fish. . . . . . .
5)   kill somebody with *a knife*. . . . . . .
6)   cut the meat *into slices*. . . . . . .
7)   to cover a wall *with paper*. . . . . . .
8)   spread *butter* on the bread. . . . . .

5   †*Conversely, a process is sometimes expressed periphrastically by a verb of general meaning such as **be, get, take, put**, and the support of a PrepG, e.g.*
1)   The car skidded.   The car went into a skid.
2)   His health is declining.   His health is . . .
3)   The police control the situation.   The situation is . . .
4)   They contacted me.   . . . . . .
5)   The UNO favours a referendum.   . . . . . .
6)   You must consider every possibility.   . . . . . .
7)   I don't trust him very much.   . . . . . .

6   †*In the following sentences, classify the italicised words as prepositions or adverbs. Can you spot the one which is neither a preposition nor an adverb?*
1)   The children had left their toys *about* all over the floor.
2)   Our friends live just *across* the road from us.
3)   It's cold on deck. Why don't you go *below* to your cabin?
4)   Some people have the telly *on* all day.
5)   Keep *on* walking.
6)   Keep *on* the right side.
7)   We usually go to a little pub *up* the street.
8)   Come on, drink *up* your beer!
9)   Tell me all *about* what happened.
10)   I'll run *off* enough copies for all the students.
11)   Everything is going to change in the *near* future.
12)   In debates he puts his ideas *across* very well.
13)   Some plants can live at temperatures *below* freezing.
14)   The picture is not finished yet, but I'll paint *in* the sky later.
15)   There were just a few light clouds high up *in* the sky.
16)   We're a long way *off* understanding the real causes of this situation.

Module 59
1   †*Consider the examples of **under** in 59.1 and **by** in 59.2.1. What part of the linguistic context of each example governs its contextual meaning: a preceding NG, VG, AdjG or its own completive?*

2   †*Read again the paragraph in 59.2.1 regarding the different contextual meanings of the preposition* **round/around**. *Can you suggest similar bundles of semantic features for each of the following uses of the preposition* **over**?
1)   They built a bridge *over the river*.
2)   We live *over the road*.
3)   I weigh *over 80 kilos*.
4)   He looked at the blue sky *over his head*.
5)   We had to climb *over the wall*.
6)   She laid a blanket *over his bed*.
7)   The baby fell *over a toy*.
8)   The thief knocked me *over the head*.

3   *Work in pairs or small groups, as follows:*
1)   Choose *one* of the simple, frequently used prepositions, e.g. *for, at, from, with, through, on*, etc.
2)   Collect a good number of examples of the use of the chosen preposition, by consulting various dictionaries, periodicals, books or spoken sources.
3)   Arrange the examples in groups that have a common and reasonably definable meaning.
4)   Study the groups and observe how close the meanings are: (a) within each group; (b) between the groups.
5)   In the light of your observations, try to formulate a prototype or core meaning, either for the general meaning of the preposition or for the meaning of each group.

4   *Work in pairs or small groups as before:*
1)   Choose one of the 55 sets of prepositions proposed in 59.5.1, 2, 3, containing four or more members.
2)   Collect examples of their use in the general sense assigned to the set (superiority, period, reason, etc.).
3)   Test the prepositions for substitutability one for another, and try to explain in what ways and to what extent they differ in meaning and use.

5   a)   †*There are many fixed Prepositional Groups in common usage. Can you formulate for each of the following four sets a prototype meaning relating the preposition to the five completives?*

at once	on duty	out of work	in a hurry
at times	on purpose	out of practice	in the money
at sea	on business	out of fashion	in pocket
at work	on time	out of sight	in labour
at war	on holiday	out of breath	in charge

b)   *Which of them tend to be used in construction with verbs, and which can also be used as qualifiers of nouns? Give examples of each type.*

6.   *Make a short list of the types of spatial, temporal and abstract references of the preposition* **for**. *Then underline its uses in the following news item from a British newspaper, and complete the tasks given below:*

> Animal welfare groups have attacked London Zoo's owners for setting up vast trophy-hunting reserves for tourists in southern Africa. There are also fears that the reserves planned for South Africa, Botswana, Swaziland and Mozambique could encourage a revival of ivory trading, which has been banned for at least a year now.
>
> There is a great potential in these countries for the mass minibus tourist market. The reserves will be primarily for high-quality photo-tourism, but trophy-hunting will play an important part. The company founded to run the commercial reserves has already paid a large sum for an option on several hundred thousand hectares in Mozambique, and Mr Jones, a trustee of the World Wide Fund for Nature has stressed that the Zoological Society would not be putting money into the reserves for profit. The reserves would provide much needed income and employment for the local population, he argued. For all that, the Wildlife Officer of the Royal Society for the Prevention of Cruelty to Animals condemned the Zoological Society for supporting trophy-hunting, saying that it was a barbaric practice.
>
> This new controversial venture has horrified the British zoo-going public, who fear for the ecological future of natural wildlife in Africa. At the same time, it seems to be damaging the financially-troubled London Zoo, whose attendance figures for the last few years show a decrease from 3 million to 1.5 million per year.

The Sunday Observer, 18 August 1991.

Tasks
1)   Write out a list of the PrepGs headed by *for* in this text.
2)   Study the list of prepositional sets and their members given in 59.5.1, 2, 3; write the list of 11 types of meanings which can be expressed by *for*.
3)   Say which of these types of meanings are expressed by *for* in the text. How many have spatial or temporal reference, and how many have abstract reference?

7   †*The following sentences all express processes taking place in a period of time. Can you explain the different semantic relations between process and period which motivates the choice of a different preposition in each sentence:*
1)   I have worked here *for* two years.
2)   I have been happy here *over* the two years.
3)   We have had problems *during* the two years.
4)   We have lived *through* two years of problems.
5)   There has been steady progress *throughout* the two years.
6)   The building will be finished *in* two years.
7)   The building will be finished *within* two years.

8   *Choose any set of prepositions included in 59.5 and compose sentences to show the differences in contextual meaning between the different members of the set.*

9   *Use the following in sentences to show the difference in meaning between the two members of each pair:*
in view of   in search of   in contact with
in the view of   in the search for   in our contact with

Module 60

1   *Add units to the following PrepG elements so as to realise them recursively:*

The head:
1)   There's a garden in front and also _____ of our block of apartments.
2)   The agency provides a coach to take you to _____ the airport.

The modifier
3)   The population is slowly _____ increasing every year.
4)   Our train arrived surprisingly and _____ at its scheduled time.

The completive
5)   'Shelter' is an organisation for obtaining accommodation and
     (V-*ing* _____) for persons who are in need.
6)   I bought this leather jacket on a trip [_____ [_____ [_____]]].

2   †*Express these sentences differently, beginning each one as indicated.*
     1)   I am most interested in the ecological consequences of this project. –
          It is the . . .
     2)   You must be particularly careful about your money when walking in the
          streets. – *What you must be . . .*
     3)   I haven't yet paid for the meals. – *What . . . The meals . . .*
     4)   I find it difficult to talk to my parents. – *I find my . . .*
     5)   In what do you believe then? *What . . .*
     6)   On which flight did you say we are booked? *Which flight . . .?*
     7)   We are collecting this money in aid of the refugees.*Who are you . . .?*
     8)   I told you that they gave us this medal in return for the clothes we sent
          them after the earthquake. *What did you say . . .?*
     9)   Caracas is the capital of Venezuela. *Which country . . .?*
     10) The caretaker said that this is the parking place of the Dean. *Who did
          the caretaker . . .?*

3   †*Consider the extract from Dirk Bogarde's letter and describe the expansion by coordination and embedding of the five numbered Prepositional Groups.*

4   *Try writing a paragraph of roughly similar structure to Bogarde's, but giving
    different details:*
    Got back here just before _____ after _____, nothing but _____
    and _____, and, late in the afternoon, a _____
    who _____ with _____. It was a day of
    _____. I have never _____
    _____.

Key of Selected Answers

Chapter 1

Module 1

1. 1) participant; 2) participant; 3)circumstance; 4) circumstance;
5) participant.
2. 1) Adjunct; 2) Subject; 3) Direct Object; 4) Subject; 5) Adjunct.

Module 2

3. 1a) No; 1b) Yes; 1c) No; 1d) No; 2a) No; 2b) No; 2c) Yes; 2d) No.
4. 1) independent; 2) minor; 3) dependent non-finite (as in *Not being a tele-viewer myself, I have no preferences as regards programmes*); it could also
be embedded, as in *Not being a televiewer myself does not worry me*;
4) dependent finite; 5) independent; 6) abbreviated; 7) minor; 8) dependent
finite; 9) dependent finite; 10) independent.
5. 1) NG; 2) AdjG; 3) PrepG; 4) AdvG; 5) VG; 6) AdjG; 7) NG with elliptical
head; 8) PrepG; 9) NG; 10) AdvG.

Module 3

6. 1a) finite independent are 3, 4, 5, 6, 10; 1b) finite embedded are 7, 8;
1c) abbreviated are 1, 2; 1d) minor is 9; 2) 1 and 2; 4 and 5; 7 and 8; 3) 1,
2, 5, 8, 9; 4) All the coordinated elements are recursive. These include, as
well as the clauses: coordinated colour nouns as c in PrepG (of *reds and
blues, golds and silvers, greens and purples*); adjectives as modifiers in
NG (*louder and louder* yes; *bold, exotic and decidedly unnatural* colors);
mixed modifiers in NG (*inexpensive, temporary, hair-coloring* products;
shocking British and American punk emblem); nonfinite *-ing* forms in VG
(*streaking, squiggling and dotting*).
   Possibly, the use of elements of equal syntactic status in this text
provides, first an element of suspense by means of the conjoined
abbreviated interrogative clauses, followed by a cumulative effect of
movement and colour which mirrors the notions expressed, and is therefore
to some extent iconic.

Chapter 2

Module 4

1. 1) (since my father's day); 2) –; 3) (briefly) (to Mrs Davies); 4) (at the time); 5) –; 6) –; 7) (in the park); 8) (in silence); 9) –; 10) –.

Module 5

1. Clearly fulfilled criteria for Subject are: (a) presence and position in declarative clauses; (d) pronominal Subject forms *I* and *he*. Less clearly fulfilled are (e) number and person concord, which are manifested only in: *there isn't, I am, it is, the Americans are.* Not illustrated at all are (b) position in interrogative clauses, (c) tag questions and (f) concord with Subject Complement.

3. 1) the use of caves for smuggling; 2) there (Subject place-holder), half a dozen men (notional Subject); 3) the light of a torch; 4) what the critics failed to understand; 5) the list of people who she says helped her; 6) it (anticipatory) to meet him before he died (extraposed Subject); 7) the wind coming down from the snowfields above; 8) it (anticipatory) to tell the neighbours you are going away on holiday (extraposed Subject); 9) it (anticipatory) that there is no real progress (extraposed Subject); 10) there (Subject place-holder) no way of knowing what goes on in their minds (notional Subject).

4. 1) It surprised us that Pam is seeking a divorce. 2) It was bad manners, really, to leave without saying goodbye. 3) It doesn't interest me who she goes out with. 4) It's not my idea of fun to swim in a cold lake. 5) It is obvious that recognising syntactic categories at first sight is not easy.

5. 1) anticipatory; 2) referring (to *Wimbledon*); 3) prop, prop; 4) anticipatory; 5) referring (to *the heat*).

Module 6

1. 1) the no-sales-on-Sunday trading laws (NG); 2) the door (NG); 3) that foreign doctors were not allowed to practise in that country (finite *that*-clause); 4) very little (quantifier as head of NG); 5) what (pronoun); 6) a classical rendering of Shakespeare's text (NG); 7) what they believe to be sunken treasure (nominal clause); 8) that many will survive the long trek over the mountains (finite *that*-clause); 9) what is the use of all this (*WH*-interrogative clause); 10) a ton of gravel (NG).

2. All the verbs in **1.** can passivise.

3. 1) Recipient; 2) Beneficiary; 3) Beneficiary; 4) Recipient; 5) Recipient; 6) Beneficiary; 7) Recipient; 8) Beneficiary; 9) Recipient; 10) Beneficiary.

Module 7

1. 1) *alone* Cs (AdjG); 2) *fit for the task* Co (AdjG); 3) *a multi-million pound industry* Cs (NG); 4) *what* Co (pronominal head of NG); 5) *where it's at* Cs (finite clause); 6) *a series of accidents* Cs (NG), *what he thinks* Cs (finite clause); 7) *accessible to a wide public* Co (AdjG); 8) *laughing* Co (non-finite clause); 9) *unexpectedly cold* Cs (AdjG); 10) *a bit stronger* Co (AdjG); 11) *an animal-lover working in a department dedicated to cancer research* Cs (NG); 12) *for the stage door* Co (PrepG); 13) *rather disconcerting* Co (AdjG); 14) *what colour* Co (NG); 15) *self-defeating* Cs (AdjG).

2. 1) *any in Europe* Cp; 2) *of what we are doing* Oprep; 3) *over a million pounds* Cp; 4) *of illegal possession of fire-arms* Cp; 5) *into this house* Oprep; 6) *to snooping* Cp; 7) *at him* Oprep; 8) *how to tackle this problem* Cp; 9) *discretion* Cp; 10) *for his pipe* Cp.

Module 8

1. 1) *for five years* (A); 2) *for two nights* (A), *at a magnificent hotel on the coast* (A); alternatively, *on the coast could be analysed as a third Adjunct;* 3) *under the barbed wire* (Cp); 4) *in the nurses' hands* (A); 5) *off the standard price for this car* (Cp).

2. 1) *the gang's hideout* is Direct Object, *without much difficulty* is Adjunct; 2) *the gang's hideout* is Direct Object, *more elaborately equipped with technology than they had expected* is Object Complement.

3. //The sun / never / sets / on the tourist empire.// But //
    S   A   P   A   (conj.)
    NG   Adv. VG   PrepG
travel pictures, business contracts and sports programmes/
                           S
    NG   +   NG   (conj.)   +   NG
don't tell / the full story:// getting there / may be / no
    P   Od   S   P
    VG   NG   clnf.   VG
                 (appositive clause)
fun at all.// Aircraft / perform / flawlessly,// but/// what/
    Cs   S   P   A   (conj) S
    NG   NG   VG   Adv   WH
happens / to passengers, flight crews and cabin staff?//
    P   Cp
    VG   PrepG + (ellipted prep. + 2 NGs)
Jet lag.// A mass phenomenon, almost as universal as the
minor cl.   minor cl.
  NG   NG   minor cl.
common cold. //

Chapter 3

Module 9

1. 1) b; 2) a; 3) b; 4) a; 5) a; 6) a; 7) b; 8) a; 9) preferably a; *dresses himself* is grammatically possible, but little used; 10) a; 11) b; 12) a; 13) b; 14) a; 15) b; 16) b (one with another).

2.   Objects unexpounded by social convention may be postulated for (1), (3), (7) and (15). Objects ellipted because the referent has already been mentioned occur in (9), (11) and (13). Reciprocal participation occurs in (16).

3.   1) *reason with: Cecil can't be reasoned with*; 2) *dispose of: Old, broken furniture is not easily disposed of*; 3) *call on: The Minister of Defence will be called on . . .*; 4) *aim at: The target that is being aimed at . . .*; 5) *keep to: Your schedule should be kept to. . . .*

5.   2) I doubt whether we have enough petrol to reach Barcelona. 3) Who knows whether/if there is an emergency kit in the building. 4) I asked where the nearest Metro station was. 5) We have all agreed (on it) that you keep/ should keep the keys. 6) The Under-Secretary can't account for the fact that some of the documents are missing. 7) I suggest he look/should look/looks/ in the safe. 8) The spokesman confirmed what we had just heard. 9) We must allow for the fact that he has been under great strain lately. 10) Will you see to it that these letters are posted today, please?

6.   1) indirect interrogative; 2) nominal relative; 3) embedded exclamative/ indirect interrogative; 4) indirect interrogative; 5) nominal relative; 6) indirect interrogative; 7) nominal relative; 8) indirect interrogative; 9) embedded exclamative; 10) nominal relative.

Module 10

1.   2) Most teenagers/ attach/ great importance/ to their peer group. SPOdCp; 3) Support for the party/ dropped/ five points/ in May. SPCpA; 4) Has/she/ made/ you/ one of those strange concoctions of hers? SPOiOd; 5)His uncle/ has left/him/ a large fortune. SPOiOd;6) I/ ran/ some cold water/ into the kettle. SPOdCp; 7) They/ granted/ all the prisoners/ a reprieve. SPOiOd; 8) She/ thanked/ the lost-property officer/ for the trouble he had taken. SPOdCp; 9) They/ can pressurise/ you/ into doing what you'd rather not do. SPOdCp; 10)The Olympic committee/ has commissioned/ a Japanese architect/ to build one of the stadiums. SPOdCp or SPOdA.

2a.   Suggested verbs might be: 1) *protect*; 2) *assured*; 3) *persuaded*; 4)₁*show*; 5) *beg*; 6) *cook*; 7) *announced/read*; 8) *convince*; 9) *explained*; 10) *signalled/indicated*.

2b.   1) *you* is Od; 2) *us* is Od; 3)*the actress* is Od; 4) *me* is Oi, *your invitation card* is Od; 5) *you* is Od; 6) *both of us* is Oi, *a curry* is Od; 7) *the results* is Od; 8) *them* is Od; 9) −; 10) −.

Module 11

1.   1) complex transitive; 2) complex transitive (with anticipatory *it*); 3) ditransitive OdCp; 4) complex transitive; 5) complex transitive; 6) complex transitive; 7) complex transitive; 8) monotransitive non-finite clause + Subject; 9) complex transitive; 10) monotransitive + Adjunct; 11) complex transitive (with anticipatory *it*); 12) complex transitive; 13) complex transitive; 14) monotransitive; 15) complex transitive.

Chapter 4

Modules 13 and 14

1. 1) material; 2) mental; 3) relational; 4) mental; 5) material; 6) relational; 7) mental; 8) material; 9) both relational; 10) relational.

2. 1) Subject-filler; 2) participant (the sum of $10); 3) participant (the baby); 4) Subject-filler; 5) participant (the bicycle); 6) Subject-filler; 7) participant (the kiwi); 8) Subject-filler; 9) participant (the brake pedal); 10) Subject-filler.

3. Suggested participants might be: 1) a strong wind; 2) waves; 3) tide; 4) river; 5) landslide.

5. 1) Effected; 2) Affected; 3) Effected; 4) Effected; 5) Effected; 6) Affected; 7) Affected; 8) Effected; 9) both Effected; 10) Affected.

6a. 1) Recipient; 2) Recipient; 3) Beneficiary; 4) Beneficiary; 5) Recipient.

7. 1) Yes; *Most Prime Ministers age prematurely*; 2) No; 3) No; 4) Yes; *The sky darkened*; 5) No; 6) Yes; *His brow wrinkled*; 7) Yes; *New techniques in pig-breeding are developing*; 8) Yes; *The camera clicked*; 9) Yes; *The load of sand tipped onto the road*; 10) Yes; *The company's sales have doubled*.

Module 15

1. 1) a property expressed; 2) acted upon; 3) *your letter* is acted upon; 4) a property expressed; 5) acting; 6) acting; 7) a property expressed; 8) a property expressed; 9) acting; 10) acted upon.

Module 16

1. 1) cognition, entity; 2) perception, entity; 3) cognition, fact; 4) affectivity, situation; 5) perception, entity, or rather, an event, 6) cognition, doubt; 7) cognition, fact; 8) affectivity, situation; 9) perception, entity; 10) affectivity, situation.

2. 1) The members of the commission were not pleased by either of the proposals. 2) We were amazed at/by his presence of mind. 3) The government is alarmed at/by the dramatic increase of crime in the cities. 4) She is worried by the fact that she seems unable to lose weight. 5) Will your wife be annoyed by the fact that you forgot to phone?

Module 17

1. 1) attributive; Carrier–process (intensive)–Attribute (identifying); 2) possessive; Carrier/possessor–process (possessive)–Attribute/possessed; 3) circumstantial; Carrier–process (intensive)–circumstance; 4) possessive; Carrier/possessor–process (possessive)–Attribute/possessed; 5) attributive; Carrier–process (intensive)–Attribute; 6) circumstantial; Carrier–process (circumstantial)–circumstance; 7) circumstantial; Carrier–process (intensive)–Circumstance (place)–circumstance (time); 8) attributive; Carrier–process (intensive/perception)–Attribute; 9) possessive; Carrier/possessor–process (possession)–Attribute/possessed; 10) attributive; Carrier–process (intensive/transition)–Attribute.

Module 18

1.   1) reported directive; 2) reported statement; 3) reported statement;
4) reported question; 5) either a reported question (expressed by a *WH-*
clause) or a reported directive (expressed by a *to-*infinitive clause);
6) either a reported statement (expressed by a *that-*clause) or a reported
directive (expressed by a *to-*infinitive clause); 7) reported statement or (if
suitably modalised) a reported directive; 8) reported statement; 9) reported
directive; 10) reported statement or (if suitably modalised) a reported
directive.

3.   *There* could be omitted from (4) and (5) since each has a 'presentative'
locative Adjunct in initial position.

Modules 19 and 20

1.   1) time (distribution); time (location); 2) manner (means); 3) contingency
(concession); 4) contingency (cause); 5) accompaniment (additionality,
positive); 6) extent in time + end-point; 7) contingency (reason); 8) role
(capacity); 9) manner (means); 10) matter; extent in time.

2.   1) Instrument; 2) Range; 3) Range; 4) Instrument; 5) Range.

Module 21

1.   1) *We chatted for a long time*; process is realised as Thing (*chat*),
circumstance (*for a long time*) as part of Thing. 2) *X continued to drop
bombs (on Y) throughout the night*; process as Thing (*bombing*). 3) *An
election campaign that would last for 50 days was launched in Canada last
weekend*; circumstance of place (locative) as Thing (*Canada*), process as
Thing (*launch*), new process *see*, circumstance (extent in time) as part of
Thing (*50-day*). 4) *Because he (Franz Josef Strauss) was obviously
intelligent and spoke exceptionally well in public, Konrad Adenauer
appointed him minister without portfolio in his cabinet in 1951*; Attribute as
Thing (*his obvious intelligence*), circumstance (reason) as Thing
(*exceptional oratory*), both of these being causative Agents in the
metaphorical version *won him a place*. 5) *X was released after people in
Washington had been increasingly expecting throughout the day that the
hostage who would be released would be Professor Steen, aged 48*;
processes as Thing (*release* and *expectations*), circumstance as part of
Thing (*rising*).

2.   1) Most of the companies in the motor industry have manufacturing
interests outside the production of cars, commercial vehicles and
components. 2) During the inter-war years a number of companies
gradually diminished their secondary activities or else ceased vehicle
production / manufacturing altogether. 3) In this way, a process of
specialisation set in / ensued. 4) The continuation of this process since
1945 has led to a fall / drop / decline in the number of companies engaged
in vehicle manufacturing. 5) In addition, mergers and take-overs of
companies have led to an increase in the degree of concentration in certain
areas.

3. 1) Recipient (e.g. *you / them*) in a material process; 2) Attribute (e.g. *fresh*) in a relational process; 3) Affected (*the ball*), Recipient (*her opponent*), Affected (*it*, i.e. *the ball*) in material processes; 4) Range (e.g. *mathematics*), Effected (e.g. *pictures*) in material processes; 5) Phenomenon (e.g. *you / what you are saying*) in a mental process.

Chapter 5

Module 22

2. 1) interrogative (exclamation); 2) declarative (prediction); 3) exclamative (exclamation); 4) interrogative (question); 5) declarative (question); 6) declarative (offer/question); 7) imperative (directive); 8) declarative (directive); 9) declarative (exclamation/question/protest, etc.); 10) declarative structure + performative verb 'warn' (warning).

3. 1) indirect; 2) indirect; 3) direct; 4) direct; 5) indirect; 6) indirect; 7) direct; 8) indirect; 9) indirect; 10) direct.

4. 1) yes, *WH*-interrogative, question, but also disapproval, as is clear from (8); 2) no, answer, statement; 3) yes, declarative, statement (+ aggrieved protest); 4) yes, declarative, apology; 5) yes, declarative, explanation/ excuse in answer to (3); 6) yes, declarative, explanation of (5); 7) no, acceptance of explanation; 8) yes, declarative, statement + disapproval; 9) no, invitation.

5. 1) goods and services, (a) *Oh, thanks*, (b) *I don't need one*; 2) information/ opinion, (a) *Yes, I do*, (b) *No, not really*; 3) goods and services, (a) *All right, I will*, (b) *No, I won't*; 4) information, (a) *Yes, I'm afraid they have*, (b) *Oh, surely not*; 5) information, (a) *I wonder*, (b) *I've no idea*.

6. Possible illocutionary acts will be suggested here; possible social contexts and speakers are open to discussion. 1) acceptance of offer/service with thanks; 2) aggrieved protest; 3) promise; 4) warning/advice; 5) request for confirmation; 6) reminder/protest (not giving new information, since *you know* implies that the addressee already knows); 7) prohibition; 8) request for assurance; 9) suggestion; 10) compliment.

Module 23

2. 1) *ever, anything*; 2) *any*; 3) *any*; 4) *any* (also assertive *some*); 5) *anything*; 6) *any*; 7) *any* (also assertive *some*); 8) *anything* (also *everything*); 9) *anyone*; 10) *anything/any house, property*, etc.

3. *ever* (clause contains hypothetical *should*); unstressed *any* (after the implicitly negative lexical auxiliary *fail to*); stressed *any* after the lexical verb *question*.

Module 24

2. The starred forms (*ever, anybody, anything*) are non-assertive items, which are not in themselves negative. They cannot, therefore, initiate the scope of negation.

3. Possible illocutionary forces are suggested; the contexts may be discussed: 1) with rising intonation, a question carrying negative expectations; with a high fall tone, an indignant exclamation; 2) either seeking information or a tentative request, or both at once; 3) disbelief (the possibility of the action occurring is negated); 4) dismissal by negative statement; 5) promise; 6) negative statement, implicit complaint; 7) advice; 8) prediction (transferred negation); 9) warning; 10) disclaimer of responsibility.

Module 25

2. 1) information-seeking/request; 2) request for information; 3) criticism/directive (= Don't leave your bicycle out in the rain); 4) offer; 5) exclamation; 6) request; 7) directive (= Please remove it); 8) request for information, or for the newspaper; 9) invitation; 10) equivalent to negative statement (= I could say nothing); 11) rhetorical question; 12) refusal to give an informative answer; 13) request to borrow the book; 14) suggestion; 15) exclamation.

Module 26

2. 1) vocative; 2) Subject; 3) Subject, vocative, Subject; 4) vocative; 5) Subject, vocative; 6) vocative; 7) Subject; 8) vocative.

3. Suggested illocutionary acts are as follows: 1) invitation to confide; 2) warning; 3) encouragement; 4) refusal to comply with an order; 5) (rather impatient) advice; 6) request for clarification/suggestion that speaker and addressee straighten something/playing for time when at a disadvantage; 7) condition of promise; 8) condition of threat; 9) attention-seeker, request/order; 10) (soothing) advice; 11) suggestion; 12) considering a possible happening.

Module 27

2. (The suggested responses do not exhaust all possibilities.) 1) wòn't you. Yes, I will. No, I won't. 2) is there. No, there isn't. Well, we could. ... 3) isn't it. Yes, it is/Yes isn't it. Do you think so? 4) are you. Yes, I am. No, I'm not. 5) have you. Yes, I have. No, I haven't. 6) shall we. Yes, let's/all right. No, I'd rather not. 7) is there (either falling or rising intonation, according to the positive or negative attitude of the speaker). Well, there might be. No, I'm afraid there isn't. 8) did he (intonation as in (7)). No, he didn't. Yes, he did. 9) shall we. O.K. Oh, I don't know. ... 10) mightn't it (intonation as in (7)). Yes, it might. Oh, I don't think so.

3. 1) opening/resuming a work session, etc. *Let's get down (to business)*, imperative; 2) information-seeker, *Is there (anything, etc.)*, interrogative; 3) giving an opinion/warning, *It/he/she (sounds nasty to me)*, declarative; 4) rhetorical question or equivalence to a negative statement = 'It is not necessary to apologise', *(Why) should I/you/he, etc. (apologise)*, interrogative; 5) exclamation, *What awful weather it is*, exclamative.

Chapter 6

Module 28

2. 1) *Paul*, unmarked; 2) *Abruptly*, marked, Adjunct; 3) *Is he*, unmarked;
4) *High quality consumer goods*, marked, the nominal part of the Adjunct;
5) *One of the most popular artists of this century*, marked, Subject
Complement; 6) *meet*, unmarked; 7) *In the American soft-drink industry*,
marked, Adjunct; 8) *Celebrating her victory today*, marked, non-finite part of
Predicator + predication; 9) *For months*, marked, Adjunct; 10) *Absolutely
dumbfounded*, marked, Object Complement; 11) *Another thing*, marked,
Direct Object; 12) *How*, unmarked; 13) *Never again*, marked, negative
Adjunct; 14) *Ludicrous*, marked, Subject Complement; 15) *Crazy*, marked,
Object Complement.

3. 1) *all of these*; 2) *fun*; 3) *most of it*; 4) *Government spokesman*; 5) *Riding on
a donkey at the seaside*.

4. 1) Predicator Complement, *her father's foreman*.

5. 1) (i) notional Subject; (ii) Direct Object; (iii) Subject; (iv) Direct Object;
(v) Direct Object; 2) No; 3) –; 4) Possibly, the noises, the sweepers, the
scavenging-carts, no boy in the street, any boy and the men are basic-level
Topics. The rubbish and the glamour are, possibly, subordinate Topics.
5) Any boy . . . he; the men . . . they, maintained until the end of the paragraph.

6. 1) (i) *Paxos* is Subject and Topic, but not Theme; (ii) *It* (Paxos) is Subject
and Topic, but not Theme; (iii) *the rugged islanders* is Subject, Topic, not
Theme; (iv) *Antipaxos* is Subject and Topic, but not Theme.

8. 1) and 2) (i) *For even the only remotely fashionable* (Adjunct); (ii) *indeed*
(conjunctive Adjunct), *so heinous* (Subject Complement), the whole clause
being thematic to the clause complex; (iii) *but* (conjunction), *stonewashing*
(Subject); (iv) *which* (Subject); (v) *developed by Nova Nordisk, the Danish
chemical giant* (dependent *-en* clause); (vi) *a cupful of cellulase* (Subject);
(vii) *as a result* (conjunctive Adjunct), *Levi, Wrangler and the other denim-
makers* (Subject); 3) The conjunction and conjunctive Adjuncts have a
connective function.

Module 29

3. SAY; KNOW; HEAR; ANYthing; TOLD; ROOM; CARE; DO; TALK; ALways;
2) marked focuses are CARE, DO and ALways.

4. The intonation nuclei could be assigned as follows: EGG; YOU; YOU;
YOU'RE; I; NO; ARE; COOKing; yourSELF; THAT; I'LL; I'LL; DO; NO; DON'T;
YOU; EAT.

5. Possible intonation nuclei are as follows: LUcky; inHErit; arisTOcracy;
IMmigrants; SEcond; WELL; LOOKS; CHOsen; AnOINTment; initIAtion;
PASSport; IS; selECtion; SOMEthing; BRAGging; BLESSED; HARvard.

6. 1) can; 2) have/have done/'ve done so; 3) haven't done/haven't done so;
4) would/would like to; 5) how/how to; 6) it; 7) did/did so; 8) so/it was; 9)
not/it doesn't; so/it does; 10) wasn't.

Module 30

2. 1) It is on the recycling of plastic that experts are working; The ones who are working on ... are experts; What experts are working on is ...; 2) It is fatal diseases that smoking can cause; what smoking can cause is fatal diseases; what can cause fatal diseases is smoking; 3) It's for the evening that this kind of garment is best reserved; when this kind of garment is best reserved for is the evening; what is best reserved for the evening is this kind of garment; 4) It was some icecream that she bought the children; what she bought the children was some icecream; the ones she bought some icecream for were the children. 5) It is your help we are counting on ...; what we are counting on is your help ...; the ones who are counting on your help ...; 6) it was because he didn't reach the station in time that John ...; (the reason) why John wasn't on the train that crashed was because ...; 7) It's by reading and listening to the radio that I unwind last thing at night; how I unwind ... is ...; when I unwind by reading ... is ...; 8) It's against viruses that the computer industry is fighting/It's the computer industry that is fighting ...; what the computer industry is fighting against is viruses; 9) It's at 12.30 p.m. that I .../It's to Marks and Spencer that I .../It's for a sandwich that I ...; when I nip down to Marks and Spencer is ...; where I nip down for a sandwich is ...; 10) It was shortly after I got home that I realised that ...; what I realised shortly after I got home was that ...; when I realised that I had lost my purse was ...

3. Sentence 5; then.

4. 1) a + c; 2) a + c; 3) a + c; 4) a + b; 5) a + c.

5. (i) 1b) The first kindergarten in the United States was founded ...; 2b) no passive; alternative: Milwaukee residents have traditionally benefitted from ...; 3b) Four-year-old kindergarten has been as much taken for granted as ...; 4b) The unthinkable has been proposed by ...; 5b) Are property taxes to be raised or is four-year-old kindergarten to be kept; these are the choices that may have to be made ...; 6b) The dilemma has been produced by ...; The proportion of ... is reduced by the budget, and cost controls are imposed on local district spending by the budget.

Chapter 7

Module 31

1. The first paragraph of the Dylan Thomas text consists entirely of Nominal Groups. The second consists of one clause complex made up of a main clause (with a projecting verb *remember*) and a non-finite dependent clause. The third consists of three clause complexes. The first of these has basically the same structure as that of the previous paragraph – a main clause followed by a non-finite dependent clause; the second and third consist of minor clauses followed by a main finite clause.

Module 34

4. 1) adversative (*yet*); 2) concessive (*although*); 3) adversative (*yet*);
4) replacive (*instead*); 5) replacive (*instead*).

Module 35

6. (1), (2) and (3) are instances of paratactic enhancement; in each case,
there is a finite secondary clause conjoined to the primary clause by the
conjunctive combination *and + then*. The circumstantial meaning
expressed is that of time, but also, implicitly, one of cause and effect. (4) is
an instance of hypotactic enhancement, in which the primary clause is
followed by a finite dependent clause introduced by the conjunction
before. Again, the circumstantial meaning is that of time, together with
implicit cause and effect. The parallel or similar organisation of these
clause complexes, together with the same explicit and implicit meanings in
each, contribute considerably to the force of the argument expressed.

Module 36

2. Possibly (a) *There was no mistake*, in which a reporting clause such as *He
realised* has been omitted; (b) From *The pale, tired face* to the end of the
second paragraph. *Now* in the second clause of this paragraph indicates
the switch to 'free indirect thought'. Similarly *And now a cough*, followed by
a direct *WH*-interrogative. The tense forms are back-shifted as is
characteristic of indirect speech or thought.

3. 1) Annie said she was sorry/Annie apologised for interrupting us/them in
that vital discussion. 2) I asked the EEC official what exactly his job was. 3) X
demanded whether I realised that the press would be printing something
that wasn't true. I agreed with a smile that indeed it would be frightful.
4) Annie inquired about Duncan and asked whether he would be
recommended./Annie asked Desmond whether he would recommend
Duncan. Desmond said he wouldn't/flatly refused to do so. 5) Humphrey
stammeringly/in a stammering voice accused the Prime Minister of lying.

4. 1) Annie invited the official to sit down for a minute. 2) Fiona suggested to
Godfrey that he (should) wear a sports jacket. 3) The Prime Minister
suggested that he could sort of put on his glasses and take them off while
he gave his speech. 4) Luke exclaimed in horror and begged/pleaded not
to be sent to Israel, claiming that his career would be at stake. 5) I told him
briskly not to be silly, and pointed out that it was an honour and could be
considered as promotion.

5. 1) (i) is an instance of paratactic projection (quoted speech), with the
projected clause placed before the projecting one. The tense form (*is*) in
the projected clause is not back-shifted, but the inverted commas
characteristic of quoted speech in written English have been omitted. (ii)
consists of two finite clauses, the second with an ellipted Subject *the blue-
green algae*, joined by *and* (paratactic extension). This clause complex
may also be interpreted, within its co-text, as two projected clauses

containing quoted material, the projecting clause being understood from (i). (iii) consists of one finite clause followed by a non-finite dependent clause, the semantic connection not being made explicit. An elaborating connector such as *specifically* could be inserted before *warning*; alternatively, the non-finite clause may be interpreted as having a circumstantial meaning of 'means' (*by this means*). (iv) consists of a projecting clause containing the verb *claim* (meaning 'declare to be true') which introduces a reported statement. This statement is itself a clause complex in which the dependent clause (*once drinking supplies have been filtered*) provides temporal/concessive enhancement to the primary clause *there is no threat to public health*.

Chapter 8

Module 37

2. 1) one-element VGs: *whizzed, startled, fell, shouted, turned, said, are, asked, scrambled, pick, changed*; 2) two-element VGs: *was crossing, was clutching, can't . . . be, was pedalling, was lost, had fallen, was rolling*; 3) three-element VG: *could have injured*; 6) *are* in (i) is, experientially, Finite + Event while syntactically it functions as a main verb.

3. suggested combinations are as follows: 1) is supposed to be; 2) are (un)likely/bound/sure to; 3) is . . . due to; 4) had better; 5) is likely/sure to; 6) was about to; 7) are apt/liable to be; 8) have to/would rather/sooner; 9) will . . . be able to; 10) is . . . to.

Module 38

2. 1) oxv, present, modal, progressive; 2) oxv, past, lexico-modal; 3) oxv, present, perfect, passive; 4) oxxv, modal, perfect, passive; 5) ov, past, passive; oxv, past, progressive; 6) oxv, past, progressive, passive; 7) ov, past, progressive; oxv, past, perfect, progressive; 8) ov, present, progressive; 9) oxv, present, perfect, lexico-modal; 10) oxv, present, modal, progressive.

3. 1) was being taken; 2) had been being instructed; 3) must have been using; 4) can't have been using; 5) must have moved; was being taken; 6) will be being developed; 7) are likely to be sold; 8) are sure to have been bought; 9) is being shot; 10) must have been being shot.

4. Suggested combinations are as follows: 1) needs repainting/should be repainted; 2) had better be trimmed; tidied up; would/would be certain to brighten up the place; 3) would look; 4) falling out/starting to fall out; had been/were hung up or stacked away; 5) hadn't we better clean; wouldn't/mightn't it have been; 6) could/would/might be improved/would be bound to be improved; couldn't/wouldn't be seen; 7) haven't been decorated; haven't been used/haven't been being used; 8) must have been (last) cleared out; will/would/is bound to take; are/were allowed; 9) has been worrying; have had to be prepared; 10) can't get involved.

5. (Text for Modules 37 and 38 combined) 1) There are only three occurrences of states: the stative verbs (*is, sees, sees*); all the rest are dynamic, showing actions; 2) Finite is fused with Event in *flash, sees, is, take, panics, heads, hold, comes, goes, misses*; Finite is realised by an operator in *is passing, (is) having, can't get, 'll spill, 'm braking, honking, flashing*; 3) Yes: *coming, getting, to make* (sure); 4) Present; 5) five progressive choices, the rest non-progressive; 6) one instance of *can't* meaning inability or impossibility, one instance of *will* with a predictive meaning; 7) one instance of negative polarity, the rest positive; 8) one instance of emphasis (*COMES*); 9) Briefly, the non-progressive forms are used to express a series of actions presented as complete and, in this text, sudden and for this reason alarming. The sense of imminent danger is heightened by the use of emphasis (*COMES*) and by modalising the declarative in two cases. The interjection (*Christ Almighty*) and exclamative force of the following clause, indicated by punctuation, also contribute. The progressive forms at the beginning of the extract plunge the reader into the scene by presenting an action in the process of happening, not yet completed (the car with a trailer is passing and having trouble getting back in lane); a later sequence of progressives (*I'm braking, honking, flashing*) represents iterative actions (see Module 42), here conveying an impression of urgency. The overall use of positive polarity, with one exception, together with the use of Present rather than Past tense in the narrative effectively convey the impression of a series of events which happened, rather than, for instance, a speculation on events which didn't happen or might have happened.

Module 39

2. 2) happened to be/chanced to be; 3) neglected to; 4) trying . . . to pass; managed to do so; 5) seems to be; 6) hastened to; 7) tend to be/tend to be being; 8) tried to; proved to be; 9) hesitate to; keep on; 10) stop; get.

Module 40

1. 1) from the bottom of the hamper; on to the bank; with a pocket-knife; in the tin; with the spiky end of the boat pole; between the boat and the bank; into two feet of muddy water. 3) intransitive phrasal verbs: *went up, went back, rowed away*; transitive phrasal verbs: *took . . . out, brought. . . out, gathered up, brought . . . down, took . . . off, beat . . . out, beat . . . back, threw . . . away, caught . . . up*; prepositional verbs: *hammered at, went at, looked at, rushed at, got into*; phrasal–prepositional verbs: *got off with*.

3. 1) a; 2) a; 3) b; 4) a; 5) a; 6) e (with this meaning *knock off* does not fulfil the criterion for transitive phrasal verbs of allowing the NG Direct Object between verb and particle; 7) a; 8) c; b; 9) e; e; 10) d; 11) a; 12) a; 13) a; 14) b; 15) b; 16) a; 17) a; 18) e; 19) e; 20) d.

Chapter 9

Module 41

2. 1) event, repeated; 2) state; 3) *face* temporary state, *decide* bounded durative process. Both are presented here (in a newspaper headline) as if instantaneous, *decide* referring to a past event, while *face* represents a situation which is no doubt still operative; 4) state; 5) events, historic present (stage directions); 6) events, past, historic present (anecdote); 7) state; 8) event, repeated; 9) state; 10) *plug in* event, instantaneous; *is* state; (demonstration); 11) past event, referred to by means of the 'historic present'; 12) both verbs refer to states; 13) *prove* event, repeated, past (reported information still valid); *leads* event, timeless present; 14) event, repeated; 15) event, future.

5. 1) Past, Past. *Early* suggests that the speaker is visualising the event as occurring at some specific time in the past. The coordinated sequence of events suggests Past in both, although in the second the Perfect is marginally possible (*have left*), in which case the car is still by the bridge; 2) Perfect in both: *Get* here could mean 'grasp' in either its literal sense or its figurative senses of 'understand' or 'discover'; in either case continued possession of what has been grasped is more likely than definite possession (*got*) followed by a gap in time; 3) Past, necessarily, since the referent of 'he' is obviously now dead; 4) Past, for the same reason as in (3); 5) *woke up* (Past), since the waking is clearly over, with a gap in time between the waking and speech time; *haven't had* (Perfect) since no gap is established; 6) Past (*did you say*), since the action of saying is seen as occurring at some specific time in the past; Past (*was*) with back-shift, or preferably Present (*is*), since 'your name' is presumably still the same; 7) Perfect because no specific time is implied, and there is no disconnectedness, the addressee still being present; 8) Past, a specific point in time being implied; 9) Past, a specific event being visualised; 10) better Perfect in both, since the interpretation of connectedness is the more likely: 'you are still in the wrong group'. The Past in both would imply that the situation described no longer holds.

Module 42

2. 1) punctual, agentive; 2) durative, agentive; 3) durative, unmotivated agency (Force); 4) *banged, rang* and *went out* are all punctual, non-agentive; 5) punctual, agentive; 6) durative, non-agentive; 7) both *ran* and *plunged* are here punctual and non-agentive; 8) *made* is here probably bounded durative, agentive, but it depends how the action is visualised; 9) both *graze* and *come down*, with *cattle* as Subject, could be analysed as durative and agentive (or at least partially so); 10) punctual, non-agentive.

3. 1) bounded; 2) ambiguous, bounded or unbounded; 3) unbounded; 4) unbounded; 5) unbounded; 6) bounded; 7) unbounded, probably iterative; 8) bounded; 9) bounded; 10) unbounded; 11) bounded; 12) both *dropped* and *pick up* are bounded; 13) unbounded; 14) both *know* and *feel* are unbounded; 15) bounded.

4. 1) *was driving* stretches out the durative process before the end-point *home*; 2) *was sizzling*, limitation of a durative process so that it includes orientation time; 3) *were jumping* + *up and down* gives an iterative meaning; 4) *was trying*, limited duration; 5) dynamic use of a normally stative verb, *is seeing* (= 'visit'), future reference; 6) *was crackling*, limited duration; 7) *were photographing*, stretching the process or iterative; 8) *am shivering and coughing*, iterative; 9) *was pulling up*, stretching out the stage before the end-point; 10) *was stooping* and *was lying* will be interpreted as limited states.

Module 43

2. 1) In (b) the standard set up still prevails, whereas in (a) this is not necessarily the case. 2) The implication in (a) is that I am no longer a colleague of his, nor in the same department, whereas in (b) the situation still holds. 3) (a) asks about the point at which you stopped some time in the past; (b) asks about the point at which you are now. 4) (a) asks about a destination in the past unrelated to the present, whereas (b) connects the destination to present time, with inferences of recency or the (unfulfilled) obligation to have been where the speaker is. 5) In (a) the action is over, in (b) it is recent and its effects are probably still felt or visible. 6) is similar to (5). 7) In (b) mobile phones are still popular, whereas no such implication exists in (a). 8) In (a) the action of giving is recent, in (b) there is no such implication. 9) In (b) the query is oriented towards the project as still on-going, whereas (a) only asks about its continuation at some time in the past, but without continuing up to speech time. 10) In both (a) and (b) the process is incompleted (indicated by the progressive), but (b) situates the explaining as recent, while (a) places it in the past.

Module 44

1. 1) will/'ll; 2) can't/won't be able to; 3) can't; may; 4) must; can; 5) will; 6) should; 7) are bound/sure to; 8) can't; 9) must; 10) need/don't have to.

2. 1) ambiguous: with volitional meaning, *wouldn't wait*; with predictive meaning *won't have waited*; 2) must have been mistaken; 3) can't have been listening/couldn't have been listening; was saying; 4) should have taken; 5) could hear; 6) were able to capture; 7) may have been; 8) had to have ... vaccinated; 9) would have telephoned; had been able; 10) oughtn't to have been talking / shouldn't have been talking.

3. 1) *will* expresses a strong prediction, *may* a possibility; 2) *may* expresses the possibility that many grants will be too low, whereas *will* expresses a strong prediction; 3) *ought*; 4) *must, has to*, intrinsic necessity; 5) *will*, prediction; *may, might, could*, extrinsic possibility (it is possible that it will have ...); 6) *can/are able to*, it is possible for them to do so; 7) the same as (6) (intrinsic possibility); 8) *should*, merges two meanings: (a) it is to be expected that this third aspect worries the government most; (b) it is the government's obligation to worry most about . . .; 9) *likely to*, probability.

Chapter 10

Module 45

4.   1a) qualifier; 1b) temporary situation; 2a) classifier; 2b) gender;
3a) epithet; 3b) objective; 4a) classifier; 4b) functional; 5a) head;
5b) animate entity; 6a) epithet; 6b) objective quality; 7a) epithet;
7b) objective material quality; 8a) head; 8b) abstract entity;
9a) determiner; 9b) non-exact quantity; 10a) qualifier; 10b) circumstantial.

8.   *Questions 1 and 3*: 1) cataphoric reference to the next clause;
2) exophoric reference to speaker and anaphoric reference to *Pam*;
3) the same as (2); 4) reference to speaker or *Pam*; 5) ambiguous: either anaphoric reference to the mentioned situation or relationship, or cataphoric reference to the Complement *nature* as the cause of the relationship (impersonal use of *it*); 6) exophoric reference to *anybody* (impersonal use of *you*); 7) exophoric (ostensive) reference to speaker's gesture; 8) exophoric (ostensive) reference to speaker's hand;
9) exophoric reference to speaker; 10) exophoric (ostensive) reference to speaker's other hand; 11) anaphoric reference to *Pam*; 12) anaphoric reference to *this* and *that*; 13) anaphoric reference to *people*;
14) exophoric reference to speaker.
Question 2: 9) normal use of objective form of pronoun at Cs under phonological stress of end-focus; 11) the same as (9) for *her*;
14) ungrammatical use of objective form of pronoun instead of subjective form.

9.   1) Ambiguous: either *this whole sequence of events*, or *this last event* (i.e. 'the stopping of work at the city's maternity and children's units');
2) Analyse as pronoun.

10.   In these colloquialisms *it* denotes either an unspecified referent implied in the context, or the whole situation itself. Paraphrases therefore vary with the context. The following are possible, but generalised: 1) There is nothing left. There is now no possibility or solution. 2) I don't understand the situation or what has been said. 3) an expletive of anger (colloquial): 'Damn' derives from 'to condemn'; *it* refers to the event or the situation.
4) *it* = 'wonderful' or 'the most important person'. 5) *that* = things related to that activity (building). 6) spontaneously, immediately; *like that* is often expressed with a click of the fingers. 7) *it* = 'the right way to do something'.

Module 46

2.   5) and 7) are acceptable, the rest unacceptable. Reasons: 1) An exception, not covered by the six proposed degrees of countability (see 46.3). *Brains*

(= intelligence) has mass reference but plural form, and accepts only countability markers nos. 1, 2, 8. It cannot be quantified by '*many*'. We say *He has brains* or *He has a good brain*. 2) *The car* is specific; the meaning is generic. We say *by car*. *Camping* has mass reference to the activity of 'camping', and cannot be pluralised. We say *camping sites*. 3) *Progress* has mass reference and is not normally individuated by *a*. 4) *Information* has mass reference and does not admit count markers such as *every* (singular determinatives). 6) *Outskirts* is a partially count noun used only with markers 7 and 8 (set D). It has only plural form and cannot be singularised or individuated by *a*. We say 'We live in a quiet part/district of the city', or 'in the quiet outskirts of the city'. 8) *Police* is a partially count collective noun (set D) which has only singular form but plural concord; it is invariable in form and very rarely individuated by *a*. A member of the police is *a policeman* or *policewoman*. We say 'reported by the *police*' (collective count) or 'by *a policeman*' (singular count).

3. 1) singular count noun *hat* determined by the typically mass quantifier *a lot of*: produces a comic effect; 2) similar syntactic treatment accompanied by the metonymic transfer of meaning from *knife and fork* to food; 3) similar use of a singular count noun with a mass quantifier; 4) unusual pluralisation of the mass noun *weather*; 5) acceptable though not frequent individuation of a mass noun (treason) with the meaning of 'a kind/type of'; 6) pluralisation of certain mass nouns (e.g. *snow, mist*) occurs occasionally in certain institutionalised expressions; 7) de-verbal nouns (e.g. swim, walk, attempt, go, etc.) usually have count reference and so can be pluralised: they refer to individual occurrences of the process; 8) de-verbal noun used as an individuated count entity; 9) plural de-verbal noun determined by a plural quantifier (several); motivated by the metonymic transfer from verb *find* to *object found*. 10) de-verbal count noun (*throw*) determined by an ordinal quantifier (*third*).

4. The following are used in the text as: 1) *mass NGs*: one's nature, material comfort, childhood, outer space, humanity, the common sense; 2) *count NGs*: a habit, the cosmonaut's denial, terrestrial comforts, the satisfaction, the scientific achievement, the impact, our planet, a painter, the sight, atomic flames, all cosmonauts, members, one family, my space experience, the people who live on our planet.

5. 1) *definite nouns*: *The Don* (proper noun); *the age* (identified by its qualifier); *the village* (identified by its qualifier); *the son* (identified by its qualifier); *the man* (identified by its qualifier); *the young boy* (identified anaphorically by inference from 'the son' and 'the age of twelve'); *the new land* (identified anaphorically by inference from 'America'); *the few gestures* (identified by its qualifier); 2) *indefinite nouns*: *a real man* (marked by *a* as indefinite–specific); *strange men* and *friends* (marked by zero article as indefinite–non-specific); *some time* (marked by some as indefinite–specific).

6. *the backdoor*: by inference that it is the backdoor of the speaker's house; or of a house which will be identified later in the text; *the moon*, exophoric reference to the earth's only moon; *the dark hump of the hillside*, identified by inference, as what the speaker saw from 'the backdoor'; *the smoke, the moon, the night*, identified by inference as the view from 'the backdoor' and 'the moon', which shines at 'night'.

7. Genericity could also be expressed by the following forms: 1) Liquids have no shape. 2) A gas has no shape. 3) Human beings need the company of others. 4) A war is politics carried out by violent means. 5) An animal that lives in captivity plays with its food . . . 6) A television (set) is a mixed blessing. 7) A bicycle is a cheap form of transport. Bicycles are a cheap form of transport. 8) Computers have revolutionised business methods.

8. 1) generic; 2) indefinite; 3) indefinite; 4) generic.

9. (a) 1) must be corrected: *Money makes the world go round* (a mass noun with *the* has definite, not generic references). 2) and 3) are acceptable as generic statements. 4) Proper nouns do not admit *the*. Poor King Charles . . . 5) Both are acceptable, but with different references. *Lions* has generic reference. *The lions* has definite reference to some specific lions (e.g. in a specific zoo or other place). (b) Either an indefinite but specific Frenchman; or, any man who is French (indefinite–non-specific).

Module 47

1. 1) subjective; 2) objective; 3) locative; 4) temporal; 5) extent; 6) objective; 7) subjective; 8) subjective; 9) subjective; 10) source.

2. 1) I should like *another doctor's* opinion. 2) Have you read *the chairman of the examination committee's* report? 3) The *Regional Training Scheme's* failure was inevitable. 4) My *next door neighbour's* dog barks all night. 5) Preferably no change, in order to avoid *in my class's grandmother*. 6) Preferably no change, for similar reasons to (5).

3. 1) *Every* member . . .; 2) . . . *hundreds* of butterflies; 3) . . . *some/sm/* very good news; 4) *Some/s ʌ m/ people* . . .; 5) *Most* of their energy . . .; 6) *None* of this work . . .; 7) . . . *such an* opportunity; 8) *Half* my friends. . . .

4. The following are examples: 1) *the usual* five dollars . . .; 2) *double* the price; 3) *Many of our* friends . . .; 4) *any* of *those* books . . .; 5) *Other* Europeans . . . *their former* political beliefs; 6) . . . *whichever* bedroom . . .; 7) . . . *one* of *his typical* remarks; 8) . . . *half an* hour.

5. *Aries*:   Not many important things will happen. Live quietly. example: Is *one* number greater than *another* number? *Each* operation is small; for example: multiplying *a three* figure number by *a five* figure number, producing *all* print on *a* word processor or changing *the* position of letters in *certain* data in *its* memory. *The* computer goes through *a* lengthy series of small steps as *its* programmer instructed it to do, perhaps repeating *some* steps *several* times with very *few* changes. A medium-sized computer can execute *a thousand* instructions in *two* seconds at *a* cost of about *five* cents. It will normally make *no* errors in *their* execution.

The result it obtains is better than *any* human can obtain, because *no* person has *the* patience or time to perform *such an* operation.

Module 48

1. (a) modified by epithets: *Europeans*; modified by classifiers: *building, policy, power, Parliament, week, questions*. The qualifiers of *students* and *attitudes* are of a classifying type. (b) modified by epithets: *animals, world, day, sky, rocks, trees, life*; modified by classifiers: none. The noun *animals* is qualified by postposed adjectives which are not of a classifying type.

2. Despite the fact that the Attributes *good, effective, persuasive, optimistic, sound* are adjectival and appear to be epithets describing the ideal person for the job, they are also essential types of the qualifications: the examination record must be 'good', the commitment to work must be 'optimistic', etc. They therefore have a classifying besides an attributive value. The modifier *mental* is clearly classifying. The 'outstanding benefits' are classified administratively: *non-contributory* (pension), *personal* (loan), *company* (car), *career* (development), except for the epithet *excellent*.

5.

Aries:	Not many important things will happen. Live quietly.
Taurus:	You should be bold and active during this month.
Gemini:	Many surprising things will happen in this month.
Cancer:	Very little will happen during this month.
Leo:	You will have several delicate problems to solve.
Virgo:	An emotional month. Or: You will move to another house.
Libra:	A good luck month.
Scorpio:	A baffling month.
Sagittarius:	A get-rich-quick month.
Capricorn:	A thrifty month.
Aquarius:	A watch-it-carefully month.
Pisces:	An extravagant month.

6.

inherent	**non-inherent**
non-inherent	**inherent**
inherent	**non-inherent**
inherent	**non-inherent**
non-inherent	**inherent**

7. 2), 3), 4), 7), 8) need correction. 6) might be accepted by some speakers but not by others.

11.

classifier	ambiguous
ambiguous	classifier
classifier	classifier
classifier	epithet
epithet	classifier
epithet	classifier
classifier	epithet

Module 49

1. 1) restrictive; 2) restrictive; 3) non-restrictive; 4) non-restrictive; 5) non-restrictive; 6) restrictive; 7) restrictive; 8) restrictive; 9) non-restrictive; 10) non-restrictive.

2. 2) journeys of such length; 3) a person of considerable enterprise; 4) the month having the most rain/the greatest rainfall/the greatest amount of rain/when it rains most; 5) his period of greatest creativity.

4. 2) an appositive, elliptical NG, expressing an Attribute of *daughter*; 3) an appositive NG, expressing a definition of *inflation*; 4) PrepG expressing circumstantial information; 5) non-finite verb expressing a process; 6) PrepG expressing circumstantial information; 7) non-finite clause expressing an attributive process; 8) PrepG expressing circumstantial information; 9) PrepG expressing a locative circumstance; 10), 11), 12), 13), 14) PrepGs expressing different types of circumstantial information (locative, attributive); 15) non-finite clause expressing an attributive process; 16) and 17) PrepG expressing a locative circumstance; 18) finite clause expressing a circumstantial Attribute; 19) non-finite clause expressing an attributive process; 20) PrepG expressing an attributive feature.

Module 50

3. (b) 1) land-based multiple-warhead missiles; 2) intermediate-range nuclear-type weapons; 3) an all-European home-robots exhibition; 4) a classic-style night-blue velvet lady's evening suit; 5) a two-year-old Maltese honey-coloured stone farmhouse.

4. 1) ... (I'm) a/professional/first-category,/massed-start/racing/cyclist (structure: *d c c c c h*); 2) ... (we saw) a tiny/really exquisite/but slightly damaged/early Greek/statue/which my sister said she would like to steal (structure: *d e e e c h q*); 3) ... (a need for) fairly concentrated/other discipline oriented/foreign language teaching/methodology/courses (structure: *e c c c h*); 4) a/grotesque/and frightening/typical/Star Wars/character (structure: *d e e c c h*).

5. 1) Three subjective epithets: place first the shortest, and last the one which you prefer to emphasise; separate them by commas. 2) Most speakers would say: *We heard a mysterious, faint tinkling sound*; that is: subjective + short objective + longer objective epithets. Place a comma only after *mysterious* because *faint* and *tinkling* are referentially more closely related to each other. 3) Place shortest first, longest last; also in order of ascending 'dynamism': *her long slender artistic hands*. Commas are optional. 4) Long sequences usually require bracketing or admit several arrangements: (a) *She had penetrating and absolutely bewitching/ deep round black eyes* (2 subjective + 3 objective), or (b) *She had deep, round, penetrating/and absolutely bewitching black eyes* (objective + subjective/subjective + objective). 5) The most natural order is: size + colour + material: *The toilet was a smallish brown wooden box. Wooden* is placed last for reasons of communicative dynamism; that is, it is surprising that a toilet is a 'wooden' box, but not that it is 'smallish' or 'brown'. Commas optional. 6) The most likely order is: 2 subjective + 2 objective epithets, each according to the norms mentioned in 50.5.3: We drove through the *dark threatening, wooded, granite mountains*. No comma after *dark* (threatening because dark).

6. 1) Both orders (*rich but a miser/a miser but rich*) are logically possible and differ only in emphasis. 2) same as (1). 3) Reverse order is possible, but expresses a different geographical situation. 4) Same as (1) and (2). 5) Same as (1), (2), (4). 6) Reverse order is illogical: one cannot complain (by telephone) before telephoning. 7) Reverse order is illogical for socio-cultural reasons: he could not marry again before his (first) wife died. However, *my grandfather (a widower) married again and his wife died* would refer to his second wife. 8) Reverse order is possible but unlikely. 9) Reverse order is possible but less likely. 10) Reverse order would produce *a demo, which they took*, that is, separating the relative clause from its antecedent and making it non-restrictive. This is possible but less likely. 11) Impossible to separate the AdjG qualifier *very odd* from the antecedent pronoun. 12) The sequences *The woman in hospital* and *whose life you saved in hospital* imply different situations. 13) Same as for (11). 14) Same for the adverbial qualifier *back* as for the adjectival qualifiers in (11) and (13). 15) Reverse order changes the meaning from *the officer that came* to *the general that came*.

7. (a) If there is no comma after *neck* it seems that it is his neck that is in evening dress; moreover one would normally perceive the whole evening dress before the chain round the neck. (b) *it* is here placed too far from its presupposed NG *a clear fire*, and appears to say that he is 'standing with his back to his own evening dress'. (c) It also appears that 'his face is spread out in both hands'. Rearrange the sentence as follows: *A clear fire burned in a tall fireplace, and an elderly man, standing with his back to it in evening dress and with a chain round his neck, glanced up from the newspaper he was holding spread out in both hands before his calm and severe face.*

11. 1) *his taste in women*: **Od** of *describing*; 2) *the famous baby doctor, Benjamin Spock*: **S** of *said*; 3) *Benjamin Spock*: **q** of *doctor*; 4) *rather severe women*: completive (**c**) of the preposition *by*; 5) *their severity*: **c** of the preposition *despite*; 6) *The model for these women*: **S** of *was*; 7) *his own mother*: **Cs** after the copular verb *was*; 8) *his early eighties*: **c** of the preposition *in*; 9) *a most exceptionally charming man*: **Cs** after the copular verb *is*; 10) *the wish to win over his mother*: **S** of *may help*.

12. 1) *this tour*: **S** of a clause; 2) *the space of nine days*: **c** of a PrepG; 3) *much of the glory of the Highlands*: **Od** in a clause; 4) *An added attraction*: **S** of a clause; 5) *a visit to the incomparable 'Winged Isle' of Skye, the most fascinating and perhaps most beautiful island in Great Britain*: **Cs** of a clause; 6) *the most fascinating and perhaps most beautiful island in Great*

Britain: appositive qualifier in NG (5); 7) *Long days*: **S** in a clause; 8) *the wonderful scenery of Scotland*: **Od** in a clause; 9) *new and stimulating sights*: **c** in a PrepG; 10) *loch side and mountain pass*: **c** in a PrepG; 11) *glens*: **c** in a PrepG; 12) *enchanting wooded valleys*: **c** in a PrepG; 13) *heather-clad moors where the red deer roam*: **c** in a PrepG; 14) *the coach*: **S** in a clause; 15) *places of outstanding beauty and memorable interest*: **Od** in a clause.

Chapter 11

Module 51

2. 1) He had a *bearded* face. His face was *bearded*. 2) You have been very *enterprising* in setting up this firm. 3) The newspapers have published *detailed* reports of the case. Newspaper reports of the case were very *detailed*. 4) Conflicts often arise between *neighbouring* countries. 5) We live in an ancient *walled* town. 6) *Flowered* dresses are no longer in fashion.

7. The compound adjectives are: 1) hair-raising; 2) time-consuming; 3) home-made; 4) breath-taking; 5) airborne; 6) wind-swept; 7) award-winning; 8) labour-saving.

10. 1) *crumbling* (material process); *fancied* (mental process); *mounting* (material process); *trackless* (state); *unfathomable* (evaluation); *grubbing* (material process); *bright* (quality or state); *long* (evaluation); *secure* (evaluation); *flag-flying* (quality); *dry-throated* (state); *well-prodded* (material process); *gaping* (state); *old* (quality); *black* (quality); *slimy* (state); *dry* (state); *crowded* (state); *rotting* (material process); *silent-roaring* (state–process); *grub-captured* (state); *dead* (state); 2) simple: *bright, long, secure, old, black, dry, dead*; affixed: *crumbling, mounting, grubbing, gaping, rotting; fancied, crowded; trackless, unfathomable, slimy*; compound: *flag-flying, silent-roaring; dry-throated, well-prodded, grub-captured*; 3) a baby's first encounter with the horror of death and decay in our physical world.

Module 52

In this module, Tasks 1, 2, 4, 5, invite free answers. Tasks 3 and 6 require only reference to the text book. Task 7 requires only reference to a good dictionary for some items, and then the free composition of examples. For these reasons, no key is offered.

Module 53

2. Introduce your PrepGs with the following prepositions: 2) (*delighted*) at; 3) (*satisfied*) with; 4) (*opposed*) to; 5) (*white*) with; 6) (*expert*) at; 7) (*tired*) of; 8) (*keen*) on; 9) (*ill*) from; 10) (*good*) at.

Chapter 12

Module 54

1. *where* (space, position); *down* (space, position); *up* (space, position); *just* (degree, intensification); *well* (modal, attitude of acceptance); *there* (space, position); *away* (space, direction); *yet* (time, relation); *up* (degree, intensification); *along* (space, direction); *up* (degree, intensification); *behind* (space, position); *all round* (degree, intensification); *back* (space, direction); *back* (space, direction); *even* (focusing by reinforcement); *just* (focusing by reinforcement); *again* (time, frequency); *about* (space, indeterminate position); *back* (space, direction); *even* (focusing by reinforcement). Comment: the preponderance of circumstantial (space and time) adverbs (13) reflects the normal preponderance of these types of adverbs. The good number of intensifying, focusing and modal items (8 in all) reflects the extent to which the writer introduces his personal attitudes and feelings into the narrative.

2. In this passage, the adverbs are distributed as follows: circumstantial: *elsewhere, anywhere*; modal: *incredibly, perhaps, probably*; focusing: *especially, even, too* (= also), *alone*; degree: *roughly, about, approximately, enough, quite, so*. Comment: the passage contains argumentation about space rather than its description, and therefore contains only two 'spatial' adverbs. No subjective attitude is expressed; the adverb *incredibly* is not emotive in this context, where it means little more than *very*. The modal, focusing and grading meanings of the other 13 adverbs express, not personal feelings, but a hesitant approach and cautious assessment of the arguments concerning a relatively undocumented scientific matter. The observation of this one linguistic feature (use of adverbs) in two different kinds of text (personal experience and objective exposition) shows how subject matter and its mode of treatment by an author always affects the choices of language forms in which a text is written or spoken.

Module 55

2. (a) Affirmative answers: 1) Yes, it's *already* time. Oh yes, it *already* is. 2) Yes, I've *already* had it. Yes, I've had it *already*. 3) Yes, I *still* love you. Yes, I *still* do. Yes, I love you *still*. 4) Yes, I'm *still* studying it. Yes, I *still* am. 5) Yes, it's *already* ten. Yes, it *already* is. Yes, it's ten *already*. 6) Yes, I've *already* been there. Yes, I've been there *already*. Yes, I *already* have.
(b) Negative answers: 1) No, it is*n't* time to go *yet*. It is*n't yet* time to go. 2) No, I have*n't* had it *yet*. I have*n't yet* had lunch. 3) No, I do*n't* love you *any more/any longer*. I *no longer* love you. 4) No, I'm *not* studying it *any more/any longer*. No, I'm *no longer* studying it. 5) No, it's *not* ten o'clock *yet*. No, it's *not yet* ten o'clock. 6) No, I have*n't* been there *yet*. No, I have*n't yet* been there.

3. 1) We *sometimes* take long holidays abroad. We take long holidays abroad *sometimes*. *Sometimes*, we take long holidays abroad. 2) Women are *often* successful in business. *Often*, women are successful in business. 3) He works hard *abroad*. *Abroad* he works hard. 4) They gave a concert *yesterday*. *Yesterday*, they gave a concert. 5) I gazed *longingly* at the brightly coloured fish in the aquarium. *Longingly*, I gazed at the brightly coloured fish in the aquarium. 6) *Perhaps* you'd better take an overcoat with you. You'd better take an overcoat with you *perhaps*. 7) We shall *probably* leave tomorrow. We shall leave tomorrow *probably*. *Probably*, we shall leave tomorrow. 8) *Hopefully*, they have arrived at their destination. They have arrived *hopefully* at their destination. Comments: (a) the above keyed examples show first the preferred unmarked positions, followed by the alternative positions which are also possible, and which are mentioned in the five subsections of 5.2; (b) the different positions an adverb may occupy determine the scope of its reference. Within the clause, it focuses mainly on the Predicator and so is placed closely before, after or within the Predicator: *sometimes take, are often, gaze longingly, shall probably leave*. Other elements are sometimes focused, for example by restrictive adverbs: *He alone, only for them*. In end-position, the scope of an adverb may range over all of the preceding elements of the clause, with a variable degree of end-focus, sometimes very little, even as if it were an afterthought: *We shall leave tomorrow probably*. In initial position, the scope extends to the whole clause and so conditions the way in which it is to be understood. For example, we may note the difference in meaning between: *They have arrived hopefully* (= they are hopeful) and *Hopefully, they have arrived* (= It is to be hoped that they have arrived). (See 55.2.5)

Module 56

5.

	Adverb	**Function**	**Semantic type**
1)	*terribly*	modifier of *new*	intensification
2)	*at all*	qualifier of anything	attenuation
3)	*really*	Disjunct	modal, judgement
4)	*much*	modifier of *the same*	intensification
5)	*still*	Adjunct	time relation
6)	*out*	Adjunct	spatial direction
7)	*so*	Conjunct	result
8)	*well*	Conjunct	concession
9)	*scarcely*	Adjunct	attenuation
10)	*really*	Disjunct	modal, judgement
11)	*so*	Conjunct	result
12)	*a bit of*	modifier of heavy	attenuation
13)	*really*	Disjunct	modal, judgement
14)	*just*	Adjunct	restriction
15)	*sort of*	Adjunct	attenuation
16)	*entirely*	modifier of *separate*	intensification

17)	*only*	Adjunct	restriction
18)	*Anyway*	Conjunct	concession
19)	*really*	Disjunct	modal, judgement
20)	*A bit*	modifier of *awkward*	attenuation
21)	*through*	Adjunct	spatial direction
22)	*so*	substitute	clausal
23)	*even*	Conjunct	focus on *if*
24)	*together*	Adjunct	manner
25)	*just*	modifier of *ideal*	intensification
26)	*really*	Disjunct	modal, judgement
27)	*really*	Disjunct	modal, judgement
28)	*So*	Conjunct	result
29)	*out*	Adjunct	spatial direction
30)	*never*	Adjunct	time, frequency
31)	*since*	Adjunct	time, relation
32)	*at all*	qualifier of *not*	intensification
33)	*really*	Adjunct	modal, emphasis
34)	*a little*	modifier of *unpleasant*	attenuation
35)	*sort of*	modifier of *unpleasant*	attenuation
36)	*rather*	modifier of *unpleasant*	intensification

Comment: some common adverbs may be interpreted semantically in more than one way. For example, 13) (*really*) may be considered as an Adjunct having intensifying force instead of as a Disjunct expressing a judgement of the truth value of the statement. Similarly 14) (*just*) may be interpreted as expressing attenuation rather than restriction. Discussion of the other adverbs in this task may well reveal further examples of this semantico-syntactic fluidity.

Chapter 13

Module 57

2. 1) NG; 2) noun; 3) noun; 4) pronoun; 5) pronoun; 6) Clnf; 7) NG; 8) NG; 9) Clnf; 10) NG; 11) Clnf; 12) pronoun; 13) NG; 14) NG; 15) pronoun; 16) NG; 17) NG; 18) NG; 19) NG; 20) *WH*-Clf; 21) *WH*-Clf; 22) NG; 23) Clnf. Comments: (a) distribution of these completive forms is as follows: NG (12), noun (2), pronoun (4), Clnf (4), *WH*-Clf (2); (b) AdjG, AdvG, PrepG (0). 9) consists of two coordinated non-finite -*ing* clauses, the second containing a PrepG whose completive is also a non-finite clause. 13) is a NG containing a finite relative clause qualifier which itself contains a PrepG whose completive is a NG containing another PrepG whose completive is a NG (14). 17) is a NG whose qualifier contains a finite relative clause, itself containing a PrepG with a NG as completive (18). 20) and 21) are coordinated *WH*-finite clauses, functioning together as a complex completive of the preposition *to*.

Module 58

4. The verbs are: 2) to bottle milk; 3) to iron clothes; 4) to bone a fish; 5) to knife somebody; 6) to slice meat; 7) to paper a wall; 8) to butter the bread.

5. The periphrastic forms are: 2) be on the decline; 3) be under control; 4) be in contact with/make contact with; 5) be in favour of; 6) give consideration to; 7) put one's trust in.

6. 1) adverb; 2) preposition; 3) adverb; 4) adverb; 5) adverb; 6) preposition; 7) preposition; 8) adverb; 9) preposition; 10) adverb; 11) not an adverb, nor a preposition; 12) adverb; 13) preposition; 14) adverb; 15) preposition; 16) preposition.

Module 59

1. *under:* 1) the verb *sleep* governs the meaning 'position under'; 2) the verb *walk* governs the meaning 'movement under'; 3) the verb *crawl* can indicate either position or movement; 4) the completive *an hour* governs the meaning 'under, less than'; 5) all the meanings are governed by the completives: caused by; subject to; has received; in a state of; given/in the present; has a (contract). *by:* 1) the verb *sit* governs the meaning 'proximity'; 2) the verb *walk* governs the meaning 'movement', and *the Post Office* governs the meaning 'place'. *By* expresses 'proximity'; 3) the verb *type* governs the meaning 'agency'; 4) the completive *tomorrow* governs the meaning 'before'; 5) the verb *sent* and the completive *registered mail* governs the meaning 'by, mode of transport'; 6) the verb *measures* and the NGs govern the meaning of 'multiplication'.

2. 1) path; extending from one side to the other; without contact; 2) position; on the other side; contact with surface; 3) more than a mentioned quantity; 4) position; extension; higher than; without contact; 5) movement from one side to the other; involving also movement up and then down; with contact; 6) extent; covering a horizontal surface; with contact; 7) movement downwards from an upright position; caused by an obstacle; making contact with the obstacle; 8) indeterminate position of a blow on an object. Comment: some different semantic features can be expressed by the preposition *over* in other contexts; e.g. *to fall over a cliff; to be over an operation; to be over the worst; all over the world; conversation over lunch; over the years; over the telephone; to take a long time over something; to have difficulties over something.*

5. 1) Only very general descriptions of prototype meanings can be formulated, such as: *at:* related to points in space (*sea*), time (*once, times*), and engagement in an activity (*work, war*); *on:* related to a state or activity; *out of:* related to a lack of, or absence of something; *in:* related to a state.

7. 1) *for* is the preposition most often used for the simple expression of the extent of a period; 2) *over* expresses the feature 'during the whole period'; 3) *during* refers to points or short periods at different times during the whole period; 4) *through* expresses the notion of continuity; 5) *throughout* intensifies the notion of 'the entire period' and 'constant activity'; 6) *in* means 'at the end of the next two years'; 7) *within* means during the next two years or a period not longer than two years.

Module 60

2. 1) It is *the ecological consequences of this project* that I am most interested *in*. 2) *What* you must be particularly careful *about* when walking in the streets is your money. 3) *What* I haven't paid *for* yet is the meals. *The meals* haven't been paid *for* yet. 4) I find *my parents* difficult to talk *to*. 5) *What* do you believe *in*, then? 6) *Which flight* did you say we are booked *on*? 7) *Who* are we collecting this money *for*? 8) *What* did you tell me they gave us this medal (in return) *for*? 9) *Which country* is Caracas the capital *of*? 10) *Who* did the caretaker say this is the parking place *of*? Comment: Sometimes discontinuous PrepG structures are better avoided. For example, the *of* construction in (10) is unnatural and cumbersome and better replaced by a non-prepositional group structure such as: *Whose parking place did the caretaker say this is*?

3. 1) Two asyndetically coordinated PrepGs: *just before dusk – after a superb day on a three-mile long beach at Piera*. In the second one, the completive contains an embedded PrepG whose completive contains another embedded PrepG (*at Piera*). 2) In the PrepG *but miles*, the completive contains an embedded PrepG as qualifier (*of silver sand and mangrove*) whose completive consists of two coordinated NGs. 3) In this PrepG the completive of *apart from* consists of a NG (*one old shepherd*) whose qualifier is realised by a non-finite clause which itself contains a PrepG (*on a rangy horse*). 4) This unit begins with two asyndetically coordinated PrepGs: *along the beach* and *with a huge basket*. The completive of the second (*a huge basket*) is qualified by two embedded and asyndetically coordinated units: a PrepG: (*... basket*) *on her head*; and a Clnf: (*... basket*) *filled with every kind of fruit you could imagine*. The Clnf contains a Prepositional Group Adjunct (*with every kind*) whose completive (*every kind*) is qualified by two embedded and asyndetically coordinated units: a PrepG: (*every kind*) *of fruit*; and a Clf: (*every kind*) *you can imagine*.

Index